Stomp Off, Let's Go

A serious Louis Armstrong, Chicago, c. 1923.
Author's personal collection.

Stomp Off, Let's Go

The Early Years of Louis Armstrong

Ricky Riccardi

Oxford University Press is a department of the University of Oxford.
It furthers the University's objective of excellence in research, scholarship,
and education by publishing worldwide. Oxford is a registered trade mark of
Oxford University Press in the UK and certain other countries.

Published in the United States of America by Oxford University Press
198 Madison Avenue, New York, NY 10016, United States of America.

CIP data is on file at the Library of Congress

ISBN 978–0–19–761448–8

DOI: 10.1093/oso/9780197614488.001.0001

Printed by Sheridan Books, Inc., United States of America

For the women in Louis Armstrong's life: Catherine Walker, Josephine Armstrong, Mary Albert, Beatrice Armstrong, Tillie Karnofsky, Daisy Parker, Lillian Hardin, Alpha Smith, and Lucille Wilson.

And for the women in mine: Margaret, Ella, Melody, Lily, and my Mom.

Praise for *Stomp Off, Let's Go: The Early Years of Louis Armstrong*

"Louis Armstrong is quite simply the most important person in American music. He is to 20th-century music what Einstein is to physics, Freud is to medicine, and the Wright Brothers are to travel. In this indispensable and thrilling book, Ricky Riccardi guides us through the period of Pops's own creative Big Bang, the first decades. Stunning!"

Ken Burns, award-winning documentary filmmaker

"Ricky Riccardi has artfully researched and presented the early years of Louis Armstrong's life to teach us the story of the man who changed music forever. The narrative, with illustrations, moves at an even tempo, offering everything needed to create a playlist and embark on this phenomenal journey. From the beginning, love and soul invited scholarship to liberate the treasure."

Maxine Gordon, author of *Sophisticated Giant: The Life and Legacy of Dexter Gordon*

"Riccardi handles the legacy of our greatest musical icon with care, laser precision, and staunch integrity. This early accounting of Louis's community and work is an extremely important chronicle of world history. Amazing work!"

Jon Batiste, GRAMMY Award-, Oscar-, and Emmy Award-winning multi-instrumentalist, bandleader, composer, and New Orleanian

"Ricky Riccardi has written, with love, passion, and respect, the most thoroughly researched biography of the most influential musician in American history."

Wendell Brunious, New Orleans bandleader and trumpeter

"Riccardi has made a monumental contribution to American history with his biographical work on Louis Armstrong, and this may be his finest volume. *Stomp Off, Let's Go* presents Armstrong the jazz genius, Armstrong the agent for cultural change, and Armstrong the man—all told with masterful technique, swinging style, and a full, warm tone. This is a book worthy of its extraordinary subject."

Jonathan Eig, Pulitzer Prize-winning author of *King: A Life*

"Nobody knows Louis Armstrong like Ricky Riccardi. Nobody loves Louis Armstrong like Ricky Riccardi. He generously shares both the knowledge and love with his readers and has delivered the definitive guide to this seminal American musician."

Ted Gioia, author of *The History of Jazz* and *The Jazz Standards*

"I have waited for this culminating volume in Ricky Riccardi's magisterial trilogy on Louis Armstrong with the same heightened expectations that some folks might reserve for the World Cup. I am happy to report, it does not disappoint! Riccardi brilliantly guides us into the creative vortex of Pops' early decades, a time during which Armstrong made some of the most electric, joyful, revolutionary music known to mankind. Read *Stomp Off, Let's Go* while listening to early Armstrong recordings. Your life will be immeasurably enriched!"

Matt Glaser, Artistic Director, American Roots Music Program, Berklee College of Music

"Ricky is one of the foremost scholars on the subject of Armstrong that I've ever encountered. The love he feels for Pops is palpable. Whereas so many completists take pride in hoarding information, Ricky literally invites people into Armstrong's home and makes them feel comfortable. His joy is in sharing whatever his findings are with whomever is genuinely interested. He curates Armstrong's archives at the level of channeling, which gives you a glimpse into the passion of Pops."

Nicholas Payton, "The Savior of Archaic Pop"

"Riccardi's deep research has new stories going off like firecrackers on every page. Even better, this book subtly yet powerfully charts Louis Armstrong's human development. The growth of the phenomenal artist is all here, and more: the man creating himself 'in the cause of happiness.' Louis would be delighted by this 'history book': its accuracy, its empathy, its irresistible swing."

Michael Steinman, author of the *JAZZ LIVES* blog

"This eagerly awaited third installment of Ricky Riccardi's dazzling Armstrong trilogy proves beyond a whisper of doubt two things: that Ricky understands Louis better than anyone on the planet. And that Louis' is a story not just about a jazz genius, but of the soul of 20th-century America."

Larry Tye, journalist and author of *The Jazzmen: How Duke Ellington, Louis Armstrong, and Count Basie Transformed America*

"Riccardi has Mr. Armstrong on speed dial. This is the only way to explain the richness of the details. Either that or he has the finest time machine on the market. Either way, everybody wins because we better understand why Satchmo is the man!"

Sacha Jenkins, filmmaker and director of *Louis Armstrong's Black and Blues*

I'd like to see some of these same people who label Pops a "Tom," "Remus" and all that, I'd like to see some of them have to come through the changes that he had to come through in order to emerge as the great man he is and see which direction they would have gone, see where they would be. They would probably still be picking cotton!

Clark Terry, in conversation with Jack Bradley (1970)[1]

We was very poor. Very poor. My brother Louis died a rich man, but he went to school bare-footed. Yes he did, went to school bare-footed, and he didn't have nothing. But when he got to this here music, he just kept on trying.

Beatrice "Mama Lucy" Armstrong (1973)[2]

I was raised with him and stayed with him, and I remember one time Louis told me, he said, "Israel, if I ever get my hands on these three valves of the trumpet, I wants to be the Talk of the Town."

Israel Gorman (1961)[3]

It's really amazing because we had no idea in the beginning that jazz was going to be that important, that someday people would want to know how we started and what we did and what records we made. And it's amusing to read in books that people tell you why we did this. I'm glad they know because we didn't!

Lillian Hardin Armstrong (1969)[4]

You get hungry, you'll do it!

Louis Armstrong, when asked how he came up with his scat improvisations (1970)[5]

Contents

Prologue: "My Whole Life, My Whole Soul, My Whole Spirit"

The lavish new Empire Room opened at the Waldorf-Astoria in New York City on September 18, 1969, after a $250,000 renovation. The space, bathed in apricot hues with silver accents, now boasted three crystal Marie Therese chandeliers and a 30-foot stage; the hotel promised "no posts or obstructions anywhere in the room."[1]

Louis Armstrong opened a two-week engagement at the Empire Room on March 2, 1971. He, too, had been through quite a renovation to even get to that point. In September 1968, he showed up at Beth Israel Hospital, suffering from kidney failure brought about by losing weight too rapidly. Dr. Gary Zucker admitted Armstrong into intensive care, where he would remain for the next two months. On October 8, an ailing Armstrong grabbed a piece of paper and scrawled out a note to Dr. Zucker:

> Doc, it has just dawned on me. Man I really don't know how I stood so much miserie [*sic*] for such a long time (+ so young.) When I was (15) years old, I drove a (ton) truck full of Hard stone coal. I had to load the truck myself. And diliver [*sic*] it to the white folks' homes. Go back to the Coal yard and repeat the same thing. I would finish this job at 5 o'clock with my back so weak until I would stretch out for just a few minutes with my Back hurting so badly, I would scream. Then I would pick up my trumpet and go to the Honky Tonk and Blow the Blues all night, for the whores + pimps who really loved me Doc – The way that I blow those Blues for them. I finish the Honky Tonk and right back looking that old mule in the face again. Anyhow, that's why I have a very weak Back. My spine is bad. Both sides of my Back is weak. P.S. All three need looking into. Love.[2]

Armstrong would make it out of intensive care, only to be sent back in February 1969 with more heart and kidney issues. Once out, he spent much of the year convalescing at his home in Corona, Queens, warming up every day in hopes of being able to perform in front of an audience again. He finally received the okay from Dr. Zucker to return to performing in the fall of 1970, making his comeback at the International Hotel in Las Vegas.

However, during a return to Vegas at the end of the year, Armstrong wrote a letter to Zucker concerning the "shortening of my breath."[3] His return to the stage was clearly hindering his health but it did not stop the Waldorf from offering Armstrong a contract in January 1971 to do a two-week engagement—two shows a night, five nights a week—beginning on March 2.[4] The engagement would pay well—$15,000 a week (the equivalent of $117,000 a week in 2024)—but Armstrong didn't need the money; he needed to play his trumpet for an audience.

Dr. Zucker knew that playing the Waldorf was a potentially fatal mistake. During Armstrong's visit to Zucker's office on January 14, Zucker told him, "Louie, I don't think you'll be able to do it. There's a risk that you'll die on the stage." He never forgot what happened next:

> [Armstrong] said he doesn't care. And there he is in his shorts and he assumes the position of holding a horn and looking up at the ceiling and he says to me, "Doctor, you don't understand," he says, "My whole life, my whole soul, my whole spirit is to bloooooow this hooooorn!" He says, "My people are waiting for me, I cannot let them down," or words to that effect. And I must tell you, a chill went up and down my spine, I got prickly all over my body. It was almost like a religious experience.[5]

Zucker noted that Armstrong had "no fear" of dying on stage, but such a prospect frightened Armstrong's wife, Lucille, as well as his management at Associated Booking Corporation. Zucker told Armstrong to check into a hospital first, but he refused. Zucker finally relented and allowed Armstrong to sign the contract to appear at the Empire Room, but under one condition: "I made the deal with him. I said, 'I'll tell you what. If you would get a suite at the Waldorf, I will come to see you twice a day, morning and afternoon, and treat you as if you were in the hospital. I'll give you the medicines and I'll supervise your diet and if you need anything else, I'll take care of you in the Waldorf and then you can do your two [shows a night].'" Armstrong agreed and signed the contract on January 18.

Any frailties were not overly apparent on opening night at the Waldorf, as Armstrong received a positive review from John S. Wilson in the *New York Times*. "Looking slim and trim in a light-blue suit, Mr. Armstrong sings with the deliberate, toothy emphasis that is his trademark and blows his trumpet sparingly but with enough emphasis to let it be known that he is back at the old stand," Wilson wrote.[6] Syndicated columnist Earl Wilson also attended and noted that Armstrong "got a standing ovation (he always does)."[7]

Meanwhile, between shows, Zucker was doing his best to tend to the trumpeter's rapidly failing heart. "I did just what I said and was able to make him feel better and get rid of some of the heart failure," he recalled. Armstrong invited Zucker and his wife to attend the performance on Wednesday, March 3, dedicating "What a Wonderful World" to him after telling the audience how Zucker "saved my life three times in the intensive care unit at Beth Israel Hospital in New York."

But as the two weeks wore on, Armstrong began breaking down. Musicians in his band later remembered him needing oxygen, needing help to walk on stage, vomiting in the elevator; one remembered him defecating in his pants and needing to change clothes before a performance. Yet he never canceled a single show and managed to play the trumpet each night. He had spent much of the previous two and a half years resting at home, semiretired. He had money, he loved his neighborhood in Corona, he had a good doctor, and could have easily lived 10 or more years—if he had just agreed to put down the trumpet for good. And that was something he just could not do.

Eventually he made it to the final bell, the second show of the night on March 15, 1971. He opened with his theme song of 40 years, "When It's Sleepy Time Down South," thinking of home and his beloved mother, Mayann, as he sang about "when ol' mammy falls on her knees." A kid who grew up eating food plucked from garbage cans then sang "What a Wonderful World." Hardened souls rolled their eyes at the sentimental message of that song, but Armstrong lived it and could deliver it with conviction; the stage of the Empire Room was a long way from "The Battlefield," the neighborhood where his life began.

In between, he played trumpet on "Indiana," most assuredly leaning on the lessons he had learned firsthand from King Oliver, whose own chops had diminished before Armstrong's eyes. Road manager Ira Mangel said Armstrong "played as he never played before" during this show. He relived hit records like "Mack the Knife" and "Blueberry Hill" and "Hello, Dolly!"—the latter had knocked the Beatles off the top of the charts at the height of Beatlemania. He told stories of his days as "Ambassador Satch" in the 1950s. He indulged in his love of comedy in a riotous duet with Tyree Glenn—wearing a woman's hat like Zutty Singleton used to do back at the Savoy in Chicago in 1928—on "That's My Desire." And he sang his own composition "Someday You'll Be Sorry," perhaps reminding some in the audience that "the way you treated me was wrong."

But he saved the best for last, closing with "Boy from New Orleans," an autobiographical take on "When the Saints Go Marching In" that told his entire life story from birth to the present day. Each chorus ended with the phrase "New Orleans," repeated over and over, drilling it through the audience's head that this is where he was from, this is who he was, this is what he represented. He name-dropped Jane Alley and Rampart Street and King Oliver and all the names and places that made him who he was. He thanked his fans for being "mighty kind" and closed by scatting a six-note lick that's omnipresent in his discography: Franz Drdla's light classical number "Souvenir." Louis first heard a woman violinist play it at a concert in Chicago he attended with his second wife, Lillian Hardin Armstrong, in the 1920s. "He heard it once and remembered it," Lil recalled.[8] Perhaps Louis thought of Lil as he scatted it one last time.

"He had tears in his eyes as he walked off the stage during his last night at the Waldorf," Mangel said afterward. "In all my years with him, I have never seen him cry before." Photographer Eddie Adams noticed a crowd of autograph seekers waiting for Armstrong, who obliged each and every one of them. "The crowd disappeared, Pops disappeared," Adams wrote. "At the far end of the lobby the light was reflected from his horn. It made me look up. I saw Pops walking away alone. He seemed in a daze, swaying as he walked. I thought he was going to go to his room. His doctor answered the door. . . . No one but Pops knew. He would never play publicly again."[9]

Armstrong walked off stage on Sunday night and was admitted to intensive care at Beth Israel Hospital on Monday night, March 16, for a "cardiac irregularity." Reports to the press were positive, with stories of the trumpeter singing and cracking jokes to nurses, but truthfully, he was in dire shape, unable to sit up and eat until Sunday, March 22. A few days later, his heart stopped beating for 30 seconds, requiring an emergency tracheotomy to save his life. It would be a long road to recovery and Armstrong would not be able to leave Beth Israel until May 8.

Visitors were limited, but Louis did make time for one special person: his sister Beatrice Collins, better known as "Mama Lucy," who flew in from New Orleans. "And I went up to that hospital there and Louis was so sick," she recalled in 1973. "I had to leave out there 'cause he looked up at me and asked me how *I* felt. I couldn't answer." While in New York, Mama Lucy stayed with Lucille at their home in Queens. Two years later, she excitedly told trumpeter Yoshio Toyama about the guest bedroom ("And that bed is gold top, yeah, gold!"), the downstairs bathroom ("It's all mirrors. You see yourself 20-something times!"), and Louis's den ("And his music room where he have all his tapes and things like that, it's beautiful!") When Toyama asked, "He didn't have that down here [in New Orleans]?" she scoffed, "He had nothing down here—he had *nothing*. He was making a living, you understand? He didn't get famous until he went up there, he didn't get famous here." Giving credit where it was due, she added, "And Lil pushed him up front."

Back at the hospital, Louis had an interesting proposition for his sister. "You see, before he died, when I was up there when he was sick, he told me he wanted me to come back and we was going to talk about being children. And I know he was going to tape all of that, you see, and find out that I know about some of those things, you understand? And he said he wanted me to come back and spend a while with him when he get out of the hospital."

Both Mama Lucy and Louis Armstrong made it back to their respective homes in May. When Mama Lucy returned to New Orleans, she immediately noticed a funeral parade and asked, "Who's that dead?" She was told it was Peter Davis, Louis's first cornet teacher at the Colored Waif's Home for Boys, who passed away on April 29. All Mama Lucy could remember was how Davis "used to come out and tell Mama how Louis was doing and not to worry about him." Now Mama Lucy was the one worried about Louis. When she called him on his birthday on July 4, knowing her brother was still sick and had spent his life helping others, she asked, "You want me to send you two or three thousand dollars?" A shocked Louis could only ask, "Mama Lucy, where you get all that money from!?"

Louis also asked her when she was coming back to New York. She told him September. Two days later, Louis passed away in his sleep at home in the early hours of July 6, 1971. "I always regret that," she said of not coming back to New York to tape her reflections on life with Louis. "That thing hurts me so bad." Mama Lucy lived a quiet life until passing in 1987 and only left two extended interviews about her early days, neither ever published in full.

Her brother was different, of course. Louis left home in July 1922 and spent the next 49 years telling anyone within earshot about his days in New Orleans. He wrote books about it, and letters about it, and he sang songs about it. Those years taught him about music, about race, about women, about food, about society. They shaped every inch of his core. And he was in no rush to ever go back. Reminisce? Yes, every day. But to relive those early days in the South? The hunger? The poverty? The racism? Never again.

The journey of Armstrong from a "Boy from New Orleans" to the "Ambassador of Goodwill" on the Waldorf-Astoria stage was a remarkable one. After a backbreaking youth, plagued with "miserie," he had spent the bulk of his adulthood spreading joy. "They know I'm there in the cause of happiness," he once told *Life* writer Richard Meryman about his audience. "To Louis, no doubt, that date—his first at the Waldorf—was a kind of pinnacle, a very specific measurement of the distance from squalid [Jane] Alley," Meryman wrote after Armstrong's passing. "For that—and for him—I am much more happy than sad."[10]

It's quite likely that the majority of those who went to see Armstrong at the Waldorf were unaware or uninterested in his early days as a trailblazer; they just wanted to hear the hits and be entertained, and Armstrong made sure they were satisfied on both fronts. But to a later generation of jazz writers and musicologists, the Armstrong of 1971 bore no resemblance to the innovator who set about shaping the sound of American popular music through the power and swing of the trumpet solos and vocal stylings of his youth. To such critics, the 1920s represented Armstrong's peak, a young genius not yet tainted by the lure of commercialism, the pure soul who would never stoop to singing a "Hello, Dolly!" or a "What a Wonderful World" or hamming it up on stage and screen. The 1920s *do* represent the height of Armstrong's innovations—but they're also the years in which he performed comic sermons, did routines in drag, danced the Charleston, covered Broadway showtunes, played slide whistle, scatted through a megaphone, and fell in love with the sounds of Guy Lombardo. In other words, there's a consistency throughout Louis Armstrong's career that might not be readily apparent at a cursory glance, but his musical and entertainment values scarcely changed from his days in the honky-tonks of his hometown through that final performance at the Waldorf.

It's true that Armstrong's Hot Five and Hot Seven recordings had an incalculable influence on an entire century of music that followed. Recordings such as "Cornet Chop Suey," "Struttin' With Some Barbecue," "Potato Head Blues," "West End Blues," "Heebie Jeebies," "Weather Bird," and "Tight Like This," are still studied by up-and-coming musicians around the world as they provide the foundational language necessary to master the art of improvisation, as both a soloist and a vocalist.

But to some of Armstrong's critics, the last of that series of recordings—"Tight Like This," recorded on December 12, 1928—truly represented the beginning of the end—and the end of the beginning, a definitive closing of the door on Armstrong's perceived earlier "pure" style. With its humorous banter, tongue-in-cheek "Streets of Cairo" "snake charmer" trumpet quote, and melodramatic solo, "Tight Like This" was viewed as an abandonment of earlier principles. "Finally, on 'Tight Like This,' we hear the already-noted tendency toward commercialism, now at a more advanced stage, manifesting itself in an increasingly saccharine sentimentalism and a grandstanding high-note final chorus," Gunther Schuller would write.[11] Biographer James Lincoln Collier titled the post–"Tight Like This" chapter of his book "The Fork in the Road," while Thomas Brothers went one step further and called it "The White Turn." According to this view, as soon as the mythical year of 1928 ended and the wax was dry on "Tight Like This," Armstrong made the decision to embrace "commercialism" and comedy, sacrificing his supposed artistic ideals for cash and the adulation of white audiences.

The truth is Armstrong's performance values had not changed since New Orleans. He found his own voice on the trumpet and developed into a virtuosic soloist in Chicago, but he never stopped valuing the importance of tone, of melody, of playing the lead. His comedic antics could be traced back to his early days singing in a vocal quartet in New Orleans, but he also danced with King Oliver, did Bert Williams impressions with Fletcher Henderson, and brought down the house with a drag routine with Zutty Singleton in Chicago. Singing was in his blood before he picked up a cornet thanks to the encouragement of the Jewish Karnofsky family, and he was confident that he had a "million-dollar talent" in that voice of his that neither Oliver nor Henderson had cashed in on. He believed a musician should play "all kinds of music," which he first demonstrated back on the riverboats with Fate Marable. In Chicago, he played classical music, featured himself on the "Intermezzo" of *Cavalleria Rusticana*, improvised variations on Noel Coward's Broadway tune "Poor Little Rich Girl," and learned the latest popular hits introduced by Paul Whiteman and Guy Lombardo. If he had "gone commercial," perhaps it happened when he first learned pop tunes in the Colored Waif's Home or with his vocal quartet.

Thus, if anything, the Hot Five and Hot Seven recordings, as important as they are in the development of 20th-century music, actually presented Armstrong in a limited setting. Blazing trumpet solos and daring scat vocals in a New Orleans–inspired ensemble helped to establish his greatness, preserved on record for future generations to study, but they only scratched the surface compared to what he was doing night in and night out in New Orleans, New York, Chicago, and on the Mississippi River.

This is the third—and final—entry in my personal attempt to tell Armstrong's story and spotlight the artistic values that were consistent in each decade of his career. As in my other books, Armstrong's own words will carry the most weight here. This book is not meant to replace the musicological work of Brian Harker's *Louis Armstrong's Hot Five and Seven Recordings* or the sociological work prevalent in Thomas Brothers's *Louis Armstrong's New Orleans* and it especially isn't an excuse to forget about *Satchmo: My Life in New Orleans*. Part of the goal is to go deeper, when possible, than Armstrong did, bringing in the voices of the musicians he played with, his sister Beatrice, his second wife, Lil, and others who were there to create a chronological narrative closer to the actual history than his sometimes-faulty memory allowed. "People ask me about things happened fifty years ago," he told New Orleans historian Al Rose in the 1960s. "I can't remember what happened yesterday."[12]

This didn't stop Armstrong from devoting much of his adult life to sharing stories about his early days. On more than one of his private reel-to-reel tapes, he talked about doing it all "for posterity." He personally supplied Belgian author Robert Goffin with multiple handwritten notebooks containing stories from his life—and Goffin turned it into the melodramatic, dialect-heavy, almost "fan fiction" biography *Horn of Plenty*, which was widely panned by critics at the time of its publication in 1947. Though he never stated it, it does seem that at that moment, Armstrong came to the realization that he should be the one in charge of his own legacy. Armstrong never lost his humility, but he always remained very aware of his importance to the 20th century.

Once, after passing out hundreds of dollars to down-on-their-luck friends in Chicago in the 1950s, Armstrong was chewed out by his manager Joe Glaser for giving all his money away.

"What do I need money for?" Armstrong responded. "They're going to write about me in the history books one day."[13]

He was right.

1

"A Firecracker Baby!"

1901–1906

Let's begin with an irrefutable fact:

Louis Armstrong was born.

On that much, everyone can agree; after that, matters become murkier. A follow-up statement shouldn't stir up much controversy:

Louis Armstrong was born in 1901.

Hopefully most readers are still with me at this point, but there might be some who have "July 4, 1900," so ingrained in their minds that 1901 sounds peculiar.

But try this:

Louis Armstrong was born on July 4, 1901.

Cue the controversy.

Perhaps a summary is needed about the Louis Armstrong birthday fiasco. Armstrong first formally gave his birthday to the United States Draft Board on September 12, 1918, offering the date as "July 4, 1900."[1] Though far from stardom and not even yet a full-time musician, Armstrong continued to use this birthday for the rest of his life—except when filling out his social security application on May 25, 1937, when he told the government he was born July 4, 1901.[2] This discovery wasn't made until decades later and escaped public consciousness, which stuck to 1900.

Enter Tad Jones, a brilliant historian and scholar from New Orleans who was hired by Armstrong biographer Gary Giddins to conduct research on his behalf in the 1980s. Giddins admittedly "became obsessed with getting to the bottom of the birthday business,"[3] intrigued by a single line in Robert Goffin's "extremely problematic" 1947 Armstrong biography *Horn of Plenty*: "The next day little Louis was taken in his grandmother's arms to Sacred Heart Church to be christened."[4]

"So I went to Sacred Heart," Jones said, "and just walked into the rectory and said, 'Do you have a baptismal certificate for Louis Armstrong?' They said, 'Yes, we do.' They had a card catalog and they went through it. They said: 'Armstrong, Louis. The father's name is William Armstrong, the mother's name is Mary Albert.' It took about ten minutes."[5] The birthday on the baptismal certificate was August 4, 1901.

Around this time, Jones also discovered that the census records from April 1910 gave Armstrong's age as eight, disqualifying the 1900 birthdate. "The baptismal certificate and the 1910 census record backed each other up," Giddins wrote in an August 1988 *Village Voice* column titled "Happy Birthday, Pops." "Armstrong was, in fact, one year and one month younger than he said. All the parts fit." Almost overnight, much of the jazz community and most Armstrong fans around the world made the switch over to August 4, 1901, as the "real" birthday.

I personally have enjoyed and taken part in many August 4 celebrations in Armstrong's honor, but for the record, though I agree he was likely born in 1901, I believe August 4 was a meaningless date to Armstrong and the only birthday he ever knew and believed—and the one that might be the actual date—is July 4.

For one thing, Louis insisted July 4 was the date his mother, Mary "Mayann" Albert, told him as soon as he was cognizant, and it was the only date his sister Beatrice remembered celebrating during their childhood. When asked if Mayann would wish Louis a "Happy Birthday" on July 4 or tell him, "This is your birthday," Beatrice responded matter-of-factly, "Yeah, she'd tell him."[6] Louis once told British biographer Max Jones that it was "a blasting fourth of July, my mother called it, that I came into the world and they named me a firecracker baby."[7] The invocation of his beloved mother is an important one—why would Mayann lie about such a thing?

One sticking point comes right at the start of Armstrong's autobiography, *Satchmo: My Life in New Orleans*. "Mayann, told me, the night I was born, they had a great big shooting scrape in James Alley, and both guys killed one another," Armstrong wrote on page 1 of his manuscript.[8] Tad Jones took that clue and searched all the daily newspapers and the homicide reports of the New Orleans Police Department and the best match he could find was a fatal shooting that took place on July 16, 1901, on South Rocheblave between Gravier and Perdido Streets, just a few blocks away from where Armstrong was born on Jane Alley.[9]

Jones used this discovery as more evidence for August 4, arguing that even though the homicide occurred 19 days before that date, Mayann would have associated it with Louis's birth. "By all evidence, Mary Albert could neither read nor write," Jones said in 2001. "It was common for those who could not relate to the written word to record major events in their lives by marking time by some extraordinary circumstance or event. As the years passed and her memory faded, discrepancy of time is easily explained."[10]

This seems a bit unfair to Mayann, who, according to the 1900 and 1920 census and Louis himself, "could read and write a little."[11] The July 16 shooting occurred closer to July 4 than August 4; wouldn't it make more sense for her to recall this shooting taking place with a 12-day-old baby in her arms—leading her to tell Louis it happened when he was a newborn—rather than if she was eight months pregnant in the New Orleans summer humidity? As Michael Steinman has written, "Although Mayann's formal education must have been limited, I believe that she wouldn't confuse July and August when remembering her delivery."[12]

But the shakiest bit of evidence for the August 4 date is the actual baptism itself, which did officially take place on August 25, 1901. The registry is written in Latin and lists Armstrong as the 70th entry, giving his birthday as August 4. But what about the child baptized just before Louis? Entry number 69 was reserved for baby Dominic Martina, born to parents Antonio Martina and Rosalia Garlo and given a birthday of August 15. Dominic Martina's life can be charted thoroughly through census and government records, and he was consistent in giving his birthday—as *June* 15, 1901, the date on his World War II draft registration card and the date listed in the Social Security Index, among other places.

Thus, both Armstrong and Martina were given August birthdays at Sacred Heart, yet each man lived into the 1970s claiming birth months of July and June, respectively. Perhaps it was a humid August day and the priest was tired, or maybe there was a language barrier or, 25 days into the month, he just assumed all babies being brought in that day were August babies and besides, who is going to care 125 years from now? And am I the only person skeptical enough to find the August 4/July 4 conflation a little too tidy?[13]

To bring it back to the beginning, how did Robert Goffin even know about the Sacred Heart baptism in the first place? Jones believed Armstrong told Goffin, "When I was three weeks old, my grandmother took me to be baptized at Sacred Heart Church,'" Jones told *Offbeat* in 2002. Armstrong did supply Goffin with copious amounts of material, but in no surviving document does he mention being baptized at Sacred Heart—nor does it come up in any of his other autobiographical writings, published or unpublished. So where did Goffin get the information if not from Louis? The only logical answer would appear to be Louis's paternal grandmother, Josephine, whom Goffin likely interviewed while in New Orleans researching his 1945 book *La Nouvelle-orleans, Capitale Du Jazz*. Josephine supplied information that even Louis didn't know about—how many people can immediately recall the details of their own baptism?—but Goffin's work, even with Louis and Grandma Josephine's cooperation, still stuck with a July 4 birthday and even alluded to young Louis adding a year to make himself appear older, lending even more credence to the date of July 4, 1901.

In summary, did Louis add a year and fudge the 1900 portion of his famous birthday? Almost certainly. And do I state that Louis Armstrong was definitively born on July 4, 1901, no questions asked? Absolutely not. After all of this, could he have been born on August 4, 1901? Sure—but I just have too much skepticism to embrace a date that only appears one time in an era when such documentation was frequently riddled with errors. And if forced to choose, I'd prefer respecting the date Louis and his family went by over one jotted down by a Catholic priest who had already made one mistake that day. Tad Jones truly believed Armstrong secretly knew he was born on August 4, but when asked why Armstrong would have chosen July 4 instead at such a young age, Jones responded, "Beats me."[14]

Perhaps New Orleans trumpeter Gregg Stafford put it best. "My feeling was always that, okay, if Louis Armstrong celebrated his birthday all his life on the Fourth of July, he must have known that—they must have told him that," Stafford says. "It's as if to say that he was lying around his birthday. He wasn't around to challenge it, so what are you going to do, change his birthday because of a paper that says another date?"[15]

Louis Armstrong, born on the Fourth of July, 1901. Maybe he was, maybe he wasn't, but that's the date this book will follow. In the end, it's all irrelevant; the bottom line is Louis Armstrong was born and that alone is something to celebrate.

All of the foregoing is not to discredit the late Tad Jones; his discovery of that baptismal record is perhaps the most monumental Armstrong find of the 20th century and was still what Jones was best known for at the time of his untimely death in 2007. But Jones's impeccable research skills turned up many more discoveries about Armstrong's genealogy and years in New Orleans, work that has been expanded on by Dan Vernhettes and Bo Lindstöm in their outstanding *Jazz Puzzles* series of books, along with some recent discoveries by the author of this book, all of which are combined into the following brief summary of Armstrong's ancestry.

Jones was the first person to trace Armstrong's ancestry back to a slave in Richmond, Virginia, named Daniel Walker, born circa 1792 in Africa, though the exact region has not been identified. On May 18, 1818, French colonist and banker Jean Baptiste Moussier sold the 26-year-old Walker to Antoine Turcas in the Parish of Orleans for 1,200 plastres (roughly $600), one of 18 slaves Turcas bought and sold between 1815 and 1818. Turcas was born in southern France but, according to the 1822 Soards's City Directory, was living in New Orleans at 166 and 72 St. Ann Street, on the corner of Burgundy.[16]

Daniel Walker eventually fathered a son, also named Daniel Walker, who was most likely born in the late 1820s. He later married a slave named Catherine Washington, born either as early as 1835 or as late as 1844, according to conflicting census records. Washington grew up on a plantation in Madison County, Mississippi, and was auctioned off with her mother and sister to New Orleans, where she met the younger Daniel Walker. By the time of the 1870 federal census, Walker was living with Washington in New Orleans and working as a drayman. Though they didn't legally marry until September 2, 1884, Daniel and Catherine Walker already had three children, Septine, Josephine, and Daniel Jr.

(Perhaps this is a good time to address the three generations of Daniel Walkers that lend credence to the "Daniel" that often appears in Louis Armstrong's name, as either Louis Daniel Armstrong or even Daniel Louis Armstrong. The "Daniel" doesn't appear on the baptismal certificate and doesn't even appear in print until a 1934 *Melody Maker* story about Armstrong's childhood.[17] "Daniel Louis" started showing up in the 1940s, gaining traction after being used in *Time*'s 1949 cover story, but when questioned about it by young fan Marion Gustowski in the 1950s, Armstrong was adamant that his name was not Daniel and seemed miffed about it.[18] He usually just gave his name as "Louis Armstrong" but at one point in *Satchmo: My Life in New Orleans* he did refer to himself as "Louis Satchmo Daniel Armstrong," opening the door to it being a middle name.[19] Toward the end of his life, he told Max Jones, "I was born Louis Armstrong. The Daniel came later from somewheres 'down the line.' It came out of the clear blue skies, I guess. I don't remember Mayann ever calling me Daniel. It's not important anyway."[20] But it *is* on his death certificate as his middle name and should probably be taken seriously, given the amount of "Daniels" in his lineage on his father's side.)

Middle child Josephine Walker was born on August 19, 1866, according to her birth record and the 1870 census.[21] She would go on to give birth to Louis Armstrong's father, William (b. 1881), a daughter, Liza Elizabeth (who died at 18 days old on September 29, 1883), and two more sons, Joseph (b. 1886) and Oliver (b. 1891). The paternity of these children has long been a mystery, but Tad Jones discovered the death certificate of Liza Elizabeth, listing her as the daughter of Josephine and "Ephram" Armstrong.[22] Jones also discovered, in a "Record of Bodies Deceased" at New Orleans's Charity Hospital in March 1890, a record of a 41-year-old Ephraim Armstrong, born in Mobile, Alabama, but living in New Orleans in the Liberty and Perdido Street neighborhood, where little Louis later grew up. Ephraim died on March 17, 1890, of cirrhosis of the liver.[23]

A great deal of speculation is needed when trying to untangle the family tree of Louis Armstrong's mother, Mary Estelle Albert. She hailed from Boutte, Louisiana, a small town located about 25 miles from New Orleans, and though her birth name was Mary Estelle, folks knew her as Mary Ann, or as Louis called her, "Mayann." The 1900 census gives Mary Albert a birthday in January 1885, corroborated by the 1910 census, which gives her age as 25. However, the 1920 census gives her age as 37, something that carried over to her record in the Illinois Death Index, which gives a birth year of 1883.

Nothing has ever been mentioned about her parents, but perhaps some clues can be found when examining the life of her maternal grandmother, Florentine Johnson. According to the paperwork that accompanied the purchase of the property at 723 Jane Alley on December 21, 1897, she was listed as "Mrs. Florentine Johnson, widowed by first marriage to Prince Albert and widowed of second marriage to Thomas Johnson."[24] Going back to the 1880 census, one finds 30-year-old Florentine living in Boutte with her husband, 35-year-old Thomas Johnson, and their three children, 15-year-old Jules, 9-year-old Frances, and 1-year-old Aaron. Living right next door was her first husband, Prince Albert, originally from Mississippi, now married, coincidentally enough, to a 31-year-old housekeeper named Mary Albert. They had a son, also named Prince Albert, who married Mary Davis of Boutte, Louisiana, in 1882.[25] There isn't any information on Mary Davis after that date, and the 1900 census lists 42-year-old Prince Albert as a convict at the Louisiana State Penitentiary in Baton Rouge; perhaps they were Mary Albert's parents?

There is one more bit of confusion to add to all of this. Florentine and Thomas Johnson's daughter, Frances, eventually married Isaac "Ike" Myles, who would play a large role in young Louis Armstrong's formative years. When George Avakian asked Louis in 1953 exactly what Isaac Myles's relationship was to Mary Albert, Armstrong responded, "Ike Myles was her brother-in-law, see. We called him Uncle Ike." That means that Louis grew up believing that Frances Johnson was Mary Albert's sister or half-sister, which couldn't be possible—unless Florentine Johnson was actually Mary Albert's mother instead of grandmother.[26]

Louis never bothered trying to figure out his mother's genealogy. "She came from a slave," he said in 1969. "She never told me much about her parents. We was so busy struggling she didn't have time to reminisce. But she had it rougher when she was a teenager comin' up."[27] It does feel like there are some answers buried somewhere within the street in Boutte, Louisiana, with the Johnsons living next door to the Alberts.

What's not disputed is that by 1895, Florentine Johnson was living in New Orleans, listed as "Flora Johnson" at 515 St. Ann Street in that year's Soards's

New Orleans City Directory. She remained there until December 1897, when she purchased a new home at 723 Jane Alley—Louis Armstrong's eventual birthplace.

Jane Alley was one block in length, bounded by Perdido, Gravier, South Broad and South White streets. Only two houses were on the street in 1896, but it had grown to 10 by 1900. The property at 723 Jane Alley was originally purchased by John Maltry, a white cigar maker, in January 1897. In December that same year, Maltry sold the residence to Flora Johnson for $400. Segregation was the law of the land, especially after the landmark "separate but equal" *Plessy v. Ferguson* trial in New Orleans in 1896, but that didn't stop Johnson from being the first African American to purchase property on that street.

In January 1898, Johnson was joined at 723 Jane Alley by her daughter, Frances, and Frances's husband, Isaac Myles,[28] born in 1857 and according to the 1900 census, a Black laborer who could not read or write. Frances and Isaac Myles were married in 1887 and had four children by 1900: Jeremiah (b. 1890), Louise (b. 1892), Sarah (b. 1895), and Edward (b. 1896). Flora Johnson passed away in March 1900, leaving the house to Isaac and Frances, who eventually received help with the rent from two boarders: Mary Albert and Willie Armstrong.[29]

How and when Mary and Willie met is lost to posterity, but they could not have courted for long before conceiving baby Louis. According to the 1900 census, 15-year-old Mary began the year living with her grandmother, Rosa Marshall, and two young siblings, 7-year-old brother Samuel and 6-year-old sister Sarah at 614 St. Phillips Street. But at some point, she ended up at 723 Jane Alley and met Willie Armstrong, "a tall nice looking guy," in the words of his future son. "Brown skinned, with holes in his face—indications of healed small pox."[30] Mary Albert would have been pregnant by the end of the year for Louis to have been born in the summer of 1901.

What kind of home was 723 Jane Alley? A nearby property at 731 Jane Alley was advertised as a "Cozy Single Cottage" in January 1901.[31] Tad Jones described Louis Armstrong's birthplace as follows:

> The house, like many others on the alley, was a wood frame with a slate roof often referred to as a box house. There were three rooms for living with a wooden partition dividing the house with a brick fireplace for cooking and heating, drinking water supplied by rain drained from the roof in a large wooden cistern. There was no electricity. Light was supplied by oil lamps. Behind the house was a small backyard with a two-hole privy and a stable. Washing was done outside in large metal tubs. The house was set back 20 feet from the street, was raised with small steps

> going up to the front door. Gutters were dug and grated along the flat mud street that connected Gravier to Perdido. . . . There were no saloons or grocery stores in the neighborhood, only a few small businesses.[32]

The actual makeup of the neighborhood of Jane Alley is something that has been seemingly exaggerated with each telling of Armstrong's tale. Robert Goffin was the first to describe it as something resembling the seventh circle of hell in *Horn of Plenty*, a "cutthroat alley," "truly a tragic and bloody lane[, a] fearful hiding place for the dregs of the city's Negro population." Goffin also described it as the scene of constant brawls and knife fights. "Women scream

Figure 1.1 Two unidentified boys sit on the front steps of Louis Armstrong's birthplace at 723 Jane Alley in 1963, the year before the home was bulldozed by the city of New Orleans.

Credit: Photo by Dr. Edmond Souchon, Courtesy of the New Orleans Jazz Club Collection of the Louisiana State Museum.

as they try to defend their men," he wrote. "Suddenly a rending cry ends in a gruesome death rattle; a man lies in agony, dying like a dog; and over the dark earth flows the dark blood of a dark man."[33]

Louis Armstrong remembered so little of Jane Alley that he spent much of his adult life not knowing its actual name. "From the day I was born in James Alley," he wrote in 1950, quickly adding, "some say Jane but to me it is just plain ol James Alley."[34] In the manuscript to his autobiography, *Satchmo: My Life in New Orleans*, Armstrong took a stab at describing the neighborhood that seemed to borrow from Goffin, writing, "James Alley was right in the heart of the Battle Field...It was named the Battle Field because those bad charactors [*sic*] would shoot and fight so much." Describing the makeup of the street, he added, "In this one block there were, Church People, Gamblers, Hustlers, Cheap Pimps, Thieves, Prostitutes, and lots of children,..Infact, people of all walks of life lived in James Alley......There were several bars, honky tonks, and Barooms [*sic*], and Saloons.... Lots of women walking the streets, catching tricks taking them to their pads....meaning their room."[35]

But upon a closer examination of the 1900 census, there were 36 residents occupying the eight wood frame houses on Jane Alley, 14 white, 22 Black. They included James Johnson, a white carpenter, with his wife and three children at 719 Jane Alley; Frank Poole, a Negro laborer and widower, with three children at 725; German-born Joanna O'Rourke, keeping the home for a family of three at 731; Matilda Gibson and Christine Hutchinson, Negro washerwomen, at 733; Thomas Grant, a Negro screwman, at 743; and Mary Peterson, a washerwoman of Swedish and Irish ancestry, with her four children, at the end of Jane Alley. "Not only was the Alley racially integrated, but there were a variety of nationalities and occupations," Tad Jones said. "There are no police reports, no homicide reports, no reports of shootings, and knifings, no newspaper accounts, no crime reports, no eyewitness accounts, no oral history, there's nothing. . . . The inhabitants at the Alley were lower and middle class people, many were homeowners, and most were employed and productive citizens."[36]

One can't blame Armstrong for romanticizing the "Battlefield" aspect of Jane Alley since he really had no possible way of remembering anything accurately about the state of Jane Alley at the time he was born. By the end of 1901, the three-bedroom structure was home to nine people: Isaac and Frances Myles and their four children and Mary Albert, Willie Armstrong, and baby Louis Armstrong.

But by the time the 1902 Soards's Directory was published, Willie Armstrong was giving his address as nearby 824 South Dupre Street, the residence of the Walker family; Daniel Walker Jr. gave this as his address in the 1901 Soards's Directory. But, more important than Daniel Walker, this address was the residence of Josephine Armstrong and Catherine Walker, Louis's grandmother and great-grandmother—and soon it was the residence of young Louis Armstrong. "I lived with my great-grandmother back o' town, about two blocks from James Alley," Louis recalled in 1969. "It was like the wilderness, nothing but shacks."[37]

It's assumed that Mary Albert was raising baby Louis at 723 Jane Alley in this period, but it's quite possible that she was living with Willie at 824 South Dupre in 1902. It's also possible Willie left Mayann almost immediately after Louis was born to live with another woman, as Louis wrote: "After two years, my father quit this other woman and he and my mother Mayann got together again and tried to make another go of it."[38] Sure enough, at some point in the early part of 1902, Willie and Mayann conceived another child, Beatrice Armstrong, born January 9, 1903.

The reunion was short-lived; Willie left for good shortly after the birth of Beatrice. "The man who Mayann told us was our father left us the day we were born," Louis wrote shortly before he died, the "us" meaning him and Beatrice.[39] Louis once said that Mayann "married Willie Armstrong" but caught himself and quickly added, "I mean, I'm only going by what they telling me along them lines because as long as I could remember, they weren't together. Mayann carried me and [sister] Mama Lucy, I never seen him. I never seen them live together. They must have separated before I could understand what the hell was happening."[40] Willie moved uptown and out of Louis and Beatrice's life, eventually working at the American Turpentine & Tar Company, which opened in the fall of 1905, and marrying a woman named Gertrude Nolan in March 1906, starting a new family of his own.

Mayann wouldn't be far behind. "My mother went to live in another fast neighborhood, down to Liberty and Perdido (a cheap, storyville section)," Armstrong wrote. Frances Myles gave birth to another daughter, Flora, in 1902 but passed away shortly after on June 13, 1903. After her death, Isaac Myles packed up his many children,[41] left 723 Jane Alley, and moved into a flat in a tenement building known as "Brick Row" at 1305 Perdido Street. Mayann and baby Beatrice would eventually join them in the room next door at 1303 Perdido. For her part, Beatrice didn't have any memories of Jane Alley except for its proximity to the House of Detention. But she remembered why she left: "My mama took me out [of] James Alley in her arms," she recalled in 1983, using the same name for the street as her brother. "She had been running my daddy, run him out. Yeah, he was a terrible man."[42]

Looking back at this period in his life, Louis wrote, "My mother went away, to another neighborhood, leaving me with my grandmother....And my father he went another direction, to live with another woman....So that left me, practically an infant, without a mother and father . . . " Or as he wrote another time, invoking his sister's nickname, "Mama Lucy + I were bastards from the start."[43]

All Louis could remember, from when his earliest memories began to form, was the care of Josephine Armstrong at 824 South Dupre Street. "I stayed with my grandmother so long until I'd begun to call her mother, as I grew up," Louis wrote, adding, "From a baby, I have always had great love for my grandmother... Quite naturally, she spent the rest of her days raising me. Teaching me right from wrong, in the most important [time] of a young kid's life...."[44] This included lessons about discipline. "When ever I would do something that grandma thought I should get a whipping for, she would send me out to get a switch-from that big old chinaball tree she had in her yard, so she could whip me," Louis wrote. "She would say to me, you have been a bad boy, now go out to that tree and bring back a switch off of it, and come here and get your whipping... Huh...with tears in my eyes, I would go to that tree and get the smallest switch I could find...She would laugh and let me off—most of the times...." Other times, Louis didn't get off as easily. "But if she was real angry," he wrote, "she would whip me, and give me a lick for every thing I had done for weeks..."[45]

Louis also got his first lessons in the Jim Crow South from his grandmother, a former slave. "Look, Pops, I come out of a party of the South where it ain't no way in the world you can forget you're colored," he told *Ebony* in 1964. "My own mother went through hell down there. My Grandma used to have tears in her eyes when she'd talk about the lynchings and all that crap."[46] Louis never forgot the bitter words of Grandma Josephine, understandably beaten down from a life of oppression. He shared with his friend Jack Bradley in 1967, "My grandmother told me when I was a little boy, 'A Nigger ain't shit!" Of the years that followed, he added, "I always believed that."[47]

The question remains: why did Mayann take her infant daughter and leave her son behind? It was probably interference from the Walkers and Armstrongs, who were protective of little Louis—and opposed to Mayann's rowdy lifestyle. Robert Goffin spoke to Josephine Armstrong in the 1940s and quoted her advice to young Louis: "Them that kicks over the traces too quick forgets that I seen the day when we was sold on the hoof like dumb cattle. Them that goes too fast gets nowhere. Them that shines and makes a lot of fuss in Perdido are goners. Them gamblers, them drunkards, them no-good women, them pimps, they'll all be in jail before you grows a beard."[48]

If the recollection of such advice is accurate, Josephine Armstrong most likely had Louis's mother in mind as, over on Perdido Street, Mayann was drinking heavily and living it up. The protective Louis later wrote, "Whether

Maryann was hustling, I could not say," but she most definitely was.[49] Mayann's lifestyle caught up with her on September 3, 1905, when she and Annie Reed were arrested on Lafayette and Girord Streets "relative to Drunkenness and Disturbing the Peace." Mayann gave her name as Mary Ann Albert and her age as 21; she was living at the time with the 28-year-old Reed at 728 South Liberty Street. Both Albert and Reed were listed as "prostitutes" in the First Precinct's arrest book. After an evening in jail, they were sentenced by Judge John T. Fogarty—a legendary figure who became immortalized in the lyrics sung by Jelly Roll Morton on "Buddy Bolden Blues"—to either pay a $10 fine or spend 30 days in the House of Detention. Unable to come up with the money, both women were sent to the House of Detention. Presumably, two-year-old Beatrice stayed with Uncle Ike and his children for the next month.

Once released, Mayann went back to a life of prostitution—and heavy drinking—and eventually wound up at 1303 Perdido Street, next door to Ike Myles. That property was still possessed by one Mamie Lewis on April 24, 1906, when the *Daily Picayune* reported that a man was shot there.[50] Lewis would eventually move to nearby 431 South Franklin Street, opening up the room for Mayann to inhabit by the summer of 1906. It was around this time that she fell ill and needed help—help watching baby Beatrice, help making ends meet, help while she was sick and couldn't earn her regular money on the streets. She needed help from her five-year-old son, Louis.

Louis connected his reunion with his mother to a time when "they had what was called a drought...No water to be found anywheres...It hadn't rained for ages . . . "[51] New Orleans was indeed ravaged by a major drought in the spring of 1906. "After sixty-four days, with a precipitation during that time of only 2.20 inches, New Orleans is to-day experiencing one of the most serious [droughts] that has occurred in this vicinity in years," the *Times-Democrat* reported on June 1.[52]

According to Louis, when "On this particular day I was helping out getting this water along with the rest of the neighbors of James Alley, an elderly lady (a friend of Mayann) came to my grandma's house with a message from Mayann, saying she was very Ill and she and Willie (my dad) had broken up again."[53] Grandma Josephine had "tears in her eyes" as she dressed Louis, telling him, "I really hate to let you out of my sight." Louis, with a "warbly throat," responded, "I am so sorry to leave you too, Granny." "At five, I broke down and cried," he remembered.

Louis continued crying until Mayann's friend snapped at him. "Louis, if you don't be a good boy and stop crying, I will have to put you in the house of detention, where they keep the bad men and women," she threatened. "Now you don't want to go there do you?" Louis stopped crying immediately.

Once on the streetcar, Louis had his "first experience of the 'James Crow' at five," as he later put it in a striking story that opens *My Life in New Orleans*. Unable to read, he didn't notice the "FOR COLORED PATRONS ONLY" sign and sat in one of the seats in the front of the car reserved for white people. "Come here, boy," Mayann's friend scolded him, "and sit where you belong." Louis instead started "acting cute," until the woman "snatched me up by the hand so fast, it made my head swim....And quick as a flash, I was sitting in the rear seat, as far back as she could get me....My goodness, that lady was so frightened, she changed colors." Louis asked what the sign said only to be met with, "Boy, don't ask so many questions, and SIT DOWN DAMIT."[54]

They got off the streetcar at Tulane Avenue and Liberty Street and walked two blocks toward Perdido Street. After five years, Louis was about to make his very first memories of his mother.

2

"Everything Happened in the Brick Row"

1906–1910

"You did come to see your mother, didn't you?" Mayann asked her son.

"Yes, mother," Louis responded, holding back tears, not knowing how to feel. He couldn't help but notice the poverty-ridden living conditions of this "Brick Row" home. Mayann had just enough room to sleep, take care of baby Beatrice, and wash and dry her clothes in their one-room apartment. Louis would make a lot of memories in this location, good and bad. "Oh everything Happened in the Brick Row," he once wrote.[1]

"I was afraid Grandma wouldn't let you," Mayann stated frankly before admitting, "After all, I realized I haven't done what I should by you. But Son, Mama will make it up."

Suddenly, she thought of Willie.

"If it wasn't for that no good father of yours, a no good bastard, I am sure everything would [have] been better."

She calmed down and resumed comforting her son. "I try to do the best I can," she said. "I am all by myself here with my baby."

It might have been overwhelming for young Louis to see his own mother—whom he didn't know—bashing his father—whom he didn't know—while crying out for help. Looking back at it 50 years later, he wrote, "Although I remember the situation until this minute, I didn't know whether that was good or, was it BAD." He didn't have time to process it and simply decided, "All I know, I was with my mother, whom I'd always loved the same as I did my grandmother."

Louis also recalled that in the next breath, Mayann imparted wisdom Louis would live by for the rest of his life: "Always remember, when you're sick, ain't nobody's gonna give you nothin....So try to stay healthy....Even without money, your health is the thing........" Mayann then made her son promise her one thing: "I shall see that you take a physic at least once a week," she vowed. "And I want you to promised me that you will take a physic, as long as you live."[2] No son has ever taken his mother's advice to heart as much as Louis Armstrong did on this matter.

After taking three Coal Roller Pills, Louis soon felt a pain and ran outside to an outhouse in the yard. "And they had one toilet—well, they wasn't toilets, they was old privies," he said. "Outhouse now, but privies in the early days. Like I tell you, when you go there, you're liable to see a turd on that seat, God, it looked like a trombone! . . . They don't to try to adjust themselves, they just shit all over the fucking seat!" Armstrong also recalled there was no toilet paper and the residents of Brick Row used pages from Sears and Roebuck catalogs.[3] Coal Roller Pills were purchased over the counter, but for much of Louis's childhood, Mayann saved money by doing it herself. "My mother used to go over the railroad tracks and pick up that same shit, they used to call it pepper grass, Senna leaves, all that shit was in Swiss Kriss," Armstrong said, referring to the laxative he began taking in the 1950s. "And mama would bring that shit home and boil it and give it to us, boy, shit, you'd have thought it was Sousa's Band! Remember that intermezzo?" At that moment, Armstrong began scatting "Stars and Stripes Forever," interspersed with sounds of flatulence. "Every morning!" he added emphatically.[4] After taking a nap, Mayann gave Louis 50 cents and sent him to J. O. Zatarain's grocery store at 361 South Rampart Street to purchase salt meat, red beans, and rice, and asked him to stop at Frederick Staehle's bakery at 406 South Rampart to pick up two loaves of bread for a nickel. This section of Rampart Street, stretching from the 200 block to the 800 block, was known as "Black Storyville" or the "Colored Red-Light District," a place for African Americans who were not welcome on nearby Canal Street. Most of the businesses on South Rampart were owned by Sicilian and Jewish immigrants, in addition to a small Chinatown section, which helped inspire Armstrong's lifelong love affair with Chinese cuisine.

Prostitution was an integral part of the scene, too, especially on South Franklin Street, where it was assuredly practiced by Mayann. Over on the corner of South Franklin and Gravier Street was one of the saloons that regularly featured gambling, which often ended with outbursts of violence that were only stopped when the police showed up. They didn't have far to travel; across from the saloon was an imposing sight that made a lasting impression on the young Louis. "The court house, parish prison, police station, and the morgue, all in one square of buildings, were direct across the street from the honky tonk," he would later write.[5]

This would be young Louis's first time exploring the neighborhood he would call home for the next several years. Contrary to any clouded memories about the perceived dangers of Jane Alley, his new Third Ward "back o'town" neighborhood was the real "Battlefield."

"Hey you—are you a mama's boy?" taunted the "big bad bully" known as "One Eye Bud" after he spotted the new kid on the block in his prissy Little Lord Fauntleroy outfit. When Armstrong questioned the meaning of such a term—he had been reunited with his actual mother literally moments earlier—One Eye Bud soiled Armstrong's clothing with a handful of mud. Armstrong responded by launching a right cross to his tormentor's mouth. "I had his nose and his mouth bleeding plenty," he later wrote. "You know how a guy can fight when he's scared?" The bullies took off and Armstrong thought about running after them but admitted, "Then too—I didn't want to."[6]

That was little Louis Armstrong's introduction to his new neighborhood. "As bad as James Alley was I could see the [difference] in the kids," he said. "There were no kids in the Alley as bad as this Liberty and Perdido gang."[7] A bigger threat was waiting for him at home, where Mayann "gave me a good flogging for getting my nice suit dirty, can you imagine that?"[8]

It wouldn't be the only time Armstrong had to prove his toughness in his new neighborhood, leading to a bit of a reputation as a "bad boy." Asked about this by Max Jones in 1970, Armstrong responded, "All boys were bad in those days—you'd better believe it," adding: "You must realize it was very shaky all the time during my days coming up in New Orleans. Especially those early ones. They were rough. You had to fight and do a lot of ungodly things to keep from being trampled on. Sure I had fights and did a number of rough things, just so I could have a little peace or elbow room as we used to express it."[9]

Bullies aside, Armstrong found a lot to embrace in this part of town, including exposure to a completely multiethnic neighborhood. "All of the saloon keepers are Italian," Tad Jones said. "A lot of them had phonographs and they would've been playing Italian operas and arias. He's a few blocks from Chinatown. All of the shopkeepers on Rampart are German Jews, speaking Yiddish. He hears the French language on a daily basis. He's exposed to every language imaginable during that time period. So this is going to impact him for the rest of his life."[10]

With a saloon on every corner employing bands of all sizes, the biggest impact this neighborhood had on Armstrong was its vibrant music scene. "Music has been in my blood from the first day I was born," he later declared.[11] He might have heard some solo piano playing at venues near Jane Alley, "But at Liberty and Perdido, Franklin and Perdido, Gravier and Franklin, Poydras and Franklin, all within one square, and a honky tonk on each corner, they all had musical instruments in them," he wrote, almost with a sense of wonder. "Real live instruments . . . "[12] Though not called "jazz" yet, the music Louis would devote his life to was developing rapidly right in Armstrong's backyard—almost literally.

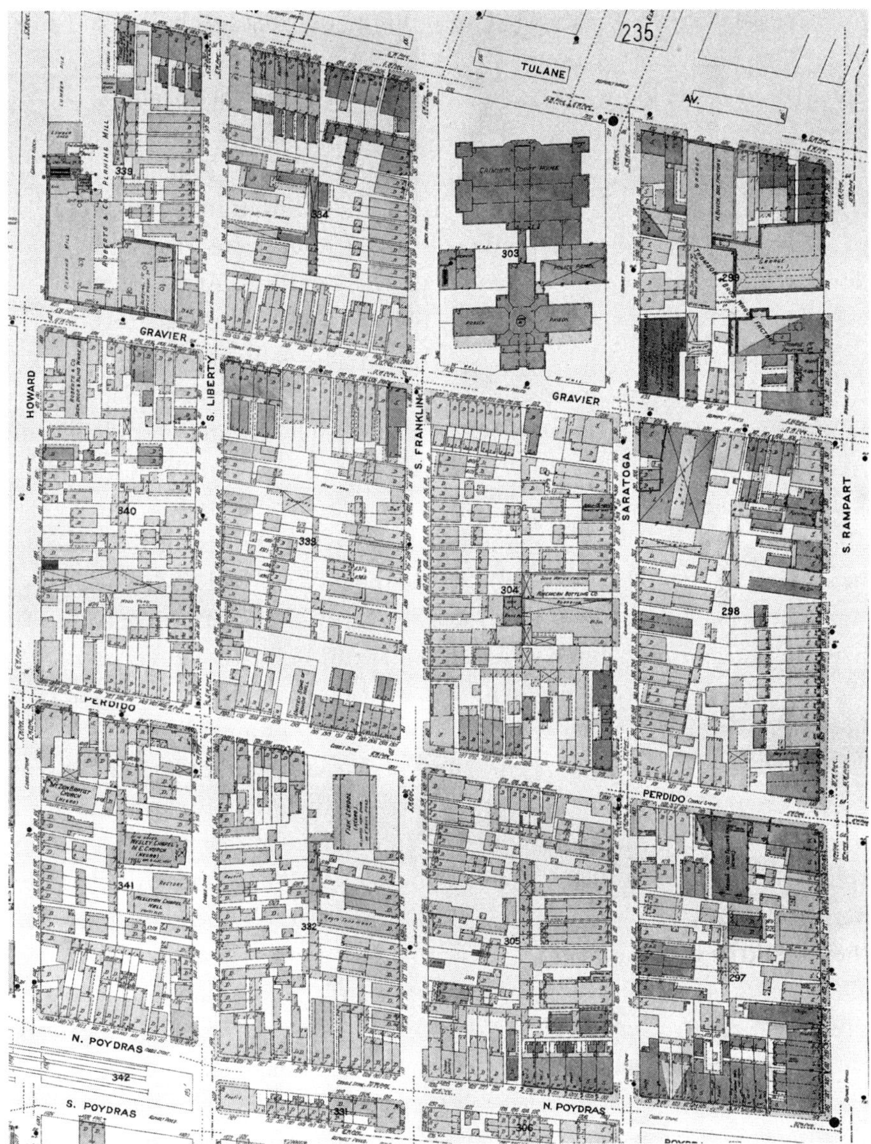

Figure 2.1 1908 Sanborn Fire Insurance Map of Armstrong’s Third Ward neighborhood, including touchstones such as his Brick Row residence at 1303 Perdido, the future home of Henry Matranga’s honky-tonk across the street at 1233 Perdido, Elder Cosey’s Mt. Zion Baptist Church on Howard Street, the prostitute’s cribs on South Franklin Street, the backdrop of Parish Prison and the police station, the two-block walk to South Rampart Street, and much more.

Credit: Library of Congress, Geography and Map Division, Sanborn Maps Collection. Composite of four separate maps created by Matthew Rivera.

Cornetist Charles "Buddy" Bolden, still generally thought of as the "Father of Jazz," made his reputation with his lowdown performances at the Union Sons' Hall—better known as the Funky Butt Hall. And with an address of 1319 Perdido Street, Armstrong—residing at 1303 Perdido Street—couldn't avoid hearing Bolden's band, at least outdoors. "I remember hearing Buddy Bolden when I was five years old," he recalled in 1956. "In those days they used to play in the Funky Butt Hall, see? They'd play a half-hour in front of the Hall, you know, outside, then they'd go in and play. Well, when they'd play that half, we kids could . . . dance and I was in my little old dress, you know? And I'd be wailing and having a ball!"[13]

How much Armstrong actually absorbed of Bolden's playing, though, is up for debate. Armstrong chastised Bolden for blowing "too hard," but that seems to be an opinion he formed in later years. When asked in 1939 by William Russell if Bolden blew too loud, Armstrong tellingly responded, "Yeah, that's all they ever tell me."[14] And if he indeed returned to his mother's care around June 1906, he would have heard Bolden at the tail end of his career, as Bolden was institutionalized in 1907 and from then on lived the last 24 years of his life in an insane asylum.[15] But even if he only heard Bolden for a few months in 1906 and didn't even realize who he was, the fact remains that he was happy to just be dancing and responding to the music in his "little old dress."

And though Bolden might be best known as the "Father of Jazz" and for his mastery of the blues, Armstrong remembered hearing different types of music in this period. "The Funky Butt gave me quite a bit of my ear for music and inspiration," he wrote in 1950. "They would play Ragtime, Fox trots, Waltzs [*sic*], Tangos, Mazookas [*sic*—Mazurkas], Scottische in fact all kind of tempos which helped me through the years to play with different orchestras, symphany [*sic*], show music etc."[16] Armstrong's exposure to different types of music made a deep impression early on and inspired musical values that would last a lifetime.

Of his new neighborhood, Armstrong wrote, "The kids were bad but the good music made up for it and after all I had proven to myself I could look out for little Louis."[17] He'd be looking out for himself for the foreseeable future.

Back at Brick Row, Louis was introduced to his many new cousins, Ike Myles's children in the flat next to his mother's. "My uncle's wife was dead so he had to struggle with all of those kids alone," Louis recalled. "He was a good Joe, in spite of the hard times he worked all he could to help feed all of us because May-Ann was having a pretty tough time herself."[18]

Louis quickly learned that he would do a lot more than just occasionally eat meals with his cousins; Uncle Ike's apartment became something of a second home during these early years. "If it wasn't for Uncle Ike a lot of times, I don't know what Mammy Lucy and I would have done," Louis wrote. "Because when ever Mayann would get the yen to go out and have a good time, we might not see her for days an days...And she too would dump us right into Uncle Ike's [lap]."[19] Clearly, a combination of her work as a prostitute and her propensity for alcoholic benders kept Mayann out of the picture for days at a time, perhaps even longer, making Uncle Ike's a place of welcome refuge.

Both Louis and Beatrice remembered the sleeping situation at Uncle Ike's, with Louis sleeping between cousins Aaron and Isaac Jr. and Beatrice sleeping between Flora and Louise. As for Uncle Ike, Mama Lucy recalled, "He'd take two chairs and put an iron board [across them], you know, that's where he used to sleep. Louis, too, all of us, too. Some of us laying under the bed, in the bed, he had but one bed."[20] Having everyone piled together led to some uncomfortable incidents. Once, annoyed by Isaac Jr.'s constant poking from behind, Louis elbowed him in the stomach and said, "Hey there, Isaac, remove your finger and stop that playing." "Hmmm," Isaac replied, "This ain't my finger and I ain't no playing."[21]

This would be Louis Armstrong's life over the next year, basically living as a five-year-old street urchin, running errands to Rampart Street for his mother, absorbing any music he heard along the way, and sleeping with his cousins when his mother disappeared. Since he would not be able to enroll in school until October 1, 1907, this also meant a lot of time was spent at home looking after his baby sister, Beatrice, who now went by a new nickname: "Mama Lucy."

Even that moniker was a result of Mayann not being the most attentive mother. A lady lived nearby who was "losing her mind" according to Beatrice. "If Mama turn her back, she'd come in and take me out the house, bring me to her house," she said. One day, the lady stole baby Beatrice and brought her to her home to make her a meal—which turned out to be nothing but a big pot filled with a lime inside, possibly nabbed from the backyard privies. "And the lady next door heard her say, 'Come on, Mama Lucy, I'm going to cook us some dinner,'" Beatrice recalled. "The lady peeped through the fence and there she was, stirring that lime to feed me and her with that. And they called me 'Mama Lucy' ever since."[22]

It didn't take long before Louis acquired a nickname of his own. The little boy with the big mouth became a frequent sight on the streets, eventually getting the attention of the old gamblers in the neighborhood. "See, all your names derive from some name you resent when it first starts," Armstrong said. "Well, quite naturally, like the cats used to call me 'Dippermouth' and they had an old gambler that I used to like to hear him say [*sings*] 'Dipppeeeeeer! Dippermouth!'"[23]

Louis began attending Fisk School in October 1907, a segregated school located at 507 South Franklin Street, directly across the street from Brick Row. In June 1900, the Orleans Parish School Board announced that because "barely ten per cent of attendance in colored schools go to the grammar grades and nearly 9 per cent go into the primary grades," African Americans would no longer be permitted to attend school past the fifth grade.[24]

"I realize from my limited observation that to teach the negro is a different problem," assistant superintendent Nicholas Bauer said in 1902. "His natural ability is of a low character and it is possible to bring him to a certain level beyond which it is impossible to carry him. That point is reached in the fifth grade of our schools."[25] When Bauer visited Fisk School in 1906, he described the conditions as "frightful," with overcrowded classrooms run by underpaid, underprepared teachers in an out-of-date, poorly ventilated building.

Armstrong didn't let the poor conditions affect him adversely. "I was an active youngster and anxious to do the right thing, and I did not stay in the kindergarten long but was soon in the second grade," he wrote in his autobiography. "I could read the newspaper to the other folk in my neighborhood who helped mama to raise me."[26] No records have survived from Fisk School so it's impossible to know if Armstrong skipped a grade, but he did seem to

Figure 2.2 Armstrong's "Back o' Town" Third Ward neighborhood, as photographed in 1938 for the Annual Report from the Office of the Mayor. Armstrong's "Brick Row" residence of 1303 Perdido Street can be seen in the foreground on the right. The building next door with the tower on top is Funky Butt Hall. The two-story structure across the street is Fisk School.

Credit: Courtesy of The City Archives & Special Collections, New Orleans Public Library.

take to both reading and writing early on, hobbies that lasted until the end of his life.

Armstrong's fondest memories were of the school's caretaker, Carmelite Martin, who lived a few doors down at 515 Franklin Street. Her husband, Ovide, a cooper by trade, died in 1904, leaving Carmelite to take care of their eight children by herself.[27] "She always had some kind of consolation for the under dog, who would rapp [*sic*] on her door and ask advice, etc., or food for the hungry...with all of those kids she would find a piece of bread from somewheres to give," Louis wrote of her.[28] Many of the Martin children stayed in the family business, working in the schools into the 1950s. "They were loved by everybody in the neighborhood," Armstrong wrote of the Martins. "Several generations, grew up with all of their children."[29]

But there was also a musical streak in the family, with pianist and guitarist Casimere making a reputation—a "superb musician" in Louis's eyes—using the nickname "Coochie" (or "Koochy") and Henry Martin growing up to be a drummer in Kid Ory's pioneering jazz band. Apparently one of the older brothers, James, was a "fine violinist" according to Louis and "the best musician of all of them," but he got caught in the East St. Louis race riot of 1917 and was never heard from again.[30] Hearing the music coming out of the Martin household might have subliminally planted some seeds, though it wouldn't be easy for Armstrong to do anything about it since Fisk School didn't offer any music classes of any kind.[31]

Most of Armstrong's memories of his time at Fisk revolved around food. Reminiscing on *The Mike Douglas Show* in 1970, Louis paid tribute to Mayann: "My mother could take fifteen cents and go to the Poydras Market and come back and cook a meal," he said. "I mean, a big [meal]—and lick your fingers, it was so good. . . . In those days, you could take a newspaper, and I'd go to the market, a fish market, and buy a whole newspaper full of fish heads. Just plain, chop it off, fish heads that they wouldn't use, they'd put it aside." When Douglas asked, "Yeah, that'd be garbage for them, wouldn't it?" Louis responded, "Well, they just ain't got time to do what we did. My mother would get them fish heads and take them home and cook them and clean them . . . and put a lot of tomatoes, canned tomatoes, in them and call it court-bouillon. A Creole dish, and serve it on top of some rice. Boy, you talking about beautiful food. And delicious."[32]

The quality of Louis's school lunches improved when Mayann began dating a man named Tom, a cook at the DeSoto Hotel, a white establishment at Barrone and Perdido Street. Tom was one of many "stepfathers" Mayann brought home in this period of instability. "Every time I looked around, I had a new step 'pappy,'" Louis wrote.[33] Sometimes Tom's feelings for Mayann spilled over in uncomfortable ways, especially in a one-room apartment. "We both had gotten old enough to know when Mayann and Tom were getting a little nookie," Louis said. "After all we both had ears. And the room was dark, so there was nothing for Mama Lucy and I to see. We played asleep. Hmmm. Oh those grunts. Some time I wondered if they were angry with each other—silly boy."[34]

Tom would bring home leftover food scraped off the plates of hotel guests and Mayann would transform it into a "wonderful lunch" Louis could bring to school. "I would have some of the very best steaks, chops, chicken, and eggs, scrambled all kinds of ways," he wrote, adding, "And the kids knew, I had the best lunch, they would beg me just like a bunch of hungry wolves."[35]

Those kids included the neighborhood bully One Eye Bud, who changed his tune when Armstrong offered him and his gang a piece of his sandwich one day. "After that, I was a very good friend to all of them," Armstrong wrote. "And they never did bother me again.......And nobody else better not bother me either.....Gee, they were tough kids.........And to think that they thought, I was tough, just tickles me pink, right until this day....."[36]

Louis remembered playing "war" with his new friends one day, saying of One Eye Bud, "He (like Hitler) appointed himself the General of the Army." The game ended when a big piece of slate flew off the roof of a nearby house and hit Louis in the head. Suffering from lockjaw, Louis was attended to by his mother. Mayann, "with TEARS in her eyes—worked frantically, with her Erbs and roots, and stuff—all boiled up Along with a glass of [laxative] pluto water. She put me to bed—sweated me out real good overnight. Shucks—the next morning I was on my way to school Just like nothing happened." Louis summed it up by quoting an old saying he was fond of, "The Lord take care of fools."[37]

That was far from the only time Mayann had to serve as her son's doctor. "When I was a kid, Mama used to give me a whole lot of little old crazy remedies," he recalled. "For a sore throat she cooked up a lot of cockroaches, strained off the water, and give you a teaspoon of water."[38] Mayann would also rub Sweet Spirts of Nitre all over her son's face and lips. The substance, a concoction of alcohol and ethyl nitrate, was usually used, according to the Food and Drug Administration, "to reduce fever, treat cold sores, relieve muscle spasms, reduce belching and abdominal pain and promote the production and excretion of urine."[39] "Mama used to give it to me in hot water, with a little sugar, to cut a cold," Louis said. "Put it on your lip, you want to grab four bedposts and everything—but it relieves. And I had to learn all that."[40] Louis swore by Sweet Spirits of Nitre for the rest of his life, especially after he later began playing the trumpet, though he died before the FDA banned it in 1980.

Louis continued getting in fights, even though Mayann would beg him, "Son, don't fight, don't fight." One time, he dared a bully to hit him. "And he did—right in the eye," he said. "Damn near blinded me." Armstrong eventually got his revenge, saying, "I swung on that so-'n'-so's jaw and head and etc. From that time on I got the name of being a bad boy."[41]

Fights were not just confined to the school grounds; Louis sometimes witnessed—and got involved in—them at home. One of Mayann's other boyfriends, remembered by Louis as "Albert," was "one of the lowest of guys I've ever seen in my whole life." Albert had an argument with Mayann that ended with him calling her a "black bitch," and shoving her into the Old Basin Canal, walking off without even turning around. Little Louis was playing by himself when he witnessed it. "And my God, was I frantic," he later wrote. "With Maryann, screaming, with her 'Chops'—all busted, and me—hollering the top of my voice,—HELP—HELP, HELP—HELP, —people came running from every directions.......Oh, God, whatta moment.....I've never forgiven that man for doing that to my mother...And said then, ever I see that man on this earth again, I'll sure kill him...I've never seen him to this day......And thank God I didn't."[42]

Another boyfriend only remembered as "Slim" "wasn't much better" than Albert, in Louis's estimation. "He could really play piano," according to Mama Lucy, but he "was very jealous" and "didn't want anyone to touch my mama."[43] After the incident with Albert, Louis felt the same way. One day, while Louis was at school, Slim and Mayann got into an altercation at Kid Brown's Saloon at the corner of Gravier and Franklin Streets that soon turned into a street fight. Word spread quickly in the neighborhood, eventually reaching Louis's friend "Cocaine Buddy" Martin, who delivered the news to Louis while he was at recess at Fisk School. "I drop books and everything, and, tore out towards the battle," Louis wrote. "When I got there they were still at it, and fighting their way back out into the streets, when all of a sudden, Slim turned his back to me just as I got there...Seeing what I did see-I started crying, 'Leave My Mother Alone—Leave My Mother Alone.....'"[44]

Louis spotted a pile of bricks in the street by a barn door and began hurling them at Slim. Word reached Mama Lucy, still too young for school, who ran over and saw a crowd of people cheering, "Look at Dipper, there! Look at that little boy throwing bricks!" "Louis was *chunking* some bricks up in there!" she remembered.[45] "I taken, good aims, and didn't waste a brick," Louis recalled. "Yessir—Satchel Paige didn't have a thing on me for pitching.....Slim's side commenced to hurting...... Then, he had to stop fighting Mayann."[46] The bricks eventually landed Slim in the hospital and Louis never saw him again. "Yes, he hit that man in the stomach, I don't think that man got well after that cause he always did suffer with his stomach," Mama Lucy recalled.[47]

Such outbursts of violence never felt right to Louis, who was not proud of his reputation as a "bad boy" and did his best to shake that image. "I stayed in my place as a kid," he said. "I respected everybody...I never was a sassy child."[48] Mama Lucy agreed with that assessment of her brother, calling him "a very humble lad" who "wasn't no sassy boy." "He didn't want no violence," she said. "You see, he was good like that."[49] Looking back at this aspect of his childhood personality, Louis knew who to give the credit to: "Mayann and my Grandmother taught me that." He was quick to add, "Of course my father didn't have time to teach me anything...He was so busy chasing the chippies...."[50]

It's possible that in a different situation, not infused with the systemic racism prevalent in his hometown, Armstrong could have excelled as a student. Toward the end of his life, he found himself in intensive care, his mind swirling with negative thoughts as he reflected on the shortcomings of his childhood. He didn't blame the system that failed him and he didn't blame Mayann. ("She had to struggle with us until we both grew up.") Instead he blamed the men in his neighborhood "who might be gambling off the money he [*sic*] should take home to feed their starving children or pay their small rents, or very important needs, etc."[51]

Some have read this intensive care manuscript as simply an indictment of his own race, but more specifically, it's an indictment of Armstrong's absent father and all the no-good "stepfathers" Mayann brought home. "[They] never tried to get together and to show the younger negroes such as my self to try and even to show that he [*sic*] has got ambitions," he wrote. Then arguably the most influential and famous musician on the planet wrote these words: "And with just a little encouragement—I could have really done something worthwhile."[52]

The bitterness most likely came from the fact that because Mayann couldn't support Louis and Mama Lucy on her own and because she couldn't depend on her boyfriends, Louis, a promising student, had to go out and start working while still in elementary school.

Armstrong was consistent in describing his first paying job as selling newspapers for a boy named "Charles," most likely Charles Wilson, who was born in 1889 and lived at nearby 733 Girod Street in the Third Ward, giving his occupation in the 1920 census as "newsboy" in the "daily papers" industry. According to Robert Goffin's research, Armstrong continued going to Fisk and would stop off at Wilson's newsstand after school ended, selling copies of the *New Orleans Item*, *Times-Democrat*, and *Daily States* until the evening, sometimes getting home long after dinner was served and his mother and sister had gone to sleep. For this work, he'd make 50 cents a day.[53]

Though he was now working nights, Louis never seemed to resent Mayann for a minute in his life, though she was growing less dependable—and present. Mama Lucy remembered times when Louis had to cook just for the two of them. "We didn't even have a furnished stove like that, no indeed," she said. "Louis would build bricks out in the yard. Yeah, yeah. *Poor.* Build the bricks out in the yard, I don't know what he would do, he'd cook them beans all right, call me to eat."[54]

Mayann's frequent disappearances remained an issue as Louis grew older. On August 22, 1909, a drunken Mayann was arrested after publicly fighting with her then-boyfriend Lou Patterson outside of Spano's Original Saloon at South Franklin and Poydras. Once again, Judge Fogarty gave Mayann a choice—pay a $20 fine or go to the House of Detention for 20 days. Both Mayann and Lou Patterson opted to go to jail, leaving Louis and Mama Lucy to fend for themselves for nearly three full weeks.

It's possible this was when Louis went back to Grandma Josephine and great-grandmother Catherine Walker, once staying "for several months" around the age of seven, according to Goffin.[55] Walker was elderly but still able to come to the rescue of a hungry Louis and Mama Lucy. "I ain't never forgive my papa's mama," Mama Lucy said of Josephine Armstrong in 1973. "She didn't give us enough to eat." Mama Lucy would then appeal to Walker, who would ask Louis if what she claimed was true.

"Mama Lucy's always talking about eating, you know," Louis began. "But Grandma, she don't give us enough to eat." Catherine Walker would respond by going into her kitchen and making "a big ol' pan of pudding," Mama Lucy said. "It was all right as long as it was hot, you know? The pudding get cold, me and Louis would ball it up and chunk it at one another. . . . But that helped to fill us up because we didn't have nothing. We was very poor. Very poor."[56]

In *Satchmo: My Life in New Orleans,* Armstrong associates his grandmother with going to church and Sunday school, placing it in the time he lived there before his reunion with Mayann, but he was most likely far too young to enroll in Sunday school at that age. Goffin specifically wrote of Louis visiting Grandma Josephine on Sundays, making it more likely that it was during this 1909–1910 period that Louis was attending the nearby Mount Hermon Baptist Church with his grandmothers (his uncle Joseph Armstrong married Lillian Richardson there in February 1907) and attending Sunday school classes taught by Reverend Arthur P. Orlage.[57] "Of course I went to church constantly," Louis wrote. "Quite naturally, you know I would. With grandma being a Christian woman, as well as my great grandmother...Between the two, they kept me in school, church, and Sunday school."[58]

But Louis was back home with his mother and a different "stepfather," Thomas Lee, when an enumerator showed up at 1303 Perdido Street on April 23, 1910, collecting information for the 1910 census. Lee, listed as the head of the house, was born in Jonesville, Louisiana, on December 20, 1885, spent much of life at sea, working as a laborer on a schooner in 1910 and still on the river at the time of his World War II registration in 1942.

Next the enumerator recorded Mary Albert, not using the Armstrong name and listed as Lee's "companion." The 25-year-old Mayann gave her occupation as "laundress," following in Grandma Josephine's footsteps. "Maryann could always find a job," Louis recalled. "Every white family she worked for wether [*sic*] they were rich or poor they all were satisfied with her work and gave her good recomendations [*sic*]. She kept them very much contented."[59] Finally, Louis was listed as being eight years old—strengthening the case for a 1901 birthday—and attending school at that time. However, according to the enumerator, Thomas Lee, Mayann, and Louis all could not read or write, contradicting Louis's memories of proudly reading the newspaper to the older folks in his neighborhood at a young age.[60]

One person is missing from this 1303 Perdido census, however: Mama Lucy. A deeper search of the 1910 census finds Beatrice Armstrong at nearby 781 Franklin Street, living with a 52-year-old "roomer," Mary Williams. Asked in 1983 if she used to go to church with her mother and Louis at this time, Mama Lucy said she didn't, adding, "I used to be with my godmother most of the time. Because I used to go more than Louis and his mama, you see?" Mama Lucy also said that her godmother christened her a Methodist and was named Mary Williams.[61]

Seven-year-old Beatrice was probably better off living with her godmother in this period, because on June 8, 1910, Mayann was one of five women arrested for fighting and disturbing the peace outside 1301 Perdido Street. All of the women—including Sarah Myles, Ike's daughter—gave their occupations as "washerwoman" or "cook" but were quite possibly working as prostitutes at the time of the arrest. Mayann once again had to serve time in the House of Detention.

She was released in time for her son's birthday on July 4, though he didn't have much time to celebrate as he was busy selling newspapers for Charlie Wilson's newsstand. July 4, 1910, was also the day of the big heavyweight championship bout in Reno between Jack Johnson, the first African American champion, hated by many for the color of his skin and his taunting and flaunting persona, and former champion James J. Jeffries, the first "great white hope." Asked for a prediction before the fight, Jeffries had said, "That portion of the white race that has been looking to me to defend its athletic superiority may feel assured that I am fit to do my best."[62]

Jeffries's best was no match for Johnson, who knocked Jeffries out in the fifteenth round, battering and humiliating the older man from start to finish. Word of Johnson's victory spread quickly, resulting in race riots across the United States as angry white fans sought to take out their frustrations on any African Americans in sight. As Armstrong approached Charlie's newsstand, he recalled, "I met a gang of colored boys, running like mad towards me,.... I immediately asked them what was the trouble?"

"If you knew like we do, you'd run, too," came the response from one of the out-of-breath youngsters. "Because Jack Johnson has just knocked out Jim Jefferies, and the white boys are really sore about it, and taking it out on us colored boys."

"They didn't have to say another word," Armstrong remembered. "I immediately, made an about face, and started running right beside them."[63] But once Armstrong got to his home turf, he strangely felt safe from the threat of "the canal street fellows." "They turned around at our street because they knew they would have to run into DANTES INFERNO or a reasonable facimile [*sic*]," he wrote. "We knew the boys were from the canal street gang because all the white boys in our neighborhood were fine fellows."[64]

Armstrong was well aware of what would have happened to him had he been caught by the mob after the Johnson-Jeffries fight, as he'd seen it happen before. "At ten years old I could see—the bluffings that those old fat belly stinking very smelly dirty White folks were putting down," he wrote toward the end of his life.

> It seemed as though the only thing that they cared about was their shot guns or those old time shot guns which they had strapped around them. So they get full of their Mint Julip or that bad whiskey, the poor white trash were guzzling down, like water, then when they get so dam drunk until they'd go out of their minds—then it's nigger hunting time. Any nigger. They would'nt give up until they would find one. From then on, Lord have mercy on the poor darkie. Then they would torture the poor darkie, as innocent as he may be. Then they would get their usual ignorant [Cheshire] cat laughs before they would shoot him down—like a dog.[65]

Coincidentally, Armstrong was spared such a fate due to the police squashing any attempted riots after the Johnson-Jeffries fight. "The next day, everything had blown over with the assistance of the 'Peelers,'" he wrote.

"Thats, what they called the Policemen in those days....Because they were known to 'Peel' your head, when they arrest'd you...."[66]

The police might have helped Armstrong out that day, but it wasn't always the case. Once when asked if he had ever been scared when growing up in New Orleans, Armstrong responded by remembering the times he would play "a little African dominoes"—dice—with his fellow newsboys until they'd be discovered by the police. "That's as scared as I've been because when the cops would get behind us, don't look like your feet was carrying you fast enough," he said. "And you got to make one of those fences with one hand. And all those days, those were scary days because in those days, the cops would whip your head and then ask your name afterwards, you know?"[67]

Armstrong had avoided conflict with the police as best he could to this point in his life, but they eventually caught up with him, leading to his first arrest. He was 9 years old.

3

"Like a Human Being"

1910–1911

On October 17, 1910, the Chinatown section of Louis's Third Ward neighborhood was rocked by a fire that started in a bundle of hay in the Tulane Stables and traveled by wind toward South Rampart Street. The fire department eventually put out the flames there, but the surrounding area continued burning, causing $20,000 worth of damage.[1] The burned buildings were a beacon for looters, including 15-year-old Henry Smith, who targeted one such location filled with brass objects that could potentially be resold for a profit. "He could not get it out fast enough without help, so he hired five negro boys to help him," the *Daily Item* wrote. "Before he got the job completed he was served with an injunction by the officers, who took him and his laborers to jail."[2] All of the boys were arrested as "dangerous and suspicious characters"; among them was "Louis Armstrong, of Perdido, between Liberty and Franklin Streets."[3]

Armstrong was taking a chance by joining Smith's crew, but the lure of making money off some stolen brass was too good to pass up. A few dollars from a junk shop or pawn shop and Armstrong and his family could eat comfortably for a week. Instead, Louis would be sent by Judge Andrew Wilson to the Colored Waif's Home for Boys on October 21.

This institution had been run since 1906 by Captain Joseph Jones, a man whose coworkers called him "probably the greatest Negro leader New Orleans ever had" at the time of his death in 1957.[4] A New Orleans native, Jones was born on July 5, 1880, and had the luxury of an eighth-grade education before the city limited the African American schooling experience to fifth grade in 1900. (Jones even spent a ninth grade at New Orleans University.) He enlisted in the service and immediately saw action in the Spanish-American War of 1898 and the Philippine-American War, which lasted from 1899 to 1902. Jones was discharged on July 2, 1902, and married 16-year-old Manuella Duplessis on December 30, 1905.

Captain Jones was troubled by the problem of juvenile delinquency, especially in the African American community. A Waif's Home was opened on Clio Street in 1893, a year and a half after the formation of the Society for the Prevention of Cruelty to Children, but it did not admit Black children; any young African Americans caught committing a crime were sentenced to prison to serve alongside the adults. "There were six black juveniles in the Orleans Parish prison in 1904," Will Buckingham later wrote. "Though their living quarters were separate from the adult population, the children were forced to share facilities and intermingle with adult inmates during the day."[5]

Upon discovering this, Captain Jones devoted his energy to changing the system. "In those days," Jones said, "there were a great many youngsters in the city who were supposed to be 'bad,' but it seemed to me they were just kids who never had a chance."[6] Jones's first response was to work it out with the juvenile court judge to have convicted Black juveniles stay with him and his wife in their home instead of going to prison. Eventually, Jones found an abandoned building between Rosedale and Conti Streets and established the Colored Waif's Home in November 1906. Funding came in from the Society for the Prevention of Cruelty to Children, as well as from the African American community. "In the Waifs' Home they attend school, and in the shops are taught the rudiments of various occupations that will assist them in earning a livelihood," the *Times-Democrat* reported one month before Armstrong's arrest.[7]

Figure 3.1 Postcard of the Colored Waif's Home in 1913, with an inset of Captain Joseph Jones.

Credit: Courtesy of the Louis Armstrong House Museum.

Such a stable routine might have appealed to Armstrong, but almost as soon as he arrived on October 21 he was gone, having been discharged into the care of a mysterious "aunt" on November 8. Little Louis's 18 days in the facility were enough to make an impression on Manuella Jones, who accurately remembered his first time at the Home in 1910 when asked about it by Richard B. Allen and Mike Casimir in 1971.[8] Armstrong seemed to have blocked this arrest from his memory, never mentioning it in interviews or in his writings—"Maybe my memory's bad," he told Max Jones when asked about it in 1970; "it has been so long"[9]—but he did admit that hanging around with the wrong crowd did get him into trouble during these years. "Many a time I would be with kids in my neighborhood and they would play Follow the Leader," he said. "So if they would get into any kind of trouble, I would be in trouble also. If they would steal something and get caught, I was in trouble the same as they. Savvy?"[10]

His mother had been arrested and sent to jail twice in the last two years and now Louis himself had been arrested and spent 18 days in a juvenile detention home. He might have continued attending Fisk School sporadically, but now, it was time to go to work. The Karnofsky family was hiring.

The story of Louis Armstrong and the Jewish Karnofsky family has become legend, to the point where it has been completely distorted in the age of social media, with viral posts loaded with false claims such as that the Karnofsky family adopted little Louis and taught him to speak fluent Yiddish. The true story is more interesting and inspirational.

Though Louis believed the Karnofskys were from Russia, patriarch Louis Karnofsky's birth certificate shows he was actually born Ziskind-Leib Karnovsky in Vilkija, Lithuania, on August 13, 1864.[11] He eventually settled with his first cousin, Esther Kauffman—born about October 20, 1871, and soon to always be known as "Tillie"—in Vilkija and the couple left for New York City on September 20, 1886. They married on October 21, 1889, Louis listing his occupation as "Peddler" on the marriage certificate. Between 1890 and 1910, Tillie gave birth to ten children, the last four being born after the family's move to New Orleans in 1901.[12]

Louis Karnofsky first shows up in Soards's City Directory in 1906 in the "Junk Dealers" section, giving the address 1304 Girod Street, two blocks away from Louis Armstrong's residence at 1303 Perdido Street, an easy walk straight down South Franklin Street. But trying to figure out exactly when Armstrong first showed up at the Karnofsky residence is a mystery.

Armstrong is partially to blame for the confusion. In 1941, he told Leonard Feather that he worked on a coal wagon with Louie and Tillie's son Morris Karnofsky "somewheres around the year of 1915 and early 16."[13] That meshed with the manuscript for *Satchmo: My Life in New Orleans*, where Armstrong introduces Morris "Karnoffsky" [*sic*] on a page with the heading "1916–17."[14] But in between, Armstrong wrote an article for *True* magazine in November 1947 in which he stated, "I couldn't hardly wait until I would get out of school in the evenings, looklike. . . . I wanted to get on that wagon with Morris Karnoffsky [*sic*] and help him deliver that stone coal."[15] Armstrong's school days were over by 1913 so it's possible, even probable, that he worked for the Karnofskys during his Fisk period and again as a teenager.

For all his melodramatic tendencies and fabricated, dialect-heavy quotes, Robert Goffin usually had a good handle on the chronology of events in young Armstrong's life. Goffin described Armstrong selling newspapers for Charles Wilson until his job was given to someone else. His friend "Cocaine Buddy" told a dejected Louis, "I heared [*sic*] my paw say they was a job at Konowski's, the coal man." Goffin couldn't quite pick up the spelling of "Karnofsky," but he got the job right. In this version, Armstrong was nine years old, but Goffin even offers a particularly revealing detail: Armstrong lied to the family and added two years to his age, telling them he was 11.[16] Thus, this could very well be the time Armstrong started using 1900 as his birthday as he magically went from being listed as 8 years old in the April 1910 census to being listed as 12 years old in December 1912.

However, Armstrong continued to add to confusion when he insisted late in life that the Karnofsky story took place in 1907 when he was seven. While convalescing in intensive care at Beth Israel Hospital in 1969, he heard his doctor, Gary Zucker, hum a familiar tune: "Oyfn Pripetshik," a Yiddish lullaby also known as "On the Hearth." Armstrong immediately remembered Tillie Karnofsky singing it to her baby and, with memories flooding back to him, grabbed a pen and a stack of paper and began writing "Louis Armstrong + the Jewish Family in New Orleans, La. The Year of 1907."[17]

Armstrong didn't remember the title of "Oyfn Pripetshik," instead identifying it as "Russian Lullaby," the title of an Irving Berlin composition that wasn't published until 1927, but the Yiddish lullaby had quite an impact on him. "This is the song that I sang when I was Seven years old," he wrote, "with the Konarfsky [*sic*] family when I was working for them, every night at their house when mother Kornofsky [*sic*] would rock the baby David to sleep."[18] Armstrong's insistence on placing this episode in the year 1907 has led other historians to follow suit. But for that to make sense, one must examine what is known about "the baby David."

According to the Karnofskys' "Petition for Naturalization," David Karnofsky was born on February 12, 1903. However, a deeper search shows that David's World War II draft registration, his obituary, and even his tombstone give a birthday of September 20, 1904![19] Either way, by 1907, David would have been a toddler, not quite a baby that needed to be rocked to sleep.

Thus, it's my belief that the older, ailing Armstrong actually had one of the Karnofskys' other children—Sarah, born in 1907, Eva, born in 1908, and Samuel, born in 1910—in mind. If Armstrong was singing to baby Samuel instead of David, everything lines up quite nicely: Samuel born in March 1910, Louis being discharged from the Waif's Home in November 1910, adding a year to his age to begin working with the Karnofsky family, and starting to show up in early 1911 when the family was still singing lullabies to baby Samuel.

Armstrong would get to know the Karnofsky residence almost like a second home over the next few years.[20] "They put their shoulders together and did a fine job fixing up that house," he wrote in 1969. "They had a pretty good size yard. So they started a little business in no time at all. That's where I came in with little money that they had."[21]

Figure 3.2 The Karnofsky Family, c. 1916. Standing, left to right: Morris, Lillian, Harry Meyer, patriarch Louis, Gussie (Golde), Aleck. Seated, left to right: David, Sarah, matriarch Tillie, Samuel (also known as Nick), Eva, Hyman.
Credit: Courtesy of Judge Jacob Karno.

The Karnofskys ran multiple businesses from 1304 Girod Street. In addition to the junk business, which son Alex helped with (14 years old in 1910), they also ran a coal wagon, operated by Morris (16 years old in 1910). In the two aforementioned 1947 publications—Goffin's *Horn of Plenty* and Armstrong's *True* magazine story—Armstrong stuck to tales from the coal wagon, but in his 1969 manuscript he spent more time discussing the junk wagon. It seems likely that Armstrong worked both jobs from the start. "I alternated with the two sons," he wrote of Alex and Morris, adding, "Alex would go out early in the mornings on his junk wagon—stay out all day. Me—right along side of him. Then I would help Morris at night. The first job that I ever had. So I was very glad over it."[22]

If that's the case, Armstrong's new job began before the school day started, as he recalled meeting the family at five o'clock in the morning. The junk wagon was up first and it allowed Armstrong to have an early experience making music. "We used to go on the wagon and pick up and buy bottles and things from the kids and had a little horn that long, like they celebrate with, you know, and took the top off and man, I could play some weird Blues with that thing. . . .And them kids would be running with them bottles and old pieces of brass or something."[23] Armstrong eventually learned how to play popular songs on the tin horn and was gratified by Alex Karnofsky's encouragement, applauding Louis and complimenting him on his "beautiful tone." "Just think," Alex said, "if you could play a real Horn as well."[24] A seed was planted but it would still take some more time to grow into something special.[25]

The time spent in the Karnofsky home between jobs provided more everlasting memories for Armstrong. "I liked their Jewish food very much," he wrote. "Everytime we would come in late on the little wagon from buying old rags and bones, when they would be having 'supper' they would fix a plate of food for me, saying you've worked, might as well eat here with us. It is too late, and by the time you get home, it will be way to late for your supper. I was glad because I fell in love with their food from those days until now."[26] Such regular sustenance was not a guarantee when Armstrong got back to Mayann's house, so he learned to relish every bite he took with the Karnofskys. "If it wasn't for the nice Jewish people, we would have starved many times," Armstrong recalled. "I will love the Jewish people, all of my life."[27]

After dinner, Armstrong joined in with the family as they sang Yiddish lullabies to the baby, even though he couldn't speak the language. "I always enjoyed everything they sang and still do," he wrote. "Of course I sang the Lullaby Song with the family—I did not go through every song they sang. But I was a good Listener. Still am."[28] Armstrong might have forgotten the name of the song, the year he met the Karnofskys, even the name of the baby he sang to, but he never forgot the way the Karnofskys made him feel. "They were always warm and kind to me," he wrote toward the end of his life. "Which was very noticable [*sic*] to me—just a kid who could use a little word of kindness."[29]

For the Karnofskys, the feeling was mutual. "In New Orleans, we didn't say this is a nigger section or a colored section," Samuel Karnofsky—who later changed his name to Nick Karno—said in 1992. "We didn't treat black people like black people. They were just people. They ate with us and they slept with us."[30] Armstrong went one step further, stating, "They so warm, and made a little Negroe boy such as me feel like a human being."[31]

After waking up early, riding the junk wagon and blowing his tin horn, going to school if he had the time, getting back on the junk wagon, having dinner, and singing with the family, the highlight of Armstrong's day was about to begin: his evening shift delivering coal with Morris Karnofsky. Armstrong seemed to associate the coal wagon with school, so it's possible that he continued going to Fisk School after 1910, albeit with spotty attendance, something alluded to by Goffin. After getting hired by the Karnofskys, Goffin wrote, "On the next day, a Tuesday, Mrs. [Martin] missed Louis at school which did not strike her as strange since many little Negroes started to work young."[32] Fisk School could not compare to the new exciting world the Karnofskys were opening Armstrong's eyes to: the world of Storyville.

Storyville was the name given to New Orleans' official red-light district, a 38-block area sanctioned by City Councilman Sidney Story in 1897 to offer legalized prostitution in a controlled surrounding. The government even published "Blue Books" for out-of-towners to use as a guide to Storyville's best bordellos and prostitutes. Armstrong didn't know the name "Storyville" when he was growing up; "During the days that I'm talking about—there weren't such a name," he wrote in 1947. "Storyville was called by that name in the later years. . . Just to kinda polish it up a bit—so it wouldn't sound so bad to the younger Hep Generation. . . Tee Hee . . . "[33]

Crossing Canal Street into the world of Storyville was taboo for Armstrong—unless accompanied by a white man. "Since the Red light District were stricly [*sic*] all white—we Negroes were not allowed to buy anything sexy," he wrote in 1969. "Some of those girls who were standing in the doorway of those cribs they looked just like a bunch of girls who had just finished High School or just received their Deplomas [*sic*] from college they looked so young. They all had pimps to give their money to. As long as I was working for the White man—I could wittness [*sic*] all of this."[34]

Armstrong and Morris soon devised a system. "Morris would drive through Storyville and when somebody would call for different amounts of buckets of coal—I would be the one to deliver them and Morris would sit and watch the wagon and the stone coal," Armstrong wrote.[35] Memories of those deliveries to the prostitutes remained fresh in his mind 60 years later. "Well, quite naturally they're standing there with nothing on but a shimmy—well, they called them teddies at the time, you know," he said. "So they'd have me, a little boy, 'Put some coal on the grate,' you know. Quite naturally, I'd have to take a mug [look] real quick! If they'd see me, they'd slap me down!"[36]

Armstrong also witnessed the protection that working with Morris Karnofsky gave him when it came to the police. "Even the tough cops didn't bother me and believe me they were really tough," he remembered. "They were known to whip heads so fast until one would think that they had an electric stick. The whores had to have heat. So that's where I came in, and was safe and nobody bothered me."[37]

After making the rounds of Storyville, Armstrong would finally make his way back home. He never divulged just how many days he performed this nonstop routine or for how many years he did it, but he was now caught up in a life of nearly nonstop work that would not really stop until he found himself in intensive care roughly 60 years later. Even when discussing the poverty-ridden aspects of his childhood, Armstrong always stressed, "But we were happy."

But how happy could he have actually been, basically violating every child labor law in existence by working so hard at such a young age? "Again, when thinking about Armstrong's relationship with the Karnofskys we must be blunt," Dalton Anthony Jones has written in his examination of Armstrong's 1969 manuscript. "We are not just talking about any kind of labor—we are talking about *child* labor with all of its attendant vulnerabilities and estrangements. Whether or not he found sanctuary or work with the Jewish family at such a young age . . . this appears to be one of the main engines driving the tension of the document. Furthermore, whether or not his experiences with child labor took place with the Karnofskys, it is fairly certain that such labor left an indelible mark on his psyche."[38]

Jones continues: "He is not only drawing attention to the lasting consequences of a life torn between institutional exclusion, structural violence, and economic exploitation; I contend, rather, that since we are essentially reading his deathbed reflections, he is revealing the origins and residual effects of a life spent performing affective labor: a life in which his emotions, along with his physical work, were appropriated, that is to say alienated, as a mechanism for the production of someone else's surplus value."

Jones's points should not be taken lightly; Armstrong's childhood was cut short by a need to go to work to support his family—and the early adoption of this lifestyle created a superhuman work ethic that clearly contributed to his failing health and the bitterness conveyed in his 1969 "deathbed reflections."

But that bitterness seems to have been more fueled by a fear that he was going to die and African Americans would remember him as nothing but an old Uncle Tom. He was certainly not bitter over working for the Karnofsky family, even if at a young age. "Being a helper for those boys made me very proud and happy," he wrote in the same manuscript. "I began to feel, like I had a future and it's a wonderful world after all."[39] Once out of the hospital and reenergized by the prospect of playing the trumpet in public again, Armstrong pushed back against any attempts to inject his life with pity. "Now I must tell you that my whole life has been happiness," Armstrong wrote to Max Jones in 1970. "Through all of the misfortunes, etc., I did not plan anything. Life was there for me and I accepted it. And life, what ever came out, has been beautiful to me, and I love everybody."[40] This was corroborated by his sister, whose upbringing wasn't much different from his. "Louis was lovely with *everybody*," she insisted in 1973. "Everybody. Didn't low-rate, didn't scorn nobody. He was just happy with everybody, hugging, playing with you, going on, seeing someone else playing with someone else. He's happy with everybody."[41]

But even if *that* is true, it's only natural to ask —how? Armstrong would be the first to disavow any attempts at portraying him as a saint and that is not my intention here. Yet there he was, abandoned by his father, working two jobs, going to school, no shoes on his feet, sometimes with nothing to eat, living in a single-room flat, smack in the post-Reconstruction Jim Crow South—"Oh, danger was dancing all around you back then," he once said—yet he still remained devoted to "the cause of happiness." It's no surprise that other writers, critics, and biographers have had a tough time believing it, searching instead for ways to prove he was secretly tortured within. Because if someone who grew up like that could lead a happy, fulfilled life, what excuse do the rest of us have?

A big part of the answer to this riddle seems to be held in the influence of his mother. In a passage in the manuscript of *Satchmo: My Life in New Orleans* that didn't make it into the published version, Armstrong reflected on his childhood and the other kids he grew up with, never taking it for granted that he emerged the way he did:

> It would take, pages + pages for me to call names of all the unfortunate youngsters who did not get the real chance to rough it out like we kids—the kids whom I grew up with. Of course, it wasn't no fault of mine, that my parents were poor as JOBE' S Turkey, etc. and we kids didn't have everything that we wanted through life. Like the kids who families were better situated. But—After Suming [*sic*] it all up, from the

> lessons of good Common sense, that my Mother who did not have an awful lot of learnings herself, taught my Sister + I -the real Routaments [rudiments] in life, I feel, right to this day that we both "Sis + I" have gotten the very best of the deal. In life that is.[42]

Young Louis was now the breadwinner in his house, combining his income with that of Mayann. According to Louis, in this period, Mayann "had a job at a beat up paper place where they bonded up old news papers and make bales with them and sell them to some other company. She was paid (50c) a day and [with] my little (50c) from each [Karnofsky] brother we managed pretty good."[43] It's quite possible that Mayann did have such a job at some point, but on July 25, 1912, Mayann was one of 15 people arrested for "disturbing the peace" at 756 South Franklin Street, and was once more listed as a "prostitute" in the First Precinct's arrest books. Mayann served 30 days at the House of Detention for this arrest.[44]

With Mayann incarcerated, Mama Lucy eventually had to start working as a child, too. It's not much of a surprise to reveal who she first worked for; asked in 1973 for her earliest memory, she remembered: "Them prostitute womens, I'd go scrub for them, you understand? We used to sell red bricks. . . .It's good luck if you put something in it."[45] On many Saturdays, she was joined by her brother, who wasn't shy to explain the "something" the prostitutes put in it. "Every Saturday they scrub their steps down with pee and then they throw the brick dust on the sidewalk in front, and that brought them luck Saturday night," he recalled. "That was their superstition."[46] With the money, Mama Lucy remembered, "Every Sunday I had me a new dress. It wasn't no fancy dress, gingham, something like that, someone would make it for me, you understand." She added, "These were very poor people," before stressing, "But one thing: we had a full, full stomach."[47] Louis agreed, writing, "We at least had lots to eat, and roof over our heads and Mayann could realy [*sic*] cook, good. Ooh she could cook. On small money."[48]

Mayann would sometimes leave money for her children to go out and buy groceries, though Mama Lucy didn't always prove trustworthy in this endeavor, often using her dime to buy a piece of cake for herself! Mama Lucy roared with laughter when telling this story but when asked if Mayann got mad, she exclaimed, "Yeah! Ooo-weee, get mad!?"[49] She left it at that, but her brother wasn't shy about describing their mother's disciplinary tactics. "Mama Lucy, I seen my mother hit her like [boxer Jersey Joe] Walcott hit [Ezzard] Charles, so help me God," Louis said. "Knocked her right on her ass." Louis used this story as an example of his mother's effective methods, saying, "So Mama Lucy ain't nobody's damn fool today. You know what I mean? That's what I mean. Same with me. Of course, I didn't require as many whippings cause to see how she beat the shit out of her, I said, 'Well, I didn't want to go through that.' "[50] Not that Louis avoided it entirely. Asked by Mike Douglas how Mayann disciplined him, he replied, "Oh, I mean, she'd just, like, whip the hell out of us. Man, she hit like a man!"[51]

These were not easy years for young Louis, working multiple jobs to support his family, yet there was something that made it all worthwhile. "We were poor and everything like that, but music was all around you," he said. "Music kept you rolling."[52] Especially the music of his two biggest formative influences: Bunk Johnson and Joe Oliver.

4

"Nothing Could Stop Him"

1911–1912

Cornetist Willie "Bunk" Johnson is one figure who earned his nickname. He claimed he was born on December 27, 1879, but historians Lawrence Gushee and Peter Hanley discovered *six* different birthdays in the public record, with the pair leaning toward 1885, though not ruling out 1888 or 1889.[1] He claimed he joined Buddy Bolden's band in the mid-1890s, but Bolden biographer Donald Marquis concluded that Johnson didn't play with Bolden at all.[2] And he claimed to have been Louis Armstrong's cornet teacher, prompting Armstrong to respond, "Bunk didn't teach me shit."[3]

Yet there's no denying that Johnson was a major formative influence on the young Armstrong. "Bunk, when he played, he never blasted, he played full, but he had ideas," clarinetist Albert Nicholas said. "Louis got a *lot* of Bunk. He learned a lot from Bunk."[4] Armstrong agreed about Johnson's penetrating sound. "You take Bunk, there's no amount of musicians can drown him out because he had tone," Armstrong said in 1956. "I'm speaking about the days when he was a young man, about 25 years old. He just had a lazy way of playing his trumpet, but his tone was so beautiful, could nobody drown him out and you could always hear Bunk."[5]

Johnson originally made his reputation in the Superior Band but was fired for excessive drinking. "For months and months, Bunk didn't go home, would sleep on a pool table until it was time to go play," bassist Pops Foster said. "All the trouble Bunk that ever got in was himself, see, just drinking."[6] In 1911, he joined the Eagle Band, the group Bolden led until he became institutionalized. "I used to hear him in the Eagle Band, with [trombonist] Frankie Duson," Armstrong told William Russell in 1939. "Did that band swing!" Armstrong admitted he became enamored with Johnson at that impressionable time. "How I used to follow him around. Parades. Funerals. He could play funeral marches that would make you cry." Asked about his style, Armstrong began fingering an imaginary trumpet, answering, "His tone! His fingering! Man, what a tone he had! He used his hand like I do. Used the same kind of fingering. I might say he played a swing lead."[7]

Figure 4.1 The Superior Band, c. 1910, featuring the cornet playing of Willie "Bunk" Johnson. Standing, left to right: Buddy Johnson, trombone; Bunk Johnson, cornet; "Big Eye" Louis Nelson Delisle, clarinet; Billy Marrero, string bass. Seated, left to right: Walter Brundy, drums; Peter Bocage, violin and leader; Richard Payne, guitar.
Credit: The William Russell Jazz Collection at The Historic New Orleans Collection, acquisition made possible by the Clarisse Claiborne Grima Fund, acc. no. 92-48-L.243.

Armstrong learned about phrasing from hearing Johnson play, plus he was gaining an appreciation for the repertoire of the Eagle Band, namely Johnson's specialty, "Maple Leaf Rag." "Take a tune like 'Maple Leaf Rag,' that was written by Scott Joplin," Armstrong said. "Now there's a man, way back there, if he was a good enough musician that he could just play his music note for note, he was swinging."[8]

Even though Armstrong admittedly followed Johnson through the parades and yearned to hear him play in his neighborhood, he didn't get close to him. "Bunk, in the days of the honky tonks, I was just a little ol' kid and Bunk didn't know me, for sure," Armstrong said. "But I stayed right in front of that horn, that port wine was coming out of the bell!"[9]

But delivering coal in the red-light district with Morris Karnofsky did allow Armstrong to have his first interactions with the next great "King" of New Orleans cornetists, Joe Oliver.

Joe Oliver was most likely born on December 19, 1885, though his World War I draft registration card lists a date of December 19, 1881, many history books offer May 13, 1885, and his marriage certificate and the 1920 census seems to lean toward December 19, 1884.[10]

Oliver's mother, Virginia "Jinnie" Jones, born in Florida in September 1854, was enumerated in the 1900 census as living at 1105 Nashville Avenue in New Orleans' more affluent Garden District with 21-year-old daughter Fanny Davis, 16-year-old daughter Adel Hadford, and 14-year-old son Joseph Oliver. Jinnie Jones was listed as widowed and, judging by the three different surnames of her children, most likely had divorced or separated from Joe Oliver's father, Nathan Oliver, by 1900.[11]

The enumerator left the residence at 1105 Nashville Avenue on June 1, 1900; on June 13, Jinnie Jones passed away.[12] Though the census listed Joseph as a "day laborer" and noted he had gone to school and could read and write, the music bug seems to have bitten Oliver around this time, perhaps as a way of coping with the loss of his mother. Bunk Johnson remembered a man named "Mr. Kenchen" who hired Oliver to play in a children's brass band in "about 1899 or 1900."[13] In this instance, Johnson's memory appears to have been spot on; the New Orleans *Daily Picayune* reported on September 25, 1900, about a 38th anniversary celebration of the Emancipation Proclamation at Union Bethel A.M.E. Church featuring "music by the youths' band, J. M. Kinchen leader."[14] Using that as a lead, one can find the records of Jackson M. Kinchen, born in New Orleans on January 12, 1869.[15]

Bassist Wellman Braud recalled that Oliver was about 14 years old when he started playing with Kinchen's youth band—perhaps the Emancipation Day celebration was his first public gig—and that it was Kinchen who "taught them to play [and] took them on the road" around 1900.[16] Oliver might have been playing with a band, but everyone who heard him in this period did agree on one thing: he was far from a musical prodigy. "Now Joe was a poor cornet player a long time," Bunk Johnson maintained.[17]

In fact, Oliver first started on trombone, but according to his future wife, Stella Oliver, "he played too loud for the trombone" and "the man took him off of it." Eventually Kinchen gave Oliver a cornet. "He didn't know much about cornet, but he was determined to learn," Stella said. "So he started rehearsing, practicing, and he did fairly well."[18]

After one tour with Kinchen's brass band, Oliver returned to New Orleans bearing a scar over one eye that impaired his vision for the rest of his life. Braud told William Russell that Oliver found himself in a fight "with a gang of river bullies" while still with Kinchen and received "a good lick on his head" from a boy wielding a broomstick.[19] Banjoist Clarence "Little Dad" Vincent remembered attending a performance of the Kinchen band in Baton Rouge, saying, "I was standing right by Joe Oliver when a fellow, a drummer named Buddy Sally hit him in the eye with a wheelbarrow handle."[20] Though he was now blind in one eye and would have to deal with derisive nicknames such as "Monocle" and "Bad Eye," Stella Oliver insisted her husband "wasn't a fella to complain much about being sick or feeling bad."[21]

After his mother's passing, Oliver chose to earn a steady paycheck rather than pursue music as a full-time career, working for several years for the German-Jewish Levy family at 2502 Magazine Avenue, located on the corner of Second Street in the Garden District. "Well, that was a fancy neighborhood in them days," according to Sister Bernice Phillips, who remembered Oliver from this period. "Bonton people lived all out there in them days."[22] Though many remembered him as a "butler," Stella Oliver recalled her future husband did the work of a "yard boy, they used to call him then. They'd clean the yard around it, and he could get off anytime he wanted. . . . [T]hey were very good to him." She added that the Levy family "didn't pay much of a salary, but they raised him. They raised him."[23] It's ironic that Louis Armstrong is thought by many to be the one who was raised by and lived with a Jewish family but those details are more appropriately applied to the man who would eventually become his mentor.

Oliver continued his efforts on the cornet, occasionally enlisting the help of Bunk Johnson. "[Drummer] Walter Brundy and I, we used to go up to Second and Magazine where he was working on the premises, and I used to help Joe a great deal in his cornet playing," Johnson recalled. "The music that Joe had was too hard for him to play."[24] Oliver worked on his reading, studying with violinist Johnny Brown and getting some formative experiences with the Melrose Brass Band and Henry Allen Sr's Brass Band, but he did not possess the confidence to play with a ragtime band.[25] "When I first got Joe Oliver, he only could play brass band music," bassist Eddie Dawson recalled. "He couldn't play no dance music. . . . And I went to hire him to play a dance up on St. Charles Street with me, I had the job, and he told me he wasn't able to play no dance music."[26]

Eventually, Oliver attempted to sit in one night with Frankie Duson's Eagle Band, whose members improvised their parts. He was immediately in over his head, playing "so loud and bad they sent him home" according to pianist Richard M. Jones. However, Jones added, "But he kept on tooting away."[27] Oliver began to regularly fill in with the Eagle Band before accepting steady work with guitarist Louis Keppard's Magnolia Band, which also included bassist Pops Foster.[28] Foster later remembered "the band jumped sky high the minute he joined us."[29]

Figure 4.2 Portrait of Joe Oliver.
Credit: Courtesy of the New Orleans Jazz Club Collection of the Louisiana State Museum.

Off the bandstand, Oliver did run afoul of the band after collecting $15 from each member to order new uniforms, which he failed to do. "So Joe was shooting pool with our money, see, drinking up and eating up and giving us some excuse," Keppard said. "He ain't got the money, he spent our money!"[30] Eventually the band threatened Oliver. "If you don't get our uniforms, we're going to throw you in the river!" Oliver eventually cobbled together enough money to get the band their new dark green uniforms, but his greedy ways would not dissipate over the years.

Initially, the Magnolia band stuck to dance numbers like "Bag of Rags," "Frog Leg Rag," "Maple Leaf Rag," and "Champagne Rag," but they had to adapt their sound to the rougher crowds that would show up in the second half of the dance. "They wanted you to play slow blues and dirty songs so they could dance rough and dirty," Pops Foster recalled.[31] Oliver soon began to master the blues at these dances. Asked if he liked to play the blues on his cornet, Oliver's wife Stella responded, "Ohhhhh, he love it, he loved it, yes."

Oliver married Stella Dominique on July 13, 1911, and moved in, with her two daughters, Bernadine Phinazee (b. June 22, 1904) and Ruby Frazier (b. circa 1907), to a new home on Dryades Street. Oliver felt confident enough in his musical abilities that he quit his job as the Levy's butler and began accepting any music-related jobs that came his way, including subbing for Bunk Johnson, who was sometimes too drunk to make his engagements. He was improving but was not thought to be among the upper echelon of cornetists in the city. Louis Keppard admitted, "[Oliver] used to knock that cornet's tune out, knock the tone exactly out." Keppard's brother, popular Creole cornetist Freddie "King" Keppard, used to give Manuel Perez, leader of the Onward Brass Band, hell for using Oliver, telling him "you can't do nothing with that kid."[32] Future trombonist Preston Jackson remembered a time when cornetist Mutt Carey got the best of Oliver in a parade by "playing some grand stuff. Joe couldn't take it long. He just threw his horn away and went into a pawnshop and bought another."[33]

But Oliver soon began to show improvement when he began performing in a place where cornetists were heretofore unwelcome: the red-light district.

Many early histories of jazz have overemphasized, romanticized, and borderline fetishized the role Storyville played in the development of the music. "The District" was a haven for pianists such as Jelly Roll Morton, who made his reputation playing for the prostitutes, and the occasional string band, but ragtime outfits with cornets, clarinets, and trombones were prohibited from performing there for a very long time.

Sometime around 1910, bassist Eddie Dawson was playing with a small group at Harry Parker's Dance Hall on Franklin Street in the District, between Iberville and Bienville Streets, when cornetist Freddie Keppard stopped by after playing a job. Parker hadn't ever seen such an instrument before and asked Keppard to play something. "Oh boss, I can't play nothing, it's a violation of the law," Keppard told Parker. "I'm afraid. But if you protect me, I'll play it." Parker agreed, even promising, "I'll go see the mayor to get a permit." He did just that and Keppard became the first cornetist to play the District, creating quite a buzz in the process.[34]

Other Storyville establishments followed suit and soon, Oliver and the Magnolia band found themselves performing at 1401 Iberville, which many of the other musicians of that era referred to as "Hunt's" or "Hunt's and Nagel's," a corruption of the name of the venue's co-owner, Hans Nagel. The formal name of the saloon was Nagel and Groshell's, giving equal billing to co-owner Edward Groshell; it first turned up in Soards's Directory in 1911. "They were two Jew guys and were good guys to work for," Pops Foster said, adding, "We were the best-paid band in the District. You could live real good on it and save money."[35]

By 1912—most likely the year Armstrong spent a lot of time in the District delivering coal with Morris Karnofsky—Storyville was jumping with the sound of the ragtime bands. "Things were right on top of each other in the District," according to Foster. "Freddie Keppard was at Billy Phillips's on one corner, Manuel Perez was on the same corner at Rice's. Our band was on the next corner at Hunts and Nagels at Custom House and Liberty. . . . When all of us were playing the District, we couldn't wait for night to come so we could go to work. Most of us loved the District and tried to stay there as much as we could. Sometimes I didn't go home for weeks."[36]

Eddie Dawson sometimes played guitar or bass with the Magnolia Band and said of Oliver, "He had a glass eye, but he was a wonderful sight reader. But he couldn't play much. At that time he couldn't play no head music. He could read."[37] Oliver's reading came in handy as the Magnolia Band began playing arrangements out of a new book, *Standard High-Class Rags*, published by the Stark Music Company in St. Louis in 1912 and known among musicians as the "red back book of rags" for its red cover. "That's the time we used to use that Scott Joplin music," Louis Keppard said of the Magnolia Band's repertoire at Nagel and Groshell's. "That's what they called the Red Book."[38] But Keppard also recalled the band playing "Panama," "Egyptian Rag," and "Black Smoke," three popular pieces that were *not* in "The Red Back Book," probably learned by ear to play for dancers. This marked a turning point for Oliver. "Then after he picked up that dance music, he was able to play without the [sheet] music," Dawson said.[39]

As he made a reputation, Oliver began playing other spot jobs around the District at venues such as the 101 Ranch, John T. Lala's Big 25, and Abadie's saloon. "Joe Oliver, practically overnight, woke up and started playing," said pianist Richard M. Jones.[40] Jones's "Four Hot Hounds" band performed regularly at Abadie's, a "whites only" saloon located at 1501 Bienville and run by brothers Eugene and Oliver Abadie.[41] One evening in 1912, Jones hired Oliver on cornet, resulting in a legendary moment Jones relished retelling until his passing in 1945. Here is how William Russell jotted it down in the version that eventually was published in *Jazzmen* in 1939:

> "One night they were playing. Perez was playing up at Rice's. Keppard playing at Lalas. Oliver was at the [Abadie] Brothers, at Bienville and [Marais]. Wooden Joe playing on the clarinet. Ernest Rogers beating on the drums. Oliver had always been sort of underdog. All these guys had always talked about Keppard and Perez. He was afraid to blow out strong because of these other guys. But this night,

> something got his goat and he got his dander up. He said, Jones, beat out B Flat. Oliver picked up his horn. The band got going. Oliver took his cornet and walked out on the sidewalk. Started walking up towards Rice's, pointed his cornet up the street and kept walking and playing. Jones kept beating it out in B Flat. Oliver played like he never had before. And before long the crowds came out of Rice's and out of Lala's. Old King, he turned around, like the Pied Piper, and led them back into [Abadie's]. Walked in there and threw his cornet down and said, 'There.' He had shown them. From then on, nothing could stop him."[42]

Could little Louis Armstrong have been passing by on Morris Karnofsky's coal wagon at the moment Oliver made his defining stance? He never said so, but it's possible since Armstrong's 1911–1912 period of working with Karnofsky coincided with both the rise of ragtime bands in the red-light district and the rise of Oliver as a cornetist of note. Armstrong was still under the spell of Bunk Johnson, but he would notice Oliver during these trips to the District and soon began to spot him playing parades with the Onward Brass Band. Actually playing a cornet might have seemed like a pipe dream at this point, but that wasn't going to stop Armstrong from starting to make music of his own—with his voice.

5

"Blessed Assurance"

1912

Armstrong's punishing schedule of balancing his work with the Karnofsky family, his home life with Mayann and Mama Lucy, and occasionally attending school continued into 1912—but now with a lot more singing. "I used to sing for my Boss, some of those good ol good songs and he would enjoy them so well, he would applaude [*sic*] for me, so earnestly until I would feel just like I had just finished a Cornet solo in the French Opera House—A place where Negroes were not allowed," Armstrong wrote of his early coal cart days with Morris Karnofsky. "Funny thing about it, I did not have or play a Cornet at the time."[1] He looked forward to those evenings spent singing with the Karnofsky family, and the encouragement that came with it. "The Karnofsky Family kept reminding me that I had talent—perfect [intonation] when I would sing," he remembered.[2]

Armstrong initially began singing when he'd attend church with his grandmother Josephine and great-grandmother Catherine, later writing it was there that he acquired his "singing tactics I guess."[3] Those "tactics" were now flowering in the Karnofsky's home. "When I reached the age of eleven I began to realize that it was the Jewish family who instilled in me singing from the heart," Armstrong recalled. "They encourage me to carry on."[4] When members of the Karnofsky family would insist, "You should sing more," Armstrong would sometimes respond, "Well, I sing in church with my mother Mayann."[5]

The church Armstrong was referring to was the Mount Zion Baptist Church at 512 Howard Street near Perdido Street, right across from the Fisk School. According to Louis, this was "Elder Cozy's Church...He was, at that time, the most popular preacher in the neighborhood."[6] Armstrong never quite got the reverend's name right; he was referring to William Mark Cosey, who, according to his World War I draft registration card, was born on March 25, 1878, and was employed as a minister at the Mount Zion Baptist Church.

Louis's confidence in singing continued to grow at Mount Zion, especially with his mother by his side. "I used to enjoy going to church with my mother and you could hear me singing over everybody," he told Mike Douglas in

1970. "Veins would be coming because I wanted my friends to hear me outside." When asked by Douglas, "Why did you want your friends to hear you outside?" Armstrong responded, "Well, I'm going to let them know I could sing better than everybody in the church, you know?"[7]

Soon enough, Armstrong found some like-minded friends and entered into his first official musical venture: a vocal quartet. According to Mama Lucy, the quartet originally began as something much larger, an offshoot of the "second line" that followed every street parade. "The second line consist of anybody who want to follow the parade or the funeral," Armstrong wrote. "They could be Doctors, Lawyers, Hustlers, or, etc, Anybody who might hear the music, and the spirit hit them, to follow and see whats, happening."[8]

"You know what they used to do at night around the neighborhood?" Mama Lucy continued. "Like he'd get old tubs, old dish pans and buckets and everything, had about 15 or 20 of them little boys, just coming on, just beating, you know, harmonica and everything, singing all along the street just like a second line . . . Yeah! All that night, the people would be running to see that."[9] Out of such gatherings, a formal quartet was formed. Armstrong would be the youngest member and, given the fact that his later gravel-voiced efforts inspired a million impersonations, his role in the group might sound surprising. "I was a tenor singer at that time," he said in 1953. "Was putting my hand behind my ear [sings a high note] 'Yessssss!' Man, I used to holler!"[10]

The other charter member was James William Bolton, also known as "Red Happy" or "Redhead Happy." Bolton is another figure with a mysterious age; the 1910 census lists him as a 15-year-old living with his family at 449 S. Liberty Street. But when he got married on May 23, 1917, he gave his age as 20 years old, and his draft registration card of September 12, 1918, lists a birthday of March 25, 1900![11] To Armstrong, the multifaceted Bolton, who would later become a top drummer, was "the greatest showman of them all... He wasn't only a great showman, he was also a good pimp."[12]

"Little Mack" Lacey sang lead tenor and also grew up to be a drummer, but research has not turned up his real first name; however, a George Lacey Jr. born in the Third Ward in May 1896 does seem like a good fit. Similar speculation can be used regarding the group's bass vocalist whom Armstrong always referred to as "Big-Nose Sidney." In this case, the 1910 census does list a 13-year-old African American named Sidney Johnson, living at 431 Franklin Street, right in Louis's neighborhood; there's no mention of the size of his nose.

George Gray Jr. sang baritone in the group and would also later become "an ace drummer, hard to beat," in Armstrong's estimation.[13] He was born on December 20, 1894, and was living with his family at 412 Saratoga Street according to the Soards's City Directory of 1911, the time the quartet was most likely formed. Looking back in the 1950s, Armstrong said, "It's a funny thing, there was three of them, three drummers in that outfit."[14] It shouldn't come as a surprise then when asked if he ever wanted to play in a band when he was a kid, Armstrong replied, "Yes, I wanted to be a drummer."[15]

Robert Goffin's New Orleans research did turn up some interesting insights into the quartet that did much more than just sing—this group also represented Armstrong's first forays into dancing and comedy. "At this period, Louis knew only one kind of dance," Goffin wrote. "He would buckwing his way into the center of the group of kids, and imitate a hunch back or a lame man, then straighten up abruptly and dance a lively jig. In order to excite him to greater efforts the other kids sang ragtime songs, clapping their hands so as to stress the rhythm. Then another would take his place and Louis would join the singers."[16] Young Henry "Kid" Rena recalled that Armstrong played his first instrument with the quartet. "Louis had a 'gitbox' made of a cigar box, four strings, copper wire, piece of flatwood for handle," Rena said.[17]

At first, dancing and singing with his friends was simply a source of great amusement—but Armstrong soon realized their fun could generate a profit after a fateful trip delivering coal for the Karnofsky family. "On his rounds with the coal vendor, Louis had noticed groups of three or four Negro children who sang and danced for the amusement of the public in well-to-do sections, and then passed the hat," Goffin reported.[18] Armstrong and his friends began seriously rehearsing an act so they could follow suit.

Armstrong would do his comic dancing and Little Mack Lacey apparently was an expert at gymnastics. Red Happy Bolton's natural showmanship would come to the forefront when he would impersonate instruments with his voice; they didn't have a word for it but decades later, after they did, drummer Paul Barbarin said of Bolton, "Yeah, he did a lot of scat singing."[19] Armstrong possibly joined in on this nonsense singing, but he had another way of contributing musically to the group: whistling. Richard M. Jones vividly remembered the quartet, and said in 1939, "Maybe this is something you don't know: Louis used to whistle all this stuff that he plays [today] when he was a kid."[20]

According to Goffin, "the quartet's big hit was a side-splitting scene in which Louis Armstrong made passionate love to Redhead Happy. While the three others were blowing a discreet accompaniment, Louis declared his love in passionate terms and rolled his eyes in a simulation of desire." Armstrong's performance inspired "shouts of laughter and approval from the audience," especially as he would break into a minstrel song, "Everybody's Gal is My Gal (and Your Gal is My Gal, Too)."[21] Armstrong proved to be a natural comedian and honed certain performance characteristics that would take him around the world later in life. "When you get a chance, you can ham it up," he said in a 1962 interview. "That's about what I do when I ever put the horn down, just singing and being assured. Blessed assurance."[22]

Asked in 1953 what kind of songs the quartet sang, Armstrong responded, "Oh, we sang the usual songs of those days, like 'My Brazilian Beauty' and 'Shine On Harvest Moon' and 'When the Saints,' things like that."[23] Armstrong frequently named "My Brazilian Beauty" as the group's theme song and would often sing a few bars for delighted interviewers in his later years. Though "My Brazilian Beauty" was the first line of the song, its actual title was "Down on the Amazon," written by Billy Johnson and published in 1903. Goffin also reports the group did folk material like Stephen Foster's "Swannee River" and a vaudeville song from 1903 that turned into something of a traditional folk song of its own, Smith and Bowman's "Mister Moon (Kindly Come Out and Shine)."

Too young to attend vaudeville shows and too poor to own a phonograph, how would the members of Armstrong's quartet learn such songs? They likely heard other similar quartets perform them on the streets. Though pop culture has associated "barbershop quartets" with visions of white men with handlebar mustaches and straw hats, historians such as Lynn Abbott and Vic Hobson have definitively argued for the African American roots of the form. In his influential 1992 article "'Play That Barber Shop Chord': A Case for the African-American Origin of Barbershop Harmony," Abbott writes, "For the male population, at least, it was nothing less than the black national pastime" and quotes New Orleanian Dr. Laddie Melton—who was singing in schoolyard quartets the same time Armstrong was—as saying, "We used to love to get together. It was typical, almost for any three or four Negroes to get together and, they say, 'Let's crack up a chord! Let's hit a note!'"[24]

Armstrong couldn't have known it at the time, but harmonizing with his friends developed his ear and provided an invaluable music education that would last a lifetime. Though he rarely liked to get into the nuts and bolts of music theory, in one interview from 1954, Armstrong shared advice he gave to a young trumpet player who struggled to improvise. "I said, 'Well, all you gotta do is think of you singing in a quartet and if somebody's playing the lead on a trumpet, you just play the second to every note he hits, the same as if you're singing a duet,'" Armstrong related. "He said he never thought of it that way. That's the only way to look at it."[25]

Thus, for the rest of his career as both a vocalist and a trumpeter, Armstrong fell back on the lessons he learned in the quartet. When he needed to play or sing lead, he always had the melody front and center in his mind; when he needed to blend in an ensemble, it was never a problem; and even when he was improvising, the lead would be running through his head at all times, allowing him the freedom to create new melodies as if he was "singing a duet." Historians and critics have long debated whether Armstrong played like he sang or sang like he played but the truth is both were connected to the same soul. "You make the same notes, you know, like the horn," Armstrong explained about his singing. "That's why we could scat and do things like that. I always would sing. I was singing before I played the horn, see."[26] Armstrong's later bassist Arvell Shaw once said of him, "He would have been a singer regardless if he had played trumpet or not."[27]

The quartet soon began performing regularly—and making money, too. "Had a nice little taste every night," Armstrong reminisced. "Dollar-and-a-half a night. Right there, twelve, thirteen-years-old, can you imagine? That's a lot of money."[28] But he quickly added, "The nights Happy didn't take it—he was the bully of the quartet." Of Bolton, Armstrong once said, "Happy would throw bricks at his own mother, you know." At the end of some nights, Bolton would take a look at the collection and announce, "I'll take this tonight." "Can't do nothing about it, see," Armstrong said.

But one night, he got help from an unexpected source: his nine-year-old sister, Mama Lucy. "So Mama Lucy heard of it and man, if she didn't whip the hell out of Happy!" he remembered. "I said, 'Whip him, sis! Whip him, sister! Whip him!' I didn't care for all that old [fighting], you know what I mean?"[29] Mama Lucy didn't mention Bolton but she did admit to carrying "a little rusty knife" when she was "about 9, 10" and remembered seeing a Black man talking to her brother in an animated fashion before it looked like he smacked him. "I took that knife and I stuck him," Mama Lucy recalled with a laugh. "That's when he run. . . . I stuck that knife and there was blood. And do you know what Louis did [to] me? Louis went home and told Ma, 'I told you you gotta do something about Mama Lucy. She cut that man!' "[30] On the nights Red Happy behaved himself, the quartet continued to improve and began to get noticed, soon performing in tent shows produced by the vaudeville team "Mack and Mack"—Billy and Mary McBride. "Louis, then, and this Little Mack, and little Georgie Gray, and Happy, they had a little quartet," Billy McBride said. "Now, at this time, none of them were playing drums, or horns. They'd go up there and sing amateur nights—some night when I'd have them—and that's where I first met Louis."[31]

In the audience for one of these shows was a 13-year-old named Arthur Singleton from Bunkie, Louisiana, who recently moved to New Orleans. "The first time I ever saw Louis was when he was about 12, 13 years old," Singleton recalled. "He was singing with three other kids in an amateur show at Bill and Mary Mack's tent show in New Orleans. Louis was singing tenor then, and they broke it up that night."[32] Singleton's nickname was "Zutty"—Creole patois for "cute"—and he would be seeing much more of Armstrong in the years to come.

But perhaps most exciting, Armstrong was beginning to be noticed by the musicians around town—including Bunk Johnson. Johnson often played with clarinetist Sidney Bechet, born May 14, 1897, and already an established professional at the age of 15. One day, Johnson told Bechet, "Sidney, I want you to go hear a little quartet, how they sing and harmonize." Bechet, admittedly "crazy about singing harmony," went to see the group and had his first meeting with Armstrong. "They were real good . . . they had a way," Bechet remembered, adding, "I went many a time to hear this quartet sing and I got to like Louis a whole lot, he was damn nice."[33]

Soon after, Bechet invited Armstrong's quartet to come to his house for dinner and to sing for his family. Bechet was living at 1716 Marais Street in the Seventh Ward, about a mile and a half from Armstrong's neighborhood. "Look, Sidney," Armstrong told the older teen, "I don't have any shoes . . . these I got, they won't get me there." Bechet gave him 50 cents to get his shoes fixed and waited for Armstrong to appear. "Well, I don't know what it was, but he never showed up," Bechet recalled, still bitter about it toward the end of his life. "It's a little thing, and there's big things around it, but it keeps coming back. You're playing some number and it starts going—sometimes it goes right back to the street and [it's] played about those shoes."[34] Bechet was not about to forget the perceived slight, and its repercussions would spark some of the most exciting—and combative—jazz ever captured on wax.

But in addition to encouraging his vocal work with the quartet, both Bechet and Bunk Johnson are connected to Armstrong in another way during this period: they each remembered him playing the cornet at this time, *before* his life-changing return to the Colored Waif's Home.

"During that time [1912] Louis started after me to show him how to blow my cornet," Johnson stated in *Jazzmen*, stating it happened at Dago Tony's saloon on Perdido and Franklin Street. "Louis used to slip in there and get on the music stand behind the piano. He would fool with my cornet every chance he could get until he could get a sound out of it. Then I showed him just how to hold it and place it to his mouth and he did so and it wasn't long before he began getting a good tone out of my horn."[35]

"Of course, Louis was playing the cornet a bit before he went into that Jones school, but it was, you know, how kids play," is how Bechet remembered it, referring to the Waif's Home by the surname of its founder Captain Joseph Jones. "The school helped, it really started him up; you know, it's like at home if you have an instrument around all the time—it helps a boy make up his mind what he will do if you give him an idea."[36] In addition to Johnson and

Bechet, Henry "Kid" Rena, who sometimes sang with Armstrong's quartet and would soon reunite with him at the Colored Waif's Home, "confirmed Bunk Johnson's story that Louis already played cornet when he arrived at the Waif's Home," according to a 1940 story.[37]

For much of his adult life, one person denied these rumors wholeheartedly: Armstrong himself.

Armstrong's answers to the question "When did you first start playing?" were remarkably consistent throughout his life. "When I went to the orphanage," he said in a 1956 interview, referring to the Waif's Home. "I was about thirteen."[38] "In the orphanage," he repeated in 1968. "Yeah when I was thirteen years old."[39] In between, he must have answered the same question in the same fashion at least a thousand times.

But then came his problematic 1969 manuscript "Louis Armstrong + the Jewish Family." While chronicling his work with the Karnofsky family at the supposed age of seven, Armstrong wrote, "Sure enough, I saw a little Cornet in a pawn shop window—Five Dollars—My luck was just right—with Karnofsky loan me on my salary—I saved 50c a week and bought the horn. All dirty—but was soon pretty to me. After blowing into it awhile I realized that I could play Home Sweet Home—then here Come the Blues. From then on, I was a mess and tootin away." Armstrong then delivered this jaw-dropper: "People thought that it was my first horn that was given to me at the Colored Waif's (Home for Boys. —The Orphanage) but it was'nt."[40]

But like the rest of that document, this new twist must be handled with care. "I kept that horn for a long time," he wrote of this cornet. "I played it all through the days of the Honky Tonk." Armstrong's "days of the Honky Tonk" are indisputably 1916–1918, which means that in 1969, he claimed he had one cornet from 1907 through 1918, something that simply wasn't the case.[41] There's also evidence that the Karnofskys did help him purchase an instrument—after his stay in the Waif's Home, closer to those honky-tonk days.

Perhaps most baffling is the fact that Armstrong still stuck to the Waif's Home story *after* he wrote the Karnofsky manuscript. In November 1969, he told the BBC his usual story about the Colored Waif's Home—"So they gave me a little cornet, taught me how to play 'Home Sweet Home' on it and everything," he said at one point—while holding the Karnofsky manuscript *in his hands*, even reading from it later in the interview!

This pattern continued into 1970. Asked by David Frost in February 1970, "When did you first play an instrument?" Armstrong answered, "Well, I was in a boys Waifs' Home."[42] In July 1970, Armstrong told George Wein, "I didn't play that cornet until I got out of the orphanage in 1913."[43]

Only on his very last television appearance on the *Tonight Show Starring Johnny Carson* on March 1, 1971, did he offer up his new story, telling Carson, "Well the first [cornet], I was seven years old and I used to work for some Jewish people that . . . had a little junkyard and we'd go out and pick up old rags and bones and all, and in one of those pickups, they had a little cornet there, and Morris Karnofsky, the little son that I worked for, gave me the horn, you know, and that was my first one."[44]

Now *that* is a different story. Finding a cornet in the garbage while working on the junk wagon is not the same as advancing him money to buy one from a pawn shop, but it's possible that both events occurred, just at different times. This story is corroborated by an unlikely source, one Jacob Karnofsky, who later became a popular film and television actor using the name James Karen. When Karen met Armstrong and told him he was a Karnofsky descendant, Armstrong touchingly replied, "You're my cousin!" He then offered up another spin on the story: "They bought me my first trumpet! I had found one in the trash. The valves didn't work but I was playing it and they heard me play it. They said, 'You're good Louis and you should have a good trumpet' and they bought [me] the trumpet."[45]

Trying to untangle this mystery is a fool's errand, but perhaps the most believable story is as follows: Armstrong found an old cornet in the garbage while working on the junk wagon with the Karnofsky family at the same time he fell under the spell of Bunk Johnson. It was a beat-up old horn and Johnson didn't formally give him lessons, but he remembered him trying to play it, as did Bechet and Rena. Whatever playing he was doing in this period was not enough for anyone to think of him as a prodigy, but it was enough for him to enter the Waif's Home with enough rudimentary knowledge of the instrument to rapidly progress on it.

But all of this would be moot—and perhaps the sound of American popular music would have progressed in an entirely different way—if not for the events of December 31, 1912.

New Year's Eve began "raw and chilly," but by the evening, "the climatic conditions softened until it became an ideal night for the celebration."[46] It was a noisy night, the *Times-Democrat* mentioning "the tremendous cannonade of numerous bombs, fireworks and the shouting which burst spontaneously from a joyous holiday mob."[47] The *Daily Picayune* reported that outside of D. H. Holmes's dry goods store on Canal Street, a man pulled out a revolver and fired it in the air. "Women actually screamed," according to newspaper coverage. "This demonstration was dangerous and unlawful, but it added spice to the event. The man quickly replaced the weapon in his pocket and when two policemen hurried to the spot they found nothing."[48]

Over on South Rampart Street, another young man was walking around with a revolver: Louis Armstrong.

The events of this New Year's Eve might constitute the most oft-told story of Armstrong's life. Different versions featured different embellishments so an accurate report of just how it went down is hard to piece together, but the gist of the story remained consistent.

According to the manuscript of *Satchmo: My Life in New Orleans*, written in the 1950s, Armstrong was already packing heat when he hit the streets that night. "The people down in New Orleans celebrates with roman candles, torch lights, etc.," he wrote. "They also shoot their shot guns, pistols, or anything that can make a noise...They aren't supposed to shoot their guns and pistols, etc., out in the opening [*sic*], but they do." Armstrong soon found his noisemaker. "I found this old sawed off 38 pistol in the bottom of Mayann's old cedar trunk," he wrote. "She didn't know I had it when I went out to sing with my quartet on this particular night."[49]

The "quartet" that night consisted of five members: Armstrong, Redhead Happy Bolton, Georgie Gray, Little Mack Lacey and Big Nose Sidney. In each version of the story, it was another boy with a "little 'tinny' six shooter" that started the trouble while Armstrong's group was singing on Rampart Street. "We heard this thing go— Dy Dy Dy Dy Dy Dy, —while we were singing," Armstrong wrote. The other members of the quartet looked at him and said, "Go get him, Dipper." He continued: "When they said that to me, I immediately reached down into my 'busom' where I was 'toating it' (carrying my gun) and I raised my hand up into the air, and let her go,—'Ye'yoom- 'Ye'yoom'Ye' Yoom'Ye'Yoom'Ye'Yoom......And my boys all of them rejoiced..And patted me on the back, while the lad with the six shooter, 'cut out' and was out of sight before one could say Jack Rabbit....We all laughed about it....And was having a wonderful time, singing as we walked along........"[50]

Armstrong also alluded to the initial aftermath of his discharging the revolver in his earlier 1936 autobiography, *Swing That Music*. "Merry-makers were going along the street and when that old cannon let loose in my hand, and sang out so loud, they stopped short and looked back," he wrote. "There was one pretty big party of them. They stood still a minute, then they all burst out laughing. They laughed a lot and then they called, 'Happy New Year,' and went on. I must have looked funny to them, a little kid with such a big gun in my hand, standing there scared half to death at all the noise I'd made."[51]

But in Robert Goffin's version, there's very little laughter. To Goffin, "a little darky popped off his cap pistol in Louis Armstrong's face," causing the other members of the quartet to tell Louis, "Go on, Dipper, yo' can't swallow that!" At this point, Armstrong wished aloud that he had his "Pa's thirty-eight" and ran home, past Mayann, to find the weapon "in the bottom of a trunk." Back on Rampart Street, Armstrong spotted the original troublemaker standing on a porch.

"Get him, Louis, go get him, Dipper!" urged the quartet.

"Louis loosened the safety catch, aimed at the porch, and pulled the trigger," Goffin wrote. "He was stunned by the recoil and the loud report. With yells of rage he continued to press the trigger. The people of Perdido scurried to safety. A wench fled into the Eagle Saloon. Georgie Gray applauded wildly."[52]

Goffin's version is the only one that paints Armstrong pulling the trigger with "yells of rage" as he shot towards the porch where the other boy stood, arguably attempting murder. With the Belgian Goffin, one must always consider the language barrier that could have led to misunderstandings, as well as his book's tendency to dramatize many situations; at the same time, he did supply many unique details about Armstrong's quartet, which means that he might have been able to interview one of the surviving members—possibly Georgie Gray, since he's named—to get a different perspective.[53] Thus, it's possible that Armstrong really was out for blood, something he would downplay in later airings of the tale once he was a superstar.

Armstrong also changed the identity of the gun's original owner. In *Swing That Music,* Armstrong wrote of his weapon, "My mother had an old '38' gun and when time came along towards New Year's she hid it away because she knew I'd get in trouble with it."[54] But in the published version of *My Life in New Orleans*, he refers to the weapon in Mayann's trunk as "my stepfather's revolver," perhaps as a way of disassociating his mother with the incident.

After Louis died in 1971, Mama Lucy set the record straight. "I know about that gun, too," she said. " 'Cause I done seen that big ol' gun my Mama had. . . .That's my mama's gun. She had it in a trunk. And that New Year's Eve, Louis went in that trunk and got it. And that's what started the ball a-rolling for him."[55]

Louis didn't remember it happening quite so immediately. "Further down on Rampart street, I re-loaded my gun," he wrote in the manuscript for *Satchmo: My Life in New Orleans.* "And no sooner than it was re-loaded, I commenced to shooting up into the air again.....My little companions still enjoyed the thrill....."[56]

This time, shortly after discharging the revolver, Armstrong was spotted by Detectives Edward Holyland and George Dillman. Coincidentally, Holyland and Dillman were returning from the First Precinct, where they had just arrested 24-year-old Louis Malachia, who owned a retail shop at 434 South Rampart Street, for "discharging fire arms" at Rampart and Perdido at 11:05 p.m. Now, closer to midnight, here was the young Armstrong doing the same thing in almost the same spot, directly in front of the Eagle Saloon at 401 South Rampart. Holyland and Dillman wrestled Armstrong to the ground, causing him to break down in tears and begin screaming "all kinds of excuses."

"Mister! Please don't arrest me! I won't do it anymore! I want my momma!"

"All of this through tears, mind you," Armstrong stressed. "But still, that man just wouldn't let me go . . . Oh, I cried myself sick."

The paddy wagon soon showed up and took Armstrong to Juvenile Court, located about a half mile away at 823 Barrone Street. "According to the law, he could not be taken to the First Precinct station because the law stated that he could not be booked with adults for any crime as long as he was a juvenile," Tad Jones explained.[57] At the Juvenile Court, Armstrong was taken from processing downstairs to a segregated dormitory on the third floor, "a boys' cell," as he later put it. "I was so sick and dis-heartened, I slept on that hard bed, all night long," he wrote. "I had all kinds of dreams, while sleeping in there....I was wondering also 'what on earth are they going to do with me...Or, where in the world are they going to take me' [. . .] I also wondered, how much time will a boy get for having a gun let alone, shooting one....Oh, I had a million minds....And I couldn't pasify [*sic*] any of them....."[58]

The answers to those questions would come in the morning. He couldn't have known it at the time, but in some ways, getting arrested was the best thing to have ever happened to him. "Because that shot, I do believe, started my career," he reflected in 1936. "It changed my life and brought me my big chance."[59]

6

"Hooray for Louis Armstrong!"

1913–1914

A policeman awakened Armstrong at 10 o'clock the next morning, bringing him down to the Juvenile Court for his trial. The judge would be a familiar face, Andrew W. Wilson, who had previously sent Armstrong to the Colored Waif's Home when he was arrested in October 1910.[1]

As Louis's legal guardian, Mayann would have been present at her son's trial. Robert Goffin claimed that Mayann testified, pleading with Judge Wilson that the gun belonged to her "husband" and that she had unsuccessfully tried to hide it from Louis. Beatrice was also there and remembered how distraught her brother was, not so much for his own sake but because he felt he let his family down. "He was worried about his Mama and Mama Lucy, 'How are Mama and Mama Lucy going to make out?'" she recounted.[2] Louis had sacrificed much of his childhood to help his mother and sister make ends meet—how would they fare without his contribution? After Judge Wilson talked with Louis and with the detectives who arrested him, he delivered his verdict: Armstrong would be sent back to the Colored Waif's Home for an indeterminate amount of time. His case would be reviewed in six months, at which time Wilson would decide if he should stay there or be released.

The *Times-Democrat* had a reporter assigned to the Juvenile Court who turned in a short paragraph-long story that ran on January 2, 1913, with the headline "Few Juveniles Arrested." "The most serious case was that of Louis Armstrong, a twelve-year-old negro, who discharged a revolver at Rampart and Perdido streets," the article stated. "Being an old offender he was sent to the negro Waif's Home."[3] Mama Lucy specifically remembered, "They had all of that in the papers."[4] Seeing her son summed up as "an old offender" was too much for Mayann to handle. She drowned her sorrows in alcohol and caused enough of a scene to be arrested again for "fighting and disturbing the peace" with a man named Sidney Dozier at Gravier and Franklin Streets at 3:30 in the morning on January 4; in the arrest record, Mayann was still listed as a "prostitute."[5]

Louis most likely never knew about that arrest. After the sentencing, he was led into the yard of the Juvenile Court to be taken to the Waif's Home on a horse-drawn wagon that reminded him of the "Black Maria" that used to take inmates to the House of Detention near Jane Alley. Armstrong stared out of the wagon's screen window as he traveled from the Juvenile Court building to Canal Street and then five miles north to the Colored Waif's Home. The Home was located in a rural area a few blocks from City Park and was surrounded by six cemeteries. He was soon let out of the wagon and brought into the Home, where he would be reunited with Captain Joseph Jones and his wife, Manuella. Armstrong was given his uniform, which consisted of overalls during the week and, according to Tad Jones, "a brown cotton outfit with loose pants and a jacket with the words 'Boys Home' stitched across the chest."[6]

Armstrong was then taken to the dormitory on the second floor, where he was given a bunk in between August "Gus" Vanzan (born February 19, 1900), and Isaac Smoot (born June 5, 1897). It's not known what Vanzan did to get sent to the Waif's Home, but Smoot was a lifelong troublemaker who had first been arrested in March 1910 for "malicious mischief." His family paid Judge Wilson the $250 fine at the time, but by 1913, his mischievous ways had landed him at the Waif's Home for a long stay.[7]

From there, Armstrong was brought to the mess hall, where the other inmates were having lunch: a plate of "white beans (no rice)," as Armstrong put it. At home, he admitted he "would have annihilated those beans...But at this time, I only pushed them away." This pattern continued until his fourth day, when a starving Armstrong was the first one to line up for food. He looked over and saw Captain Joseph Jones "and the rest of the big wigs" laughing and applauding him. Armstrong offered back a "slight grin" but "inwardly, my sense of humor just couldn't blend with theirs."[8]

Armstrong soon got into a daily routine at the Waif's Home. Awakened at sunrise by a bugle playing "Reveille," the boys would head to the washroom and then line up for inspection, where Captain Jones and his assistant keepers would examine their heads "looking for lice, sores, or, any discomforts."[9] Jones would also inspect the boys' wardrobe, handing out "some of those fine stinging Lashes" to any of the boys who had buttons missing or who were late getting dressed. "They had quite a good system there," Armstrong wrote.[10]

From there, Armstrong and the inmates would start their chores—"That's where I learned how to scrub floors, wash and iron, cook, make up beds, and do a little of everything around the house"—before Captain Jones would conduct military training, using wooden guns.[11] Talking about these days on the *David Frost Show* in 1970, Armstrong said that thanks to Captain Jones, "I knew all about shoulder arms and parade rest, and you know, retreat!"[12]

Captain Jones was listed as the "Warden" of the Home in the 1910; his "Assistant Keeper" was Henry Alexander, born c. 1874. Aside from being another disciplinarian, Armstrong recalled, "Mr. Alexander, taught the boys how do gardening, carpeting, build camp fires, etc."[13] Captain Jones's wife, Manuella, referred to Alexander as the Home's "gardener" who "raised our vegetables, which included Irish potatoes, cabbage, and a thick cauliflower that measured almost two feet wide." Mrs. Jones and a supervisor, "Miss Underwood," oversaw the cooking, which was done on a woodstove, offering the boys three meals a day. "And we use'ta cook red beans and cabbage, things of that sort," Mrs. Jones recalled.[14]

Louis and the other inmates attended school each day from 9 a.m. until 3 p.m. During his first year, he was taught the basics of reading, writing, and arithmetic by Naomi Spriggins, born in 1891 and a recent graduate of Straight University.[15] In his second year, he would transfer to the classroom of Leontine Vignes, born in 1881 and a former public school teacher who had served as principal of the Colored Waif's Home since 1906. The overcrowded classroom conditions were not much better than at Fisk, but the year and a half Armstrong received of daily schooling formed a crucial part of his education. Asked by a radio disc jockey in 1954, "Louis did you go to high school, college, things like that?" Armstrong replied, "Well I went to high school when I was in the orphanage. . . . They had two teachers out there for the whole class and you graduate the same as if you was in the city."[16]

After evening activities, the boys would march to the upstairs dormitory, where they were allowed to talk until the lights were turned off at 9 p.m. Some of the boys continued whispering, but they were taking a chance, situated right above the keepers. "Whenever one of the Keepers would come upstairs, somebody would catch a whipping," Armstrong wrote.[17]

Perhaps all of this routine, or at least a form of it, had been in place when Armstrong had spent his two weeks in the "Jones Home" back in 1910. But the Waif's Home did offer something new in 1913: a music program, overseen by the Home's other assistant keeper, Peter Davis.

Peter Davis lived a long life, and one that was not without mystery. He became best known as Armstrong's first music teacher, giving a handful of interviews over the years, and even appearing on national television with his prized pupil. But it's not exactly known when he was born—sometime between 1880 and 1890—or how he entered the world of the Colored Waif's Home, or why he never married or had children of his own, and kept to a near hermetic lifestyle from 1949, when he retired from the facility, until his passing in 1971.[18]

He first turns up in the 1910 census, living at 622 South Johnson Street in the Third Ward right off Perdido Street, about a half mile from Armstrong's boyhood residence. Though listed as working in a furniture factory, Davis later claimed to have started teaching music at the age of 19, after studying with the renowned Professor William J. Nickerson, beginning on piano before switching to cornet.[19] Davis was hired as assistant keeper of the Colored Waif's Home in 1911. Future drummer Abbey "Chinee" Foster was in the Home at the time and recalled, "We used to take railroad spikes and play on the sides of the walls. And sometimes we would use the forks out of the kitchen; I'd use the fork and he'd use the cooking spoon and beat on the tub. And from then on, Old Man Dave [Peter Davis] got the idea of building up a band."[20] For his part, Davis said, "I entered the home with my instruments, my Cornet and my Bugle," most likely referring to secondhand instruments he brought with him to get the music program started.[21]

Captain Jones asked Davis to institute a system of bugle calls at the Home, replacing the police whistles Jones initially used to signal the boys. "It sounded too much like jail," Davis observed.[22] There was a problem, though. "In the very beginning I knew nothing about bugle calls," said Davis, "and Captain Jones would have to hum them to me. After a few times listening, I would learn to blow them on the bugle."[23]

By October 1912, the little brass band was able to perform at a rally at the Waif's Home for the Young Men's Christian Association. "The boys of the home have organized a brass band and are doing well," the New Orleans *Times-Democrat* reported.[24] A photo was taken of the small band around this time with Davis, holding a cornet, standing next to Henry "Kid" Rena on clarinet, Jeffrey Harris on baritone horn, Gus Vanzan on alto horn, Isaac Smoot on bass drum, and James Brown on snare drum.

Armstrong might have been interested in joining the band, but he did not hit it off with Davis at first. "He would whip me every time he had a chance and every time he'd whip me he'd make these remarks, 'You're one of those bad boys from Liberty and Perdido Streets and I don't like you,'" Armstrong recalled.[25]

Armstrong admitted that occasionally his behavior brought out the worst in Davis. "Oneday, I did something against the rules of the Waif's Home," he wrote. "Nothing that I would write home about...But just the same, Mr Peter Davis, gave me about fifteen hard lashes into my hand.....After that, I really was scared of him." Davis didn't mention the punishment but did recall one of Armstrong's transgressions. "He had ran away from there, left away from there and we were responsible for him if he had gotten hurt or something like

Figure 6.1 Peter Davis leads an early edition of the Colored Waif's Home band in 1913, shortly before Louis Armstrong joined. Left to right: Peter Davis, Henry "Kid" Rena, Jeffrey Harris, Gus Vanzan, Isaac Smoot, and James Brown.
Credit: Courtesy of the New Orleans Jazz Club Collection of the Louisiana State Museum.

that and we had to find him," Davis said, adding that Armstrong was missing for a full day.[26]

Fifteen lashes was getting off easy compared to the punishments given some of the other kids who ran afoul of Davis and the keepers. Davis himself recalled that when kids would get in trouble and fight, they'd be put in a little detention room he called "the dungeon," a small room on the second floor.[27] Armstrong remembered one kid who attempted to escape but was caught and had to face the wrath of Captain Jones. "[Captain Jones] had that nigger holding his naked ass," Armstrong recalled on one of his reel-to-reel tapes. "He had the biggest boys in the Home holding him for running away and he give him 105 [lashes]. And after 105 lashes, of course, the shit comes out." Like the time he observed his mother beat his sister, Armstrong concluded, " 'Well, that makes me a good boy.' And I didn't want that hard shit so I did everything right, coming from a kid."[28]

It's quite possible Armstrong was part of a more serious, disturbing punishment, but the following story has not been substantiated and comes from a unique source: Morris Grossberg, the interior decorator who worked closely with Louis and his fourth wife, Lucille, in their Corona, Queens, home for nearly 40 years. Asked if Louis and Lucille ever talked about having children, Grossberg responded in 1996, "They couldn't." He explained that when Armstrong was in the Waif's Home, one of the black inmates raped a white girl, who couldn't identify her attacker. "A terrible thing happened," Grossberg recounted. "Louie told me this story and never anyone else. They sterilized all the men in the orphanage, all the kids."[29] Grossberg was getting up in age at the time of this conversation, but this claim is clearly something that Louis or—more likely—Lucille told him. This also explains why Lucille was adamant to her dying day that Louis could not father a child with her or anyone else, once telling him, "You couldn't make a baby with a pencil."[30] It's also worth noting that many of the other inmates at the Waif's Home during this period, including Isaac Smoot, Gus Vanzan, Henry Rena, Edward Frazier, and others, never fathered any children.

Armstrong enjoyed hearing the Home's brass band but still could not conquer his fear of Peter Davis. "I was afraid Mr. Davis would say something to me, or give me a few more lashes, just he did not particularly care for me," Armstrong wrote. "I really was under the impression that he hated the very ground that I walked on."[31]

Armstrong grew unhappy in his early days at the Home. His father Willie had been out of his life for as long as he could remember, but now he visited his son in the Waif's Home on Sundays, often bringing his two sons, Willie Jr., born on February 8, 1907, and Henry, born May 9, 1909. Henry remembered Louis pleading with his father, "Dad, when you gettin' me out?" "He asked him that every Sunday," Henry said.[32] Willie Armstrong was powerless for now, just as he always had been.

The only bright spots occurred when Davis, impressed with Armstrong's work ethic and attitude, would give him "a slight smile of approval" or offer a kind word. "Gee, whatta feelin' that coming from him," Armstrong said.[33] Armstrong soon felt comfortable hanging around the band room—and showing off some of the comedy routines he perfected on the streets. "I remember Louis used to walk funny with his feet pointing out and at the first note of music he'd break into comedy dances," Davis said. "He could sing real well as a boy too, even though his voice was coarse."[34] Armstrong tried translating his experience with his homemade "gitbox" to a real guitar, but Davis said, "He couldn't do nothing with that."[35]

Instead, Armstrong formed another vocal quartet in the Home. "I'd play the piano and they'd sing," Davis said. "Anytime I'd play the piano, he'd sing and they'd go on different programs at different churches and raise little collections for them; 'cause nobody wasn't giving us nothing. . . . They allowed us to go out and beg different churches and schools to give us old clothes, something to eat, give us money and that's what we lived off."[36] In addition to Armstrong, the quartet also featured Isaac Smoot, Jimmy Brown, and Henry "Kid" Rena and allowed Armstrong to do the "buck dance" he used to do with his old quartet on Rampart Street.[37]

Armstrong clearly still loved to sing and dance, but there was another instrument that caught his attention: Davis's cornet. "I'd play the horn and he'd dance and then when I'd put my horn down, he'd pick it up and start playin' it," Davis said, lending further credence to the stories of Armstrong playing a bit before he was incarcerated.[38] Armstrong was just hamming it up for now, but Davis took note and soon after asked him a life-altering question:

"Louis Armstrong, how would you like to join the band?"

"That man had me so breathless, and so speechless, and surprised to boot,—why, —I just couldn't answer him right away," Armstrong wrote. He eventually stuttered, "Er'wa, yes, yes Mr. Dave, I would be thrilled to." Davis patted him on the back and told him, "Be to rehearsal after you wash up."[39]

Though there's a very strong possibility Armstrong had already attempted to teach himself the cornet, in the manuscript of *Satchmo: My Life in New Orleans*, he wrote, "I'd never tried to play a cornet before, but hearing that little brass band every day, and reminscing [*sic*] over my mind, thinking about Joe Oliver, Bolden and Bunk Johnson, I had an awful urge to try to learn the cornet."[40]

But he was getting ahead of himself: at his first rehearsal, Davis handed him a tambourine. "Hmmmm" Armstrong wrote. "It seemed that all of my dreams were in vain."[41] Even Davis noticed Armstrong "was a little disappointed when I put him in the band because he thought he would blow the horn, but instead of a cornet, he was playin' the tambourine."[42] Armstrong got over his disappointment and "started to whipping with rhythm along with the band... Mr Dave was so impressed, he immediately changed me from the tamborine to the drums....He must have sensed, I had the beat he was seeking, or, 'somphn.' "[43] Davis concurred with that assessment, saying, "Later, because he had good rhythm, he played the drums."[44] Armstrong succeeded on the drums, especially when he took a break—"a real good one, and a fly one at that"—on "At the Animal's Ball."

"Hooray for Louis Armstrong!" the boys shouted after hearing Armstrong's drumming. Davis nodded his approval and asked Armstrong if he was interested in learning the alto horn. "I being a singer all my life, my better judgement told me that an Alto is an instrument that sings a duet in a brass band the same as the baritone or the tenor would do in a quartet," Armstrong said. "So, I played the Alto (horn) very well indeed."[45]

Eventually, the kid who played bugle at the Home was discharged. "The minute he left the place, Mr. Dave appointed me the Bugle boy," Armstrong wrote. "My My. . . .what another thrill That was."[46] The bugle was dirty and starting to turn green, but Armstrong immediately went to work polishing it up and learning how to play it with Davis's tutelage. "They gave me the bugle and had me to learn the calls and, you know, 'Taps,' and when they go to bed and the mess call," Armstrong said. "That was my favorite one, that mess call, you know. And I used to be devilish and I'd hold it up sometime, you know, and them cats would [yell], 'Man, if you don't blow that call!' "[47]

"After a while, I commenced to being the most popular [boy] in the Waifs Home," he wrote, adding, "The whole place seemed to change."[48] Mayann and Mama Lucy would regularly visit Louis, bringing him baskets of cakes, candies, and fruit. Mama Lucy couldn't stop crying over her older brother's situation, but Louis consoled her in the Home's music room. "I was crying and he caught me by my hand and said, 'Come on, let me show you!' he say, 'I'm doing this!' He used to play piano, too. Play a little piano, go and get that big ol' thing like a guitar, beat on that thing. He say, 'Look, I'm learning! I'm learning!' He say, 'Don't cry!' "[49]

Impressed with how Armstrong was coming along on the bugle, Davis finally promoted him to the cornet. "Just think,—here I am with the ambitions, of my dreams, finally came true," Armstrong wrote. "Or, was it still a dream... Thats, what I thought to myself.... But it wasn't... It was the real thing."[50]

The first song Davis taught his new pupil on cornet was "Home Sweet Home." But once Armstrong got the melody down, he couldn't help putting a little of that Third Ward sound in his interpretation. "And by being around the honky tonks, I put in a few licks in there," Armstrong said in a 1954 interview before launching into a swinging scatted rendition of the melody. Davis was not impressed. "Don't put that stuff in there, boy!" he would shout. "Play it straight!"[51]

Davis eventually worked on teaching him how to read music, though only "a little," Armstrong said.[52] He admitted that he struggled with reading music over the next several years. "Now Professor Dave [Peter Davis], he would strictly try to learn them the music," Wilbert Tillman, who helped as an instrument cleaner at this time, recalled. "But he wouldn't stop them from playing by ear if they had that gifted talent. See, that's why they grew so fast to be musicians. See, Louis played a long time by ear until he began to see the light to read."[53]

Davis used to let Armstrong's ad hoc quartet sing in church but now he let the brass band lead the way with a very special (and humorous) selection: "We used to play 'When the Saints Go Marching In' every Sunday for the boys to march to church and I enjoyed that," Armstrong said.[54] In 1965, Davis recalled, "Then when I did get him to play 'When the Saints Go Marching In' [and] 'Put on Your Old Grey Bonnet,' there was a high note . . . at the end of the strain. None of the other boys couldn't make it. And I couldn't make it myself. But he would blow the high C above the staff to let us to know that's the end of the strain."[55]

Armstrong developed so quickly on the cornet that Davis soon came to him with a proposition:

"Louis, I am going to make you the Leader of our brass band."

"Yeeoww," Armstrong exclaimed. "I jump straight up into the air, with Mr. Dave watching me, as I ran into the mess to tell all the boys the good news.... And they too, rejoiced for me." It was exciting enough to be the leader of the brass band and to be playing his favorite instrument, but Armstrong was especially thrilled because being leader "automatically gave me chances to see, and be in the streets and see Mayann and the crowd around Liberty and Perdido streets a little more."[56]

Armstrong got his first opportunity on Decoration Day (now known as Memorial Day), May 30, 1913. When the band reached Armstrong's Liberty and Perdido neighborhood, they were cheered on by "all the whores, pimps, gamblers, thieves, beggars, infact, everybody who was anybody were watching the parade, because they knew they'd see Mayann's boy, Dipper and the brass band," Louis wrote. "And they'd never visualize me with a cornet in my hand, blowing as good as I did." Apparently Mayann was sleeping "real hard from a night job she had," but neighbors woke her up just in time to see her son leading the band.[57] Even Mama Lucy remembered, "And that's when people's running to get Mama for her to come stand and see Louis."[58]

Finally, someone in the crowd asked Davis, "Can we give little Louis some money?"[59] Davis, used to sending the boys out to beg in the church, nodded his approval, not expecting much. "Huh," Armstrong remarked. "Those Sports people gave me so much money into my hat, I had to borrow several boys caps in the band to accept all of that money... They gave me so much money until, Mr. Dave taken it and bought, all new uniforms and new instruments for everybody who played in the band."[60] Armstrong had spent most of his days before the Waif's Home scraping together every cent he could earn from selling newspapers, delivering coal, working on a junk wagon, singing with a quartet, grinding up red bricks for the prostitutes; now people were stuffing his hat with money, probably more money than he had ever seen before in one place, all because he was the leader of a kids' brass band. Music might have already been in his blood but suddenly, it now represented a way out.

Figure 6.2 The Colored Waif's Home brass band of late 1913 or early 1914, with an arrow pointing to leader Louis Armstrong, third row, center. Peter Davis is seated in front of Armstrong.
Credit: Courtesy of the Louis Armstrong House Museum.

The *Times-Picayune* was at the Decoration Day parade and devoted a solid portion of their coverage to the Colored Waif's Home Band, even listing its personnel, beginning with "Louis Armstrong, leader."[61] In less than five months, he had transformed from Louis Armstrong, "old offender," to Louis Armstrong, "leader."

There was no going back.

The designation of "Louis Armstrong, leader" doesn't make it clear whether Armstrong also played cornet at the Decoration Day parade or was made leader only because of his personality, comic dancing, and ability to work a crowd. The *Times-Picayune* did mention two cornetists, Sam Johnson and Henry Rena; Rena would figure prominently in Armstrong's life over the next several years. Rena (pronounced *ren-nay*) arrived in the early days of Peter Davis's brass band, first gravitating toward the clarinet and then, like Armstrong, eventually the bugle and the cornet.[62] When *Down Beat* reporter

John Lucas talked with Rena in the early 1940s Rena relayed his memories of "how he and Armstrong tried their best to imitate Bunk after Louis had persuaded Rena to give up the clarinet for the trumpet."[63]

Born on August 30, 1898, Rena was older and more experienced and already making a name for himself with his ability to play high notes. "We used to take the mouthpiece and go on the pavement and flatten it," his brother Joseph Rene explained. "A lip could stay there. You want to get it in there, man, and hook up in there and stay there. That's what you want. That was my brother's secret to making high notes."[64] Kid Rena was alive at the time Robert Goffin conducted his research for *Horn of Plenty* and is quoted as warning Armstrong that "he would blow himself out" by practicing all day, trying to hit high notes.[65] This led Armstrong to borrow a file to scrape notches into his mouthpiece to fit better on his lips. "Louis copied behind my brother," Joseph Rene concluded.[66]

"Go get them kids," was a common refrain whenever a social club or private party needed music, and the Waif's Home brass band was happy to play for any and all occasions.[67] Not all of these engagements were without incident. During a break at "a white folks picnic" on the water at Spanish Fort, the band's drummer, Jimmy Brown, went for a swim. When he stood up, his bathing suit fell off! "Oh—you never saw such scramblin to pick up a bathing suit in all your days," Armstrong wrote. "Especially when the white fellow from the camp facing us [went] inside and got his shot gun, and pointed it straight up Jimmy Brown's 'Rusty Dusty'—saying, you black 'Sommitch' 'cover your black ass, or I'll shoot........ At those words, we all help Jimmy pick up his trunks, as we ran like mad up the stairs." Armstrong admitted they were "scared stiff," even after the white folks started laughing and joking about the incident. "Hmmmm. . . .," Armstrong wrote. "We kids weren't any more good the rest of the day......... But we weren't so scared, that we did not eat all the spaghetti, and beer they served us, after they'd finished eating theirs...Was good."[68]

Armstrong was definitely playing cornet when the Colored Waif's Home band hit the streets on Labor Day, September 1. Trombonist Kid Ory, then leader of one of the hottest ragtime bands in town, was asked in 1957 about the first time he heard Armstrong. "On a parade, on a Labor Day," Ory replied. "He was in the next band, parading with a little kid band, you know, from the [Waif's] Home. . . .He and Kid Rena." Ory's band was marching directly in front of the kids' band when he heard a cornet with a "nice, good, solid tone to it." Ory called a break to get some beer and sandwiches, stopping to watch Louis. "And he's blowing," Ory recalled.

"Come here, I want to tell you something, you're doing a good job," Ory told the youngster.

"Thank you, Mr. Ory," Armstrong replied.

"You're going to be all right some day," Ory said. "You keep that up."[69]

These parades provided many New Orleans musicians—including future trumpeter Don Albert and drummers Minor Hall and Louis Barbarin—with their first memories of Armstrong. Arthur "Zutty" Singleton, already impressed by hearing Armstrong sing with the quartet at a Mack and Mack tent show, soon heard a buzz about the new cornet player at the Home. "Then I saw Louis playing in a band at a picnic," he said. "He was marching along with the band, so we got up real close to him to see if he was actually playing those notes. We didn't believe he could learn to play in that short time. I can still remember he was playing 'Maryland, My Maryland.' And he sure was swingin' out that melody."[70]

"Maryland, My Maryland" was a popular march that dated back to 1861 (featuring the same melody as "O Tanenbaum") and apparently a staple of the Waif's Home band's repertoire. On Christmas Day, the group performed it at the Pythian Temple at an event sponsored by the *Times-Democrat* to give toys out to 9,000 poor Black children. Later that same day, they performed in front of 3,000 more Black children at a similar event held by the Mystic Order of Hobgoblins, a recently formalized social aid organization that had paid an earlier visit to the Waif's Home "with a wagon load of toys and clothing for the inmates."

The *Daily Picayune* complimented the "excellent music" of the band, noting, "Hymns were mingled with other selections."[71] "The band played 'Little Bunch of Shamrock' [*sic*], 'Dixie,' 'Maryland, My Maryland,' 'America' and other selections," added the *Times-Democrat*, offering us an early Armstrong set list. "At the close a 'nickel collection' was taken among negro citizens present, and the musicians received a veritable coin shower."[72] "Dixie" went back even further than "Maryland, My Maryland," having been published in 1859. But "America" was from 1910 and "Little Bunch of Shamrocks" was a brand-new popular song, published in 1913. It might be the first example of Armstrong performing one of the latest popular hits of the day; it would be far from the last.

Armstrong's family was too poor to give gifts at Christmas time; he later told his fourth wife, Lucille, that he never had a Christmas tree until he was in his forties. But now at the Colored Waif's Home, he was receiving toys and clothes from charitable organizations, and performing in front of over 12,000 people in a single day as the cornetist and leader of the Home's brass band. His life had changed immensely in the previous year. His case came up before Judge Andrew Wilson every six months and Wilson chose to keep Armstrong in the Home into 1914. Armstrong did not complain.

He now had structure, for one thing. He attended school daily, ate three meals a day, wore clean clothes, performed chores, and even played sports. "The place seemed more like a health center, or a boarding school, than a boys jail," Armstrong wrote.[73]

On Davis's night off, he would sometimes take Armstrong into town with him or even take him back to his home, where Armstrong became "real Chummy" with Davis's 14-year-old niece, Ida E. Robinson, who sang hymns with Armstrong and played piano while he played cornet. Davis would continue to give Armstrong lessons during these overnight stays, the two returning to the Home in the morning.

Armstrong continued to impress Davis, who had vivid memories of a parade that occurred on Fireman's Day, March 4, 1914. Each year, George Palmer Homes, a one-time volunteer fireman known as "Fireman George," would dress in "spectacular costuming," hire a band, and "sally forth and parade the streets of the business section," taking up a collection as he did so. On this day "Fireman George," now 73 years old, got in costume and began parading with the Waif's Home band behind him, but he soon collapsed. "In consternation his band ceased playing," the *Times-Democrat* reported. "The cornetist picked up the aged negro and carried him to the sidewalk." Minutes later, Fireman George was pronounced dead.

"This indeed saddened Louis very much," Davis recalled. "I must say that Louis could smile and forever appear gay even if there was [nothing] to be gay about, but when it comes to showing respect for a love [*sic*] one he also knew how to be serious. Without my advising him he struck up the hymn, 'What a Friend We Have in Jesus.' The boy was very pathetic and hurted over the death of Fireman George."[74] The *Times-Democrat* reported the hymn as "Nearer My God to Thee," writing, "The darky band struck up the tune, discordantly perhaps, but nevertheless solemnly and sincere" in an article with the headline "'Nigger' George Makes Last Parade and Answers Roll Call in the Beyond."[75]

Armstrong was showing his maturity as a musician and as a man, continuing to impress his elders. But in June 1914, the fairytale ended and a nightmare began; he would be leaving the Waif's Home to move in with his father.

7

"I Would Gladly Live It Over Again"

1914

Willie Armstrong had been working for the American Turpentine Company since it opened in 1905 and proved himself to be a hard worker. When his son's case came before Judge Wilson again in June 1914, Willie brought his boss, who promised Wilson that Louis would be happy living with his father, stepmother, and half-brothers. That was good enough for Wilson; Louis would be released on June 16.

When Louis got the news, his first thought was, "Wonder what my father would say if I asked him to let me stay right there in the Home." He had never lived with his father before and worried about whether he would ever see Mayann and Mama Lucy again. "I already knew how happy I'd become in the Home," he said. "Everybody there loved me and I was in love with everybody."[1]

Louis noticed that even the Home's staff looked sad as he began packing his clothes. The brass band played and Armstrong joined them for one last time. "I played several numbers, with them for my father's approval, which he was very much elated, at his son's advancement through the world," he wrote. His half-brother Henry remembered, "When he got out he said he was glad my daddy made him stay back there, made a man out of him."[2] Louis kissed Mrs. Jones goodbye and shook hands with all the kids, Henry Alexander, Peter Davis, and Captain Joseph Jones. "I wasn't happy at all, leaving the Home, to go home," he reflected.[3]

Mayann wasn't happy either. As she did when her son was arrested, Mayann went off the rails upon learning that Louis was now going to be living with his father. It all caught up with her on July 21, 1914, a month after Louis was discharged, when Mary Albert was arrested at 1:50 a.m. for disturbing the peace at 420 South Franklin Street, a tenement house used as a "crib" for many of the prostitutes in the neighborhood. The police report listed her as being 30 years old—the first example of the 1883 birthday she'd use for the rest of her life—and her occupation was again described as prostitution. Mayann would have to pay a $2.50 fine or spend 30 days in the House of Detention.

Figure 7.1 Tinted portrait of Willie Armstrong, which hung in the home of Beatrice "Mama Lucy" Armstrong until she gave it to Lucille Armstrong in 1973. It is now part of the permanent exhibit of the Louis Armstrong House Museum.
Credit: Courtesy of the Louis Armstrong House Museum.

The police report simply stated, "FINE NOT PAID." Mayann went off to jail, leaving Mama Lucy without her mother again.

Mama Lucy was now 11 years old and beginning to notice things, though she, like Louis, remained protective of her mother. "Maybe I'd seen it going on and didn't know what it is," she said in 1983. " 'Cause I was a really green girl. And if she did . . ." At this point, she paused before continuing, "But all I know, Mayann *worked*, you understand! I don't know what made her do it. But when a woman got children, and ain't got nobody to take care of 'em, she got to . . ." Again, her voice trailed off. " 'Cause she sure used to have plenty company," she said. "Plenty company." She remembered a friend of her mother's, "Miss Lily," who would come over and "get it on all the time" with men in one of the rooms in her mother's home. "And I was peeking, I wanted to see what was going on," Mama Lucy remembered. "And so the lady opened the window and vomit. I called my mama and I didn't know what they doin.' "[4]

Thus, Louis might have been sad to leave the Waif's Home and sadder to not be with his mother, but it was probably best for him to be living at Willie Armstrong's home on Poydras and South Galvez Streets, a solid mile away from Mayann.[5] Louis's new residence wasn't exactly the lap of luxury; the home had only two bedrooms and a kitchen, no indoor plumbing, and no electricity, leading the family to use kerosene lamps for light. The neighborhood was the third of three different neighborhoods Armstrong lived in that were called at one time or another "The Battlefield." "That's what they used to call it," Henry Armstrong said. "Yeah, so many people used to get killed over there."[6]

Louis settled in and soon met his stepmother, Gertrude, "a very fine woman," he said, "And treated me just the same as if I was her own child... I will always love her for it." Both Willie Armstrong Sr. and Gertrude Nolan worked during the day, so Louis's full-time job became housekeeper and babysitter to his half-brothers. He grew close with the younger Henry, but Willie Jr. was a troublemaker. "Sometimes I felt just like taking a whole pot of beans and throw it on him," Louis said.[7] It might have been better than working on a coal cart or junk wagon, but raising two young boys was still not an ideal situation for a 13-year-old boy. Looking back at this period, Mama Lucy said of her brother, "Louis was the oldest child, see? But he was a little boy, too."[8]

Louis soon learned that his half-brothers might have been small, but they had large appetites. "And Louis get to cookin' and when he get through cookin' he had nothing to eat," Henry Armstrong remembered. "Me and my brother ate it all up."[9] Louis finally "got wise to them" and would eat a full portion before ringing the dinner bell for his half-brothers.[10] "And so Louis tricked us one time, he was cookin' and eating," Henry remembered. "We had nothing."[11] Louis's propensity for nicknames also led him to give Henry a moniker that would last the rest of his life. "Louis told my mama, 'Henry like bread so much I'm gonna name him 'Baker,' " Henry said. Even his 1991 obituary referred to him as "Mr. Henry (Baker) Armstrong."[12]

As usual, there are conflicting reports about this period in Armstrong's life relating to a very serious subject: music. In a 1931 profile, the *New Orleans Item* accurately summed up Armstrong's time in the Waif's Home before adding, "But when he was discharged as a reputable youngster a year and a half later, it never occurred to him to stick to music. Instead, seeking to support himself, he became a newsboy, selling *Items* in a lusty voice at the corner of Poydras and Baronne streets. This went on for about six months during which time Louis and cornets were complete strangers."[13] Writing his life story five years later in *Swing That Music*, Armstrong lengthened the time, saying he left the Waif's Home at the age of 14 and "I can remember just as well, I was seventeen years of age before I decided to pick up my cornet again."[14] Robert Goffin spent several pages chronicling Armstrong's time with his father and the various odd jobs that followed, writing that "Louis gave little thought to music" during this period.[15]

But in *Satchmo: My Life in New Orleans*, Armstrong wrote of his half-brothers, "As much as they laughed, when I'd practise [*sic*] my cornet, they began to kind of listen (casually)and give little comments, etc, as kids go..... Then we began to understand each other....."[16] Henry Armstrong concurred and actually remembered it as a very musical home. "My brother was playing trumpet, I was playing drums, my mother used to play guitar, my daddy used to play guitar, and my daddy's brother—one of them—used to play the sliding trumpet, another one of them had a big horn, the kind you put around your neck [sousaphone], you know?" he said. "All of us used to play music, but Louis was the only one who kept it up because he went to that Home."[17]

If Louis was indeed playing a cornet at his father's home, where did he get it? The best possible explanation is it was a gift from Captain Joseph Jones. "The story goes that it was bought in a pawn shop by Capt. Joseph Jones of the Waifs' Home once they realized how talented this kid was," said New Orleans Jazz Museum curator Steve Teeter. "It was bought to encourage him. When he left the home, Jones loaned it to him, telling him to bring it back once he'd earned enough money to buy his own horn. He did, and as his fame grew, they kept it as a treasure."[18] It does seem almost common knowledge that Jones gave Armstrong a horn. Multi-instrumentalist Manuel "Fess" Manetta recalled that Armstrong "come out Jones Home with an artificial lead horn, you know, that old man Jones gave him."[19]

There was also the question of Peter Davis, who lived nearby. Asked if Louis continued to see Davis after he got out of the Waif's Home, Henry Armstrong answered, "Oh yeah. . . . His shack was right there by that gym, Earhart [Blvd.] and Broad [Street]. It wasn't nothing but a dump with high weeds, couldn't see the little shack for the weeds. . . . And he had a house and had tar paper on his floor, you know, you used to make for your house. And he had every instrument you wanna name. So he would call us all around there, all the boys around the neighborhood and learn us how to play."[20] But asked if Davis ever loaned out his instruments, Henry replied, "Well, no, you couldn't take it out of his shack. You had to go over there and play."[21]

It's hard to imagine Armstrong giving "little thought to music" after the life-changing experiences he had at the Waif's Home. Whether or not he regularly was practicing during this period, he was stymied by the location of his father's residence, far away from the hustle and bustle of the ragtime bands that provided the soundtrack to his Perdido Street neighborhood. He'd be back sooner than he expected.

One day Louis entered his father's home and saw a surprising sight: his mother Mayann sitting there. Willie Armstrong said to his son, "Louis, I'm sending you home to live with your mother. Is it alright?"

Louis knew why he had to leave: "Because my father came to a conclusion that his expenses were heavy enough with his original family... And with me along, kind of made it real heavy."

He was "thrilled inwardly" at the turn of events, but didn't want to hurt the feelings of the man who had abandoned him shortly after he was born. "Afterall, he did try his best to make me happy the whole time I live with him, mother Gertrude, Willie and Henry," Louis later wrote, accentuating the positive. "And for that and their kindness, I was ever so grateful."[22]

He must have been in a forgiving mood when he wrote the above words as it went down a bit differently in Mama Lucy's memory. She recalled that it was Louis who initiated the move, reaching out to Mayann and telling her, "Mama, I don't want to stay there. Papa said that he can't make ends meet." Mayann was incensed. "Wait 'til that son of a bitch come this way," she said of Willie before demanding that Louis come back and live with her. "He come and walk all the way," Mama Lucy said. "Yeah, he walked home."[23] Mama Lucy's telling is probably more accurate; though Willie Armstrong lived until 1933, Louis rarely saw his father again.

Louis was gratified to be back home with Mayann. "All this time I was living with Mama and we always poured our troubles into each other," he reflected in 1965. "She was a stocky woman—dark, lovely expression and a beautiful soul. And she instilled in me the idea that what you can't get—to hell with it. Don't worry about what the other fellow has. Everybody loved her for that, because if you live next door and you got the world, that's all right. Just don't mess with her little world. I think I had a *great* mother. She didn't have much power, but she did all she could for me—grabbing little knicknacks here and there and everything, and we put it all together."[24]

Louis knew that being back home with his mother and sister meant he would have to go back to work, leading him back to Charlie Wilson's newsstand. "I sold papers for him a long time," he wrote.[25] Stock footage even survives from 1915 of an African American newsboy with a smile that's uncannily reminiscent of Armstrong's.[26]

Armstrong learned to do whatever he could to help support Mayann and Mama Lucy, writing that "some time when things were rough," he would go to the produce places in "front of town" and wait for them to throw their "potatoes, onions, cabbage, chickens, turkeys" in the garbage. "Before the garbage wagons would come, we would get to those barrels, with what ever was in them, if it was half spoiled chickens, turkeys, ducks, or a flock of goose, or geese," he continued, "we would cut the bad parts, off, boil them real good, dress them up nice, put them in a basket (looking like new) and sell them to those fine places, for what ever amount the proprietor would offer us."[27]

A haul from one of these garbage cans led to a story that both Louis and Mama Lucy loved telling for the rest of their lives. Louis told it in detail in the manuscript of *Satchmo: My Life in New Orleans* but it was cut from the published edition. Mama Lucy told it in both of her surviving extended interviews, too; the following has been pieced together from all three versions.

The story begins with Louis "looking into those waste barrels," finally spotting "a great big spoiled turkey, laying there doing nothing." Louis admitted it smelled terribly, but he brought it home and had Mayann parboil it. Mama Lucy observed the scene and asked if she could come along to help her brother sell the turkey to a restaurant. "Personally I didn't particularly care to have her come along," Louis thought to himself, "Because she laughs too much... And might spoil the whole sale of my turkey."

Mayann said it was fine by her, so Louis and Mama Lucy headed to a "swell restaurant on St. Charles Street." Mama Lucy said the turkey was "stinking so bad we could hardly stand it," but she remembered Louis holding her hand the whole way, imploring, "Mama Lucy, don't you laugh!"

"I ain't gonna laugh," she responded.

Once they arrived at the restaurant—"We went in through the rear (of course)," Louis noted—they found the proprietor and Louis went into his sales pitch.

"Mister, do you want to buy a turkey?"

Mama Lucy remained quiet but Louis "could see the expression on her face...And that (to me) meant laughter somewheres soon."

"How much do you want for it?" the proprietor said.

Louis stammered, "Er'wa, a dollar and a half."

"Okay, let's see it," the man said.

"By that time," Louis said, "everybody in the place had turned around, looking at us."

The owner of the restaurant reached in Louis's basket.

"And as he pulled the napkin back, the fumes—the odor ——Famine—the smell—all hit the Proprietor in the face—at one time," Louis recalled. "The place (by this time) was as quiet as a church mouse..... After the proprietor had gotten his [senses] back again from being gassed to death, he looked at me with disgust."

"Boy," the man said, "if you don't get out of here with that rotten turkey, I will have you arrested."

That was too much for Mama Lucy to handle.

"I fell out," she said, breaking into laughter all over again in 1983. "The geese were smelling strong! And I fell out."

"Mama Lucy, immediately fell to the floor, laughing as hard as she could—holding her side," Louis said. "I went out in the street—real salty at her... And went home without her."

Mama Lucy also added one more detail about the proprietor's wife entering the room, "smelling and smelling" as she walked closer to the turkey. "When she put her hand on that sack, honey, I fell out! And the lady said, 'Whew!' " At that point, she remembered Louis grabbing her by the hand as the two raced out of the restaurant together.

Mama Lucy also added a postscript to her version of the story that spoke to her brother's determination. "And Louis stopped, picked up that [turkey], honey, and sold it right underneath for us for 35 cents," she said. "A lady named Mrs. Laurelton bought it for 35 cents, asked us if we had any more." Asked when this took place, Mama Lucy said, "I think he was in his teens back then, you know? But he used to be a good boy."

For his part, Louis ended his story by writing, "My sister sure used to make me so angry" before adding, "But I was deeply in love with my sister and mother... We three struggled together pretty near all our lives.... And, even at that, I would gladly live it over again."[28]

With her two children back home, Mayann seemed eager to reform her ways a bit and made it a point to take Louis with her to Mount Zion Baptist Church every Sunday to hear Elder Cosey. But even in such a sacred space, the two managed to have some laughs. "She's sitting in church one time—I used to go to church with Mama, she's always a lot of fun—preacher said, 'Well, since everybody enjoyed my sermon' and blah blah blah, Mayann says, 'I ain't heard nothing,' " Louis recounted, bursting into laughter at the memory. "Yeah, I mean, she was awful sarcastic but she could pull that shit."[29]

Louis had been doing comedy on the streets with his quartet and in the Waif's Home, but now he had an opportunity to win some laughs in church, impersonating the preacher, conducting the choir, and even doing a Bert Williams routine. "They all but give me applause in the church!" he recalled of the reaction to his exploits.[30] It was most likely around this time that Armstrong won an Amateur Night competition at the Iroquois Theater by dipping his face in flour and doing a routine in whiteface.[31]

Armstrong's foundation of singing and comedy was secure, but he hadn't had any real opportunities to hear good ragtime since he left the Waif's Home in June 1914. Finally, back in his neighborhood, Armstrong couldn't wait to hear his old favorite Bunk Johnson with a fresh pair of ears.

The fact that Armstrong sought Johnson out is undeniable. "And me and Louis, sometime we used to go down, they used to call them tonks, go down there and wait for Bunk Johnson," banjoist Clarence "Little Dad" Vincent recalled. "And Bunk used to like to drink and buy us a little drink. . . . Well, that's where Louis learned all of his stuff from Bunk Johnson, you see, after he come out of the Home."[32]

Johnson claimed to have given Armstrong some pointers in 1911, but said that Armstrong's favorite song to hear him play was "Ballin' the Jack"—a tune that was published in November 1913. Thus, if Johnson's claims were true, he might have remembered the little kid fumbling with the cornet in 1911, but it was more likely that Armstrong would have asked him for advice after his stay in the Waif's Home—though not for long. Johnson's biographer Christopher Hillman wrote that between 1914 and 1917, Johnson "generally worked outside of New Orleans."[33] Mike Hazeldine and Barry Martyn agreed in their book on Johnson. "He never liked New Orleans much to stay in and, in fact, never liked to stay any place too long. He called New Orleans a 'dirty old hole,'" they wrote.[34] In their chronology, Hazeldine and Martyn had Johnson leaving New Orleans in 1914, though there are also stories of him playing the 1915 Mardi Gras.

Thus, it appears that Armstrong fell under the spell of Johnson's cornet when he was playing with the Eagle Band and in parades throughout Armstrong's neighborhood in 1911 and 1912 and, after his year and a half in the Waif's Home, sought him out for tips and inspiration in late 1914 before Johnson left New Orleans, most likely in the first part of 1915. With access to the cornet Captain Jones likely loaned him when he left the Waif's Home, it would have been exciting for Armstrong to hear Johnson play, then go back home and try to figure out how to replicate the older man's tone and ideas.

But that's as far as it went. Johnson soon left town, as did another New Orleans cornet "King," Freddie Keppard, who left in 1914 to go on a pioneering vaudeville tour with Bill Johnson's Original Creole Band. That left one figure, a future "King," for Armstrong to seek out for inspiration.

"So forget Bunk's statement," Armstrong wrote. "I did learn to play the cornet in the Colored Waifs Home for Boys. And after I got out Papa Joe Oliver took over, quite naturally. He was always my idol. I liked the way he did things (musically anyway). My man Joe—God Bless him."[35]

Armstrong's nickname for Oliver made sense to his sister, Beatrice. "Called him 'Papa Joe,'" she reflected in 1973. "Did more for him than his papa did."[36]

8

"Destined to Be Great"

1914–1915

After Louis returned to Perdido Street in late 1914 or early 1915, he most likely reconnected with Morris Karnofsky. In his 1969 manuscript "Louis Armstrong + the Jewish Family," Armstrong placed all of his Karnofsky stories before the Waif's Home, writing, "As I came into twelve years old I became a little large for the job with the Jewish people."[1] In *Horn of Plenty* from 1947, Robert Goffin also claimed that Armstrong reached out to Morris Karnofsky when he got out of the Waif's Home and Karnofsky rejected him as being too big to be a helper.[2] But in 1941, Armstrong reunited with Morris in New Orleans and reminisced in a letter to Leonard Feather about "working on his Coal Wagon," adding, "It was somewheres around the year of 1915 and early 16."[3] And in the manuscript for *Satchmo: My Life in New Orleans*, Armstrong writes about Morris in a section with the heading "1916–17." This would suggest Armstrong did go back to work for the Karnofskys for a short period of time after the Waif's Home, which makes sense when one considers the trajectory of the career of Joe Oliver.

Freddie Keppard held the plum gig at Pete Lala's in the District until he left town in the summer of 1914, opening the door for Oliver to take his place at the hefty salary of $25 a week. Oliver had worked hard to earn this opportunity and it showed. He did not possess the tone of Manuel Perez or Bunk Johnson, but discovered something unique when he started experimenting with different mutes, making him stand out from the other cornetists in town. "He was the greatest freak trumpet player I ever knew," cornetist Mutt Carey said. "He did most of his playing with cups, glasses, buckets and mutes. He was the best gut bucket man I ever heard."[4]

Preston Jackson agreed, stating, "Later on, about 1914 I should say, Joe began to improve a lot. He used to practice very hard. I remember he once told me that it took him ten years to get a tone on his instrument. He used a half-cocked mute, and how he could make it talk! He played the variation style too; running chords I mean. His ear was wonderful—that helped a lot."[5]

The timing was fortuitous; just as Oliver was hitting his stride at Pete Lala's, Louis found himself back in the red-light district on the coal wagon. Though Armstrong was there for Oliver, he recalled the actual leader of the band being pianist Buddy Christian. When interviewed by William Russell in the 1930s, Christian called it "the greatest all-star band that ever existed," adding that they "played for about three years at Pete's place . . . they played there from around 1914 to 1916," lending further credence to Armstrong's recall of being there after his stay in the Waif's Home.[6]

The impression Oliver made on him in this period lasted a lifetime. "How he used to blow that cornet of his down in Storyville for Pete Lala," Armstrong wrote. "I was just a youngster who loved that horn of King Olivers... I would delight delivering an order of stone coal to the prostitute who used to hustle in her crib right next to Pete Lalas Cabaret... Just sos I could hear King Oliver play... I was just too young to go into Pete Lalas at the time... And I'd just stand there in that lady's crib listening to King Oliver... And I'm all in a daze . . . " The prostitutes would sometimes have to snap Armstrong out of the stupor he was in while listening to Oliver play songs like "High Society" and "Panama" but it was worth it. "So I'd go home very pleased and happy that I did at least hear my idol blow at least a couple of numbers that really gassed me to no end," Armstrong reflected.[7]

Armstrong called Pete Lala's "the most important" cabaret in the District and once stressed, "I didn't go around any other place at all. Because I was always a King Oliver deciple [*sic*], ever since I could tell the sound of a note or one note from another." But truthfully, Oliver wasn't the only cornetist Armstrong heard while working in the District. "There's Buddy Pitit [*sic*] whom I admired again on the cornet—He used to play right up the street from King Oliver in Storyville," Armstrong wrote in 1947. "Of course, Joe Oliver was the 'baddest' 'Sommitch' in Storyville on Cornet—'Blieve that'... But it was something that I liked also... And in the later years he too—gave me lots to do musically."[8] In his rush to always prop up Oliver, Armstrong downplayed the influence of Buddy Petit, but Petit indeed gave Armstrong "lots to do musically" in more ways than one.[9]

Petit was inspired by both Bunk Johnson and Freddie Keppard, but his big contribution seemed to be his harmonic knowledge, his way of breaking up chords, and his use of chromatic runs. "Yeah, Buddy was a wonderful trumpet player, at mostly making them diminished chords," trumpeter Ernie Cagnalotti recalled.[10] Clarinetist Edmond Hall, who later played with Armstrong in the 1950s, worked with Petit in his younger days and said, "He's the first trumpet player I ever heard spoke about different chords, minor, major augmented, you know." Hall also tellingly compared Petit's style to that of the white cornetist Bobby Hackett, who later became one of Armstrong's very favorite musicians.[11] That gibes with Punch Miller's description of Petit's style: "Round, pretty, he didn't make high notes. Everything he made was clean."[12]

Petit's lack of range wasn't seen as a drawback at the time. "As for Buddy Petit, I think he was the sweetest little variation trumpet player, because he'd make the cutest things on his trumpet that you'd ever listen to," trumpeter Amos White said. "They were cute. He had no great range. But who wanted a range? When you went out of the familiarity of the trumpet, you would be going into the clarinet family or some other family. Nobody wants that."[13] At least not yet they didn't.

Armstrong might have been soaking in the music of Joe Oliver and Buddy Petit, but musicians weren't the only kinds of people Armstrong began spending time with during his trips to the District. "I was so small until I had to put on long pants when ever Mr Karnoffsky would go down in the District to sell his stone coal (as we called it then) Five Cents a Water Bucket," Armstrong reminisced in 1941, adding, "Oh I really thought I was somebody down there amongst those Pimps-Gamblers, etc."[14]

Indeed, 1915 seems to also be the year Armstrong really started hanging with "the sporting crowd" as he called it. In a 1959 manuscript, Armstrong typed "1915" and wrote about how when Oliver finished work at Pete Lala's, he'd head to the "Big 25"—formally known as the 25 Cabaret—on Franklin Street, where "They used to have some mighty big games there with the Pimps and Hustlers, who gambles nightly and also killing time waiting until their Women get through Hustling."[15]

The band at the 25, which sometimes included future Armstrong associates such as Clarence Williams and Sidney Bechet, was led by pianist Louis Wade and the place was managed by his brother Thomas Wade, who went by the nickname "Clerk."[16] In Armstrong's estimation, Clerk Wade was "the sharpest pimp of them all," known for wearing diamonds and solid gold clasps in his garters, along with a "solid gold belt buckle" and "the very best clothes." "All the women went wild over Clerk," according to Armstrong.[17]

Wade was a dangerous man, first mentioned in a newspaper on August 4, 1910, for stabbing Joseph F. Ingram twice in the left breast and then escaping before the police arrived.[18] But it all caught up with Wade on April 27, 1915, when he was killed by Lillian Smith after a quarrel.[19] "When he died, his funeral was the largest New Orleans had witnessed at that time," Armstrong wrote. "Everybody turned out... Even to the people who did not know Clerk Wade, turned out at his funeral...."[20]

Armstrong couldn't help but observe the love a pimp like Wade received. Armstrong was now in his teenage years and beginning to think about sex. He would still hang out with Isaac "Ike" Smoot from his Waif's Home days, noting, "He was a very handsome child... And lot of the whores would try to make him.... But he and I were sort of afraid of those bad strong women..... Our mothers always told us about fooling around with women that was too strong-for-us sexually... So, we would hang around the joints, but we didn't think about sex... Not to the extent that it was detrimental to us... We wanted to learn all we could about life... Mostly music."[21]

At Wade's funeral, music came in the form of Manuel Perez's Onward Brass Band with Joe Oliver on second cornet. "There was one band I'd always follow," Armstrong said in 1956. "I don't care how many bands there were on the street. That was the Onward Band with Joe Oliver and Manny Perez in that band.... Them cats would play a tune like 'Panama,' and the second liners, you know, the guys that follow the parade—raggedy guys, you know, on the other side of the street—they would applaud, and old Joe Oliver had to play an encore on 'Panama.' And I was this kid, diggin' all this."[22]

Armstrong recalled a time when the baseball team from his neighborhood, the Black Diamonds, traveled to Algiers to play a local team. In the middle of the game, those present heard the sounds of the Onward Band playing as they headed to the Canal Street Ferry. "They struck up, 'It's A Long Ways From Tipperary,' " Armstrong said. "Man, you ain't never heard so much horn blowing! Old Joe Oliver reached up in that second cornet—[scats] doot, deet, doot, deet, you know, he hit them kind of notes like that and broke up the game! Cats were dropping bats, balls, following the parade!"[23]

"It's a Long Way to Tipperary" achieved worldwide popularity after Irish tenor John McCormack recorded it in November 1914, a few months after the start of World War I. The Onward's choice of "Tipperary" is yet another example of men like Oliver and Perez playing the most popular songs of the era, a lesson not lost on Armstrong. Oliver's playing wasn't lost on him either; the two-note phrase he scatted when recreating Oliver's playing on "Tipperary" is identical to what he would later play on immortal records such as "Cake Walking Babies from Home" in 1925 and "Stomp Off, Let's Go" in 1926. Oliver's playing was now firmly implanted in his brain.

Armstrong soon began getting closer to Oliver—figuratively and literally. "I used to carry his cornet in the parade because the policemen can't run me out if I had King Oliver's cornet, you know," Armstrong told Johnny Carson in 1968. A few seconds earlier, Armstrong was telling Carson about seeing Oliver at Pete Lala's, saying, "I used to put on long pants to stand outside the window and hear him blow, you know, till the police come around and run you away."[24] Now, just by holding Oliver's cornet, "the police couldn't run me out of the parade then."[25] It was as if the cornet had magic powers, allowing him the freedom to experience this life and this music without any fear of police repercussions.

Such incidents must have heavily impacted Armstrong's desire to be a cornetist, but there hadn't been very many chances to blow in public since leaving the Waif's Home. He continued taking lessons with Peter Davis, who claimed, "When Louis left the home, he had no place to go so I took him with me to live there and complete his music course."[26] Neither Henry Armstrong, Beatrice Armstrong, or Louis himself ever alluded to him actually living with Davis, but it's possible that those sleepovers Louis wrote about as happening when he was living at the Home actually happened when he got out.

Davis began inviting Armstrong back to the Waif's Home as a special guest musician. Future bassist Chester Zardis was living at the Waif's Home in 1915 and remembered, "Louie was there, but they wouldn't keep him there. He come and give us lessons like; you know what I mean. But he don't stay there.... On his way, when he'd be going, he'd come over by us first and gave us instruction, our lesson, and different things like that. Then he'd say, 'Well boys I'm gonna have'ta go.' "[27]

Davis would sometimes call on Armstrong and other ex-pupils when the Waif's Home band had a public gig, such as the dedication of the Thomy Lefon Playground—the first playground for Black children "in the south" according to newspaper reports—on Magnolia and Sixth Streets on August 28, 1915.[28] Armstrong's playing made a distinct impression on those in the crowd, including cornetist Lee Collins, born on October 17, 1901, who noticed that "Louie had a similar touch of Bunk" to his own.[29] Preston Jackson was also present and never forgot his first time seeing Armstrong perform. "Louis was playing more jazz than the average fellow is now," Jackson said. "You couldn't help noticing him. There was something about him and his playing that was out of the ordinary. Everyone had their eyes on Louis, he was so wonderful. I remember that the band played 'My Maryland,' in which Louis took a cornet obligato that set the people on fire."[30] Years later, Jackson enthusiastically told this story to William Russell, stressing, "Honest, he was destined, he was destined to be great, Bill! He was destined to be great! You could see it in him then."[31]

By the time of the playground dedication, young Louis had to worry about another mouth to feed in his family: his cousin Flora Myles had given birth to a son named Clarence Hatfield on August 8. Both Louis and Mama Lucy were close with Flora, who was born in 1902, the last of Uncle Ike's brood. But in her early teenage years, she began running with the wrong crowd and eventually met a white man Louis only remembered as "Copper Cent John" Hatfield, though his sister remembered him as Joseph Hatfield. "He would have these colored girls, come up to his house, which was an old beat up one—and ask them an unfair question... (you know what I mean?)... Hmmm?... Well, if you don't get it,... You can just figure it out when I tell you that my cousin Flora Miles, became pregnant... we all did not know what to do about it," Louis wrote.[32] "That was a white man's baby," Mama Lucy said of Clarence.[33]

Flora gave birth to baby Clarence on August 8, 1915; the family never heard from his father again. "Everybody was telling old man Ike Miles, Flora's father, to have Hatfield arrested," Louis wrote. "But that did not make sense at all.... The first place, Mr. Hatfield was a white man, and the judge would have thrown it all out in the streets, including Clarence the baby, if we would have tried to make an attempt to have him arrested... So we threw it out of our minds [and focused on] the next best thing... And that was to try and struggle through that, and take care of Clarence myself..... And believe you me, that my friend, was really a struggle....."[34]

As he got older, Louis associated Clarence's birth with "The Great Storm of 1915," a ferocious hurricane that hit New Orleans on September 29 and lasted through October 1. Louis never forgot how afraid he was trying to make it back home while the storm was blowing slates off the roofs of the homes in his neighborhood. When he finally reached home, Louis, his mother, and his cousins all hugged each other, "crying at the same time."[35]

"My cousin Flora Miles, was never the same," he wrote. "I am sure the shock from the storm and the birth of Clarence, had something to do with her death... Then too, in the south, especially in those days, it wasn't very easy to get to a doctor... Or, it wasn't very easy to get 'money to go to a doctor... We could not offord [*sic*] a doctor at two dollars per visit...Nay Nay.... We needed that money to eat off of. Ofcourse we did everything we could for Flora before she died ... But, that wasn't enough."[36]

Armstrong made it appear that that Flora died in the aftermath of the Great Storm of 1915, even writing that they couldn't get her into Charity Hospital because it was filled with storm victims. However, there's no death certificate for Flora Myles in 1915 or 1916—but there is one for Flora Meyers, passing away on September 24, 1924, at the age of 22. The spelling of her family's surname commonly fluctuated between "Myles" and "Miles" but there's also multiple examples of "Meyers" that crop up, especially on the World War I draft registration cards of her brothers. Her death also coincides with the moment Clarence was sent to Chicago to live with Louis in the fall of 1924. Flora also doesn't appear in the 1920 census, but Clarence does. Flora's whereabouts between Clarence's birth in 1915 and her death in 1924 might never be discovered—perhaps she was in the House of Good Shepherd, where she served some time with Mama Lucy, or perhaps something about being raped and forced to give birth at the age of 13 resulted in unspeakable psychological trauma that rendered her unable to raise her child—but Louis thought it better to make his public believe she died after childbirth than to reveal the truth.

Taking care of baby Clarence was now added to Louis's list of responsibilities. "My whole family was poor all my life, since I can remember," he recalled. "When Clarence was born, I was the only one who was making a pretty decent salary.. And that was [not much]... But I was doing lots better than the rest of the family.... I was selling papers, playing a little music on the side."[37]

The music wasn't quite paying off yet, however. Drummer Christopher "Black Happy" Goldston remembered a band being formed mostly made up of veterans of the Waif's Home with Louis and Kid Rena on cornet, George Washington on trombone, and Joe Rene on clarinet. They used to rehearse, even though "none of them know how to read," according to Goldston. "They just played this juke music, that sound, tonk numbers."[38] Drummer Dave Bailey also remembered an early musical experience from this period. "Louis played with us when he first came out of Jones, my brother [bassist Ernest "Duck" Johnson] was the first one who grabbed him," Bailey said. "He had a little old brass horn, all bent. He couldn't play over 4 or 5 numbers."[39]

The part that jumps out of Bailey's recollection is the mention of Armstrong's "little old brass horn, all bent." Which horn could this be? The "much used" "artificial lead horn" Captain Jones bought for him was no longer making the grade in 1915. Clay Watson, one-time curator of the New Orleans Jazz Museum, explained, "Later, when [Armstrong] had saved enough to buy a new trumpet he gave the old one back to Jones."

But how did Armstrong save money and when did he buy this "bent" cornet? In 1965, he told Richard Meryman, "Then I found a little nickel-plate cornet for $10 in Uncle Jake's pawn shop—all bent up, holes knocked in the bell. It was a Tonk Brothers—ain't never heard of them. Charlie—he was the ofay fellow supplied me with papers when I was a newsboy around there—he lent me the money. I clean that little horn out, scalded it good. It was all right. Made a little living with it."[40]

"Uncle Jake's pawn shop" was Jacob Fink's Loan Office, located at 401 South Rampart Street, a short walk from the Karnofsky family's new residence/business at 427 South Rampart. In 1951, Dr. Edmond Souchon profiled Fink's establishment for *The Second Line*, with details provided by Dave Frank, who worked there in the teens. "Intermittently, (at first just on Saturday nights, then more often as time went on), Uncle Jake's place was frequented by a short, husky Negro boy of 14 or 15 years," Souchon wrote. "Bashfully, almost apologetically, one of the cornets, with a stuck valve was rented for 'four bits' a night and returned early next morning." Naturally, the boy was Louis Armstrong. Elsewhere in the story, Souchon stressed, "The year would *have* to be 1915—and so it is."[41]

Louis's sister, Beatrice, remembered this part of her brother's life, too. "Louis was in Jones's home about a year and a half," she recalled. "When he came out he found a hock shop where he could rent a horn cheap, put on long pants and started playing the tonks. Sometimes, Louis wouldn't even make as much money as it cost him to rent the cornet."[42] Her brother agreed, saying, "I couldn't get enough money together to even talk about a horn of my own—used to rent one for each gig."[43] But eventually, he was able to afford an instrument of his own, thanks to his clear-eyed recollection about Charlie Wilson lending him the money to buy one from Uncle Jake's—that is, until this claim was undone just four years later by Armstrong's notoriously un-clear-eyed manuscript "Louis Armstrong + the Jewish Family," where he claimed it was the Karnofsky family that went to Uncle Jake's and helped him buy a cornet before he went in the Waif's Home. But in 1983, George Finola, curator of the New Orleans Jazz Museum and a man who had befriended many older musicians of Armstrong's generation, said of Captain Jones's cornet that Armstrong "returned it when Karnovski [*sic*] bought him a new horn."[44]

The story of the Karnofskys buying a cornet for Armstrong would not be widely known until Gary Giddins published it in his 1988 book *Satchmo.* Thus, Finola's statement does seem to tie everything together: in late 1914 or early 1915, Armstrong returns to live with Mayann, works on the coal cart with Morris Karnofsky and selling newspapers for Charlie Wilson, falls under the spell of Joe Oliver at Pete Lala's, spots a cornet at Uncle Jake's pawn shop near the Karnofskys' new residence at 427 South Rampart, gets the Karnofskys to advance him the money for the instrument, and pays it off with funds earned from both the coal wagon and from selling newspapers.

However it happened and whenever it happened, Armstrong never forgot the importance of the Karnofsky family in his early life. "As I said before I must have been born with talent," he wrote in 1969. "All that I needed was a little encouragement to bring it out of me. And they did thank God. I was just a kid trying to find out which way to turn. So that Mayann and Mama Lucy could feel proud of their Louis (me). Not trying to be too much, just a good ordinary horn blower. The Jewish people sure did turn me out in many ways."[45] Armstrong would wear a Star of David around his neck for much of his adult life, a way of remembering the impact the Karnofsky family made on him.

Armstrong likely left Morris Karnofsky's employment sometime in 1915, but almost immediately found himself back in the coal business thanks to a job provided by one of Mayann's new beaus, a coal cart driver for the C. A. Andrews Coal Company.

"The nicest one of the step fathers, which I can remember at least (six) to me, was my step father, 'Gabe,'" Louis wrote in the unedited manuscript to *Satchmo: My Life in New Orleans.* This was most likely Gabriel Woods, born in Lambert, Mississippi, on March 26, 1894, listed as a coal cart "Driver" in Soards's 1916 City Directory, and living at nearby 1327 Perdido Street according to his World War I draft registration card. When he began working with Woods, Louis remembered beginning their day "at Ferret and Perdido streets."[46] Sure enough, C. A. Andrews had their office at 1515 Perdido Street, but in August 1915, they moved their operation to 315 Carondelet.[47] Thus, Armstrong would have started working with Gabriel Woods for C. A. Andrews by the summer of 1915.

"From seven in the morning until five o'clock in the evening I would be hauling stone coal (hard coal) for fifteen cents per load.... And loved it," Armstrong wrote of his new steady day job. "I was fifteen years of age then... And I thought I was a real man, when I could lift up one of those big, wide shovels and load up my own coal cart, which held a ton. Being a small and young as I was, I could not make over five loads a day...."[48] Loading up the coal cart was only half the job. With his mule leading the way, Armstrong "had to deliver that coal maybe across the city, and you make a little extra taste if you put the coal in the bin, maybe 40 cents and a sandwich," he said. "They call that 'cakes throwed in.' Then I'd come home, put the mule up and sum up my coal money—75 cents. By the end of the week you get about $5.00."[49]

Trumpeter Ricard Alexis had very distinct memories of Armstrong's coal cart days. "I remember Louis Armstrong when he was driving a coal cart for a dollar-and-a-quarter a day, barefooted," Alexis said. "Coal dust beneath his nose and all between his toes. I remember them days. A dollar-and-a-quarter a day delivering stone coal with a dump cart and a mule. He was in his teens."[50]

"I was so young and strong, and had all the ambitions in the world," Armstrong said about this period in his life. "And I also wanted to help Mayann and Mamma Lucy, and do a whole lots, for them."[51] Armstrong's ambitions would soon help his family in a whole new way: he was about to embark on his first regular job as a musician.

9

"The Memory of the Bullies and Trouble Makers"

1916

The Armstrongs had moved by early 1916, leaving their "Brick Row" flat at 1303 Perdido Street for what appears to have been an even smaller dwelling at 334 South Liberty Street, about a block and a half away. Soon after the move, Armstrong had a chance encounter with his old friend from school "Cocaine" Buddy Martin,[1] who was then working at Joe Segreto's "Grocery, Saloon, and Honky Tonk" at 457 South Liberty. Martin told him that "one of the biggest pimps in the red light district" was opening a saloon across the street from Segreto's and "he wants a good cornet player." Armstrong always referred to this proprietor as "Henry Ponce," but his name was actually Andrew H. Pons. He later described Pons as a "goodlooking French Pimp from the good old Storyville days," though it seems more likely Pons might have been from Spain, "Pons" being derived from the Catalan word for "pont" or bridge.[2] Pons opened his new establishment at 1332 Perdido Street, on the corner of South Liberty, applying for a license to operate it on January 18, 1916.[3]

Armstrong borrowed a pair of long pants and headed down to Pons's place, where he would be joined by a man nicknamed "Boogers" (or "Boogus," as Armstrong typed it) on piano and Sonny Garbie on drums.[4] To Armstrong, "the first night I played my first job, it was more than [*sic*] a hustle than anything else."[5] Armstrong's use of the word "hustle" could refer to something Goffin reported: Armstrong's lips became sore after 10 minutes, forcing him to fall back on his singing, sticking to the blues for the entire evening.

Both Louis and Mama Lucy vividly remembered the aftermath of this first gig. Mayann had promised to give Mama Lucy a nickel when Louis came home, but when he arrived, Mama Lucy heard her brother tell their mother, "Yeah, Mama, that's all they give me, fifteen cents." From under the covers, Mama Lucy shouted, "Mmm! Blow your heart out all night long for fifteen cents! I want my nickel!"

"Mama just fell out," Beatrice recalled, admitting, "I just hollered like hell!"[6]

"I wanted to kill her," Louis wrote. "Mother had to seperate [*sic*] us from fighting that morning."[7]

Louis paid his sister no mind and would continue working at the coal yard with Gabriel Woods in the daytime and at Pons's honky-tonk on Saturday nights. It didn't pay much but at least for one night of the week, he could put on some long pants and get lost in his music. Mayann would fix Louis a big "bucket lunch," which would come in handy for the gig's long hours, starting at 8 p.m. and sometimes not finishing until 10 or 11 a.m. Sunday morning. Playing at Pons's gave him serenity—until it almost got him killed.

When Cocaine Buddy Martin told Armstrong about the job playing for Pons, he left out a crucial bit of information: Pons and Joe Segreto were staunch enemies. Pons was far from the only pimp to run a saloon in Armstrong's neighborhood. "Not only did Joe Segretta [*sic*] envy Henry Ponce, but all of the Tonk owners did," Armstrong wrote. "They all were Pimps, some time or other." Armstrong figured owning saloons would serve as "a good alibi" for the police, proving "they were in business instead playing the whores."[8]

The drama between Pons and Segreto came to a head on January 23, 1916. Armstrong was talking to Pons by the front door about "some new blues" he had played earlier when he looked over to Gaspar Locicero's grocery on the opposite corner at 501 South Liberty and suddenly noticed "several colored guys" who usually hung around at Segreto's, identifying two of them as "Sun Murray," and "Dry Bread."

Armstrong remained oblivious. "And I'm talking to him, getting ready to leave, and all of a sudden, I say, 'See ya, man,' and boom, boom, boom! I said, 'What the hell?' "

"Well, I'll be god damn," Pons exclaimed, "those black 'sommbitches' are shooting at me!" Pons started firing back, over and around Armstrong. "And every time that man shot his pistol, you'd hear, 'Oh lord, my leg!' Yoom! 'Oh, Jesus!' That's how good Henry Pons was with a pistol," Armstrong said. He remained frozen until someone rushed up to him and asked, "Are you hurt!?" "And goddamn, I fainted!" Armstrong recalled, breaking into uproarious laughter as he told this story among friends in 1953.[9]

When Armstrong came to, he could still hear the sound of gunshots. When the scrape was over, Pons "had carried me home to mother Mayann," Louis wrote.[10] However, it appears he possibly misremembered this part of the story. Mayann had been arrested for "fighting and disturbing the peace" along with another prostitute named Anna Hart at 2:30 in the morning that same day; the arrest of Andrew H. Pons for "shooting and wounding [with a] gun" took

Figure 9.1 The corner of Liberty and Perdido Streets, photographed by William Russell in 1948, looking more like the Old West than the French Quarter. The saloon on the right, facing Liberty Street, was Joe Segreto's Grocery and Bar—the property across the street would have been H. Andrew Pons's short-lived saloon in 1916.
Credit: The William Russell Jazz Collection at The Historic New Orleans Collection, acquisition made possible by the Clarisse Claiborne Grima Fund, acc. no. 92-48-L.273.

place at 8:40 p.m., logged just a few pages after Mayann in the First Precinct's "Report of Arrests."

Other than the mention of his mother, Armstrong's memory was incredibly accurate for the details of the Pons incident. "Four negroes were shot, one of whom is dangerously wounded, when negroes and Italians engaged in a pistol battle at Liberty and Perdido streets late Sunday afternoon," the *Times-Picayune* reported. In their telling, though, the shooting began when African American Curtis Coleman—possibly "Dry Bread"—began firing at "Sunny" Murray. Murray took cover in Pons's saloon. "Pons, the proprietor, ran out of his place with a loaded revolver and he was greeted with shots from Murray's weapon," the paper continued. "Pons returned the fire, chasing Murray to a coal yard in the neighborhood, where the negro made his escape." Soon, Vincent Segreto showed up and began firing at Pons. "Bullets were flying in all directions and men, women and children rushed into houses and hid behind doorsteps, until the arrival of Sergeant Ray and a detail of patrolmen from the First Precinct station," the *Times-Picayune* continued. No mention was made of Armstrong fainting.

Armstrong returned to Pons's job on Saturday nights, but now he was looking over his shoulder. "I worked for quite some time after that, always on the alert.... Thinking something would jump off, most any minute," he wrote.[11]

He was lucky he wasn't present for the next violent outburst, which took place on a Friday night, April 7, 1916, when Vincent and Joseph Segreto visited Pons in his saloon and "stabbed Pons in the shoulder following an altercation, without cause," according to newspaper coverage. "Bleeding profusely, Pons ran behind a counter, secured a shotgun and fired upon the Segretto [*sic*] party, without effect. Pons reloaded his gun and fired another volley as the Italians fled down the street. Again he missed."[12]

These incidents seemed to be enough to drive Henry Pons off Perdido Street, possibly as early as May 1916. On June 5, Pons applied for a license to operate a new establishment on 1329 Magazine Street; Louis Malain was the next person to apply for a license at 1332 Perdido Street on July 26, meaning Pons was officially out. "Anyway, it certainly was a drag to see him close down and go away from the neighborhood," Armstrong wrote of his one-time boss. "Because he was such a good man, to us colored people."[13]

By this point, Armstrong had begun to form a small addiction to his neighborhood's nightlife. Many nights when he was done at the coal yard, he would go home, wash up, have supper, put on his "tuxedo and long pants" ("I had saved up a long time to buy and finally made the grade") and meet up with his old friend Isaac Smoot. "And we two silly kids would just go from one honky tonk to the other, and dig that jive," Armstrong wrote.[14]

Armstrong's Waif 's Home friends were not always the best influences. "In the Juvenile Court Saturday Isaac Smoot, a sixteen-year-old negro boy, was arraigned for throwing coal from a car of the Belt Railroad," read a report from December 4, 1914. "The police say that Isaac threw at least a ton of coal off before he was arrested."[15] Smoot was just getting started; once described as a "well known pickpocket," he was arrested multiple times in ensuing years, serving two sentences in Sing Sing Prison in New York.[16]

Henry "Kid" Rena was also trying to make it as a musician, but he too was running afoul of the law, arrested for "petty larceny" on April 1, 1916, at Liberty and Perdido; April 1 was a Saturday so it's possible he was at Pons's saloon, watching his friend play cornet. Rena was also getting a reputation for his consumption of alcoholic beverages. "Yeah, I tell you, he drank himself to death," Christopher "Black Happy" Goldston said. "Rena could drink, boy. He'd get so drunk, he couldn't play."[17] "He used to do some awful things when he was drunk," Joseph Rene said about his brother.[18]

In his book and on radio and television appearances, Armstrong loved to tell the story of "Red Sun," a boy who was sent to the Colored Waif's Home multiple times for stealing. On *The Mike Douglas Show* in 1964, Armstrong almost lost his breath from laughing so hard at the story of Red Sun heroically returning to the Waif's Home to show off a new horse he was riding—only to be sent back to the Home the next day, arrested for stealing said horse! But in 2018, journalist James Karst discovered that "Red Sun" was really Arthur Brooks, a troubled figure who would go on to be arrested several more times for stealing, for throwing a rock at a woman, and for shooting a pistol at an ice cream parlor. The tragic end of "Red Sun" came on January 3, 1918, when he was caught trying to steal a brass handle from a door on a train and was shot in the back of the head by a private guard.[19]

Armstrong was now at a crossroads and he could have easily ended up like one of his old Waif's Home friends if he had made the wrong choices. He got a taste of what could have been on September 25, 1916, when he was arrested for loitering at Dryades Street and Jackson Avenue.This was just a few blocks away from Joe Oliver's residence at 2712 Dryades and quite a distance from Armstrong's Third Ward neighborhood. He was arrested along with a man named George Jackson, who lived near him at 528 South Liberty Street. A glance at Jackson's police record yields numerous arrests over the years for fighting, disturbing the peace, reckless driving, and multiple other charges of loitering. That vague term often gave police an excuse to round up Black people for seemingly just existing, but it was sometimes applied to the world of prostitution, specifically used for pimps waiting for their whores to finish their work. Could this have been an early foray by Armstrong in an attempt to be a pimp?[20]

Armstrong never mentioned George Jackson in his various writings, but he always remained fascinated by the colorful criminals in his neighborhood with their equally colorful names. "All them bad characters came in to gamble where I was playing in the honky-tonk," Armstrong said. "They didn't bother with kids like us—but I knew Red Cornelius carried anything he could get to cut you or shoot you. George Bo'hog another one. There was Dirty Dog, Brother Ford and Steel Arm Johnny, Aaron Harris and Black Benny—always in trouble."[21]

Armstrong enjoyed writing about "The Memory of the Bullies and Trouble Makers" often, but he usually left out the actual sordid details of their lives.[22] Here's a quick rundown:

"Red Cornelius" was born Cornelius Crowley on March 4, 1891, according to his World War I draft registration card, and lived at 2060 Poydras Street during Armstrong's teenage years. "When Red got tired of cutting you he would take out his gun and shoot you a little," Armstrong wrote.

Red Cornelius lived up to his reputation according to his many mentions in the newspaper. "Louis Moore . . . was shot in the left hip last night by Cornelius Crowley," read one story from 1907.[23] A year later, Crowley was arrested again for "assault, shooting and wounding."[24] After serving in World War I, Crowley made headlines in July 1922 for shooting and killing Jacob Bell after demanding that Bell salute him. "Bell saluted twice, the police said, but Crowley was dissatisfied with the execution of the command, whipped out a pistol and shot him through the stomach," the *Times-Picayune* reported.[25] Crowley died less than two months later.

Aaron Harris, born in 1880, was "no doubt, the most heartless man I've ever heard of or ever seen" according to pianist Jelly Roll Morton.[26] A good example was Harris killing his own brother, William, in 1910, beating the charge by claiming "self-defense."[27] The following year, police were also certain that Harris murdered Vincent Richards, who was "shot in the upper part of the body three times, his skull was beaten to a pulp, his throat was cut from ear to ear, and he had been stabbed under the left arm," but Harris beat that charge too.[28] Harris met his downfall in 1915 because of a run-in with the next man on Armstrong's list.

"George Bo'hog" was an older man, born around 1876. Newspapers referred to him as "George Robinson, alias Boar Hog" after a 1912 arrest, though his surname was more likely Robertson.[29] While working as a watchman for the Frisco Railroad Company, Robertson witnessed Aaron Harris stealing goods and ratted him out to the police, leading Harris to swear vengeance. This "fatal moment of bravado" came on July 14, 1915.[30] "George Bo'Hog is a bad man, too," Armstrong wrote. "He wouldn't fight [Harris] face to face. He waited until he turned on Tulane Avenue and Franklin and [killed] him. Yeah, bad son-of-a-bitch, man."[31]

"Steel Arm Johnny," the alias of one Ferdinand Poree, refers to his way with a knife. On June 4, 1918, Poree was arrested for disturbing the peace along with an African American named Joe Crader. While waiting together in the dock of the First Precinct police station, Poree pulled out a knife he had concealed and "buried the knife twice in Crader's body."[32] Poree also most likely stabbed a white man, Louis Bricknackle, during a fight in 1916, but that time, Bricknackle retaliated by shooting Poree in the back.[33] He survived that wound but the end came for him in 1920, when he was shot in the head on New Year's Day. He was 27 years old.

"Dirty Dog" and "Sore Dick": Joseph "Dirty Dog" Williams was born in 1895 and earned his nickname "from fighting dirty," according to Armstrong.[34] He was arrested in May 1917 for "fighting and disturbing the peace and gambling with dice" and sent to jail where he quarreled

> with Louis "Sore Dick" Johnson, born in 1890, "boss of [the prison] yard" and "the toughest of them all" in Armstrong's eyes.[35] Once out, the two men met at Perdido and Dryades Street on Sunday, December 2, 1917, when "Dirty Dog" shot and killed "Sore Dick" with an .88 caliber revolver.[36]

The prostitutes were just as dangerous in Armstrong's neighborhood. In his handwritten list of "Bullies and Trouble Makers" he included a subcategory, "The Females":

> Big Vi Green
> Mary Meat Market
> Funky Rella
> Boote Mama
> Cross Eyed Louise
> Mary Jack the Bear
> Alberta

Armstrong loved to tell the story of the bloody street fight between the last two names on his list, "Mary Jack the Bear," "the toughest woman in all the tonks" in his estimation, and "Alberta."[37] "Mary Jack the Bear" was Mary Francis, who was arrested nearly 60 times in this period; the police frequently used her alias in their arrest books. Francis, who lived for a time next door to Mayann at 1307 Perdido, lived up to her reputation, with numerous arrests for "disturbing the peace," "fighting," "shooting at with intent to murder," "cutting and wounding," and "stabbing with intent to kill." Though fights between prostitutes were a normal part of the landscape of The Battlefield, the battle of Mary Jack the Bear and "Pretty Alberta" over the affection of a pimp made a lasting impression on Armstrong. "Every time, one would slash the other, the crowd would go, 'Huh-My Gawd,' " Armstrong wrote. "This [fight went] on for a fullhalf an hour...... Finally they both commenced to getting weak in the knees.... And slowily taking wacks, at each other, still in the face. They both were streaming blood when they fell to the ground."[38]

In his original 1950s manuscript, Armstrong noted that Alberta was still alive. That was enough to make his editor at Prentice-Hall change Alberta's name to "Deborah," but a search of the First Precinct's police records for "Alberta" doesn't clear up the mystery.[39] It could have been the very dangerous, frequently arrested Alberta Coleman, but Louis mentions her alias of "Sister Pop" separately and tells of her murdering his boyhood friend Harry Tennyson, on November 26, 1919, shooting him through his brain with a .45.

There's Alberta Monroe, arrested for fighting with four other prostitutes at Franklin and Gravier Streets on February 7, 1917. Another prostitute, Alberta King, was arrested for fighting on Perdido Street three days later. Alberta Hopkins of Gravier Street was arrested for cutting and wounding on Rampart Street in 1914. Alberta Jackson was arrested numerous times in Armstrong's neighborhood, including for cutting and wounding on Perdido Street in March 1915. One of these Albertas was the one who fought Mary Jack the Bear but all of them were probably intimidating figures to the young Armstrong.

Those names just scratch the surface of the dangerous characters who made their presence in Armstrong's formative years, but he saved the most important one for last. Joe Oliver might have been the figurative angel on Armstrong's shoulder, inspiring him to devote more time to learning his craft, but there was another man who was perhaps equally influential, though with a devilish flair.

That man was Black Benny Williams.

"Now, let me tell you some more about Benny because every story I write about New Orleans, to me, he's my star," Louis Armstrong said during a 1958 interview. "I think he's the greatest of all of 'em. He had a good heart and he had guts. He wasn't afraid of nobody."[40]

Benjamin Williams was born in the Third Ward on March 21, 1890, old enough to serve as something of a guardian angel to Armstrong and the boys of his generation. "The things he did for kids, he always protected the underdog, that's one thing," Armstrong said about him.[41] In one telling of the famous story where the Waif's Band paraded through Armstrong's Liberty and Perdido Street neighborhood, Armstrong said he spotted Black Benny and "all those tough characters that practically raised me."[42]

Kid Ory's drummer Henry Martin taught Black Benny how to play and he soon became a fixture on the parade scene. The visual of Black Benny playing "with that big cigar in his mouth" left an impression on drummer George Williams, who called Benny "the best in the city."[43] In one interview, trumpeter Punch Miller demonstrated Williams's style, scatting a funky bass drum pattern that would be the heartbeat of all future New Orleans drumming. "That's the man that started all them funny beats on the bass drum," Miller said.[44]

But Williams had a violent side, too, which also came out during the parades. "He used to like to fight," trumpeter Ricard Alexis said. "He'd put the bass drum down and be all out on the second line there, knocking fellows out."[45] Many of the musicians found humor in this side of Williams. "Well, he was comical," Albert Francis said. "He'd be playing the bass drum and he'd be

Figure 9.2 "Black Bennie" Williams, smoking a cigar and dispensing a larger-than-life smile during the 1923 Zulu Social Aid and Pleasure Club parade.
Credit: *The Jazz Archivist* 2010, p. 47, published by Tulane University, New Orleans, LA.

fighting while leading the band! Black Benny was tough."[46] "A character, boy!" is how Paul Barbarin described him. "He'd hit you with that mallet if you got too close to the bass drum."[47]

Williams found a better use for his fists when he began dabbling in boxing, becoming the king of the battle royal in the process. "The battle royals were when they'd put five men in the ring, one in the center, and blindfold them," guitarist Danny Barker explained. "The bell would be hit, and everybody would start punching. Whoever stayed the longest won the prize—five or ten dollars. . . . You'd have to be an awful brave man to get in that ring. And Black Benny won them all."[48] Barker could be prone to hyperbole—he once famously described Williams as "six foot six—nothing but muscle," whereas police reports describe him as 5 foot 9, 155 pounds—but he was not kidding about the battle royals, which sometimes made the newspapers: "Benny Williams won the battle royal, which lasted nearly a quarter of an hour, proving himself best of five placed in the ring at the start."[49]

But Williams's violent tendencies sometimes came out in a much darker fashion. "Arthur Smith, of 524 Howard Street, is in a serious condition as a result of a row with Benny Williams, of Franklin and Poydras," read one report from 1909. "Williams was at a wake and made a lot of noise, and Smith asked him to quit. Williams became angry and threw a brick at Smith, which hit him on the head, fracturing his skull. Williams escaped."[50] Williams occasionally mixed it up with other characters from Armstrong's story, even getting shot by Red Cornelius in September 1913.[51]

Women especially weren't safe from Black Benny; he was arrested on July 3, 1913, for "having carnal knowledge" in February of that year, accused by a prostitute named Amelia Bogle and her 15-year-old daughter, Gertrude. He beat the rap by marrying Gertrude Bogle on July 5 and the case was dismissed on July 8.[52] But in November, the *Daily Picayune* described Williams as a "Beastly Black Boxer" and reported he was arrested for "assaulting and wounding" 16-year-old Mrs. Eugene Hendricks with a pistol and sentenced to pay $100 or spend 6 months in the Parish Prison.[53]

Armstrong was present when Black Benny got arrested on August 3, 1915. Armstrong recalled Black Benny having a quarrel with his "wife," Nelly, during a parade, removing his bass drum and chasing Nelly until he spotted a piece of heavy marble. Armstrong said Williams "dropped the whole thing direct in the middle of Nelly's back." Those present thought it would paralyze her, but instead, Nelly pulled a large knife and "sliced ass as long as she could see him."[54] The police report for this particular arrest adds more details: "Nelly" was Nellie Farrell, a 17-year-old cook living at 429 Howard Street, and not only was she arrested for "fighting and disturbing the peace at Perdido and South Liberty" but so was her 48-year-old mother, Emma Farrell, and Gertrude Williams, Black Benny's now 19-year-old wife. Armstrong's account provided a punchline for the whole incident regarding Benny and Nellie: "When they were released, they went home together smiling at each other, just like nothing that happened...Tch Tch."[55]

This would be the downside to Black Benny's influence on young Louis—imparting his "wisdom" about the opposite sex, which Armstrong would relate in a 1955 letter to his manager Joe Glaser: "Always remember, no matter how many times you get married—always have another woman for a sweetheart on the outside," Armstrong wrote, giving Benny credit for this line of thinking. "Because, mad day might come, or she could be the type of woman who's ego, after realizing that you care deeply, may-for no reason at all, try giving you a hard time. And with no other chick whom you're just as—[fond] of—on the outside—two chances to one you might do something 'rash' which is a mild word."[56] Such advice led Armstrong to matter-of-factly write, "Benny never did serve over thirty days, at any time... Mostly for a fighting and disturbing the peace, or, some minor thing, such as beating the hell out of his Ol lady, Nelly . . . "[57] Armstrong would later act upon Black Benny's advice—sometimes with disastrous results.

Black Benny lived right in the neighborhood at 1316 Perdido Street, and even worked for the C. A. Andrews Coal Company at the same time Armstrong did; he remembered a time "a bunch of kids were being beat up by some elderly guys, just as Black Benny was passing by ... And Benny immediately jumped off of his coal cart he was driving for C.A. Andrews, the same company I was driving for at the time....Huh....Black Benny made a real stew of those guys."[58]

Armstrong also vividly recalled a fight between Black Benny and "Nicodemus," the alias of one Joseph Moore who lived at 1214 Perdido Street. "Nicodeemus was a good gambler, and also was the best dancer the honky tonks ever known," Armstrong wrote, noting that he was taken with the way Moore "would mug and make some of the funniest expressions...Especially when he was dancing, with a sharp chick."[59] Nicodemus also had an "awful temper," which would sometimes come out during his card games with Black Benny. During one such game, an angry Nicodemus stormed out and headed home to get his gun. A calm Benny hid in an ally, wielding a piece of pipe. The entire neighborhood, Armstrong included, grew "quiet as a church mouse" as Nicodemus approached the honky-tonk. "Out of the alley Benny came, and before Nicodemus could turn around to see what was happening, Black Benny had already swung on Nico's jaw, with this iron, and knocked ol' Nico out, cold," Armstrong wrote.[60] Police soon arrived and arrested both Black Benny and Nicodemus. Black Benny did not fear the police; the "Report of Arrest" from August 8, 1915, notes that while both Williams and Moore were arrested for "disturbing the peace," Williams was also arrested for "using obscene language and reviling police and tearing an officer's uniform."

But aside from the fight, there was a moment in the aftermath that particularly stuck with Armstrong years later. "When Black Benny knocked out Nicodemus cold, the crowd who were standing around watching the fight, they all made a mad rush to Nicodemus's pocket, and taken his gun and hid it some place where the Peelers (the cops) couldn't find it on him when they arrived," Armstrong wrote. "And believe you mee—they looked high and low for the gun.... But, not a soul saw it.... That's what I call sticking together even in their fighting moments."[61]

Yet, for all his dark and violent episodes, those who knew Black Benny said he always protected three types of people: musicians, underdogs, and children. In Armstrong, he found someone who embodied all three.

Black Benny was too old to be in the Colored Waif's Home—Parish Prison was more his speed—but he liked hiring "all little bitty fellows" as cornetist Charlie Love put it, including Armstrong, Kid Rena, and Louis "Shots" Madison.[62] Sometime in early 1916, Williams put together a band with Armstrong, Madison, and teenage cornetist Lee Collins to play a street parade for the Zulu Social Aid and Pleasure Club. The Zulus started as a marching club in 1909, but according to Charles Chamberlain, "In 1916, the club incorporated and gradually gained a legion of supporters with their Mardi Gras antics."[63] Those "antics" included the appearance of King Zulu himself, wearing a grass skirt, black turtleneck and tights, a wig of straight black hair and gold-painted boots, not to mention blackface makeup, all done as a way of satirizing the white Mardi Gras king Rex. Armstrong was immediately inspired by the Zulus. "The members were coal-cart drivers, bartenders, waiters, hustlers, etc.—people of all walks of life," he wrote. "Nobody had very much, but they loved each other . . . and put their best foot forward making a real fine thing of the club."[64] Being in a brass band "playing all of that good jumping music for the members to march by" was an honor Armstrong would not soon forget.[65]

Armstrong was steadily improving to the point where Black Benny felt he could sit in with trombonist Kid Ory's popular band. Ory was playing with cornetist Mutt Carey at National Park when he noticed a peculiar sight: Black Benny had Armstrong "tied to his wrist, like a handcuff, so he wouldn't get lost in the crowds."[66]

Williams asked if Armstrong could play a number with the band. "I remembered the kid from the [1913 Labor Day] street parade and I gladly agreed," Ory said. "Louis came up and played 'Ole Miss' and the blues, and everyone in the park went wild over this boy in knee trousers who could play so great. I liked Louis' playing so much that I asked him to come and sit in with my band any time he could."[67] "Ole Miss"—sometimes known as "Ole Miss Rag" or "Ole Miss Blues"—was a multistrain piece written by "The Father of the Blues," W. C. Handy, and published in 1916, the same year Mutt Carey left to go to Chicago. Thus, this would have been a brand-new tune, another example of Armstrong learning the latest popular songs. Ory's banjoist at this time, Johnny St. Cyr, reflected that the New Orleans bands "played all popular numbers . . . as fast as they come out. . . . We play them and play them in our old style."[68]

Armstrong's way with the blues left a deep impression on cornetist Carey. "Now at that time I was the 'Blues King' of New Orleans and when Louis played that day, he played more blues than I ever heard in my life," Carey recalled. "It never did strike my mind that blues could be interpreted so many different ways. Everytime he played a chorus it was different and you knew it was the blues—yes, it was all the blues what I mean. When he got through playing the blues I kidded him a little. I told him, 'Louis, you keep playing that horn and someday you'll be a great man.' I always admired him from the start."[69]

Aside from sitting in with Ory and Black Benny, Armstrong didn't have many opportunities to play music in mid-1916, so he found a new way to pass the time: playing the card game Cotch with the "old-timers," soaking up every word of their conversation. "I know I would get broke cause I was just glad to sit among them and hear them talk," he recalled in a private conversation in 1959. "The kids didn't have nothing to say except me. Oh, a motherfucker be playing the drums on the steps with sticks and [get in] your face for laughs. That's how stupid kids were. See, but what them niggers told me was real shit."[70]

Black Benny was a fixture at these Cotch games when he wasn't playing a parade—or going to the Parish Prison. On August 1, 1916, he was jailed for "resisting arrest" at Howard and Perdido Streets, possibly the occasion for one of Armstrong's favorite tales. It began when Benny won enough at Cotch to afford to get his best clothes out of the pawnshop. "He was a tall handsome black boy," Armstrong said, "pink shirt, had the cuffs of his box-back shirt turned up like we used to, them pointed high-button shoes—man, if you paid $26 for a pair of Edwin Clapps, you really had a pair of shoes."[71]

Armstrong remembered Benny was "sitting on one of them old beer boxes on the corner, telling lies and everything and here comes this [policeman]... And why this son-of-a-bitch come after him, he must have been older than baseball."

"Nigger come around, they want you down at the station," the officer said. "I've come to get you."

"Man, I ain't had this outfit on for a whole year," Black Benny responded. "I ain't going to jail today for nobody."

The officer lunged at Benny. "Shit," Armstrong said, "Man, he grabbed Benny and Benny didn't try to fight him or anything, he just tore out. He was the runningest son-of-a-bitch you've ever seen."

"I told you I wasn't going to jail—not today anyhow," Benny shouted as he dragged the officer through the muddy streets. "Tomorrow I'm going to give myself up. But I ain't had these clothes on in a whole year!"

Even though Black Benny had just dragged a cop through the mud and was back in jail, Armstrong observed that the police "liked him so well didn't any of them whip his head (when they'd arrest him) like they did the other guys."[72] Being behind bars also didn't interfere with Benny's parade work. "And any time he went to jail, the bands would ask the warden to let him out to play at a funeral," Armstrong added.[73]

Such an occasion took place shortly after this particular arrest when tragedy struck in Armstrong's life: Arthur Brown, one of his classmates at Fisk School, was accidentally shot and killed on August 8, 1916.[74] A band would have to be hired for the funeral and Armstrong and his friends knew there was only one choice. "The brass band we hired was the finest brass band I'd ever heard... It was Onward Brass Band, with Joe (King) Oliver, and Emanuel Perez, blowing the cornets," he wrote, adding that Black Benny played the bass drum on this occasion.[75]

The New Orleans funeral tradition went back to long before Armstrong's birth, but he was eloquent in summing it up as it related to the passing of his friend: "When the Onward Band, stuck up the funeral march, when they'd began to bring Arthur Brown's body from the church to go to the Grave Yard (cemetary [*sic*])-it was a real sad moment... Everybody cried, including me.... Black Benny would [beat] the base [*sic*] drum with a soft touch, while the snare drum (Babe Mathews) put a handkerchief under his snare drum, to deaden the tone... The band played, Nearer My God to Thee... Real touching...."

Armstrong also noted, "It has always been the tradition in New Orleans, to rejoice over the dead." He continued: "But after they lower the brother, etc, in the ground (six feet) and the minute that band strike up one of those good ol, good ones, such as Didn't He Ramble, they leave all the worries behind them..... Especially, when King Oliver commenced to blowing the last [chorus] in the high register, but good.... Everybody starts swinging and swaying from one side of the street to another (especially) the Second Line."[76]

With Joe Oliver playing those high notes and Black Benny on the bass drum, Armstrong must have felt like this was where he belonged, not just dancing with the second line or holding Oliver's horn, but playing with the band—and it's quite possible he did so. Writing about Arthur Brown a few years later, Armstrong claimed, "I played his funeral in Joe Oliver's brass band...His Cornet [player] whom were working in the day time, couldn't get off."[77]

It's impossible to know if Armstrong did or did not play at the funeral of Arthur Brown, but it's not inconceivable to imagine Oliver giving the young man a chance to blow in such a cacophonous setting. If he did play, he must have passed the test, because Oliver was about to call on him again in an entirely different yet no less exciting setting.

10

"My Fairy God Father"

1916–1917

Armstrong was always coy about his young crushes and infatuations with girls like Wilhelmina Martin and Peter Davis's niece Ida Robinson, but at some point, most likely around late 1916, he fell in love with a prostitute named Irene Jones and experienced the real thing. "I, being on the inexperience side, I did not know how to even treat the woman, but [. . .] she showed me the ropes, and taught me things, that I until this day, still remembers," he wrote. "We fell deeply in love with each other."[1]

Irene's health took a turn for the worse when she developed an "awful illness" and "stomach trouble" in Armstrong's words. Almost overnight, he found himself in a serious relationship, living with an older woman, working multiple jobs, still supporting his mother, sister, and cousin, and now, caring for an ailing girlfriend. He still wore short pants and liked to play baseball with his friends, but any vestiges of a normal childhood—if he ever had one in the first place—were gone.

While heading to the Poydras Market, Louis said, "[H]ere come my fairy god father (Papa Joe Oliver)." After Louis told him about Irene's plight, Oliver said, "You need money for a doctor," and demanded that Armstrong work in his place for two nights at Pete Lala's.[2]

"Papa Joe, I appreciate your very kindness, but personally I do not feel that I am capable of playing in your place," Armstrong responded.

"Aw—Go 'wan, and play in my place," Oliver replied with a sigh. "And if Pete Lala say anything to you, just tell him, that I sent ya."

"As bad as I actually needed the money, I was scared to death," Armstrong recalled. Pete Lala—real name Pete Ciaccio—was known for being tough on Oliver's subs and Armstrong was fearful that Ciaccio would tell him, "Since Joe isn't here, we will do without a cornet player tonight."

Armstrong put on his long pants and went over to Pete Lala's the next night. He could feel Ciaccio staring him down as he opened his cornet case.

"Where's Joe?" Ciaccio asked.

"Er'wa, he sent me to work in his place," Armstrong stammered.

Ciaccio let Armstrong play but after a few minutes, he walked over to the bandstand, dragging his gimpy leg, and shouted, "Put that bute in that horn!"

Armstrong didn't know what he was referring to, so he kept playing his blues, unaffected. But five minutes later, he heard it again.

"Boy, I told you to put that bute in that horn," Ciaccio insisted.

Armstrong finally realized Ciaccio meant "mute," so he did what he was told and made it through the rest of the night. But at the end of the evening, Armstrong's prophecy came true.

"Tell Joe we will do without a cornet," Ciaccio told Armstrong, ending any chances of him returning the next night.

"I told Papa Joe Oliver what had happened," Armstrong remembered. "So he paid me for the two nights anyway.... He knew I really needed the money... Then to—Joe Oliver is just that way, especially with someone he really likes."[3]

In Armstrong's version, that's where the story ends—Irene recovered and soon afterward, Oliver quit Pete Lala's. But banjoist Johnny St. Cyr, who was hired by Oliver to play in the Magnolia Band for much of 1916, recalled that it was he who recommended Armstrong when Oliver needed a sub—and that Armstrong filled the role numerous times.

St. Cyr first saw Armstrong playing with Boogers and Sonny Garbie in "the toughest part of town" and was impressed with his appearance. "Louis was always so clean and neat," St. Cyr said. "He would get all cleaned up and dressed up to go to his job." St. Cyr liked the way Armstrong played the blues, as well as another song that Armstrong himself had written, a bawdy number he could sing for the pimps and whores to give his sore lips a break. Everyone who heard him in this period vividly remembered the tune, but they all gave it different titles.

To St. Cyr, it was "Who Threw the Bricks on Katy's Head."[4] Kid Ory remembered Armstrong performing it with his band at National Park as "Get Off Katie's Head." Manuel Manetta mentioned it in several interviews, always giving it a different spin, once calling it "Take Your Fingers Out of Katie's Hair," another time "Take Your Finger Out of Katie's Head," and yet another time as "Take Your Fingers Out of Katie's Ass."[5]

St. Cyr also remembered Armstrong needing to use a mute after midnight at Pete Lala's because they had to keep the noise down. "Well, the waiters and everybody around there liked to hear Louis 'get off,' so they would talk him into taking the mute out of the cornet," St. Cyr said. Hence Pete Ciaccio's frustration.

Armstrong still didn't know too many tunes, but his natural brand of showmanship won him some new fans, especially when he took aim at Ciaccio. "Now, old man Lala had quite a limp and he would come across the floor, limping and shaking his finger at Louis, when he'd take the mute out of the cornet," St. Cyr recalled. "After he had turned his back, Louis would go into a little dance which would end up with him taking a few steps with a limp and shaking his finger, just like the old man. This, of course would bring the house down. Louis was always a comedian and he was always coming up with something."[6]

Armstrong's days as Oliver's sub ended when Oliver quit Pete Lala's in late 1916 and joined Kid Ory's band. Oliver had been trying to get into Ory's band for years, without success, as Ory felt Oliver played "loud and wrong."[7] But Oliver had greatly improved in recent years and with Mutt Carey's departure in 1916, there was now an opening.

The star power of having Oliver and Ory together in the same group was enough for Ciaccio to immediately offer the band a regular spot, hanging up a big sign advertising "Joe Oliver, Formerly of the Magnolia Band, Now with Kid Ory's." Oliver quickly adapted to the Ory band's repertoire and style, which made great use of dynamics, adding his "freak" trumpet sounds and fiery improvisations to an already exciting combination—one that almost immediately set out to "cut" every other band in its path.

"Kid Ory and Joe Oliver, got together and made one of the hottest jazz bands to ever hit New Orleans," Armstrong wrote. "When ever they appear on the corner in the tail gate wagon, advertising for a dance, etc, and run up on another band in another wagon, advertising for another dance or what ever they were advertising for, Joe and Kid Ory would throw a whole lots of that Mad, good music under their belt while the crowd would just go wild."[8] Once the other band was officially "cut," Ory and Oliver added insult to injury by dedicating a song to the defeated band as their wagon rode away: "Kiss My Fucking Ass!"[9] Reworked into the more family-friendly composition "Do What Ory Say," it became one of the band's most popular numbers.

Armstrong followed the Ory and Oliver band wherever they played, including Pete Lala's. Manuel Manetta was playing violin in the group and remembered Armstrong "when he was playing three tunes in 1917, and we had Ory and Oliver's jazz band." Asked to name the three tunes, Manetta said one was the aforementioned "Take Your Finger Out of Katie's Ass," while another was an Armstrong original called "Wind and Grind" that Oliver and others picked up on in that period but apparently was never recorded (at least not by that name). Armstrong's third piece, Manetta said, was "just the old blues. Real common New Orleans blues."[10]

Armstrong got along with everyone in the band except the drummer, Red Happy Bolton, the "bully" of Armstrong's old vocal quartet. When Armstrong would get his chance, Manetta said, "Happy would get so jealous of all that."

Things came to a head when they got off the bandstand. "Louis goes down there, there go Happy, and they're fighting like bulls," Manetta said. The only way he could get the fight to stop was to threaten to tell Joe Oliver. "But anyway he had a chance, he would hop on that boy, because the people made [a fuss] over Louis with his three tunes more so than them over here in the regular band!"[11]

Red Happy, perhaps recognizing Armstrong's ability in spite of himself, also lifted Armstrong's material. When the Ory and Oliver band started regularly playing for dances at Tulane University's gymnasium, Dr. Edmond Souchon recalled that Red Happy Bolton was "the guy that used to sing the dirty songs. . . . One of them was 'Take Your Hand Out of Katie's Ass.' "[12]

The impact of this band, and particularly Oliver, made a deep impression on Souchon, a Tulane student at the time who went on to become a respected jazz guitarist and historian (born October 25, 1897). Years earlier, Souchon snuck into the Big 25 to hear Oliver play, remembering the music as "hard-hitting, rough and ready, full of fire and drive."[13] But of Oliver's playing at Tulane, he said, "I remember Oliver as impressing me even more up there because I think to me that was when he was at his peak. . . . He could take one note and sustain that through a whole damn chorus of the band doing the changes behind him. Just one, he'd just hold it just as clean and pure as you ever heard. I never heard that on a record."[14]

Another musician who was transformed by hearing Oliver at Tulane was white cornetist Johnny Wiggs (born July 25, 1899). "I'll never forget how Joe hit me up at those Tulane gym dances," Wiggs recalled. "I just stood up there with my mouth open. I just couldn't imagine music being like that."[15] Of Oliver's personality, Wiggs said, "He was a very supercilious Negro, you know. He knew what he had. He was a big boy in music in New Orleans. He had all the jobs tied up, you see, and he took nothing from nobody." Any time Oliver was asked what the name was of the song he'd just played, Wiggs remembered he would always answer, "Who Struck John?" "You know he was a real sassy nigger, I'm telling you, cute as hell," Wiggs said in 1962. "Mean, too, boy. He was. . . . It still was fun to watch that guy. I mean he had that band under control, too. Boy, he was the boss. He was the boss."[16]

When Oliver and Ory would get a call to play a Saturday night dance at Tulane, that left an opening at Pete Lala's. Oliver grew more comfortable sending Armstrong in as his sub, along with Steve Lewis on piano, Morris French on trombone, Louis Prevost on clarinet, "Old Man" Francisco Ferdinand Valteau on violin, and Alfred Williams on drums. Williams, born in 1900 and a schoolmate of Armstrong at Fisk, recalled how it still wasn't easy for them to get to work in that part of town. "Cause I was a kid, I couldn't go down in the District, you know," he said. "When I went down to play, police stopped me and Louis two or three times, wanted to put us in jail. But I told them I had a mother and didn't have no father, you see, and I had to try to help my mother make a living. So he let me slide. Me and Louis was the youngest one[s] in there you know."[17]

The core of this band of substitutes soon formed a six-piece band of their own, co-led by Armstrong and "Little Joe" Lindsey, born on September 7, 1899, and "a very good drummer when we were kids" in Armstrong's estimation.[18] This band quickly became known for their ability to substitute in a pinch for the bigger names on the scene. "We played all of Joe Oliver's dates, Buddy Petit's dates, things that they couldn't fill, you know," Armstrong recalled.[19] He also noticed that when "Joe Lindsey had the deposit, we didn't get nothing." Armstrong quickly came to the realization that he wanted no part of the business side of the music business. "That was one reason why I never cared to be a band leader," he said after watching Lindsey wheel and deal. "I just wanted to blow my horn peacefully.[20]

Armstrong still wasn't a great reader, but it didn't matter at this time. "When they get to our little band, we didn't need but one man to read and all he had to do was go down to Krauss's department store, where it was [on Canal Street], and buy the sheet music," Armstrong said. "And he played the lead and we had such beautiful ears. Every Sunday we had a tune, that's how we got all the crowds. Then after we got through cutting them on the corner, we play Ory's tune, you know, [sings "Kiss My Fucking Ass"] and the crowd would go wild!"[21]

Well, not every crowd. Armstrong and Lindsey's band occasionally played one of the Saturday night dances at the Tulane gym—but only when those who booked the dances were feeling desperate. "Now, Armstrong, who was just the kid coming up at the time then, we never hired him unless we were absolutely broke and couldn't get anybody else because he blew false and he blew too loud," Souchon remarked. "And he was a rough, rough character in his youth."[22] Regardless of Souchon's opinion, Armstrong remained proud of his group, saying, "And, believe me when those six kids would spread out and start to swinging, one would swear it was Ory and Oliver's jazz band."[23]

That is, until they ran into Ory and Oliver's jazz band. Armstrong knew that Oliver "would never do anything that would make me look small (musically) in the eyes of the public" so they worked out a system: if Armstrong's band was on a wagon and came across the Ory and Oliver band, Armstrong would just have to stand up and show himself. It worked the first few times; Oliver would see Armstrong, play a short number and head out in a different direction.

But a day came when Armstrong wasn't feeling good and forgot to stand up. "Ump Ump Ump.... What a licking those guys gave us," he wrote. "And-'Sho'nuff Kid Ory played his get away tune ["Kiss My Fucking Ass"] at us, and the crowd went mad." When Oliver saw Armstrong later that night, he asked, "Why in the hell didn't you stand up?"

"Papa Joe, it was my fault," Armstrong responded. "And I won't ever do that again."

Armstrong and his bandmates were embarrassed by the thrashing, but they retained their confidence. "Because, couldn't no other band do it to us," Armstrong wrote. "We were (for youngsters) the closest things, to the Ory band." He accurately predicted that "a new generation was about to take over."[24]

Part of that new generation was reflected in the name of the band, which, depending on who you asked, was either "Kid Lindsey's Jazz Band," the "Maple Leaf Jazz Band," or most often, the "Brown Skin Jazz Band." But each name had something in common: the use of the word "jazz." Armstrong grew up hearing this music described as "ragtime," but even he later admitted, " 'Ragtime' was going out when I was coming in. See, that word, 'ragtime,' Buddy Bolden and them boys used that." Asked when he first heard the word "jazz," Armstrong said he didn't exactly remember but immediately called attention to the name of the Maple Leaf Jazz Band, adding, "See, [jazz] was a modern word in my times."[25]

The use of "Brown Skin" was also an attempt to latch on to a current popular hit song in New Orleans, "Brown Skin, Who You For?," written by pianist Clarence Williams and violinist Armand J. Piron in 1915.[26] After they published the sheet music, recordings were made of it for Columbia and Victor Records and Williams received a check for $1,600. "I believe it was the most money anybody ever made on a song in New Orleans." Williams said. "After that, everybody was writing songs down there."[27]

For his next opus, Williams turned to the Ory and Oliver band. Their "Kiss My Fucking Ass" anthem had already been sanitized into "Do What Ory Say" but now Williams and Johnny St. Cyr transformed it into "Mama's Baby Boy," giving Williams another hit, much to Ory's chagrin. "On both 'Brown Skin, Who You For?' and 'Mama's Baby Boy,' I used the words, 'Jazz song,' on the sheet music," Williams said. "I don't exactly remember where the words came from, but I remember I heard a woman say it to me when we were playin' some music. 'Oh, jazz me, baby,' she said."[28] The word soon caught on. "Theatrical journals have taken cognizance of the 'jas bands' and at first these organizations of syncopation were credited with having originated in Chicago, but any one ever having frequented the 'tango belt' of New Orleans knows that the real home of the 'jas bands' is right here," the *Times-Picayune* reported on November 16, 1916.[29]

The sounds of New Orleans music were originally spread across the country by Bill Johnson's pioneering Original Creole Band, with Freddie Keppard on cornet, during a series of high-profile vaudeville tours that began in 1914. To get the message across, the band had to wear costumes, do comedy, and appear in a plantation setting, but the response to the music was so great that it opened the door for white bands from New Orleans to follow in their footsteps. Tom Brown's Band from Dixieland was first, opening at Lamb's Café in Chicago in May 1915 before changing their name to Brown's Jass Band. Stein's Dixie Jass Band followed at Schiller's Café in Chicago in March 1916, causing a sensation. After retooling their personnel and adding Larry Shields on clarinet, the Dixie Jass Band opened at Reisenweber's Cafe in Manhattan in January 1917 and were an instant smash.

The success of these bands, and the Dixie Jass Band in particular, led to an explosion of the use of the words "jass" or "jazz" in early 1917. The Steamer Sidney excursion boat began featuring "Fischer's ragtime jass band" in January.[30] On January 28, Dugan's Piano Company, located at 914 Canal Street, ran an advertisement for multiple piano rolls, including "Once in a While" ("one of the latest Jazz Fox Trots"), "Butterfly" ("Jazz Arrangement"), "I'm Glad You're Sorry" ("Special Jazz Arrangement"), "If You Ever Get Lonely" ("Jazz Fox Trot") and a new song called "That Funny Jazz Band from Dixieland."[31] Two weeks later, the *Times-Picayune* covered the success of the Dixie Jass Band, "said to have come from New Orleans."[32]

RCA Victor finally recorded the Dixie Jass Band on February 26, 1917, releasing the results—"Livery Stable Blues" backed by "Original Dixieland Jass One-Step"—in April. The New Orleans department store Maison Blanche ran a descriptive advertisement for the record, even featuring a photo of the group, now billed as the Original Dixieland Jass Band. Maison Blanch smartly emphasized the New Orleans connections of the band and the music, saying it was "Made by New Orleans musicians for New Orleans people. . . . It has all the 'swing' and 'punch' and 'pep' and 'spirit' that is so characteristic of the bands whose names are a by-word at New Orleans dances. It is more proof that New Orleans sets the pace for 'wonderful' dance music—a fact that is recognized and commented upon the country over."[33]

This special brand of innovative New Orleans music was finally available on record—as played by a white band.[34] It's not exactly a secret where they picked up their sound. In praising the greatness of the Ory and Oliver band, trombonist Preston Jackson noted, "The La Rocca boys of the Dixieland Jazz Band used to hang around and got a lot of ideas from [Oliver's] gang."[35] "You know they, LaRocca, and those boys, used to stand on the walkways out at Lake Pontchartrain and pick up everything we were doing," Kid Ory said. "I saw them. They played a lot of old New Orleans tunes and put their names on 'em. Like 'Tiger Rag.' "[36]

Making matters worse, Nick La Rocca grew old and bitter over the years, often flaunting opinions that were flat out racist. "Any white person that says they're fit to integrate, I say they're stepping down and lowering the morals of the white race," LaRocca said. "All you have to do is read Louis Armstrong's book. He had nine daddies; he says he didn't know who was his right daddy. He didn't know, but he had nine daddies. That's what they're trying to force on you, these minority groups."[37] According to LaRocca, Joe Oliver "was just an ignorant negro that didn't know no better, like these ignorant white crumbs who [are] supposed to be historians from New Orleans."[38]

Such statements make it difficult to listen to the music of the Original Dixieland Jass Band objectively in the 21st century. Yet it cannot be denied that their recordings had a major impact on what was happening musically in New Orleans—with both black and white bands. For instance, before the Original Dixieland Jass Band , most Black New Orleans bands featured a similar instrumentation. "We did not use pianos, in those days," Armstrong said, before giving the standard lineup: "Cornet-Clarinet-trombone-Drums-Bass Violin-Guitar."[39] Armstrong and Lindsey's Brown Skin Jazz Band followed that template, as did the Ory and Oliver band—until the Original Dixieland Jass Band recordings were released. "Some of us saw that band [the Original Dixieland Jass Band] doing very well with only five pieces and cut our own bands back to five," Ory said. "I did that for a while."[40] Ory moved Manuel Manetta from violin to piano and released bassist Bob Lyons and guitarist Lorenzo Staulz "to follow the suit of the Dixieland Jazz Band," Manetta said.[41] Almost overnight, the violin was no longer considered an integral part of the front line.

From a repertoire standpoint, Armstrong later said, of the Original Dixieland Jass Band's recording of "Tiger Rag," "between you and me, its the best," and he soon began playing it himself.[42] Trumpeter Punch Miller heard Louis around 1918 and said, "He's the first one I heard play [the Original Dixieland Jass Band's] 'Clarinet Marmalade,' Louis Armstrong."[43]

Armstrong admitted he listened to the Original Dixieland Jass Band's records and never said an unkind word about them, even when goaded to, though he also avoided overt praise. During a 1953 conversation, George Avakian said of the Original Dixieland Jass Band, "I never heard anybody from New Orleans who ever felt they were so hot" and asked Armstrong if he listened to them. "Yeah, I bought their records, 'Livery Stable Blues' and all of those—well, shit, man . . . that's the first records of jazz or Dixieland anything that start selling!" Armstrong stated emphatically.[44] Over a decade later, he told *Life*, "Big event for me then was buying a wind-up Victrola. Most of my records were the original Dixieland Jazz Band—Larry Shields and his bunch. They were the first to record the [kind of] music I played."[45] The bottom line is Armstrong bought their records and enjoyed them, and he was probably far from alone.[46]

But just as the Original Dixieland Jass Band's popularity exploded, Armstrong and Lindsey's Brown Skin Jazz Band disbanded in the first part of 1917. Joe Lindsey was developing quite a reputation as a drummer, but according to Armstrong, Lindsey became more interested in becoming a pimp than playing music for a living. Lindsey "ran into a goodlooking prostitute named Neeta at a picnic where we played and they fell madly in love," Armstrong said; in the 1920 census, Lindsey is shown as married to a woman named Anita. "So he automatically left me and the rest of the youngsters to be a big time Pimp and hang out at (25) with the rest of the big timers."[47] It was the end of the Brown Skin/Maple Leaf Jazz Band.

It was also the end of Armstrong's relationship with Irene. Watching the fractious relationship between Joe and Anita Lindsey—"My God, did she give him a bad time," he remembered—Armstrong decided to tell Irene that "she should get an older fellow. Because I am so wrapped up in my horn, I wouldn't make a good mate for her." Irene appreciated his sincerity and agreed to part ways—for now.

Armstrong cleared his mind by taking a job in Houma, Louisiana, about 45 miles south of New Orleans, in a band organized by an undertaker named "Bonds."[48] It was a little upsetting to be "around all them dead people," Armstrong said—Bonds conducted his business where he lived—but overall he enjoyed his break from the coal cart and said Bonds "was so nice to me, until I stayed longer than I went there to stay."[49] He stayed for two full weeks but was the worse for wear when it was time to go back home. "They'd feed me and then they give me so much [money] and I'm young, dig that little change, and I was gambling and fooling around, just a phase, you know, beat me down," he said.[50]

Armstrong was thankful to run into Joe Oliver on his way back from Houma. Armstrong "looked so bad," inspiring Oliver to give him a speech about how "You've got to take care of your health."[51] Oliver soon began inviting Armstrong over to his house. "He was very young," Stella Oliver said of Louis. "He used to run errands for us. He'd come to my house, nothing but a boy, he'd come to my house and make errands for us. And he followed Joe every step Joe went around. And Joe was fond of him, he was fond of Joe, and I used to always call him 'my boy.' "[52]

The errands soon turned into meals, providing memories Armstrong always treasured. "When I ate red beans and rice with him at his house and he had a big tin bucket full of sweetened water, just sugar and water—he didn't want coffee and all that, just a big bucket of sweetened water to rinse them beans down," Armstrong reminisced in 1968. "His wife, Mrs. Oliver, made me a bucket too, like the three little bears. I had my little bucket, too. Because Joe Oliver, whatever he did, I wanted to do."[53] Eventually, Oliver began offering lessons, charging Armstrong 50 cents, which Armstrong thought "was real great in my estimation."[54] Of the lessons, Armstrong said, "He gave me lessons out of an exercise book—then we'd run down little duets together."[55]

Armstrong went back to his coal cart job during the day, but with the disbanding of the Brown Skin Jazz band he was out of a steady opportunity to play. But that would soon be rectified when he entered a honky-tonk in his neighborhood run by a man whose family is credited with starting the Mafia in the United States: Henry Matranga.

11

"Just Wasn't My Time to Die, Man"

1917

Growing up in the Third Ward, Armstrong became accustomed to the many Sicilians and Italians that populated his neighborhood. After emancipation, many newly freed slaves left New Orleans and the South in general as quickly as they could, leaving the many planters in the area requiring new workers to carry on the jobs of the slaves. They found a solution in Sicily, flaunting promises of the great American dream if they'd move to Louisiana. Thousands of Sicilians came to Louisiana between 1884 and 1924 but once they arrived, they basically assumed the role of the "new" slaves, treated poorly and paid very little for their grueling work on the plantations.

Many of these immigrants left the plantations as soon as they could and headed to New Orleans. They weren't exactly welcomed with open arms. "They were described in the press as 'swarthy,' 'kinky-haired' members of a criminal race and derided in the streets with epithets like 'dago,' 'guinea'—a term of derision applied to enslaved Africans and their descendants—and more familiarly racist insults like 'white nigger' and 'nigger wop,'" according to Brent Staples.[1]

On October 15, 1890, popular New Orleans police chief David Hennessy was shot on the corner of Girod and Basin Street. As he lay dying, he let it be known that he was shot by "dagoes." That's all the police needed to round up every Sicilian they could find in the neighborhood, arresting 19 in all. But when none of the defendants was convicted, an angry mob formed and lynched 11 of the Sicilians on March 14, 1891. One of the only Sicilians to escape death was an immigrant named Charles Matranga, most likely the mastermind of the killing of Hennessy. In the aftermath of the lynchings, Matranga formed what is known as the first "Mafia" crime family—Charles Matranga's Black Hand—not just in New Orleans but in the United States of America.

Twenty-five years after the lynching, Matranga was still in control of New Orleans's underworld and at war in Armstrong's neighborhood with the Segreto family. But one member of the Matranga family stayed out of trouble: Charles's nephew Henry, born in December 1882. Henry wasn't a stevedore like his father, Joseph, brother, Salvadore, and uncle, Charles Matranga. Henry was listed as an "Ice Dealer" in the 1915 Soards's Directory and then as running a saloon with A. J. Scaffino at 1201 Poydras Street the following year. When Matranga wanted to branch out and run a saloon of his own, he applied on October 18, 1916, for a license to operate an establishment at 1233 Perdido Street.

Matranga's first hire was Oscar Johnson, "alias Slippers, a notorious negro burglar and ex-convict" according to the press, as bouncer.[2] Born in 1886, Johnson was a fixture in Armstrong's Third Ward neighborhood, a tough troublemaker who once refused to go to the hospital after being shot in the shoulder.[3] Slippers would also partake in the gambling that went on in Matranga's back room. On October 15, 1916, during the same week Matranga applied for his license, Slippers was one of five African Americans arrested for "gambling with cards for money at Perdido and Franklin." He was released quickly, only to be arrested again on November 7 as a "dangerous and suspicious" character "pending investigation of a robbery." On and on it went: arrested on March 5, 1917, for "fighting and disturbing the peace"; arrested on May 1 for being "dangerous and suspicious"; arrested again on May 15 for "breaking box car seals and larceny of flour"; arrested November 23 "relative to flim-flamming"; arrested December 3 for being "a well known thief."

Armstrong praised Slippers's tough nature, saying "he's not only a bad man on the pistol and on the draw...But he really can 'Duke' [i.e., fight] awhile." But Armstrong also stressed that Slippers was "as nice a fellow, that God ever died for.... I admired him so well until I loved him just [like] a father of mine.... I as a youngster, felt so secured when ever I was around fellows such as Slippers or Black Benny..... And just to be in their company, was just like heaven to me."[4]

After Matranga's original cornetist quit, Slippers recommended Armstrong for the job. "At first Mr. Matranga was a little in doubt about my ability to hold the job down, because the fellow who had just quit, was a pretty good man," he wrote. Armstrong put on his long pants, reorganized his trio with Boogers on piano and Sonny Garbie on drums, and made his debut at Matranga's. As he began to blow, Slippers excitedly cheered him on, shouting, "Listen to that little sommitch blowing that quail!" Slippers never learned the actual name of Armstrong's instrument, once telling him, "Boy, if you keep on, you're gonna be the best Quail Blower in the world, mark my word." "And that coming from Slippers, made me feel real grand," Armstrong said, "Because Slippers did not say those words to anybody."[5]

Armstrong worked steadily at Matranga's throughout the rest of 1917, once saying "it was same as Carnegie Hall to me."[6] But he had to balance that feeling of pride with a feeling of constant terror born out of the dangerous atmosphere of the honky-tonk. "Boy, you talking about three guys (musicians) being scared to death, that was us," Armstrong wrote of his trio.[7] When the Cotch games in the back room turned violent, Slippers would draw his gun and expel any troublemakers. Sometimes they shot back, as Armstrong vividly recalled in a 1953 conversation: "Now the bullets, I'm always in the way of them. They say the Lord take care of fools—he's sure looking after me! Those bullets are whizzing past and I'm just blowing the blues. I always had that saying, 'You've got to go down with the ship' or some shit like that. But I never did get hurt."[8]

"Our bandstand was right by the door, and if somebody start shooting, I don't see how I didn't get hit," Armstrong said on another occasion. "Just wasn't my time to die, man."[9]

When things got bad at Matranga's, the police would sometimes raid the place and take everyone they could find—especially if they were Black—to jail. "Sometimes I'd be in a few days, sometimes more, until the owner (Henry Matranga) came down to pay the fine or get us all out on bail," Armstrong said.[10]

In *Satchmo: My Life in New Orleans*, Armstrong provided details from one such visit to prison, vividly recalling the presence of Louis "Sore Dick" Johnson, which means that this incident took place before Joseph "Dirty Dog" Williams killed Sore Dick on December 3, 1917. Armstrong might have been nervous with bullets whizzing by him on the bandstand, but in prison, surrounded by people he grew up with, he felt oddly relaxed—until he heard someone yell, "LOOK OUT!" "I noticed about Twelve Brooms sliding towards my direction," Armstrong said. "And about three of them wrapped around my legs tripping me to the ground... When I looked up, I look straight into Sore Dick's face." As Sore Dick stared, Armstrong got the hint and began sweeping the yard, realizing that was Sore Dick's "way of letting the new comer know who was the boss of the yard."[11]

Armstrong was relieved when Matranga got him out, learning a valuable, if demoralizing, lesson in the meantime. "If you didn't have a white captain to back you in the old days—to put his hand on your shoulder—you was just a damn sad nigger," Armstrong said. "If a Negro had the proper white man to reach the law and say, 'Why the hell you mean locking up MY nigger?' then—while naturally—the law would walk him free. Get in that jail *without* your white boss, and yonder comes the chain gang! Oh, danger was dancing all around you back then."[12] The hours were tough at Matranga's, too. "Well, we start about, say about 10 or 11 o'clock, play until 5, on an ordinary morning," Armstrong said. "Mind you, I used to get off from there and go to that mule. Sure. I'd just take a nap between mealtime." But Armstrong didn't complain. "We'd think nothing of it, especially with them whores coming in there with their stocking full of money, you're trying to beg something out of it," he continued, offering a window into one of the perks of the job. "They give you tips to play the blues. Being I was a little boy, they used to sit me on their laps and everything else."[13]

Armstrong did pick up one trait from watching the older men woo the women at the honky-tonks that would result in his adopting perhaps his most iconic stage prop after his trumpet: a white handkerchief. "See, when we was kids in New Orleans, teenagers, we'd go to a dance where King Oliver or Bunk Johnson and some of them cats blowing, and we're dancing with a chick, you know?" Armstrong recounted on *The Mike Douglas Show* in 1970. "And cats don't take their hat off, no way, you know. No, no. Just go and dance with the chick and when they get the chick in the corner, talking to her, you know, put the hat back and wipe their brow, you know." At this point, Armstrong took out his white handkerchief and almost seductively mopped his brow with it, recreating the move from those humid, New Orleans nights and eliciting laughter from the studio audience. "That was something else, huh?" he said, chuckling at the memory. "How can I forget it? The choice days of my life, man."[14]

Even armed with his new handkerchief, Armstrong's face would turn red and he'd get "hot in the collar," when he'd talk to the prostitutes. Internally, he thought, "I am too young to even come near of satisfying a hard woman like her." Admitting he always felt "inferior" to the pimps, he eventually decided that if he couldn't beat them, he would join them. "As I said before, I have always been, from a very small kid, a great Observer. And, I would noticed [*sic*], the youngsters, whom I ran with, they all had a woman, who were prostitutes," Armstrong wrote. "They did not get much money from them... But the notoriety among them were great."[15] Only in New Orleans could the "notoriety" achieved from being a pimp—as evidenced by the lavish funeral of Clerk Wade in 1915—be something Armstrong could aspire to.

One night at Henry Matranga's, Armstrong noticed a "hustling" girl with the nickname "Nootsy" and realized this could be his shot at "notoriety." "She wasn't very much to look at," he later wrote, describing her as "short, nappy hair'd and buck teeth." Even with her homely appearance, Armstrong decided he would work as Nootsy's pimp. Armstrong had to admit that Nootsy "made good money . . . That is, I thought it was big money in those days." But since he was already working all day and playing at night, he also admitted that he "didn't take Nootsy serious"; any income she generated was purely supplemental.

Nootsy didn't feel the same way. Though Armstrong later made it clear that they had had sex regularly, he seemingly had no interest in any other duties that came with being a pimp, such as protecting her and even living together. "One day, Nootsy wanted me to go home and spend the night with her, and I told her, I wouldn't think of staying away from May'ann and Mama Lucy, not for one night," he recalled. "I hadn't ever did it before and I won't do it now."

"Aw hell," Nootsy taunted him, "you are a big boy now. Come on and stay."

"No," Armstrong said flatly.[16] Later in the same manuscript to *Satchmo: My Life in New Orleans*, Armstrong added that in addition to not wanting to leave his mother and sister home alone, he turned her down "because I wanted to go home and practice my cornet instead of going to her house."[17]

That was enough for Nootsy to realize that Armstrong was too soft to be a real pimp. Her pride already wounded, Nootsy decided to end the relationship—and perhaps Armstrong's life along with it. Before he knew what was happening, Nootsy had taken out a penknife and stabbed him in the left shoulder. "I saw this blood streaming down my shoulder and all over the back of my shirt," he said. All he could think of was he was afraid to tell his mother about it when he got home.

Sure enough, once Mayann spotted the blood, she began shaking him violently, asking, "Who did it!? Who did it!?"

"Er'wa, Nootsy did it," Louis said with his usual nervous stammer.

"Nootsy did? What right have Nootsy cutting on you."

Louis later said he told his mother "the whole thing, with fear in my eyes," but it's not quite certain if he went into detail about his foray into pimping. Instead, he seemed to stress the fact that Nootsy wanted to make love to him and he was "afraid of her" and "hated to hurt her feelings."

That was enough for Mayann. "The minute I told what happened, she pushed me aside, and made a beeline, to Nootsy's house," he recalled. Mayann knocked and knocked until Nootsy answered. "The minute Nootsy opened the door, May'ann grabbed her by the throat," Louis said, remembering his mother with tears in her eyes.

"What you stabbed my son for?" Mayann demanded. "Huh!?"

"And before Nootsy could say a word, 'May'ann was choking her to the ground," Louis said. He believed that Mayann was going to choke her to death right then and there, but suddenly, Black Benny appeared.

"Don't kill her, Mayann!" Benny pleaded with her. "Nootsy won't do it again!"

Mayann let up and told Nootsy, "[You] better not ever bother my boy again."[18]

Louis never forgot the way Mayann fought for him. "There she was fighting my battle," he later wrote. "She was always in my corner. So there was nothing too good for my mother."[19]

Armstrong's days as a pimp were over almost as soon as he started, but now he had a scar to remind him of Nootsy. He showed it off to George Avakian during a visit to his home, saying, "This is a penknife scar, man. Right here." He still associated the moment with Mayann, remarking, "Like Nootsy, now I'm sleeping with the woman but [Mayann] saw this blood, she go and whip her for me! ....She'd just go mad seeing that blood." But then Armstrong added an interesting detail: "And the more blood [she saw], she must have digged that [wound], and knocked out four detectives on their ass. Well, quite naturally, we was getting in a spot there then, you know. The more that would come, it got to be hell around there with them cats with them pistols [i.e., detectives], too—they wasn't going to stand for that shit. So they had to quiet it down."[20]

Armstrong seemed to associate Mayann knocking "four detectives on their ass" with the Nootsy incident. This tantalizing reference makes this an appropriate place to discuss one of the big mysteries of Armstrong's early years, specifically, what on earth happened on March 1, 1917?

According to the First Precinct's Record of Arrests, two patrolmen descended upon the Armstrongs' home, at 334 South Liberty Street and began arresting all present for disturbing the peace. This included Louis, mother Mayann, and for the first time, 14-year-old Beatrice Armstrong. But somehow, Willie Armstrong was also there, traveling all the way from his residence nearly two miles away at 3336 First Street. Also present was a man named Duncan Anderson, then living with Louis, Mayann, and Beatrice. The previous year, on April 2, 1916, Mayann had been arrested for disturbing the peace along with 43-year-old "Dunk" Anderson, then living at Saratoga and Perdido Street. Now Anderson was living with Mayann—yet, for the first time, Mayann told the police she was married and her name was Mary Armstrong!

But two more people were arrested during the March 1 incident and their presence only adds to the mystery of it all: Irene Jones and Charley Wade. Irene Jones was "Irene," the prostitute Armstrong had fallen in love with the previous year and broken up with before going to Houma. She gave her age as 21—Louis gave his as 18, adding a few years for good measure—and listed her address as 336 South Liberty, right next door. That could be a mistake, as even Louis later told Robert Goffin, "She's the girl whom I was living with—as we express it—it's called Common Law-Man + Wife."[21]

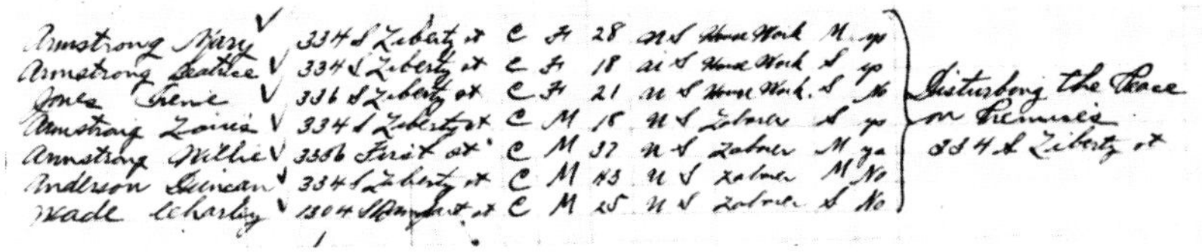

Figure 11.1 Excerpt from the First Precinct's "Report of Arrests," detailing the arrest of Louis Armstrong, his family, and other associates—including prostitute Irene Jones and her pimp, Charley "Cheeky Black" Wade—for disturbing the peace at 11:45 p.m. on March 1, 1917. Willie Armstrong and his daughter, Beatrice, gave their correct ages but Mayann, who was in her early thirties, told the police she was 28, and Louis, who was 15 or 16, gave his age as 18.
Credit: Sourced from Ancestry.com.

But who was Charley Wade? Wade lived a few blocks away at 1322 South Rampart Street but was a frequent presence in the First Precinct, arrested numerous times over the years for everything from being a "well known thief" to "associating with prostitutes." In many of his arrest records, the police noted his alias: "Black." Thus, there's a strong possibility that Charley Wade was Irene's pimp, "Cheeky Black," a "Real Bad Spade" in Armstrong's mind. Armstrong reunited with Irene while playing Matranga's, but before they could get down to business, Armstrong asked about Cheeky Black. "Oh no, I am no longer going with him," Irene assured him.

"The minute we undressed and gotten into bed we heard a knock on the door," Armstrong related. "A real Hard Knock at that."

"Who is that?" Irene called out "in her little voice."

"It's me—Cheeky Black," came the response.

"Uh uh," Armstrong said to himself. "Here's where there's going to be trouble."

"I have company, Cheeky," Irene responded, which was code in those days for a prostitute to let her pimp know that she was in the process of earning money.

But it didn't work; Cheeky Black kept knocking. Armstrong was nervous but knew he had locked the door behind him.

"But Shucks just like a Flash of Lightning Cheeky Black Broke the Door Down—Irene Screamed and ran out into the streets justa Screaming. And Cheeky Black pulled out his razor and started cutting at 'Irene's Rear,'" Armstrong wrote. "Whether he really cut her—I really can't say—I was so busy putting on my clothes trying to get out of there before Cheeky Black came back looking for me." He added, "I heard later that Irene was saved when a 'Cop' came along just in time—ooh wee—what a Close Shave that was."[22]

Thus, could March 1, 1917, have been the date of the "Cheeky Black" and Irene incident? Or was this the time Mayann beat up Nootsy and "four detectives" came to "quiet it down"? Did Willie Armstrong fight Duncan Anderson? Could "Nootsy" really be an alias for Irene?

The answers will never be known. Armstrong's memory offered no concrete answers, even regarding the times he spent in jail. "Now you can see why I don't remember just how many times that I went to jail," he said in 1970. "It was a common thing in those days."[23] But it's undeniable that Armstrong got himself involved in the sordid world of pimping and prostitution for a time in 1917 and was lucky to live to tell about it.

Toward the end of his life, Armstrong summed up this phase by telling a reporter, "Needed money so bad I even tried pimping, but my first client got jealous of me and we got to fussing about it and she stabbed me in the shoulder. Them was wild times."[24] He could not have predicted which direction his career would head, but he surely would have been flabbergasted to know that such a quote would one day appear in his *New York Times* obituary.

Louis had now tried pimping, had been stabbed, and had been arrested at least twice in the year leading up to his seventeenth birthday celebration in 1917. Mayann realized that even though her son hadn't had much of a childhood, he wasn't quite a man yet—especially after he got drunk for the first time and vomited in his own bed.

"Son, you have to live your own life," Mayann told him after this incident. "And also, you have to go out into this world someday all by your lone self. And you need all the experiences you can get, such as what's good for you and what's bad. I cannot tell you these things. You have to witness them for yourself."

Mayann told Louis that she wasn't going to scold him for "a few nips" of liquor and admitted, "I drink all the liquor [I] wants to and I get pretty tight some time. Only thing, I am more experience than you as to how to carry my liquor to keep from getting sick."

In *Satchmo: My Life in New Orleans*, Louis devotes several pages to the tale of the night Mayann took him out on the town to "show you how to really enjoy good liquor." It's one of the most entertaining passages of the book, but it does have a dark underbelly. Louis would never admit it, but his mother was an alcoholic who frequently disappeared on drinking benders during his young days and got arrested at least 10 times between 1905 and 1917, often choosing to go to the House of Detention rather than pay a fine. He also didn't admit—or didn't know—that Mayann's drinking was slowly killing her.

When Louis and Mayann arrived at Henry Matranga's, the proprietor gave them each a drink on the house and told Mayann, "You have a fine boy and he is well liked by everybody who comes to my place. And they, as well as I, predict he will be a very fine musician some day. His heart is in it."

"Thank God," Mayann, responded, sticking her chest out with pride. "Because I was never able to give my son a decent education like he deserved. I could see he had talent within him from a wee youngster. But I could not do very much about it. Just pray to the Lord to guide him and help him in the things that he alone would undertake. And the Lord has answered my prayers greatly."

Mayann thanked Matranga for allowing Louis to work there "knowing he did not have the experience needed" and closed by stressing, "With all of you people pulling for Louis the way you all are doing, he just can't miss, that's all."

Slippers came out to say hello to Mayann and insisted they have a drink with him, even though they were getting pretty "tight" by this time. Mayann's voice was "slightly warbling," but she told Slippers, "I'm proud of that boy. He's all I've got. He and his sister. His sister Mama Lucy. I have struggled hard for those two children. Of course his no good father have never done anything decent for those children. Only their Step Fathers. Good thing they had good Step Fathers, or else I don't know what those two children would have done." It's probable that Mayann didn't utter those words exactly in that manner, but there's no doubting that Louis did not forget his mother's pride in his accomplishments, even if that meant just playing the blues for the prostitutes all night and trying not to get shot.

Armstrong's story ends with Gabe Woods coming to rescue Louis and Mayann—who by that point literally embodied the expression "fall down drunk"—helping them up as a crowd laughed at their antics. Duncan Anderson was living with Mayann by March 1, 1917, and Gabe Woods married Julia Washington on July 14, 1917, so if Armstrong's memory is correct, this was another event that took place in early 1917, an action-packed year if there ever was one—especially overseas.[25]

"The Kaiser [was] getting worse with his drastic antics," Armstrong noted. Indeed, the United States was about to enter World War I in April 1917. No one might have known it immediately, but this event would soon herald the end of the red-light district.

The music scene in Storyville had already been in decline for several years, beginning on March 22, 1913, when a feud between two rival dance hall proprietors had ended in bloodshed, leaving Billy Phillips of the 102 Ranch and Harry Parker of the Tuxedo Dance Hall dead and several others seriously wounded. Police Superintendent James W. Reynolds went on the offensive, issuing an edict "calling for the prompt closing of all dance halls in the city and revoking all permits thereto."[26] However, Reynolds had trouble enforcing his edict. "The cabarets were among the first to get it in the neck, but they didn't die without a struggle," a *Times-Democrat* reporter noted in a November 2, 1913, story. "Orders would go out at 6 o'clock to close the cabarets at midnight; at 9 o'clock the orders would be countermanded."[27]

But by 1915, the police were making progress, getting an order passed to shut down the cabarets after that year's Mardi Gras. "The performers realize this fact and a big exodus has set in ever since the first arrests were made," the *Times-Picayune* noted. "The performers are going away, bag and baggage, satisfied that the cabaret business as operated in New Orleans is dead."[28] Indeed, between 1913 and 1917, pioneers of New Orleans jazz such as Freddie Keppard, Manuel Perez, Mutt Carey, and others left the city entirely. On January 19, 1917, the *Times-Picayune* reported, "The death-knell of the cabarets was sounded by Commissioner [Harold R.] Newman Thursday when he ordered police to take up their music permits. Without music there will be no dancing, which was one of the lures."

Pete Ciaccio continued to keep Pete Lala's afloat, but it was becoming more and more difficult as 1917 began, leading him to start closing his establishment at midnight—a move that ended up having quite an impact on Armstrong's life. "I used to play in the honky-tonk and [Joe Oliver] come from down in the Storyville and come up there where I played because he got off at 12:00 at night and see, they threw the key away where I played," he said. "He come up there and sit down and listen to me play, then he'd blow a few for me, you know, try to show me the right things."[29] Not only did Oliver come down to listen to and sometimes play for Armstrong, but one night, he announced, "I'm sick of looking at the beat-up cornet. I'm going to give you a horn." "So one night he gave me an old York he'd had," Armstrong recalled. "Oh, my! I drooled all over the place. 'Thanks, Papa Joe, thank you Mister Joe.' I always knew, if I'm going to get a little break in this game, it was going to be through Papa Joe, nobody else."[30]

Oliver soon found another excuse to regularly use Louis as a sub. Proving that he, too, succumbed to some of the same feelings toward women as Black Benny, Oliver had fallen in love with singer Mary McBride, who was part of the team of Mack and Mack with her then husband, Billy McBride. After the United States entered the war in April 1917, Pete Ciaccio knew that the red-light district's days were numbered and opened a "First Class Theatre" at 419 North Claiborne Street, hiring Clarence Williams as manager.[31]

Oliver wanted nothing more than to accompany Mary Mack at Lala's new theater, but he still had responsibilities with Kid Ory, including Monday night dances at Economy Hall. Oliver's solution was to send Armstrong in his place from 8 to 11, coming back to finish off the night after he was done at Lala's theater. Oliver agreed to advertise the dances on the wagon during the daytime, guaranteeing a large crowd, but when the spectators spotted Armstrong playing "the same three tunes," "nobody come in," Manuel Manetta said.[32]

But now, armed with the cornet Oliver gave him, Armstrong became determined to improve, practicing every chance he could at home. Asked about her brother's practice habits, Mama Lucy said he would "Just blow, blow, blow all the time when he was at home. Blow all the time." Asked what he practiced, she responded, "All kinds of music, all kinds of songs. And he'd sing, stamping on the floor and sing[ing] by hisself."[33]

Curious about what her brother was up to, Mama Lucy said, "I used to go peep through a little hole there, you know." She saw her brother in a pair of long pants, rolled up so he could walk, playing a cornet, and creating a stir. "They used to be hollering, 'Oh, blow it, Dipper!'" she recalled. "They'd say, 'Blow it, Dipper!' And he'd be playing that [cornet], his face would be out like that. He worked hard."[34]

The hard work was paying off. Armstrong later said he "commenced to get known" at Matranga's."[35] When clarinetist Sidney Bechet needed to hire a cornetist for a job, Black Benny suggested Louis, saying, "You think you can play. But I know a little boy right around the corner from my place, he can play 'High Society' better than you."

"High Society" was an old Porter Steele march that Joe Oliver transformed into a popular dance tune up at the Tulane gym. It originally featured a piccolo part that was adapted to the clarinet by Alphonse Picou and soon became the test piece for all New Orleans practitioners of that instrument. "And I'll be doggone if he didn't play 'High Society' on the cornet," Bechet recalled, adding, "It was very hard for clarinet to do, and really unthinkable for cornet to do at those times. But Louis, he did it. So I was very pleased about it."[36]

Armstrong was impressed with Bechet, too, having heard him play with Oliver for several years. "Oh whatta clarinet player he was," Armstrong said of him.[37] Bechet remembered the trio playing on the wagon, advertising twice a week for a movie theater, the Ivory Theater, while Armstrong remembered them on the wagon advertising for a boxing match. Whatever the circumstance, both men retained fond memories of their time together, Bechet recalling that they bonded over some "Poor Boy" sandwiches, which consisted of "a half a loaf of bread split open and stuffed with ham. We really had good times."[38]

For all of Manuel Manetta's repeated claims about Armstrong only being able to play three songs, the fact that he was able to execute the fast fingering of the "High Society" clarinet solo shows that he was becoming technically proficient on his instrument. Punch Miller also remembered Armstrong playing

Larry Shields's demanding clarinet part on "Clarinet Marmalade," making it clear that Armstrong's early style was heavily influenced by the fleet-fingered clarinetists of his hometown. By studying those solos, Armstrong became proficient at executing arpeggios on his instrument, gaining much dexterity in the process.

There was also the influence of Buddy Petit, whom Armstrong still admired and now sometimes played alongside. Petit never recorded, but to those who heard him, certain characteristics of his style lived on in Armstrong's playing. "When you hear Louis Armstrong now, you'll hear Buddy," clarinetist Emile Barnes said. "But the difference between Louis Armstrong and Buddy, Louis goes up and Buddy never go up. But when he makes that chromatic in there, that's Buddy over and over."[39] "Louie used to hang around with Buddy Petit and Buddy Petit showed him a lot of stuff and he picked up Buddy Petit's style," Paul Barnes, Emile's brother, concurred.[40] Between the influence of Petit and the clarinetists, Armstrong said, "I played all them variations—I thought I was a clarinet!"[41]

However, one man started feeling that Armstrong was gaining *too* much dexterity at this time: Joe Oliver.

"So Joe would come by [Henry Matranga's] after 12 and he'd sit down and listen to me awhile and then he'd come up and say, 'Listen boy, you play some more lead!,'" Armstrong recalled.[42] He would later relate this as some of the most important advice he ever received—but fast fingering and variations would remain a part of his early style for several more years to come.

Oliver had more time to spend with Armstrong after the red-light district was finally shut down on November 12, 1917. Its proximity to the city's four naval bases, coupled with the murder of four soldiers in the district early in the war, officially ended the Storyville era 20 years after it began. To Armstrong personally, it was no big deal. He'd spend much of his life telling tales of Storyville to anyone who asked, but except for working on the coal cart with Morris Karnofsky and the infrequent times Joe Oliver sent him to Pete Lala's as a substitute, he had spent very little time performing in the district. He still had his regular job at Henry Matranga's, of which, he said, "It seemed as though the law hadn't [shut] them down along with Storyville, because it was just a third rate place."[43]

Armstrong would continue the pattern of working odd jobs during the day and playing Matranga's and anywhere he could at night well into 1918, but by the summer of that year, he would find love, get the biggest break of his musical career—and say goodbye to his beloved mentor.

12

"Had to Eat"

1917–1918

As Armstrong's confidence and reputation grew in late 1917 and early 1918, he was put to the test any time he came up against his old friend from the Waif's Home, Henry "Kid" Rena. Except for the occasional reunion for Peter Davis or a parade with Black Benny, Armstrong and Rena had mostly gone separate ways since leaving the Waif's Home because, as Armstrong explained, "Rena, who was a Creole, went downtown, and since I was not a Creole, I went uptown."[1] Rena's proficiency in the upper register had only improved since their early days playing for Peter Davis. "When it comes to high notes I don't believe anyone could beat Kid Rena," trumpeter Herb Morand said. "He could blow higher than Louis at one time."[2] To clarinetist Albert Nicholas, Rena "was a creator. Kid Rena is the first one making high notes. Louis started making high notes *after* Kid Rena. He was inspired by Rena."[3] For his part, Armstrong said in 1950, "Like myself, Rena had a very high range on his horn, and today these youngsters think they're making high notes, but I tell them, they'll never hit the high notes that Kid Rena and I used to, when we were in our teens."[4]

Now, the two friends were turned rivals and often met on opposing advertising wagons. "Kid Rena and I used to have some awful battles!" Armstrong remembered. "When I was young, I always had my tone and a good sense of phrasing, so that alone would protect me in all of my battles, and I seldom lost."[5] Others, however, felt the battles between Armstrong and Rena were split decisions. "When he was at his best, he'd give Louie—when Louie was at his best—all Louie wanted," Preston Jackson said of Rena.[6] Drummer Christopher "Black Happy" Goldston stated, "To tell you about the facts, Rena was a better cornet player than Louis Armstrong."[7] Cornetist Tony Fougerat agreed, saying Rena "could play as much trumpet as Louie played. In fact, he played prettier than Louie played."[8] Paul Barnes praised Rena but added, "The onliest one that could outblow Rena or anybody else, that was Louis Armstrong."[9]

Preston Jackson called Armstrong and Rena "keen rivals" and recalled a time when Armstrong performed some subterfuge to protect one of his friends and overcome Rena at the same time:

> One day, Lee Collins was with a band advertising a picnic. Louis was with him, not playing but just riding around. Lee saw Rena coming from the opposite direction in a wagon. Lee was afraid because Henry Rena could outplay him. Louis hid in the bottom of the wagon, so that Henry did not see him. Rena tied his wagon to Lee's so that he couldn't get away. Then Louis Armstrong jumped up and grabbed Lee's horn. The battle was on and they played until dark. Louis made Rena give up.[10]

Armstrong could emerge victorious in such one-on-one battles, but he still knew his limitations as a musician. Drummer Bill Matthews remembered a time the Excelsior Brass Band had Arnold Metoyer and "Old Man" George Moret on trumpet but they needed a third man to play a parade. "Why don't you try Dippermouth?" Matthews asked. "Oh man, he can't read," came the response. Matthews paid them no mind and asked Armstrong if he wanted to play the parade. "Oh man, you know I can't make that, I can't make no brass band, not with the Excelsior Band," he responded. Matthews argued that it would give him great experience "to learn how to play that music." Armstrong finally agreed, but on the day of the parade, a thirsty Armstrong bought a bottle of Jumbo soda for a nickel and drank it down too fast. "We had to lay Louis out," Matthews said. "Louis got overheated and had the cramps from that Jumbo bottle! He stayed right there. So we went and played on through without Louis."[11]

But Armstrong would eventually get another chance to prove himself in a brass band setting, when Joe Oliver suggested him to replace an ailing Oscar "Papa" Celestin in the Tuxedo Brass Band.

"I didn't know Louis," trombonist William "Bebe" Ridgley, the band's coleader, recalled, but he "was just glad to have any cornet player." The older men in the band were standing around drinking beer before the parade began when they saw a peculiar sight.

"We were all on the job waiting for Louis and I saw a boy coming, had on a police cap looked like it was too large for him, a little old blue coat and he had a little bag under his arm with his cornet in it," Ridgely said.

"Mm, what am I going to do?" Ridgley thought to himself. He met Armstrong and began asking him if he knew the different tunes the band played.

"Yeah, I can play it, I can play it," Armstrong responded confidently each time Ridgely named a song.

Once the band started playing, Ridgely was shocked that "Louis could play them all better than we could!" Armstrong soon became a regular sub for Celestin with the Tuxedo Band and impressed everybody with his playing. But Ridgley also called him "a devilish boy. When he was small, he was the devil. . . . [H]e came from that rough part of town with all them bad, devilish boys, and they used to just follow him up, get right by him. They'd walk along and they'd call him everything they could think of, I'm telling you."

"Cause you're playing with the Tuxedo Band, you think you're somebody!" Armstrong's friends would taunt. Armstrong would "break off and run them down the street about half a block," Ridgley said. "Just funny! He's just funny like that. Good kid."[12]

Oliver most likely couldn't make that parade because he was so busy playing with Ory. Of this period, Ory said he was playing "five nights a week in one of the yacht clubs, hotel work, parties up and down St. Charles and funerals. I had my own dance hall."[13]

But everything came to a crashing halt on June 19, 1918.

Ory and Oliver were packing them in at the Winter Garden on South Rampart and Gravier, taking crowds away from the nearby Pythian Roof Garden at Gravier and Saratoga. "The owner of the Roof Garden was very unhappy about this and did the usual thing," Ory recalled. "He called the cops." Around 11 o'clock in the evening, a group of police officers raided the Winter Garden and rounded everyone up for disturbing the peace—including the band. "So we all went to jail and then through night court and everyone who had it or could get it paid $2.50 bail," Ory wrote. Arrest records survive for Ory, Johnny Dodds, and Oliver.[14]

For Oliver, the inhumanity of being thrown in jail while trying to earn a living playing music was too much to overcome. "Joe thought it was terrible," his wife, Stella, said about the raid. "He said a man working for, making an honest living, they could raid him and take him to jail, and that's why he left New Orleans."[15]

"The Great Migration" of African Americans from the South to northern cities such as Chicago had been happening for years, turning the "Windy City" into a haven for New Orleans musicians looking to escape the South. In 1917, the year the red-light district closed, more New Orleans musicians migrated from New Orleans than in any previous year: Wellman Braud, Sidney Bechet, Johnny Dodds, Lawrence Duhe, Fred "Tubby" Hall, Minor "Ram" Hall, "Sugar" Johnny Smith, Preston Jackson, Herb Lindsay, Clarence Williams, Jimmie Noone, and others all headed to Chicago in that year alone.

Some of those musicians, such as Noone and Dodds, returned in 1918 and probably talked up the city's burgeoning jazz scene. Ory was offered work in Chicago but wasn't interested. "I was making between $300·and $400 a night off my dances, and working all the rest of those stands," he said, "so I said why go out of business and go work for somebody for nothing, go to Chicago?"[16]

But Oliver, just when he wanted to get away from New Orleans, received not one but two opportunities. The first offer came from bassist Bill Johnson of the Original Creole Band, then in the process of putting together a band to play the opening of the Royal Gardens, located at 31st Street and Cottage Grove Avenue in Chicago. Johnson had already hired Paul Barbarin, a young drummer who had just arrived from New Orleans, where, Barbarin later said, "There was nothing happening. . . . The music had got to a standstill."[17] Johnson attempted to lure Buddy Petit to Chicago to take the cornet chair, but Petit refused to leave home. Barbarin then told Johnson about how much Oliver had improved since Johnson had left town in 1914 and Johnson offered him the job.

Coincidentally, Ory's old cornetist Mutt Carey also reached out to Oliver around this time to see if he could fill in for two weeks in clarinetist Lawrence Duhe's group at the Deluxe Café in Chicago, which featured all New Orleans musicians except for a pianist from Memphis named Lillian Hardin. With multiple opportunities waiting for him, Oliver's decision to go up north was an easy one to make. He would live another 20 years and would never set foot in New Orleans again.

Oliver's impact upon Chicago was immediate. "The first night we played a blues that Oliver and Ory used to play down here [in New Orleans]," Barbarin said. The song was "I'm Not Rough" and it was a feature for Oliver's muted style. "People never heard nobody with a mute, I mean, make a mute cry or anything like that," Barbarin said. "Joe's playing the blues and we started playing soft that night, see. And Joe started talking on the horn, see, he took the little mute and he's working his hand and . . . man, the people start screaming, man, and throwing their hats in the air. A lot of women was just taking off their hats and going wild, man." After the number, the Royal Gardens emcee,"King" Jones, "came up and crowned 'King' Joe Oliver, 'King' Oliver," Barbarin recalled. "That's how he got his name. The very first night! Man, that man was a sensation."[18]

Oliver was clearly going to thrive in Chicago, but he had left Ory without a cornetist and broken up one of the great early partnerships in jazz. Oliver didn't want to leave Ory in the lurch so addressed the situation before boarding the train to Chicago.

"Joe told me before he left that he could recommend someone to take his place," Ory remembered. "I told him I appreciated his thought but that I had already picked out his replacement."[19]

Louis Armstrong was also at the train station that day to see Oliver off. He called it "a sad parting" but also summed it up as "that's Show Business for you." He had no time to sulk because he had to go to work. "The minute the train pulled out, I was on my way out of the Illinois Central Station to get back up on my cart, and continue to deliver my load of coal, when Kid Ory called to me," Armstrong recalled.

Ory told Armstrong he "had heard a lot of talk about Little Louis" and that the boys in the band "told him to go get Little Louis to take Joe's place," Armstrong recalled.[20] "I went to see him and told him that if he got himself a pair of long trousers I'd give him a job," Ory said.[21]

Louis was ecstatic and immediately ran home to share the news with his mother. "I had been having so many bad breaks, until I just had to make a bee line to Maryann," he wrote. "She was the one who had always encouraged me to carry on with my cornet playing, since I loved it so well." "Within two hours, Louis came to my house and said, 'Here I am. I'll be glad when 8 o'clock comes. I'm ready to go,'" Ory said. Looking back, Ory reflected, "There were many good, experienced trumpet players in town, but none of them had young Louis' possibilities."[22]

Armstrong's whole life had seemingly been building up to this moment. Shooting off the gun on New Year's Eve, learning the cornet in the Waif's Home, playing for Ory at the Labor Day parade, the encouragement of the Karnofskys, the lessons and mentoring of Oliver, the protection of Black Benny and Slippers, the countless hours of playing honky-tonks such as Pons's and Matranga's with the countless bullets sizzling past him, the excitement of the Brown Skin Jazz Band, the battles with Kid Rena, all of it had led him here.

He was ready.

"The first night I played with Kid Ory's band, they were so surprised, they could hardly play their instruments for listening to me blow up a storm," Armstrong said. "And, I was not frightened one bit. Because I lived Joe Oliver from the word say go... And tried to do everything he did anyway." This didn't only apply to Oliver's musical offerings. Armstrong had become accustomed to seeing Oliver drape a large bath towel around his neck, opening up his shirt collar before he'd blow. "So, from the first night on, [I] did the same thing," Armstrong said.[23] Ory was not impressed by the beat-up cornet Armstrong was playing, even if it was one of Oliver's old ones; he bought his new man a new instrument.

However, it is quite possible that this entire early experience with Ory's band was nothing more than a false start. New Orleans police had arrested hundreds of prostitutes in the preceding months, part of the continued battle to limit access to vice during the war. Now they were coming for the music.

"With the stroke of twelve Saturday night in every cabaret within the city limits the snare drum rolled forth its last note," the *Times-Picayune* reported on July 7. "The sliding trombone gave vent to its last moan. The pianist touched the last key, and the voice of the singer was silenced—for the lid had descended on cabarets and for the duration of the war it will remain clamped down."[24] The effect this had on Ory's band is not known; they were likely able to continue playing country clubs and private dances unaffected, but the lack of steady work would lead them to temporarily disband for stretches at a time until the end of the war which was still raging overseas. The original June 1917 draft targeted men between the ages of 21 and 30 but on September 12, 1918, the government expanded the range of ages to include men between the ages of 18 and 45. Joe Oliver now had to register, giving a Chicago address for the first time, along with an 1881 birth year so as to appear four years older.

Back in New Orleans, Armstrong chose to register on that date, too. But did he have to? The card represents the first time he ever gave his birthday as July 4, 1900, in effect telling the government he had just turned 18 and was ready to be drafted. If he had stuck with a 1901 birthday, he could have avoided any chance of going to war altogether. But even if he felt it was his duty to report for the draft, all he had to do was identify as a coal cart driver, which would have been considered an essential occupation and exempted him from service. Thus, he had not one, but *two* ways to avoid going to war.

Instead, Armstrong listed his occupation as "Musician." It might have been important to him to have an official piece of paper that stated he was an 18-year-old musician instead of just a coal car driver—but what if this decision actually got him drafted? For years, this decision has baffled many historians; why would such a seemingly passive figure as Armstrong suddenly want to potentially put himself in harm's way defending his country? But Armstrong himself admitted that that was what he wanted to do. He wrote that he "tried to slip into the Navy" during the 1917 draft but was only stymied when they checked his birth certificate, an elusive document that must have existed at one time (and yes, could have displayed a July 4, 1900, birthday).[25] When the 1918 draft rolled around, Armstrong wrote, "I went on down to the draft board and registerd [*sic*]... I sure was a proud fellow when I could feel back there in my hip pocket and feel my draft card, expecting to go to war any minute, and fight for Uncle Sam." But then he added an important afterthought: "Or. Blow for him."[26]

REGISTRATION CARD

SERIAL NUMBER 928 ORDER NUMBER 4177

1 Lewis Armstrong.
(First name) (Middle name) (Last name)

2 PERMANENT HOME ADDRESS:
1233 Perdido st. N. O. La
(No.) (Street or R. F. D. No.) (City or town) (County) (State)

Age in Years 3 18 Date of Birth 4 July 4th. 1900
(Month.) (Day.) (Year.)

RACE

White	Negro	Oriental	Indian	
			Citizen	Noncitizen
5	6 ✓	7	8	9

U. S. CITIZEN / ALIEN

Native Born	Naturalized	Citizen by Father's Naturalization Before Registrant's Majority	Declarant	Non-declarant
10 ✓	11	12	13	14

15 If not a citizen of the U. S., of what nation are you a citizen or subject?

PRESENT OCCUPATION 16 Musician EMPLOYER'S NAME 17 Peter Lala.

18 PLACE OF EMPLOYMENT OR BUSINESS:
150 Cont st. N. O. La.
(No.) (Street or R. F. D. No.) (City or town) (County) (State)

NEAREST RELATIVE Name 19 Mary. Armstrong mother
Address 20 1233 Perdido st N. O. La
(No.) (Street or R. F. D. No.) (City or town) (County) (State)

I AFFIRM THAT I HAVE VERIFIED ABOVE ANSWERS AND THAT THEY ARE TRUE

P. M. G. O.
Form No. 1 (Red) 6—6171 (Registrant's signature or mark) (OVER)

Louis Armstrong.

Figure 12.1 Louis Armstrong's World War I draft registration card, filled out September 12, 1918.

Credit: From the Records of the Selective Service System (World War I), Record Group 163. National Archives at Atlanta.

That seems to be the key. When one considers Armstrong's life up to this point, the only time he had structure was at the Colored Waif's Home. Since being released in 1914, it was four years of working on coal carts, digging through garbage cans, pimping, playing honky-tonks, doing whatever he could to survive. It's quite possible—even probable—that the thought of joining the service enticed Armstrong as a possible way to regain some structure in his life. And by insisting he was a musician, instead of a coal cart driver, perhaps that was the ultimate dream: to play in a military band.[27]

The rest of Armstrong's draft card doubles and even triples down on the role music played in his life. For "Employer's Name," he listed Peter Lala (he most likely never knew Lala's real last name was "Ciaccio"). For "Place of Employment," he gave 1500 Conti Street, a confusing mashup of Lala's cabaret at 1500 Iberville Street and his theater at Conti and North Claiborne Streets. And for his and Mayann's address, he listed 1233 Perdido Street—Henry Matranga's saloon. Mayann had begun working for Matranga's family at his private home at 425 South Saratoga Street, so it's possible the Armstrongs moved into an apartment above the honky-tonk around this time in exchange for Mayann's services. Mayann's impact can also be felt in another way on the draft card, which spells Armstrong's name as "Lewis," indicative of the way he pronounced it. "My mother always called me Louis," he said in 1947, "not Louie."[28]

Ironically, there wasn't any music being made at Matranga's when Armstrong registered for the draft. When the *Times-Picayune* published a list of 24 cabarets that were shut down in July 1918, the very last one at the bottom of the page simply read "Saloon, 1233 Perdido"— Matranga's. Armstrong even noted that on the same day he went down to the draft board in September he "dropped into Henry Matrangas one night for a drink...A bottle of beer...the tonk wasn't running, just the saloon."[29] The honky-tonk days were over and even Kid Ory had to take a day job. "With the war still going in full blast, the orders were, still work or fight," Armstrong wrote. "And, since I was too young to fight, I kept on working."[30]

Looking back at this time in his life in 1965, Armstrong reflected, "I don't see why I got any strength left at all. But at that time I was enjoying it, being around the cats I wanted to be with, and as a kid I didn't know no better. I had to help Mama and sister. My stepfathers—you know stepfathers—they just going to do so much. Had to eat."[31]

Driving a coal cart for C. A. Andrews Coal Company was still his number one job, but it was far from the only one he held down in this time. "When I wasn't down at the coal yard, I was unloading banana boats," he recalled.[32] This job must have also come about through Armstrong's connection with Henry Matranga, as the "Matranga Brothers, stevedores at the Thalia street wharf of the United Fruit Company," oversaw a banana boat operation.[33] One day a "great big rat (from the old country)" ran out of a bunch

Armstrong was carrying; he quit right then and there. "From that day on, I never cared for bananas," he said. "I wouldn't eat one right this day, if I was starving."[34]

For a time in 1918, Armstrong helped his friend "Sweet Child" by "Hopping Bells at the saloon on my corner in the third ward." "Sweet Child" was the alias of Robert Cook, who was arrested six times between 1912 and 1920, giving a different age each time, but his World War I draft registration card gave a birthday of December 25, 1896. Though the words "bellboy" and "bellhop" now have hotel connotations, Armstrong explained that in those days, it referred to a young man who would deliver beer to the "hustling gals." "Bellboy!" they would shout. "Bring half a can! Bring a whole can!"[35] Armstrong enjoyed the job, "Because you could have a chance to go into the houses and see what everybody's doing"—"everybody" meaning the prostitutes. "Finally Sweet Child came back for his job," he wrote. "Dornit... He never did lay off again... Dornit....."[36]

Armstrong also worked for a time delivering milk for the Cloverland Dairy Co., which boasted "The Only Pasteurizing Plant in Louisiana" according to a 1907 ad.[37] Armstrong couldn't remember the name of the driver of the milk wagon, describing him only as a "very fine white boy" and "a very kind boss." It's quite possible the driver was David W. Carraway, who listed his occupation as a driver for the Cloverland Dairy in 1918. Mama Lucy remembered that Mayann once worked for a lady named "Miss Carraway"; if the Carraways were related, then there's a good chance Mayann's connection helped her son get this job.[38]

"Early in the morning I used to hop off the wagon and bring the milk to the back doors," Armstrong reminisced.[39] But one morning, still working barefoot, while attempting to hop back on, he missed his jump and the wagon wheel ran over his right foot. His big toe was torn wide open and he had to be rushed to Charity Hospital. After fixing up his toe—"You can imagine the agony I was in," he wrote—he was asked if he was going to sue Cloverland. "No sir," he said, "I think too much of my boss for that." He also realized that if he did sue, the lawyers would "take the best portion of it...You know?—the south...."

When he did get his paycheck from Cloverland on Friday mornings, he would go around the corner to Scandaliato's Saloon at 502 South Telemachus Street and shoot dice with the other helpers. "I sure was a very lucky boy, in that crap game," he recalled. "Yes I was....I used to come home with all of my pockets just loaded with all kinds of dough." He took the money and went to Canal Street to buy "real sharp outfits" for his mother, sister, and little Clarence, as well as "a pair of tailor made (short pants) for myself." However, he ran out of money before he could buy a new pair of shoes, shrugging it off by telling himself he was used to living barefoot anyway.[40]

Armstrong put himself in harm's way when he started working a short while "for a house wrecking company." "And another thing, the way some of those buildings would fall toward us, so they were going to crush me to death," he wrote. "I would think to myself, how in the world am I going to play my cornet, looking up under these monstrous looking buildings all around me looking just like mountains."[41] He would be hired as needed, then let go again when the dangerous work was complete—he didn't mind the layoffs.

Armstrong teamed up with his old Waif's Home buddy Isaac "Ikey" Smoot to help Smoot's father, Frank Smoot, a painter, whitewash a building in the "front of town" section of the city.[42] Once again, this job didn't last very long—Armstrong's services were again no longer needed once the building was finished. And once again, he was most likely relieved to be let go because he didn't like meeting Smoot's family at their home near the Irish Channel district. "I dreaded going up there to the old man's house, for fear I'd run into some of those bad Irishmen coming out of a saloon, or something," he wrote. "And, don't think for once that they won't bother you, because you're mistaking [*sic*] if you do."[43] In later years, Armstrong liked to tell a story to friends about waiting for a streetcar in the Irish Channel when he saw "one of them big fine Irish cops."

"How do, officer?" Armstrong asked. "Will you tell me what time it is please?"

"And that son-of-a-bitch took out a big black stick and hit me across the head. Wham! He said, 'Just about one!' "

"I said, 'Thank you, officer—I'm glad I wasn't here around 12 o'clock!' Jesus Christ!"[44]

Armstrong had a much more enjoyable time during his two weeks as a dishwasher at J. P. Thompson's "modern restaurant" on St. Charles Street.[45] "What [knocked] me out with this job, I could eat all the cream puffs, doughnuts etc, that my little heart wanted... And any time I wanted, I could dig down in the Ice Cream Freezer and get a large scoop, and fill up one of those soup bowls and even get an encore if I wanted to," Armstrong said. "Oh, for the two weeks I work there I would'nt eat anything at home." But after those two weeks, the thought of such food began to "nauseate" him, so he quit.[46]

As the war raged on, the government turned to New Orleans for help. "The United States Government is erecting its great Army Supply Depot at Poland and Dauphine Streets and between 5,000 and 6,000 men are already employed on this tremendous undertaking," the *Times-Picayune* reported.[47] The contractor for this project was George A. Fuller, who began running ads in the newspapers in August 1918. One such ad from August 28 read:

> WANTED
> AT ONCE
> 12 CARPENTERS
> 54 CENTERS PER HOUR
> 400 Negro Laborers
> Day and Night Shifts
> 30 CENTERS PER HOUR
> Time and Half After 8 Hours
> GEO. A. FULLER CO.
> New Orleans Army Supply Depot
> Poland Ave. and Dauphine St.[48]

Armstrong heeded the call. "I was rather proud of that big yellow button I were for my identification, to enter the gate, to go to work, and on coming out of the yard."[49]

Armstrong also wasn't the only musician working at the Supply Depot. "You can imagine how rough things were, when, even Kid Ory was down there at the same time as me," he wrote. "He was a carpenter...That's his trade anyway...And a good one at that." This would seem to lend credence to the Ory band being on hiatus in the fall of 1918, after the city closed down the cabarets in July.

Armstrong also had a reunion with his old drummer from the Brown Skin Jazz Band, Joe Lindsey, whom he hadn't seen since Lindsey had quit the band. On September 1, the *Times-Picayune* reported New Orleans was being considered for "planning the construction of a fleet of steel boats and barges."[50] Once in effect, Armstrong and Lindsey went to work on that project, too, even attempting to recruit cornetist Lee Collins to work with them, but without success. "Oh, man, it was rolling cement up on where they were buildin' ships," Collins said, adding, "Shucks, I didn't care if it paid $50 a day, I didn't want no part of it."[51]

Armstrong did manage to play an occasional musical engagement in this period. On October 8, he performed at an "Old-Fashioned Liberty Loan Rally" and "Patriotic Gala Mass Meeting" at White Brothers' jewelry shop at 624 Canal Street. The *Times-Picayune* promised "That Original New Orleans Jazz Band Will Entertain." Photographer Charles L. Franck snapped a photo of the outdoors event, which ended up in the National Archives and eventually turned over to Wikimedia. During the Covid-19 pandemic, New Orleans jazz historian and disc jockey Dan Meyer discovered the photo online, zoomed in, and was shocked to find the slightly obscured face of young Louis Armstrong on the bandstand, wearing a hat, white shirt, and an apprehensive look on his face.[52]

He might have worn that expression because the October 8 event was held during the time the "Spanish Flu" hit New Orleans in the fall, killing 3,362 people in the city between September 8, 1918, and March 15, 1919. Schools closed, church services were suspended, motion picture houses and theaters went dark. After 4,000 cases were reported on October 14, the *Times-Picayune* reported, "The question of closing every saloon in Louisiana and many of the soft drink places, to further prevent the spread of influenza, is under consideration."[53] It was decided not to close all restaurants and saloons, but the paper reported, "In many of the restaurants, soft drink places, and in one case, at least, the attendants in a tobacco establishment were wearing influenza masks Wednesday."[54] Still, Dr. Oscar W. Dowling, president of the State Board of Health, remained frustrated. "There is one way and one only of stamping out the epidemic; that is for the people to stay at home," he said. "If they would stay away from each other for three days the disease would practically be stifled. People will not realize the seriousness of the situation, despite our efforts, and it seems that publicity is the only thing that arouses them."[55]

Armstrong had vivid memories of the 1918 influenza epidemic. "And then [too], there was a very serious sickness spreading around in New Orleans call the Flu," he wrote.

> Everybody was down with it...Everybody except me... That's because I was always physic minded, and kept my self open at all times... I never in my life, missed a week without taking, some kind of physic...And that alone, kept all kinds of sickness out of me.....Anyway, just when the Government was about to let the crowds congregate again, which would have given us a chance to play our horns again, they clamped down, tighter than ever before... That made me go back to working, from one job, to another.... With everybody around me suffering with the Flu, I had to work and also play the part of a doctor to everyone in my family and friends of my neighborhood... Which, if I have to say it myself, I did a good job in curing them.....[56]

Though the epidemic hit its peak in October 1918, the number of cases ebbed and flowed into March 1919; Kid Ory's sister Lizzie died from the flu on January 1, 1919. It's almost miraculous that Armstrong didn't contract it—how would the sound of the twentieth century have changed if he had?

Whenever one of Armstrong's various jobs ended in 1918, he'd go to C. A. Andrews's coal yard and his mule, Lady. "That's when I wrote the song Coal

Cart Blues," he noted of this period.[57] Writing songs during his backbreaking day jobs was further proof that music was never far from his mind. "I wasn't making no great sums so I kept on delivering coal, unloading banana boats, selling newspapers—though there never was any doubts I would follow music at that point," he reflected in 1967.[58]

It's hard to believe Armstrong didn't have any doubts in October 1918, when the flu epidemic was raging and his musical boss, Kid Ory, was still working as a carpenter at the Army Supply Depot. But then came November 11, 1918: Armistice Day.

Armstrong was unloading a load of coal—"sweating like mad"—at Fabacher's Restaurant on St. Charles Street when someone told him the news. "When he said that to me, it seemed as though a bolt of lightning strucked me all over," Armstrong said. "I must have put about three more shovels of coal into the wheelbarrow, to take inside, when all of a sudden a thought came to me... The war is over, I am here monkeying around with this mule... Huh... I immediately dropped that shovel, slowily [*sic*] put on my jacket, I looked at the Lady and said—so long my dear, I don't think I'll ever see you again... And cutout, leaving mule cart, load of coal, an' everything that was connected with it... I haven't seen them since."[59]

13

"Nothing but Fuck and Fight"

1918–1919

Upon hearing about the armistice, Louis made a beeline for home to tell Mayann the news.

"The war is over and I quit the coal yard job for the last time," he told his mother. "Now I can play my music, the way I want to and when I want to."

Louis remembered "the lights went on again" in New Orleans "the very next day," but the city didn't lift the ban on music in the cabarets until December 7. "Matranga called me to come back to play in his honky tonk but he was too late," Armstrong said. "I was looking forward to bigger things...Especially since Kid Ory had given me such a chance to really play the music I wanted to play, and that was, all kinds of music, from jazz to waltzes."[1] Once again, this was Armstrong stating his credo; he would always be devoted to jazz but he was more determined to master "all kinds of music."

With the cabaret ban, the "Work or Fight" period, and the Spanish Flu behind them, Armstrong and Ory would spend the next six months performing together regularly, often with clarinetist Johnny Dodds joining them in the front line. "After he joined me, Louis improved so fast it was amazing," Ory said. "He had a wonderful ear and a wonderful memory. All you had to do was to hum or whistle a new tune to him and he'd know it right away. And if he played a tune once, he never forgot it. Within six months everybody in New Orleans knew about him."[2]

"Now, I began to get real popular with the dance fans as well as the musicians," Armstrong corroborated. "All the musicians came and hired me to play in their band, the nights I wasn't engaged by Kid Ory."[3] One night Armstrong got the call to fill in with the Silver Leaf Band, a group that "read a lot of music." Armstrong wasn't a great reader, but wasn't worried: "I had an ear that was like a living ass [i.e., great]....They didn't worry about whenever I had to play with them."

The Silver Leaf Band featured the intimidating Sam Dutrey (born in 1888), on clarinet, whom Armstrong admired—until Dutrey greeted the young cornetist with an angry "What are you doing up here, boy!? Get out of here!"

"Yes sir!" Armstrong responded, quickly packing up his horn. The rest of the band laughed and Dutrey let on that he was only joking. "But shit, I didn't feel good all night long," Armstrong recalled in 1953. "He tried to make up to me, man and I'd see it, but I was scared of him. I always did have a little scare of Sam—even right now!"[4]

Some establishments were less than optimal, such as the Brick House, which Armstrong once called "the toughest joint I played in."[5] Located in Gretna, about six miles outside New Orleans, the Brick House was a redux of Henry Matranga's, finding Armstrong playing the blues all night long with a trio for an audience of "whores, pimps and gamblers."[6] It was there where Armstrong met a woman he called "the biggest whore in Gretna."[7] Her name was Daisy Parker and she would soon become Mrs. Louis Armstrong.

Without a birth certificate, pinning down a date for birth for Daisy Parker is difficult. Louis claimed she was 21 when they met in 1919 and always said she was older than him, but when she died in 1950, her age was reported to be 45. She must have shaved a few years off by that point; when arrested in 1922 and 1919, she told the police she was born in 1897 and 1899, respectively. Her social security application, filled out in July 1940, might be the most accurate of all, listing her birthday as July 11, 1896.

Whenever she was born, Louis filled in some of the details of her upbringing, saying she was "spoiled" by her parents, who didn't care if she played hooky from school. "Later I found out, she could not read or write," he said.[8] Daisy turned to a life of crime and eventually prostitution. "Mathilda Harangue, Daisy Parker and Olivia Smith, negroes, are being held in the parish jail at Gretna without bond on a charge of grand larceny," the *Times-Picayune* reported on April 5, 1916. "They are accused of taking $125 from Peter Ramon, an engineer on an oil ship lying at Gretna."[9]

At the Brick House, Armstrong wrote, "For about three Saturday nights straight, I kept noticing one of the gals looking at me with the stuff in her eyes while I played. And started to giving her that righteous look in return." They flirted and agreed to get down to business after work. "She stated her price which wasn't much in those days," Armstrong said.[10] Once upstairs, Daisy undressed and revealed that she was wearing "sides," as Louis called them, to enhance her shape. "I didn't know what to do then but my dick stayed hard, so I just didn't worry about the sides—and tried to get what was inside!" Armstrong laughed as he made his pun, but then revealed a serious truth: "Once I got in there, it cost me four years."[11]

All Louis and Daisy had in the beginning was sex, the two going upstairs every time Louis played the Brick House, making love from 5 in the morning until the afternoon. "We had several sessions after that, and Daisy and I commenced to falling deeply in love with each other," Louis wrote. "So we cut the payin proposition out."[12] Daisy soon invited Louis to visit her at her home in nearby Freetown—without ever telling him she was not only dating another man but living with him! "Well, shit, man," Armstrong said of the time he made this discovery. "We're there kissing and everything and here comes some nigger open the door and walk in the back. And when she went back there, I heard [*imitates a gunshot*] 'YOOM!' I hauled ass, man! I hauled ass for that ferry!"[13]

As Armstrong made a break for it, he could hear Daisy's boyfriend punch her in the jaw. He was not about to fight for her; it was the situation with Cheeky Black and Irene all over again and once more, he was lucky to make it out alive. Armstrong would put the Brick House—and Daisy—behind him soon enough. "And since Kid Ory had signed [a] Contract to play at New Orleans (rich folks) Country Club, every Saturday night, I put the Brick House down, quicker than I put that mule (Lady) down the day the War ended," he wrote.[14]

Daisy eventually showed up in Louis's Liberty and Perdido neighborhood to confess her love to him—and to also show off her skills with a razor. "She come over here in my neighborhood and she never been over here before," Louis said. "And she's got that razor, you know, and I'm hauling ass, Lord. And she say, 'Wait a minute, I'm lost!' I said, 'Well, shit.' She said, 'Look, I'll throw it away.' She throw the razor out in the street and we went on back home."[15]

Daisy would soon move to New Orleans, living with friends Emma and Henry Vance in a tiny flat at 754 Dryades Street, across from the St. Louis Cemetery. It was while living there that she got arrested at 12:10 in the morning on Sunday, January 26, 1919, for "fighting and disturbing the peace." Louis wasn't mentioned, but Daisy was arrested at 419 North Claiborne Street, a few feet away from Pete Lala's theater at 425 North Claiborne. It doesn't take much imagination to assume Daisy saw another woman flirting with Louis—or Louis flirting back—and created a ruckus.

If Louis needed another sign that getting mixed up with Daisy could potentially be hazardous to his health, it came in the form of a violent knife fight that took place between two prostitutes in March 1919. "Annie Sweezer, a negro, 450 South Franklin street, was taken to the Charity Hospital, late Wednesday night suffering from four stab wounds in the back, inflicted, the police say, by Alberta Frowner, 441 South Franklin street," the *Times-Picayune* reported. "The two women, with Myrtle Hamilton, the police say, were engaged in a free-for-all fight, when the Frowner woman drew a knife, using it on Annie Sweezer."[16] This was business as usual on the 400 block of South Franklin Street, a notorious spot inhabited by many prostitutes in Armstrong's neighborhood. (Mayann was arrested at 420 South Franklin in 1915.) The blood of two knife-wielding prostitutes was probably still fresh on the street when Louis made the decision to marry razor-toting prostitute Daisy just days later on March 24, 1919. On the marriage license Daisy gave her age as 20 while Louis gave his as 21, so as to appear to be an adult even though he was only 17.

Back in his neighborhood, word of Louis's marriage spread fast. All the old "gossipers" ran to Mayann, asking her, "Are you going to let that boy marry that whore?"

"Well, that's my son and he has to live his own life," Mayann replied with a shrug. "And he love the women enough to marry her, that's his business, and they both have my blessings. And I will also try my best to make her as happy as I can."

When she finally confronted her son, Louis insisted, "I've never been surer of anything in my whole life as my love for Daisy. She has convinced me that she's the woman for me."

"Well, I hear she hasn't much of a learning," Mayann said, hinting at Daisy's lack of education.

"Well, mother, what's that got to do with our being in love with each other?" Louis pleaded. "You must realize that I didn't go any further than fifth grade in school myself. But with my good common sense and mother wit and knowing how to treat and respect the feelings of other people, that's all I've needed through life. You taught me that, mother. And I haven't done so bad at it. Ain't that right?"

"I guess you're right, son," Mayann said, shrugging again.[17]

In the end, Mayann proved to be right. Looking back 35 years later, Louis vented about Daisy, "She didn't read nothing. She couldn't read! Nothing but fuck and fight, that's all she did—and she did a whole lots of that!"[18]

Now married, Louis and Daisy moved in together in "a two room flat, over an upholstering place," in Louis's words, at 2009 Melpomene Street, scene of one of the most harrowing moments of Armstrong's early life.[19] Louis and Daisy were watching Louis's three-year-old cousin Clarence Hatfield, who spent much of his time playing with toys in their back room. Eventually, Clarence made his way onto the rain-soaked back porch without being noticed. Louis and Daisy soon heard Clarence crying and ran outside to see what was wrong.

"I was real frightened when I looked on the porch and I did not see Clarence," Louis said. "But I could hear him Crying (real loud) then I looked down to the ground, and there was Clarence (a little fellow) coming up the steps crying and holding his head... He had slipped off the porch, by it being

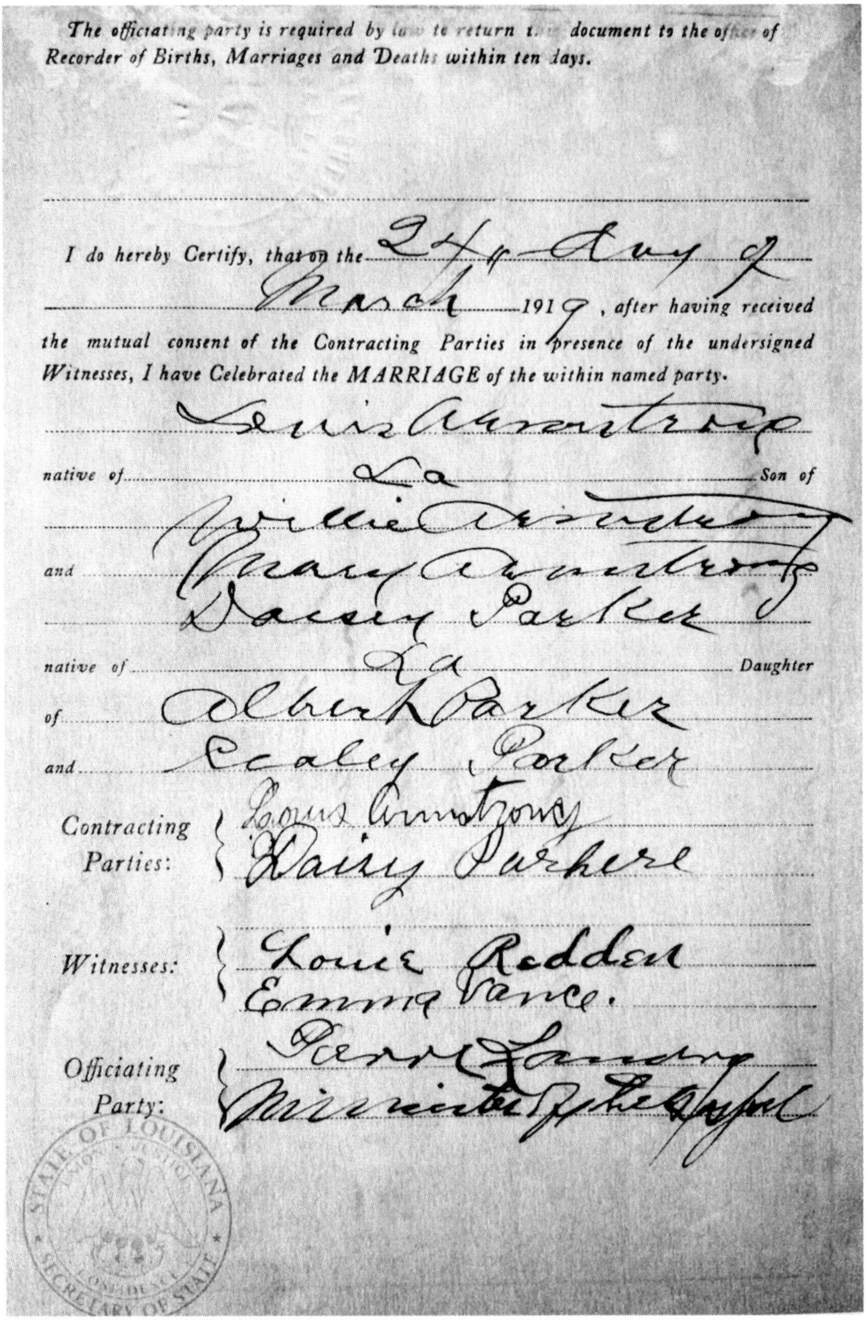

The officiating party is required by law to return this document to the office of Recorder of Births, Marriages and Deaths within ten days.

I do hereby Certify, that on the 24th Day of March 1919, *after having received the mutual consent of the Contracting Parties in presence of the undersigned Witnesses, I have Celebrated the MARRIAGE of the within named party.*

Louis Armstrong

native of La *Son of*

Willie Armstrong

and Mary Armstrong

Daisy Parker

native of La *Daughter*

of Albert Parker

and Cealey Parker

Contracting Parties: Louis Armstrong
Daisy Parker

Witnesses: Louie Redden
Emma Vance.

Officiating Party: P. Henry Lanauze
Minister of the Gospel

STATE OF LOUISIANA · UNION · JUSTICE · CONFIDENCE · SECRETARY OF STATE

Figure 13.1 Louis Armstrong and Daisy Parker's marriage license from March 24, 1919. The license lists Louis's parents as Willie and Mary Armstrong and Daisy's as Albert and Cealey Parker. Witnesses were Louie Redden and Emma Vance and the officiating party was P. Henry Lanauze.

Credit: Louisiana State Archives.

so wet, he lost his balance and fell to the ground." The fall left Clarence developmentally disabled for the rest of his life. "I had some of the best Doctors anyone could get to examine Clarence and they all agreed that the fall he had caused him to the feeble minded," Louis said. "That's what they all said that's why Clarence's mind [was] four years behind the average normal child."[20]

However, two years after Louis passed away, Mama Lucy told a very different story about what happened to Clarence. "This poor thing," she said of him. "See, when he was a baby, see like the platform when you're going down a step, and the guy was sitting up on that platform, a man, a drunk. He tied a rope around Clarence and the other end on a dog. The dog pulled him all the way down the steps. He got nervous, and he's been nervous ever since.... He ain't been right since that man tied that rope around that child's neck and that dog pulled him down the steps."[21] Could this have been the actual incident that caused Clarence's disability? Or was he unlucky enough to suffer two separate, traumatic injuries in his youth? Though the "rainy porch" story casts Louis in a negative light, not paying attention to his three-year-old cousin, he still thought it was more palatable for his public—and for Clarence himself—than to recount Mama Lucy's far more disturbing story.

In the aftermath, Louis began thinking of Clarence as more of a son than a cousin, and never let his disability get in the way of his unconditional love for him. "As Clarence grew up, that same fall kind of hindered him through life," Louis declared. "But he's my Son, so what happened to him, I was still with him."[22]

Outside his chaotic home life, Armstrong enjoyed plenty of opportunities to play with Kid Ory's band in early 1919, though his confidence was momentarily shaken by the arrival of a new cornetist in town, Ernest Burden, later and better known as "Punch" Miller. Born in Raceland, Louisiana, in 1894,[23] Miller arrived in New Orleans after serving in the army during World War I. He headed to the Big 25, where the Ory band was playing with Armstrong, Johnny Dodds, his brother Baby Dodds on drums, and—returning to the band after Ory's Original Dixieland Jass Band–inspired phase—guitarist Lorenzo Staulz and bassist Bob Lyons. Miller sat in with the band and played two songs he'd learned during the war, the pop tune "Smiles" and the patriotic anthem "Over There." Of the latter, Miller said, "I really could play that piece."[24]

Armstrong didn't know either song and didn't respond kindly when the band kidded him about it. "Louis got mad, boy!" Miller recalled. "He told them, 'You just take him, I'll just go ahead on, just take him in the band.' They said, 'Oh no, man, we're just kidding.'" As Armstrong's bruised feelings faded, he became an admirer of Miller's style. One of Miller's tricks was to hold a note for a long time while playing a blues. "I could hold it from the beginning of a chorus to the end, that's 12 bars," Miller said.[25] Dr. Edmond Souchon remembered Joe Oliver doing something similar at the Tulane dances, but Miller never heard Oliver in New Orleans. Whether he got it from Oliver or Miller, the notion of holding a single note for an entire chorus became an attractive idea to the young Armstrong.

Speed was the name of Miller's game, dazzling all present with the fluidity of his playing. Asked by Richard B. Allen in 1960, "Who was the best with that fast fingering?" Miller coolly responded, "Well, I believe I was. That ain't no joke." Of Armstrong, Miller said, "Well, Louis was already here but he didn't finger much. But Louis could make some stuff that was different from all of the rest of us." Asked for an example, Miller picked up his trumpet to demonstrate how Armstrong would play Larry Shields's technically demanding clarinet part from the Original Dixieland Jass Band's record of "Clarinet Marmalade."[26]

Armstrong was able to learn pieces like "Clarinet Marmalade" because he had bought his first Victrola soon after marrying Daisy. The impact of this purchase was something he'd speak about for the rest of his life, telling Richard Meryman, "Big event for me then was buying a wind-up Victrola." In addition to the Original Dixieland Jazz Band, Armstrong said, "I had Caruso records too, and Henry Burr, Galli-Curci, Tetrazzini—they were all my favorites. Then there was the Irish tenor, McCormack—beautiful phrasing."[27] A January 1919 ad for Victrola included a list of 29 "great artists," including Caruso, Galli-Curci, McCormack, and Tetrazzini. These were the hottest new records on the market and Armstrong was listening closely.[28]

Opera had always had a rich tradition in New Orleans, starting with the opening of the French Opera House in 1859. Amelita Galli-Curci came to New Orleans and performed at the Athenaeum on April 25, 1919. "Not once did she fall short of expectations," the *Times-Picayune* wrote in its review. "Her perfect modulations, her clearness of enunciation, her prolonged notes of splendid strength and quality, all blended into a simplicity which is the acme of finish."[29] One year later, on June 26, 1920, Enrico Caruso himself performed at the same venue. "Caruso has constantly improved in his work as the years have passed," Noel Strauss wrote. "His art is more perfect and his voice more mellow than it has been before." Of his closing performance of "Vesti La Giubba," Straus wrote, "This has always been one of his triumphs and in it he is unrivalled for dramatic intensity and fervor."[30]

African Americans weren't allowed inside the French Opera House until 1913 and it's doubtful that Armstrong ever attended a performance there before its destruction by fire in December 1919. It's also extremely doubtful he was at the live performances of Galli-Curci and Caruso at the Athenaeum.

But thanks to the miracle of recording technology, he could now buy their records and study Caruso's "Vesti La Giubba" and the way Galli-Curci sang the melody of Verdi's "Bella figlia dell'amore" from *Rigoletto*, the quartet of voices blending on that one like the front line of Kid Ory's jazz band. Kid Rena might have inspired Armstrong to play high notes on his cornet, but the recordings of Caruso, Galli-Curci, Luisa Tetrazzini, and the other opera stars of the day would instill "prolonged notes of splendid strength and quality" and "dramatic intensity and fervor" in his playing for the rest of his life.

Armstrong wasn't exactly singing opera with Ory's band. He was still doing his bawdy song, which Ory remembered as "Get Off Katie's Head." When he used to perform it at Pete Lala's, Armstrong said, "Man, it was like a sporting event. All the guys crowded around and they like [*sic*] to carry me up on their shoulders."[31] Pianist Clarence Williams was the manager of Lala's at the time and after the success of "Brown Skin, Who You For" and "Mama's Baby Boy" in 1916, he and Armand J. Piron were looking for new compositions to publish—and claim as their own. Williams soon approached Armstrong with an offer.

"They stole 'Sister Kate' from me," Armstrong later said. "Clarence Williams and Piron. See what I mean? I'm seventeen years old and wrote that song, playing it in the wagons with Kid Ory and everybody, Pops Foster, all of them. And they offered me fifty dollars, and fifty dollars to me at that time, seventeen years old, [was] like a thousand, well, quite naturally. Yeah! No contract—what the hell do I know about a contract?" Asked specifically who offered him the money, Armstrong said, "Clarence Williams" and continued venting, "They don't think enough to even put my name on the song."[32] But if Williams did indeed pay Armstrong for the song in 1917, Williams didn't do anything with it at the time.

According to the August 9, 1919, *Chicago Defender*, Williams was "visiting his people in New Orleans, La," one of whom must have been Piron.[33] By the end of the month, Piron had transformed Armstrong's opus into something a little more palatable for the public, "I Wish I Could Shimmy Like My Sister Kate," copyrighting it on August 28, 1919, when the "shimmy"—"a vulgar 'cooch' dance" in the words of *Variety*—was all the rage.[34] Still, Williams sat on the composition for three full years and didn't start pushing the sheet music and recording it until 1922—at which point the song became a sensation.

Armstrong was miffed at this for the rest of his life, but Piron shrugged it off, telling historian Al Rose, "Of course, that's not Louis' tune or mine. . . . That tune is older than all of us. People always put different words to it. Some of them were too dirty to say in polite company." Piron's attempt to downplay Armstrong's involvement is contradicted by Williams's gesture of paying

Armstrong for the song; if the song was truly "older than all of us," why would Williams need to pay Armstrong at all? There was clearly something novel about Armstrong's performance; even after downplaying Armstrong's claim of authorship, Piron was still able to recall one of Armstrong's lost stanzas, pointing out that "the way Louis did it didn't have anything to do with his Sister Kate":

> Gotta have 'em before it's too late,
> They shake like jelly on a plate.
> Big 'n juicy, soft an' 'round
> Sweetes' ones I ever found.

"That's the way Louis sang it, his words," Piron continued. "Well you know, there's just so many places you could do a number like that. Not in *my* band, you know." Rose noted that Piron's attitude toward Armstrong was "patronizing, but understanding."[35]

The "patronizing" attitude was common among Creoles such as Piron, who generally looked down on Third Ward Blacks such as Armstrong. Armstrong returned the favor in his own way, omitting all mentions of Piron in his autobiography. However, he did mention Piron's biggest Creole competitor, bandleader John Robichaux, whose popular society orchestra was adept at playing waltzes, marches, cakewalks, schottisches, quadrilles, and early ragtime. When Robichaux was short a cornet player and trombone player for a funeral job in 1919, he begrudgingly hired Armstrong and Ory, neither of whom were known as good sight-readers.

"Kid Ory and I noticed, all of those stuck up guys giving us, lots, of ice (meaning) they did not feel that we were good enough to play their marches, etc... and for that reason, they did not have much to say to us at all," Armstrong wrote. But when it was time to play, Armstrong claimed he and Ory played the written music "with much more ease than they did" and when it came time to perform something swinging for the march back to the hall, "those old fossils just couldn't cut it, swingingly." Armstrong and Ory took charge on "Panama," with the second line demanding an encore. "Those guys hired us several times after that incident," Armstrong said. "Afterall, we proved to them that any learned musician can read much, but truly all can't swing... Nice lesson for them."[36]

Armstrong couldn't have known it at the time, but he was about to become a "learned musician" himself.

14

"They Loved Us"

1919

In the spring of 1919, Louis Armstrong showed up at Co-operator's Hall on North Liberty Street for one of his regular weekly gigs with Kid Ory's band, probably not expecting anything special. But if he looked out into the audience, he would have noticed some unusual patrons among the venue's usual clientele. There was Peter Bocage, a light-skinned Creole who doubled on cornet and violin, perhaps best known for his tenure in Armand J. Piron's orchestra; there was also a light-skinned Black man with reddish hair named Fate Marable, whose calliope playing had provided part of the soundtrack of Armstrong's life since he'd sold newspapers as a boy; and there was a white man named Verne Streckfus, one of four sons of Commodore John Streckfus, respected head of the Streckfus Steamboat Company.

Armstrong could not have known the supposedly normal night with the Ory band was actually an audition for one of the biggest opportunities of his career. Midway through a rousing performance of Chris Smith's "Down in Honky Tonk Town," Marable knew he had found the next cornetist for his riverboat band.[1] Verne Streckfus remembered that "the minute they heard Louie play, why, we didn't have to stay there very long, they wanted him." There was a problem though; Streckfus said that Armstrong "wouldn't come work on the boat and play for white people. So we had to go get him."[2]

The name "Streckfus" had been synonymous with Mississippi River steamboats since the nineteenth century. Commodore John Streckfus Sr., born in 1856, originally ran the Acme Packet Company, based in St. Louis and set to deliver goods up and down the Mississippi River from St. Paul, Minnesota, to New Orleans. When speedy freight trains began taking business away from his steamboats around the turn of the twentieth century, John Sr. converted his fleet into excursion boats, enlisting the help of his sons Joseph, Roy, John Jr., and Verne, all of whom worked their way up to becoming captains. All four brothers were also trained musicians who formed a band to entice customers into dancing on the boat, but when this endeavor didn't prove successful, they ended up hiring professional musicians—including young Fate Marable.

Born in Paducah, Kentucky, on December 2, 1890, Fate Clifford Marable grew up in a musical household; his mother, Lizzie, worked as a music teacher. Classically trained as a pianist, Marable graduated from high school in June 1907, even performing "Oh! Believe Me" from *La Somnambula* at the commencement ceremony.[3] Shortly afterward, he took a job on the excursion boat *J.S.* (for John Streckfus). "It sailed to New Orleans that year with me at the piano and a white fellow playing the violin," Marable recalled. "That's all we had. Each year we added one more piece until we had what we thought was a great big band. Four pieces—piano, violin, trumpet, and drums. All of them were white boys but me, and playing strictly ragtime."[4]

In addition to his piano playing, Marable became proficient on the steamer *Sidney*'s steam-powered calliope. By 1912, he was referred to in newspapers as "Fate Marable, the demon calliope artist, who is generally conceded to be the premier harmonic tooter of the Mississippi."[5] Marable's calliope soon became a familiar sound around New Orleans. "That cat could swing that thing, too, man," Louis Armstrong said of Marable's calliope work on the *Sidney*. "I used to sell newspapers and used to hear him play that thing and I used to go out and look at him sometimes from a distance."[6]

But the music of New Orleans was having a similar effect on Marable. "We were going in and out of New Orleans all the time," Marable said, "and I began to notice the type of music they were playing there. It just got under my skin."[7] More important, the Streckfus family began to notice it, too. One of the very first printed uses of the word "jass" in the New Orleans *Times-Picayune* was in a description of the music being performed by "Fischer's ragtime jass band" on the *Sidney* in January 1917, one month before the Original Dixieland Jass Band recorded.[8]

But Fischer's band was a white band. Marable began lobbying the Streckfus family to let him put together a band of African American musicians from New Orleans. The "Kentucky Jazz Orchestra" debuted in March 1918, made up of musicians from both New Orleans and Paducah, but ultimately, it was a failed experiment. "The Paducah boys were fine, but they couldn't play jazz the way the New Orleans fellows played it," Marable said. "I knew if I wanted to play real jazz I had to have New Orleans musicians."[9]

"You've heard talk of Fate Marable?" drummer Albert Francis asked. "He was like a baseball manager. If he want a man in his band, he'd go around and scout you, see, and pick out who he want."[10] It took some time, but Marable soon solidified a world-class outfit with Johnny St. Cyr on banjo, Pops Foster on bass, Baby Dodds on drums, David Jones on mellophone, and Peter Bocage, and Joe Howard on cornet, among others. On November 17, 1918, the *Times-Picayune* reported, "The Sidney's new jazz band, under the direction of

Fate Marable, made a decided hit with the dancers and many encores had to be played to each of the eighteen numbers."[11]

When it was time for Marable's band to begin excursions outside New Orleans in May 1919, Bocage decided he wanted to stay home.[12] But he had a suggestion for a replacement, one that had the whole band buzzing: Louis Armstrong. "We all had our eye on Louis Armstrong as the coming man on this instrument in New Orleans," St. Cyr said. "So we were all bucking to get him in the band."[13]

Armstrong later claimed he "jumped at the opportunity" to join Marable, but the memories of Verne Streckfus tell a different story.[14] "He lived up on Rampart Street at that time," Streckfus said, referring to his home with Daisy which was on the corner of Melpomene and South Rampart. "We had to go up and get him out of his home to bring him where the boat was, he was so scared about coming down."[15] "Louis was playing with the Ory band," drummer Baby Dodds said. "So was my brother, John. So I was fighting to get Louis on the boat, and my brother was fighting to make him stay with Ory."[16]

Older musicians warned Marable that he was "wasting his time" by asking Armstrong to leave New Orleans, since the cornetist rarely left home except to play "little country towns" such as LaPlace and Houma. But Marable still invited Armstrong to perform on some of the band's regular moonlight excursions in New Orleans before offering him the role of featured cornetist. Armstrong accepted, later saying he did so as "an advancement towards my musical career... Because Fate's band had to read, and they did read music, perfectly... And Ory's band didn't." Of Ory's band he admitted, "nobody living [could] outplay them... But, to me I wanted to do more than just Fake the music all the time... Theres more to music than just playing just one style."[17]

Louis ran home to share the news with Daisy, assuming she would "rejoice" for him. "But instead, she gave me a disgusted looked," he wrote, "as if she thought I only agreed to leave New Orleans in order to get away from her." Louis was devastated—"my feathers fell something awful"—but launched into an impassioned speech about how much this opportunity meant to him.

"Well Daisy, darling this is my one big chance to do the things that I have been wanting to do all my life," Louis told her. "And I'm afraid if I should turn this one down, the same as I have been doing, I will be stuck here forever, with nothing happening."

It's telling that Louis would later write hundreds of pages about these early years in New Orleans, but deep down he knew that even though he'd worked his way up from the Colored Waif's Home to the first cornet chair in Kid Ory's band, he felt that "nothing" was happening and he was in danger of being "stuck here forever."[18]

Daisy wasn't the only person upset by his decision; Baby Dodds remembered that "Ory was furious."[19] Ory had taken a chance, replacing King Oliver with a little-known teenaged cornetist, and less than a year after he started, Armstrong was leaving him. When Armstrong had joined the band, Ory had procured a brand-new cornet for him to play, and Ory wasn't done paying it off when he learned about the Marable opportunity. "If you go on the boat, I'm going to take my horn," Ory warned him.[20] The cornet would now go to Armstrong's replacement, Henry "Kid" Rena.

Before departing, Armstrong nervously sought out St. Cyr.

"Pops, I don't believe I can make it," he told the banjoist.

"Why?" St. Cyr asked.

"Well, Ory said if I go on the boat, he's going to take his horn," Armstrong replied.

"Well, you come on the boat," St. Cyr insisted. "We'll talk to the captain after rehearsal."

St. Cyr let Marable know about the problem first. "He don't have to worry about no horn," Marable said. "The captain will buy him any kind of horn he wants."

Marable took Armstrong to meet Captain Roy Streckfus, "a very rough speaking fellow," according to St. Cyr.

"Can the man play?" Streckfus asked insistently. "Can he play? Can he play?"

"Yeah, he can play all right!" Marable answered emphatically.

"Well, he oughtn't worry about the horn," Streckfus said before turning his attention to Armstrong. "Son, we'll buy you any kind of horn you want. You want to make the trip? You want to go with the boys?"

Armstrong replied, "Yes sir."

"We'll buy any horn you want," Streckfus stressed. "Just be here Tuesday morning to catch the train to go to St. Louis."[21]

Before arriving in St. Louis, the band would stop for one night in Paducah, Kentucky, to join the musician's union, since there was no union for African American musicians in New Orleans. This was not only Armstrong's first time leaving his home state but also his first time riding on a train. "I had to take a lunch on the train so my mother went to Pratt's restaurant and brought me a big old trout loaf to take with me and a bottle of olives," Armstrong recalled in 1956.

> David Jones, who was the mellophone player in the band, he went along with me. And he's one of them dicty cats, you know, he'd been playing it all the big circles and things like that and he didn't particularly care about me taking a sandwich with me. But I mean, I didn't know the difference; my mother wanted me to eat.

> But the payoff came when we was changing trains in Galesburg, IL. Well, I had to get on the train with all these bottles in my hand and my beat-up suitcase and the station was crowded with people. When the train came and everybody made a rush, these olives dropped out of my hand and fell to the ground and the olives were running everywhere. The bottle had broken and David Jones left me like he never knew me before. I didn't say nothing to him. But when we got to St. Louis, and on our way to the boat, it was real hot that day and I noticed everybody was laughing at him because he had on an overcoat and a straw hat! Oh, those were kicks in early days.[22]

Once they reached their final destination, Armstrong admitted, "I wasn't no better than he was because I was looking at all them tall buildings in St. Louis and them flats and things and I thought they was all universities and colleges because I didn't see buildings that tall in New Orleans before!" When he made this observation out loud, Marable responded, "Aw boy, don't be so damn dumb."[23]

Armstrong and Marable headed straight for the Streckfus's main office, where a secretary shared that Captain Roy Streckfus had instructed Armstrong to go a local music store to "pick out the horn you want and we'll take care of it." Armstrong picked out a Harry B. Jay model cornet along with a new mouthpiece.[24] "[Armstrong] reported for boat rehearsal with his feet half out of his shoes, and had no trumpet," Captain Joseph Streckfus recalled. "He had been using [Kid Ory's]'s trumpet and [Ory] was mad at Louie for leaving him, for the first time. We bought new shoes for Louie and let him use a silver trumpet we had on hand. Later we bought him a good trumpet." It wasn't exactly a gift; Streckfus recalled later buying Armstrong a second cornet that cost $225 and noted, "Louie repaid us in full."[25]

From St. Louis, the Marable band headed to Davenport to pick up the *St. Paul* to begin their regular daily performances. Once there, Armstrong got a chance to try his new horn out at the band's first rehearsal. "And Louis liked to blow the bell off that horn," St. Cyr said, remembering Armstrong blowing furiously on one number before coming to an abrupt stop.

"What's the matter, Louis?" Marable asked.

"Man, I had to stop and let some of them notes get out this horn!" Armstrong said, breaking everyone up.[26] "From the first note on, we had one of the best bands on the Mississippi," Armstrong fondly recalled.[27]

Newspaper reports began covering Marable's new band in Davenport, announcing the group's new name: the Metropolitan Jaz-E-Saz Band. "Of all the different kinds of jazz music played by the various famous bands, there is none that can compare with the Jaz-E-Saz as played by the famous Metropolitan band," the *Quad-City Times* reported.[28]

For much of May, the Metropolitan Jaz-E-Saz Band brought the sounds of jazz to Davenport, Iowa; Alton, Dallas City, and Rock Island, Illinois; La Crosse, Wisconsin; and Winona and St. Paul, Minnesota—in other words, places where authentic New Orleans jazz had not yet traveled, especially as played by an all–African American band. "I shall go as far as to say, that we (Fate Marable's Band) sort of broke down a few barrier[s], in other wordes [*sic*], we sort of deserve a little credit for breaking down that mean ole James Crow...(jim crow) and segregation... Yea," Armstrong wrote, adding, "We were the first colored band to play in most of those towns (the little ones, especially)."

They weren't always welcomed with open arms—at first. Here's how Armstrong related it in his manuscript of *Satchmo: My Life in New Orleans*, a passage that was cleaned up considerably upon publication:

> Quite naturally, the Ofays (the white folks), wasn't used to seeing us—Er-rr- colored boys, blowing those horns...And playing all of that fine music for them to shake a leg (dance to)-so, at first, we ran into a lot of ugly moments while we were on the band stand... Such as, come on thar—black boy, etc... We (most of us) were from the South anyway—and being used to that kind of jive—we'd-just keep on making it swinging just like nothing happened.... And before the nights over after we've ignored all of that mad jive they'd layed on us the first part of the evening, and beating out that fine music for them in fine fashion - hmmmmm, They Love us, -do you hear me????—they Loved us... We couldn't turn for them singing our praises, etc....Telling us to hurry up and come back...... Cute?[29]

Armstrong's repetition of the phrase "they Loved us" signifies that this was another major event in his life, akin to the time he realized that just because he was carrying Joe Oliver's cornet, the police would leave him alone. He still had to deal with the same kinds of ignorant comments he regularly heard in New Orleans, but now he noticed the impact his music was having on such small-minded folks, winning him respect by evening's end. The cornet's magical powers knew no ends.

Not that every evening ended up as a giant antiracist lovefest. "The first year we went up the river we didn't do good at all," Baby Dodds recalled. "It was pitiful. We played up the Missouri River and I think people used to come on the boat more for curiosity than anything else. And they sat down and looked at us. They'd advertise before we got there that we were colored. So people wouldn't be disappointed." In Hannibal, Missouri, Dodds noted, "Nobody danced. We'd take an intermission, go off, come back, and they'd still look at us." He admitted it was "embarrassing," but somehow didn't get dismayed, telling himself, "Well, I'm doing something big or else there wouldn't be such astonishment." However, when the band returned to Hannibal, Dodds said, "My God, you couldn't get them off the boat; the boat was packed to capacity. I think the first time it was a surprise for the people. They had never before seen Negroes on the boat. They saw Negro roustabouts but had never seen a Negro with a tie and collar on, and a white shirt, playing music. They just didn't know what to make of it. But they really liked it. They were the dancingest people I ever found on the boat."[30]

These first nights with the band were not easy for Armstrong, musically speaking. At an early dance in Paducah, the local musicians laughed when they spotted his cornet-blowing technique. "I used to puff," he said in 1953. "I used to blow right up." Soon, local musicians greeted him with, "Here come old Jaws!" "So they commenced to calling me 'Jaws' and laughing at me, you know?" Armstrong said. "And I looked in the mirror and it *was* funny. And I just kept on lookin' in that mirror til I cut it out....That's all I had to do, and I mean, it wasn't no effort. I said 'I'm gonna break myself of the habit,' and did it."[31]

More urgently, Armstrong was also struggling with reading the band's arrangements.

"Louie Armstrong played by ear," Captain Verne Streckfus said. "When he came with us, he couldn't read a note. . . . The band would play the piece through it first and then he would listen. He'd say, 'I have it' and then he could play it. That's how it went."[32] Armstrong began spending his free time studying with multiinstrumentalist David Jones, who played saxophone, cornet, and piano in addition to mellophone. Jones was a "phenomenal musician" in the words of fabled New Orleans guitarist Danny Barker, who added that Jones "was running all kinds of . . . strange changes and everything. And I think he . . . was some help to Louie because Louie could see from David Jones what could be done with that horn. Cause nobody had taken the liberties and variated on the horn other than clarinet players, but here was David Jones doing these things on the mellophone."[33]

"Bre'r Jones (as I learned to later, call him) he would teach me how to devide [*sic*] those notes," Armstrong wrote. "So, when ever Fate would throw a new arrangement on us I could easily Cope with it (or) get with it, and wouldn't have to sit down with my cornet in my hand and wait for Joe Howard (a fine fellow) to play the tune on down 'once' then turn it over to me."[34] The invocation of cornetist Howard calls to mind Pops Foster's assertion that "Joe Howard was the one who taught Louie how to read."[35] "Between them two

[Jones and Howard], Louis being a likable youngster, younger than them, they give him skills," Barker said. "Well, you got all day. Some days you do nothing but stay in your quarters on the boat and practice."[36] "Within no time at all, I was reading everything Fate Marable put in front of me," Armstrong said.[37]

What constituted "everything"? The answers varied. Pops Foster stressed it was a reading band but when asked to describe their style, he answered, "Ragtime. Same thing that they call Dixieland today."[38] "Now, the music we played — how the band sounded — this would be more like a swing band than the New Orleans type jazz band," St. Cyr recalled.[39] Armstrong summed it up by saying, "Oh, we played all kind of music. We had to play waltzes and rhumbas, fox trots. You know, there was all types of people."[40]

But the musicians all agreed that the Streckfus's were calling the shots—and the numbers to be played. "Streckfus had a standing order with the music

Figure 14.1 The 1919 edition of Fate Marable's Metropolitan Jaz-E-Saz Band, aboard the steamer *Sidney* in New Orleans. Left to right: Warren "Baby" Dodds, William "Bebé" Ridgley, Joe Howard, Louis Armstrong, Fate Marable, Davey Jones, Johnny Dodds, Johnny St. Cyr, and George "Pops" Foster. The man standing behind Johnny Dodds has been identified as a fan of the band named Sam Rosenbaum. Johnny Dodds was not a regular part of the band and was just filling in for Sam Dutrey, who was not able to be present when this photo was taken.

Credit: Courtesy of the New Orleans Jazz Club Collection of the Louisiana State Museum. Photo restoration by Nick Dellow.

publishers and they shipped him all the new arrangements right off the press," St. Cyr said. "He just paid them by the month. We just played the arrangements as they were, we never changed them. We had no staff arranger, no special jazz arrangements. The other bands used the same music we did. We just had that feeling, that rhythm, that swing."[41] "The Streckfus people were funny to work for," according to Pops Foster. "You play music to suit them, not the public. As long as they were happy you had the job."[42] Pianist Marge Creath worked on another Streckfus boat, the *J. S.*, and summed up the Streckfus sound by saying, "If you played on those steamboats, you had to play dance music. But a swinging dance music!"[43]

However, Baby Dodds added that one style of music was out: the blues. "The white people didn't go for blues like they do now," he said, adding, "In New Orleans we used to play the blues and the very lowest type of dancers used to love such things. They were played very slow and fellows and their girlfriends would stand almost still and just make movements."[44] That was not going to be tolerated on the *St. Paul*. "The Streckfus people always wanted us to play music at a tempo of 60 beats [per minute] or up," Foster said. "When you got down around 40 or 45, guys would be out on the floor doing nothing but shaking their butts very slow and dirty. The boats had floorwalkers looking for guys who were twisting themselves all up like that."[45]

After nearly a month of these tours up and down the Mississippi, the *St. Paul* pulled into St. Louis on Decoration Day, May 30, its home base until August. Pay went up from $35 a week to $55 in St. Louis, as the band would play excursions to Alton, Illinois, both in the daytime and at night. "The first season in St. Louis we worked from 9 o'clock in the morning until 6 p.m., with an hour off at noon," St. Cyr remembered. "Then back from 8 p.m. 'til 12.15 a.m. for the night trip."

St. Louis was a major city with a rich musical heritage, steeped in ragtime and the blues, but the real New Orleans jazz did not make an impact on that city until the Marable band arrived in the summer of 1919. Asked what kind of music they were playing in St. Louis, St. Cyr responded, "Well, they were playing popular numbers, but they had no jazz outfits there. They weren't playing hot."[46]

Not all St. Louis musicians welcomed the Marable band with open arms. "The white musicians didn't want us there" is how St. Cyr put it. Sensing possible danger with his Black musicians walking around the city unprotected, "Streckfus just hired a lot of guards, take you up the hill," St. Cyr said. "To let you catch the streetcar. After you got on the car, then you were all right, see. . . . And they used to watch us. Nobody worried us but the white musicians were hard on us."[47]

Black musicians were more welcoming, if still a little defensive. The *J.S.* featured the music of cornetist Charles Creath, whose sister, pianist Marge Creath, argued that "the real blues were played in St. Louis different from New Orleans."[48] Creath "had set St. Louis on fire," according to trumpeter Bob Shoffner.[49] Understandably protective of her brother, Marge said audiences in St. Louis thought Charlie Creath "was the greatest trumpet player in the world. . . . In those days folks didn't think about Louis Armstrong, it was Charlie Creath."[50]

Trumpeter Dewey Jackson originally felt that way, especially after getting hired to play with Creath's outfit on the *J.S.* in 1919. One day, the *J.S.* broke down and the *St. Paul* had to be sent to rescue her passengers. "Before this me and everybody think Creath's the best trumpet there is," Jackson said, "but as that boat come near I hear a trumpet playing in the band on the St. Paul. Man! I never forget that trumpet! They playing 'High Society' and the trumpet takes four, five choruses, and *hot*! I never know anybody play a trumpet like that. Later on I find out it's Louis playing with Fate Marable's band. I say to Creath, 'Sorry, Charlie, but *there's* the greatest trumpet player in the world.' "[51]

The Marable band was especially popular on Monday nights, the only evening African Americans were allowed on the *St. Paul*. "Then we'd play what we want, we'd have fun, we'd drink, smoke, we used to wish for Monday night to come," Foster said.[52] "It gave us an altogether different sensation because we were free to talk to people and the people could talk to us, and that's a great deal in playing music," Baby Dodds said. "We were less tense because it was our own people."[53]

Future saxophonist Greely Walton, born October 4, 1904, first heard Armstrong on one of these Monday night excursions in St. Louis. "He was terrific then!" Walton said. "He played that same style that he always played, you know, that he continued to play after all those years." Asked if Armstrong was "head and shoulders above the rest" of the members of the Marable band, Walton laughed and said, "Head and shoulders and ten feet tall! Yeah, he was terrific. He was ten feet above all the rest of them, really."[54]

Those four months made a new man out of Armstrong—in more ways than one. "I think it was on the riverboat where Louis developed his gravel voice," Dodds said. "He had a cold all the time and we used to kid him around, laughing and joking. . . . He got rid of the cold but the voice had developed like that and he's been like that ever since."[55]

The cold ended up affecting more than just his voice. Armstrong only weighed 140 pounds when he joined Marable in May, living up to the "Little Louie" moniker that had followed him around since he was a kid. But once sick, Armstrong began taking Scott's Emulsion, a tonic made up of cod liver oil, which increased his appetite. By August, he claimed to have gained between 30 and 50 pounds![56] “Why I had gained so much weight I had to buy a fat man’s trousers,” he said in the early 1950s. “From that time on— I never did get back to my good ole, fighting weight again.”[57]

Armstrong didn’t mind his new portly shape, especially after observing David Jones for a few months. “That son of a bitch bought a cotton field, you know, when that was so plentiful, the war, and Uncle Sam was buying that shit,” Armstrong said of Jones. “And that nigger wouldn’t even buy a solid meal. We out there, I’m eating pork chops piled up like cordwood, man. Rice and peas. . . . And there’s Davey Jones eating an apple. An apple. One fucking apple. And he did that all season, and just when he’s supposed to make money on that cotton field, the boll weevils ate up all the shit.” Armstrong kept his eye on the despondent Jones as he’d wander around the boat. “And every intermission, I tell Fate, ‘You better go get Davey Jones, he’s standing by that rail again looking at that water. Getting ready to jump any minute,’ ” Armstrong continued. “Went in bad health and everything else, over money. He ain’t never been the same.”[58] Right then and there, Armstrong developed a new mantra: “I won’t probably ever be rich,” he said to himself, “But I’ll be a fat man.”[59]

Armstrong received a nice surprise upon arriving back in New Orleans at the end of the summer season: Captain Joe Streckfus had been holding back five dollars a week from each man during the season and now gave it to them as a lump sum bonus. “Real swell people, those Streckfus’s,” Armstrong recalled.[60]

With his pocketful of money, corpulent physique, and new gravelly voice, Armstrong said, “When I went back to New Orleans after that first season, I could walk all over Rampart Street, and didn’t anybody recognized me.”[61] Armstrong headed straight for his old Liberty and Perdido Street neighborhood and ran into Black Benny at Joe Segreto’s saloon.

“Well, if it ain’t Ol’ Dipper,” Black Benny said, staring at Armstrong. “Come heah you little sommitch. You been up north blowing dat horn of yours. I know you’re sticking,” slang for having lots of money. “Come up heah to this bar and buy me a drink.”

“Well, after all, who am I to refuse the great Black Benny a drink,” Armstrong thought to himself. Armstrong ordered a round of drinks, paying with a $20 bill. As the bartender went to hand him his change, Black Benny interceded.

“I’ll take the change,” Benny said.

“So he did,” Armstrong wrote. “As he put it into his pocket, I smiled all over my face...What else could I have done... Black Benny wanted that money, and that was that.......Then too— I was so fond of Benny, it didn’t matter anyway.” However, in a sign that he was maturing, Armstrong added, “Only thing—I do

Figure 14.2 Studio portrait of Louis Armstrong, his mother, Mary Albert, and sister, Beatrice "Mama Lucy" Armstrong, taken by Villard Paddio in New Orleans most likely in late 1919 or early 1920.
Credit: Courtesy of the Hot Club of New York.

believe, if he had not strong armed me out of that change, I would have given him lots more money than that...Because I had eyes for it... I was thinking about it in a big way on the train coming home from St Louis... But since he did it the hard (tough) way... I declined the idea." Armstrong "disgustingly" waited for an opportunity to leave, leaving his one-time hero to go home to his wife.[62]

Louis had a rare happy reunion with Daisy and a big reunion dinner with Mayann, Mama Lucy, and Clarence, whom he dubbed "the wrecking crew" for how much they could eat. "My mother just stood up and looked at us with pride," Louis recalled.[63] Mayann was going through an era of relative peace. Both of her children were married—16-year-old Beatrice had wed an older man named George Donald on May 30, 1919, just two months after Louis and Daisy. Mayann hadn't been arrested a single time since 1917 and had found religion to the point of getting baptized.

Louis chose to document this moment of bliss by taking his mother and sister into the photo studio of 27-year-old African American photographer Villard Paddio to have their first—and only—family portrait taken. Seated in a chair, Mayann looks strong and dignified, wearing a long, ruffled dress and clasping her hands together. Though recently married, Mama Lucy does look like a 16-year-old kid, skinny, her posture noticeably rigid. The now slightly chubby Louis wears a suit with the jacket unbuttoned. With his hair parted down in the middle, he stares into the camera without a trace of the smile that would one day ingratiate him to millions. "I was a pretty serious fellow by then, as you can see by my picture taken when I came home from playing on the riverboats and got my mother, Mary Ann and my sister, Beatrice, to have this made," Louis said while fondly looking at the family portrait with Inez Cavanaugh in 1945.[64]

The closeness he felt with his family was probably a big part of the reason he chose to stay in New Orleans instead of taking an offer from his old boss, Kid Ory, to come to California. Like Joe Oliver, Ory was tired of having his dances raided and even his life threatened and chose to head to Los Angeles. Armstrong promised to join him if there was work for him, but when Ory sent for him, Armstrong got cold feet and Mutt Carey went in his place.[65] Armstrong admired Ory but was not ready to go to California at this juncture. He was content to remain with Marable on the riverboats where every trip away from home was guaranteed a return trip back.

15

"Descending the Sky Like a God"

1919–1921

When the Marable band returned to performing their daily excursions on the *Sidney* out of New Orleans in the fall of 1919, Captain Joseph Streckfus noticed a change. In his effort to impress the St. Louis dancers—and musicians—with their new style, Marable had started goosing the tempo of many of their signature arrangements. "With faster tempo, the band had lost that syncopation and the beat they used to have," Streckfus concluded.

Streckfus began insisting the band utilize medium tempos but was initially met with resistance. "Fate, Louie, and the band thought I was wrong," he said. Streckfus's advice was ignored for the next two weeks until one afternoon trip, he looked down and noticed the boat's headlight and pilothouse shaking. Upon hearing shouts of approval, Streckfus went down to find "the dancers were going off." A smiling Armstrong approached him and said, "We's got it." Asked to explain, Armstrong responded, "We played it slow like you wanted it, and I's put in a little swing, and did they like it!"

"From that time on, our band put out the best dance music ever," Streckfus said. "St. Louis tempo was just 20 beats faster per minute than New Orleans, and it took Louie Armstrong's ability and his trumpet to play the syncopation, which was possible at the slower tempo, but at the St. Louis fast tempo was an impossibility. Louie Armstrong was always ready and willing to try out anything for the good of the band."[1]

Armstrong looked forward to his steady work with Marable on the *Sidney* in New Orleans as a respite from the daily drama that played out with Daisy. "My wife Daisy turned out to be such a jealous woman, until, when ever we would have a fuss or fight (as much as I hated it)—I would put my clothes—and Clarence's clothes into my charcoal sack (the sack that I sold charcoal in) and move back down to my mother's house...Clarence right behind me," Louis said. "We would stay with May'ann with the intentions of never leaving."[2] Eventually, Louis got his wish.

On January 9, 1920, a census enumerator showed up at a boarding house at 1408 Perdido Street, owned by neighborhood grocer Gaspar Joseph

Locicero, and found 37-year-old Mary Armstrong, living with a new boyfriend, George Money; she gave her marital status as "widowed" even though Willie Armstrong was alive and well.[3] Also living there was her 19-year-old son, Louis, working as a "musician" in the "theater" industry. Louis was listed as being "married" but Daisy does not appear anywhere in the 1920 census. One month later, on February 13, 1920, Daisy took her husband to court for desertion, with Louis ordered to pay his estranged wife $2.50 per week in support. For the rest of 1920, they would remain separated.[4]

What could have led them to the breaking point? Armstrong's reflections on his tumultuous first marriage provide some clues:

> She was twenty-one years old and I was eighteen at the time [we got married]. And the way those tough men such as gamblers, pimps, etc., got along with their wives and whores, that was the same way that I had to get along with Daisy. That was to beat the hell out of her every night in order to get some sleep. That was suppose to be love. And the Lord was with me. She was so mean and jealous. And to my surprise I awakened one morning and Daisy had a big bread knife laying on my throat, with tears dropping from her eyes, saying, "You black son of a bitch, I ought to cut your God dam throat." Hmm. That's why I always said the Lord was with me. Many times she and I went to jail from fighting in the streets, and my boss would have to come get me out.[5]

Perhaps the most violent and harrowing of all the Louis-and-Daisy stories occurred when Daisy caught Louis talking to an old female friend, Rella Martin, at a funeral. "Sure enough, Daisy starts that shit about Rella, you know," Louis said. "One word and another, 'Well, go fuck yourself,' and shit, out with that razor." Louis jumped into a ditch to avoid Daisy's razor, causing his new John B. Stetson hat to fall off his head. Daisy "took that hat and cut it to ribbons," Louis said. "Oh shit. And then it was on, you know."

After the funeral, an angry Louis reached their Melpomene Street home, unaware that Daisy was waiting for him at a second-floor window—armed with a stack of bricks. "I unlock the door and bricks are hitting me, 'Yoom!' 'Boom!' She was throwing them fucking bricks!" Louis remembered.[6] When Daisy ran out of bricks, "she came down stairs to actually fight it out with me," he wrote. "As she came nearer and nearer to me, I—quick like a flash, stooped down and picked up one of the bricks that she had been throwing at me from upstairs, and I took a straight aim at her, cocked up my right leg as if I was going to pitch a strike for the home team, (with a brick in my hand) I let go, and hit Daisy direct in the middle of her stomach."

"Oh, you've killed me!" Daisy screamed in agony.

A neighbor called the police, who arrived at the scene, sirens blaring, as Louis made his escape. "I Tore out for the back fence," Louis said. "I was so frightened until I Scaled that wall with only one hand... And I didn't even touch the fence." Daisy didn't have it so lucky. While still "hollering and screaming and cursing," Daisy took a swing at one of the officers. "Ooh God," Louis wrote. "That cop got so angry with Daisy, he hit her up beside her cute little Creole head with his lickoricestick [*sic*], (his police club) which made her head bleed, terribly... But she wouldn't dare report it to the Captain of the police force... Because when she would have gotten out of jail, the same cop would have laid for her and given her another head whipping... That was the custom of the cops in New Orleans in those days."

But with Daisy in jail, Louis "softened up right away" and reached out to the Streckfus brothers, who called the police and had Daisy paroled immediately. Back home, Louis claimed to have attempted to "call it quits," causing Daisy to burst into tears, screaming, "Don't leave me!" "So we made up and toughed it out a little while longer together," Louis said.[7] But when 1920 began, Louis was living back home with Mayann and Daisy was going to court to get financial support. Even separated, there'd be more rocky moments ahead. As he once put it, "Our marriage lasted four years and there wasn't a dull moment the entire time."[8]

Later in life, while reflecting on the loss of his beloved John B. Stetson hat that Daisy sliced up, Armstrong lamented, "Hurt me to my heart, man. Rather lose her than that hat."[9]

The next excursion season kicked off in May 1920 on the newly renovated steamer *St. Paul* in Davenport. "Enjoying the same popularity of the excursion queen is the Metropolitan Jaz-E-Saz band, incomparable in its renditions of jazz music and it is that very music that makes fans root hard for the *St. Paul*," the *Quad-City Times* reported on May 13.[10]

It was most likely around this time that Armstrong met a teenaged cornetist from Davenport, Leon "Bix" Beiderbecke, born March 10, 1903. In the manuscript of *Satchmo: My Life in New Orleans*, Armstrong claimed to have "met the almighty Bix Beiderbecke, a great cornet Genius" during his first trip to Davenport in May 1919, but when further questioned by Beiderbecke biographer Phil Evans in 1955, Armstrong moved it up a year.[11] "Man, 1920 sounds right," he told Evans. "Bix would come aboard the steamer, listen, then go home and practice what he heard."[12] Norman Mason joined Marable on cornet in 1920 and remembered meeting Beiderbecke on the *St. Paul* "the first year I played up there."[13] That same year, the *Capitol* began featuring a white band with future members of the New Orleans Rhythm Kings, including cornetist Paul Marris and saxophonist Jack Pettis. "Bix used to come down to the boat when they were in Davenport and hear both their band and Louis's," Pettis recalled.[14]

The *St. Paul*'s home base was again set up in St. Louis beginning on May 30, but this season there would be a major change. After playing both the daytime and nighttime excursions in 1919, Johnny St. Cyr said "the union had brought a law, there had to be two bands to play that job. It was too much for one band. They had to have a day orchestra and a night orchestra."[15]

With more free time during the day, Armstrong sometimes sought out local bands to rehearse with to enhance his reading ability. One such band was the Pilgrim Brass Band, of which teenaged trumpeter Louis Metcalf was a member. After rehearsing with the band, Armstrong invited the musicians to hear him on the *St. Paul* that evening. "And I heard that man's sound, nobody, I mean, no trumpet player, has had the sound that Pops had," Metcalf said in 1980. "Because nobody had his kind of heart. . . . When I heard this man, I fell in love with him."

Armstrong soon returned to rehearse with the Pilgrim Brass Band with a gift for Metcalf. "He gave me my first instrument," Metcalf said, still audibly touched over 60 years later. "And Louis told me how to work the keys, what went first, second, third and so forth like that. And he taught me my scales and everything, and I listened to him. I loved him so much that anything he said was tops with me. He couldn't make no mistakes, as far as I'm concerned. And that's where I started."[16]

Armstrong clearly enjoyed spending time with fellow cornetists, but he was beginning to have even more fun spending time with members of the opposite sex. "I was a very popular boy in the Grand Central Hotel in St Louis," he wrote. "I being the youngest in the (Fate Marables, band) and single too, all the maids made a lot of fuss over me.... Uh, I thought I was real hot stuff, with the gals, arguing with one another...Saying, he's my man ... I saw him first, etc, and Blaa Blaa ... But, I was so interested in my music, and trying to get to point of playing it to my own satisfactions, I turned deaf ears to all that Jive.....Most of it anyway."[17] Armstrong's use of the word "single" alluded to his and Daisy's separation; even without a formal divorce, he was free to indulge in some of the extramarital activities encouraged by Black Benny, starting a pattern that never really stopped until he ended up in intensive care at Beth Israel Hospital nearly 50 years later.

Pops Foster recalled an evening in Paducah when he and Armstrong "picked up two chicks" and brought them back to their rooms. They heard the milkman delivering buttermilk, so Foster and Armstrong each bought a big can for a dime. "I go to bed with my chick and I look out the door and every two minutes, I could see Louie running to the toilet, man!" Foster said. "That buttermilk gave him the shits! And as soon as he'd get ready to go to bed, man, he had to run to the toilet from drinking all that buttermilk!"[18]

One of the reasons Armstrong was drinking buttermilk was that Prohibition had gone into effect on January 17. "They put the lid on it by the time we got to St. Louis," St. Cyr recalled. "Oh man, it was plenty tough." But with Prohibition came the rise of bootleg alcohol—and bootleggers in general. One day during the summer of 1920, some members of the band were approached by a man carrying a suitcase he claimed was filled with bootleg liquor. "So Fate, Louis and I made a deal with him for the suitcase," Baby Dodds said. "He was asking $75.00 which made 25 apiece but when the time came to get up the money Louis and Fate paid him but I was broke. Well, I had the laugh on them, because when they opened the suitcase, there were three bricks wrapped up."[19]

Dodds had the last laugh on that occasion, but Armstrong never forgot a time in Keokuk, Iowa, when the band had some downtime and Dodds left the boat and got drunk at a party. He was late getting back on the boat and his playing immediately suffered from his inebriation. The musicians tried covering it up, but Dodds got insulted and started calling his bandmates "a gang of black bastards."[20] Marable immediately called an intermission and took Dodds downstairs to try to talk some sense into him, without success. "He wanted to put drums on people's heads!" Armstrong said. "He was swinging around, wild. I was afraid I'd get hit in the chops and put me out of business."[21]

At that point Captain John Streckfus Jr., "a big strong, six feet tall man" in Armstrong's words, entered to calmly tell Dodds to at least stop swearing. "Baby told Captain Johnny where to go and what to do," Armstrong said.[22] Streckfus chose to take matters into his own hands. "He leaned down and took hold of Baby's throat and choked him right down to his knees," Armstrong told William Russell. "Tongue hanging out. We're all standing around." Armstrong was disturbed, but he learned a valuable lesson that night, which he shared with Russell: "A musician should drink when he's through work or maybe before he comes to work, if he can get a nap in between. He should not drink on the job."[23]

The Marable band eventually switched from the *St. Paul* to the *J.S. Deluxe* in September to close out an excursion season newspapers reported as "the most successful in history."[24] Upon returning to New Orleans, they left the smaller *Sidney* behind in favor of the Streckfus's newest and biggest boat, the *Capitol*, which could hold 3,000 passengers.[25]

By the fall of 1920, Captain Joe Streckfus was noticing a shift in popular music tastes away from the New Orleans–infused sounds of the Original Dixieland Jass Band. "Is the passion for freak dance music going the way of other popular fads?" the *New York World* asked in an editorial that was picked up in newspapers around the country. "Perhaps the worst is over. Perhaps the pendulum is now about to swing the other way. . . . Certainly a return to normalcy in dance music will be hailed by most people with a delight they have not known under the infliction of jazz."[26]

That "normalcy in dance music" was now exemplified by the more cohesive, saxophone-heavy stylings of white dance bands such as those led by Joseph C. Wright, Paul Whiteman, and especially the San Francisco–based drummer Art Hickman. Captain Joseph Streckfus was paying attention. "Personally, I believed if [Marable's] band played more variety, they could become the best band in New Orleans," he said.[27]

The moment of awakening for Streckfus occurred when he heard an Art Hickman Columbia record that featured a medley of "Avalon" and "Japanese Sandman," with each side alternating between the choruses of each song. Advertised as "the dance sensation of the country,"[28] Streckfus remembered it "was the first record of its kind." Inspired, he bought a Victrola and other Hickman recordings, including "Love Nest" and "Young Man's Fancy," and began playing the sounds of "dance music that they never heard before" for Marable's musicians. "Louie Armstrong, with his trumpet in his hand, came down alongside of a Victrola and would pick up on his trumpet the notes in the several chords in the modulation," Streckfus said, referring to a part of the arrangement that changed keys. "That evening we had approximately 1200 dancers, and when the band played 'Avalon,' they stopped the show. Folks crowded around the orchestra stand and applauded and applauded. They never had heard music like that." After that first night, Streckfus felt "it was not hard for the band to continue rehearsing and learning the music played by Hickman's band. That I believe was the start of the success of Louie Armstrong and Fate Marable."[29]

To emulate Hickman's influential reed section, both David Jones and Norman Mason began doubling on saxophone, as did the band's new violinist, Boyd Atkins. Streckfus had new photos of the Marable band taken on the *Capitol*, with Armstrong the lone cornetist. "Of course, the music on the boat changed, you see, from what they called ragtime because after . . . they switched from where they had trumpets playing lead to where they had the saxophones, the whole style of music changed," Mason said.[30]

On that same influential recording of "Avalon," Hickman also played slide whistle, a sound he became associated with to the point that some referred to the novelty instrument as the "Hickman Whistle." One of Hickman's greatest disciples was bandleader Paul Whiteman, who found great popularity with a Hickman-styled ensemble, leading to a series of recording sessions for Victor. On August 23, 1920, Whiteman recorded "Whispering" and featured a full

Figure 15.1 Fate Marable's Orchestra aboard the *Capitol* in St. Louis in 1920. Left to right: Henry Kimball, Boyd Atkins, Fate Marable, Johnny St. Cyr, David Jones, Norman Mason, Louis Armstrong, Norman Brashear, and Warren "Baby" Dodds.
Credit: Courtesy of Nick Dellow.

chorus of slide whistle. The record was issued on October 6—the same day the *Capitol* pulled into New Orleans—and sold over one million copies.

One of those sales was to Joseph Streckfus, who immediately sought to add that novelty sound to the Marable orchestra. "I'll never forget the first time the Captain bought a song whistle for Louis and he . . . used to play that piece, 'Whispering,'" Norman Mason remembered, also noting that Armstrong played slide whistle on "Love Nest," another song recorded by both Whiteman and Hickman in the fall of 1920. Streckfus soon began buying more "trick instruments," including a slide trumpet, which Mason remembered Armstrong playing on "Wang Wang Blues," yet another selection Whiteman recorded for Victor.[31]

Streckfus next introduced the band to "La Veeda," a "Castilian Fox-Trot" recorded by the Green Brothers' Novelty Band and released on Victor in June 1920. Armstrong chose to perform it as a duet with Marable. "Louie Armstrong stood up alone and played his first trumpet solo accompanied with the piano," Streckfus said. "This was the first time. The applause and requests were so outstanding, they repeated the number."[32]

In addition to his cornet, slide whistle, and slide trumpet solos, Armstrong was also now letting his personality flower in the band's nightly performances, especially on the song "Don't Take Away Those Blues," published in June 1920. "Anyway, the Captain used to insist on somebody singing and of course, Louis tried to sing on there one day," Mason said. "And he got to sing the words and of course, he forgot the words and that's where he start doing all that garbling up and scatting!"[33] Armstrong probably hadn't done this type of nonsense singing since his days with the quartet, but it made an impression on the dancers—and quite possibly on the band's violinist/saxophonist, Boyd Atkins.

Armstrong's personality also came out in different, non-musical ways. "Louis also had a lot to do with the popularizing of jazz words," Dodds said. "He used certain expressions on the riverboats, like 'Come on, you cats,' and 'Look out, there, Pops,' and the like. These were his own ideas. I had never heard such words as 'jive' and 'cat and 'scat' used in New Orleans."[34]

Armstrong also dusted off his old comedic talents from the quartet days. "On the boat, he used to dance, shadow-box, everything," trombonist William "Bebe" Ridgely said. "[It was] just in him. The Lord just gave Louis that talent."[35] All of these facets of the new, more confident Armstrong would soon flower in his hometown in one of the few remaining night spots to feature his kind of music: Tom Anderson's.

During the halcyon days of the red-light district, Thomas C. Anderson was known as the "Mayor of Storyville." Though he served as a state legislator in Baton Rouge for 16 years and was one-time president of the Liberty Oil Company, his heart belonged to the District. After years of running Anderson's Arlington Annex, named after the celebrated madam Josie Arlington, he opened a restaurant at 125 North Rampart, using the property to run a brothel upstairs. In 1919, Anderson became one of three cabaret owners charged with "operating an immoral resort within ten miles of a naval camp," the others being Harry Brooks of the Pup and Joseph Crucia of the Cadillac. Anderson claimed he had no knowledge of such an operation and was discharged after two highly publicized trials, with the *Times-Picayune* calling it a "nauseous episode."[36]

Anderson celebrated his victory by bringing music back to North Rampart Street in May 1920. "Jazz music and the 'shimmy' were trumps Friday night at 'Anderson's,'" the *Times-Picayune* reported. The owners of the Pup and the Cadillac were also acquitted in their trials and quickly followed suit. "Opening of 'Anderson's' is to be followed, rumor says, by a general 're-jazzing' of other cabarets which formerly comprised the 'gay white way' of New Orleans," the *Picayune* continued.[37]

Anderson's restaurant featured the music of the Maple Leaf Orchestra, which included young clarinetist Albert Nicholas. This was a reading band, still using the "red back book" of ragtime arrangements that had been popular in the city for nearly a decade. "I was amazed when Louie came off that boat and come around to Tom Anderson's and sat in with us," Nicholas said. "We had that red book, man. He didn't miss a note!" Nicholas didn't know Louis Armstrong personally but had been following his progress since first spotting him with the Waif's Home band. "When he came out [of the Waif's Home], he couldn't read nothing," Nicholas continued. "When he come off that boat, he was reading his ass off."[38]

Anderson's also featured a quartet with violinist Paul Dominguez, drummer Albert Francis, his wife Edna on piano, and Arnold Metoyer on cornet. When Metoyer left, Francis lobbied to get Armstrong, having heard about his reputation with Marable. "He was on the river there playing on the Steamer *Capitol*, when the captain, he'd go out there and he'd get them records, you know, and he'd want them to play like them records," Francis said. "He'd play it once and Louie heard it—and that's all. And the band would be around there playing, and you see the trombone player miss his part, Louie would grab his horn and make it for him. He heard it. I'm telling you, he was wonderful. Louie was wonderful."[39]

Tom Anderson himself was keeping a low profile after two trials, so Armstrong mainly worked for Anderson's son-in-law George Delsa, who reminded him of comedian Lou Costello; in fact, for a time, newspapers reported the name of the establishment as "the Delsa, former Tom Anderson's."[40] "We used to make more tips than our salary," Armstrong said of working there. He had come a long way since the days when he would dig food out of garbage cans for his family, but he wasn't too proud to refuse the leftovers of Anderson's wealthy clientele. "I being a dear friend to all the colored waiters in the house, and they had to pass the bandstand as they brought those dead soldiers (left overs) to the kitchen, they would look straight into my eyes as they passed, and I would give them that well known wink," he remembered. "Wow......When we would take intermission, I would make a bee line straight to the kitchen, and there would be, all of this fine food waiting for me to partake....Yum Yum."[41]

Armstrong was also happy from a musical perspective. "We played all sorts of arrangements from the Easiest to the Hardest-And from the Sweetest to the Hottest," he said of this band."[42] He felt Dominguez was "the best violinist in town" and said Edna Francis and her later replacement, Wilhelmina Bart, both "played a whole lot of piano. Much better than some men I've heard through the years."[43] "Paul Dominguez was good, my wife was good, all of us could read," Albert Francis said. "All of us could read. I used to get them piano copies, you know I'd write for them, you know, just drop it down. [Armstrong] read good there."[44]

As for his own contributions, Armstrong said, "They featured me in trumpet solos."[45] He had clearly grown confident in his solo abilities since joining Marable and was now comfortable being the only horn in the ensemble. "Yeah, he was always good," Francis said. "He don't make no mistakes. Every note he made, he's going to make something to correspond with it. He got a good ear. He'd play 15 choruses, all of them are going to be different. He know his self."[46]

It's not known exactly when Armstrong began playing at Anderson's, though it had to have been when he was stationed in New Orleans between October 1920 and May 1921. "During the times I wasn't playing on the boat, I would take odd jobs, here and there," he wrote before specifically dating his time at Anderson's as "the year of 1921."[47]

Armstrong continued to play excursions on the *Capitol* in New Orleans in early 1921, and that was where he met a 16-year-old white trombonist from Vernon, Texas, named Jack Teagarden. Teagarden, in town looking for musicians to join Peck Kelly's band in Texas, described this life-changing moment in 1944:

> In the small hours, a friend and I were wandering around the French quarter, when suddenly I heard a trumpet in the distance. I couldn't see anything but an excursion boat gliding through the mist back to port. Then the tune became more distinct. The boat was still far off. But in the bow I could see a Negro standing in the wind holding a trumpet high and sending out the most brilliant notes I had ever heard. It was jazz; it was what I had been hoping to hear all through the night. I don't even know whether it was "Tiger Rag" or "Panama." But it was Louis Armstrong descending the sky like a god.[48]

Armstrong and Teagarden didn't get to play music together during this brief meeting, but they would rectify that in a major way in the ensuing decades, becoming musical brothers in the process.

Armstrong's third summer season with Marable was spent almost entirely in St. Louis, where he had a happy reunion with Joe Oliver before the older man headed to California in June.[49] "When Joe Oliver Came from Chicago down to St Louis to hear me play the trumpet, and spend four days of his vacation with me as my personal Guest, [Captain Joseph Streckfus] got a big boot - out of watching Joe Oliver's expressions and admiration, as he watched me play," Armstrong fondly recalled.[50]

But according to Stella Oliver, her husband had an ulterior motive: "He went to try to coax Louis to leave the boat," she said. Louis demurred at this time, telling Oliver that "he would come if he got a good job," but in honesty, he was probably apprehensive about going to California, having already turned Kid Ory down in 1919. While discussing this St. Louis visit, Stella said, "I have a picture of it here of Louis and Joe," producing a famous studio photo of the two that had long been assumed to be taken later in Chicago.[51] Multiple prints of the photo were made and it's possible that Armstrong kept one, too, using it to remember where he came from—while daydreaming of a potential future opportunity to once again make music with his mentor.

Oliver was clearly in a poaching mood during this trip; David Jones would soon join him in California and Baby Dodds would follow in September after he quit Marable. Yet Armstrong didn't—even though he quit around the same time they did.

Figure 15.2 Famous studio portrait of Louis Armstrong and Joe Oliver, which, according to Stella Oliver, was taken in St. Louis while Oliver was visiting his protégé on the riverboat in the spring of 1921.

Credit: The William Russell Jazz Collection at The Historic New Orleans Collection, acquisition made possible by the Clarisse Claiborne Grima Fund, acc. no. 92-48-L.331.956.

Armstrong never offered a sufficient explanation of why he chose to quit Marable's band, but Baby Dodds did. According to Dodds, the Streckfus brothers once again tried to interfere with the sound of the band, but this time they went too far.

In the summer of 1921, there were whispers of a new dance craze, the "toddle." Famed "dancing master" Arthur Murray initially refused to teach it, but he gave in, publishing a long treatise on the subject, complete with photos, during the first week of July. Murray noted that both the one-step and the waltz had "lost favor" because they were "tiresome and very strenuous compared with the 'Toddle.'. . . In 'toddling,' you take the regular Fox Trot step, then rise up and come down at the finish of each step. The bouncing movement comes after the step is taken."[52]

The always astute Streckfuses must have picked up Murray's article, possibly reading it in the *St. Louis Star and Times* on July 3, and decided to act, demanding that the Marable band introduce "toddle time." "It was really two-four time but he wanted four beats to the measure," Dodds said. "It's what they are doing today. To me, four beats was all wrong. It has a tendency to speed up the music. But for the older people it was easier since instead of dancing to a step they would just bounce around." The band struggled during rehearsals. "I just couldn't do this toddle time on my drums," Dodds said, adding, "Louis couldn't do what they wanted him to do either." They appealed to Fate Marable to no avail. "Well, Fate Marable had been with Streckfus so long that anything Streckfus asked for he'd tell us to do, even if it meant breaking our necks," Dodds said.[53]

Dodds and Armstrong took stock of the situation and made what must have been a very difficult decision. "Well, we were the stars on the boat and we felt that if we were the stars, why monkey with us," Dodds said. "We had already made a reputation with our music and the people were satisfied. So finally Louis and I left the boat together after handing in written resignations. That was about the first of September, 1921." Losing Armstrong and Dodds was a tremendous blow to the Marable band, but the Streckfuses were determined to get their way. When Marable left the *Capitol* in September, they were replaced by the Ten Capitol Harmony Syncopators, who billed themselves as "The Toddle Kings of the Mississippi."[54]

"Toddle-time" was likely not the only reason Armstrong and Dodds left. Johnny St. Cyr also quit the band in 1921, later saying, "And that year, Fate got ugly with the boys." St. Cyr had been with the band since 1918 and told Marable, "When you were trying to induce us to come on the boat, you didn't talk that talk. You was very nice." St. Cyr had grown especially tired of Marable always threatening "Captain Joe is on the boat!" anytime the musicians were relaxing or laughing. "I've been used to playing music, laughing, and joking," St. Cyr told Marable. "When it gets to a place where I've got to sit up like a stale pie with a frown on my face like I was going to somebody's funeral, I just can't play music in that mood."

The detailed explanations St. Cyr and Dodds gave of why they left make Armstrong's silence especially conspicuous. Only in *Swing That Music* did he state, "But I was getting tired of the routine on the boat and ready for a change, so I decided to join the orchestra at Tom Anderson's cabaret."[55] But Albert Francis, the drummer in the band at Tom Anderson's, recalled, "And they had a humbug so Louie quit [Marable] and we hired Louie." Francis even remembered a letter Marable wrote to Armstrong, stating, "Out of all the cornet players, you're the best I've got. I'll give you everything in the world to come back and play this job." "Louie said no," Francis said. "Louie wouldn't go."[56]

"There was a saying in New Orleans," drummer Zutty Singleton once said. "When some musician would get a job on the riverboats with Fate Marable, they'd say, 'Well you're going to the conservatory.'"[57] Armstrong's three seasons with Marable represented his conservatory years in every sense of the word. He entered the world of the riverboats in 1919, armed with only a trout sandwich and a jar of olives, unable to read arrangements, too bashful to take a featured solo, derided for puffing when he blew, all while doing his best to ignore racist comments from ignorant passengers. By 1921, he was reading, soloing, singing, scatting, dancing, playing slide whistle and slide trumpet, doing comedy, coining slang, inspiring youngsters, and "descending the sky like a god" in the words of Jack Teagarden.

Armstrong knew how far he had come. "I had played on the boat for two full years by then, and traveled about five thousand miles in all," he said. "Playing and practicing day and night, and the experience of playing to hundreds of crowds, had done a lot for me. I could read music very well by now and was getting hotter and hotter on my trumpet."[58]

Marable would continue leading bands for the Streckfus company until his passing in 1947, with several great musicians passing through his ranks, including Earl Bostic, Jimmie Blanton, Gene Sedric, and Clark Terry. But Armstrong's departure—and the departure of Dodds, St. Cyr, David Jones, and Pops Foster—marked the end of his greatest era. "I often think what a shame it was that our riverboat band never recorded," Baby Dodds said. "If they had, people would really have heard something pretty."[59] St. Cyr agreed, saying, "If this band ever recorded I am sure the records would still stand up today." In St. Cyr's estimation, the only recording "that sounded much like we did" was Fletcher Henderson's 1924 version of "Mandy, Make Up Your Mind," with Armstrong featured on cornet. It's telling that Henderson, for his reputation as a cutting-edge pioneer of African American dance music, was just catching up to the sounds of what the Marable band was doing five years earlier.

As for Armstrong, he was once asked during a radio interview in 1953, "Tell me one thing about the early days, your first big job—was that in New Orleans or in Chicago with King Oliver?"

"Well, no," he replied, "I'd say the big-time job for me was in 1919, when I went on the boat."[60] Armstrong would go on to have some major experiences in the music business, but never forgot that those years with Marable truly represented his first taste of the "big-time."

16

"Son, You Got a Chance"

1921–1922

Armstrong must have known he was taking a risk by leaving the secure employment of the Marable band. With the closing of Storyville and the onset of Prohibition, the jazz scene in New Orleans was not the same in 1921 as it had been just a few years earlier. Many of Armstrong's friends and contemporaries were now living and playing in either Chicago or San Francisco. Only the "Tango Belt" section of town, consisting of cabarets such as Tom Anderson's, the Cadillac, and the Orchard, regularly featured his style of music.

Armstrong thought about going back to Tom Anderson's but said it "had closed down for repairs" in this period.[1] He had at least saved up a little money from his riverboat days that could last him until he could get back on his feet. "Things were rather slow all during the year of 1921," he wrote. "Other than my last season on the excursion boats, which gave me a few dollars to kind of Skate on until something decent happened..."[2]

Those "few dollars" allowed Armstrong to live opulently for perhaps the first time in his life. "I went over to Louis's house," Arthur "Zutty" Singleton said. "He was unpacking his suitcase [from the riverboats] and showed me some underwear he got in St. Louis. All the colors you could think of, red and blue and green, and all of them with a big 'A' crocheted on the chest. Man, that was the sharpest underwear I ever saw."[3]

Singleton was now playing drums regularly, though he had recently been fired for fighting at Tom's Road House. While carrying his drums home, he ran into Norman J. "Butsy" Hernandez, proprietor of the Orchard Cabaret—also known as the Orchid—at 942 Conti Street. Hernandez was a larger-than-life New Orleans figure, known as the city's "greatest barefisted street fighter," the owner of over 100 thoroughbreds, the founder of the Terminal Taxicab Company, the bodyguard of Huey P. Long, an associate of Al Capone, and much more.

Hernandez asked Singleton to put together a four-piece band to play regularly at the Orchard. Singleton immediately signed up pianist Udell Wilson and, fresh from the riverboats, Johnny St. Cyr and Armstrong. However, according to drummer Rudolph Beaulieu, Hernandez was auditioning different bands and asked Beaulieu to put together a combo, too. Beaulieu did so and performed two numbers for Hernandez. "So the next band that comes in is Louis Armstrong," Beaulieu said. "Well, I certainly knew I was out of work now! It's all over. I know he was going to get the job, you know. . . . I ain't never heard trumpet playing like that before in all my days, not even as yet."[4] Armstrong quickly won Hernandez over, too. "Old Butsy Hernandez, boy, he loved Louis," Singleton said."[5] The feeling was mutual, as Armstrong later referred to Hernandez as "one of the nicest fellows alive."[6] In a 1972 profile on his many accomplishments, Hernandez claimed he "got [Armstrong] started in show business."[7]

The Orchard Cabaret engagement solidified the close friendship between Armstrong and Singleton. "We would meet every morning and get our doughnuts and root beer," Singleton said. "We would walk uptown. He would go to see his girl and I would stand outside and wait."[8]

Though not explicit, it's quite probable that Louis's "girl" was not his wife, Daisy Parker.

Daisy had taken Louis to court in February 1920 to receive financial support during their separation, but on January 12, 1921, she wrote a letter to the district attorney withdrawing all charges against her husband.[9] They might have temporarily reconciled at this point, but it's also plausible that they never lived together full-time again. In their eventual divorce papers, Louis claimed that "on or about" February 15, 1921, Daisy "willfully and without any reasonable cause therefore deserted and abandoned [Louis], and wholly refused to live and inhabit with him any longer as husband and wife," stating that they had not lived together "for the span of 2 years and upward."[10] Daisy responded that her husband had it backward and that on February 15, 1921, he was the one who "had deserted and abandoned the defendant and that his testimony to the contrary was false and perjured."[11]

Armstrong never referenced these separations directly, but he hinted at them between the lines of his writing. For example, he wrote, "During this year [1921], my wife Daisy [adopted] a little girl by the name of Wila Mae Wilson," instead of "we adopted."[12] Willie Mae was born in Plaquemine, Louisiana, in 1908 and moved in with Daisy after her mother died. Louis referred to Willie Mae as his "godchild" when she visited him at his Queens home 1953, but when it came to Daisy, he maintained, "That's who raised her."[13]

"Daisy was very fond of Wila Mae... which was a surprise to me," Louis wrote. "Because Daisy never did take to anybody very much...She did not care for people very much...Lots of times, she did not care very much for even mee...But I loved her and she loved me...So that was it."[14] Though it's almost assured that Louis and Daisy had occasional reunions of an intimate nature, Louis spent the better part of late 1921 and early 1922 avoiding his wife at all costs. Singleton recalled playing a "big parade" with Louis and the Tuxedo Brass Band. "Louis had a girl, Daisy, very, very bad and tough," Singleton said. "The parade was supposed to pass in front of her house. He left the band at the corner, run around the block, and joined us at the next corner."[15]

Aside from avoiding Daisy, Armstrong was honored to be asked to join Oscar "Papa" Celestin's Tuxedo Brass Band in the "latter part of 1921" after serving as a sub for a few years. "Yes...I became a full fledge member," he wrote. "A treat I 'still cherrish [*sic*]....I really felt that I was somebody...And I also had gained to the hight [*sic*] of one of my real ambitions."[16] Armstrong felt a sense of pride working with Celestin, saying, "When ever I had a funeral to play with the Tuxedo Brass Band—I'd feel just as proud as if John Phillip Sousa or Arthur Pryor or one of those boys would have hired me."[17] Armstrong admitted he did not have "too much brass band experience" but was excited to put his much-improved reading ability to the test. "When they would pass out the brass band music, on those cards, so's you could read the music as you walk along, and when they'd hand me my book, Geeeeee—I felt important," he said. "As young in the game as I was, I saw to it that I played my part very much right, and did not miss a note."[18]

Amos White was in the Tuxedo Band and remembered Armstrong frequently declaring, "I want to learn to play the music." "And he really scrambled hard to learn to play," White said.[19] To those who heard the band, the effort paid off. "I remember when Louis Armstrong was here, he was playing in the Tuxedo Brass Band at that time," trombonist Joseph "Red" Clark remembered. "And they used to play 'Panama' and he used to make that high note."[20] Drummer Abbey "Chinee" Foster said Armstrong's playing was "what helped make that Tuxedo band."[21] Rudolph Beaulieu remembered the Tuxedo Band playing "The Sheik of Araby," a brand-new pop tune that was published in December 1921. "Ain't nobody ever played 'The Sheik of Araby' like that," Beaulieu remembered. "[Armstrong] covered Papa Celestin and that other trumpet man they had, I believe it was Peter Bocage from over the river, he covered them two when he pull up his horn. Ooh! I never heard a trumpet man like that since I've been playing and never before. Gentlemen, I'm telling you, that was murder."[22]

Armstrong's big sound and ability to "cover" the cornetists in the band—including its leader, Celestin—created a stir. Bassist Joseph "One Eyed Babe" Phillips said, "Louis was so strong, people used to tell him all the time that he should be blowing the first trumpet." Armstrong had too much respect for

Celestin to show the older man up or ask to play first. "I can't go be a boss under that man," Armstrong told Phillips. "I just want my money."[23]

As Armstrong's reputation grew, he became an in-demand sub with the city's other popular brass bands, always making an impact—and always gaining food for thought—with each parade he played. "They were musicians among musicians," he said in 1950. "You'd get in some of those brass bands, sometimes you didn't even know who you were going to play with. But they'd give you that part and you'd instill your heart in it."[24]

One of the bands Armstrong sometimes played with in this period was the Excelsior Brass Band, led by cornetist George Moret, known as "Old Man" Moret because he was born around 1868. "And that old man was one of the strongest, prettiest, tone trumpet players you ever listen to in your life," cornetist Amos White said, "but couldn't fake a dot. And he couldn't improvise nothing. He played it just like it was."[25]

Armstrong was especially inspired by Moret's ability to hit high notes. "That man was in his sixties and every time that band stopped, he had that top note. I admired that."[26] Armstrong also picked up one of his future trademarks from watching Moret closely. "And I used to notice every time he was gonna hit a high note, he would just slightly look up and here come that note, see?" Armstrong said. "And I admired that so well that I adopted the style myself. So, anytime I want a high note, I usually [visualize imaginary] shelves. Say, there's a D, there's an E, there's an F, and things like that, I live by that and that's the way I play today. And that's why I very seldom miss them!"[27] Thus, the iconic image of Armstrong looking skyward while reaching for a high note was simply a case of him emulating Moret.

Punch Miller remembered a parade with Armstrong, Kid Rena, and himself on cornet that, one could argue, changed the course of New Orleans brass band music. "After one big parade one day, we come back playing, you know, the usual stuff on the street . . . and [drummer] Henry [Martin] decided to play some blues, play them fast, you know, up, up," Miller said. "And we come back playing the blues at an uptempo you know where you could walk right along with it, see. And boy, boy, boy, after that, all the bands started playing blues on the streets!" Over 100 years later, the blues remains a staple of New Orleans brass band repertoire, but Miller stressed that "it started with Henry Martin and Black Benny, they're the ones that started that. They told us to light out on a blues and we did it."[28]

In addition to his drumming, Black Benny now served as a reminder of Armstrong's old Liberty and Perdido Street neighborhood, where not much had changed in terms of crime; Black Benny alone was arrested five times between September 18 and November 15, 1921, including once for "disturbing the peace, using obscene language, reviling the police." During his teenage years, Armstrong marveled at how Black Benny could travel to any part of the city and "nobody would dare bother him." To Armstrong, Williams accomplished this feat because "He was just that tough, and was not afraid of a living soul."[29]

Armstrong envied that kind of freedom, but he wanted to earn it through his music, not his toughness. Thanks to his popularity with the Tuxedo Brass Band, he claimed that by 1922, he "could go to any parts of New Orleans playing my cornet, and nobody bothered me." As he later put it, "From the toughest to the nicest, they all loved me."[30]

Armstrong's gregarious sense of humor also went a long way toward making friends. "All of my life from a kid, I could always see the humarous [*sic*] side of life," he said. He fondly remembered the moments he'd spend eating poor boy sandwiches with the older members of the Tuxedo Brass Band as they waited to play a funeral. "And I would have them holding their side, laughing at my sayings, matched with theirs," he said.[31] "He was wonderful," Albert Francis said of Armstrong. "And never get angry. Calm, always happy. Always happy."[32]

Armstrong's generous spirit was also in place by the age of 21. He reunited with Francis at Tom Anderson's around this time, leaving Zutty Singleton and the Orchard Cabaret. "Louis quit me to make more money," Singleton said. "We were making $21, and he quit for $23, and went to Anderson's."[33] The $23 salary was just a start; Anderson's clientele also tipped exceptionally well. "I made so much money I didn't know what to do with it," he said of working at Anderson's, now also known as "The Real Thing." "I'd go down town to some big store and buy a lot of things just to be buying... Checker boards and such silly stuff like that... And give them away to some poor enthusiastic kid of my neighborhood—who couldn't afford to buy a 'poor boy sandwich' let lone things of that sort."[34]

Such generosity would be a hallmark of Louis's character for the rest of his life. "If you had a hard luck story and you needed something and you came to Louis, you got it," his fourth wife, Lucille, recalled. She added:

> But this is a throwback. It's been instilled in him in the old days in New Orleans when Louis was a youth coming up. Because that's what they did, not because they didn't have that kind of money, but if a person had five or eight or ten dollars—which was a lot of money back in 1914 and '15—they would . . . give you a dollar or fifty cents. It had happened to Louis. He had been given. It was a way of life down there. They were all poor. And the one that had a little more than the other saw to it that the one that has less had a little bit. So he never outgrew it.[35]

Armstrong's generous spirit, quick wit, pleasing personality, and prodigious work ethic—and talent—made Mayann Armstrong prouder than ever of her son; she couldn't say the same of her daughter, who was now regularly involved in the Third Ward's dangerous gambling scene, carrying a Barlow pocketknife to protect herself. On March 10, 1922, Beatrice Donald—her married name since marrying George Donald in 1919—was one of 11 people arrested at 1316 Girod Street "relative to gambling with cards for money."

But a gambling arrest was nothing compared to what lay in store for her. On September 2, 1923, Mama Lucy was arrested for "fighting and disturbing the peace." She gave her address as 445 South Franklin, among the row of boarding houses used for prostitution where her mother had once been arrested. The police noted her alias as "Mama Lou" and now listed her occupation as "Prostitute." Aside from following in her mother's footsteps, Mama Lucy was back in jail less than a month later—and this time, in the newspapers as well.

"NEGRO SHOT BY NEGRESS" blared the headline in the *New Orleans Item* on October 1, 1923. "Henry Gray, negro, 21, 445 South Franklin street, was shot at three times, one bullet taking effect in his left leg by Beatrice Donald, 20, 445 South Franklin street. According to the police Beatrice was jealous. She was arrested and charged in the first precinct with shooting and wounding. Gray was taken to the Charity hospital where his condition was reported not serious."[36] Once free, Mama Lucy didn't learn her lesson and was arrested again on July 29, 1924, "relative to shooting and wounding." Arrests followed for fighting and disturbing the peace on July 6, 1925, and April 2, 1926; both times she was listed as a prostitute, the second time with a note of her "Alias, Mama Lucy."

By 1927, Beatrice and George Donald had moved to Pensacola, Florida, where Mama Lucy got work cooking and cleaning at a sawmill. Of course, she also found an outside source of income. "They had a little gambling session down there, making all kinds of money," Louis said of his sister and brother-in-law.[37]

For her part, Mayann wasn't doing much better in the early 1920s. After she passed four relatively peaceful years without getting arrested, the police nabbed her for "loitering" in the early hours of April 24, 1921. She gave her occupation as "cook" but a closer read of the police record shows that she was arrested along with two women who identified, respectively, as "launderess" and "house keeper" and that all three were arrested for "loitering" after midnight on South Franklin Street. Perhaps Mayann was working as a cook in the daytime, but she still needed to turn to prostitution in times of need.

But here was Louis, working steadily, earning good money, making friends, excelling at his instrument. Mayann did not want her son to waste this opportunity.

"Son, you got a chance," she told him. "Don't blow it."[38]

Louis would soon get such a chance—and he wouldn't take it.

History was made inside the brand-new radio station WGV in New Orleans on April 21, 1922. "Every shoulder twitched and every foot beat time Friday evening among the people who crowded the rooms of WGV, The Item-Interstate radio broadcasting station, when Ethel Waters, the nationally known negro singer, and her famous Black Swan jazz masters opened up on the radio transmitter," the *New Orleans Item* reported.[39] This marked the first time jazz music was broadcast over the airwaves in New Orleans—and perhaps anywhere. Waters was in town to play the Lyric Theater with her "Black Swan Troubadours," capitalizing on the popularity and success of another recent cultural breakthrough: "race records."

In 1920, Fred Hager of OKeh Records had heard Mamie Smith sing in Harlem and had an epiphany. "I believe that the Colored people would like to have phonograph records of singers like this," Hager said. "They would like to hear their own stars sing in their own way."[40] On August 10, 1920, Smith recorded "Crazy Blues," backed by Perry Bradford's Jazz Fools. The result was not only a smash hit from a sales perspective but represented a significant shift in African American culture. "Mamie was famous overnight," the *Chicago Defender* wrote. "Never before had it been possible to obtain phonograph records of real Race music, and Mamie became the country's darling the moment her first record was heard."[41]

Thanks to the success of "Crazy Blues," African American songwriters Harry Pace and W. C. Handy began seeing a bump in their music publishing business, requiring them to hire a pianist to serve as a song demonstrator. The man they chose was Fletcher Henderson.

Born on December 18, 1897, in Cuthbert, Georgia, Fletcher Hamilton Henderson Jr. had an upbringing that could be considered the polar opposite of Louis Armstrong's. Both of Henderson's parents were accomplished classical pianists, and his father, Fletcher Sr., was a distinguished professor, proficient in mathematics and Latin. Fletcher Jr. started piano lessons at the age of six but was more interested in chemistry, graduating with a Bachelor of Arts degree from Atlanta University in June 1920. Henderson hoped to continue his chemistry studies at Columbia University but while in New York City, he got a job as a pianist on a riverboat, subbing for a sick friend who couldn't make the gig. After becoming the band's regular pianist, Henderson began working for Pace and Handy, heralding the end of his chemistry career.

Henderson was in the right place at the right time for the boom of race records. "Colored singing and playing artists are riding to fame and fortune with the current popular demand for 'blues' disk recordings and because of the recognized fact that only a Negro can do justice to the native indigo ditties such artists are in great demand," *Variety* stated, noting that major labels such as Victor and OKeh were now regularly recording African American talent.[42]

Harry Pace was watching this trend intently and believed African Americans should have a label of their own. In January 1921, he withdrew from his partnership with Handy and formed Black Swan Records, instituting Henderson as his musical director. After some ragtime and novelty numbers failed to make an impression, Henderson discovered vocalist Ethel Waters and asked her to record for the label. Her recording of "Down Home Blues" and "Oh Daddy" sold over 118,000 copies, making it Black Swan's first smash hit.

Pace now figured that if the public was excited to buy recordings of African Americans, they would be even more excited to see them perform in live settings. He booked Waters, Henderson, and a small band of "Black Swan Troubadours" on an extended tour that began on October 17, 1921. The group reached New Orleans in April 1922, breaking the box office record at the Lyric, billed as "America's Largest and Finest Colored Theatre."[43]

In their off-hours, Henderson and Waters hit the town in search of good music, eventually finding one musician who possessed something unique enough to potentially shake things up back in New York. "It was back in 1922, down in New Orleans, when I heard this young man playing the trumpet in a little dance hall," Henderson recalled. "I was accompanist for Ethel Waters, who was the headline attraction of the Lyric theater [*sic*], and I decided that that youthful trumpeter would be great in our act. I asked him his name and found he was Louis Armstrong."[44]

Henderson described Armstrong as "just a nice, enthusiastic youngster, blowing a great horn in a small band in New Orleans" and said, "the power and imaginativeness of his horn immediately made me want him for my band."[45] The scene of this moment must have been Tom Anderson's as it was clearly remembered by Albert Francis. "And a woman came here, Ethel Waters, wanted to take [Armstrong] off," Francis said. "She had Fletcher Henderson playing piano."[46] Henderson said, "So right then and there I offered him a job."[47]

This was a potentially life-changing opportunity, but Armstrong didn't immediately accept; instead, he bought time by coming up with an excuse. "Louis told me that he would have to speak to his drummer, because he couldn't possibly leave without him," Henderson said.[48] The drummer in question was not Albert Francis but Zutty Singleton. "I had another gig with Zutty, we was playing at Butsy Hernandez's place, Fletcher sends me a wire to come join the band, and I wouldn't go because he didn't take Zutty," Armstrong said.[49] Singleton remembered it the same way. "Fletcher Henderson sent for Louis and Louis showed me the telegram that Fletcher wanted Louis to join him in New York," he said. "And old Louis told me, he said, 'I'm not going if you don't go.' So we went to the telegraph office and we sent Fletcher a night letter, see, explaining everything to him."[50] Henderson finally wrote back, "Well, I've got my own drums," rescinding the offer.[51]

The question remains: if Henderson said yes to Armstrong and Singleton, would they both have left New Orleans? Or was it a ploy by Armstrong to demand something he knew would result in a rejection so he wouldn't have the burden of turning down the opportunity himself?

Deep down, Armstrong knew that there was only one man who was going to get him to leave New Orleans and it was not Henderson or Singleton. "I wouldn't leave New Orleans until Joe Oliver sent for me," he said.[52]

Oliver had kept in touch with Armstrong since leaving for California in June 1921, sending him a publicity photo of his band taken in San Francisco in September of that year. Armstrong spotted Oliver's pianist, Lillian Hardin, and wrote back, "Tell Miss Lil I like her."[53] Oliver might have also shared some details about his California sojourn, which likely relieved Armstrong, as he had made the right decision by not joining him.

Oliver performed an extended engagement at the Pergola dancing pavilion in San Francisco. That city was already home to Art Hickman's popular, reed-heavy dance band and Oliver knew he'd have to compete with that sound. He expanded from the sextet he fronted in Chicago to an octet at the Pergola, adding violinist James Palao and saxophonist David Jones. It wasn't enough. "And as famous as the band was, the people didn't understand our music and they couldn't dance by it," Hardin remembered.[54]

A low point occurred during a date at the California Theater. Oliver was billing his band as "King Oliver's Creole Band," a nod to the one-time popularity of Bill Johnson's old Original Creole Band. Drummer Baby Dodds had recently joined the band and remembered hearing "some little smart guy in the audience shout, 'I thought you said those guys were Creoles. Those guys are no Creoles. Those are niggers!' "[55]

Soon afterward, as the band continued struggling, some members went back to Chicago, while others stayed behind to grab any work they could find. For a time, Kid Ory and Oliver reunited to perform twice a week at a dance hall in Oakland. In April 1922, Oliver even connected with pianist and composer Jelly Roll Morton, who had been out West since 1917. Soon afterward, Oliver received "the highest salary ever known to a cornet player for a night's work" for a single evening's performance at the Hiawatha Club in Los Angeles, as described by "Ragtime" Billy Tucker in the *Chicago Defender*: "As an extra added attraction we are featuring 'King' Joe Oliver, the world's greatest cornetist, who is in town en route to Chicago. . . . I'll 'chirp' to the whole continent he set Los Angeles on fire. The public says he is the greatest that has ever been in Los Angeles, and some mighty 'hot babies' have had the good fortune to visit Los Angeles in the past year. You'll have to hand it to King Oliver."[56]

After a turbulent year out west, Oliver, accompanied by Baby Dodds, Johnny Dodds, and San Francisco–born pianist Bertha Bookman, headed back to Chicago to perform at the refurbished Royal Gardens, now known as the Lincoln Gardens. Trombonist Honore Dutrey agreed to return to the fold and Bill Johnson would join on bass.[57] As Tucker's report made clear, Oliver, "the world's greatest cornetist," was apparently still blowing strong horn. But as he prepared for his return to Chicago, a thought crossed his mind that perhaps employing a second cornetist would strengthen his band. He knew who to ask: Henry "Kid" Rena.

"Kid Rena had a bigger reputation than Louis Armstrong," Alexander Bigard remembered. "Just [said] he didn't want to go away. He had the best opportunity of his life. They were begging him to come to Chicago. King Oliver wanted to send for him instead of Louie."[58]

At least that's the way Bigard remembered it. But if Rena indeed was offered the opportunity and turned it down because he didn't want to leave home, that left an opening to be filled by only one other cornetist: George "Little Mitch" Mitchell.

Born in 1899 in Louisville, Kentucky, Mitchell had sat in with Oliver at Dreamland in Chicago before moving to Milwaukee in the early 1920s. "And that's where [Oliver] enlarged his band and he didn't know where I was," Mitchell said. "He said he would have, when he was enlarging his band, he was going to put me in there. . . . [T]hat's before Louis come. But [Oliver] didn't know where I was at that time, I guess, when he was looking. But afterwards, why, he sent for Louis."[59]

If the stories Bigard and Mitchell told are true, they raise more questions than they answer. Stella Oliver was certain that her husband visited Armstrong on the riverboat to "coax" him to join his band in 1921. And Armstrong himself recalled that Oliver "kept sending me telegrams and letters to come up to Chicago, join his band, and play second cornet to him."[60] But when it came time to officially hiring a second cornetist on his return to Chicago, there's a strong possibility Oliver didn't ask Armstrong first. Why the hesitation?

The simplest answer could be a combination of ego and self-doubt. Oliver was now the "King" and in his mind, Armstrong may have still been "Little Louis," the barefoot kid who would come to his house for lessons and hold his cornet during parades. He might not have been fully aware of how much his protege had improved since he'd last heard him. White cornetist Paul Mares had played on a Streckfus riverboat opposite Armstrong before he moved to Chicago in the early 1920s and formed the New Orleans Rhythm Kings. One day Mares went up to Oliver and told him, "There's a kid down there in New Orleans. If he ever comes up here, you're dead."[61] He was referring to Armstrong.

Perhaps that was enough to give Oliver pause. He was already starting to have some trouble with his teeth—what if Armstrong came up to Chicago and outplayed and outgunned the "King"? That might have inspired Oliver to ask around about the availability of other cornetists he might have viewed as non-threatening. But in the end, he knew the right choice was Armstrong, and he sent him a telegram in early July—possibly on his birthday, July 4—asking him to join the band on July 8, 1922.

Armstrong was making good money at Tom Anderson's and staying busy with the brass bands, but he might have sensed that he had gone as far as he could in his hometown. For one thing, with Prohibition raging, the number of police raids of cabarets and other nightspots was increasing. "Police swept through the 'tango belt' below Canal Street and toward Rampart Street Saturday night and Sunday, sending sixteen women to jail," the *New Orleans States* reported on July 3, around the time he received the telegram from Oliver. "Other raids will follow until a general moral cleansing of the Quarter is effected police intimated."[62]

On top of that, he and Daisy had one last brawl on May 16 that resulted in the arrest of not only Daisy and Louis but also Mama Lucy, all three ending up in jail for "disturbing the peace" at Lafayette and Rampart at 2 p.m. Louis and Daisy were still separated at the time of the May arrest, with Daisy telling the police she lived at "Gravier and Franklin," while Louis gave a new address for the first time, 547 Dryades. The details of this incident have not survived, but the police report does note that Louis and Beatrice were discharged quickly, while Daisy was not.

Thus, there was no hesitation when Oliver reached out this time. It was time to leave home.

Armstrong always remembered where he was when he received the fateful telegram: in Algiers, playing the funeral of Henry Vincent, father of Original Creole Band trombonist Eddie Vincent, who had passed away on July 2, 1922.

Armstrong remembered being there with the Tuxedo Brass Band, but cornetist Maurice Durand remembered Armstrong subbing for Manuel Perez in the Onward Band. Durand was uncertain about who was going to show up in Perez's place, until he saw Armstrong coming and shouted, "Here come Dipper!"[63] Armstrong and Durand reminisced about the job in 1951, Armstrong saying, "I remember it just as well because the last hymn we placed was 'Abide With Me' when they was bringing the body out of the house."[64]

When Armstrong started talking about Oliver's offer, some of the musicians present warned him that he was making a mistake.

"You shouldn't go to Chicago because King Oliver's band is out of the union now and they're scabbin'," one told him.

"Whatever King Oliver's doing, I want to do it, too," Armstrong responded.[65]

The way Armstrong told it, he got the telegram, played the funeral, and rushed to the train station, the band going with him to see him off. But Durand remembered that after he paid him, Armstrong left to perform at Tom Anderson's that evening with Paul Dominguez, Albert Francis, and Luis Russell, a piano player from Panama who had arrived in town the year before and would become a close friend and musical associate of Armstrong in the decades to come.[66] Of Armstrong's final night in New Orleans, Albert Francis clearly remembered that "Joe Oliver sent for him" and "He was playing with me that last day."[67]

Armstrong also stopped by the Orchard Cabaret to say farewell to Zutty Singleton. "Zutty, I got to go," Armstrong told his friend. "King Oliver sent for me from Chicago. Man, Baby Dodds is drumming with King Oliver. Man, so I got to go up there. I got to leave you." "I sure hated for him to leave," Singleton recalled.[68] Armstrong might have also shared the news with Butsy Hernandez. In a 1972 profile, Hernandez claimed to have "staked Satchmo to his trip to the big time in Chicago," perhaps insinuating that Hernandez gave Armstrong some money to get on his feet once up north.[69]

Armstrong eventually headed to the train station, joined by many of the city's finest musicians. He knew that some of them disagreed with his decision. "Of course they did not care so much for me to play second cornet to Joe Oliver," he said. "They all thought that I was good enough to go on my own."[70] This is a point Albert Nicholas made in a 1967 interview, saying, "Louis was the greatest thing in New Orleans when [Oliver] sent for Louie. He wasn't doing Louie a favor."[71] Armstrong disagreed. "All my life was wrapped around Joe Oliver," he said. "I lived for Papa Joe. So his calling for me was the biggest feeling I ever had musically."[72]

With some of Armstrong's rival trumpet players, there was also a hint of envy. "We always was playing alike, wasn't no different," Punch Miller said.

"And King Oliver wanted a second trumpet player and instead of me or Buddy Petit and them, he sent for Louis. . . . But any of us who would have went up there would have made it the same time."[73]

Aside from musicians, Armstrong remembered that Mayann was among the crowd that gathered to see her son off, having once again packed him one of her fish sandwiches for the journey. Oscar "Slippers" Johnson, the tough bouncer from Henry Matranga's, also approached Armstrong to deliver a "pep talk." "Look here, son, I like the way you blow that quail," Slippers said, still unaware of the name of Armstrong's instrument. "Now, you go up north and always have a white man behind you to say, 'That's my nigger.' "[74] Armstrong had been through enough in New Orleans—and had called in such favors from Henry Matranga and Captain Joseph Streckfus to get him out of jail—that he probably didn't need such advice, but it was good to be reminded of it one last time before he got on the train.

"Standing there waiting for the train to pull out, many thoughts ran through my mind," Armstrong recalled. "Thoughts that I shall never forget as long as I live."[75] Decades later, he would write these thoughts down and immortalize the "bullies and troublemakers" of his neighborhood, whose only shot at posterity would have otherwise been the reports of their dastardly deeds in newspapers and arrest records of the time. Armstrong managed to humanize them and let the world know that he was a product of his community, and he would not forget or apologize for where he came from.

He had just celebrated his twenty-second birthday, though he was most likely 21, a legal adult who had been working steadily for almost 15 years. He might have been nervous leaving home, but he must have had a sense of satisfaction that he had survived. Survived the broken home, the neglect of his father, the alcohol-fueled disappearances of his mother, the brutality of the police, the racism of the Jim Crow South, the abuses of One Eye Bud and the other bullies, the multiple arrests, the jail time with Sore Dick, the Colored Waif's Home, the food dug out of garbage cans, the street parades in the hot sun, the flying slates hurled by the Great Storm of 1915, the coal cart, the banana boats, the house-wrecking job, the dairy wagon that ran over his foot, the Spanish Flu, the bullets that whizzed past him in the honky-tonks, the knife wound from Nootsy, the vengeance of Cheeky Black, the bricks thrown by Daisy. Not only had he survived, but he had somehow thrived, becoming one of the most respected cornetists in the city.

Armstrong was leaving with a musical education that would get him through the rest of his career. "He was gathering knowledge all the time," Danny Barker said of Armstrong's New Orleans years. "When Louis went to Chicago, Louis was prepared."[76] His cornet style now dipped into four separate buckets: the tone of Bunk Johnson, the fire of Joe Oliver, the high notes of Henry "Kid" Rena, and the harmonic knowledge of Buddy Petit. He had mastered their styles, mastered what was called "jazz," mastered the blues, which he played for countless hours in the honky-tonks.

But there was so much more to his musical upbringing than just blues and jazz: the experience of playing ragtime from the "red back book"; playing waltzes, rhumbas, foxtrots for dancers; learning Art Hickman and Paul Whiteman arrangements directly from the records; interpreting the latest pop music hits in every band he played in; singing and harmonizing with his quartet; scatting and playing slide whistle and slide cornet on the riverboat; instilling his heart into funeral marches with the Tuxedo and Excelsior Brass Bands; humming along with the Yiddish lullabies sung by the Karnofsky family; gobbling up the operatic stylings of Enrico Caruso, Amelita Galli-Curci, and Luisa Tetrazzini on his Victrola; reciting Bert Williams's comedic monologues; singing all those songs about "Katie" and her assorted body parts. Armstrong's goal was to be a complete musician, one who could master every style, and he achieved it by the age of 21.

When a friend spotted him at the train station and asked, "Where are you going, Dipper?" Armstrong responded with pride: "Yeah man, I'm going up to Chicago to play with my idol, Papa Joe."[77]

17

"I Always Played Pretty under Him"

1922

"I arrived in Chicago about eleven o'clock the night of July 8, 1922, I'll never forget it, at the Illinois Central Station at Twelfth and Michigan Avenue," Armstrong recalled in 1947.[1] He had enjoyed the 25-hour train ride as he'd lucked out and found an empty seat next to a woman who was a friend of Mayann—and who was carrying "a big basket of good old southern fried chicken" for her family. Louis "lived and ate like a king, all the way to Chicago."[2]

"All out for Chicago, last stop!" the conductor hollered.

"A funny feeling started running up and down my spine," Armstrong said. By waiting until the evening, he had already missed the early morning train Joe Oliver had told him to take—what if Oliver wasn't waiting for him at the station? He couldn't hide his anxiety. "If anyone would have been watching me closely, they could have easily seen, that I was a country boy from the way my eyes were wide open and looked," he wrote.[3]

He waited by himself at the station for over an hour before a policeman asked if he needed help.

"Yes sir," Armstrong responded. "I came in from New Orleans. I am a cornet player. And I came up here to join Joe Oliver's Jazz Band."

"Oh, you're the young man who's to join King Oliver's Band at the Lincoln Garden," the officer responded with a smile.

Armstrong was perplexed for a moment, hearing his mentor's royal moniker. "In New Orleans it was just plain Joe Oliver," he recalled.

The officer explained that Oliver had been waiting for him earlier in the day but had to go to work, leaving word to be on the lookout for his new cornet man. He set Armstrong up in a cab and sent him on his way.

"I thanked the cop for being so kind," Armstrong said. "Something a little different from the cops down south. They usually whip your head and then ask you questions."[4]

Armstrong's cab eventually pulled up to 459 E. 31st Street on the corner of Cottage Grove, home of the Lincoln Gardens. A painted canvas sign hung outside advertising "King Oliver and His Creole Jazz Band." Armstrong could hear the music from the street and became consumed with self-doubt. "My Gawd, I wonder if I'm good enough to play in that band," he thought to himself.[5]

The venue's huge lobby felt like it was "a block long" as he nervously navigated the crowded hallway before entering the colorful cabaret. Once inside, he would have been gobsmacked by the big crystal ball that hung from the center ceiling—a precursor to a later generation's "disco ball." "A couple of spotlights shone on the big ball as it turned and threw reflected spots of lights all over the room and the dancers," frequent visitor and future drummer George Wettling remembered. The ceiling was lowered with chicken wire, across which "great bunches of artificial maple leaves" were hung.[6]

Perhaps the first person to spot Armstrong was trombonist Preston Jackson. The New Orleans native had moved to Chicago several years earlier and had spent many nights shadowing Oliver's trombonist Honore Dutrey. "I was sitting on the stand," Jackson said of Armstrong's arrival. "I'll never forget it, he had on a sailor [straw hat] with a brown suit, tan shoes."[7]

Oliver was in the middle of passing out sheet music to the other members of the band when he spotted his protégé. "And My My My... One would have thought that 'Hell' broke loose," Armstrong wrote.[8]

About Armstrong's appearance, Oliver later told trombonist Clyde Bernhardt, "Everything was all right about him but the way he looked. He was just as greasy as a pig!" Oliver also said Armstrong "had a suitcase, it was so raggedy, it had ropes all tied around it to hold it together."[9] Oliver's pianist, Bertha Bookman, recalled that Armstrong was "carrying his cornet wrapped in a black bag."[10]

Armstrong was thrilled to be reunited with fellow New Orleanians, including drummer Baby Dodds from the Fate Marable band, clarinetist Johnny Dodds from Kid Ory's band, and trombonist Honore Dutrey, brother of clarinetist Sam Dutrey. He probably didn't remember bassist Bill Johnson, who had left home when Armstrong was still a boy, but he knew of Johnson's reputation due to the success of the Original Creole Band. But looming above everyone was Oliver. "Gee Son, I'm really proud of you," Oliver said.[11]

Oliver told Armstrong to take a seat and enjoy the floor show, which was introduced by emcee Collwell "King" Jones, "a little fellow with a great big voice" who spoke with a comedic West Indian accent but, according to Armstrong, was actually from Mississippi. The *New York Amsterdam News* later referred to Jones as "one of the greatest laugh provokers on the continent" and a "remarkable humorist."[12] Though remembered for malaprop-heavy monologues that probably reeked of minstrelsy, the bespectacled Jones represented Armstrong's first taste of a certain kind of performer in Chicago.

"Truly, he has a personality that has its effect upon both the orchestra and onlookers," the *Chicago Defender* reported, adding, "He believes in himself, and a little more self-confidence will put a lot of us over."[13] These lessons would not be lost on young Armstrong.

At the end of the evening, Oliver introduced Armstrong to the owner of the Lincoln Gardens, an older white woman named Florence Majors, who didn't say much but had stuck by Oliver through his issues with the musicians' union, and the venue's manager, a 44-year-old African American man named Charles "Bud" Redd.

"Joe, where in the hell did you get that little country sommitch?" Redd asked, breaking up the band in the process.

"Don't kid that boy, Budd, he don't know anything about that kind of ribbing." Oliver responded. "You might frighten the kid."

"Joe was right," Armstrong later admitted, "Because the whole time I worked there, I was a little shaky of Budd."[14]

Armstrong and Oliver left the Lincoln Gardens together and headed to Oliver's apartment, located right around the corner at East 32nd Street and South Vernon Avenue. There Louis had a joyous reunion with Stella Oliver and her daughter Ruby over a big meal. "[Stella] fed me the same way she'd feed Joe a big dish of red beans and rice, a half a loaf of bread, and a bucket of good ice cold lemonade," Louis remembered. "Yum Yum...."[15]

Oliver had taken the liberty of setting Armstrong up with an apartment at 3412 South Wabash Avenue, where the landlady was a "goodlooking middle aged Creole yellow gal with pretty big eyes" whom Armstrong remembered as "Filo." A quick search of the property records shows that she was Philo Atkins, originally born in New Orleans and the wife of trombonist Ed Atkins, who would go on to record with both Armstrong and Oliver the following year.

As they rode the cab to Philo Atkins's apartment building, Oliver told Armstrong his room would have a private bath.

"What's a private bath?" Armstrong asked.

"Listen, you little slew-foot sommitch, don't be so damn dumb," Oliver said with a "funny" look.

"But he had forgot, that he must have wondered the same thing when he first came up north," Armstrong reflected. "Because in New Orleans the neighborhood we lived, we never heard of such a thing as a bath tub Period,.. Letlone a private bath....Savy?"[16]

After catching up on some sleep, Armstrong took advantage of his new private bath, got dressed, and went out for a long walk, stunned by the beautiful African American neighborhood he found himself in. "The reason why I was so amazed over South Parkway is because, such a street in New Orleans, with all those highpowered homes and apartments, nothing but white folks lived on a street like that... And nothing but the Filthy Rich ones at that," he wrote. "I just could not get [over] the idea, that it was a little difference between the north and the south (a little differnt [*sic*] anyway) and the colored people were a little more respected and appreciated."[17]

A touching moment occurred when Armstrong passed Olivet Baptist Church, located almost next door to the Lincoln Gardens. One of the last songs he had played in New Orleans at the funeral for Eddie Vincent's father had been the hymn "Abide With Me." "The first Sunday I was in Chicago, I took a little stroll, you know, trying to look the city over, especially in my neighborhood as much as I could see," he said. "And I happen to pass by a church at 31st and South Parkway. Olivet Church, I'll never forget it, it was about 7:00 in the evening and what I want to make clear was a coincidence: the choir was singing 'Abide With Me.' Isn't that funny?"[18]

Armstrong was also comforted by numerous friends from New Orleans he met as he strolled through Chicago. "Now with so many New Orleans Boys and Gals I knew I could not get homesick as I had done so many times before when I left New Orleans," he wrote.[19] He was experiencing the effects of the Great Migration right before his eyes, squashing any trepidations he might have had about moving up north.

After a nap, Armstrong got dressed, putting on his old "Roast Beef"—"P.S. that was what we called an old ragged Tuxedo," he later explained. "Of course, I had it all pressed up and fixed so good that no one would ever notice it, unless they were real close and noticed the patches here and there. Any way-I was real sharp, at least I thought I was anyway."[20]

Armstrong arrived at the Lincoln Gardens and said hello to Mrs. Major, Bud Redd, and King Jones before taking his place on the bandstand. Baby Dodds said the band lined up in a row in the "New Orleans tradition." Bill Johnson was farthest to the left, standing next to Bertha Bookman's piano. Johnny Dodds was next, with Armstrong taking his place in the center next to Oliver. Honore Dutrey would be to the right of the cornetists and Baby Dodds's drumset would be on the far right. "The lineup at the Lincoln Gardens bandstand was arranged in such a way as to make the music sound better," Dodds said. "In other words, it gave good balance and improved the sound."[21]

After he took his place on the stage, Armstrong's nerves acted up again. "It's a funny thing about the music game and Show Business," he later reminisced, "no matter how long a person has been in the profession, their opening Night always seem to give the feeling that you have little Butterflies moving around in your stomach."[22]

Any butterflies disappeared as soon as the music began. "We cracked down on the first note and that band sounded so good to me after the first note that I just fell right in like old times," Armstrong wrote. "Papa Joe really did blow that horn. The first number went down so well we had to take an encore." Armstrong was content to take a back seat to his mentor, later writing: "I did not actually take a solo until the evening was almost over. I never tried to go over him, because Papa Joe was the man and I felt any glory that should come to me must go to him. I wanted him to have all the praise. To me Joe Oliver blew enough Horn for the both of us. I could just sit and listen to him and play second to his lead. I never dreamed of trying to steal the show or any of that silly rot."[23]

Armstrong did get a few moments in the spotlight that night, but only alongside Oliver when the two men discovered a new way to join forces. "During my first night on the job, while things were going down in order, King and I stumbled upon a little something that no other two trumpeters together ever thought of," he recalled. "While the band was just swinging, the King would lean over to me, moving his valves on his trumpet, make notes, the notes that he was going to make when the break in the tune came. I'd listen, and at the same time, I'd be figuring out my second to his lead. When the break would come, I'd have my part to blend right along with his. The crowd would go mad over it!"[24]

In that crowd was something Armstrong wasn't accustomed to seeing in New Orleans: white musicians. "King Oliver and I got so popular blending that jive together that pretty soon all the white musicians from downtown Chicago would all come there after their work and stay until the place closed," he wrote. "Sometimes they would sit in with us to get their kicks."[25] On his first night, Armstrong recalled, "This was the time I met Louis Panico who was the ace Trumpeter (white) at that time."

Panico, a featured sideman in Isham Jones's popular Chicago-based orchestra at the time, did more than just visit the Lincoln Gardens. "Joe was teaching this boy, this Italian boy—yeah, he was teaching Panico," Preston Jackson said. "Joe, he'd taken a whole lot of time up with them young musicians, you know, I mean as far as teaching them and telling him this and telling him that."[26] Panico was working on a book, eventually published in 1923 as *The Novel Cornetist,* that according to David Sager was "filled with many novel mute effects that seem to have come directly from the King himself. These included imitations of a baby crying, laughing, sneezing and even the so-called sing song character of Chinese."[27]

Panico was far from the only white musician to learn directly from Oliver. Cornetist Paul Mares was now leading the New Orleans Rhythm Kings at the Friar's Inn in Chicago but spent as much time as he could at the Lincoln Gardens. "They were the most inspired band of all," he said of Oliver's Creole Jazz Band. "They actually killed you."[28] Preston Jackson remembered, "The New Orleans Rhythm Kings were there every night too. It was common to see musicians writing on their cuffs in those days. [Leon] Rapollo, the Rhythm Kings' clarinetist, was always writing—and his numbers are still played today."[29]

They might have been present on Armstrong's opening night when Oliver played J. Russell Robinson's 1912 composition "That Eccentric Rag," "the one where Papa Joe took a lot of breaks," Armstrong wrote. On August 29, 1922, less than two months after Armstrong's arrival, the New Orleans Rhythm Kings got the opportunity to record for Gennett Records in Richmond, Indiana. The first song they recorded was "Eccentric," with Mares doing his best to replicate Oliver's muted breaks. Oliver would never get the opportunity to record his own version of his showpiece.

Armstrong might have been put off by such events a few years earlier. Baby Dodds recalled that on the riverboats he and his fellow musicians would call white musicians "alligators. "That was the way we'd describe them when they'd come around and we were playing something that we didn't want them to catch on to," he said. "We'd say 'watch out, there's an alligator!' "[30] But seeing Oliver patiently teaching and encouraging his white disciples inspired Armstrong to follow his lead. He soon befriended the members of the New Orleans Rhythm Kings and encouraged them before their record dates, later noting that "they would come to my house and rehearse when they would go to make a record."[31]

The Rhythm Kings were popular but even their most ardent white fans switched allegiances when confronted with the sounds of Oliver's band. Tenor saxophonist Bud Freeman, born in 1906, said of the Rhythm Kings, "It was something that we had never heard or felt before. We didn't know what it was . . . didn't even realize that it was to any extent Negroid. All we knew was that it had a feeling to it and that we liked it and wanted to play like that." But one day drummer Dave Tough, born in 1907, insisted Freeman and their circle of friends—later known as the "Austin High Gang"—go hear Oliver at the Lincoln Gardens. "At first we didn't understand the music," Freeman said. "We didn't know if we liked it or not. It was a more vigorous music than the Rhythm Kings and it was really quite a lot different. Although we were at first confused by Joe Oliver's band, we soon decided that it was the thing so we took up their style and dropped that of the Rhythm Kings."[32]

Freeman and Tough were far from alone. Cornetist Muggsy Spanier said both Oliver's band and the New Orleans Rhythm Kings were "wonderful bands and they were both swinging," but admitted, "I liked Joe Oliver's band better cause they were more original." Spanier referred to himself as one of the "privileged few" who got to sit in with the Oliver band and was even gifted a Conn silver-plated "doorknob" mute by Oliver himself, which Spanier used for the rest of his career.[33]

Oliver's music had an equally life-changing effect on the number of young Black musicians who frequented the Lincoln Gardens, such as clarinetist and violinist Darnell Howard, who said, "To me this was the greatest band I'd ever heard up to that time—and since! The greatest—period!"[34] "That's when the climax came, when Joe sent for Louie," tenor saxophonist Happy Caldwell added. "They didn't have nothing written out, all those breaks." Caldwell and Preston Jackson were soon hired by cornetist Bernie Young to play in a small group inspired by the Creole Jazz Band. Asked if Young was directly trying to imitate Oliver's sound, Caldwell said, "At that particular time, yes, they were patternizing [*sic*] the ideas and the sounds because . . . King Oliver, he was the king, and most of us were following in his trend."[35]

Oliver was the King but later admitted to Clyde Bernhardt that Armstrong "actually played more than he was expecting for him to play. . . . He upset that house, he played so much. He had to pat both of his shoulders!"[36] Armstrong himself remembered Oliver kidding him, "Can you imagine this lil so and so coming up here and blowing all that horn."[37] Orchestra leader and composer Dave Peyton remembered Armstrong as a "green looking country boy, with big forehead, thin lips and robust physique," but noted "this newcomer brought us an entirely different style of playing than King Joe had give us."[38]

Yet the question remains: just how much was Armstrong featured with Oliver? "Joe didn't let Louis . . . [take] a solo because Joe kept Louis [under wraps]," Preston Jackson said. "I don't know if it was intentionally, but he did it." However, he added, "Louie was just as great a second trumpet player as he was a first—or maybe greater, because it's harder!"[39] "My opinion is I think Louis stole the show from . . . Joe, although he was playing second to Joe," saxophonist Lester Boone said. "Joe was playing, but Joe didn't have the power and the conception and the variety of ideas that Louie had at that time."[40]

For his part, Armstrong was proud of the way he blended with Oliver. "And I never did try to over-blow Joe at no time when I played with him," he said in 1950. "And it wasn't no show-up thing like a youngster would do today.... He still played whatever he wanted to play, and I always played pretty under him."[41] Baby Dodds eventually asked Oliver if he would ever let Armstrong play lead. "It's my band," Oliver firmly stated, ending any speculation. "What am I going to do, play second?"[42]

Armstrong himself did fondly recall that Oliver let him play "my rendition of the Blues" on his first night with the band but such instances were few and far between.[43] "After Louie had been here about a month or so, people down in the audience used to say, 'Give the kid a break, Joe! Give the kid one of them breaks!' " pianist Glover Compton remembered. "And Joe started giving Louie those breaks."[44] But those occasional short four-bar breaks were all Oliver would concede. "Until I left Joe, I didn't tear out," Armstrong quietly said.[45]

He never resented his lack of features, though; playing in Chicago with his heroes was more than he could ever ask for. "Often I would say to myself, This can't be me here playing with all of these masters," he wrote. "To play with such great men was the fulfillment of any child's dream, and I had reached that point in Music."[46]

Armstrong was in awe of each member of the band, marveling at the way Baby Dodds "sort of shimmied when he beat his sticks," he wrote. Armstrong was also happy to reunite with Johnny Dodds, remarking "those variations of his were still mellow and perfect."[47] Of Honore Dutrey, Armstrong admired his "beautiful tone. He always played cello parts which used to really knock

Figure 17.1 King Oliver Creole Jazz Band publicity photo, taken at Daguerre Studios in Chicago in the spring of 1923. Left to right: Baby Dodds, Honore Dutrey, King Oliver, Louis Armstrong, Bill Johnson, Johnny Dodds, and Lillian Hardin.
Credit: Courtesy of Archeophone Records.

me out." Dutrey had been gassed during World War I and suffered from "a bad case of asthma," according to Armstrong. "And every time he had one of them solos, he had to kind of pump something up his nose. But after he got through pumping, he'd really blow a lot of horn. Although he's gone, he'll always be remembered, especially by old Satch."[48]

To Armstrong, Bill Johnson was "a really good bass man" with an "unlimited" sense of humor.[49] When Oliver would make his cornet cry in imitation of a white baby on "Eccentric," Johnson would gently say, "Don't cry, little baby." But when Oliver would blast out the exaggerated wails of a Black baby, Johnson would impatiently shout, "Shut up you lil so and sooooooo." "Then the whole house would thunder with laughs and applause," Armstrong recalled.[50]

Johnson was also responsible for taking Armstrong to what would become one of the seminal events of his formative years: a performance by dancer and entertainer Bill "Bojangles" Robinson. Robinson opened at the Palace Music Hall (also known as the Erlanger Theater) on North Clark Street as part of an Orpheum circuit vaudeville bill on September 7, 1922. Armstrong had heard about Robinson in New Orleans, so Johnson took him to a matinee performance. Armstrong recalled what happened next during a privately recorded conversation in his motel room in 1967:

> And here come Bill Robinson, always kept that beautiful physique and that weight, and he had on a gabardine suit, I'll never forget it, brown derby, *sharp!* Tell you the truth, I never saw a colored man in my life that sharp. New Orleans, they're wearing box backs and all of that, button shoes and all that shit. And here's this son-of-a-bitch, walks out and after all the applause died down, he say, "Give me a light—my color." All the lights went out! Moment of truth. "Give me a light—my color," boom! The house went dark. Isn't that something?...And he did that dance and at that time, he used to go off the stage, you know, like they used to do ice skating and you couldn't hear a sound and that fractured the house. And then he come back and tell jokes and everything. And that suit![51]

Armstrong had fallen under the spell of Bert Williams while a teenager in New Orleans and though he never saw him perform live, he was familiar with the many Williams-inspired blackface comedians who performed in his hometown. But seeing Robinson changed something in Armstrong. "He didn't need black face to be funny," he wrote. "Better than Bert Williams. I personly [*sic*] admired Bill Robinson because he was emackly [immaculately] dressed- you could see the quality in his clothes even from the stage-stopped every show. He did not wear old ragity [*sic*] top hat and tails with the pants cut off—black cork with thick white lips, etc. But the audiences loved him very much.”[52]

The impact of Robinson on Armstrong’s eventual stage persona would not be fully realized for a few more years, but the sound of laughter made up a big part of the soundtrack of his life in Chicago. “People would see us, the band as a whole, laughing and joking and playing,” said Baby Dodds, who called Armstrong “the comical man in the band.”[53] But perhaps the funniest member of the band was King Oliver himself. Asked if Oliver was as “stern” as he appeared in photos, Clyde Bernhardt responded, “No! He used to laugh a lot and he was a great teaser!”[54] “He was a man who had a joke to tell all the time,” Baby Dodds said of Oliver. “He was kidding and joking all the time.”[55]

The parallels between Oliver and Armstrong were many. Asked what kind of person Oliver was, Darnell Howard said, “I would describe him as lovable and human. He was also a big joker who liked to laugh a lot.”[56] To Bernhardt, Oliver “was a great man, but he was just a plain down-to-earth man.”[57] Both men also carried on the New Orleans tradition of handing out nicknames to friends. “He give me a nickname, he called me Skunklefoot,” drummer Freddie Moore said. “Cause when I drum, I used to drum in my bedroom slippers.”[58] And when asked about Oliver’s reputation as a legendary eater, Preston Jackson shouted, “Oh my goodness, red beans and rice!”[59]

Armstrong was still invited to the Oliver’s apartment for red beans and rice feasts cooked up by Stella. “He idolized Joe and Joe was crazy about him,” Stella said of their relationship. “They’d come home and I’d fix red beans for them. . . . But they were funny, to be together, they had a lot of fun together.”[60]

Oliver also occasionally took Armstrong out on the town to hear Chicago’s other jazz bands. One night they ended up at Bill Bottoms’s Dreamland Cafe, where the orchestra was led by violinist Mae Brady. Oliver pointed at the band’s pianist and told Armstrong, “That there is Miss Lil.”

Oliver couldn’t have known it at the time, but that simple gesture would change the sound of twentieth-century music—and eventually drive Louis Armstrong out of his band.

18

"The Hot Miss Lil"

1922–1923

"Miss Lil" was Lillian Hardin, born February 3, 1898, and raised in "the largest and most pretentious house in the Negro section of South Memphis."[1] Her father, William Hardin, died of tuberculosis when Lillian was three and a half. She had never seen an adult cry, so she "laughed loud and long" when she saw her mother, Dempsey—lovingly known as "Decie,"—crying. "I, as a child, had absolutely no sympathy for anyone or anything," Lillian admitted. She frequently battled Decie, demanding she get what she wanted, even if it meant being punished. "I developed a desire for expensive things at a very early age and I would examine the price tag on all my clothes," she said. When she discovered her mother had bought her an Easter hat that only cost 25 cents, Lillian refused to wear it, getting a beating for her "obstinance." "These beatings and punishments never changed anything within me and Decie finally gave up trying to make me understand what she could and what she couldn't afford," she said.

However, Lillian did proudly identify her "one good characteristic" from her early years: "I took a delight in improving on things or people and then standing back to watch them show off, not wanting anyone to know that it was I who helped." This was a quality that would not soon go away. "There were many times when I made up my mind to concentrate on myself and forget about others but then something would come up and I was again directing someone else here or there," she continued. "I have never been able to change, I always had a knack for showing others how to improve themselves and people, most of the times, seem to trust my judgement and follow my instructions."

From a musical standpoint, young Lillian discovered an old organ in the corner of their parlor and soon "kept that organ groaning and sighing most of the day," to the consternation of her family. Her mother eventually hired third grade teacher Violet White to come to the house and give her lessons on the organ. Lillian became good enough to start playing marches during recess at school and hymns for Sunday School at church. "Oh, how I played those marches!" she recalled. "I had the kids strutting like little toy soldiers, I was really giving them the beat. I didn't spare the church that rhythmic feeling in my bones either. I played 'Onward Christian Soldiers,' 'Bringing In The Sheaves,' and 'There's Sunshine In My Soul Today' with such a beat that the preacher, the Reverend R. J. Petty, would give me a questioning look over his spectacles."

Lillian soon demanded a piano to play at home instead of the organ. She later wrote, "Decie's chest was just bursting with pride and with her Lillian being hailed as a child prodigy, the smartest kid in school, how could she possibly refuse me a piano?" She couldn't.

Decie's pride in Lillian grew when she became a star pupil at Miss Hook's School of Music. But when Decie discovered the sheet music for W. C. Handy's "St. Louis Blues" in her daughter's collection, "she beat me with a stick," Lillian said. "That was the worst thing that had ever happened to me. . . . The fact was that Decie hated the Blues in any form, she felt that it was vulgar music, only fit for vulgar people."

Lillian graduated valedictorian of her high school class, though her school only offered three years of education. She soon set her sights on attending a college for her fourth year. "I found out that Fisk University was the place where all wealthy Negroes sent their children and would not even consider any other school after that," she said. Decie had to take on extra work to cover the high tuition costs, with Lillian promising to some day repay her.

But at Fisk, Lillian sputtered when her music professor told her she had been poorly trained and gave her second grade material to study. "I, the pride of Memphis, Decie's prodigy and genius, being told in just so many words that I was nothing!" she recalled. "I was crushed and I never fully recovered from this blow to my pride although I now know that it was entirely justified." Back home, she tore up her diploma from Miss Hook's School of Music.

Her second year at Fisk represented a major improvement over the first, but in the summer of 1917, Lillian moved to Chicago with Decie and her new husband, John Miller. Lillian soon found work as a music demonstrator at the Jones Music Store at 3409½ South State Street, run by Mrs. Jennie Jones, earning 3 dollars a week. Decie wasn't pleased, but Lillian told her it was only temporary until she could return to Fisk—a return that never came. For all of future husband Louis Armstrong's claims that she was valedictorian of her class at Fisk, Lillian only completed two years of studies there and never graduated.

At the Jones Music Store, Lillian quickly established herself as the "Jass Wonder Child," playing everything from Bach to the previously forbidden "St. Louis Blues," gaining an increase in salary to 8 dollars a week in the process. A buzz was created when Jelly Roll Morton entered the store and began to play. "I had never heard such playing before," she said. "Jelly Roll sat down, the piano rocked, the floor shivered and the people swayed as he attacked the keyboard with his long, skinny fingers, beating out a double rhythm with his feet on the loud pedal. I was amazed and thrilled. Finally he got up from the piano, grinned and looked at me as if to say, 'Let this be a lesson to you.'" It was; Morton remained Hardin's prime influence for the rest of her career.

A short time later, clarinetist Lawrence Duhe's New Orleans Creole Band came to Chicago and performed in the store, opening with the Original Dixieland Jazz Band's hit "Livery Stable Blues." "I had never heard a real jazz band before and their music made goose pimples break out all over me," Hardin said. "They played loud and long, weaving in and out of the melody with such ease and rhythm, and seemingly enjoying every minute of it." Jennie Jones helped the band find work at a nearby Chinese restaurant, an establishment that had a piano. The New Orleans Creole Band didn't use a piano, so Jones sent Lillian over to play with them.

Once there, Lillian asked for her part and was told there was no sheet music. When she asked about a key, they told her to just listen and "hit it" after the leader counted off. "When I heard the two knocks I struck as many of the keys as I possibly could at one time because that way, I thought to myself, whatever key they'd be in, I'd be in it too!" she remembered. Her ploy worked and she eventually grew comfortable with the formulaic chord structures of the songs she was asked to play.

A move to the De Luxe Cafe came with a salary increase to $22.50 a week, but Lillian began telling her mother she was working nights playing at a dance school rather than confessing she was playing with a jazz band. The ploy worked until a friend told Decie, "I saw your little girl at the cabaret last night." "As hard as I have worked and slaved to make you nice and lady-like," Decie told Lillian during the ensuing screaming match, "you end up in a cheap, vulgar low-down cabaret."

Decie and John Miller went to hear their daughter play at the De Luxe, where she was billed as "The Hot Miss Lil." "What do they mean, chopping your name off like that?" Decie said. Lillian later admitted, "I didn't like that too much myself and, to this day, I don't exactly relish being called 'Lil.'" But it was clear that she was thriving and when the manager of the De Luxe told Decie, "Just listen to that applause—the world will soon be at her feet," Decie's chest began "swelling with pride." "Decie never really forgave me and she never came back to hear me play," Lillian recalled, but Decie no longer tried to stop her—she'd remain "The Hot Miss Lil" until her dying day.

Hardin was playing with the New Orleans Creole Band with Freddie Keppard on cornet in the summer of 1918 when they heard the rumor that

Figure 18.1 Eighteen-year-old Lillian Hardin in Chicago in 1916, well on her way to becoming "The Hot Miss Lil."
Credit: The Lil Hardin Armstrong-Chris Albertson Collection, Louis Armstrong House Museum.

another top cornetist from New Orleans was due to arrive: Joe Oliver. "On his very first night in town, he visited the De Luxe and walked straight to the bandstand," Hardin wrote "I'll never forget it, you'd think God had stepped down from heaven, and the sight of him made the boys play better than I'd ever heard them." Though "everybody in the place went wild," she admitted, "Frankly, I thought Freddie Keppard was better."

But when Hardin was offered the opportunity to join Oliver's new band at the lavish Dreamland Cafe, she jumped at the chance. "On opening night you could scarcely walk in the place, the people were literally hanging on the chandeliers," she said. "I'm telling you, the 'King' played music fit for kings and peasants alike." Hardin and Oliver added a second job at the Pekin, an after-hours cabaret that catered to entertainers, and spent much time bonding together offstage. "Although Joe appeared quiet and reserved, he could keep you in stitches saying funny things under his breath," she said. "He sat next to the piano and, at intermission or between sets, he would tell me jokes. Nasty ones, clean ones and some true ones." Hardin also learned another important life lesson while observing Oliver and the other New Orleanians in his band: "I soon found out that New Orleans men were as great at philandering as they were at playing music."

Hardin went to California with Oliver for his band's six-month engagement in San Francisco in the summer of 1921, but she chose to return to Chicago at the end of the year, joining violinist Mae Brady's band at Dreamland. It was there that Hardin met a "young, good looking singer from Washington D. C." named Jimmie Johnson. After a short courtship, they married on August 22, 1922, at Olivet Baptist Church and announced their union at Dreamland that night.

Louis Armstrong had been in Chicago for about six weeks by that point and was anxious to meet Hardin when Oliver finally brought him to Dreamland. For her part, Hardin had heard the New Orleans musicians talk about "Little Louis" for years and was curious to meet the new cornetist in town. Any chance of love at first sight disappeared immediately. "I looked Louis over quickly but thoroughly, and was not a bit impressed with what I saw," Hardin said.

> As a matter of fact, I was very disappointed. Everything he had on was too small for him, an atrocious tie dangled down over his protruding stomach and, to top it off, he had a hairdo that called for bangs—and I do mean bangs—that jutted out over his forehead like a frayed canopy. Well, my feathers really fell. Having heard so much about "little Louis" from Joe and the other fellows, it was quite a shock to see him weighing every bit of 200 pounds and then some. I began to wonder how he ever got that name, and when I saw how small his clothes were I figured maybe he once was little.

Matters got worse when Hardin sat down at the piano and rolled her stockings down below her knees for circulation. "And the first thing Louis spied was my knee," she recalled. "And he was looking and I said, 'This guy's got ideas he'd better not put in words!' "[2]

Armstrong didn't let a disastrous first impression get in his way. "I guess I didn't look too friendly, but Louis knew just what to do—he gave me one of his broadest and most effective smiles, his teeth gleamed like pearls and I was so flattered by the look he gave me that I forgot all about his awful outfit and smiled back at him," Hardin wrote. Armstrong and Oliver were unimpressed with Brady's band, but Armstrong liked Hardin's piano playing and continued to seek her out over the coming months.

"During those early days with Louis, I flirted with him a bit, but I had no serious romantic ideas as far as he was concerned," Hardin said; she was recently married. But that would soon change when she made her next career move: rejoining King Oliver's Creole Jazz Band.

On December 2, 1922, the *Chicago Defender* ran a photo of pianist Bertha Bookman with the headline "Gone West," announcing that she returned home to San Francisco at the end of November."[3] Oliver approached Hardin about returning to the band and she immediately accepted. "I particularly enjoyed Lil that night, with that four (4) beats to the bar," Armstrong wrote of his first time playing with Hardin. "For a woman I thought she was really wonderful."[4]

One of Lil's regular jobs was to go over published arrangements with Oliver so he could be familiar with the routines before rehearsing them with the rest of the band. "And I was very happy to have him to confide in me, you know, I thought that was being real grand," Hardin said.

During one of these conversations, Oliver suddenly broached the subject of his new cornetist. "You know this Louis, he's a better trumpet player than I'll ever be," Oliver told Hardin. "But as long as I keep him playing second with me, he won't get ahead of me. I'll still be the king."

Hardin replied, "Oh yeah?"

"It didn't mean anything to me because Louis didn't mean anything to me either," she recalled of the conversation. Her curiosity piqued, she did admit, "But I started listening to try to see if there was any difference, but I couldn't tell any difference because they played their solos together and Louis would play a second to everything he played exactly, the phrasing, everything. Oh, you couldn't tell."[5]

Hardin might not have been able to detect what made Armstrong so special, but she liked spending time with him off the bandstand. "After I joined the band again, Louis and I became real close buddies, he called it 'nibs,' and that's what we were, real nibs," Hardin said. Her marriage was on the rocks, with Johnson once shouting at her, "They told me you'd be hard to handle." Hardin didn't disagree and after spotting him around town with various white women he met at Dreamland, she packed her belongings and moved back in with Decie.

Meanwhile, Louis was struggling with a new girlfriend who always seemed to make excuses to avoid going out with him. "We started going everywhere together and I started to take a slight romantic interest in him because I felt sorry for him," Hardin said. "I should have known that feeling sorry for a man could easily lead to something more serious, and that's exactly what happened."

Both newly single, Armstrong and Hardin began "Running together after work," Armstrong said. "She would take me to the Dreamland Cafe, lots. I liked very much to go there and give May Alix and Ollie Powers money to Sing for me. I'd give them each a Dollar-Shucks-I thought I really was a *grand Sport*—And be with great Lill."[6] Oliver was unimpressed when Armstrong told him about his exploits, only grunting, "As if he wanted to say, 'Why you country so and so.' "[7]

For all the fun Armstrong and Hardin were having together as friends, they still weren't officially a couple. But when they finally did become a couple, it wasn't because of Joe Oliver or Freddie Keppard or Ollie Powers or Mae Alix or anyone else in their immediate orbit.

The person who inadvertently brought them together was Mayann Armstrong.

During a cold winter's night in late 1922 or early 1923, King Oliver's Creole Jazz Band was preparing to swing out at the Lincoln Gardens when they were interrupted by a commotion in the audience. Armstrong looked up and suddenly saw his mother running toward him, carrying various bags. "I was speechless," he said. "When my mother reached me, across the Band Stand, I hadn't closed my mouth and it had been open [ever] since I spied her."

"How is my boy?" Mayann greeted him. "How are you doing?"

"I realized my mother was actually there before me, in Person," he wrote. "Everything was real great. Oh! my sucha hugging and kissing."

Louis had kept in touch with Mayann regularly since he left, sending frequent letters, always with money attached. But "some cat" he never identified had returned to New Orleans from Chicago and told Mayann that her son was "in real bad shape," "was not working," and was "broke, sick and hungry." He claimed that he had asked Louis why he just didn't return home, and told Mayann, "Louis just held his head down and cried." "She didn't take time to send me a wire or nothing," Louis said. "She got the very first train that she could get and started for Chicago."[8]

Seeing her son wearing a tuxedo and performing with Oliver eased her mind. Some laughs were even had at Joe Oliver's expense as he liked to always kid Louis that he was his real father. With Mayann in the room, Louis whispered to his boss, "Well, Papa Joe—Mother's here—shall I tell her what you've been saying?" "Oh Gosh you should have seen Papa Joe blush all over the place," Louis wrote.[9]

Louis was thrilled to have his mother up north and offered to rent a room for her, but she planned on leaving the next day, telling him, "Son, I don't think

I like up north with all of these new fangled gadgets." Not willing to take no for an answer, Louis enlisted the help of his "very good friend" Lil Hardin to help pick out a place for Mayann to stay.[10] They found a large apartment building at 43rd and St. Lawrence Avenue and chose a three-room flat on the fifth floor for Mayann. "While we looked over the place I was reminded of New Orleans," Louis wrote. "May-Ann had been so wonderful to me. She and Mama Lucy had done everything they could do for me. Now was my turn to prove how thankful I was for the sacrifices she had made for me."

While furnishing the apartment, Louis and Lil's eyes met while they stood on each side of an empty bed. "We both, thought, Hmmm—nobody here but the two of us," Louis wrote. "And, it seemed like we both came to a conclusion at the same time... That we should, play a little tag, right this minute.... And we did... Yes we did........" Louis and Lil made "violent, but beautiful love" right there on what was Mayann's soon-to-be bed. "And, from that moment, until the day we were married, we fell in love with each other," he remembered.

When they surprised Mayann with the finished apartment, she cried tears of joy.

"Son, I've never had an apartment of my own in my whole life," she told Louis.[11] She even gave Lil a big kiss and said, "Thanks Son + my future daughter in Law."[12]

Mayann would remain in Chicago for close to a year, but more important, Louis and Lil had consummated their relationship and now went public with their love. Louis remembered the boys in the band being "suspicious," as they all had taken turns making a play for Lil before a "Real Country 'Sommitch' come up here, and take her from right under our noses—Shucks.' "[13] "And the musicians, soon as they found out that Louis and I were dating, they all quit speaking to us almost," Lil said. "Oh, they didn't like that at all because they knew I was going to start something."

Icy feelings notwithstanding, from a musical perspective, the Oliver band remained the rage of the South Side of Chicago in 1923. Only one member of the band remained apathetic toward the excitement they were generating: Lil. She would notice a bunch of white musicians crowding the bandstand to listen, but didn't know who they were, only to be told later that these crowds included musicians ranging from superstar bandleader Paul Whiteman to the young cornetist Armstrong had met back in Davenport when he was with Fate Marable, Bix Beiderbecke. "And I used to wonder to myself what they were listening at, what particular thing they were listening [to]," Lil said. "That's how much I knew about what we were doing, eh?"

Lil did remember one fellow who became "quite famous: Hoagy Carmichael," she said. "I remember he came and sat in with the orchestra one night at the Garden."[14] It was equally memorable for Carmichael, who vividly described a marijuana-fueled scene that found him replacing Lil on "Royal Garden Blues." "It wasn't marijuana," he wrote. "The muggles and the gin were, in a way, stage props. It was the music. The music took me and had me and it made me right." Carmichael named Armstrong as Beiderbecke's idol and remembered "Bix was on his feet, his eyes popping," when Armstrong and Oliver "slashed" into "Bugle Call Rag."

"Why," Carmichael moaned in the middle of it all. "Why isn't everybody in the world here to hear that?" Looking back in 1982, he wrote, "I meant it. Something as unutterably stirring as that deserved to be heard by the world."[15]

The world was about to get such a chance—King Oliver's Creole Jazz Band was due to make their first records.

19

"He's *Got* to Be Better"

1923–1924

Located about 225 miles outside of Chicago and only a few miles removed from the Ohio border, Richmond, Indiana, might not immediately spring to mind as a candidate for a "cradle of jazz," but considering it is where Louis Armstrong and King Oliver made their first recordings in 1923, its stature in the music's history is secure. Beginning in 1872, Richmond was the home of the Starr Piano Company, one of the most popular piano manufacturers in the country. By the early 20th century, Starr was being run by Henry Gennett and his sons, Henry Jr., Clarence, and Fred. The piano business was strong enough on its own to keep Starr in the black for many years, but by 1915, the family began to take notice of the burgeoning popularity of records and began selling phonographs. The move was so successful, the Gennett family decided to make their own records to sell alongside their pianos, phonographs, and sheet music. The family put their own name on the label and Gennett Records was born in 1916.

For its first five years, Gennett only recorded out of New York City, but in 1921, they built a small, 125-by-30-foot studio in the back of their piano factory in Richmond to begin making even more records, this time almost literally in their backyard. Numerous Gennett sessions were derailed by the sound of passing trains; railroad tracks were located about three feet from the studio's front door.

The label hadn't recorded much jazz until Frank Higgins, a manager of one of the Starr Piano showrooms in Chicago, let Fred Gennett know about the popularity of the New Orleans Rhythm Kings at the Friar's Inn. Gennett recorded 16 sides by the group of King Oliver's white disciples between August 1922 and March 1923, selling enough copies to persuade Gennett to record more jazz—including music made by African Americans.

"Race records" had been selling steadily since the success of Mamie Smith's "Crazy Blues" in 1920, but there seemed to be a prejudice against bands of Black musicians from New Orleans; after the success of the Original Dixieland Jazz Band's first records in 1917, no Black bands from New Orleans got the opportunity to record until Kid Ory cut some sides in California in May 1922.

But 1923 seemed to represent a shift, possibly brought on by the success of the New Orleans Rhythm Kings; by the end of the year, Black New Orleanians such as Clarence Williams, Richard M. Jones, Sidney Bechet, and Jelly Roll Morton would make their first recordings. And on April 5, 1923, thanks to another tip from Frank Higgins, Gennett would be the first label to record King Oliver's Creole Jazz Band.[1]

After the nearly five-hour train ride from Chicago to Richmond, Oliver and his musicians were greeted by Gennett's main recording engineer, Ezra Wickemeyer. Wickemeyer would have to make some adjustments to the band's sound: the primitive acoustic recording technology could not pick up Bill Johnson's bass, so Johnson would have to resort to playing bass lines and chords on a louder six-string banjo. The same technical limitations prevented Baby Dodds from using his full kit, relegating him to sticks on a woodblock, with occasional hits of a tom-tom or cymbal.

"Of course everybody was on edge," Dodds said. "We were all working hard and perspiration as big as a thumb dropped off us. Even Joe Oliver was nervous; Joe was no different from any of the rest. The only really smooth-working person there was Lil [Hardin] Armstrong. She was very unconcerned and much at ease."[2]

Oliver seriously prepared for this opportunity, sketching out arrangements with Hardin and leaving nothing to chance. "Joe decided which tunes we would record," Dodds continued. "They were all numbers which we had worked out many times on the bandstand."[3] Asked if the band rehearsed in the studio, Armstrong said, "Well we'd rehearse that on the job, you know. By the time we get to the studio all they got to do is kind of cut it up and time it."[4] "Everything we played was organized so well under Oliver," Hardin added. "You notice all the numbers we played, everybody knew what they were supposed to do. We used to rehearse."[5]

A surviving Gennett Records contract sheds light on the label's recording methods: "We start work by making a short test which is immediately played back to the performer from the wax and from that we begin to judge positions and tone and arrangement of music and everything that is necessary to make a good record."[6] The band took their positions and made a test record of the first song to be recorded, Oliver and Bill Johnson's composition "Just Gone." What happened next would eventually go down as part of jazz lore.

"And at this recording session was, well, we all had to blow in this great big horn, the old style," Hardin recalled, referring to the recording horn that was used to capture sounds before microphones were invented. "And in trying to get the balance, Joe and Louis stood right next to each other as they always had." After finishing the test recording, the musicians and Wickemeyer immediately listened to the playback. "And you couldn't hear a note that Joe was playing and only could hear Louis," Hardin said.

"Well, we've got to do something," Wickemeyer wondered aloud before coming up with a solution.

"So they put Louis about 15 feet away over in the corner from the band," Hardin said. "And Louis was . . . standing in the corner looking all sad. You know, he thought it was bad for him to be separated from the band. I saw, I looked at him and smiled to reassure him that he was all right, you know." At the Lincoln Gardens, Hardin hadn't really noticed much of a difference between Armstrong and Oliver, but after hearing that playback, she experienced an epiphany. "And then I said to myself, 'Now, if they had to put him that far away in order to hear Joe, he's *got* to be better,'" she said. "Then I was convinced."[7]

He might not have wanted to admit it, but Louis himself sensed something had changed in Oliver, too. "The man was failing when he was making records," Armstrong said in 1950. "He wasn't in his prime then, like he was before he sent for me. See, now, when we made Gennett records, let me show you how powerful, how much stronger I was than Joe. The horn, you know them old [recording] horns—Joe would be right in it, blowing. And I had to stand at the door and play second trumpet!"[8]

Even standing by the door, Armstrong makes his presence felt throughout the second tune recorded that day, "Canal Street Blues," joining forces with Oliver on the harmonized introduction, call-and-response melody, and closing tag, plus a chorus of blues based on the part of the religious song "The Holy City." Singer Alberta Hunter had fond memories of hearing the Oliver band in Chicago and said of Oliver, "He and Louie played a thing, you know 'The Holy City'? [*sings*] 'Jerusalem, Jerusalem.' They used to play that as a duet. It would make hair rise on your head as they play it, just the two of them."[9]

It's the ensemble that steals the show on "Canal Street Blues," especially in the song's rocking final choruses. It's tempting to listen to it as another example of freewheeling polyphony, but the four horns actually take on the roles of "sections" toward the end with the two cornets leaning into a riff, Dutrey responding with trombone smears, and Johnny Dodds harmonizing the riff in addition to playing his own countermelodies. In just a few years, these roles would be performed by a trumpet section, trombone section, and reed section, something Oliver was clearly foreshadowing.

On "Chimes Blues," the fifth song recorded that day, Armstrong took his first solo on record, his tone cutting through the primitive recording methods to grab the listener between the ears. Though steeped in Oliver's tutelage, when the spotlight hit him for the first time, Armstrong fell back on another formative influence: "That's Bunk," Sidney Bechet said of this solo, further evidence of the inspiration of Bunk Johnson on Armstrong's playing.[10]

After listening to "Chimes Blues" on a Voice of America broadcast in 1956, Armstrong lamented that Oliver "missed the boat" by not featuring him more. "You notice all these records, you hear more harmony because his lead was weak," he said. "That's why I had to get back to the door to play the second when he should've put me to play the lead, knowing that I had that first chair tone. And it would still have been Joe Oliver's records but bigger, you know?" Armstrong would have gladly sacrificed any name recognition if it helped Oliver sell more records and garner more fame. "Even this solo in 'Chimes Blues' sold this record, oh, a gang of them," he said. "Just think of all the records I made with Joe Oliver on the Gennett and the OKeh, they'd all be priceless, which they are, you know—to an extent."[11] Armstrong proved his point the next day, when he was given the opportunity to play lead for one chorus on Jelly Roll Morton's "Froggie Moore," his bright tone and the fluidity of his lines making an immediate impression.

But Oliver reminded everyone why he was still the King on "Dipper Mouth Blues," a performance that established him as one of the first great soloists in jazz, living up to all the hype heaped on him in later years by his protégé.[12] Midway through the performance, Oliver got right up into the recording horn and proceeded to take a plunger-muted solo that is still emulated over 100 years later (though perhaps "solo" isn't the right word as the other three horns never stop playing in the distance the entire time). For three choruses, Oliver talks, shouts, moans, and cries the blues, bringing to mind Mutt Carey's description: "Joe could make his horn sound like a holy roller meeting. God, what that man could do with his horn!"[13]

Already immortalized by Oliver's solo, the aura around "Dipper Mouth Blues" only grew when Baby Dodds was supposed to take a short break—and promptly forgot his part. Sensing that Dodds was "unsettled," quick-thinking Bill Johnson shouted, "Oh, play that thing!" "That was an on-the-spot substitution for the solo part which I forgot," Dodds said. "And that shows how alert we were to one another in the Oliver band. The technician asked us if that was supposed to be there and we said no. However, he wanted to keep it in anyway and ever since then every outfit uses that same trick, all because I forgot my part."[14] Over 100 years later, no performance of "Dipper Mouth Blues" is complete without an invocation of Oliver's solo and a joyous shout of "Oh, play that thing!"

With eight songs completed, Oliver had not adequately showcased the two-cornet breaks that made the group's reputation at the Lincoln Gardens. With the clock probably ticking on the session, Oliver called "Snake Rag," a selection that inspired the most spontaneous and exhilarating playing of the date.[15] As the band starts to wind down after two exciting ensemble choruses of the blowing strain, Oliver storms into a seemingly unplanned, euphoric third chorus, allowing the Lincoln Gardens magic to play out before our very ears. In bars 6 and 11, Oliver plays phrases that oscillate between a concert B natural and C, most likely exchanging a look with Armstrong as if to say "Remember that." This would give Armstrong roughly four seconds to read Oliver's mind, figure out the break he's about to play, and devise a second part. When the break hits, Armstrong locks into Oliver, and plays a perfect harmony part to the King's lead, all of which was hinted at on the fly just seconds earlier. There would be no need for a second take.

After the session, the Oliver band posed for multiple new publicity photos at Chicago's Daguerre Studios. The photos showcase the usual seven musicians who made up the band in the first part of 1923, but thanks to the prominence of Bill Johnson's banjo on the records, Oliver soon added a regular banjoist to the mix in the form of New Orleanian Bud Scott.

Most of the photos taken simply lined up the band in different formations, each member staring almost grimly into the camera, with Oliver always looking a bit off in the distance to shield his bad eye. But the most striking photo from the session is an action shot, with each member posing while performing on their usual instruments—except for Armstrong, who is kneeling down and playing a slide trumpet. "I used to play that with Joe Oliver," Armstrong said. "Oh yeah, it's just like a trombone."[16] Trombonist Roy Palmer verified this, saying, "Joe Oliver tried to play one, too," but added, "They didn't do no good, though. I don't know why but they couldn't make good on those sliding trumpets."[17]

Aside from the unusual choice of instrument, there's a story being told with Armstrong's placement, dead center, looking away from the camera, blowing, but also deep in thought. Over one shoulder is Oliver, cutting an imposing figure, blowing with fire, his left hand holding a mute in place in the bell of his cornet. But on the other side is Lil, staring intensely into the camera with a calculating look as her raised left hand prepares to smash down on the piano keyboard. Like the cartoon trope of an angel hovering over one shoulder while the devil dispenses advice over the other, Armstrong was now stuck in the middle, trying to figure out who was who.

Bill Johnson also appears in the photo, strumming a banjo and looking away from the drama taking place in the center. Even with the success of "Chimes Blues," Oliver's pride would not allow the younger man any more opportunities in the spotlight. "Joe wouldn't give Louis a chance," Johnson recalled. "Louis was playing more cornet than Oliver. Oliver would say that as long as he had Louis with him, he couldn't hurt him. Oliver admitted Louis was better."[18]

Oliver had made similar comments to Lil Hardin, who also could not get the events of Richmond out of her mind. She fell deeper in love with Louis and called it quits with husband Jimmie Johnson. One can chart the acceleration of Louis and Lil's relationship by simply checking the copyright registrations for the song "Just Gone." Oliver originally registered it on April 11, 1923, crediting "Lillian Johnson" with the arrangement. But on May 21, he registered it again, this time crediting the arrangement to "Lillian Harding [*sic*]." Jimmie Johnson was out and Louis Armstrong was officially in.

The release of the first four Gennett sides in May 1923 created enough buzz for the Creole Jazz Band to be invited to perform at the National Association of Music Merchants convention at the Drake Hotel in Chicago on June 7 in front of over 2,000 music dealers from around the country.[19] After performances from white bands such as Isham Jones's group, the Benson Orchestra, and Frank Westfall's Rainbow Garden Orchestra, Oliver closed the show and broke it up. "The 'dark horse' orchestra of the bunch was sure dark," *Talking Machine World* stated after the performance, before publishing one of the first references to Armstrong in print: "Especially the little frog-mouthed boy who played the cornet. These babies worked hard and collected a mob of admirers around them even at 3 a.m."[20] *Talking Machine World* was still writing about this moment two months later, noting: "On the night of the frolics this organization was the last on the bill and was scheduled for twenty minutes' playing, but the applause was so great and Oliver was so good-natured that the band did not leave the hotel for nearly two hours."[21]

In the audience were representatives of OKeh Records. After three years of successfully recording Black artists in New York, OKeh sought to expand their "niche market" to Chicago. Ralph Peer of the General Phonograph Corporation, maker of OKeh discs, would team up with Elmer A. Fearn of the Consolidated Talking Machine Company, an OKeh distributor in Chicago, to record African American talent at Fearn's studio at 227–229 W. Washington Street. They chose Erskine Tate and King Oliver, recording both in late June.

King Oliver's Jazz Band—dropping the word "Creole"— recorded seven songs over two sessions for OKeh, including exciting, faster-paced remakes of both "Snake Rag" and "Dipper Mouth Blues." The latter was the first of the Gennett sides to be released, instantly immortalizing Oliver's solo. Oliver believed in performing his recorded solos in public performances, something he expected out of his sidemen, too. "He didn't like for nobody to change their solos from what they had on the record," Clyde Bernhardt said. "Because back in those days, you know, I was young and sometimes new ideas would come to me and I thought it was better. He'd say to me, 'Why in the hell did you change that solo, boy? You were playing a damn good solo. Now you had to go change it!' "[22] Oliver must have repeated his down-home solo on OKeh's "Jazzin' Babies Blues" enough times that it became a favorite of Armstrong, who would replicate it multiple times throughout his career.

Aside from the two remakes, Oliver's June output is most notable for documenting some nearly lost sounds of New Orleans. On "High Society Rag," Oliver showcased the swinging arrangement he had been playing since the Tulane Gymnasium days, giving Johnny Dodds the opportunity to be the first to record the tune's famous piccolo-turned-clarinet solo. According to trumpeter Punch Miller, the reharmonized trio strain featuring Dodds and Armstrong was something originally devised by Buddy Petit, who never got the chance to record.[23] And on "Sobbin Blues," Armstrong broke out his slide whistle for the first time on record, illustrating the beautiful, almost haunting sound that was popular on the riverboats with the unrecorded Fate Marable band of 1919–1921, as well as at the Lincoln Gardens. When Melrose Music published the sheet music for this piece, they used one of the band's new publicity photos on the cover.

OKeh knew they had something special and put their promotional muscle behind the Chicago recordings. On August 28, a convention of the Improved Benevolent Order of Elks brought over 200,000 African American spectators to Chicago. *Talking Machine World* ran a photo from the event of the Oliver band playing on the back of a truck with a large banner proclaiming the "special release" "Dipper Mouth Blues" backed by "Where Did You Stay Last Night." Armstrong can be seen wearing a natty cap, his leg hanging over the top of the banner, directly in the middle of the word "Dipper." How surreal this must have seemed: his photo in a major music magazine, his Third Ward nickname plastered on the side of a truck, a banner proclaiming not one, but two of his compositions, his mentor/father figure "Papa" Joe Oliver situated a few feet away, his new girlfriend Lillian Hardin seated next to him. On the surface, the photo seems to capture the end of a fairy-tale story.

But that same image also contains evidence of the transition Armstrong was going through in his musical—and nonmusical—life. The lead song being advertised, "Dipper Mouth Blues," was credited to Armstrong and Oliver, but "Where Did You Stay Last Night" was written by Armstrong and Hardin, their first joint composition (the title seemingly winking toward a question both had probably asked their respective first spouses—and one they would eventually come to ask each other). Oliver is staring at the camera with a proud, warm smile on his face, but Hardin is staring at Armstrong. And though almost all the men in the photo are wearing similar caps, there's a strong chance that Armstrong's wardrobe was picked out by Hardin—much to the chagrin of Oliver.

As the pair grew closer, Lil's first order of business was to change Louis's wardrobe. "You don't look right," she told him. "You've got to change your clothes."

"Where's your money?" she asked.

"Joe keeps my money," Louis replied.

"Well, Joe doesn't need to keep your money," Lil answered. "You keep your own money. You go to Joe and get your money."

"Well, I'd rather Mister Joe [keep my money], you know," Louis demurred. "He sent for me and looks out for me."

"No, I'm going to look out for you from now on," Lil declared.[24]

Armstrong did as told and approached Oliver about letting him handle his own money.

Figure 19.1 King Oliver's Creole Jazz Band advertising their latest OKeh release on the back of a truck at an Elks' convention in Chicago, August 28, 1923. Louis Armstrong is seated on the left, with his leg hanging over the banner.

Credit: Author's personal collection.

"Well, you're a big fool, fooling with that little ol' gal," Oliver told Armstrong. "She stays at home with her parents. She doesn't have to pay any money at home and she won't do a thing but make you throw away all your money on clothes like she does."

"In the meantime, I had already made Louis spend $200 for a hat and a coat, which was unheard of then!" Hardin said. When Oliver saw him with his new hat, he just said, "Mm-hm, what did I tell you?"

Armstrong dropped his head and let Oliver say what he needed to say. But according to Hardin, "Louis didn't care because he liked the way he looked himself. He looked better to himself."

When Lincoln Gardens manager Budd Redd spotted Armstrong's new look, he broke into laughter and shouted, "I knew if you fell for that little ol' gal that she was going to change your ways! Look! Look at him! Look!"

"So Joe didn't like that at all," Hardin said.[25]

Oliver assuredly wouldn't have liked Louis and Lil's next move, if he had known about it: on August 30, just two days after the photo was taken at the Elks convention, Louis filed for divorce from Daisy Parker, claiming Daisy had "abandoned" him "on or about the 15th day of February A.D. 1921."[26]

Louis knew Daisy well enough to know that his actions would incur her wrath. He had the summons sent to 2508 Melpomene Street, an address she apparently never lived at. By October, the court ordered that "Daisy Armstrong come into court here and plead, answer or demur to the said bill of complaint," but she didn't know it existed until it was too late.[27] After a default was entered against Daisy on November 15, an official decree of divorce was granted to Louis on December 18. Daisy was officially out as the first Mrs. Louis Armstrong and Lillian Hardin was well on her way to becoming the second.

The success of Oliver's sides led him to receive offers to record for Gennett, OKeh, and Columbia in October 1923 alone. Oliver wasn't going to turn down any opportunities, even if it meant hurting some feelings along the way.

Banjoist Johnny St. Cyr came up from New Orleans for these sessions, making his recording debut at a Gennett session on October 5—the same day the Ku Klux Klan hosted a celebration that drew a crowd of over 30,000 people to Richmond.[28] "A number of fiery crosses borne on machines and trucks were in evidence," the *Richmond Item* reported. "Ten or twelve bands and rum corps provided music and cadence during the march . . . while the binding words were being pronounced, two large crosses in the background were ignited and blazed up, lighting the entire field. The American flag was prominent at all times."[29] None of the musicians present ever discussed this Klan parade; being from the South, it's possible they weren't phased. They had work to do, recording eight songs for Gennett just a few miles away from the burning crosses and the prominent American flag.

Ten days later, Oliver recorded the first of two sessions for Columbia, replacing Dutrey with trombonist Ed Atkins and Johnny Dodds with clarinetists Jimmie Noone and Buster Bailey, a move that would eventually have major consequences. In addition, Armstrong was buried in the recording balance and not given any solos or breaks of his own.

That changed when the Oliver band "proper" was finally reassembled on October 25 and 26 for two final OKeh sessions, with Honore Dutrey and Johnny Dodds back in the fold, plus the addition of Charlie Jackson's booming bass saxophone in the rhythm section. Armstrong hadn't been featured in quite some time, but he got a few moments in the spotlight during these dates, taking a slide whistle solo on "Buddy's Habit" and executing nine scintillating solo breaks on his and Lil's "Tears." On "Mabel's Dream," his second cornet work even momentarily steals the spotlight from Oliver's diminished lead, a short but priceless example of how Armstrong "played pretty under" Oliver.[30] On the concluding "Riverside Blues," Oliver steps aside and allows Armstrong to shine on a surging 12-bar-blues chorus over stop-time backing, even closing the record with an effective coda.

Armstrong was frustrated when listening back to some of these sides in the 1950s. Of "Tears," he told the Voice of America, "everybody's wailing, but you don't know what the tune is because Joe's lead is overshadowed."[31] Oliver might have been faltering, but he was far from finished. Trumpeter Louie Metcalf, who was inspired by Armstrong during his days in St. Louis with Fate Marable, came to Chicago in December with Jimmy Cooper's 10-piece band, specifically to challenge the Oliver band. "We knew that Louie Armstrong was a powerful man on cornet," Metcalf recalled. "We had heard him playing on the boat in St. Louis. So we knew what we were to expect from him. But what really surprised us was that we thought Joe Oliver was through and were we surprised to see that he was playing more cornet than Louie. With the two of them together we got our lumps."[32]

That side of Oliver was captured during a December 24 session for Paramount, especially on a new version of "Mabel's Dream" where he eliminated Armstrong's duet chorus and remained in the forefront throughout, sounding particularly passionate in the final chorus. And though Armstrong still got to take his climactic solo chorus on a remake of "Riverside Blues," this time Oliver joined him for a harmonized coda, the perfect punctuation mark on one of the most important series of recordings in the history of recorded music.[33]

Any remaining harmony in the band vanished as the band's October records started to be released and Johnny Dodds and Honore Dutrey realized that Oliver had made records without telling them. Preston Jackson surmised: "The trouble started the break-up of Joe's band."[34]

Money issues also expedited the breakup of the band. The Lincoln Gardens gave Oliver a raise to pay each member $95 a week, but he didn't tell them and continued paying them each $75. "So oh boy, it was bedlam on the bandstand that night," Hardin said when the others found out. "All of them threatened to beat Joe up, you know—everybody but Louis. Louis, he just sat quiet and he didn't say a word." Oliver realized he had to protect himself against his own sidemen. "Joe had to bring his pistol to work every night with him in his trumpet case, because they threatened to beat him up when they found out he'd been stealing money from them," Hardin continued in a 1969 interview. "But it didn't faze Louis. He didn't care. Joe could do no wrong as far as Louis is concerned. He still can't."[35]

When Oliver announced he was booking a tour of one-nighters outside Chicago, that was enough for the Dodds brothers and Dutrey to quit and join Freddie Keppard's band at Bert Kelly's Stables. "I talked with the others and by the time I got through talking they all felt like I did, and we decided to disband," Baby Dodds said. "It was a sad thing. I felt awful blue about seeing that band break up. . . . It seemed as though something was missing from my life. It was pretty bad for a while."[36]

However, William Russell got to know Johnny Dodds before his untimely passing in 1940 and reported a different reason for the breakup from the one brother Baby offered. "Johnny said the real reason he thought [the band broke up] was they wanted Louie to play trumpet lead," Russell said "They said his tone was much better than Oliver's and they said a good tone would cover up a bad tone and could be heard farther and easier."[37]

Armstrong himself didn't seem to buy any of the aforementioned excuses for the breakup of the band and claimed the other members simply didn't want to go on tour. Yet he was still sorry for this era to end. "Boy that was a real [sad] day for all of us," he wrote. "We had been together for a long time and to break up almost killed us."[38]

Only two musicians remained with Oliver as he planned his tour: Louis and Lil. Oliver had never been in favor of their romance and was dealt a blow on February 5, 1924, when his second cornetist and pianist joined in holy matrimony to become husband and wife.

"After the Lincoln Gardens let out the first night Lil and I got married," Louis wrote, "we made the Rounds to all of the After Hour spots. And everywhere we went - Everybody commenced throwing a lot of Rice on us. My My - I often wondered - where on EARTH did they find so much Rice."[39]

On February 7, the newly married Armstrongs celebrated with a reception at the Ideal Tea Room on South Michigan Avenue. The *Chicago Defender* covered the reception, even printing separate photos of the bride and groom wearing equally serious expressions. Among the guests listed were Joe Oliver, Stella Oliver's daughter Ruby, drummer Fred "Tubby" Hall, cornetist Tommy Ladnier, and Oliver alumni Baby Dodds, Johnny Dodds, and Bill Johnson.[40]

One name was conspicuously absent from the list of guests at the wedding reception: Louis's mother, Mayann, who had returned to New Orleans several months earlier, but not before receiving a whole new wardrobe, purchased by her son.

"Son, now that I know you are all right and I have these fine clothes, I just can't stay another minute," she told him. "I must go back to New Orleans and show these things [off]."

"The night before she left Chicago we made the rounds of all the Night Clubs, + Dances, etc," Louis wrote, adding, "And the police had to show Both of us where we lived the next morning—Coming from those places. Mother + I laughed over that event a lot of times."[41] Louis might have had fond memories, but his mother's drinking was not getting any better. Soon after arriving back in New Orleans, she fell back into old habits and was arrested for "fighting and disturbing the peace" on November 18, 1923. She gave her occupation as "house keeper" but her address of 445 South Franklin Street told another, sadder story: that she had gone back to prostitution.

Louis and Lil did not go on a honeymoon after their marriage, instead choosing to stay in Chicago to prepare for the upcoming tour with Oliver. The decision almost proved disastrous thanks to a scarier-than-usual trip to the movies.

In early February, the Auditorium Theater in Chicago screened D. W. Griffith's controversial 1914 film *Birth of a Nation*, which glorified the role of the Ku Klux Klan during the Civil War, leading to a revival of the Klan. Writing in the *Chicago Tribune*, Mae Tinee celebrated the rerelease of *Birth of a Nation*, calling it "the greatest picture ever made." "Some one has suggested that perhaps its revival may be Ku Klux Klan propaganda," Tinee wrote. "Maybe but I doubt it. Three cheers for *The Birth of a Nation*!"[42]

By screening it, the Auditorium was ignoring a law passed in 1917 that stated it was unlawful to present any film "which portrays depravity, criminality, unchastity, or lack of virtue of any class of citizens of any race, color, creed, or religion and exposes them to contempt and danger in riots." The *Chicago Tribune* argued that such a law was unnecessary, writing, "But the *Tribune* did

MISS LILLIAN HARDIN IS BRIDE OF LOUIS ARMSTRONG

Miss Lillian Hardin, daughter of Mrs. Dempsey Miller, 3320 Giles Ave., was married to Louis Armstrong of New Orleans, La. They gave their reception at the beautiful Ideal Tea room, 3218 S. Michigan Ave., on Thursday evening, Feb. 7. The bride was beautifully attired in a Parisian gown of white crepe elaborately beaded in rhinestones and silver beads and Miss Lucille Saunders, a lifelong chum of the bride, who was her bridesmaid, wore orchid chiffon with silver trimmings.

Mrs. Armstrong

Oscar Young's seven-piece orchestra furnished music for the occasion. Mr. and Mrs. Armstrong are both members of King Oliver's Creole band, who are recording for the Gennett, Okeh and Columbia records. They will leave on Feb. 22 for an extended tour on big time. The guests present were: Misses Lucille Saunders, Mae Gilbert, Laura Watson, Clara Gunn, Anna Ecton, Ruby Oliver, Myrtle Villavasso, Pauline Kinner, Laura Rawlyns, Messrs. Arthur Rockford, William Spratley, Louis Bustill, Val Harvey, James Hollins, Clarence Lee, Willie Saunders, Fred Hall, Warren Dodds, John Dodds, Bill Johnson, Lawrence Guidry, Dr. Owen Williams, Mr. and Mrs. William Gunn, John Miller, Willie King, Joseph Oliver, Tom Ladinier, Raymond Whitsett and Capt. A. Pitts. The couple received many beautiful presents.

Louis Armstrong

Figure 19.2 Newspaper announcement of the wedding of Louis Armstrong and Lillian Hardin, with details on their reception at the Ideal Tea Room, featuring appearances by musicians such as Johnny Dodds, Baby Dodds, drummer Fred "Tubby" Hall, cornetist Tommy Ladnier, and King Oliver.

Credit: Courtesy of the Louis Armstrong House Museum.

not agree that a law was needed to ban the film, writing, "Such a law could be used to interfere with the artistic and intellectual freedom of people. . . . No intelligent person likes to see the principles of free speech within the bounds of public decency restricted for adults, and if we were all sensible adults it would not need [to] be. Sensible adults do not require censors."[43] Nevertheless, after two days of showings on February 5 and 6, the police turned up on February 7, arresting the theater management and stopping the screenings. After a week of protests and court testimonies, the film was officially banned a few days later for violating the 1917 law.

Somehow, in the middle of getting married on February 5, playing the Lincoln Gardens at night and planning for a wedding reception on February 7, Louis Armstrong made time to attend one of the screenings of *Birth of a Nation* at the Auditorium. He remembered it as follows:

> So I went on in there and I got my seat and . . . just before the picture went on, the lights went up and I look around and there's about 5,000 white people sitting there and I'm the only Negro in the crowd. So that didn't move me at all. So when this spade run that white gal off that cliff, you could hear a mouse—you know what I mean? [*mimics audience responses*] "Good God," "My God," you know. They didn't say nothing but I could feel them eyes, you know, out the side and everything. And it was terrible there until they captured this Negro. Then the house come down, applause, and everybody started applauding at *me*. And I could hear them saying, "Well, what are you doing in here?" I'm the only colored man in the place, Pops. And when I got out there, I just took my time, walking with the crowd, I was doing everything, you know, that fresh air hits you and I could see that streetcar coming up Wabash Avenue. So I wouldn't *run* to get that car, but I sure did walk slow very fast![44]

Louis was probably glad to get out of Chicago at such a tense time, as the Oliver tour was due to start February 22.[45] Oliver had to build a new band almost from scratch, hiring Charlie Jackson, who played bass saxophone on some of the band's late 1923 sides, and from New Orleans, the flashy left-handed drummer Clifford "Snags" Jones and trombonist Alvin "Zue" Robertson.

But Oliver now had an opportunity to again expand his ensemble with the addition of not one, but two reedmen, Buster Bailey and Rudy Jackson, who were then causing a commotion with their playing as members of Carroll Dickerson's Orchestra at the Sunset Café.[46] "By Rudy and Buster playing together at the Sunset and Joe and I taking the Duet, we didn't have too much trouble getting together," Louis wrote. "There wasn't too much music to remember, so after a few rehearsals we were kicks to each other.”[47]

After a few successful weeks playing for dancing and on radio broadcasts throughout Ohio and Iowa, the Oliver band’s tour took on new significance on March 13, when the brand-new Music Corporation of America, cofounded by Jules Stein, took over the booking, making Oliver “the first Colored Band ever Booked by that company,” according to Armstrong.[48] Almost immediately, the nature of the band’s publicity began to change, referencing the popular Louis Panico in ads declaring, “King Oliver Taught Isham Jones’ Cornet Player Plenty of His Stuff.” MCA also capitalized on the hysteria caused by the discovery of the sarcophagus containing the coffin of Egyptian King Tutankhamen on February 3, placing advertisements in various cities simply stating, “King Tut is Gone—King Oliver is Coming.”

Figure 19.3 Publicity photo of the 1924 edition of King Oliver’s Creole Jazz Band, taken at Daguerre Studios in Chicago just before their tour. Left to right: Charlie Jackson, Clifford “Snags” Jones, William “Buster” Bailey, Joe “King Oliver,” C. Alvin “Zue” Robertson, Lillian Hardin Armstrong (seated), Louis Armstrong, and Rudy Jackson.
Credit: Courtesy of the New Orleans Jazz Club Collection of the Louisiana State Museum.

Back in Chicago for a short time in early April, Oliver made some changes to reflect an even deeper New Orleans flavor in the band, replacing Charlie Jackson with New Orleans–born bassist John Lindsay and sending to New York for Oliver's old boss at Pete Lala's, pianist Buddy Christian, to join on banjo. Over in the reed section, Armstrong remembered Bailey and Jackson trying to emulate the two-cornet breaks without much success. "The first time they, Buster + Rudy tried it, we were in Madison Wis," Armstrong wrote. "And we had to laugh - because when the break came, Buster + Rudy were in a big argument saying- no man - you started on the wrong note - etc. Ha Ha - They never did try it again."[49]

But Jackson remembered it differently, telling Charles Chilton that he and Bailey surprised Oliver by executing a two-saxophone break perfectly one night. "This shook Joe Oliver considerably and he told Jackson and Bailey to 'cut it out,'" Chilton wrote. "He was the leader of the band and if he wanted the clarinets to play breaks together he'd tell them when to do it."[50] Once they got back to Chicago, Oliver replaced Bailey with Albert Nicholas, who had been leading a noteworthy band at Tom Anderson's in New Orleans. To Nicholas, Oliver gradually increasing the size of his band since sending for Armstrong in 1922 was a sign of his willingness to stay with the times. "He wanted to change to get out of these New Orleans six-piece deals," Nicholas said. "He wanted to build his band up to what he did, to an 8- or 9-piece band, get sort of modernish at the time, you know, with reeds."[51]

With the success of Paul Whiteman's Aeolian Hall concert of February 12, 1924, still making headlines in the music world, Oliver knew the era of the "New Orleans six-piece deals" was coming to an end. The 37 sides he made in 1923 were a punctuation mark, a summation, a literal record of the first 25 years of what became known as New Orleans "traditional" jazz. He had set the gold standard for this music but would not be content to stick with a style that was no longer in vogue. In an article for the *Etude*, Whiteman—billed as "The Millionaire Emperor of Super-Jazz"—discussed the new appeal of the saxophone, calling it "the Caruso of the Jazz Orchestra."[52] If saxophones were in, Oliver would employ multiple reeds and gradually rework his organization into a hot dance band.

Among folks devoted to that original sound of early New Orleans jazz, Oliver's choice to modernize his sound was met with derision. Dr. Edmond Souchon, who booked Oliver at the Tulane gymnasium and later became president of the New Orleans Jazz Club, lamented, "Hearing him again in Chicago, he had completely changed his style. He was trying to play like a white band, even the adding of instruments, a couple of saxes and all. They had lost it. And people went nuts about it."[53]

Young Louis Armstrong was observing all of this from the bandstand. He, too, would one day be faced with decisions about staying up with the times or staying true to his roots. He found ways to accomplish both goals simultaneously, often angering critics and traditional jazz fans like Souchon in the process. But as with Oliver, the "people went nuts about it," and that was all that mattered.

The copious amount of recordings the Creole Jazz Band made in October 1923 began hitting stores in February, just in time for their tour. Tellingly, OKeh chose "Tears" as the first selection, lending credence to Armstrong's belief that if Oliver had featured him a bit more, the records could have been more successful and Oliver still would have gotten the credit. That same day, OKeh also released "Riverside Blues," climaxed by Armstrong. The Paramount version had been issued the previous week so Armstrong's solo was all over the market. The release of these sides so close to each other seems to represent something seismic, Louis Armstrong's true coming-out party to the world. His name wasn't on the records, so it was impossible to identify him unless you frequented the Lincoln Gardens. But there was no denying that the cornet playing on these records represented something both different and dramatic.

These releases also put Oliver in a bit of a spot, as he was now getting requests to play songs that had featured Armstrong on the records. For perhaps the first time, Oliver ceded the spotlight to Armstrong. The *South Bend Tribune* shared a rare set list from a radio appearance in April 1924, noting that the Oliver band performed "Dipper Mouth," "High Society," "St. Louis Blues," and "Eccentric Rag," followed by a duet on "Tears" by "the Armstrongs."[54] Oliver wouldn't be able to hold Armstrong back much longer.

Oliver continued featuring Armstrong more during the second half of the MCA tour of April, May, and June 1924. "Finally when I went on tour with the great King Oliver Jazz Band - he decided to let me do everything and anything that I choose," Armstrong wrote. "The customers really went for it in a big way."[55] In a later interview, Armstrong added further details, saying, "I used to do my little dance.... Yeah, I used to fall and slide, you know." After chuckling at the memory, he exclaimed, "Always a showman!"[56]

Saxophonist Rudy Jackson remembered that this turn eventually created some tension with the leader. "Louis' humor, singing and playing were a great attraction, and before long people were suggesting that Louis should lead the band," Charles Chilton wrote after a conversation with Jackson. "This upset Oliver considerably as, although he was very fond of Louis, he did not like the idea of his attracting so much attention. However, Oliver found that quite often when he was booked for a date he was not wanted unless Louis accompanied him. Louis, eager to please Joe, purposely toned down his playing and took a back seat."[57] The last thing Armstrong wanted to do was show up Oliver. "After all—I was in there with him with all my heart," he said. "Because I loved Joe Oliver—And would do anything in the World to make him Happy."[58]

As the tour continued through Indiana, Michigan, and Pennsylvania in May and made its way back to Chicago in June, Louis probably felt this was the beginning of a new phase of the musical partnership he had with Oliver—but in Lil's mind, this was the end.

20

"Second Trumpet to No One"

1924

As the Oliver tour came to an end in June, Lil delivered an ultimatum: "When we came back off the trip, I told him, I said, 'Now I don't want to be married to a second trumpet player.'"

"What are you talking about?" Louis responded.

"Well, I don't want to be married to a second trumpet player," Lil repeated. "I want you to play first."

"Well, I can't play first!" Louis nervously answered. "Joe's playing first!"

"Well, that's why you've got to quit," Lil calmly told him.

"I can't quit Mr. Joe!" Louis said, growing almost hysterical. "Mr. Joe sent for me and I can't quit him!"

"Well, it's Mr. Joe or me!" Lil told him with finality.[1]

Rudy Jackson remembered that it was on the train ride back to Chicago that Lil and the other members "persuaded Armstrong that it was to his advantage to leave Oliver and try his luck elsewhere." Jackson said it took "an hour or two" to convince him but once they did, Louis "couldn't pluck up the courage to tell him." Jackson was chosen to deliver the news to Oliver, who was sleeping in his seat. Jackson thought Oliver would "go raving mad," but instead he "merely sat up quietly, as though he wasn't really quite awake, and said he knew how much better Louis was than himself and that it was lucky Louis liked him enough to have stayed with him for so long. This, probably the biggest blow Oliver ever received, he accepted in the calmest possible manner."[2]

Lil remembered that she wrote his notice for him and that Louis copied it and gave it to Oliver himself, but the reaction was the same in her version. Oliver "didn't say a word," she said. "He just sat there."

Oliver eventually approached Lil and said, "Louis gave me his notice tonight—I didn't get yours."

"No, I'm not quitting," she told him matter-of-factly.

"Well, why is Louis quitting?" Oliver asked.

Lil offered a noncommittal reply, breaking into laughter as she recalled it 45 years later. "I didn't say yes, I didn't say no," she said. Oliver just shook his head, puzzled.

"Well, don't worry," Lil confidently told Oliver. "He'll be back with us soon."

"And I said to myself, 'Over my dead body he will.'"[3]

Looking back in 1970, Louis said, "You know how much I love Joe Oliver, regardless of all that other crap, but still in all, he did make a statement to Lil during a conversation. He said, 'As long as Little Louis is with me, he can't hurt me.' When she told me that, that did it."

"With a thought like that in King Oliver's mind, as much as you idolize him, daddy, you must leave him immediately because King Oliver and his ego and wounded vanities may hurt your pride," he remembered Lil telling him. "It's all indications that King Oliver's trying to hold you back."

"I must have been very quiet because I didn't say a mumbling word," Louis reflected. "Even after she told me, I didn't say nothing. I just split, that's all. Lil spoke and that was it."[4]

Louis often recalled the advice Oliver drilled into him during their nights together on the bandstand at Henry Matranga's: "Listen boy, you play some more lead!"[5]

Now, after two years of playing second cornet to Oliver, Lil gave him similar advice, but changed the wording in a very calculated way.

"I listened very carefully when Lil told me to 'Always play the lead,' " Louis said. " 'Play second trumpet to no one. They don't come great enough.' And she proved it. Yes sir, she proved that she was right, didn't she?"

"You're damn right she did," he said, answering his own question.[6]

Armstrong could respond with such confidence 46 years later after a long career as one of the most influential and popular musicians of the 20th century. But the day after he quit the Oliver band, he was just another unemployed musician, unsure of what his next job would be.

"Well, now that I quit, now what do you want me to do?" he asked Lil on his first day off.

"Well just go on out!" she told him. "Go around to musicians, find out who needs a trumpet player—and a first one."

"I think you're crazy," Louis said.

The first place he visited was Joe Glaser's Sunset Café, where Sammy Stewart and His Ten Knights of Syncopation held forth. "They were the first negro organized orchestra playing special arrangements to hit Chicago," Stewart's saxophonist, Roy Butler, later said. "They were not known for playing 'hot' or jazz music, but more on the sweet, semi-classical style, with which Paul Whiteman later made headlines."[7]

According to trombonist Albert Wynn, Stewart and his light-skinned musicians "looked down on the type of bands that we're talking about [from New Orleans]. They were what we called the 'dicty' bands. They tried to play pretty and everything, one of those kinds of things."[8] Butler agreed, even using the word "dicty"—slang for "snobbish," or "high class"—to describe Stewart.

"The first time the members of our band saw Armstrong and Oliver at the Lincoln Gardens, we thought they were funny," Butler said. "We didn't know that we were listening to something important. Louis always kept his music on the seat of his chair and stood up and played a second voice to everything that King Oliver blew out of his horn—he never looked at the music. Louis was showing signs of genius but we didn't recognize it at the time. The importance of jazz had not seeped through yet to 'dicty' colored folks. They just made fun of it."[9]

When Armstrong heard Stewart was looking to hire a new trumpet player, he went to the Sunset Café in hopes of playing for him. Stewart wasn't interested.

"Well, I mean, let me blow a few notes there, you might like it," Armstrong told Stewart upon meeting him. "You know, maybe I'll fit in."

"No, we don't think you should blow," came Stewart's curt reply.[10]

Louis remained hurt by Stewart's rebuke for the rest of his life; as late as 1970, he wrote to Max Jones, "I wasn't 'dicty' enough, regardless of how good I played, I wasn't up to his society."[11]

Louis went home to Lil, still in a stupor.

"He didn't even turn around to speak to me," Louis said. "Just snapped at me and said, 'No, I don't need anybody.' "

"Don't worry about them," Lil insisted, "they'll soon be eating at your feet!"[12]

Lil wasn't wrong; today, Stewart remains an obscure name, as he was eventually overwhelmed by Armstrong's popularity—something Armstrong was not afraid to point out. "Two years later, he's still kicking himself for it—but I mean, I done feel like kicking him, too!" Armstrong said in 1953. "But to not at least listen, you know? And right now he's in oblivion, you don't even hear of him no more."[13]

Back to the drawing board, Lil took more of a role in shaping her husband's sound. She recalled teaching him "classical stuff" and said she "used to take Louis around to some of the churches to play. He used to get so afraid and would sweat like anything before he went on. Would get so nervous and excited before he played the solo."[14]

Louis was still fixated on his mentor and once worked for an entire week to try to play Oliver's "Dipper Mouth Blues" solo and "Then got so disgusted, Louis gave it up as impossible," Lil said. "Couldn't work his hand on the wah-wah stuff."[15] She also recalled that Louis would say, "You should have heard this fellow Bunk play," and would sing and whistle Bunk Johnson's phrases. She soon became enamored with her husband's whistling. "I could hear Louis coming home whistling for, oh, much more than a block away," she said. "He had the most beautiful shrill whistle and all those riffs that he later made in his music, he used to whistle them. . . . Such beautiful riffs and runs and trills and things you know. And I said, 'Maybe some day that guy'll play like that.' You know, crazy thoughts but it turned out all right. You never know when you're crazy the right way, huh?"[16] Taking notes on a 1938 conversation with Lil, William Russell wrote, "So finally she figured out that Louis was wasting his time trying to copy Oliver and not so good at it, and she said, 'Go ahead and play your own way,' the way he whistled and like the way that Bunk used to play, and that is where the great Louis Armstrong began to emerge."[17]

It must have felt surreal for Louis to have a wife who was in his corner encouraging him instead of someone like Daisy, who was more prone to throw a brick at him. Another figure from his New Orleans days who was settling down in this period was drummer Black Benny Williams. "Just had changed over to a nice style life didn't he, married a good-looking gal and they were settled down and everything," Louis said in 1953, before chuckling and adding, "After he got through hitting a cat in the chops with about three cueballs!"[18] Indeed, Black Benny might have domesticated to an extent, but he still resorted to his old ways when necessary, getting arrested for fighting and disturbing the peace on November 15, 1923.[19]

But overall, Williams was doing well and working regularly as the drummer at the Lyric Theater when he entered Benny Ventrola's "soft drink establishment" at 1234 Gravier Street in the early hours of July 2, 1924, with two women, 19-year-old Eva Paul and 22-year-old Hazel Minor. When 24-year-old prostitute Helena Lewis entered the venue, Black Benny asked her to dance to the music of pianist John Churchill. While dancing, Lewis stepped on Paul's foot and an argument broke out. Black Benny struck Lewis—who had a knife hidden in her hand. Lewis opened the knife and stabbed Black Benny in the heart. "Benny Williams walked to this Station where he was taken to the Charity Hospital . . . where Williams was pronounced as suffering from a 'penetrating stab wound of the left chest near the heart (later diagnosed as of the heart) condition serious and probably fatal,'" the homicide report stated.[20]

After being stitched up and transfused a pint of blood from his sister, "Black Benny woke up and began to talk," James Karst wrote.[21] The miracle was short-lived, though, and Williams developed an infection, which ended his life at 4:10 p.m. on July 6, 1924. Williams's age was given as 32 at the time of his murder, but based on his World War I draft registration card and his various arrest records, he might have been 34. "I've never seen a funeral in my life like he had," drummer Joe Watkins recalled. "I think they had three or four bands. And on top of the hearse . . . they had his bass drum up there. His real bass drum, they had it up on top of the hearse. I never will forget it."[22]

Just days later, Helena Lewis, free on bond, was shot and killed by a woman named Mary Sewell, right in Armstrong's old Gravier and Franklin Street neighborhood. "Woman Slayer of Black Benny Shot to Death" a headline blared. The Wild West had nothing on the Third Ward.

Armstrong did not return to New Orleans for Black Benny's funeral, but he heard all about it. "I'll show you how he died now," he later told friends. "They was getting ready to fight and she stabbed him in the heart running away from the man. And he lived a whole week with his heart split open. Just think if he had been up this way in a good hospital, man—see, that Charity Hospital was loaded with people. I mean, they were lucky to get to you. If he had a private doctor, he probably would have made it. Strong constitution."[23]

Armstrong's writings would ensure Black Benny's immortality in some ways, but he was now a long way from home and was not planning on returning any time soon.

As Louis continued looking for work, Lil was back at the Lincoln Gardens with King Oliver, who was still in a state of disbelief over Louis having left him. "What does Louis think he's gonna do there, all by himself, without us?" Oliver would ask Lil. "He'll find out, he'll have to come back."[24]

Lil wouldn't hear of it. In early July, she sent Louis to audition for drummer and vocalist Ollie Powers's new band that would soon debut at the Dreamland Café. This time, Louis was met with open arms and passed the audition.

"Well, I'm going in the Dreamland with Ollie Powers," he told Lil.

"Oh yeah, Ollie Powers is good," a pleased Lil responded. "That's good!" She then asked the burning question: "So how many trumpet players are in it?"

"Just one," Louis said.

"Oh, then you'll be first," Lil happily concluded.

"Girl, you're sure crazy!" Louis told his wife.

Louis would spend the summer of 1924 with Powers's Harmony Syncopators. Because there are no recordings from this period, this band is sometimes given short shrift when discussing Armstrong's development. But according to Lil, this was when he really made his reputation as a cornetist in Chicago. "Because when Louis was the only trumpet player he played what he had in himself. He wasn't playing second to Joe or anybody else," she said. "And I think [as] soon as he started playing by himself, all those ideas that were in his head came out because he wasn't copying anybody."[25]

Such ideas would create quite a buzz after Armstrong was confronted by one of the most famous trumpeters in the country, Johnny Dunn.[26]

Though mostly forgotten today, the Memphis-born Dunn was the first African American star trumpeter on records. He originally came to New York as a member of W. C. Handy's band and began recording steadily for Columbia with his "Original Jazz Hounds," creating a sensation with his version of "Bugle Blues." To Black musicians outside New Orleans and Chicago, Dunn's recordings were quite influential. Trumpeter and saxophonist Adolphus "Doc" Cheatham was born in 1905 and grew up in Nashville, where there wasn't much of a jazz scene. "Johnny Dunn made quite a few records and we'd begin to hear those once in a while but that was about all," Cheatham said. "I think everybody was excited over his recording of 'Bugle Blues.' I thought he was great, too."[27]

Dunn even had an impact in New Orleans. Joe Oliver might have pioneered the use of different mutes to achieve his "freak" sounds, but there was one that eluded him in his early days: the plunger. Punch Miller remembered Dunn performing at the Lyric Theater with Mamie Smith in the early 1920s and said, "After that, when he come here with that plunger, everybody started getting them." Miller also recalled that the first time he heard a trumpeter play an obligato behind a vocalist was on Dunn's May 19, 1922, recording of "Mammy, I'm Thinking of You" with Edith Wilson. "Boy, you talk about something!" Miller said when recalling it. "That was the only thing I liked about the whole song, [what] he put in there."[28]

However, Miller wasn't impressed by Dunn's jazz style. "This fellow Johnny Dunn played a nice horn, but he wasn't a swing man," he said, adding, "Because he didn't do nothing but play behind singers, see. . . . But just playing swing out like that, he wouldn't do any of that. He couldn't do it, he didn't know how to do it."[29]

New Orleans aside, Dunn was a star by the end of 1923, having toured Europe with *Lew Leslie's Plantation Revue*, starring Florence Mills. *Variety* even published a large photo of Dunn with his elongated "coach" trumpet, surrounded by various mutes. While Louis Armstrong was getting the occasional rare solo on King Oliver's recordings, Dunn recorded "Dunn's Cornet Blues" with just banjo and piano backing on April 11, 1924. "It remained for Columbia to release a 'cornet' record, and in doing so they selected Johnny Dunn, the one man who can do more with a cornet than a monkey can do with a cocoanut," the *Chicago Defender* wrote on June 14, 1924.[30]

"The importance of Johnny Dunn to early Negro blues and jazz in New York City cannot be more stressed," trumpeter Louie Metcalf said. "When I came to New York everybody was playing like Johnny—trumpeters, saxes, pianists and even banjoists were copying Dunn. He was perhaps the first Negro blues-jazz style in New York City which really caught on big. In fact it was hard for you to get a job playing jazz if you didn't catch on to the tricks of Johnny."[31]

Dunn was now preparing for the next big Lew Leslie show, *Dixie to Broadway*, which would once again star Florence Mills and debut on Broadway in the fall of 1924. On August 17, 1924, Leslie began presenting previews of the new show in Chicago, staging it at the Great Northern Theater and the Shubert Garrick, where it drew capacity crowds. Though the saga of Armstrong and Dunn was often placed in different venues and different eras, Armstrong maintained it happened at the Dreamland Café on a night when the dance team of Herbert Brown and Mary McGraw were on the bill. Brown and McGraw were "riots at the Dreamland nightly," according to the August 23 *Chicago Defender*, definitively placing this moment in late August 1924.[32]

Armstrong twice told this story on tape, once to the editors of *The Record Changer* in 1950 and again in conversation with Zutty Singleton in 1971. In both instances, he disparaged the New York scene. "I noticed them big shots [from New York] would come to Chicago with them big shows," he said. "Them people, they were so carried away with that phony jazz around here [New York], they thought they had everything sewn up. Then they'll come to a big town like Chicago and they'll send the hot man that they think is great up to cut you! And they did that to me with Johnny Dunn."[33]

"And Johnny Dunn was the big thing in New York with that jive he was playing," Armstrong said in 1950, breaking into a bit of very stiff scat singing to demonstrate. "And tearing up New York with that, playing the Palace and everything. And a lot of people hadn't heard of Joe Oliver.[34]

Armstrong said the cast of *Dixie to Broadway* heard about "this little cat" playing cornet at Dreamland and said, "Come on, Johnny, we'll go up there."[35] Darnell Howard was playing clarinet in Ollie Powers's band and said, "Johnny Dunn and Florence Mills's show was downtown, you know. They just got off and Johnny, he was a sharp dresser. He used to stand up there with his coat on and his cane, no hat, hair shining like an onion."[36]

When Dunn's party arrived, Armstrong was in the middle of playing for Brown and McGraw's act, of which he was an integral part. "I used to put all the notes to every step they made, just playing around and them summitches, they worked up a beautiful act," he said.[37] Howard was the first one in the band to notice Dunn. "He's looking at Louie," he said. "This was early in the evening and Brown and McGraw was out there....Johnny's standing up there with his arm on the bandstand—see, they had a railing around us, you know—and all of a sudden, he says to Louie, 'Hey, give me that horn!' "[38]

Armstrong remembered Dunn using a different phrase:

"Let me get some of that."

This immediately rubbed him the wrong way. In February 1971, just five months away from his death, Armstrong was still venting about it in his conversation with Singleton: "You know, we don't hear all that in Chicago. Everybody was *good* in Chicago. You go in any nightclub, nigger's blowing the right notes and solid, and everybody's got the right beat. But these phony cats, they got the jazz all bass ackwards—didn't they?—in New York. But they're big shots and the white folks and everything books them out there. But when they got out there [to Chicago], they had to shit or get off the pot! But they don't realize that til this night."

Armstrong could feel the tension. "So it's a big show and they're all waiting to see what's going to happen," he said.

"Let me get some of that."

"Yeah, Daddy, take it," Armstrong told Dunn as he passed him his cornet.

"I handed him the horn and when he started blowing, every valve he pushed down to play was the wrong one because I was playing in five sharps!" Armstrong said, referring to the difficult key of B major. "You ask any musician, is it hard to play in five sharps, any trumpet player. And they don't know nothing about that shit coming from New York. And that son-of-a-bitch was scuffling, saying, 'Come on, man,' yammering on, 'I-I-I can't play that.' "[39]

"And Johnny, he ain't did nothing," is how Howard remembered it.

"He can't play so he give me my horn back," Armstrong said. "I'm blowing like nothing happened."[40]

Howard never forgot the way Armstrong played after Dunn's show of disrespect. "But when that man give Louie that horn back, it was awful," he said. "I felt like hiding myself. You know it was one of them things—terrible!"[41]

"And all them niggers walked out like cut tail dogs, even the stars, [Florence Mills] and everything," Armstrong said. "Have to go through all that shit, you know."[42]

Word of the way this unknown country boy embarrassed the great Johnny Dunn traveled fast, eventually making waves in New York City—and getting the attention of Fletcher Henderson.

Two years had passed since Henderson had heard Louis Armstrong in New Orleans and asked him to join his band. "I never forgot that horn," Henderson said.[43] In 1922, Henderson was still recording director for Harry Pace's pioneering Black Swan label, but Pace had grown uncomfortable with the amount of blues and jazz being recorded. Pace was a student of W. E. B. DuBois, who served on Black Swan's board of directors and was a firm believer in the power of what DuBois dubbed “the Talented Tenth.” “The Negro race, like all races, is going to be saved by its exceptional men,” DuBois had written in 1903, arguing that if one-tenth of African Americans dedicated themselves to receiving a higher education and fighting for social change—“developing the Best of this race,” in his words—it would have a positive effect on the plight of the other nine-tenths.[44]

Twenty years after DuBois wrote those words, Pace was beginning to feel that jazz music and folk blues championed by southern African Americans migrating north was not an example of the “Best of this race.” He began recording less of these styles and turned toward Broadway material, spirituals, sacred songs, classical music, and light opera. In the January 1923 issue of *Crisis,* the magazine of the National Association for the Advancement of Colored People (NAACP), Pace took out a full-page ad imploring, “If you—the person reading this advertisement—earnestly want to Do Something for Negro Music, Go to your Record Dealer and ask for the Better Class of Records by Colored Artists.”[45] But the jazz and blues being recorded for white-owned labels such as OKeh, Paramount, and Columbia was outselling Black Swan's “Better Class of Records,” and at this point the label began floundering and was bought out by Paramount in March 1924.

Henderson had left Black Swan in 1923 and formed his own dance band soon after teaming up with a young saxophonist and arranger from Piedmont, West Virginia, named Don Redman. In the summer of 1923, Henderson added 19-year-old saxophonist Coleman Hawkins and 21-year-old drummer Joseph “Kaiser” Marshall, two future stars—and pioneers—who would remain with Henderson until the end of the decade.[46]

As Henderson began a residency at the Club Alabam in New York in January 1924, he expanded into a nine-piece band thanks to the addition of Howard Scott's trumpet, Teddy Nixon's trombone, Allie Ross's violin, Charlie Dixon's banjo, and Ralph Escudero's tuba. Though Henderson was still the leader, violinist Ross conducted the band. While an obvious nod in the direction of Paul Whiteman, this move was also inspired by the popularity of the first Black New Orleans bandleader to achieve success in New York City, Armand J. Piron.

Piron had first headed north in September 1922, along with pianist Steve Lewis, “to demonstrate his new hits,” which had been published by his longtime partner Clarence Williams, including “I Wish I Could Shimmy Like My Sister Kate.”[47] Piron's success led him to eventually send for his entire band to join him in New York in late 1923 for a series of recordings for Columbia and Victor, in addition to public performances at the Cotton Club and Club De Luxe. On May 24, 1924, they became the first African American band to play at the whites-only Roseland Ballroom, "The Home of Refined Dancing," at Broadway and 51st Street, since it had opened on January 1, 1919. However, by July, Piron and his organization headed back home to New Orleans, with *Billboard* reporting "they couldn't get their price for a vaudeville route."[48]

Louis Armstrong was watching this unfold from Chicago with almost perverse interest; he knew that Piron's band didn't go back home because of money. "There's Clarence Williams, Piron, Steve Lewis, they all went to New York at the Roseland, they had a tune," Armstrong said in 1958 before singing a few bars of "Mama's Gone, Goodbye," which Piron recorded for Victor. "Took the whole East by storm. Two months of that, they got homesick and quit right in the middle of success."

Armstrong then talked about Joe Oliver, saying, "When he went to Chicago, he could have hired good musicians out of Chicago, but he felt that he couldn't play unless he had the boys from New Orleans....So, when I come to Chicago and I looked around, I said, 'Oh my God, all these good musicians and Joe Oliver's playin' with a lot of fellas, every chance they got, they want to cut his throat.' "[49]

Oliver was struggling, placing an advertisement in the *Chicago Defender* on September 6, 1924, announcing he was "Open for Engagements in or out of Chicago."[50] After unsuccessfully testing the waters in New York,[51] he returned to Chicago and sent to New Orleans for Lee Collins to join him as his new second cornetist. After Collins's first night with the band, Oliver invited Collins to his apartment to have red beans and rice cooked by his wife Stella. "Joe seems happy now," Stella told Collins. "He got a boy sittin' beside him just like Louis, plays the ol' New Orleans stuff and he's happy again."[52] Oliver might have been happy, but business didn't improve and by October the Lincoln Gardens had cut Oliver down to only playing Wednesdays, Saturdays, and Sundays.

Armstrong summed up the situation with Oliver and Piron the same way: "They all had that little inferiority complex."

Now with Lil by his side, Louis was erasing any traces of such a complex. He was not going to solely rely on New Orleans musicians like Oliver and he was not going to go back home with his tail between his legs as he envisioned Piron did. He was determined to make it up north on his own terms.

Fletcher Henderson's band replaced Piron at Roseland in July 1924, at which time he added a new hot trombonist in Charlie "Big" Green. *Variety* caught a radio broadcast of the band and praised their "corking brand of dance music" but also predicted "serious competition in the fall from the

Arcadia," a new ballroom that would open only a block away from Roseland.[53] Roseland kicked off its fall season on September 23, using high-profile white dance bands led by Vincent Lopez and Sam Lanin before bringing Henderson back on October 13. Henderson was able to keep up with the other top white bands of the era, but he now sought to hire an additional trumpet player and reedman for his October run and wanted each man to be of the hot, rather than the sweet, variety.

Word of Armstrong's victory over Johnny Dunn in Chicago must have hit New York circles soon after Dunn left the Dreamland Cafe. The timing was perfect for Henderson, who would reach out to Armstrong soon after to ask him to join his orchestra in October. "Knowing the way that horn sounded, I had to try to get him for my band that was scheduled to open at the Roseland ballroom," Henderson said. "Truthfully, I didn't expect him to accept the offer, and I was very surprised when he came to New York and joined us."[54]

It could not have been an easy decision. On September 24, Louis's cousin Flora Myles passed away, causing Louis to immediately step into action. "I had the folks down in New Orleans whom I left Clarence to live with while I went to Chicago—I had them to put a Tag on Clarence—put him on a train and send him to me," he wrote to Robert Goffin. "It was one swell Grand Re-union."[55] Though Louis considered him his adopted son, just days after this "Grand Re-Union," Louis would leave Clarence and Lil behind in Chicago to try to make it in New York City.[56]

21

"Big Headed Motherfuckers"

1924–1925

Upon arriving in New York at the beginning of October 1924, Armstrong was greeted by two of Fletcher Henderson's men, there to take him to his first rehearsal. "Kaiser Marshall had a car and brought us downtown to meet Louis," Don Redman said. "He was big and fat, and wore high top shoes with hooks in them, and long underwear down to his socks. When I got a load of that, I said to myself, who in the hell is this guy? It can't be Louis Armstrong."[1] Armstrong wasn't entering the band with a big reputation either. Asked if he had heard any of Armstrong's recordings with King Oliver, Henderson's second trumpet player, Howard Scott, responded, "No, I had not heard any. In fact, I hadn't heard about Louis at all."[2]

Matters didn't improve when Armstrong arrived at the rehearsal, held at the Happy Rhone Club in Harlem. "The band was up on the stand waiting when he got there, and Louis walked across the floor," Marshall said. "He had on big thick-soled shoes, the kind that policemen wear, and he came walking across the floor, clump-clump, and grinned and said hello to all the boys."[3] "He had high shoes on, button shoes," Scott recalled "And a cardboard suitcase, and his stomach was way out like this."[4] Lil might have spruced up her husband's appearance during their days with King Oliver, but he stuck out like a country boy in New York.

For his part, Louis immediately felt a draft, too. "I walked in and every son-of-a-bitch saw me and looked up," he said. "Nobody said nothin', you know."[5]

When Henderson finally appeared, Armstrong introduced himself.

"How do you do, Mr. Fletcher?" he said. "I'm the trumpet player you sent for."

"Yeah, yeah," Henderson said curtly. "Your part is up there."[6]

Armstrong never forgot the first song waiting for him on his music stand: Thurlow Lieurance's composition "By the Waters of Minnetonka," recorded by Paul Whiteman on June 11, 1924, and recently released on Victor. Armstrong looked over his third trumpet part and felt confident. "I can read because I was playin' in the funeral marches in the brass band [in New

Orleans]," he said. "So I went up there and it went down. It sure did sound pretty."[7]

Armstrong's playing didn't win him any immediate friends. "Still ain't none of them sons-of-bitches didn't say nothin' to me," he noted after that first song. "Bunch of hincty cats," he thought to himself, using a slang term similar to "dicty." "I'm gettin' evil now myself. I'll put that Liberty and Perdido on 'em there."

Matters didn't improve when Marshall finally looked down at Armstrong and shouted, "Man, what you doin' with them high top shoes on?"

"I started tellin' him . . . what to do, you know?" Armstrong said. "And they just razzin' me about it."[8]

For his part, Marshall remembered the situation lightening up when Armstrong began struggling with some of Henderson's charts. "They were pretty fancy arrangements, and although Louis was a good reader at that time, he had a little trouble at first," Marshall said. "He would make a mistake, and jump up and say: 'Man, what is that thing?' Then everybody laughed and Louis would sit down and play it right the next time. After he made one mistake he didn't make it again."[9]

In 1950, Henderson was asked by two separate periodicals to pen tributes to Armstrong and both times, told a story about that first rehearsal that is possibly apocryphal—Armstrong himself never told it—but did become part of jazz lore. Henderson recalled that the band was rehearsing "a medley of beautiful Irish waltzes" that featured a section marked *fff* for fortissimo, followed by a diminuendo down to pianissimo, marked *pp* on the score.

"The band followed these notations and was playing very softly while Louis still played his part at full volume," Henderson said.

"Louis, you are not following the arrangement," Henderson said sharply.

"I'm reading everything on this sheet," Armstrong objected.

"But, Louis, how about that *pp*?" Henderson asked.

"And Louis broke us all up by replying, 'Oh, I thought that meant 'pound plenty,'" Henderson recalled. "There was no tension after that!"[10]

Both Henderson and Armstrong agreed that the tension really dissipated after the band's tuba player, Ralph "Cuba" Escudero, got into an altercation with trombonist Charlie "Big" Green. The exact details of the incident remained hazy—Henderson said Escudero's instrument fell on Green's trombone and Green yelled, "Why, you hit my horn, you S. O. B.," while Armstrong remembered Escudero leaning over and mockingly playing Green's trombone part on his tuba, before threatening, "You son-of-bitch, I cut the ass!" Regardless of the details, both Armstrong and Henderson remembered

Louis's response to the argument the same way: "I know I'm gonna like *this* band," he said.[11]

After the ribbing from his new bandmates, Armstrong realized he needed a new wardrobe for his Roseland debut. "I got me a sharp tuxedo and fell in love with it," he said. "$50 for a tuxedo in 1924! You *know* I had a sharp one."[12] He even agreed to part ways with his beloved long underwear after his bandmates constantly kidded him about it. Marshall remembered, "He had to take so much about those drawers that he finally said to me: 'All right, I'll take them off, but if I catch cold in the winter time I'll blame it on you.'"[13]

He also needed a new instrument. Though he would later date his switch from cornet to trumpet as occurring in Chicago the following year, section mate Howard Scott remembered it happening almost immediately after Armstrong arrived on orders from Henderson himself. "We met him one day and we went downtown to Conn's [at 237 W. 47th Street], we went down there and picked out a trumpet for him, went down there, [trumpeter] Elmer Chambers and myself," Scott said. "We took Louie cause he didn't know his way around, he had to find his way around New York. And he was such a likeable fellow, he was laughing and joking all the time, Louie was, all the time, about this and that."[14]

Henderson's search for a new reedman proved more difficult after saxophonists Vance Dixon and Milt Senior both turned him down. Armstrong then suggested Buster Bailey, with whom he'd played on tour with King Oliver, saying he "had confidence in the man."[15] Bailey arrived on October 6, a day before the new Henderson's new band had its first recording session for Columbia, cutting "Manda" and "Go 'Long, Mule." The new men immediately made their presence felt, with Armstrong taking poised, swinging solos on each selection, rising above the closing ensemble on the latter, while Bailey contributed exciting clarinet counterpoint throughout the date. The rest of the band's playing and the arrangements, with their warbling saxophone passages and muted "doo-wacka-doo" trumpets reflected the standard sounds of the day, but Armstrong and Bailey now gave Henderson two fresh ingredients to stand out from the pack of contemporary dance bands, white and Black.

One week later on October 13, Henderson opened at Roseland. Armstrong's playing made an immediate impression on the musicians of New York. "When he sat in the band, he just thrilled everybody," multi-instrumentalist Garvin Bushell said. "I mean, he was just sensational, and we had never heard anything like it."[16]

To Bushell, the influence of Armstrong's hometown had much to do with his impact on the New York scene. "Well, you see, all New Orleans trumpet players could swing," he continued, though he was quick to add, "No other

Figure 21.1 Fletcher Henderson and His Orchestra publicity photo, taken c. late 1924. Back row, left to right: Charlie Green, Howard Scott, Louis Armstrong, Elmer Chambers, Ralph Escudero. Front row, left to right: Kaiser Marshall, Coleman Hawkins, Buster Bailey, Don Redman, Charlie Dixon, Fletcher Henderson. According to trumpeter Yoshio Toyama, it appears that Armstrong might be holding the same Beuscher trumpet that later appears in the Hot Five publicity photos of 1926.
Credit: The Frank Driggs Collection, Jazz at Lincoln Center.

trumpet produced that kind of sound, not even those other guys in New Orleans."[17] "Nothing like that had been heard before in New York, nothing like the way Louis played," Howard Scott said, agreeing with Bushell that Armstrong "brought that New Orleans stuff here."[18]

Scott also recalled that on opening night, Armstrong was "nervous . . . about getting up there and taking solos."

"Wha-wha-wha-say, what's the matter, what do I have to do?" Armstrong would stammer. "Stand up when I take my solos? How am I going to play? And all these people out there?"

"Yes!" Scott declared. "Listen, just close your eyes, Louie, and play and forget about the people. Just play as you feel, that's all."

Scott's advice worked. "Louis played that opening night at Roseland, and my goodness, people stopped dancing to come around and listen to him," he said. "And they could hear him out in the street. And we were told that there were some people passing by that stopped, listening to him. He was so loud.

But he played. Well, that was the first night. The next night, you couldn't get in the place. Just that quick. It had gone all around about this new trumpet player at Roseland." As the band's original hot soloist, Armstrong was technically taking over Scott's role, but Scott didn't mind it. "See, I'd taken solos myself," Scott said, "but when Louis started to play—whew, that was it."[19]

Armstrong himself was somewhat surprised at the reaction he was getting because he didn't have much to do in Henderson and Redman's arrangements. "They'd got me there to blow that hot stuff," he said. "Lot of the time all I had to play in the arrangement was an 8 bar, maybe 16 bar solo. First time I did it, they went wild and I did too. Them cats all stood up and cheered. Just another night to me, you know, but it's a good feeling to know that they're satisfied that you're with them."[20] Buster Bailey inspired a similar reaction after Henderson let him cut loose one night on "Tiger Rag." "That was all. . . that WAS all!" Don Redman said. "He really broke up the Roseland that night!"[21] "And they jumped on 'Tiger Rag,' I think, one night at the Roseland," Armstrong said. "They must have given him, like, four choruses, you know, one of them things and following Buster, they had me come on, and from then on, I was in with the band."[22]

"It lifted up the band and it just made a tighter unit of the whole band, just those two men were such an addition," Howard Scott said. "And they were masters on their instruments. So they just improved the whole band 100 percent, yes. Buster and Louie. And everybody spoke about it too, all the musicians."[23]

Armstrong's transformative effects on the Henderson band are best felt when analyzing "The Meanest Kind of Blues," originally recorded on August 29 before he joined, and remade on November 14 with Armstrong front and center. On the first version, Howard Scott carries the ball with some effective plunger-muted wah-wah trumpeting, but he rarely deviates from the melody. Charlie Green's trombone is confident throughout, but Don Redman's clarinet is a bit sour and there's a stiff trumpet break at the end that might be the work of Elmer Chambers.

In November, the same selection is now Armstrong's show from nearly start to finish. He, too, opens with the melody, but phrasing it in his own relaxed fashion, filling in the cracks with his own lyrical phrases, as if playing a game of call-and-response with himself. The presence of Bailey gave Redman a new secret weapon: the clarinet trio, used to good effect here in a passage of their own. "When Buster came in and made a trio—boy, what a trio!" Scott said. In the last chorus, Redman had the clarinets set a riff under Armstrong, who hits a high F and holds it for nearly eight bars, a total of about 15 seconds. Once again, Armstrong was looking forward while looking backward; holding a note was a trademark of young Joe Oliver and Punch Miller back in New Orleans, but Armstrong was the first to record this test of endurance.

In 1950, Henderson himself admitted that Armstrong had "influenced the band greatly, too, by making the men really swing-conscious with that New Orleans style of his. The same kind of effect that Coleman Hawkins had on the reeds, that right-down-to-earth swing, with punch and bounce."[24]

Armstrong was immediately impressed by the playing of Hawkins and even introduced a new word—at least up north—to describe him, telling Bailey "that guy really swings." "That was the first time I had heard the word used that way, and I didn't dig what he meant," Bailey said. "Louis tried to explain it. He said, 'Man, he swings! He swings out of this world!' I caught on to what he meant, because after I got to work that night 1 heard Hawkins. So I knew what he meant."[25]

For his part, in 1944, Hawkins recalled a time at the Roseland when Armstrong was featured on "Shanghai Shuffle." "I think they made him play ten choruses," Hawkins said. "After that piece a dancer lifted Armstrong onto his shoulders. Fletcher Henderson kept on beating out the rhythm on his piano and I stood silent, feeling almost bashful, asking myself if I would ever be able to attain a small part of Louis Armstrong's greatness."[26]

Hawkins's remembrance of "Shanghai Shuffle" was apt, as Armstrong's solo on that particular number—done at his second session with Henderson—is one of his greatest from this period. For the first minute, the band sounds like any dance band of the period tackling a quasi-exotic number, down to Don Redman breaking out an oboe for a chorus. But then, like the sun breaking through the clouds, Armstrong enters with a call to arms and proceeds to almost will the rhythm section to swing beneath him. Not getting the support he's used to from New Orleans musicians, Armstrong turns his trumpet into a rhythm instrument, at one point repeating a single note 18 straight times, but with the swagger and confidence of a latter-day hip-hop emcee.

One hundred years later, Armstrong's "Shanghai Shuffle" still has the power to dazzle modern-day listeners. "That solo to me changed how jazz was played," states saxophonist and educator Antonio Hart. "You listen to how all those guys played right before that? When Louis Armstrong came in with that syncopation, the whole thing changed. Melody, rhythm, the groove, it makes you want to dance, it's all there. I mean, it's simplicity, you know? And it's simplicity—but then it's the highest level of maturity at the same time. It's unbelievable."[27]

Armstrong knew he had a winner. When Henderson recorded "Shanghai Shuffle" again a month later for Vocalion, Armstrong replicated his original solo in an almost note-for-note manner. As decades passed, multiple alternate takes surfaced of Henderson recordings and in almost every instance, Armstrong played nearly identical solos from take to take. This caused Henderson biographer Walter C. Allen to conclude, "Some of Louis' solos on alternate takes are so similar that he must have been reading them!"[28]

In actuality, Armstrong was just carrying over the methods of Joe Oliver and his other New Orleans mentors. He worked out his solos on the bandstand and improvised until he felt satisfied; once he perfected—and recorded—his solos, he didn't feel the need to change anything. Jazz hadn't hit the stage in its development where improvising new solos every night was seen as a crucial ingredient in the success of the music. If anything, the repetition of a favorite solo was appreciated by many in the audience. Sixteen-year-old reedman Russell Procope saw Armstrong with the Henderson band during this time at the Manhattan Casino in Harlem and remembered he played his "famous solos," including "Shanghai Shuffle." "He played like they were on the record," Procope said. "That's a good thing about it. He played them just about like they were on the record."

Procope had to see Armstrong at the Manhattan Casino in Harlem because the audience at Roseland was entirely white. Even with Armstrong's limited opportunities to play for Black audiences, Procope recalled that Armstrong's "reputation was spreading then. In conversation with all the fellas, the older fellas, they would talk about this great trumpet player, 'Fat' Armstrong. So I just had to hear him."[29]

A year earlier, trumpeter Louie Metcalf came to New York and noticed "everybody was playing like Johnny [Dunn]—trumpeters, saxes, pianists and even banjoists were copying Dunn."[30] Now, Procope said, "In those days, everybody copied Louis Armstrong solos. Everybody, the saxophone players, the piano players, the trumpet players, trombone players. They all copied Louis Armstrong solos."[31] Dunn eventually moved to Europe, where he died in Paris in 1937 at the age of 40. Howard Scott remembered Dunn as "a nice trumpet player" but added, "He didn't last long. . . . he just disappeared."[32]

Metcalf was present at another major moment, when Armstrong made his debut at the Lafayette Theater in Harlem. Cornetist Joe Smith, a disciple of Dunn, had made his reputation as a soloist with Henderson and had even been part of the Black Swan Troubadours' tour of New Orleans in 1922. Though he'd left the Henderson band before Armstrong joined, Smith was still tremendously popular in Harlem, representing the "eastern" style of jazz, whereas Armstrong represented the "western" style. "It was a real jazz feud with all the musicians taking sides," Metcalf recalled.

Smith opened by playing several numbers with the pit band and "tore the house down," Metcalf said. Henderson followed, opening up with

"Copenhagen," which had one of Armstrong's typically short solos. "And Louis' solo was so good, but different, and the audience didn't know about how much to applaud," Metcalf said. "The next number was even better and the people began to dig and were sayin', 'Here's another great trumpet player.' After the third piece, they really made their minds up. They were sayin', 'Now here's another King.' And the house was his." Metcalf felt vindicated for his devotion to Armstrong's style. "It was a real thrill for me, because Louis comin' out of New Orleans and me from St. Louis were both of the same style, and he was backin' up everything I had been tryin' to tell—only he made them understand."[33]

Making them understand was hard work; cornetist Rex Stewart noticed that Armstrong was exuding some of his old Third Ward toughness as he made his way through New York. "What he carried with him was the aroma of red beans and rice, with more than a hint of voodoo and 'gris-gris,'" Stewart wrote. "He conveyed this to the world by the insouciant challenge of his loping walk, the cap on his head tilted at an angle, which back home meant: 'Look out! I'm a bad cat—don't mess with me!' These, plus the box-back coat and the high-top shoes, all added to young Louis' facade to those days." Stewart was won over by every aspect of Armstrong, saying, "I tried to walk like him, talk like him. I bought shoes and a suit like the Great One wore."[34]

Ironically, Stewart, Metcalf, and Procope would all go on to work with Duke Ellington, then leading "The Washingtonians" at the Hollywood Club on 49th and Broadway, a short distance from Roseland. "When Louis Armstrong first came to New York, he almost caused a riot," Ellington said in 1940. He continued:

> In the first place nobody had ever heard so much horn-blowing before, and secondly he was a regular guy, he wasn't "big-head" any kind of way. He was working with Smack's (Fletcher Henderson) band, and they were sensational right on, with or without Louis. Everybody round town had been hearing about Armstrong, he'd been working out West with King Oliver's band. But nobody actually knew how much horn he could blow. So when Smack's band hit town and Louis was with them, the guys had never heard anything just like it. There weren't the words coined for describing that kick.[35]

Ellington's use of the descriptor "big-head" was eventually echoed by Armstrong himself in a 1970 letter to Max Jones: "The fellas in Fletcher's band had such big heads until—Mmm, boy, you talking about big-headed motherfuckers—such big heads until even if they miss a note, 'So what?'

Mmm!"[36] Chief offender to Armstrong was first trumpeter Elmer Chambers with his "nanny-goat sound and ragtime beat," as Armstrong told Dan Morgenstern in December 1970.[37] "You notice the weakest man in that band was the first chair man," he said.[38] Henderson wouldn't let Armstrong play first, but he did occasionally let him hit high notes "the prima donnas" like Chambers couldn't hit, always following with a patronizing "pep talk" as Armstrong called it.

"Boy, that was wonderful," Henderson would tell him. "You know one thing? You'd be very good if you'd go and take some lessons!"

"I'd say, 'Yes sir,'" Armstrong recounted, "and in my head, you know, to myself, I'm saying, 'Oh man, you go fuck yourself.' Yeah, I know what was happening. I'm for him, but he didn't dig me, so the hell with it."[39]

Though Henderson was later effusive in his praise of Armstrong—"Perhaps our greatest musician," he said of him in 1950[40]—Armstrong couldn't help but feel that the educated, light-skinned Henderson looked down on his dark-skinned, southern-fried disposition. "Fletcher was so carried away with that society shit and his education, he slipped by a small-timer and a young musician—me—who wanted to do everything for him musically," Armstrong reflected. "I personally didn't think that Fletcher cared too much for me anyway. Tush, tush. Ain't that some shit."[41]

Armstrong's feelings extended to the social circle Henderson traveled in, as well. On November 17, Henderson performed for the NAACP's annual benefit at Happy Rhone's nightclub, attended by W. E. B. DuBois, among other figures of what would later be known as the "Harlem Renaissance."[42] Jazz in its purest form was never fully embraced by artists of the Harlem Renaissance—except by poet Langston Hughes—but Henderson was admired for his more acceptable brand of arranged dance music. Armstrong would become a lifelong member of the NAACP, but he was not a fan of DuBois's "Talented Tenth" rhetoric. When Armstrong purchased J. A. Rogers's two-volume anthology *World's Great Men of Color* in 1947, he made a list of each chapter he read, including entries on Frederick Douglass, Paul Laurence Dunbar, Bert Williams, and Booker T. Washington. At the end of his list, he made sure to notate a chapter he did *not* want to read, writing "No Du Boise," underlining "No" twice for good measure.[43]

Just a few days after the NAACP benefit, *The Pittsburgh Courier* reported that Henderson had hosted a special guest from Chicago: bandleader Sammy Stewart, six months fresh from snubbing Armstrong in Chicago. "The music was delightful," the paper reported. But Armstrong and Bailey were beginning to have second thoughts about their surroundings.[44] "The first week we were both in New York we both said, let's go back to Chicago," Bailey remembered.

"There were more bands there—more everything—more money, Chicago was far ahead of New York at that time."[45]

New York did at least have a thriving race records scene and Armstrong would soon be thrust into the middle of it. Any frustrations he had on the bandstand with Henderson could at least be negated by having the opportunity to blow in small group settings, surrounded by friends from New York, Chicago, and even New Orleans.

"I knew what I could do with my horn and I proved it when I played with Bessie Smith and the Harlem people on the recordings," a confident Armstrong said when summing up this period of his life. "So I didn't let it bug me. The hell with it. Shit, they needed me, I didn't need them."[46]

Armstrong made his debut as a studio sideman-for-hire on October 16, 1924, surrounded by Henderson and other sidemen from his orchestra on a session led by vocalist Gertrude "Ma" Rainey" for Paramount Records.[47] This was Armstrong's first experience in playing cornet obligatos behind a vocalist and he proved to be a quick study, especially on a searing "Countin' the Blues," but he also seemed a bit reserved throughout the date, often letting bandmates Buster Bailey and Charlie Green overwhelm him with their own responses to Rainey's singing.

He sounded much more comfortable the following day when he made his first session for OKeh, where Ralph Peer served as the label's director of production. "Whenever we needed a New York trumpet player our first choice would be Louis Armstrong," Peer said.[48] Armstrong would often record for OKeh as a member of Clarence Williams's Blue Five, a New Orleans–flavored studio group formed as a vehicle to record compositions Williams published, often sung by his wife, vocalist Eva Taylor.

Williams began using Armstrong frequently, striking gold on November 6 with "Everybody Loves My Baby" and "Of All the Wrongs You've Done to Me." Lil Armstrong might have remembered Louis struggling to play with a mute like King Oliver back in Chicago, but this session offers definitive evidence that he had not only mastered the technique but was capable of performing even more dramatic and gripping music than his mentor. On "Everybody Loves My Baby" in particular, Armstrong tears into the melody in almost violent fashion, working over a bluesy descending motif, improvising over a stop-time bridge, and heralding the final charge with a visceral, growled lip trill.

He soon began featuring "Everybody Loves My Baby" in live settings, including a Thursday evening "Vaudeville Night" competition at Roseland. "Louis used to mug around on some of the songs we played, so we got the idea he ought to get out and sing in the show," Kaiser Marshall said. "It took a lot of persuading, but he finally said he'd do it." Armstrong chose "Everybody Loves My Baby"—playing it *and* singing it. "The crowd surely went for it," Marshall said, noting that Armstrong received enough applause to walk off with first prize. "From then on they used to cry for Louis every Thursday night, and he would play his horn and sing his songs."[49]

Drummer Vic Berton, who played with Sam Lanin's group on the opposite bandstand, remembered Armstrong revived some of his singing tactics from New Orleans during one of these amateur night performances. "I recall the first time Armstrong ever stood up and did a vocal chorus," Berton said. "The wordless vocalizing for which he is noted is something he originally did spontaneously while sitting in the band and not playing. It never occurred to him to stand up and do it for the benefit of an audience until the manager of the Roseland heard him and, after much persuasion, induced him to stand up and do it for the crowd. It was an instant success with the customers.[50]

Henderson eventually recorded "Everybody Loves My Baby" at the end of November 1924, a few weeks after the Clarence Williams version. Armstrong opens the first take by reprising a portion of his solo from the Blue Five record, as if to say, "Maybe you don't know my name but it's me, the same guy!" After the success at Roseland, Armstrong approached Henderson and asked him if he could sing on the recording. Henderson turned him down, saying, "No, you can't sing on this, man," but offered a compromise.[51] At the end of the take, the band plays some stop-time breaks, each of which is followed by a completely unique sound: Louis Armstrong's voice, captured by a recording device for the very first time. He doesn't sing, though, and instead shouts comedically to the band:

> "Uh uh, brother, don't bring me that!"
> "Aw, now you're comin' to it!"
> "Aw, that's it, boy!"

It's an inauspicious debut for perhaps the most recognizable—and influential—voice of the twentieth century, but it's still a fun glimpse of Armstrong the showman, Armstrong the ham, the kid who had been shouting and joking since quartet days in New Orleans. "My goodness—the compliments, Fletcher received, when the recording was released," Armstrong wrote, "and still Fletcher, or King Oliver, never did pick up on my vocalizing, which until this day—was nothing to write home about. But, it was Different."[52]

Armstrong went on to make dozens of recordings with Henderson, with both his orchestra and accompanying various vocalists, male and female, but was never again offered a chance to sing on record during his time in New York. "And I said, 'Well, let me sing these songs,'" Armstrong said in 1962. "'Noooo, you're not a singer, you know.' So that's the way he looked at it and I didn't bother. You know, I could have done some good things with Fletcher....but he missed the boat."[53]

Though both Henderson and King Oliver eventually let Armstrong sing more—once on the road, and away from their respective home bases of Roseland and the Lincoln Gardens—he never forgot their unwillingness to do so, later reflecting about it in his manuscript of *Satchmo: My Life in New Orleans*:

> Maybe Papa Joe...felt the same way that Fletcher Henderson did concerning my singing with the Band. Not that they weren't for it, it was just the idea that there never was a trumpet player, or, any instrument player at that time way back in the olden days, the instrumentalists just weren't singing that's all. So, I gathered that those two Big Boys, Joe + Fletcher, Just was afraid to let me sing thinking maybe I'd sort of ruin their reputations with their musical public. They not knowing that I have been singing all of my life. In Churches etc. I had one of the finest All Boys Quartets that ever walked the street of New Orleans. So you see - singing was more into my Blood than the trumpet.[54]

One figure who knew very well that Armstrong could both play and sing was clarinetist Sidney Bechet, who returned to New York in 1923 after conquering Chicago and eventually Europe. In London, he purchased his first soprano saxophone, falling in love with the instrument's louder sound, which was perfect for swatting away any cornet players who stood in his path. Back in New York, Bechet made his recording debut with Clarence Williams on July 30, 1923, unleashing a torrent of creative soprano breaks on "Wild Cat Blues" several months before Armstrong did the same on King Oliver's recording of "Tears."

Bechet's recordings announced a dynamic new voice in jazz, but like Armstrong a year later, he was originally met with some resistance from the New York musicians—Coleman Hawkins in particular. Duke Ellington's bassist Wellman Braud reported that Hawkins "remarked that New Orleans musicians can't play," leading Bechet to extend an invitation to have Hawkins meet him for a cutting contest at the Band Box nightclub. "Bechet blowing like a hurricane embarrassed the Hawk, he played and continued to play as Hawkins packed his horn and as he walked out angrily Bechet followed him outside and woke up the neighborhood, it was six o'clock in the morning," said Danny Barker.[55]

Armstrong and Bechet had a happy reunion on October 17, 1925, when they were hired by Williams to record "Texas Moaner Blues." Perhaps both frustrated with the stuffy New York scene, the two old comrades showed genuine rapport in putting Williams's composition over with passionate ensemble playing and individualistic solos. The pair even share a break, which Bechet sets up and Armstrong finishes, both men clearly on the same wavelength.

But that spirit of camaraderie started to erode the more they worked together. Bechet was the older, more experienced musician and he liked to dominate the ensembles, while Armstrong was raised to believe that the trumpet was the lead instrument—and he was determined to keep it that way. When Armstrong playfully phrased the melody to "I'm a Little Blackbird Looking for a Bluebird" in an exaggerated, herky-jerky way, Bechet immediately responded with similar phrasing in an almost mocking manner. On "Mandy Make Up Your Mind," Bechet brought a sarrusophone—a double-reed instrument that produced an even louder, deeper, and uglier sound than the soprano—to the studio to drown out Armstrong. Armstrong responded with some of his hottest playing on record to date, taking the melody up an octave, getting a break to himself, and blowing with wicked

Figure 21.2 Sidney Bechet, Clarence Williams, and Louis Armstrong, photographed during a reunion in 1940.
Credit: Photo by Otto Hess, author's personal collection.

fury, but is almost obscured the whole time by Bechet bellowing like a cartoon whale.

The tension finally erupted on "Cake Walking Babies from Home," recorded on December 22, 1924, at a Gennett session credited to the Red Onion Jazz Babies. After a vaudeville-styled vocal by Alberta Hunter and Clarence Todd, Armstrong plays a funky lip trill to announce his arrival, and the gloves come off. Armstrong's aggressive variations on the melody initially seem to catch Bechet by surprise, but the older man soon starts running arpeggios up and down his soprano, taking a fine break in the process. After more heated ensemble playing, Armstrong responds with a dazzling break of his own, dwarfing Bechet's previous effort. Feeling good, both men hold the same note and swing into the final chorus—when Armstrong momentarily stumbles and garbles up one of his notes. Smelling blood, Bechet pours it on, his virtuosity overwhelming Armstrong in the ensemble. The older man pulls out all the stops in his final break, basically snarling through his instrument. Armstrong rallies strongly with another growling trill before the horns trade blows until the final bell sounds. It's an epic recording, but in boxing terminology, honors would seem to go to Bechet by split decision.

Armstrong and Bechet would next stage a rematch on a second version of "Cake Walking Babies from Home," recorded just 17 days later as part of a Clarence Williams Blue Five date for OKeh. After Eva Taylor's lively vocal, Bechet picks up where he left off, unleashing combinations, growling through another break, and swarming Armstrong in the ensembles, unwilling to let him play the lead.

It's at that point where Armstrong seems to say "ENOUGH!" In an instant, he unleashes perhaps the angriest note of his entire career before rhythmically alternating two notes in the exact same way he once recalled Joe Oliver doing it on "It's a Long Way to Tipperary" back in the days of the Onward Brass Band. Armstrong might have been channeling Oliver's ideas, but the heat, the power, the fire, the swing, that's the Louis Armstrong who changed the world. Armstrong comes on so hot, Bechet almost completely disappears from the ensemble, resorting to quietly playing the melody and for once, staying out of Armstrong's way.

Having regained control, Armstrong takes a mind-boggling break, repeating a tricky phrase in both the upper and lower registers of his horn, executing it with thrilling precision. He doesn't let up until he reaches the song's final four-bar break, which he pounces on, daringly walking a rhythmic tightrope before ripping up to a high note and concluding with some down-home blues, all in a matter of seconds. Bechet reemerges at the very end but for all intents and purposes, Armstrong scored a knockout victory during the rematch.

While some have attempted to downplay the friction inherent on these recordings,[56] it was Bechet himself who admitted he never got over the younger Armstrong stiffing him over the money he once gave him to fix his shoes. "You're playing some number and it starts going—sometimes it goes right back to the street and played about those shoes," he wrote.[57] With thoughts of "those shoes" still fresh in his mind, Bechet was determined to show Armstrong that he was the boss—until meeting his match on the second "Cake Walking Babies."

In the years that followed, Bechet's career went into a bit of a tailspin. He spent the rest of the decade in Europe—including 11 months in a Paris jail after a shooting incident—and returned to New York at the start of the Great Depression. He worked as a sideman in Noble Sissle's Orchestra, but also opened a tailor shop in Harlem to help make ends meet. When William Russell interviewed Lil Armstrong in November 1938, he noted that Lil felt Bechet "had the soul of Louis" and "wondered why he didn't amount to anything." "Louis had gotten places," Lil said. "Nobody knows who Bechet is."[58] That would all change the following year when Bechet scored a hit with "Summertime," spawning a second career that would lead him to great fame and stardom, especially in France.

But as they left OKeh's studio on January 8, 1925, the winner and new champion was Louis Armstrong.

22

"I Know I Can Play and I Know I Can Sing"

1925

Armstrong' s recordings as a sideman made a big splash upon their release in early 1925, but without his name on the labels, many musicians were confounded by the identity of this new—or possibly old—trumpeter. He did such a credible job in invoking Joe Oliver that he fooled one of the King's disciples back home, cornetist Johnny Wiggs. "When I got that 'Everybody Loves My Baby' and 'Of All the Wrongs You've Done to Me,' I ran over to Monk Smith's house with it right away," Wiggs said. "I said, 'Listen to Joe, man! Listen to this record, will you! Oh boy!' I couldn't tell the difference."[1] Armstrong's work with the Red Onion Jazz Babies, including the first "Cake Walking Babies from Home," an even more daring remake of "Of All the Wrongs You've Done to Me," and the declarative "Terrible Blues" confounded the first group of nascent jazz historians who tried to make sense of this music in the late 1930s. "Two more records were made at this time by Oliver under the name of the 'Red Onion Jazz Babies,'" Marshall Stearns, future founder of the Institute of Jazz Studies, wrote in *Downbeat* in 1937.[2]

Besides the obvious muted work on some of these sides, one of Oliver's other calling cards that Armstrong picked up was the lip trill, a growl on a single pitch used in a break or at the end of a chorus as a way to generate heat, as heard on the OKeh "Cake Walking Babies." "Joe [Oliver] played things that hit you inside," Garvin Bushell said. "Joe also had that lip shake or trill—New Orleans trumpeters created it—that could make people jump out of their seats."[3] Armstrong relied on Oliver's lip trill frequently in the mid-1920s but eventually dropped it as he developed his own style. This choice didn't surprise Wiggs. "It takes too much of a person's lip to play like that," he said. "Oh, it's an unbelievable strain on your lip."[4]

Oliver's playing was showing strain thanks to the effects of pyorrhea in his gums, as can be heard on two duets with Jelly Roll Morton in December 1924. These sides are valuable for historic reasons but don't represent Oliver's best work on record. Still, even in pain, Oliver had enough of a reputation to be billed as the "World's Greatest Jazz Cornetist" when he was the featured soloist with Dave Peyton's Symphonic Syncopators at the brand-new Plantation Cafe in early December 1924.[5] Oliver was still leading his own band three nights a week at the Lincoln Gardens and had plans to expand it into a larger ensemble with even more musicians from New Orleans, but those plans were scuttled on Christmas Eve when a Christmas tree caught fire and completely destroyed the establishment, ending an era. It was a cruel setback that put a punctuation mark on a very tough year for Oliver, but he would prove in 1925 that his reign as King was far from over.

Oliver's fingerprints aren't the only ones that can be detected on Armstrong's sideman recordings of late 1924 and early 1925. In December 1924, he took part in three classic sessions with vocalist Maggie Jones that contained some of his most dexterous trumpet playing of this era. Armstrong sounds like he's searching for something on these sides, playing more notes than ever before in a way that Oliver would have frowned upon. His obligato work could be construed as too busy—on "Screamin' the Blues, he is so carried away that he plays over Jones's singing twice—but it's thrilling hearing him finding his voice on these sessions, of which "Good Time Flat Blues" is the highlight. He plays with great beauty from start to finish, the simple 8-bar chorus really inspiring him to take a thoughtful, well-constructed solo and to respond to Jones with great sensitivity. "Good Time Flat Blues" has often been analyzed as a choice example of Armstrong's early genius—but once again, Sidney Bechet mentioned this performance in 1938 and summed it up by saying, "That's Bunk."[6]

Without any recordings of young Bunk Johnson or young Joe Oliver, it's difficult to accurately describe their playing during Armstrong's formative years. But if musicians who *did* hear them, such as Bechet and Johnny Wiggs, are to be believed, Armstrong could almost flip a switch and channel either man depending on his mood or what he thought worked best for the song at hand.

At the same time, there are moments on these sideman recordings where he unleashes phrases that neither Oliver nor Johnson could have dreamed of. On Maggie Jones's "Anybody Here Want to Try My Cabbage," Armstrong plays one phrase that would later crop up in his iconic "Cornet Chop Suey" solo of 1926—which he had already written down and copyrighted with Lil's prodding back in January 1924. He also explores chromaticism, including one quiet, lightning-fast run that could be considered "out" from his usual melodic style. To New York musicians unfamiliar with Oliver and Johnson—not to mention Buddy Petit—Armstrong was demonstrating a different approach to improvisation. "Then the patterns that he played were just brand new because he knew more about his chords," Garvin Bushell said. "He had a great ear for analyzing the chord, the harmony of a tune."[7]

The previous month, Armstrong uncorked a sensational double-timed break on Margaret Johnson's "Changeable Daddy of Mine" that contained more than a few seeds for his later masterpiece "West End Blues." Lil later claimed the famed "West End Blues" cadenza came from "some of the classical stuff that she taught Louis," lessons that might have already been in place at this juncture since Lil moved to New York around the time of this recording. In April 1925, Louis made another classical allusion, referencing the melody of Franz Drdla's "Souvenir"—twice—during his obligato on Clara Smith's "Court House Blues," his earliest musical "quote" on record.[8]

Armstrong had always been a musical sponge, but New York was exposing him to some new sounds that made their way into his burgeoning style, including some he picked up from the other bands he'd heard at Roseland. "I used to sit down on the bandstand after we'd have intermission and Sam Lanin's band would come on," Armstrong said. "And this first chair man, Vic D'Ippolito, a little hunchback guy, he would attack them notes so beautiful and phrase, you know, just like a cat playing a solo, just an ordinary trumpet solo. And that swung the whole band, even to the first sax."[9]

Armstrong soon befriended the Lanin band's hot soloist, Ernest Loring "Red" Nichols of Ogden, Utah, who recalled, "Louis and I used to play for each other in the musicians' room downstairs [at Roseland]. We were happy to exchange ideas. He was very interested in the false-fingering idea I was working out and I showed him how it was done. The jazz musicians of that day were a kind of fraternity—all working together to promote and advance the music and each other."[10]

That fraternal spirit was not evident in the Henderson band. While Armstrong was paying attention to the playing of the Lanin band, he would look around and realize he was alone. "Well, them cats still be down there playing tonk or poker or something," he continued. "And I sit down there and whenever an incoming band, a guest band, would come in, I always heard them. I always wanted to hear the other fella."[11]

In December 1924, Lanin's band was replaced by Vincent Lopez's orchestra. Armstrong had admired Lopez for years. "I bought his records in New Orleans when he was at the Pennsylvania Hotel years ago and he'd always knock me out," Armstrong said of Lopez.[12] Lopez featured an "other fella" who would have a tremendous impact on Armstrong's sound and style: trumpeter Benjamin Albert "B. A." Rolfe. Born in 1879, Rolfe was playing in his father's orchestra by the age of 8, billed as "The Boy Trumpet Wonder."[13] By the 1920s, he was applying his prodigious technique to popular songs in the dance band style of the day, showcasing incredible dexterity and a superhuman range—all without any jazz feeling whatsoever.

The lack of jazz feeling didn't matter to Armstrong; Rolfe offered him some new ideas, which he vividly described in 1956:

> He had his horn straight up on his knee while they're playing other arrangements and things, and when it came his time, he stood up, just nonchalantly, and played a tune called "Shadowland" and he played it an octave higher with so much ease, you know what I mean? So you get food for thoughts. I was tinkering around with a tune called "When You're Smiling" then, you know, a swinging little thing. And when that man played that "Shadowland" [*sings melody*]. Now imagine how pretty that sounds an octave higher? And the next week, I went right down and recorded "When You're Smiling."[14]

Armstrong correctly remembered "In Shadowland," a new composition from 1924, but his memory played tricks on him regarding "When You're Smiling," which he did not record until 1929. However, Armstrong did record "Pickin' on Your Baby" with Clarence Williams's Blue Five shortly after hearing Rolfe and it's this number, more than any other from this period, that best represents the lessons freshly learned from the older trumpeter. After Eva Taylor's vocal, Armstrong heads into the upper register and stays up there until the end, infusing the melody with sincerity and passion, displaying tremendous endurance until the end. All of the later Armstrong trademarks are there: the throbbing vibrato, the high notes, the stately feeling, the sense of great drama, the sheer love of opera; it sounds like the Armstrong of the 1950s took a time machine back to 1925 for this one song. As years went on, he would grow tired of the fast-fingered runs and concentrate more on melody, tone, and upper register work, values all present on "Pickin' on Your Baby"—with an assist from B. A. Rolfe.

Less than a week after recording "Cake Walking Babies from Home" and "Pickin' On Your Baby" in January 1925, Armstrong was back in the studio to record with Bessie Smith, the "Empress of Blues." Born in Chattanooga, Tennessee, in 1894, Smith began singing on the streets as a child before finding success on the African American Theater Owners Booking Association—commonly known as T.O.B.A.—vaudeville circuit through the South. Smith was discovered by Clarence Williams and brought to the attention of OKeh, but according to Williams, the label originally rejected her because they simply "didn't like it, said it was coarse and loud, and they didn't want any part of it."[15]

Still, there was a buzz around Smith that eventually reached Frank Walker of Columbia Records, who had Smith record four selections in February 1923. "Down Hearted Blues" became the biggest hit, selling 780,000 copies, and overnight Smith became a sensation, billed as "The Greatest and Highest Salaried Race Star in the World" by the end of 1924. This didn't mean she was automatically accepted in New York. Fellow vocalist Alberta Hunter, who once referred to herself as "one of the dicties' entertainers," said that in New York, "No, Lord, Bessie Smith, they wouldn't think of looking at Bessie. Bessie was too raucous, although she was a good singer. But they wouldn't care how good you were, it's your background."[16]

Armstrong was most definitely a fan of Smith at the time of their January 1925 summit meeting. He once called her "the most perfect blues singer. And we ain't heard none yet to outsing what she did with the feeling in them things."[17] Smith also left a lasting impression on Armstrong for nonmusical reasons. "I'll never forget this date because one day I wanted to get change for a hundred dollars," Armstrong said. "It was the first hundred dollar bill I had and nobody had it in the band, quite naturally." Armstrong eventually asked Smith if she could break it for him.

"Sure, man," Smith assured him.

"She just raised up her dress there and there was an [apron]—you know, like a carpenter keep his nails?" Armstrong recalled, laughing at the memory. "Man, so much money—it killed me!"[18]

The first tune on the docket was W. C. Handy's "St. Louis Blues," which had already been around for some time, having been published in 1914. On the record, Armstrong, Smith, and Fred Longshaw on harmonium only get through Handy's multistrained composition—consisting of two 12-bar blues stanzas, a 16-bar minor-keyed "habanera" section, and one more 12-bar chorus—a single time in 3 minutes and 13 seconds. This is sad music, deep music, emotional music. There's no habanera here; no one feels like dancing.

Smith is a force of nature, slowly and steadily building throughout—but Armstrong is with her every step of the way. He doesn't solo, but calling what he plays an "obligato" seems limiting; it's really a duet. Unlike his cautious playing behind Ma Rainey or his constant arabesques behind Maggie Jones, Armstrong comes into his own here and really listens, maintaining Smith's mood and responding to her every move with just the right tone of commentary. He even flexes his operatic muscles in the final chorus with a bravura statement that Duke Ellington would later turn into the composition "Clarinet Lament."

If that was the only performance recorded at this January session, it would still be one for the pantheon, but incredibly, Smith, Armstrong, and Longshaw teamed up for four more selections, each one a classic. Armstrong remained in awe of how Smith "just stay in the studio and write the blues. As she finished one, just write another one."[19]

Armstrong breaks out the plunger for some emotive work on "Reckless Blues" and demonstrates Oliver's lessons on how to cry and laugh through his horn on "You've Been a Good Old Wagon But You've Done Break Down." His open horn work is quite heated on "Sobbin' Hearted Blues"—though perhaps a bit too heated for Smith's taste. He cooled it down on "Cold in Hand Blues," contributing 12 magical bars of blues storytelling that are so perfectly constructed, it's possible the solo was worked out back in the honky-tonk days in New Orleans; it would be heard again before the year 1925 was over.[20]

Armstrong and Smith would reteam on May 26 for four more numbers, all terrific, but perhaps not reaching the same heights as in January output, as Armstrong isn't as uninhibited, having to split obligato duty with trombonist Charlie Green. Nevertheless, Armstrong remained proud of his association with Smith, saying, "I think she's one of the greatest, the madam of the blues, that we are going to get for generations to come. And it's too bad she didn't live a little longer so the younger generation could have, at least, heard her in person, you know? But her records will stand up forever."[21]

In the late 1930s, the young jazz fan and future producer George Avakian befriended saxophonist Lester Young and asked him how he was able to play such perfect melodies behind Billie Holiday on their records together. "Oh, it's easy," Young responded. "I learned from listening to Louis Armstrong's records with Bessie Smith."[22]

In a 1965 interview with Richard Meryman, Armstrong reminisced about his association with Bessie Smith and said, "Everything I did with her, I *like*."[23] One person didn't feel quite the same as Armstrong: Bessie Smith herself. Bessie made it clear that she preferred the less obtrusive muted cornet work of Joe Smith, whom she didn't have to compete with for center stage. "Bessie Smith preferred Joe's playing so violently that she used to raise hell with Fletcher when he brought any other trumpeter into the studio, and that even included the great Louis," John Hammond wrote in 1937.

Joe Smith remained the best-known cornetist in New York City, and perhaps Armstrong's only true rival in town. In early 1925, Fletcher Henderson married Leora Meoux, a female trumpeter who had once been married to Joe's brother, Russell Smith, yet another trumpet player. According to Howard Scott, "Fletcher's wife liked Joe, the baby [brother]. . . . Well, she influenced Fletcher to let Joe join the band. So Fletcher sent me a notice that after this week, my services wouldn't be required." Armstrong was disappointed to see his friend leave, but left him with some advice.

"Scottie, you're a city boy," Armstrong told him. "You never been south. Don't go south, because you wouldn't understand it." Scott agreed and never traveled below Virginia during the entirety of his life. "Well, he ought to know," Scott said over 55 years later.[24]

Joe Smith rejoined Henderson's band in April 1925, just as it was transitioning into more of a hot unit. Armstrong had been bringing the heat from day one, but the band still played a lot of typical dance band arrangements, most of them stocks doctored by Don Redman, or written by other professionals such as bandleader and composer Arthur Lange. "You know, Fletcher Henderson, all you had to do was bring him Arthur Lange's arrangements and he'd pass them right out cause he'd know they're perfect," Armstrong recalled.[25] Joe Tarto, who played tuba with Sam Lanin at Roseland, said he scored "a waltz medley" for Henderson. "I used to make all his waltzes," Tarto said. "[Henderson] used to do all his jazz, and I used to do his waltzes."[26]

In the beginning, Armstrong was mainly utilized as the musical equivalent of what's known in the hip-hop world as a "hype man," there to provide short bursts of excitement with his wild improvisations. But six months in, Don Redman had come to realize that Armstrong's conception wasn't just a spice to be used sparingly but instead represented an entirely new direction for the entire band to embrace. That direction would come to be known as swing.

Redman began writing new arrangements that sounded like Louis Armstrong solos from start to finish. On material such as "When You Do What You Do" from April 1925 and "Money Blues" from May, Armstrong no longer sounds like he's visiting from another planet but blends into the group's unified concept. Up to this point, the ends of Armstrong's solos had usually felt like a switch flipping from color to black-and-white, but now the soloists, such as Bailey, Green, and Hawkins, followed his lead with appropriately swinging efforts of their own.

On May 29, the Henderson band topped itself with Redman's arrangement of "Sugar Foot Stomp," a retitled version of Armstrong and Oliver's composition "Dipper Mouth Blues."[27] According to Redman, "[Armstrong] showed [me] a little book of manuscripts, some melodies that he and the famous King Oliver had written in Chicago. . . . He asked me, 'Just pick out one you may like and make an arrangement for Fletcher's orchestra.' So I did and the one I picked out was 'Sugar Foot Stomp.' "[28]

Redman smoothed the edges, goosed the tempo, and kept things simmering on "Sugar Foot," though the overall feel lacks the earthiness of the original Gennett recording of Oliver. Armstrong would be tasked with invoking Oliver's now-famous three-chorus solo, which Lil remembered him struggling with at home. Armstrong left the plunger aside and made a personal statement of his own, retaining certain hallmarks of Oliver's original opus but phrasing them in his own fashion. He winked at Oliver with a growl in his second chorus and by holding a high note the way the King used to back in New Orleans, but this solo wasn't going to fool anyone into believing it was Oliver. This was Armstrong truly announcing his arrival as his own man.

Armstrong's solo comes fairly early in the record, which allows Redman's arrangement time to shine, climaxing when Ralph Escudero plays 4/4 time on his tuba, actually propelling the full orchestra to legitimately swing in forward motion for the first time on record.

"Now I'm sure you all know and remember the success of 'Sugar Foot Stomp,'" Redman later said. "In fact that recording was the record that made Fletcher Henderson nationally known."[29] Indeed, "Sugar Foot Stomp" received press coverage in cities far away from Roseland. "It reminds one of carefree Alabama, the cotton fields and sweet potatoes," *The Lincoln Star* wrote of it in August. "It has the 'darkie' shuffle, and is as different from other fox trots as the Danube Waltz."[30] Word reached Richmond, Indiana, where Gennett repackaged the original Oliver version of "Dipper Mouth Blues," now labeling it "Sugar Foot Stomp."[31] Even a 1931 *Pittsburgh Courier* profile of Henderson noted, "His recordings for Columbia include 'Sugar Foot Stomp,' ofttimes proclaimed his greatest hit."[32]

Armstrong had now been involved in some of the biggest selling recordings of African American music in the past year, but there was a problem—his name was not known to those buying the records. He wasn't mentioned in the publicity over "Sugar Foot Stomp," even though he cocomposed the song and took a three-chorus solo. When Bessie Smith's "St. Louis Blues" was released, a newspaper noted that Smith was "accompanied by an organ and a sympathetic cornet."[33] Author Bucklin Moon had his life changed when he heard Louis play on Maggie Jones's "Good Time Flat Blues," but admitted, "I can't even recall if I knew that it was Louis on the record when I bought it, but I doubt it. In those days Columbia did not bother to list such information on the label the way OKeh sometimes did."[34] Truthfully, OKeh was no better. They trumpeted the success of "Everybody Loves My Baby" in several ads throughout 1925, one with a cartoon depicting a cornetist who resembled Armstrong, but his name was never mentioned in association with this "record smashing OKeh Record!"[35]

On March 14, 1925, George M. Wood, "The Race's Pioneer Record Dealer," ran an advertisement in the *Pittsburgh Courier* for his shop's latest selections. "If It's a Race Artist Record, We Have It," the ad announced and listed a Margaret Johnson record, a Clarence Williams record, and three Fletcher Henderson records, a total of 10 songs on three different labels—every single one featuring solos by Louis Armstrong.[36]

Something had to change. Lil Armstrong was about to make her next move.

Lil lived with Louis for a short time in New York and even recorded with him as part of the Red Onion Jazz Babies, but she had to move back to Chicago in early 1925 after her mother, Decie, suffered a stroke. She would also have to take care of 9-year-old developmentally disabled Clarence Hatfield. In a letter to Lil from February 8, 1925, Louis showed that his ideas of raising a child were still entrenched in the world of Liberty and Perdido Streets. "Baby does he give you much trouble?" he wrote of Clarence. "Does he mind you and do what you tell him to do? Don't fail to slap the h— out of him if he don't listen to you....Nothing that I hate worse than a sassy child—ooh."[37]

Louis also alluded to some trouble in their marriage. "Baby I hope I didn't hurt your feelings for speaking the way I did, but I really don't like for you to mention such old mess as that because when you speak that way I began to think that you see another papa you want to get crazy about you like I am," he wrote. "I don't want you to think all that evil and handkerchief head stuff like some other certain women that I know and once went with—I want you to be kind and as you was when you was here with me." It's the first sign that jealousy and trust issues were seeping into Louis and Lil's marriage.

Louis also mentioned dropping a bombshell on the dance team of Brown and McGraw: "I told them that we was buying a home and their eyes stretched as large as duck eggs with surprise." He then added, "I just received another letter from May Ann, still singing the blues to come back up this way but she'll just have to sing 'em, that's all. I'll fix her up when I come home this summer, that is if I don't [accept] the job in Atlantic City."

That paragraph makes it crystal clear that not only were Louis and Lil planning to buy a home—in Chicago, not New York—but Louis was also thinking about leaving the Henderson band before they went on tour on June 1, a tour that would take them to summer resorts in New England, Pennsylvania, and Atlantic City, New Jersey. "Louis never went around much then," Kaiser Marshall remembered. "He was working hard and saving his money." Marshall, who recalled that Louis "used to write his wife every day," added, "Mr. [Louis J.] Becker, the manager at Roseland, liked Louis so much that he loaned him a thousand dollars to buy himself a home in Chicago and start his band."[38] Neither Louis nor Lil ever mentioned such a loan, but Lil did later state, "In the meantime, while he was with Fletcher I had bought the house in Chicago. And I had all the papers and everything, so I just mailed them to him here in New York and he signed them."[39] Lil had purchased a two-story Greystone at 421 E. 44th Street in the "Bronzeville" section of Chicago, moving Decie and Clarence in with her.

If Louis was going to stay with Henderson, Lil would make sure people knew his name. Lil's handiwork could be spotted in a *Chicago Defender* article, "Armstrong Toots a Wicked Cornet," that ran on May 30, 1925, complete with a reproduction of the unsmiling photograph of Louis that had originally run next to his marriage announcement.[40] In just two paragraphs, the *Chicago Defender*—through Lil—let its readers know who Armstrong was ("a noted jazz cornetist"), that he was a "big hit" in New York, and that he was responsible for the cornet work on popular recordings by Bessie Smith, Maggie Jones, and Clarence Williams, even going as far as mentioning "Everybody Loves My Baby." She now had a print article she could pass around to show how well her husband was doing. The wheels were in motion and Lil would not quit until Louis was back home.

Louis ended up staying with Henderson that summer, beginning with an extended stay at the Commodore Ballroom in Lowell, Massachusetts, in June and July before touring throughout the Northeast in August. On August 9, they performed for a dance at Paxtang Park, an amusement park in Harrisburg, Pennsylvania. In the crowd was 20-year-old Clyde Bernhardt, who would go on to become a popular trombonist and vocalist. Bernhardt had first seen Joe Smith with Ethel Waters and the Black Swan Troubadours back in October 1921 and was excited because Smith was back with Henderson. "Everybody in Harrisburg was crazy about Joe Smith," Bernhardt recalled.

Bernhardt had never heard of Armstrong and was immediately impressed—but the crowd's allegiance to Smith didn't waver. "You see, when Joe Smith would take a solo, every time Joe Smith would take a solo in Harrisburg, everybody would holler, 'Oh, play it, Joe! Play it!,'" Bernhardt said. "But when Louis Armstrong would take one, nobody would say nothing." At the performance, Bernhardt recalled that Armstrong did "Sugar Foot Stomp"—"and he played just like he did on that record"—and, more important, far away from Roseland, Henderson allowed Armstrong to sing on "Everybody Loves My Baby." "And man, he did a job on it!" Bernhardt said. "And when he finished, nobody give him the first hand." "That's when I found out Louis was very sassy," Bernhardt continued. "And he got mad!"

"I don't care that these old people here don't give me no credit for playing!" Armstrong remarked, according to Bernhardt. "I know I can play and I know I can sing! I don't care whether they like me or not. Just let them go ahead on and holler for Joe Smith. Joe Smith's right here for 'em!" Bernhardt noticed Smith was sitting right beside Armstrong. "Joe didn't say a word," he said.

Figure 22.1 Snapshot of trombonist Charlie Green, trumpeter Elmer Chambers, and Louis Armstrong labeled "The Three Musketeers," taken in Harrisburg, Pennsylvania, in August 1925.
Credit: The Frank Driggs Collection, Jazz at Lincoln Center.

After the dance, Bernhardt drove Henderson's tuba player, Ralph Escudero, back to his hotel. "Who is that short, greasy trumpet player?" Bernhardt asked. "That's Louis Armstrong," Escudero said. "Louis Armstrong?" replied Bernhardt. "Where's he been?" "He's from New Orleans," Escudero responded. "He's been playing in Chicago with King Oliver." "Man, that cat sure can blow!" Bernhardt said of Armstrong. "You think he plays as good as Joe Smith?"

"What are you talking about, boy?" Escudero said, incredulously. "There's not a trumpet player in New York that can play like Louis Armstrong. He came there and cut *all* those trumpet players. He cut all of them—including Joe Smith."

Bernhardt admired Oliver and asked, "Is he as good as King Oliver?"

"Yeah, King Oliver learned him a lot of what he was playing and now he can beat King Oliver doing what King Oliver taught him to do," Escudero said. "He's the greatest. He won't tell you he's better than King Oliver, but he's the greatest. You're going to hear a lot about him. I don't think we'll be able to keep him long."

"Why?" asked Bernhardt.

"Well, he's getting offers now to go out for himself, see," Escudero said. "He's kind of shy about leaving the band, but he's getting all kinds of offers right now. OKeh is going to sign him up to record under his name right now. You're going to hear about that guy. He's the greatest jazz trumpet player in the world!"[41]

If Bernhardt's recollection is correct—and there's no reason to doubt Bernhardt's stunningly good memory, given his incredibly accurate recall of dates, times, and places in interviews from the 1970s—Armstrong was unhappier than ever in the Henderson band. He might have admired Joe Smith's "beautiful tone," but he now resented the way Smith was the "pet" in the Henderson band, the clear favorite of Fletcher and his wife.[42] "You know, being an underdog in a band is a bad thing," he reflected in 1970. "Of course, there's always pets, and [Henderson] had them, believe me. I could call the names because that shit always comes out....You take pets, they're the ones that couldn't even blow their noses, let alone their horns. Life's a bitch, ain't it?"[43] Lil had seen enough. If she wanted her husband to return to Chicago, she was going to have to bring him back herself.

23

"The World's Greatest Jazz Cornetist"

1925–1926

Located at 3520 South State Street, the Dreamland Café was "considered the best black and tan club on the South Side" of Chicago, according to historian and civil rights activist Dempsey Travis.[1] Though Lil hadn't performed there in several years, she knew that she had a strong enough reputation to set up a meeting with its owner, Bill Bottoms, to ask him to bring Louis back from New York for $75 a week—a $20 increase from the $55 a week he was making with Henderson.

"Well, that guy, nobody knows anything about him that much to pay him $75," Bottoms replied.

Lil dug in. "Yeah, I want $75," she repeated, before adding a new demand. "I want you to put his name out in front: 'The World's Best Trumpet Player.'"

"Oh girl, you're crazy!" Bottoms said.

"Well, the people will come," Lil confidently stated. "They know me."

"Yeah, they know you," Bottoms said. "But I don't know if that guy's going to be worth that much."

"Well, you just try it," Lil demanded.

Having gotten an apprehensive Bottoms to agree, Lil wrote to Louis to tell him to put in his notice and come back to Chicago. He might not have been happy with the Henderson band, but according to Lil, living alone for such a long period had made him warm up to at least one aspect of New York. "Louis didn't want to come," she explained in 1969. "He was having a ball with that Fletcher band and the chorus girls that I found out about later!"

At the time, Louis just told Lil, "Oh no, you just want me to come home. I'm not going to get no $75 a week. I'm not coming."

"So I sent him a wire," Lil said. "I said, 'If you aren't here by such and such a date, don't come at all.' So he came on home. I had to put an ultimatum to him, you know."[2] "I was young, I didn't know about them threats," Louis reflected.[3]

Lil opened at the Dreamland Cafe on October 24, billed as "Mme. L. Armstrong's Dreamland Syncopators" with George Mitchell holding down the cornet chair until Louis finished his final weeks with Henderson.

"For a small unit they can't be beat, and they play a whole lot better than some of the 'star' cabaret bands," the *Chicago Defender* stated in a review.[4] Lil cut this clipping out and affixed it to a page in a brand-new scrapbook that would eventually document her husband's success over the next five years.

The next step of Lil's plan was to let Ralph Peer, OKeh's director of production, know that Louis was coming back to Chicago. Peer had still been recording Louis in September and October 1925, when he had taken part in three more Clarence Williams Blue Five sessions, leading thrilling ensemble passages on "Livin' High Sometimes" and "Santa Claus Blues" and once again foreshadowing his later dramatic high note style on "You Can't Shush Katie." Armstrong had even finally got to record "Coal Cart Blues," which he remembered writing while working for C. A. Andrews down in New Orleans during World War I—though cocomposer credit on the label had been given to "Lillian Harding."

"[Louis] can't stand it in New York," Lil told Peer.

"Well, now if he goes back to Chicago, I will do this for you," Peer said. "We will create an Armstrong orchestra so that we can give you some work."[5]

Peer, who would leave OKeh in December 1925, turned the project over to E. A. Fearn of the Consolidated Talking Machine Company and pianist and composer Richard M. Jones, OKeh's Race Division manager. The idea was a simple one: if Clarence Williams had success with a Blue Five, perhaps Armstrong would be willing to front a Hot Five? The answer was a resounding yes.

Louis would now have to choose the members of this recording group. Lil would be the pianist, but after a year in New York, Louis missed the special spark of playing with musicians from New Orleans. "The minute Mr. Fern (the President [*sic*] of the OKeh Company) gave me the go sign, I hit the phone and called the Musician's Union, and asked permission to hire Edward 'Kid' Ory, Johnny St. Cyr, and Johnny Dodds," he wrote.[6]

St. Cyr and Dodds were both still based in Chicago and were happy to accept Armstrong's offer to record with him, but Ory had been in California since 1919. "Louis said he had the offer of a job for a band at the Dreamland in Chicago, and also the offer to record for Okeh [*sic*]," Ory said. "He said we'd both make some money, so I decided to give up my own band, and go back East to Chicago. That was the end of 1925. I thought the world of Louis, so I was glad to go with him."[7] Thus, everything was in place by late October: Lil was at Dreamland, Ory arrived in town from Chicago, Dodds and St. Cyr were on board, and E. A. Fearn offered the date November 12 to record Armstrong's new group, the Hot Five.

Figure 23.1 Photo of E. A. Fearn, president of Consolidated Music Publishing House and the Consolidated Talking Machine Co., the man who oversaw the majority of Armstrong's Chicago recordings for OKeh in the 1920s.
Credit: Courtesy of the Louis Armstrong House Museum.

"Mr. Armstrong, the famous cornetist, will grace the first chair in the Dreamland orchestra some time this week," bandleader Dave Peyton wrote in a November 7 *Chicago Defender* column headlined "Louis Armstrong Coming Back." "William Bottoms made him an unusual salary offer to return to Chicago," he added, most likely tipped off by Lil.[8] On the following page, perhaps not wanting to appear to be cashing in on her husband's name, Dreamland ran an advertisement for "Lil Stewart's Dreamland Syncopators," an ironic, perhaps tongue-in-cheek choice of surname given Louis's history with bandleader Sammy Stewart.

"Before Louis came, they had trucks with banners with Louis' name on them going all around Chicago: 'Louis Armstrong's Coming Back to Chicago!'" trumpeter Doc Cheatham recalled. "They had a record playing all of his things. You could hear it all over the South Side: 'Louis is Coming Back to Chicago.'"[9]

All that was missing was Louis. He took part in one final session as a New York sideman on November 2, joining Perry Bradford's Jazz Phools for two songs, including the aptly named "I Ain't Gonna Play No Second Fiddle (If I Can't Play the Lead)." Though it wasn't his composition, it might as well have been his farewell song to New York, not to mention his two years with Oliver. Armstrong's days of playing second fiddle were over.

Interestingly, by the time he left New York, the initial awe that greeted his playing had died down substantially. Garvin Bushell, who had breathlessly described the impact of hearing Armstrong when he first arrived at Roseland, reflected, "After we got used to Louie's sound, we just said, 'Another fine trumpet player.' "[10] There might have been the feeling that Armstrong was going to "disappear" as Johnny Dunn had. The fast-paced city was ready for the next big thing—seemingly unaware that the next big thing was heading for Chicago.

Henderson and his band did send Armstrong off in style with a big party at Smalls Paradise, during which Armstrong admittedly "had one nip after another." At the end of the night, Armstrong went up to Henderson—"sharp as a tack in his tuxedo"—and drunkenly expressed his gratitude.

"Daddy, I want to thank you very much and . . ." Armstrong began, but didn't get much further.

"I threw all up, vomited all in Fletcher's bosom," he said. "So he's so disgusted with me, he told Buster [Bailey], 'Take him home, for God's sake.' "[11]

In some ways, thanking Henderson and immediately throwing up on him was an appropriate end to Armstrong's rocky 13 months in New York, a time in which he transformed the sound of dance band music, developed his own solo voice, perfected the art of the obligato, and took part in numerous immortal record sessions—all while feeling stifled, disrespected, patronized, and not utilized properly. He occasionally looked back on this period with fondness, other times with bitterness, sometimes both.

One such occasion occurred after Henderson's passing on December 29, 1952. Armstrong sent a piano made of flowers to the funeral and drove a great distance to attend it in person, showing up late in the process. "I wouldn't miss it for the world," he told friends during a tape-recorded conversation the following week. "And I struggled like a son-of-a-bitch getting there."

But as Armstrong started talking about Henderson, the bitterness crept back in, and he vomited out his still wounded feelings. "He done missed the boat," he said. "By playing me cheap, it kind of cut my spirits down to a helluva lot. But he's the one that cut it up. My first time in a big band, you know, and I was so elated and everything and every time I look around, 'Take some lessons.' Oh, I could have been more—and he could have been a bigger man. He missed the boat when he handed me that shit. When he was telling me, instead of just saying, 'Well, gee, that's a killer [solo], man, let's try some more of them.' Nope. All he could say, 'Go take some lessons,' and that cocksucker said—they're supposed to be virtuosos, or whatever you call those motherfuckers, he wouldn't offer *nothing*. No, they were supposed to have diplomas and all that shit but man, they was nowhere."

Yet, after calming down, Armstrong concluded, "Fletcher's my man. He did have me for the first time in the big band era. You've got to appreciate."[12]

Before leaving Chicago, Armstrong selected his own replacement in cornetist Rex Stewart, calling him personally to offer him the job. Stewart had watched Armstrong's progress in his 13 months in New York, beginning with his derided "box-back coat and high-top shoes," and reflected that "when Louis returned to his Chicago south-side stomping grounds in 1925, the youngster had changed into a worldly man, a sophisticated creator of music that people looked up to. He had arrived, and a world was waiting for the king of the trumpet."[13]

When Louis arrived back in Chicago, Lil and Clarence were waiting for him at the new home Lil had purchased. "And when he came home and he walked into the house he says, 'Really is this *our* house?' " Lil said. "I said, 'Yep, someday it'll be 'our house.' " . . . 'Oh, oh,' he said, 'you're a magician.' "[14]

For her next trick, Lil brought Louis to the Dreamland Cafe; where another surprise awaited him: the sign hanging out front that proclaimed him "The World's Greatest Jazz Cornetist"—the same phrase that had been applied to King Oliver earlier in the year.

"Girl, I think you're crazy," Louis said when he saw it.

"Well, all you've got to do is just blow," Lil said with a shrug.[15]

"You can imagine how glad that I was to join my wife Lil and her fine band," Louis said in 1970. "She had a damn good band. To me, it was better than Fletcher's. That's right. Other than those big arrangements that Don Redman was making, I wasn't moved very much with them, too much. Too much airs and all that shit."[16] Louis would spend much of the rest of his life avoiding anything that smacked of "too much airs"—eventually including his second wife.

But for now, Lil had done her job; Louis was back in Chicago, making $75 a week, and the buzz about this "World's Greatest Jazz Cornetist" brought the crowds out to Dreamland. "So we opened up and we played and all the other bands, white musicians, everybody start coming in, listening to Louis all by himself, you know," Lil said.[17] "Louis Armstrong, the greatest jazz cornet player in the country, is drawing many ofay musicians to Dreamland nightly to hear him blast out those weird jazzy figures," Dave Peyton soon reported in the *Chicago Defender*. "This boy is in a class by himself."[18]

Eventually, the hype over Louis reached other trumpet players—including old Freddie Keppard. The onetime "King" of Creole cornetists paid a visit to Dreamland one night and committed the same sin Johnny Dunn had tried the previous year on the same bandstand.

"Boy, let me have your trumpet," Keppard demanded.

When Dunn had pulled this stunt, Louis had been in Ollie Powers's band and had just done as told. This time, he looked to Lil first and waited for her to nod her head in approval, giving him permission. "So Freddie he blew, oh, he blew and he blew and he blew," Lil said. "And then the people gave him a nice hand."

A satisfied Keppard handed Louis back his horn.

"Now get him," Lil instructed her husband, playing the role of a boxing trainer sending a champion out to go for the kill.

"Oh, never in my life have I heard such trumpet playing," Lil said. "If you want to hear Louis play, just hear him play when he's angry. Boy, he *blew* and people started standing up on top of tables and chairs screaming. And Freddie eased out real slowly! Nobody ever asked Louis for his trumpet again."[19]

Having established himself at Dreamland, it was time for Louis to reestablish himself in OKeh's Chicago recording studio, located on the fourth floor of E. A. Fearn's Consolidated Talking Machine Company headquarters at 227–229 West Washington Street. Fearn initially had Armstrong record as a sideman, backing female vocalists Bertha "Chippie" Hill, Blanche Calloway, and Hociel Thomas on 10 sides before the Hot Five made their recording debut on November 12.

Once in the studio, Lil took her spot at the piano while Johnny St. Cyr took a seat on a stack of boxes near the recording horn. Louis, Kid Ory, and Johnny Dodds would stand but Fearn immediately spotted a problem when the band was rehearsing. "Johnny Dodds couldn't play without patting his foot," St Cyr said. "Fearn had to go out and get a pillow! Fearn got a pillow so he could pat on the pillow and it wouldn't make no noise, you know, it wouldn't record."[20]

Louis and Lil each brought an original composition to the date and sold both of them to Fearn for a $50 flat fee instead of arranging for any future royalties. Louis would come to regret this choice, especially when the Hot Five recordings were reissued by Columbia Records in the 1940s and 1950s. "Yeah, we wasn't paying no attention to the royalties and all that," he said in 1952. "All we wanted was money then and forget it! I wish I had held about a half-cent interest in 'em, I'd be all right. . . . They tell me Columbia bought all them tunes. [I] don't get a nickel from that. They're selling like hotcakes, too. It's one of them things, you know."[21]

For their first number, the Hot Five recorded Lil's "My Heart," which she originally wrote as a waltz titled "My Heart Will Lead Me Back to You" back in 1920. In later years, Louis liked to later claim that the group "would just make up those things" in the studio, but the group was actually a well-rehearsed outfit.[22] "When we'd get in the studio, if we were going to do a new number, we'd run over it a couple of times before we recorded it" Kid Ory said. "We were a very fast recording band, in fact the records I made with the Hot Fives were the easiest I ever made."[23] "At that time, we was just cutting masters," Johnny St. Cyr added. "Fearn wouldn't make us cut tests. Just cut masters. We used to rehearse our numbers very well, you know, time them the best we could."[24]

The rehearsal paid off on "My Heart," which included a two-bar arranged introduction, a 32-bar chorus followed by a 16-bar verse, multiple breaks, and a clarinet solo over stop-time "Charleston" rhythm. The performance also highlights the ensemble playing of Armstrong, Ory, and Dodds. Though the Hot Five would later garner a reputation for helping transition jazz from an ensemble-based music to a soloist's art form, they also represent perhaps the pinnacle of the polyphonic style due to the familiarity between the principals. "The Hot Five was actually very much like my band in New Orleans," Ory said. "Four of the five, Louis, Johnny Dodds, Johnny St. Cyr and I, played together for a long time in my band and we all knew each other's styles inside out."[25] Thus, the Hot Five recordings provide a precious glimpse of how Ory's band might have sounded back home.

In fact, Louis seemed content to defer to his elders on "My Heart," sticking to tasty lead playing and a couple of closing breaks while eschewing any trumpet fireworks. "I didn't just take the band over to be a big shot or nothing like that," Louis said. "We just played music the same as we did in New Orleans."[26] This spirit was appreciated by his bandmates. "Louis was a wonderful band leader," St. Cyr said. "One felt so relaxed working with him, and he was very broad minded. He always did his best to feature each individual in his combo. It was not Louis Armstrong, it was the Hot Five, if you get what I mean."[27]

Louis did make up for it on "Yes! I'm in the Barrel," which he had originally copyrighted back in 1923 as "I Am in the Barrel, Who Don't Like It?," a reference to losing all of one's clothes while gambling. This time, he commands attention from the outset, soloing over a minor-vamp with a plunger mute, perhaps as a nod to Oliver. But even after this dramatic introduction, Louis reverts to playing lead, helping to guide the band through the tune's tricky form, and throwing it over to Dodds for his second full-chorus solo of the day.

The two planned sides were a success, but there was only one problem—E. A. Fearn wasn't completely satisfied. OKeh made its reputation with the blues and Fearn requested that they make one up in the studio. According to St. Cyr, Armstrong's response was, "Man, we have made so many blues and they all sound mostly alike!"[28] Armstrong had been playing the blues regularly for about a decade, especially during his honky-tonk days, but beginning with his tenure with Fate Marable and continuing through the Fletcher Henderson period, he had been exposed to popular songs, waltzes, ballads, novelty numbers, exotic specialties, and much more. He had already backed multiple singers on multiple blues earlier that week and the notion of simply churning out more 12-bar blues for OKeh with his own group was not exactly an enticing one.

St. Cyr came up with a suggestion. "Well, look, I'll start off with the bass on the banjo," he said, illustrating the sound. "The banjo starting off will make it a little different than the average blues."

"All right, go ahead, try that, it might work," Fearn said.

With the introduction worked out, Armstrong decided this piece could use something of a nonmusical nature: his personality. Armstrong's extroverted demeanor had been a big part of his live performances going back to the days of his vocal quartet, but it had had been kept under wraps on the dozens of recordings he had made since April 1923. Those days were now over.

While St. Cyr played his introduction, Armstrong took over: "Oh, play that thing, Mr. St. Cyr, lawd! You know you can do it—everybody from New Orleans can really do that thing! Heeeey, hey!" This was also something new; Armstrong had become used to contributing immortal solos in session after session, only to never receive credit on a record label. Now, he would utter each musician's name, introducing an entire generation to St. Cyr, Lil ("Whip that thing, Miss Lil!"), Ory ("Blow it, Kid Ory, blow it Kid!"), and Dodds ("Blow that thing, Mr. Johnny Dodds!"). The Hot Five would become a brand and from the beginning, Louis ensured that listeners would get to know the entire cast by name.

Dodds was then chosen to introduce Armstrong, but froze during an early attempt at talking into the recording horn. "You know what that son-of-a-bitch did?" Armstrong asked in 1970. "Went right to that mike and [*stutters*] 'I-I-I-I-uh.' I said, 'Speak, motherfucker!' He said, 'Shit, I'm scared of that fucking mike!' And Ory had to take his place!"[29] Ory updated his friend's old "Dippermouth" nickname, urging him to "Blow it, Papa Dip!"

Without any time to prepare something new, Armstrong fell back on one of his set solos, in this case reprising and updating the blues chorus he had taken on Bessie Smith's "Cold in Hand Blues" earlier in the year. In the final chorus, instead of a New Orleans free-for-all, Armstrong set an earthy riff and was quickly joined by Ory and Dodds for a rocking finish.

"What shall we name it?" Fearn asked upon its conclusion.

"Call it 'The Gut Bucket,'" Louis responded. When Fearn asked what that meant, Louis brushed him off, saying it just came to him. St. Cyr later explained, "In the fish markets in New Orleans, the fish cleaners keep a large bucket under the table where they clean the fish, and as they do this they rake the guts in this bucket. Hence 'The Gut Bucket,' which makes it a low-down blues."[30]

Fearn knew he had a winner and arranged for "Gut Bucket Blues" to be the first Hot Five side to be issued, with "Yes! I'm in the Barrel" on the flip side. The Armstrongs and Ory left OKeh's studio and got some rest before returning to Dreamland that night for an "old-fashioned barn dance."[31] "It was a good sounding band, and very popular," Ory said of Lil's Dreamland Syncopators. "People lined up in the snow to get in to hear us."[32] One of those people, Erskine Tate, would be Louis's next boss.

"Erskine Tate, the subject of my article this week, is very well known to music lovers of the Middle West and will be a national character in time to come," Dave Peyton wrote on April 24, 1926. "Coming up the grade, with many obstacles in his path, this young man has won and conquered."[33] Born on January 14, 1895 in Memphis, Tate grew up in a very musical family; both of his parents were musicians and his mother, Panella, was a graduate of the Mendelssohn Conservatory of Music. Young Erskine began on drums before settling on violin, though he was also known to play piano, trombone, and mandolin; older brother James gravitated to the trumpet.

Soon after arriving in Chicago, the 17-year-old Erskine was mentioned as part of "a nice five-piece orchestra of most promising musicians" accompanying silent film screenings at the Phoenix Theater.[34] Silent movies were the rage of the nation and provided copious work for skilled musicians who could read the scores assembled to accompany each film. Tate clearly excelled at this work and eventually took over the leadership of an orchestra of his own. "There is no more popular orchestra in Chicago than Erskine Tate's Vendome Symphony orchestra, playing at the beautiful Vendome theater on State, between 31st and 32d Sts., and the work of this efficient group of young men is attracting a world of attention," the *Chicago Defender* reported in 1919.[35] "The Vendome Theater was like going to a cathedral," young saxophonist Scoville Brown later recalled. "You would go there to listen. Most of the young aspiring musicians would go to the Vendome."[36]

In addition to performing a live score for each film screened at the Vendome, the orchestra would perform a different classical overture each day. "Nothing is too heavy for them and their repertoire includes all the popular classics as well as the topical and characteristic numbers of the day, and they never fail to get a world of applause," the *Chicago Defender* reported.[37]

Now Tate was at the Dreamland Cafe to hear Armstrong blow. Satisfied, he offered him a job at the Vendome. "I like to have Fainted," Louis said of the opportunity.[38] Before accepting, he'd have to talk it over with Lil.

"Those guys are playing classical music and I don't know anything about that kind of music," Louis said. "I don't want to go on."

"Oh, they're not doing anything but greasing the music," Lil assured her husband. "Go on, you can play as good as they can."[39]

That's how Lil remembered it; Louis recalled Lil threatening, "Boy, if you don't go down there to Erskine Tate's rehearsal, I'll skin you alive."[40]

Louis went to the rehearsal, with Lil accompanying him in the manner of a parent accompanying her child to the first day of school. "So the first rehearsal I went about three rows back, you know," Lil said. "If anything come up, I was going to be an authority, you know. But all they wanted Louis to do was to play a special. . . . So after I saw he was all right, well, I left."[41] Louis got the job, and Dave Peyton announced in his December 12 column: "Mr. Armstrong is a versatile artist and will be an asset to this orchestra."[42]

Tate asked Armstrong to make one change before joining his orchestra: he would have to switch to trumpet full-time. Though Howard Scott remembered taking Armstrong to buy a trumpet shortly after he arrived in New York in 1924, Armstrong himself maintained that he didn't make the switch until joining Tate. "At the time I was playing in the symphony orchestra with Erskine Tate, he one day asked me to change from the cornet to the trumpet," Armstrong said in 1956. "Not that they don't sound good and all that, but it's just that they don't look the same, sitting in the symphony orchestra, and I'm sitting there with a little cornet beside the trumpets, you know? So, I changed and I liked it better."[43]

Armstrong's reading abilities had undoubtedly improved after his 13 months with Henderson, but this was another new experience, playing in a symphony orchestra, accompanying a film, and watching a conductor. Earl Hines, who later played piano in the Vendome orchestra, elaborated on Tate's method. "He used to get script and music sent him with the film," Hines said.

> There would be several themes about eight or sixteen bars long, which were used for changes of scene, as when a door closed and the characters went outside. These were known as one-finger theme, two-finger theme, three-finger theme, four-finger theme, and so on. If he held out his fourth finger, it meant they had to go to the fourth theme for, say, cloudiness in the sky and to get ready for a rough section of the music. The third finger would for birds flying before a love scene. The themes

> let us know we were going into a different type of music. . . . His arm and finger movements, his concentration—he was terrific and it was beautiful to watch him.[44]

"You had to watch him every minute," Armstrong said of Tate.[45] However, this proved difficult when the onscreen film captured his attention. Such an incident occurred when *The Sea Beast*, an adaptation of *Moby-Dick* starring John Barrymore, was screened at the Vendome on May 6–8, 1926. "I got this first part and I got so wrapped up in that picture, where if you're counting a few bars and you look up on the screen and you get so interested, you done lost your count!" Armstrong said. "And I'm supposed to be wailing when that whale bit his leg off. . . . And I'm looking at this picture, man, mouth wide open. Tate is directing and looks down and, 'Come on you so-and-so!' "[46]

Armstrong gained valuable experience from such moments, but he also knew why he was hired—to blow hot solos, which he did from his first night in the band. "I went down there and the opening night was sensational," he wrote. "I remember the first Swing Tune we played—Called 'Spanish Shawl.' "[47] He would be featured on many "swing tunes" during his time with Tate, including "Sugar Foot Stomp," "Panama," "Royal Garden Blues," and others. "Before the curtain would go back down and the whole theatre darkened again I would be featured in a jazz number with the entire orchestra," he added. "Boy, did we rock the theatre."[48]

Armstrong also seemed to be extra inspired by the challenge of playing classical music along with his usual hot fare. "We played everything you hear these big orchestras playing, right there in the Vendome Theatre in Chicago," he recalled, adding, " 'William Tell' wasn't nothin' after I was there two weeks."[49] In addition to Rossini's *William Tell Overture*, Armstrong recalled performing many other classical selections with Tate, offering a list to *Down Beat* in 1952 that included Gershwin's *Rhapsody in Blue*, Gounod's *Faust*, Puccini's *Madame Butterfly*, Chopin's mazurkas, Rimsky-Korsakov's "Song of India," Stravinsky's *The Firebird*, Tchaikovsky's *Romeo and Juliet*, Verdi's *Rigoletto*, Wagner's *Tannhäuser*, and Mendelssohn's *Midsummer Night's Dream*, among others.[50] But one number in particular stood out to Armstrong: Pietro Mascagni's "Intermezzo" from the opera *Cavalleria Rusticana*, which he remembered becoming "one of my biggest trumpet solos."[51]

The teenaged Armstrong, who bought opera records in New Orleans just a few years earlier, probably never could have imagined that one day he would be featured playing such music in an all-Black theater in Chicago, but this was just the next step in his journey toward being more than just a jazz musician. "A fellow didn't want to be stamped as just a jazz player or something like that,

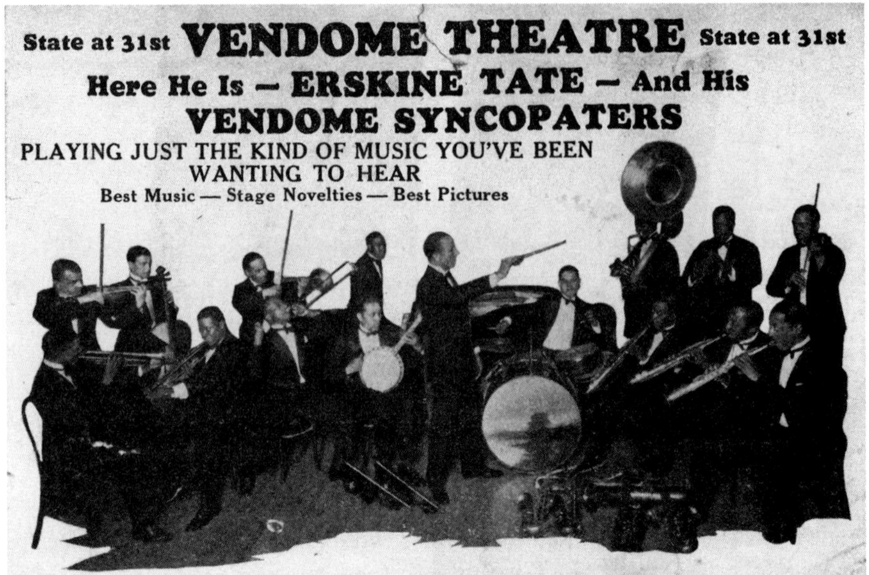

Figure 23.2 Newspaper advertisement for Erskine Tate and His Vendome Syncopators, clipped by Louis and Lil Armstrong and affixed to one of their earliest scrapbooks. Credit: Courtesy of the Louis Armstrong House Museum.

but we tried to be musicians, all-around," he said. "That's why I proved I could play in this symphony orchestra."[52]

As at Dreamland, a buzz quickly developed around Armstrong's Vendome performances, especially when he began ending one of his features with a stratospheric high F. "It got around that he was making this high note and people would come to two or three shows waiting for him to miss it one day," Lil said in a remembrance echoed by Louis.[53] "Cats lined up all around the block, man," he said. "They'd keep one picture three days and cats would come three days to see if I would miss that note!"[54]

Louis grew frustrated and vented to Lil, "Do you know people are coming to the show five times to hear me miss that F?"

"Yeah?" Lil said. "Well, make some G's at home!"

"So he started blowing around the house," Lil recalled before impersonating the sound of her husband's trumpet, emitting a sequence of high note shrieks. "Oh my God, why did I say that?" she thought to herself.

"But, you know, psychologically it was all right," she continued. "You make a G at home, you're not going to worry about an F at the theater."[55]

Once again, coach Lil was right. Asked by reporter Bill Stout if he ever missed the high note at the Vendome, Louis erupted, "Why, miss it!? I had it in my pocket all the time! I was liable to make it look hard or something in those days. . . . And I had the chops to do it. I was only 25. Man, I could jump over hurdles and do everything."[56]

Thanks to his doubling at the Vendome and the Dreamland Cafe, Louis had become the most talked-about trumpeter in Chicago at the end of 1925. He was still unknown outside the city, but that would soon change when OKeh released the first Hot Five record at the end of December 1925.[57] It sold well enough for OKeh to add Armstrong to its "Race Record Artists Night," to be held at the Coliseum on February 27. A new photo of a serious-looking Armstrong started running in advertisements for the event beginning on January 30, plugging "Gut Bucket Blues" each time.

E. A. Fearn was thrilled with the response to Armstrong's November recordings and set out to make more as soon as possible. Between February 22 and March 3, Armstrong would take part in 10 sessions as both leader and sideman, cutting a total of 22 sides—but two in particular would forever change the sound of jazz and American popular music, catapulting Armstrong to stardom and cementing his reputation as one of the most influential musicians of the twentieth century.

24

"I Got the Heebies"

1926

In the middle of a flurry of recording activity as leader and sideman, Louis Armstrong summoned the Hot Five on February 26, 1926, to record six songs. This band would have many memorable days in the studio over the course of their short history, but that February 26 session would go down as perhaps the greatest of them all.

The group made history with the first song recorded that day, Spencer Williams's "Georgia Grind," which would feature the first proper Louis—and Lil—Armstrong vocal on record. Louis shows off his half-speaking/half-shouting style, carried over from "Gut Bucket Blues," but also sings with undeniable soul. E. A. Fearn was tickled by Armstrong's vocal and wanted him to sing another one, but the other five selections the Hot Five prepared to record were all instrumentals, including the next tune on the docket—"Heebie Jeebies."

Named after an African American periodical first published in 1925, "Heebie Jeebies" was written by Boyd Atkins, Armstrong's old bandmate from the Fate Marable days. According to Johnny St. Cyr, "The composition was only an instrumental and Mr. Fern [*sic*] insisted on a vocal chorus, so Louis wrote down some words which he did not have time to rehearse or memorize, and he had to read them when it came time for him to sing."[1]

After a short rehearsal, in which they worked out a cute ending where Lil would play a "Charleston" rhythm and the fellows would each shout a line in response, Fearn asked the group to attempt a master take. The band sailed through the opening choruses before Armstrong stepped up to the recording horn and started singing, reading the words off the "slip of paper" St. Cyr recalled him holding.

Midway through the first vocal chorus, disaster struck—and history was made. "So we went ahead to making a master and Louie got to singing the 'Heebie Jeebies' and the paper slipped out of his hands!" St. Cyr said.[2] "I dropped that paper with the lyrics on it," Armstrong remembered. "So, I started to stop and Mr. Fearn . . . he kept on saying, 'Keep on! Keep on!' "[3]

There does seem to be a slight moment of panic during the tenth bar of his first vocal chorus, as Armstrong stops singing his rudimentary lyrics and mumbles something akin to "You don't dobo," sounding a bit lost. He finishes the chorus, even emitting a righteous "Yes ma'am," but with another chorus to follow and his lyrics on the floor, he had to think fast. That's when it came to him: the wordless vocalizing he first did with his quartet in New Orleans, which Norman Mason remembered him doing with Fate Marable (with Boyd Atkins present) and Clyde Bernhardt and Vic Berton remembered him doing with Fletcher Henderson. Armstrong attributed his quick thinking to his "presence of mind. And you can think of things that happened years ago in some spot like that and save the day sometimes."[4]

Armstrong transformed his voice into an instrument for the next chorus, swinging just as effortlessly as if he had been playing his trumpet, which made sense since, in his mind, it was all connected. "We [were] always music-minded in New Orleans, and every note that I'd scat on, I'm thinking about the trumpet anyway," he once said, adding, "But you can bet my fingers are going right down the horn every time I sing a note. See? So I wasn't afraid about this, Pops." The syllables flowed from Armstrong's voice so smoothly that it seemed hard to believe that this could actually be a spur-of-the-moment creation—especially when the story took on mythical status with the release of the Columbia album *King Louis* in 1940.

Produced by 21-year-old Yale student George Avakian, *King Louis* represented the first reissue of Armstrong's Hot Five output in album form. When Avakian interviewed Richard M. Jones while putting together the set, Jones went overboard with his version of the saga of "Heebie Jeebies," turning the situation into something reminiscent of a Three Stooges short, down to Armstrong and Jones conking heads while bending over to pick up the fallen lyric sheet! "Louis bent over, taking the microphone to the floor with him, singing meaningless mono-syllables as he fumbled for the words," Avakian wrote. "The recording director [Jones] jumped to the rescue and finally handed the elusive manuscript to Armstrong—upside down."[5]

Because of the improbability of it all—and the small fact that microphones weren't being used by OKeh yet in Chicago—generations of historians have never taken Louis's own version of events seriously, claiming it as an example of his perceived self-mythologizing tendencies.

But the other members of the Hot Five never completely contradicted Armstrong's version. "That was the record where Louis forgot the lyrics and started scattin'," Kid Ory said. "We had all we could do to keep from laughing. Of course, Louis said he forgot the words, but I don't know if he intended it that way or not. It made the record, though."[6] "On the 'Heebie Jeebies' when we were recording the master and it was time for Louis to do the vocal he sung half of the words and the paper dropped from his hand," St. Cyr related. "To avoid spoiling the record and having to do it all over again, he just gave out with some queer sounds such as Boo Boo Pa Doop, Boo Boo, Frinie, Nacki Sacki, and others that do not make sense, which was later known as the Scat theme. Nevertheless, we got a good laugh out of it."[7] "I don't know whether he planned to scat it or not," Lil admitted. "But I know ever since Louis had started working alone that he would always add little extra touches to things and little comical things to his work. So it must be true that he forgot the words and started scatting."[8]

In addition to the momentary stutter in the first chorus, there's an even bigger mistake at the end when Kid Ory comes in too early with his shout of "Whatcha doin' with the Heebies?" resulting in an awkward moment of silence where his voice was supposed to appear. Under normal circumstances, Fearn would have requested one more take to iron out the routine, but even he knew there was something spontaneous about that vocal that could not be replicated. "Hell, we're going to take a chance with this one," Fearn told Armstrong.[9]

In fact, there is one part of Armstrong's later versions of the story that does seem to be exaggerated: "When the record was over Mr. Fearn, he came out of the control booth and said, 'Louis Armstrong, this is where scat was born,' you see?" Armstrong later claimed.[10] It's extremely doubtful that Fearn came in and made such a pronouncement. Armstrong wasn't even the first one to do it on record; Don Redman beat him to the punch on Fletcher Henderson's 1924 recording of "My Papa Doesn't Two-Time No Time," made before Armstrong entered the band, while Cliff "Ukulele Ike" Edwards and his mentor, Ukulele Bob Williams, had already separately recorded their unique style of wordless vocalizing.

But it is feasible that Fearn's knack for marketing kicked in quickly; there wasn't a word for this type of singing until Fearn published the sheet music in late 1926, calling attention to its "skat" chorus and putting a photo of the Hot Five on the cover for good measure.

When OKeh released "Heebie Jeebies" at the beginning of May, it was an instantaneous hit. Sales figures weren't published in that era, but Armstrong estimated it sold 40,000 copies in its first few weeks on the market.[11] "This record of Louis' took all of Chicago by storm as soon as it was released," clarinetist Mezz Mezzrow said. "For months after that you would hear cats greeting each other with Louis' riffs when they met around town—*I got the heebies*, one would yell out, and the other would answer *I got the jeebies*, and the next minute they were scatting in each other's face. Louis' recording almost drove the English language out of the Windy City for good."[12]

Figure 24.1 The cover of the sheet music for "Heebie Jeebies" as published by E. A. Fearn's Consolidated Music, featuring a publicity photo of the Hot Five and using the word "skat" to describe Armstrong's nonsense vocal for the first time.
Credit: Courtesy of Rob Rothberg.

"Louie broke all this business down," New Orleans guitarist Danny Barker explained. "That's where the song stylist came in. People begin to buy records because they liked a certain personality. You could have a raspy, whiskey voice or a high soprano voice or a monkeyshine voice or anything—if people like you, they bought your records. Louis Armstrong is responsible for that. He's the first person to scat sing on a record. On 'Heebie Jeebies.' Never heard nothing like that. Scat singing they called it. He introduced that."[13]

Armstrong never put it that way, always managing to give Fearn credit for taking a chance and popularizing "Heebie Jeebies." "I didn't want to claim, you know, get the credit or nothing like that," he once said. "It was just another tune."[14]

That is, until the early 1950s, when Armstrong bought Jelly Roll Morton's Library of Congress recordings on a series of Circle LPs and heard Morton state, "Scat is something a lot of people don't understand and they begin to believe that the first scat numbers was done by one of my hometown boys, Louis Armstrong—but I must take the credit away, since I know better." Armstrong listened for a few more seconds, stopped the record, picked up a microphone and began to address Morton on his reel-to-reel-tape—though Morton had been dead since 1941.

"Of course, Mr. Jelly Roll, I'll just have to take time out and kind of let you pause a minute while I explain this situation about scat," he began. "I don't think I'll let you get away with this."

Armstrong then told his version of the "Heebie Jeebies" saga, again giving credit to Fearn for coming up with the word. "And I never heard anyone say in New Orleans even the word 'scat,'" he said. "I don't think they used that word. If they did that kind of musical gesture, it must have been another name because scat wasn't even mentioned until after that recording was made and Mr. Fearn, the president of the OKeh Recording Company said, 'Well Louis Armstrong, this is where scat was born.' I said, 'Yeah? Okay. Thank you, Mr. Fearn." Armstrong closed by noting, "I just wanted to make a little correction cause after all, I'm still in the business and you're still six feet in the ground, young man."[15] Morton was in no shape to respond.

Scatting aside, the pure vivacity of his vocal—including interjections not commonly found in 1920s pop singing such as "Yes ma'am!" and "Sweet mama!"—represented a seismic shift in the ways singers could approach a text and breathe new life into it. Armstrong claimed singing was in his blood before the trumpet and after patiently waiting in silence through his tenures with Oliver and Henderson, he managed to rewrite the rules of American pop singing with his second full vocal on record.

Next, it was time to rewrite the rules of how to solo.

Up to this point in the Hot Five series, Armstrong had been content to simply play with his elders the way they did back in New Orleans, but with his name on the label, it was time to finally showcase exactly what he was capable of doing with his horn. To accomplish this, he selected one of his own compositions, "Cornet Chop Suey," as the third tune to be recorded on February 26.

Armstrong immediately commands the listener's attention with an explosive unaccompanied introduction that calls to mind the famed clarinet/piccolo solo on "High Society," which Louis used to play on his cornet as a teenager. In fact, "Cornet Chop Suey" can be viewed as a summation of Armstrong's "clarinet" style, right down to the title, a play on the Original Dixieland Jazz Band's "Clarinet Marmalade," also a part of Armstrong's New Orleans repertoire.[16]

He then leads the front line through the very forward-thinking verse and main theme, which seem to predict the complex, snake-like melodies that would be a hallmark of bebop in the 1940s. After a thrilling stop-time trumpet solo, where every note is perfectly placed, Armstrong's virtuosity rises above the closing ensemble, manifesting in short breaks, more stop-time adventures, and a daring coda featuring a mind-boggling diminished lick played in every range of his horn.

Armstrong created something special with "Cornet Chop Suey," but the same couldn't be said for the rest of the band; Ory and Dodds hit a few clinkers in the ensemble and Lil's piano solo doesn't rate as one of her finest moments. Perhaps for those reasons—and maybe there was just *too* much trumpet—Fearn scribbled "Recommended for Rejection" on the label of the master of "Cornet Chop Suey." Only after "Heebie Jeebies" was released and became a big hit did Fearn reverse his original decision and issue the recording in the summer of 1926.

Once released, "Cornet Chop Suey" would have an effect on trumpeters and other instrumentalists similar to the effect "Heebie Jeebies" had on vocalists. Asked to name his favorite Armstrong recording, longtime disciple Louie Metcalf quickly answered, "Cornet Chop Suey," causing fellow trumpeter Doc Cheatham to respond, "Yeah, that's my favorite tune."[17] Some trumpeters learned about "Cornet Chop Suey" from hearing others emulate Armstrong's solo. Young Jonah Jones was in Kentucky at the time of its release and recalled, "My friend that sat next to me in the Sunday school band, he could do 'Cornet Chop Suey' and I couldn't get it for nothing."[18] Pittsburgh-born Roy Eldridge was patterning his trumpet style on white musician Red Nichols and the speed exhibited by saxophonists such as Coleman Hawkins. "I hadn't heard Louie Armstrong at that time," Eldridge admitted. "When I got really indoctrinated with the Louie Armstrong thing is when I got stranded in St. Louis and every trumpet player in that town could play 'Cornet Chop Suey.'. . . I never heard this kind of trumpet playing. Being from the east, I thought this was southern playing. And every Sunday, they'd come down on my gig and wash me away."[19]

"Cornet Chop Suey" even made a mark on nontrumpeters. According to Wichita clarinetist Tim Kelly, Texas trombonist Jack Teagarden "used to carry around the Armstrong OKehs of 'Cornet Chop Suey' and 'Muskrat Ramble' in his instrument case, or when there was no place else, under his overcoat. Whenever he would get near a phonograph, Jack would pull out the records and listen attentively until he had absorbed every Louis phrase."[20] Chicago pianist Joe Sullivan later listed "Cornet Chop Suey" as one of "My Favorite Records,"[21] and electric guitarist George Barnes transcribed Armstrong's solo off the original 78 and scored it for his trumpetless octet in 1950.[22]

Down in New Orleans, many of the cornet players Armstrong left behind in his hometown soon learned every note of "Cornet Chop Suey"; Lee Collins eventually made it his theme song. Others used the challenging piece for those famed cutting contests, which were still occurring after Armstrong's departure. Preston Jackson remembered such a battle between Guy Kelly, the trumpeter in Oscar "Papa" Celestin's band, and Henry "Red" Allen Jr., the trumpet-playing son of brass band leader Henry Allen Sr. of Algiers, which only ended when Allen pulled out "Cornet Chop Suey," causing Kelly to quit.[23] Allen also battled Armstrong's old Waif's Home friend Henry "Kid" Rena and bested him on the same number. "Once—just once—I cut the Kid myself—a big moment—all because I recalled two little low notes that Rena hadn't caught on Armstrong's 'Cornet Chop Suey,'" Allen said.[24]

"His ideas will never be duplicated anymore," New Orleans pianist Alton Purnell said of Armstrong in 1970. "I know not in my time will there ever be another musician with the ideas Louie had. Original. I mean, his ideas are still trying to be followed by a lot of musicians and half of them—most of them are really not following him. Like this 'Cornet Chop Suey,' there's nobody that plays these ideas."[25]

But two caveats must be mentioned when discussing Armstrong's "ideas" on "Cornet Chop Suey"—they weren't improvised, and they might not even have been his to begin with.

Soon after he began dating Lillian Hardin in 1923, Louis and Lil began writing songs together. One of Lil's duties in King Oliver's band was to help Oliver notate his tunes and submit the lead sheets to the Library of Congress for copyright purposes. Louis had been burned by A. J. Piron and Clarence Williams with the success of "I Wish I Could Shimmy Like My Sister Kate" and wouldn't let that happen again. Lil encouraged him to write down his compositions and submit the copyright deposits immediately, which he did with "Cornet Chop Suey," stamped with the copyright deposit date of January 18, 1924.

The fact that he copyrighted it two years before recording it isn't a surprise; he did the same with "Yes! I'm in the Barrel." What *is* a big surprise is that Louis notated just about everything on the recording, including both the "High Society"-inspired introduction and, most important, the entire stop-time solo, notated as a "Patter" section. While something of an anomaly—Armstrong copyrighted many other compositions and never again notated his solo before recording it—it's still fascinating that this was something he worked out and felt confident enough about to put on paper at a time when he was just a sideman in Oliver's band, rarely getting any opportunities to take a short break by himself, never mind a full stop-time solo.

But even more fascinating is that when "Cornet Chop Suey" was played for two separate aging New Orleans jazz musicians in the 1950s, they came to the same conclusion: Armstrong was channeling cornetist Buddy Petit.

Trombonist William "Bebe" Ridgeley was in the middle of telling historian Richard B. Allen about how "so many fellas tried to imitate [Petit's] style" when Allen put on "Cornet Chop Suey." "That's his style!" Ridgely shouted during Armstrong's introduction. "That's him, that's Buddy. If it ain't, that's somebody just like him, but that's his style!"[26] In a separate interview, Allen played the same recording for drummer Alfred Williams, who couldn't be fooled so easily. "Yeah, sounds like Louis in Chicago, Louis's recording," Williams said, confident from the start. But when Armstrong took the final intricate breaks, Williams exclaimed, "Now *that's* Buddy Petit's playing! See, like that? That last ending, that's Buddy Petit! That's the way Buddy used to play. Louis used to admire Buddy for that, making them diminishes, that's called diminishes. Yes indeed, he liked Buddy's playing. 'Cornet Chop Suey.' "[27]

Why would Armstrong take the time to compose a song and even write out a solo in the style of Petit in January 1924? It could be the same reason he apparently invoked young Bunk Johnson when he took his first recorded solo on Oliver's "Chimes Blues": having not fully found his own voice yet, he fell back on the styles of Petit and Johnson to set himself apart from Oliver. He was coming into his own with the Hot Five but knew that Petit's style was something different and not known outside New Orleans; Petit never made a single recording before his passing in 1931.

Thus, while "Cornet Chop Suey" remains a landmark on its own merits, it's yet another example of Armstrong immortalizing a sound of New Orleans that might have otherwise never been heard on record. Perhaps trumpeter Punch Miller put it best; asked if Armstrong had his own style, Miller responded, "He had his own style of playing, but what he did do, the stuff that he got famous with, he took it right from here. All that stuff, 'Heebie Jeebies' and all that kind of stuff, well, he got that from around there. Those boys were playing that up and down the streets here, but they didn't know what they were doing. Louie just went up there and made something out of it."[28]

Incredibly, the February 26 date was only halfway done when "Cornet Chop Suey" was finished. Armstrong followed it with another stop-time solo on Johnny St. Cyr's attractive composition "Oriental Strut." Without having two years to prepare for the moment, Armstrong created something spontaneous and dazzling, yet not quite as sure-footed as in the previous number.[29] This was followed by one of Lil's compositions, "You're Next," in which she got to showcase her classical chops during the introduction.

The date ended with "Muskrat Ramble," another soon-to-be classic, though one with a somewhat controversial backstory. According to Kid Ory, "I wrote it back around 1921 when I was playing in a taxi dancehall at Third and Main in Los Angeles. It had no name then."[30] With five songs completed, Ory recalled that "we were short of a number to finish the session and I happened to have my music with me and we recorded my number." Ory didn't have a title for it but remembered that it was Lil who told Fearn it was called "Muskrat Ramble." "I'll go for that title," Ory said, adding, "we all laughed and left the studio."[31]

Louis remembered it differently. "We start playing this tune in the studio and in fact, we all just made it up," he said, "But Ory had nerve enough to claim it! So it's Ory's tune."

Louis even explained the etymology behind the title. "See, when a kid would wet the bed in New Orleans, in those days, that's where this muskrat would come in," he said, "because his mother would fry one of them and make him eat it to stop him from, you know, messing up those sheets there. So, you had to stop it because as long as he'd keep on [wetting the bed], she'd make him eat these muskrats."[32]

Armstrong might have claimed they just "made it up" but there's also evidence that the multistrain piece had been around since the New Orleans days.[33] Louis himself reminisced about playing it "in the wagons" on a tape made with one-time brass band mate Maurice Durand in 1951.[34] Regardless of the complicated history, the Hot Five recording of "Muskrat Ramble" contains peak ensemble playing by this vaunted group, with Ory really whooping it up with his tailgate style, sounding much more comfortable here than on "Cornet Chop Suey" or "Oriental Strut." This is where the older musicians like Ory and Dodds excelled, but once the results of this very successful session hit the public, they'd slowly begin to take more of a back seat to the trumpeter—and now vocalist—leading the band.

To help promote the new series of recordings, OKeh arranged to have Armstrong and the Hot Five take a series of new publicity photos at the

Figure 24.2 Louis Armstrong's first smiling publicity photo, found in a scrapbook maintained by Armstrong and Alpha Smith.
Credit: Courtesy of the Louis Armstrong House Museum.

Woodard Studio in Chicago. Armstrong had posed for photos in the Waif's Home, on the riverboats, with his mother and sister, with King Oliver, with Oliver's Creole Jazz Band, and with Fletcher Henderson—and had never once smiled broadly for the camera. But now, knowing his face was going to help sell his music, Armstrong looked directly into the camera and unleashed a small, yet magnetic smile—the first of thousands to come.

By the time of the February 26 session, Louis and Lil's days at the Dreamland Café were over. What had started as a welcome respite after his time in New York had grown increasingly unpleasant as the months passed by. "And it was very bad because they started kidding him about me being leader of the band," Lil recalled, remembering the musicians teasing Louis, "Look out there, your wife will fire you!" Others began calling Louis "Henny," short for "henpecked." "And it made Louis angry and it embarrassed him and he became so hard to get along with at home and on the bandstand," Lil said. "I would get ready to start the band off and he would have all the musicians on one side telling them the damn joke. And I got after him about it. He said, 'Well, if they don't like it, fire me!' So I said, 'Well, this is getting nowhere.' So I just quit."[35]

The Dreamland Café band was no more, but Lil continued offering her opinions to her husband on matters musical and nonmusical. Now, however, Louis was starting to crack. He recalled "a time when one of them fucking professors be coming from Fisk University and I put a hat on the bed. Shit, she damn near run me out of the house!" Lil yelled at him about how he could do such a thing with a professor visiting, causing Louis to erupt, "Well, fuck Professor! Shit, that motherfucker better not come back here after tomorrow either!"[36] In the 1940s, Louis wrote to Robert Goffin, "But still with all of that swell Home, Lil, and I had—There was not happiness there. We were always Fussing and threatening to Break up if I sat on the Bed after it was made up. Why—Lil would almost go into 'Fits' (Spasms)—etc."[37]

Most of all, Louis was becoming disgusted by the way Lil and her mother treated Clarence, yelling at him at dinner, "Don't pick up that fork at that time! Now you take this spoon," causing Louis to lash out "That boy don't want to know all that shit."[38] "And poor Clarence my adopted son with his nervous self—used to almost Jump out of his Skin when Lil or Lil's mother would Holler at him," Louis wrote. "Most of the times it was uncalled for. Lil and her mother had some bad tempers. And it would make my Blood Boil when I'd see them Abuse, my Son Clarence. When ever they—especially Lil—would holler at me I'd tell her Just where to go. I'd say—Aw Woman—*GO TA HELL*."[39]

Figure 24.3 Louis Armstrong, second from left, and adopted son, Clarence, far right, pose with an unidentified man and his son in Chicago, c. 1926. According to a note by Jack Bradley on the back of the print, the unidentified man was a sponsor of the Zulu Social Aid and Pleasure Club Mardi Gras parade in New Orleans.
Credit: The Jack Bradley Collection, Louis Armstrong House Museum.

With their marriage showing signs of duress, Louis looked forward to his nightly engagements with Erskine Tate's orchestra. "I became quite a Figure at the 'Vendome,'" he wrote. "Especially with the Gals." He grew particularly fond of one in particular: Alpha Smith. Born in Indiana in 1907, by 1920

Smith was living in Chicago with her divorced mother, Florence. The 18-year-old Alpha would "come to the Vendome Theater twice a week," Louis wrote, adding, "Alpha used to sit in the Front Row every time she came. And She would sit Right where I could get a good look at her. And she had big pretty eyes anyway—I couldn't keep from Diggin Her."[40]

As Louis and Alpha commenced getting "Thicker + Thicker," he did his best to keep his affair hidden from Lil, but it wasn't always easy. "There were times when Lil would be in the Vendome at the same time as Alpha," he wrote. "Well—On those nights we couldn't Flirt so much." By this point, Louis was convinced that Lil "had been Running Around with one of the Chicago 'Pimps' while I was at work. So as we colored people used to say—is just as good for the Goose as it is for the Gander—meaning—if Lil could enjoy some one Else's Company, I could too."

He also couldn't shake the lessons he'd learned in New Orleans from the "ol' Hustlers and Pimps down there" who told him, "Never worry over No One Woman—no matter how pretty or sweet she may Be. Any time she gets down wrong, and ain't playing the Part of a Wife—get yourself somebody else." For now and for many years to come, Alpha would be that woman. Alpha soon bought a scrapbook of her own and began populating it with clippings about Louis—many of the same clippings found in Lil's.

On February 27, 1926, the day after their monumental recording session, the Hot Five made one of its rare public appearances at OKeh's "Race Records Ball" at the Chicago Coliseum in front of a crowd of 3,000, sharing the bill with other OKeh associates—and King Oliver.

One year earlier, Oliver had taken over leadership of a new band at the Plantation Cafe, "The Dixie Syncopators," finally getting to front his idealized 10-piece outfit filled with New Orleans musicians, including reedmen Albert Nicholas and Barney Bigard, pianist Luis Russell, and drummer Paul Barbarin, all from Tom Anderson's establishment. Kid Ory also joined Oliver full-time after Lil's Dreamland engagement ended.

Managed by Ed Fox, the Plantation soon became one of the hottest spots on the South Side of Chicago, a venue where everyone, from the band to the waiters to the hat check girl, was part of the act, as related by Albert Nicholas:

> Everybody was swinging at the Plantation. It was a bouncing place. When you come in, the waiters, they come to get your order for a drink, they got the tray going like this with the band, you know, they always in rhythm. Fox, the owner, he hits the cash register on the beat, BAM, to make change. Everything was in rhythm! That

> was a funny joint, man! Yeah, they come around here, "What are you having?" They're bouncing. "Well, I'll have so and so." And he's right with that beat. And he goes back and gets them and comes back with the drinks and the thing and that tray is swinging, lays those drinks down, picks up the money, takes it, goes to the cash register to pay Fox off, BAM, gets change, all in rhythm! The hat check girl, when you come in the door, she's like that, she's bouncing.[41]

St. Louis trumpeter Bob Shoffner was hired to play second but would occasionally have to play solos when Oliver's teeth were bothering him. "I used to feel very sorry for him," Bigard said of Oliver. "Some nights he could play, some nights he couldn't play."[42] But to Nicholas, Oliver experienced a second wind at the Plantation, where he could pace himself and just play his featured solos and let the rest of the band play for the singers and dancers in the revue. "And Joe was at the height of his career then," Nicholas continued. "That's before he had trouble with his teeth. This man was something else."[43]

Oliver was on the upswing when he encountered Armstrong in February 1926. Jack Kapp of Brunswick Records was starting a new series of electrically recorded race records on the Vocalion imprint and Oliver would record two sides on March 11, including a blues he wrote called "Snag It" that was climaxed by a spectacular, technically challenging yet supremely earthy cornet break that would soon become the rage of Chicago.

But Oliver was also perhaps feeling a bit nervous. The Sunset Cafe—the Plantation's biggest competition, located directly across the street and managed by Joe Glaser—was preparing to showcase violinist Carroll Dickerson's orchestra, just back in Chicago after a successful 42-week vaudeville tour on the Pantages circuit. Dickerson's group featured the popular stylings of pianist Earl Hines. Born in Duquesne, Pennsylvania, on December 28, 1903, Hines grew up the son of a trumpet player, eventually trying that instrument himself before gravitating to the piano. Originally classically trained, he soon heard some of Pittsburgh's jazz pianists and started formulating a style of his own, playing trumpet-like octaves in his right hand to be better heard in the noisy clubs he performed in, while daringly breaking up the time with his perpetual-motion left hand. When the Dickerson band arrived back in Chicago in early 1926, Hines established himself as the top pianist in the city and was viewed as enough of a draw to potentially take some of Oliver's crowds away.

Louis was still working regularly with Erskine Tate but with the breakup of Lil's band, he was looking for a new late-night job to play after the Vendome closed. Oliver was looking for another musician to hire to keep him on top at the Plantation Cafe. The two men talked it over and reached a decision: the mentor and the student would reunite after nearly two full years apart. "I loved Joe Oliver, and here I was back in Chicago with all these Chicago boys, and I thought I'd be more at home with Papa Joe, sitting by his side," Louis said. At least one person disapproved: Lil, who told him, "How long can you hang around Joe? It ain't doing you no good."[44] Nevertheless, Louis made up his mind and his decision was reported by Dave Peyton in the April 10, 1926, edition of the *Chicago Defender*: "Louis Armstrong will play the late watch with Joe Oliver's orchestra at the Plantation cafe, Chicago."[45]

Shortly before the reunion could commence, Armstrong stopped by the musicians' union one day and met Earl Hines for the first time, while Hines was running over some songs on the piano. "He took his horn out and began to blow," Hines said. "I always remember that first tune we played together. It was 'The One I Love Belongs to Somebody Else.' I knew right away that he was a giant. Nobody could play the horn the way he played it. He really knew that trumpet. From that time on, we began to hang out together."[46] Armstrong felt the same way, later writing, "The very first time I heard Earl play I was 'speechless.' I never heard so much beautiful Sh-t come out of a piano in my whole life."[47]

A short time later, Hines, on his way to a rehearsal with Dickerson's orchestra at the Sunset Café, ran into Armstrong, on his way to a rehearsal with Oliver at the Plantation. They stopped in the middle of the street to talk.

"Why don't you come on over with us young fellows?" Hines asked.

"I already promised Joe Oliver," Armstrong responded.

"Yeah, but you would do better to come with us," Hines said.[48]

Armstrong was at a crossroads. Should he go back "home" to Oliver and the comfort of playing with all the New Orleans musicians playing at the Plantation—where perhaps he would have to go back to playing second trumpet and maybe not get many opportunities to sing? Or should he take a risk and join Hines and the "young fellows" in Dickerson's group at the Sunset, which would be more of a challenge, but one that would place him firmly in the spotlight?

Armstrong probably agonized over the decision, but he made his mind up. Dave Peyton headed down to 35th Street and Calumet Avenue and reported his surprising findings in the following week's *Chicago Defender*: "Louis Armstrong, the cornet player, was slated to join Joe Oliver's orchestra, but switched over to Carroll Dickerson's Sunset Cafe orchestra at the last minute. Louis is in demand in the Windy City and there is a reason—he toots a wicked trumpet."[49]

Oliver must have been blindsided by the decision—but he was still King. On May 1, the *Chicago Defender* ran a large ad for his newest release, "Snag It," complete with an illustration of Oliver wearing a crown. "After you've heard this number you'll surely want to 'SNAG IT,'" the copy read. "That's what they are all doing at the Plantation Cafe where King Oliver's Dixie Syncopators play to hundreds every night."

But just underneath was another advertisement for "Heebie Jeebies," featuring Armstrong's new smiling publicity photo: "More wild jazz than you ever thought could be packed into one record is unpacked by Louis Armstrong and his Hot Five when they let loose with 'Heebie Jeebies.'"

"Snag It" would go on to become one of Oliver's biggest hits, with Dave Peyton referring to it as a "popular dance sensation" by August.[50]

But "Heebie Jeebies" would make Louis Armstrong a star.

25

"The Latest Novelty"

1926

"Carroll Dickerson's band has injected new life in the Sunset cafe," Dave Peyton wrote in his *Chicago Defender* column of April 17, 1926. "The boys are red hot. Just across the street at the Plantation cafe is King Joe Oliver and band, another hot one. The fire department is thinking of lining 35th St. with asbestos to keep these bands from scorching passersby with their red hot jazz music."[1]

With Armstrong and Oliver blowing across the street from one another, and clarinetist Jimmie Noone at the Nest next door to the Plantation, this tiny section of the South Side of Chicago became the capital of hot jazz in America. "Thirty-fifth and Calumet was jacked up every night, with Louis and Oliver and Jimmy [*sic*] all playing within a hundred feet of each other; at dawn there fell a tremendous silence," guitarist and banjoist Eddie Condon wrote. "Unless it happened in New Orleans I don't think so much good jazz was ever concentrated in so small an area. Around midnight you could hold an instrument in the middle of the street and the air would play it."[2]

Doc Cheatham, a young trumpeter and saxophonist from Nashville, arrived in Chicago and was in awe of the music he heard, but had difficulty finding work. "It was really hard because I was not a New Orleans musician and it seems that all of the work in Chicago was given to New Orleans musicians unless you were a native Chicagoan and a great player in Chicago," Cheatham said. He made the best of it though, saying, "I didn't care because it was an opportunity to play and to listen to all of the rest of the musicians. . . . The greatest jazz ever played in one city in the world at that time was in Chicago."[3]

Not all outsiders felt the same way. "Thirty-fifth Street was a bad street, and when I first went to Chicago I thought it was the worst city in the world," Earl Hines said. "It was lit up at night like Paris, and there were some of the most dangerous people in the world on it. . . . You had to *act* bad, whether you were bad or not." Of course, the dangerous characters, gangsters, pimps, prostitutes, and abundance of New Orleans musicians probably made Armstrong feel like he was back home.[4]

Cornetist Muggsy Spanier, a young white disciple of both Oliver and Armstrong, shared that he would go from the Plantation to the Sunset to "keep peace in the family." "Joe would send word over: 'Close those windows or I'll blow you off 35th street!' "[5] Spanier called it a "friendly, happy thing," but there was definitely a touch of rivalry between the two. After the release of "Snag It" in May 1926, with its climactic four-bar break, Oliver was feeling particularly cocky. According to Natty Dominique, a fellow New Orleanian who played trumpet alongside Armstrong in Dickerson's band, Oliver came into the Sunset Café one night with an arrangement for "Snag It" with his break transcribed.

"So we just looked at it, being musicians, Louie and I said, 'Stand up here, we'll play it for you,' " Dominique recalled. "And when we got to that break, we couldn't finish it. We'd run out of gas."

"Practice it," Oliver said to the two. "When you learn it, let me know."

"And he walked out and went across the street to the Plantation," Dominique said. "Louie and I got so angry, really, it was pitiful. And when he got to the door, he turned back and waved at us."

During the next intermission, the two trumpeters went into the kitchen of the Sunset Café to work on it, adjusting their breathing as necessary. "So we tried it and we succeeded!" Dominique said. "The next intermission, we went and got Joe Oliver, we said, 'You come here on your intermission, you come over here, King.' "

"Oliver was right there," Dominique continued. "When it got to the break, the trombone and the first and second trumpet, we made the break. Oliver said, 'At last, you've made it. Thanks!' And walked away."[6]

Based on the success of "Snag It," Jack Kapp asked Oliver to come back and record again for Vocalion on May 29, but Kapp was also interested in Armstrong and, on May 28, recorded him as a member of Erskine Tate's Vendome Orchestra—and with the Hot Five. Louis never had much tolerance for the business side of the music business, and seeing the way Oliver and Fletcher Henderson would record the same songs for different labels, he must have assumed OKeh wouldn't mind. To be safe, Kapp used a pseudonym: "Lill's Hot Shots."[7]

The music recorded for Vocalion was quite memorable, but not without issue. Kapp, not interested in Erskine Tate's "symphonic" side, had Tate put together a 10-piece version of his band to record two recent popular songs, "Static Strut" and "Stomp Off, Let's Go." The results were indeed scorching, with Armstrong's bravura "Static Strut" outing standing out as a highlight of his early output. There are even some Oliver-isms on "Stomp Off, Let's Go," a candidate for one of the most exciting recordings of the decade—but Armstrong also plays a couple of air notes for the first time on record. If the

May 28 recording date is correct, Armstrong would have performed with Tate the night before, accompanying the film *Irene,* starring Colleen Moore, and then played the Sunset Café before heading into the studio in the morning.[8] That tiredness came to the forefront when Lil's Hot Shots took over and played Louis's composition, "Drop That Sack." Two takes survive and though they both feature driving lead work, each attempt opens with a sloppy opening break and includes a few clams throughout, another sign of fatigue.[9] Earl Hines recalled that Louis began using a "certain salve on his lips" when his chops were sore from doubling and that sometimes a scab would develop on his upper lip. "He was always a trouper," Hines said. "He knew how to get by, but many times I knew he must have been playing in pain. He never showed it. He was all smiles."[10]

But the biggest issue surrounding the Vocalion date occurred when Louis chose to sing on Fats Waller's "Georgia Bo-Bo," contributing a rollicking vocal without attempting to disguise his voice at all. When the record was finally released, an annoyed E. A. Fearn called Armstrong into his office at Consolidated Music and played "Georgia Bo-Bo" for him.

"Louis, who played trumpet on that record?" Fearn asked.

"Gee, I don't know, boss," said Armstrong, "But I won't do it again!"[11]

Soon after Armstrong started at the Sunset Café, the venue's manager, Joe Glaser, pulled a page out of Lil's marketing book and put up a sign reading "Carroll Dickerson's Orchestra featuring Louis Armstrong, the World's Greatest Cornetist." "Surprised I was!" Armstrong said. "But that's the way Mr. Glaser wanted it."

Glaser had ties to the Chicago underworld—he ran a "chain of whorehouses" provided by mobster Roger Touhy—and often hosted members of Al Capone's gang in his establishment. Armstrong never forgot the night "one of them tough Ass Gangsters" asked Glaser, "Listen, this is a wide world—and why do you keep Louis Armstrong's name up there as the world's greatest?" Armstrong remembered Glaser "looked at him straight in the eye" and said, "Listen, I think he is and this is my place and I defy anybody to take it down."

"Well, that was that," Armstrong concluded. "Those were some fine days."[12]

Leader Dickerson, who was born in Chicago in 1895, had been playing violin since childhood but now mostly stuck to conducting—and apparently wasn't very good at it. "Carroll Dickerson used to direct with a baton, with one eye on the band, and find it way out on the floor sometime," Armstrong said. "Slipped out of his hand! He didn't realize he lost it, you know?"[13]

The Dickerson band had made its reputation on the Pantages vaudeville circuit with its "Charleston Revue" and would now reprise a bit of that at the

Sunset Café. "The Charleston was popular at that time until Percy Venable, the producer of the show, staged a finale with four of us band boys closing the show doing the Charleston," Louis wrote. "That was really something. There was Earl Hines, as tall as he is; [drummer] Tubby Hall, as fat as he was; [alto saxophonist] little Joe Walker, as short as he is, and myself, as fat as I was at that time. We would stretch out across that floor doing the Charleston as fast as the music would play it. Boy, oh boy, you talking about four cats picking them up and laying them down—that was us."[14]

While Oliver was still laying down a stomping two-beat for the dancers at the Plantation, Armstrong and Hines were working together to turn the Dickerson band into a more swinging organization. "I have made it a point to notice the increase in popularity recently of the 4/4 time with that peculiar staccato beat right on the nose," a Chicago writer pointed out. "You can find the intent, if not the real thing, in nearly every place around town now and due to nothing else than the style that Carroll Dickerson and his Orchestra have originated."[15] Drummer Baby Dodds, who performed with both Oliver and Armstrong, noted that with Oliver he played "two beats to the measure. I didn't use four." But Dodds added, "With Louis, no matter how fast you play, Louis wanted four. Four beats to the bass drum, kept filling in the time."[16] That feeling of forward momentum was thrilling; Hines said of Armstrong, "When he got through blasting his horn, and all the rest of us came up with him, that band was really swinging!"[17]

Armstrong was still best known for his "wicked trumpet" work at this time and was referred to in the press as the "iron lip cornet wonder."[18] On June 12, Fearn produced a massive event at the Coliseum, a "Cabaret and Style Show" that featured several "OKeh Race Record Stars," including the Hot Five, Richard M. Jones, Clarence Williams, and many more. Dave Peyton reported that 20,000 people showed up and called it "the greatest affair the Windy City has ever witnessed. . . . Louis Armstrong and his Hot Five broke up the big hall June 12 with their hot playing. Some jazz band. I tell 'em so!"[19] When OKeh issued "Cornet Chop Suey" in early July, their advertisement referred to Armstrong as "the sensation of the Big OKeh Cabaret and Style Show" and emphasized that he blew "the meanest cornet ever heard."[20]

However, the true highlight of the night was a performance of "Heebie Jeebies," about which advertisements promised attendees, "You Are Going to Have an Opportunity to See How It Was Done: Louis Armstrong and His Hot Five Will Actually Make an OKeh Record Right on the Stage of 'Heebie Jeebies Dance.' "[21] Fearn made good on his promise at the show, even playing the record back for the audience upon its completion.[22] Armstrong's vocals and showmanship were catching on in a big way, leading Fearn to set up two more Hot Five studio sessions on June 16 and June 23 to further capture this side of his persona.

Many serious musicologists have written off both dates, with Gunther Schuller calling them "the nadir of Hot Five recording activity."[23] The reason for this is the lack of trumpet showpieces and an abundance of comedic and novelty numbers that spotlight Armstrong's personality; he sings on nearly every number, contributes a silly vaudeville routine to the middle of "King of the Zulus" with comedian Clarence Babcock, and even breaks out the old slide whistle one last time on "Who'Sit."

Perhaps these sessions didn't change the course of jazz history, but they do provide a snapshot of Armstrong the entertainer, the showman who was steadily becoming just as popular for his singing and clowning as for his "wicked" trumpet solos. In the 1950s, producer George Avakian talked to Armstrong about one of the June selections, "Don't Forget to Mess Around," and asked if there was really a dance by that name. "'Yes, yes indeed,' he cried and leaped out of his chair," Avakian later wrote. "'Went like this!' Well, there I was without a movie camera, but be assured of one thing—Louis was a great dancer and still light on his feet. 'Used to do that every show after the vocal, and then blow two choruses. Had to dance two, three encores on Saturday nights.'"[24]

While tape recording himself and friends listening to records in his hotel room on one of his 1950s reel-to-reel tapes, Armstrong can be heard quieting down the boisterous crowd so they could hear the "West Indian" comedy sketch at the center of "King of the Zulus," saying, "this is the funniest situation" and laughing out loud at its conclusion.[25] On "Big Fat Ma and Skinny Pa," Babcock plays the role of a stiff square dance caller before Armstrong delivers an irresistible vocal, even reprising his "Hey hey!" sign-off from "Gut Bucket Blues." This became something of a catchphrase; even the normally serious Dave Peyton inserted, "Hey, hey!" into a column about the Hot Five published after the record was released.[26] OKeh positioned Armstrong as a comedian when they began promoting "this comical tune," noting in their advertising copy, "You won't know whether to let your feet do their stuff—or just sit down and shake your self with laughter."[27]

The Hot Five also recorded "Droppin' Shucks" and "I'm Gonna Gitcha," two Lil compositions that offered an almost uncomfortable glimpse into the private lives of Louis and Lil—and Alpha. And Louis didn't forget his elders either, handing "Lonesome Blues" over to Johnny Dodds for a rare clarinet feature and recording Ory's composition "Sweet Little Papa."

Thus, the June 16 and June 23 dates might represent the "nadir" of the Hot Five for those looking for trumpet solos that changed the world, but they allow modern-day listeners a taste of the Armstrong who was packing them in at the Sunset Café and the Vendome Theater, Armstrong the showman, the vocalist, the comedian, the dancer, the lady's man, the blues singer—and yes, the world-class trumpeter. In short—Louis Armstrong, period.

OKeh had now stockpiled enough Armstrong recordings to last until November. But Vocalion had the Erskine Tate and Lill's Hot Shots sides ready for release and now producer Tommy Rockwell of Columbia Records wanted a taste of the Armstrong magic. Rockwell did not want to run afoul of OKeh so he left Louis alone but instead approached Lil with a proposition: she would put together a Hot Five–type band and record eight songs for Columbia, but the songs had to be composed by Louis. Lil wrote them all herself and put Louis's name on them, recording four on July 13 as the New Orleans Wanderers and four more the next day as the New Orleans Bootblacks. For the sessions, Lil used Ory, Dodds, and St. Cyr from the Hot Five, plus cornetist George Mitchell and alto saxophonist Joe Clark from her old Dreamland Café band. The results were outstanding, with Ory and Dodds sounding particularly inspired in meshing with the steady lead of Mitchell, who didn't attempt any Louis-like pyrotechnics.

When the session was over, Rockwell paid Lil $120 per selection, which she split with Louis. Lil was pleased with the results but admitted she didn't quite understand why Rockwell had set it up the way he did, with the preponderance of compositions credited to Louis. She forgot all about it and left town a few days later to be with her ailing grandmother back in Memphis. Louis and Lil had evidently worked through their rough patch, judging by the letters Louis wrote while Lil was away. "Baby I miss you so bad until I'm about to go Crazy," he wrote on July 20. "I just can't live without [you] that's all. . . . Oh, I am a good little fat hubby, I come right straight home every night from work. I just lay here in the bed and think about my dear little wife."[28] The very next day, Louis wrote again, "I am more than glad to know that you're enjoying yourself. Just don't give my little p—sy Away and I'm satisfied. That's right honey play our records while you're there." He signed it "Papa Dip," coincidentally the title of one of the Columbia selections Lil had put Louis's name on the previous week.[29] When Lil returned to Chicago, she and Louis purchased a car and a home on the lakefront in Idlewild, Michigan, and spent two weeks there in August "hunting, fishing and 'mud crawling' " according to one published report.[30] Louis, who had been doubling since April, later said of the break, "First time I knew what a vacation was."[31]

But the good times ended in late August, when Rockwell released the first New Orleans Wanderers records on Columbia, with Louis's name prominently displayed as composer of each song. "So when the records come out, the numbers that Louis composed, his name is written on there in big letters as though he was playing on it," Lil said, finally figuring out that Rockwell's intention was to fool listeners into thinking Louis was playing on the sides.

"So Louie and I had a big argument and Louie slapped me about it," Lil said. "He said that I knew about it but I didn't know. . . . That's the only time Louie ever struck me. He slapped me, he said I had no business making the records, that he told me not to and that he already spent half the money that I gave him. Oh boy, that was a big mess."[32] Lil chose to stay with Louis and they eventually worked through it—but he began spending more time than ever on the side with Alpha and her mother in their "very Dingy Apartment" at 33rd Street and Cottage Grove Avenue. "But with all of that 'Dinginess' etc.," Louis wrote, "I was more happy Down there the nights I would stay there (sleep) with Alpha than I would if I went home."[33] He would continue leading this double life for the next five years.

Both Lil's and Alpha's scrapbooks grew fat in the fall of 1926, thanks to the success of "Heebie Jeebies." One periodical ran a photo of the Hot Five in July referring to them as "The 'Heebie Jeebies' Song Recorders." "A few months ago this organization was practically unknown, but today these harmony masters are Chicago's favorite musicians," the caption read.[34] Armstrong soon added it to his repertoire at the Vendome, sung with the aid of a megaphone. "The Heebie song was sung by Louis Armstrong who stopped the show each time he rendered the number," according to one writer who attended a show at the Vendome.[35] Bill "Bojangles" Robinson passed through Chicago in September to perform at the Palace and got caught up in the "Heebie Jeebies" mania. "Bill is said to have grown fond of the music of the Heebie Jeebies song last Friday night while at the Sunset Café when Louis Armstrong featured it with his cornet," according to one article, which added that Robinson ordered the sheet music to add it to his act.[36]

Singing, playing, and scatting was one thing, but Armstrong soon embraced an entirely different comedic character at the Vendome, breaking out the preacher impression he used to do at Elder Cosey's church as a boy in New Orleans. "He was wearing a frock coat and battered top hat, singing a kind of ring-chant tune with Louis making calls like a Baptist preacher, while the audience made the responses," Rex Stewart said of Armstrong's new routine. "Eventually one sister became confused as the mood grew more and more frantic, and her voice could be heard above the crowd. She was easily spotted because when the number ended, she rushed down the aisle shouting, 'Don't stop, Brother Louis, don't stop.' The audience in the theater broke up."[37]

Armstrong's "Preaching Blues" was regularly spotlighted in the Chicago press in the fall of 1926. "Louis Armstrong, who is one of the Heebies pet writers, led the members of this popular orchestra in a 'prayer' with his cornet," one writer reported. "During his 'offering' he wore a high silk hat, frocktail coat and smoked glasses. The fans are still giggling over the act as it was for the most amusing one ever seen here."[38] Armstrong next experimented by engaging in an "instrumental argument" with saxophonist Paul "Stumpy" Evans but soon had to return to "Preach the Gospel," with one writer noting, "This sketch was requested by many of the patrons here due to the amusing way Mr. Armstrong delivers it."[39]

When Tate added the recently published pop tune "My Baby Knows How" to his repertoire, Armstrong took his comedy one step further, with one article stating, "When Luis [*sic*] Armstrong sang 'My Baby Know How,' to Charles Harris, who slipped a wig over his head and played the role of the baby that Luis was singing about, the fans laughed themselves dizzy," the article stated. "The number was the best Tate had offered since Luis 'preached the Gospel' some weeks ago."[40]

While Armstrong continued honing his comedic skills on the Chicago stage, OKeh continued releasing selections from his June output. Though still marketed as "race records," the Hot Five recordings were also reaching a much larger international audience, leading Armstrong to be featured on the cover of Odeon Records' "Supplemento Fonotipia" catalog from September 1926, proclaiming him as "Le Ultime Novita"—"The Latest Novelty." The catalog was sent to E. A. Fearn with an accompanying letter stating, "We would suggest you giving these to Louis, showing him the tremendous amount of publicity he is securing by means of his Okeh contract, so that any time he sees fit to go to Italy, they will welcome him with open arms."[41]

Fearn next recorded the Hot Five on November 16. Lil capitalized on the scat singing craze by composing "Skid-Dat-De-Dat," a hauntingly beautiful variation on the blues with breaks for each of the horns and for Armstrong's voice, as he indulged in the most scatting he had done on record since "Heebie Jeebies." It's a gorgeous recording, but is marred by the breaks of Dodds and Ory, whose efforts pall alongside Armstrong's. After playing with Dickerson and Tate for so long, Armstrong was beginning to progress past the comfort zone of his New Orleans cohorts.

This applied in live settings as well as in the studio. Punch Miller came to Chicago in 1926 and visited Armstrong at the Sunset Café. Miller asked to sit in on "Sweet Child," a new pop tune recently recorded by Paul Whiteman, assuming they would just wing it. "Let 'em play what they want," Miller said to Armstrong when asked if the band should play an arrangement of the tune. "No, you can't do that in Chicago!" Armstrong scolded him, later accusing him of trying to "be a big shot."

Figure 25.1 The cover of Odeon Records' Italian supplemental catalog of September 1926, featuring Armstrong's publicity photo and declaring him "Le Ultime Novita"—"The Latest Novelty."
Credit: Courtesy of the Louis Armstrong House Museum.

"He just come from New Orleans where we play it by ear and it sounds good just the same," Armstrong recalled. But as Dickerson began passing out the parts of a "big arrangement," Armstrong knew Miller, who wasn't a good reader, was going to be in over his head.

"Goddamn, such a crossfire!" Armstrong exclaimed when trying to describe what ensued. "Everybody put their instruments down and started hauling ass off the bandstand and nobody sitting there but me. And I could hear Earl Hines telling one of the musicians, 'Wait for me! Wait for me!' And I'm embarrassed as anything, I said [to Miller], 'You black son of a' — oh, I called that son-of-a-bitch everything. He said, 'Who in the hell do they think they are?' I said, 'You can kiss my ass!' I was so angry."[42]

A similar incident occurred when Louis and Lil took another trip to Idlewild and Louis found out the old Creole cornetist Arnold Metoyer was in town. Armstrong had admired Metoyer since he was a teenager and hired him to substitute for him while he was gone. "When I got back, the union fined me a hundred dollars for putting him in my place!" Armstrong said. "He couldn't read!"

"That's how fast [paced] Chicago was from New Orleans," was how Armstrong summed it up to drummer Zutty Singleton, who also arrived in the Windy City in late 1926. "But we did a good job when we got ourselves in Chicago and took over anyway."[43]

The New Orleans musicians in Carroll Dickerson's Orchestra could at least play anything and read any arrangement—sometimes better than the northern-born stars of the group. Armstrong's section mate, Natty Dominique, had joined Dickerson for their earlier vaudeville tour and recalled, "Earl Hines kept telling me the New Orleans musicians wasn't good. They wasn't as good as the New York musician or the Pittsburgh, Pennsylvania musician. So I looked at him and said, 'Someday, I'll be able to find out your ability of music.' "[44]

At a rehearsal after Armstrong joined the band, Dominique noticed Hines struggling to execute a four-bar break on an arrangement of a selection from Wagner's *Tannhäuser*. Dickerson eventually performed this chart one night at the Sunset Café—with Paul Whiteman in attendance—but had to have the troublesome break arranged to be played in three-part harmony by three of the New Orleans musicians in the band, Armstrong, Dominique, and trombonist Honore Dutrey. After the performance, Whiteman complimented the musicians but did not approach Hines.

Dominique, however, did. "I'm very proud the New Orleans musicians that's here are greater musicians than you are," Dominique told him. "And if everybody in Pittsburgh is a musician like you are, I have pity for them.

Because when they taught us music in New Orleans, they taught us right."[45] Dominique, Armstrong, and the other New Orleans men in Dickerson's band were proud of the foundation they'd developed back home but had now progressed to the point where they could read the score to a Wagner opera on sight. Nonetheless, others from New Orleans, like Miller, Metoyer, and to an extent Johnny Dodds and Kid Ory, were still content to play the way they had a decade earlier, and the times were passing them by.

In addition to material like *Tannhäuser*, Armstrong remembered trombonist Dutrey's big feature was an "Irish Medley." Dutrey was still suffering from asthma and would "go in that corner with that nostril thing and say, 'Let's go,'" Armstrong said. "And he had high note duets with my horn and we used to just rock the house with the 'Irish Medley.' Boy, we'd hit that, the walls [would come down]."[46]

It was also around this time that Armstrong began using Noel Coward's "Poor Little Rich Girl" from the Broadway production *Charlot's Revue of 1926* as a feature. Pianist Art Hodes remembered Armstrong playing it for a half hour straight one evening at the Sunset Café.[47] Dominique once tried to keep up with Armstrong on this number and found it an impossible task. "He played 25 choruses of 'Poor Little Rich Girl,'" Dominique said. "I played 12 second trumpet parts under him, but I tried to play like him and I got tired cause Armstrong will kill you. He's got a powerful lip."[48]

Sadly, OKeh wasn't interested in recording Armstrong doing "Poor Little Rich Girl" or "Irish Medley" or *Tannhäuser*. But in late November 1926, Fearn did have the Hot Five record four selections—"Big Butter and Egg Man," "Sunset Café Stomp," "You Made Me Love You," and "Irish Black Bottom"—composed by Percy Venable for the latest Sunset Café revue, "Sunset Smiles." The first two sides feature roof-shaking vocals by Mae Alix, whom Louis referred to as "my favorite entertainer," setting the template for decades of future duets between Armstrong and female vocalists such as Velma Middleton and Ella Fitzgerald.[49] He exudes confidence and good humor and even shows a bit of an Al Jolson influence with his delivery of the aside "Come here, baby, and kiss me."

But it was the trumpet solo on "Butter and Egg Man" that became one for the pantheon, analyzed measure-by-measure by later musicologists such as Andre Hodier ("This entry by itself is a masterpiece; it is impossible to imagine anything more sober and balanced") and Gunther Schuller ("One could add that no composer, not even a Mozart or Schubert, composed anything more natural and simply inspired").[50] Schuller's use of the word "composed" is accurate, as this was something Armstrong most likely worked out at the Sunset Café, perfecting it before reaching the recording studio.[51]

Armstrong's "Butter and Egg Man" solo is indeed a masterpiece of construction. There are none of the "clarinet" figures that made up his landmark "Cornet Chop Suey" outing and there's no flipping a switch to invoke King Oliver, Bunk Johnson, Buddy Petit, B. A. Rolfe, or any of his other formative influences. It's melodic from start to finish but more important, it has a beginning, middle, and end, it develops motifs, it has a climax—in short, it tells a story.

Doc Cheatham was firmly under the spell of Armstrong in this era and remembered him telling musicians to "try to tell a story with your horn. Whatever you play, try to make a story out of it. Don't just go up there and blow something that . . . you don't know what you're doing, making a lot of noise. Always try to tell a little story on each thing that you play." "That has always stuck by me, right until today," Cheatham added.[52]

Armstrong heard Cheatham play with trombonist Albert Wynn's band at the Dreamland Café and was impressed, asking him to sub for him one evening with Erskine Tate. Cheatham was honored to get the call, as he had been a regular at the Vendome and was familiar with Armstrong's feature on "Poor Little Rich Girl."

Now it was Cheatham's turn to play the role of his hero:

> Then we got to Louis' solo [on] "Poor Little Rich Girl." We got to the introduction and I stood up and the spotlight hit me right here. And the people started screaming! That's the way they did with Louis. You couldn't hear one note Louis played until they stopped applauding and screaming. So they did the same thing for me—for about a second until they realized "That's not Louis." And everything just died down. Man, I felt like hell, I felt like hell! I played the number my way. It was the only way I could play. I wasn't *nothing* compared with Louis' playing in Chicago. But I played the solo.

Louis was appreciative of Cheatham's efforts and used him as a sub a few more times, which always confounded Cheatham. "There were trumpet players from New Orleans all over Chicago then," Cheatham said. "Why did he come to me?" Cheatham got his answer about 60 years later when pianist Johnny Guarnieri told him, "You know, Louis told me why he asked you. He said it was because he liked you. You were a gentleman, and all the musicians from New Orleans were very jealous of him; they envied him."[53]

It could also be that Cheatham had his own style and though he admired Armstrong, he still played "Poor Little Rich Girl" his own way. Back at the Sunset Café, Armstrong was featuring "Big Butter and Egg Man," which impressed Natty Dominique so much, he tried copying it one night. "I played that number just like him," Dominique said. During intermission, Armstrong confronted Dominique. "Listen, Greek," Armstrong said, calling him by his nickname. "Don't do that. That's a bad idea you have, playing like I play." At first, Dominique was "peeved" by Armstrong's comment but soon realized he was right, telling him, "Dip, you're the greatest and you'll always be the greatest, as long as you exist in this world. I know if anybody come here, they come in to hear you, but I'm glad that I don't copy after you anymore and I promise you, my dear friend, I'll never copy after you as long as I live!"[54] Armstrong had finally found his own, original voice and now set out to help other trumpet players find theirs.

Armstrong's singing voice, of course, was just as original as his trumpet playing and inspired just as many copycats, with varying results. "Louis Armstrong sure has the loop cornetists working hard to imitate him," one Chicago writer noted. "Some time ago we heard one trying to imitate Louis singing 'Heebie Jeebies.' All we have to say is, as a Louis Armstrong, he was a mighty flat tire."[55] "I first heard Louis' distinctive sound on records when I was a kid out of Corsicana, Texas, playing trombone with a band," Tyree Glenn later recalled. "Those jubilant trumpet notes, pure and brilliant, and that gravelly voice, just knocked out our whole outfit. We used to ride along sticking our heads out of the bus so we could catch cold and sing like Louis Armstrong. But no one ever succeeded."[56] Glenn wasn't alone; Pops Foster remembered that "[Trumpeter] June Clark stuck his head out the window to get a cold so he could talk like Louie!"[57]

"Big Butter and Egg Man" became Armstrong's biggest hit since "Heebie Jeebies" and was a smash at the Sunset, where he would perform it with Mae Alix, on whom he had a crush. "When she used to put her arms around him and look at him and sing, 'I need a big butter-and-egg man,' he would stand there and almost melt, and everybody in the band would get up and shout, 'Hold it, Louis! Hold it,'" Hines recalled.[58] Armstrong was a sensation, but Carroll Dickerson, the actual leader of the Sunset Café band, was steadily withdrawing from the spotlight. Hines remembered Dickerson's drinking became "a very bad habit," adding, "And he would never play his violin and he'd just turn around and conduct the band, and start the band off, get off the bandstand, and he's somewhere else."[59] Armstrong remembered Dickerson's love of the ladies as being the cause of his ultimate downfall. "He was looking out into the Audience who were dancing between shows, and flirting with the 'Chicks.' White Gals Of course," he wrote. "One night, Carrol Dickerson Slipped a note to one of those White Gals, and she in return, gave the note to (JOE) Glaser, and he immediately gave Carrol Dickerson a Notice (two weeks.)."

Armstrong knew that Glaser "was furious" and remembered thinking to himself, "My God, here I am up North and this Shit had to happen to me."

"So during the two week's notice, Joe Glaser, who never talked to me personally, came to me one Intermission and said—Carrol's leaving and I am going to turn the band over to you," Armstrong related.[60]

After having been a sideman for nearly his entire career, Armstrong closed the year 1926 as a bandleader for the first time since his days in New Orleans.

"The new review [*sic*] has many new features," a newspaper reported about the goings-on at the Sunset Café, adding, "even the orchestra has been changed, that is Luis [*sic*] Armstrong is now the 'owner' of Carol Dickerson's famous aggregation."[61]

In a little over a year, Armstrong had risen from sideman to leader and become a recording superstar in the process. But though the following year would feature many triumphs, he would also suffer some setbacks; his days as a sideman were not quite over.

26

"Just Keep on Blowing"

1927

Armstrong was now a bandleader as 1927 began, but there was a problem: he didn't have a great desire to actually lead a band. His first order of business was to ask Earl Hines to direct. "I put Earl as the [director] see, because he was sharp with his big cigar and he looked the part," he said.[1] However, Hines became so caught up in directing that he began spending less time at the piano and hired Willard Hamby to play while he conducted. "I used to notice Earl Hines, he wanted to be a Duke Ellington so bad," Armstrong said. "Directing and all that shit—that's where Earl made his mistake."[2] Hines would hold up the start of the revue by spending too much time on his appearance, until Joe Glaser would shout, "Put on the show, you jerk!" "Earl wouldn't hit that show until he gets straight," Armstrong said.[3]

It was a struggle for the band on some nights. In March 1927, 22-year-old Thomas "Fats" Waller came to Chicago to perform on organ at the Vendome Theater for several weeks, spending his late nights at the Sunset. "So in those days, they used to bring them orchestrations around, you know, stock arrangements, and they'd pass them out and you're supposed to cut it on sight," Armstrong said. "But this night they brought something around there, one of them funny tempos, and Fats is playing with us. So anyhow the band got lost in that second ending. So Fats couldn't stand that no longer, he looked down and said, 'Uh, what key are you all struggling in down there?' And couldn't nobody play!"[4]

Dave Peyton didn't find such struggles amusing and began taking Armstrong to task in his *Chicago Defender* column. "Louis knows how to play the cornet and he plays it well, but he should let orchestras alone," he wrote in March. "This orchestra of Louis's is way out of gear. It is noisy, corrupt, contemptible and displeasing to the ear. You have to put your ear muffs on to hear yourself talk in the place. Louis will learn in time to come that noise isn't music. He should hire a capable violin director with experience, who knows expression and orchestra conduct, and with the material he has in his line-up, the band could be whipped into efficient shape."[5]

Figure 26.1 Louis Armstrong and His Stompers publicity photo, taken at the Sunset Café in Chicago in 1927 and signed by Armstrong to drummer Zutty Singleton. Left to right: Earl Hines, Pete Briggs, Honore Dutrey, Louis Armstrong, Bill Wilson, Tubby Hall, Arthur "Rip" Bassett, Boyd Atkins, Joe Walker, Al Washington, Willard Hamby.
Credit: Courtesy of the Hot Club of New York.

Peyton regularly dispensed general criticism of certain trends and behaviors he observed in the Black music scene in Chicago. He often chose not to name names, but it's hard to believe he didn't have Armstrong in mind when he wrote a column offering advice to "Uncle Tom" musicians he felt were too willingly sharing their "jazz tricks" with white musicians. "Hold on to your ideas," Peyton wrote. "Don't show them a thing. Let's recapture our good name in the variety field of music. They have our tricks perfectly. There is the slaptongue, the brass cry, the flutter tongue, the 'wa wa' and many other tricks that our group originated and they wouldn't have had them had not our 'Uncle Toms' been so hasty in letting out the secrets by teaching them."[6]

Armstrong paid Peyton's column no mind and continued encouraging and offering advice to the white musicians who flocked to hear him. "We used to all hang around the Sunset," white drummer George Wettling said. "Louis Armstrong, Hines. . . . Tesch [clarinetist Frank Teschemacher] and Muggsy [Spanier] would sit in at the Sunset. I did too. Louis would say, 'Bring in that load of coal, George.'"[7] Spanier said one of the "thrills" of his life occurred when he had a chance to sit in and play "Big Butter and Egg Man." "Well, if you know Louis and his inimitable and indescribable belly laugh and enthusiasm, you can imagine what encouragement it was for a young fledgling, especially at the end, when I had to hit that C sharp and the rest of the fellows in the band joined Louis in the prodding," he said. "That in itself was an inspiration."[8]

"We all got a kick out of listening to each other, and we all tried to learn," Hines said of the white musicians who sat in. "We sat around waiting to see if these guys were actually going to come up with something new or different."[9] One musician who did just that was cornetist Bix Beiderbecke, then performing with Jean Goldkette's Orchestra. "He's always been my idol," Armstrong said of Beiderbecke in 1970. "We would just sit up there and blow and Bix would play so pretty and finally he started playing piano with us."[10] Hines remembered being impressed with the "unusual" chords Beiderbecke featured in his composition "In a Mist."

Clarinetist Slim Evans was present one evening when Armstrong held court with three white cornetists, Beiderbecke, Spanier, and Wingy Manone. "Hey, Pops, how do you play so many choruses the way you do?" Manone asked. "Well, I tell you," Armstrong replied. "The first chorus I plays the melody. The second chorus I plays the melody round the melody, and the third chorus I routines." Beiderbecke was "knocked out" by Armstrong's lesson.[11]

Beiderbecke often brought other members of the Goldkette band, including arranger Bill Challis. "The question has often arisen about Bix, did he copy anyone?" Challis once asked. "And I remember talking to him in Detroit one time. We were listening to some records and he said that there were only two fellas he ever copied—one was Nick LaRocca and the other one was Louis Armstrong—that he listened to and cared much about their work and probably used some of their material."[12]

Beiderbecke also introduced Armstrong to saxophonist Frank Trumbauer at the Sunset Cafe, whose name Armstrong couldn't quite master. "Glad to meet you, Mr. Trombone," he said after a few failed attempts.[13] On February 4, 1927, Trumbauer recorded a session under his own name for OKeh in New York, featuring Beiderbecke's lyrical cornet playing on the ballad "Singin' the Blues." Upon its release, the record made an immediate, lasting impression on Armstrong. "Every note he blew, he was so beautiful," he reflected in a 1970 conversation. "Like that 'Singin' the Blues,' nobody else is going to blow that like he did. I never did play that tune on account of Bix cause I didn't want to hear nobody mess with it. That's a classic and nobody else could play it like he did."[14]

At this point in the conversation, Armstrong began scatting Beiderbecke's "Singin' the Blues" chorus, still remembering every note 43 years later. "Ain't nobody else ever coped with it," he said. "They tried; I've heard a lot of cats try to play like Bix. Ain't none of them played like him yet."[15] The mutual appreciation society worked both ways and soon Armstrong would add some of Beiderbecke's "cooler" elements to his already hot palette.

The only recordings Armstrong made in early 1927 were a series of cylinders that were never heard publicly but the contents of which were notated and made available for purchase. To accomplish this, music publishers Walter and Frank Melrose set Armstrong up with white pianist Elmer Schoebel and a stack of blank phonograph cylinders. Armstrong and Schoebel recorded dozens of songs the trumpeter never recorded otherwise in this period, including "The Chant," "Grandpa's Spells," "Spanish Shawl," "King Porter Stomp," "Livery Stable Blues," and even such Oliver hits as "Someday Sweetheart" and "Snag It." "[Walter] Melrose recalled that Schoebel had quite a struggle taking the Armstrong stuff off of the old Edison cylinders," George Hoefer later wrote. "Louis made them with both eyes shut and his horn pointed at the ceiling one moment and the floor the next." Walter Melrose said, "I am sure we all had a few more grey hairs before we finally got all the material on paper, but it was worth it."[16]

The cylinders themselves were eventually lost or discarded, but not before Schoebel transcribed enough material for two books, *Louis Armstrong's 50 Hot Choruses for Cornet* and *Louis Armstrong's 125 Jazz Breaks for Hot Trumpet*.[17] White musicians such as Louis Panico had published similar books, but this was the first publication of transcriptions from a Black jazz artist. Though he was nervous about Black musicians giving away their "secrets" to their white followers, Dave Peyton approved of the move, writing, "Louis has penned in book form some of his eccentric styles of playing. This will come as good news to those who have long admired this little giant of jazz."[18]

Other than those lost cylinders, Armstrong didn't do any recording in the first part of 1927 as OKeh went through some major changes. First, their Chicago studio was overhauled to install microphones for a new electric system of recording, finally putting an end to the acoustic era. And Tommy Rockwell had left Columbia Records at the end of 1926 to oversee OKeh's entire recording operation.[19] One of Rockwell's first orders of business was to write E. A. Fearn on January 7 to solidify their arrangement with Armstrong. "You may tell Mr. Armstrong that on all future recordings, we will pay him at the rate of $150.00 per accepted selection," Rockwell wrote. "It is our understanding that Armstrong himself will not make records for any company other than our own organization, or, as a part of any other musical unit."[20]

Figure 26.2 Cover of the 1927 Melrose Brothers publication *Louis Armstrong's 50 Hot Choruses for Cornet,* featuring another magnetic new publicity photo of Armstrong. Credit: The Jack Bradley Collection, Louis Armstrong House Museum.

With that "understanding" in writing, Armstrong finally made his first official recordings of 1927 in April—for Brunswick Records.

"Well, you know, in those days, I mean, we didn't take recording that serious," Armstrong said when questioned about it in 1953. "I mean, we thought it was just like another gig." Brunswick had two dates in mind, recording Erskine Tate's drummer Jimmy Bertrand and his "Washboard Wizards" on April 21 and following up with a session by Johnny Dodds's Black Bottom Stompers the next day. Dodds approached Armstrong about appearing on both sessions, but Armstrong initially demurred. "Well, come on, man," Dodds persisted, "I'm'a play this job, you play this with me and just disguise yourself, you know, disguise your playing and your tone."

"Well, Johnny, I don't think I ought to do that," Armstrong said.

"Yeah, but I'll give you so much for it," Dodds said, obviously naming a handsome figure.

"Well, let's see, maybe I can!" Armstrong said, agreeing to do the dates.[21]

Armstrong did a decent job disguising himself on the peppy Bertrand date, but he stole Dodds's date away from him with his dark and haunting playing on "Wild Man Blues" and with a hot break on "New Orleans Stomp" made up of a quote from Verdi's *Rigoletto*, which he had listened to in New Orleans and now performed with Erskine Tate. Armstrong would later scat the same line in an interview, adding, "That's the first ending I used to make all the time."[22]

The Dodds session featured three songs—"Weary Blues," "Melancholy," and "Wild Man Blues"—published by the Melrose Brothers.[23] "Wild Man Blues" was soon added to Armstrong's repertoire at the Sunset Café, where it became a vehicle for stretching out. "And the chorus was so long, Earl could go back in the kitchen while I'm playing mine and eat meatballs and spaghetti, then I'd come back while he was playing and get a couple of pork chops and eggs!" Armstrong recalled.[24]

However, word that Armstrong made these sides with Dodds's group soon reached OKeh. Instead of getting angry, they decided to get even—they would bring Armstrong back to the studio as soon as possible, record three of the four songs Dodds did for Brunswick, and rush their releases to beat the Dodds sides to the market. With the new electric system in place, Rockwell and Fearn decided to experiment and record a "Hot Seven" instead of the standard Hot Five, adding Pete Briggs's funky tuba and Baby Dodds's slashing cymbals to the group. Lil, Johnny Dodds, and Johnny St. Cyr would also return, but Kid Ory was out of town, so the trombone role would be split between John Thomas and Honore Dutrey.

Between May 7 and May 14, the Hot Seven recorded 11 songs over the course of five sessions. The electric microphones captured Armstrong's electrifying tone better than any previous recordings. He was growing more comfortable in the upper register of his horn, too; each Hot Seven side finds him regularly climbing up to a high C—or higher—with relative ease. He leans into his New Orleans roots on "Willie the Weeper" and "Weary Blues," both of which feature euphoric final choruses booted along by Briggs's tuba and Baby Dodds's backbeat cymbal crashes. "The recording we made for the OKeh people reminded me so much of New Orleans, until I was looking direct into New Orleans when we were recording it," Armstrong said of "Weary Blues."[25]

Without the need to disguise his playing, Armstrong tore into "Wild Man Blues" with abandon, occasionally missing a note, but the daringness of it all made up for any flaws. The same can be said for "Twelfth Street Rag," a 1914 composition that was already dated by 1927, with its mechanical three-note riff drilled into the ground. Armstrong chose to slow down the tempo and tackled those three notes in the most rubato fashion imaginable, guiding his way through his chorus like a tightrope walker. This one might have been a little too "avant-garde"; OKeh rejected it and it was not released until producer George Avakian discovered it in 1940.[26]

But perhaps the greatest takeaway from the Hot Seven sides is the further development of Armstrong as a soloist. He had hit a new peak with his storytelling chorus on "Big Butter and Egg Man" the previous November and now built further on that model, most notably on his own composition "Potato Head Blues." (Once asked about the inspiration behind this title, Armstrong simply responded, "Cat got a head like a potato.")[27] This selection exudes joy from start to finish, but the main event is a stop-time trumpet solo that tells a story as compelling as any great work of literature. Armstrong is relaxed and conversational throughout, gradually building up to a climactic, earth-shaking high concert B before tumbling down with a phrase Hoagy Carmichael would use for his timeless composition "Star Dust" (which he apparently played any time he was allowed to sit in at the Sunset Café).

"Potato Head Blues" provided more fodder for musicians and musicologists in the decades to come. One of the most interesting analyses came from the late cornetist Peter Ecklund, who, Matt Glaser wrote, "says that it wasn't until he began working in salsa bands that he understood the Caribbean origin of much of Armstrong's rhythmic language. Using Armstrong's classic 1927 solo on 'Potato Head Blues,' Ecklund deconstructs the fusion of these elements. Play just the notes in straight 3/4 time, devoid of jazz feel, and it sounds like a waltz by Franz Lehar! Then play the rhythms only, on one pitch, and you hear a very hip Afro-Cuban drum solo."[28]

All of this is true, yet "Potato Head Blues" didn't seem to have as seismic an impact upon its release in 1927 as "Cornet Chop Suey," "Heebie Jeebies," or "Big Butter and Egg Man." No other bands recorded it for several decades after Armstrong and OKeh didn't even feature it in their regular newspaper advertisements after its release, only listing it for one week in October, leaving it to be rediscovered by future generations.[29]

Armstrong didn't reflect often about these sides, but when writing about "Potato Head Blues" in 1951, he did say, "Every note that I blew in this recording, I thought of Papa Joe."[30] There was a good reason for him to be thinking of Joe Oliver; the same week he recorded with the Hot Seven, Oliver left Chicago for New York, a move that foreshadowed the end of his reign as King.

Even with the troubles with his chops, Oliver was still on top of the world at the start of 1927. "Joe Oliver's Plantation orchestra still holds the position as the Kings of Jazz," Dave Peyton wrote in his December 18, 1926, column.[31] His Vocalion recording of "Someday, Sweetheart," released in November 1926, became one of the most popular records of his career, a mainstay in newspaper advertisements throughout the following year.[32] That same month, he signed a new contract with Brunswick, who promised him $275 per side, $125 more than Armstrong.[33]

Oliver began attracting attention at this time from I. Jay Faggen, who ran the Savoy Ballroom in Harlem, but Oliver wasn't interested in heading east. "The agents and everybody coming from New York had wanted to bring him in some place, *any* night club or anything like that, with his band," Armstrong said. "But Joe wouldn't leave. 'I'm doing all right here, man,' he'd tell them. You know he had a good job, he was making good tips."[34]

Oliver stayed put and continued his rivalry with Armstrong after his former pupil took over leadership duties at the Sunset. "They're shooting at one another all night long, he and Joe Oliver, see," Preston Jackson said. "It was something to see."[35] Cornetist Wild Bill Davison recalled a night at the Sunset when "in comes Joe Oliver with a brown derby on and his horn under his arms. . . . And, so, they got up on the stand together at the Sunset and they played about 125 choruses of 'Tiger Rag,' exchanging choruses. People went insane—they threw their clothes on the floor! I mean, it was the most exciting thing I ever heard in my life."[36]

Unlike the days at the Lincoln Gardens, Armstrong no longer held back when Oliver came onto his turf. "After all, we all both play trumpet," Armstrong said of himself and Oliver. "I mean, it's one of them things like Joe Louis. I mean, you're all right with Joe Louis until you get in that ring with him! Cat's all right with me until we get on that bandstand together—especially if he's got a trumpet in his hand. You know? Even if you apologize afterwards. That's the way it's got to be."[37]

In addition to the war between the musicians, there was also the war between Chicago's rival gangs, which spilled over into the scene at both the Plantation and the Sunset. A bomb was planted on the roof on the Plantation one night—some of Oliver's musicians believed the move was instigated by Joe Glaser—and though no one was hurt when it went off, it succeeded in scaring away some of Oliver's crowds. The Sunset soon began to dominate the scene. In April 1927, a letter published in the Decatur, Illinois, *Herald and Review* described "the thrill of doing both 'Sunset' and 'The Plantation' in one night," calling it an "adventure." But except for that one mention of the Plantation, the writer focused on the Sunset. "A ten piece 'nigger orchestra blows blues and beats out black-bottoms to 'who laid it,' " they wrote, adding, "At 'Sunset' there is much comedy, some pathos, often-a bit of drama, and most interesting of all, there is mystery."[38] That—plus the gangsters, police raids, and failing teeth—was too much for Oliver to compete with.

"I felt real bad when I took most of Joe Oliver's crowds away," Armstrong reflected. "Wasn't much I could do about it, though. I went to Joe and asked him was there anything I could do for him. 'Just keep on blowing,' he told me. Bless him."[39]

The bottom had fallen out for Oliver in Chicago, so he finally accepted Faggen's offer to play the Savoy Ballroom for two weeks in May 1927. Oliver was a smash, but when Faggen offered to extend the engagement, Oliver asked for too much money and the band was let go. Oliver also turned down an opportunity to perform at the Cotton Club in Harlem, paving the way for Duke Ellington to accept it and become a star almost overnight.[40] Without the prospect of any regular work, Oliver's men began leaving him one by one. Oliver disappeared from the scene for much of 1927 and 1928, managing to recruit men on the fly for the record dates he was still required to make for Brunswick, most of which ended up with rejected efforts. In the fall of 1928, dental issues forced him to put down his horn for a prolonged period of time.

Armstrong watched this play out from afar and was heartbroken, but clear-eyed about the situation. "It was his fault, too," he said unflinchingly. "Time ran out on him. He looked around, and when he came to New York—too late. From then on, he commenced to, what you call, getting a broken heart."[41] Armstrong would never stop falling back on the musical lessons Oliver taught him over the years, but Oliver's nonmusical decisions proved just as important in teaching him what *not* to do with his career.

Around this same time, Louis suffered a broken heart of his own when his beloved mother, Mayann, contacted him to tell him she was ailing. Louis's success in Chicago had little effect on his mother's quality of life back home. On December 5, 1926, Mayann was arrested for disturbing the peace, along with an older man named Jack Lambert. This time, the arrest report didn't try to hide anything; "Mary Armstrong" was listed as a "prostitute," with an added note about her "being drunk." She was back living at 1408 Perdido Street, a block away from her old "Brick Row" home, and still doing whatever it took to make ends meet.[42]

Only now her health was failing and she required her son's help. "And I had to send for her to come to me in Chicago again," Louis wrote. "This time—she was really *sick*. She suffered with the Hardening of the 'Arteries'—A Drastic thing to have."[43]

Louis had been doubling at the Vendome and the Sunset for a full year, but now, with his mother to watch over, he would have to cut his workload in half, and he quit Erskine Tate in mid-April.[44] He would never forget the impact Tate had on his career. "Of all the early leaders and the ones that I've come through, I think Joe Oliver and Erskine Tate deserve all the credit," he said in 1956.[45]

Mayann took a turn for the worse in early June and was admitted to Provident Hospital, the first Black-owned hospital in the United States. "I did everything in my power to save 'May Ann' (my mother)," Louis wrote. "I gave her the Finest Doctors-And the whole time she was in the Hospital—it Costs me over $17.00 (Seventeen) Dollars a Day—I didn't care what it Cost—As long as I could save 'Mary Ann.'"

But it was too late. In her final moments, Louis remembered that Mayann held his hand and spoke to him. "God Bless you, my son," she said. "And thank God I live to see my son grow up to be a big successful young man. Also my daughter. Thank God they are grown and can look out for themselves."

"Then she passed away," Louis wrote.[46]

The end for Mary Albert Armstrong came at 9:30 in the morning on July 6, 1927. Black Benny Williams had died on that same date in 1924—and Louis himself would pass away on July 6, 1971.

Clarence, now nearly 12, took Mayann's passing especially hard. "It broke his heart when she died," Louis said. "She was so nice to him."[47] Mama Lucy was still living in Florida and was also devastated when she eventually found out about her mother—after she died.

She had noticed that Mayann had stopped responding to her letters in New Orleans, so later that summer, she wrote to Louis and Lil, who were on one of their Idlewild vacations. Lil's mother, Decie, responded and broke the news. "Your mother seemed like she was waiting for you," Decie wrote, adding that every time she talked to Mayann toward the end, Mayann would say, "I'm all right. I'm just waiting on my daughter."[48] Mama Lucy never quite got over the guilt of not being there for her mother's final days. "My mama died, she died in Chicago," she said in her final interview. "And she was mad because I wasn't near."[49] " 'Mamma Lucy' took it terribly hard," Louis wrote.[50]

Dr. Peter Crawford filled out the death certificate, noting that Mayann had been in his care since June 6. Her official cause of death was "Heart Decompensation," but Dr. Crawford added a "Contributory (secondary)" cause: "Alcoholic Cirrhosis of Liver." Louis would spend the rest of his life telling loving stories about his mother, occasionally hinting at her excessive drinking and hard-partying ways, but he never outright discussed how her drinking ended up killing her; all references to her alcoholism—along with her various arrests and the times she worked as a prostitute—would be hidden between the lines of his carefully worded autobiographical writings.

Louis was listed as the "informant" on the death certificate, tasked with giving Dr. Crawford Mayann's occupation ("Housewife"), employer ("Herself"), and birthplace ("New Orleans," not Boutte). He did not know his mother's birthday but gave her age as 44, agreeing with the same 1883 date Mayann began using in her thirties.

Mayann's funeral was held on July 8. "And the moment that really Touched me was when the Sermon was finished and the Undertaker began to Cover up her 'Coffin'—UMP," Louis later wrote. "I let out plenty of Tears—and I just couldn't stop Crying. And 'May Ann' was laying there looking so natural—Just as though she was just taking a 'nap.' "[51] Looking back on this moment 38 years later, Louis said, "Yeah I miss old Mayann. Her funeral in Chicago is probably the only time I ever cried—when they put that cover over her face."[52] Mayann was buried in Chicago's Lincoln Cemetery, far away from home.

Louis wouldn't mourn for long—that evening, he was back on the bandstand at the Sunset Café. Asked later in life if he had canceled any performances after the death of longtime vocalist Velma Middleton, he responded, "Kiss my ass! I didn't do that when my mother and father died!"[53] Willie Armstrong would eventually pass away on August 16, 1933, while his son was on a tour of England; Louis didn't fly home for that funeral either. "The show must go on" was not just a show business cliché to Louis, it was a way of life.

When Mayann visited in 1923, she was scared that her son was struggling in King Oliver's band, possibly even sick and out of money. But in 1927, Louis was a bandleader, a featured soloist, a comedian, an innovative vocalist, a popular recording artist—a star. "Son—Carry on, you're a good boy—treats everybody right," Mayann told him shortly before she died. "And everybody—White and Colored Loves you—you have a good heart—You can't miss."[54]

Mayann was gone. King Oliver was out of town and, for the most part, would remain out of Louis's life until his passing. Even Lil and Louis were growing more distant than ever; Alpha's scrapbook is filled with ticket stubs for boxing matches and baseball games she attended with Louis in the summer of 1927. The people who shaped Louis's life and career were slipping away. They had done all they could do to get him this far. He still had a long way to go, but Mayann was right: he couldn't miss.

27

"Awful Glorious Days"

1927–1928

Louis Armstrong's Stompers remained at the Sunset Café throughout the summer of 1927, finally winning the approval of Dave Peyton. Earlier in the year, when Peyton had slammed them for being too noisy, he'd made space to compliment many of the top white bands in the country. "What is so great about the Paul Whitman, Abe Lyman, Vincent Lopez and many of the other crack popular orchestras?" he asked in May. "It is soft playing, sweet and hot. The barbarous blasting day has gone. A new era has dawned upon us. If you do not know your instrument you cannot play soft."[1] By September, Peyton reported, "Louis Armstrong and his Sunset orchestra have tamed down. They are playing softer and sweeter and are hitting the bullseye these days."[2]

That same month, Armstrong began doubling again with an orchestra at a movie house, but instead of going back to the Vendome with Erskine Tate, he went to the Metropolitan Theater to join a new band formed by pianist Clarence Jones—"the finest, popular pianist of the Race" in Peyton's words.[3] Though accompanying a silent film was a dying art—Al Jolson's *Jazz Singer* would be released in October and officially usher in the era of the talking film—Armstrong remained a popular draw on the stage; his performance of "Just Like a Butterfly (That's Caught in the Rain)" inspired applause that was "deafening for at least five minutes."[4]

But aside from pop tunes such as that one, Armstrong was still featuring early Hot Five hits like "Big Butter and Egg Man" and "Heebie Jeebies" with Jones. OKeh was hoping for similar hits, but they weren't finding them with the Hot Seven batch of recordings. The label threw its promotional weight behind the release of the instrumental "Wild Man Blues" in July, but when that didn't seem to work, they switched their strategy and began promoting the flip side, "Gully Low Blues," which featured an Armstrong vocal. In August, OKeh released two more instrumentals, "Alligator Crawl" and "Willie the Weeper," but when those didn't seem to create much buzz, they leaned on "Keyhole Blues" in September, highlighting its "scat chorus by Louis Armstrong" for the first time.

Rockwell seemed to identify the problem: yes, Louis was a star and yes, the Hot Seven created magnificent music—but the Hot Five was a "brand." It had an identity, and it had its own sound; it also had Kid Ory. Ory returned to Chicago in the summer of 1927 after King Oliver's disastrous tour in the East and began taking lessons with Jaroslav Cimera of Bohemia, which improved his technique.

Rockwell reunited the original Hot Five and booked them for two dates on September 2 and September 6. Armstrong was able to relax and use a microphone instead of shouting into a recording horn, resulting in one of his most charming vocals of the period on "Put 'Em Down Blues," even hitting some tenor notes the way he must have done in his quartet days. It's a vocal unlike anything else heard in the pop music world of 1927; popular white singers like Gene Austin, who had a hit with "My Blue Heaven," or Weston Vaughan, who sang "Charmaine" with Guy Lombardo, were quite a ways away from delivering a "sweet mama" the way Armstrong does here.

However, Rockwell rejected the other September sides, "Ory's Creole Trombone" and "The Last Time," and called a halt to the action, choosing not to record anything else until December.[5] Beginning with "Struttin' with Some Barbecue," recorded at the band's next session on December 9, Armstrong's trumpet solos would now be the undeniable centerpiece of these recordings. Though the record label credited the composition to Lil, Louis never backed down from claiming this number as his own as the years progressed, only backing down after "a big law suit," according to Lil.[6] The final product does seem to be the result of a collaboration of some sort; the melody, with its reliance on major sevenths, sounds like Louis, while Lil most likely had a hand in the verse and the cute stop-time interlude and closing routine.

Regardless of who wrote it, the recording included one of Armstrong's most dazzling trumpet demonstrations of not just the 1920s but his entire career, taking chances throughout and landing each one with aplomb. The same can be said of "Once in a While," recorded the following day and featuring another outstanding solo over stop-time rhythms. For the first time, a Hot Five record ended with a trumpet solo and not with a big New Orleans polyphonic blowout or a break.

Armstrong was feeling nostalgic when he chose to record "I'm Not Rough" on December 10, as this had been Joe Oliver's old feature in the Ory and Oliver jazz band. "So what little creations we did in the recording studio of 'I'm Not Rough'—just remember I was looking right into the Chops of my idol—the great King Joe Oliver," he wrote.[7] But aside from Armstrong, the musician who makes the biggest impact on this recording is one who was not a regular member of the group: guitarist Lonnie Johnson.

Born in New Orleans in 1899, Johnson had already crossed paths a few times with Armstrong, who recalled hearing him as far back as 1915. In 1925, Johnson won a contract with OKeh, where he became a favorite of both Richard M. Jones and E. A. Fearn, who used him in a variety of settings as leader and sideman, much as they did Armstrong. According to Louis, when the band rehearsed Lil's new composition "Hotter Than That," "The minute Mr. Fern [*sic*], who was headman of OKeh, heard it, he got Lonnie Johnson to sit in with us and play his guitar on this date."[8]

"Hotter Than That" kicked off the Hot Five's December 13 session. It is a culmination of sorts, a thrilling exploration of the past, present, and future of Armstrong's artistry. As a string of solos on a common set of chord changes found on "Bill Bailey" and "Tiger Rag," it illustrates the direction where jazz was heading. Armstrong is in command from the start, displaying some of the flashier playing, especially in his first break, that made him a star in Chicago. Dodds follows with an agitated outing that is undeniably hot, if not exactly flowing as seamlessly as Armstrong's effort.

Johnson, however, was able to get on Armstrong's wavelength and provides perfect accompaniment for his most daring scat outing to date. Armstrong's voice takes extraordinary chances with rhythm, at one point almost seemingly scatting in his own tempo, but he never wavers for a second. He then engages in a thrilling trade with Johnson, the two giants pushing and inspiring each other as the tempo disappears. Lil brings it back with a short, heavy-handed outing, followed by Ory playing an almost stereotypical tailgate trombone line, with both musicians sounding a little out of place after what just occurred.

If Lil and Ory represent the past, Armstrong is there to preview the future, entering on a dizzying, ascending break before driving the final ensemble with a two-note riff that would soon launch a million big band arrangements. The other musicians of the old Hot Five sat out the ending, leaving Armstrong to again trade with Johnson, this time with his trumpet, leading to a free-form conclusion with Johnson arpeggiating an unresolved diminished chord.

It's not known for sure if Fearn realized it right then and there or if Rockwell made up his mind when he eventually heard it in New York, but they each came to the same conclusion upon hearing "Hotter Than That": the old Hot Five had gone as far as it could go and Armstrong needed musicians such as Johnson to push him to newer, greater heights.

Even the musicians who made up the Hot Five's most ardent fans came to the same realization. "My brother [drummer] Vic [Berton] and I naturally bought them all as they were released," Ralph Berton said of the Hot Five records, adding, "We listened only to Louie (and, later, Earl). When the needle got to Johnny Dodds, Kid Ory, Johnny St. Cyr, or Lil, we simply lifted it and put it back or ahead to Louie again. In this fashion we wore out several copies of such discs as 'Potato Head'—I mean we wore out the Armstrong portions; the rest of the grooves remained more or less in mint condition."[9]

This monumental era of Armstrong's recording career came to its conclusion on December 13, 1927, with "Savoy Blues," written by Ory to commemorate the opening of the massive new Savoy Ballroom at 4733 South Parkway on November 23, 1927. After the nearly visceral intensity of "Hotter Than That," "Savoy Blues" could have been called "Sweeter Than That," as it showcases the more sensitive style then in vogue in the world of popular music. As musicologist Brian Harker has pointed out, this solo showcases the influence on Armstrong of Bix Beiderbecke's "Singin' the Blues" and other "sweet" bands of the period, as approved by Dave Peyton, yet Armstrong still manages to uncork a thrilling high-note rip and brief double-timed passage in his second chorus.

Figure 27.1 1926 publicity photo of the original Hot Five. From left to right: Johnny Dodds, Louis Armstrong, Johnny St. Cyr, Kid Ory, Lillian Hardin Armstrong.
Credit: Courtesy of the Louis Armstrong House Museum. Photo restoration by Nick Dellow.

Ory follows such beauty by blatting the blues for 12 rough-and-tumble bars before leading the ensemble in a call-and-response chorus, with Ory working over a gliss while Armstrong and Dodds answer with a riff played in unison. After a short, harmonized break, the band finally takes matters down to New Orleans for one last time, a valedictory chorus of blues with Armstrong rising to the top, taking the final break, and putting a punctuation mark on the Hot Five chapter of his career.

Though the recordings would be analyzed for generations to come, the Hot Five and Hot Seven sides represented a blip in Armstrong's life; 17 sessions made in just over two years, constituting maybe 70 total hours in the studio over the course of 25 months. It was fun making records with his wife and some old friends from his hometown, but the music they made didn't resemble what he was playing night after night at the Sunset Café and the Vendome Theater. He now felt more confident performing with the likes of Earl Hines and Zutty Singleton—and the day after the last original Hot Five session, he made his debut at Warwick Hall with those two by his side.

"The Sunset opened on Saturday night, and Louis Armstrong and his 'gang' are back," the *Pittsburgh Courier* reported on October 29—the last time the Sunset Café would be mentioned in the Black press for many months. Louis never gave any details about what happened and neither did Earl Hines, but Hines did at least state that the venue had closed and the band had not been fired or replaced. It's quite possible this was due to the exploits of manager Joe Glaser, who was arrested in February 1927 and indicted in June for raping a 14-year-old girl. With a trial coming up in February 1928, it's conceivable that Glaser decided to close his establishment indefinitely. He would beat the rap through some very duplicitous means but would not cross paths again with Armstrong until 1935.

"When the Sunset closed in 1927, Louis, Zutty and I had formed a little corporation, and we agreed to stick together and not play for anyone unless the three of us were hired," Hines recalled.[10] The "corporation" would need a manager, a role to be filled by Lil. Though their marriage might have been on shaky ground, Lil still believed in her husband's talent and star power.[11] Louis quit Clarence Jones's band and signed a one-year lease to take over Warwick Hall at 543 East 47th Street, renaming it the Usonia Dancing School and offering music for dancing on Wednesday nights, Saturday nights, and Sunday afternoons.

Yet while this was happening, all of Chicago was buzzing about the Thanksgiving Day opening of the Savoy Ballroom—located just three blocks away from Warwick Hall. Lil paid it no mind. "She got a hall rented, Warwick Hall," Singleton said of Lil. "The Savoy had just opened, with two bands, and we were going to buck the Savoy."[12] But Lil underestimated the impact the Savoy would have on Chicago. "The place can rightfully be called America's smartest ballroom," George. W. Tyler wrote in the Baltimore *Afro-American* after its opening. "Almost as many whites as colored attended the premier and the place did capacity business despite a heavy downpour of rain. Two bands offer continuous music, besides which prominent stage and cabaret stars are always on hand to supply the entertainment."[13]

The Armstrongs continued pressing ahead with their plan, forming a "Hot Six" group with Louis, Hines, and Singleton joined by Charles Lawson on trombone, George Jones on saxophone, and William Hall on guitar. It seemed like a can't-miss opportunity on paper: Armstrong, the popular OKeh recording artist, leading a small group, playing for dancing each week at a venue he personally was leasing. "He has made thousands of friends among the Chicago dance lovers and no doubt will do a thriving business in his venture," the *Chicago Defender* predicted.[14]

The prediction was wrong. "Yes, that was a floperoo, boy," Zutty recalled years later. "Talk about a floperoo." Zutty's wife, Marge Singleton, agreed: "I went up there one night with Lil and I think there were six people in the place. Oh, it was sad."[15] "We were so popular around Chicago at the time, we thought we could make it," Louis said. "But it didn't mean a thing after the Savoy opened."[16] On the final day of 1927, Dave Peyton attempted to help Armstrong out, writing, "Louis Armstrong and his dancing school will grow in attendance. Chicago is wild about Louie and his playing and when the affair is properly advertised Warwick [H]all will be packed at each session."[17]

But it was too late. "Man, we didn't do nothing!" Zutty Singleton said. "Louis lost $1900 in this hall. They sued him on the lease, and he was a long time paying."[18] Unwilling to quit, the group put their faith in Lil to help them secure more gigs. The best she could do was a series of dances on the West Side of Chicago in some dangerous, unnamed venues. Singleton recalled a time when a man and woman got into an argument in front of the band: "And he slapped her and come up with a pistol, see, and asked Louis, say, 'What's the matter, you don't like it?' And Louis said, 'Man, that's alright with me.'"[19]

For his part, Louis recalled another West Side dance that resulted in chaos:

> So we (Earl—Zootie and myself) were sitting there on the bandstand just talking over different subjects and, etc.—when in walks an old Drunken Darkie with his shirt tail all stickin out and he was as Raggity as a bowl of Slaw...Of course we didn't pay him any attention (much attention) when he entered the hall...But when that Black "Sommitch" reached down into his Pants, [and] pulled out a great big 45 calibre [*sic*] Pistol....Ump Ump Ump.....Folks you never saw a bunch of Niggers run so

> Fast in all your life as we did that night getting out of that dance hall.....Goodness Gracious....And when the Nigger pointed that big ass pistol towards the bandstand towards—Mee—Earl—and Zootie—Lawd Ta'day—It was Onn—I'm Tellin'ya—It was Onn......Honest to God—Earl Hines tried his damdest to go through that Upright Piano he was playing...haw haw haw...[20]

For all of their troubles, Armstrong, Hines, and Singleton truly bonded during this bleak time in their careers. "We were full of jokes and were always kidding each other," Hines said. "But there wasn't *that* much work and we like to starve to death, making a dollar or a dollar and a half apiece a night."[21] Armstrong referred to this period as "awful glorious days," explaining, "Why I call them glorious days also—is because although they were tough as hell—we did managed to get together almost everyday and rehearse and play to suit our damn selves and not some Jerk Arranger, or some little Ol pimple'ly face Youngster (Hep'Cat) trying to tell us how we should play our instruments. Nay Nay...we would'nt stand for in those days...Maybe thats why we nearly starved to death...haw haw haw....Huh?....Well I wouldn't care a dam we were very happy while we were at it...."[22]

Armstrong might have looked back at the failure of Warwick Hall with rose-colored glasses, but it was a tremendous blow to his confidence to suddenly find himself out of work after nearly three straight years of doubling every night. Over at the *Chicago Defender*, Dave Peyton forgot about him and began focusing on trumpeter Reuben Reeves. Born in 1905 in Evansville, Indiana, Reeves came to Chicago in 1925 and took lessons from Albert Cook, a German trumpet player who played in the Chicago Symphony Orchestra. Reeves eventually replaced Armstrong with Erskine Tate at the Vendome Theater in 1927 and was getting ready to take a featured spot in Fess Williams's Orchestra at Chicago's latest million-dollar theater, the Regal, which would open in February 1928. "Reuben Reeves, the cornetist, has taken Chicago by storm," Peyton wrote, using expressions similar to those he'd used to describe Armstrong. "He is in a class by himself. Not only a jazz artist is he, but a finished trumpeter. . . . He jazzes artistically and his work is void of blasty, sloppy tones that are sickening to listen to. Chicago has gone wild over Reuben Reeves, the hottest trumpeter yet to hit the Windy City."[23]

Armstrong was beginning to grow disgusted with Chicago. "Louis wasn't working," Zutty Singleton said. "He was thinking of having a band and making a southern tour. His records were selling good, and he figured this was the time for a tour."[24] The trio of Armstrong, Hines, and Singleton might have made a pact to stick together, but they also needed to survive. Jimmie Noone needed a pianist at the Apex Club and Hines took the job.

Not long after, Singleton received a call from Carroll Dickerson. Since leaving the Sunset Café at the end of 1926, Dickerson had straightened himself out and worked his way back toward the top of Chicago's bandleading world. "Man, if you can get Louis, I'll get the job at the Savoy," Dickerson told Singleton. "Stop him from making that trip!"

"I talked to Louis," Singleton added. "He said all right, he would [rejoin Dickerson] for awhile."[25]

Before Dickerson could get the opportunity to play the Savoy, he had to prove himself at the 1,600-seat Metropolitan Theater, by replacing violinist Jimmy Bell as director of Clarence Jones and His Hot Papas on February 6. The Metropolitan was far from the center of attention in Chicago at the time; the Regal Theater opened that same week across the street with Dave Peyton's Orchestra featuring Reuben Reeves, while the Savoy was still offering continuous music by the bands of Clarence Black and Charles Elgar. Dickerson would need Armstrong and Singleton's help to make a splash and he got it in an entirely nonmusical way.

"The next specialty which also closed the stage part of this show, was offered by Louis Armstrong and Zutty Singleton, two more men from the band, who offered a comedy routine with Singleton impersonating the 'wife' provoking huge laughter from the audience through their horse-play down the aisle as Armstrong went into his vocal on 'I Ain't Never Gonna' Play Second Fiddle," a reviewer from *Exhibitors Herald and Moving Picture World* stated. "These boys were almost as good as a professional team and were well-paid for their efforts by applause."[26]

Armstrong fondly remembered this routine and added more details when recollecting it in 1947: "Sometimes Zutty and I would do a specialty number together. It was a scream. Zutty, he's funny anyway, would dress up as one of those real loud and rough gals, with a short skirt, and a pillow in back of him. I was dressed in old rags, the beak of my cap turned around like a tough guy, and he, or she (Zutty) was my gal. As he would come down the aisle, interrupting my song, the people would just scream with laughter."[27]

The reviewer was especially impressed with Dickerson, concluding, "There is no doubt that at the present time, he is the sole attraction at this theatre that is responsible for keeping a certain portion of his audience from going across the street."[28] Dickerson remained at the Metropolitan into March, with Armstrong now being featured on Walter Donaldson's "Changes," a recent hit for Paul Whiteman featuring Bix Beiderbecke and the vocals of 24-year-old Harry Lillis "Bing" Crosby from Spokane.[29]

The combination of Carroll Dickerson's directing and Armstrong's trumpet playing, singing, and comedy finally got the attention of the management of the Savoy, who offered Dickerson an opportunity to perform at the new venue in April. Trombonist Preston Jackson was there and said, "Dickerson's band came in on a matinee and blew [Charles] Elgar's band right out of the place and got the residency. All the travelling bands played there, but Dickerson's band just blew them all out."[30]

It had been about six months since the Sunset Café closed and Armstrong's struggles began, but now he was in place as a sideman at the Savoy, Carroll Dickerson was once again leading, old friend Zutty was on drums, and the band was filled with top Chicago—not New Orleans—musicians. The only person missing was Earl Hines; according to Singleton, Hines was the first to break up the "corporation" by taking the aforementioned job with Jimmie Noone at the Apex, but Hines himself maintained, "I made a short trip to New York, and while I was away Louis and Zutty joined Carroll Dickerson's band when the Savoy Ballroom opened in Chicago. . . . When I got back I was very disappointed that our little pact was broken and they had gone off and left me."[31] The pact might have been broken, but the musical partnership between Armstrong, Singleton, and Hines was far from finished.

Dickerson and Armstrong opened at the Savoy on April 12 and, in the words of Dave Peyton, "Oh, boy, what a riot the bunch was with Louis Armstrong on the jazz cornet and a real live bunch of jazz exponents who put plenty of pep in the magnificent ballroom. Carroll knows his stuff and if given the chance will show the boys around the windy burg just what an orchestra can do in a ballroom."[32]

On April 21, the Savoy welcomed popular German-born bandleader Paul Ash, "The Rajah of Jazz," a contemporary of Paul Whiteman who was perhaps best known for the showmanship he employed as he conducted his group. The appearance of Ash broke the attendance record at the Savoy, with 1,500 people in the house, earning the venue $10,000 in one night. "Our group loves Paul Ash," Peyton said. "He has always been our great friend, and has done more than any other Nordic to advance our show folks."[33] The *Afro-American* reported that the climax to the evening was when Dickerson, Black, and Ash's orchestras battled on "Tiger Rag"—but according to Armstrong, the battle was pretty one-sided.[34]

"We used to cut every band that come in there," he said. "I remember one night Paul Ash came in there and he was famous in Chicago at that time. Spades was all in the rafters and everything. He was a popular man. But boy, when that Carroll Dickerson sit in and start swinging, you know, just playing good music now—that's it."[35]

One week later, the guest orchestra at the Savoy was Erskine Tate's outfit. After the three orchestras each played a set, Savoy owner I. Jay Faggen passed

Figure 27.2 Earl "Fatha" Hines publicity photos, inscribed by Hines: "To a real drummer who has been up against the best, Zutty Singleton."
Credit: Courtesy of the Hot Club of New York.

a note around to each leader asking if they could join forces to play Kid Ory's "Savoy Blues"; the Hot Five recording had been issued at the end of February. "This was wonderful," Peyton wrote of this finale. "The three bands, consisting of 37 players, rocked the beautiful ballroom with their scintillating music. It was Louis Armstrong, a member of Carroll Dickerson's orchestra, whom this writer has termed the 'Jazz Master,' who saved the hour. . . . The crowd gathered around him and wildly cheered for more and more."[36]

Armstrong had come a long way from playing in front of a handful of people at the Usonia just a few months earlier. Pianist Art Hodes and trumpeter Wingy Manone became regulars at the Savoy during this time. "I remember the first time Wingy took me to see Louis Armstrong at the Savoy Ballroom at 47th and South Parkway," Hodes reflected. "I can close my eyes now and still see the crowd of admirers carrying Louis Armstrong on their shoulders like a hero from the front door all the way to the bandstand. I would say there were at least two thousand people in the ballroom that night who loved Louie. I never seen as much admiration for any musician as there was for Louie during that period. That was a scene I'll never forget."[37]

Having conquered the Savoy, it was time for Armstrong to record for OKeh once again—and make history.

28

"A Record of Importance"

1928

Armstrong had not set foot in a recording studio in over six months when OKeh booked him for a series of sessions in late June and early July 1928. These recordings would once again be credited to "Louis Armstrong and His Hot Five," but Lil and the original pioneers were not invited back. Instead, Armstrong pulled together a band made up of members of the Dickerson orchestra, including Fred Robinson on trombone, Jimmy Strong on clarinet and saxophone, Mancy Carr on banjo, and Zutty Singleton on a set of "bock-a-da-bock" hand cymbals. But the biggest change occurred in the piano chair, where Lil was out, and Earl Hines was in. "The ax hit Lil and Earl took her place . . . because Earl was the talk of the town at the time," Louis later explained.[1] The ever-resourceful Lil seemed to anticipate this move and had gone back to school, earning a teacher's certificate from the Chicago School of Music in May, just a few weeks before her husband's return to the recording studio.[2] She would no longer record or perform with Louis, but was now free to focus on writing original compositions and arrangements, some of which he would record that year.

The first recording made by the "new" Hot Five was Spencer Williams's "Fireworks," which ironically featured a blowing strain over the same chord changes as "Hotter Than That" from the final session of the "old" Hot Five. The differences in approach are noticeable. Both performances are up-tempo, but the December recording rocked with that earthy New Orleans beat; on "Fireworks," the energy is frenetic from the start. Furthermore, Armstrong, Ory, and Dodds could read each other's minds in the ensembles after so many years of playing the earlier style together; Robinson and Strong were being thrown into a polyphonic situation they might not have been entirely comfortable with. Nevertheless, the Chicago feel definitely inspired Armstrong to take an even wilder solo than the one on "Hotter Than That," along with a new type of ending, slowing down the tempo to close with an operatic high A♭—the first of many such endings to come.

The highlight of "Skip the Gutter," another Spencer Williams composition, is a solid minute of Hines and Armstrong sparring. Instead of simply

Figure 28.1 Publicity photo for the "second" Hot Five, taken at Woodard's Studio in Chicago in 1928. Left to right: Zutty Singleton, Mancy Carr, Jimmy Strong, Fred Robinson, Louis Armstrong, Gene Anderson. According to Singleton's inscription on the back of the print, "Don Redman didn't show up and Earl Hines was busy," necessitating the presence of Carroll Dickerson's regular pianist, Anderson.
Credit: Courtesy of the Hot Club of New York.

exchanging musical ideas, they push each other to take risks. Hines is in the driver's seat, changing the tempo and doing his best to upset Armstrong's equilibrium, but Armstrong's responses are sure-footed and in command. It's a thrilling joust that sounds as fresh today as it did nearly a century ago.

Armstrong gave Hines a present by recording his composition "A Monday Date" next, singing it in his best crooning style of this period. The performance opens with a comedy sketch, with Armstrong interrupting Hines's piano solo to tune up the band. When Hines says it sounds "pretty good," Armstrong responds, "I bet if you had a half pint of Miss Searcy's gin you wouldn't say that sounds 'pretty good.'" Miss Searcy was Ida Searcy, who owned an apartment at 4838 South Calumet, a short walk from the Savoy Ballroom at 4733 South Parkway. "We used to all spend our intermissions over at Miss Searcy's and she made that bathtub gin," Armstrong said. Unfortunately, the recording of "A Monday Date" heralded the end of an era. "Miss Searcy, when the record come out, she wouldn't let us come in her house no more," Armstrong said. "She was scared she was going to get raided!"[3]

The Hot Five returned to the studio the next day and attempted one of Lil's new compositions, "Don't Jive Me," which OKeh ultimately rejected. It was an inauspicious start to a date that would have massive repercussions after the release of the band's second tune: "West End Blues."

King Oliver had mostly been underground since his luck had turned bad in New York City, though he hadn't forgotten Armstrong. He wrote Armstrong a letter at one point inviting him to join him out east. "You can always put dem feet in my bed!" Oliver offered.[4]

Then on June 11, 1928, Oliver found success with a recording of his new composition "West End Blues," playing well on this plaintive blues, nostalgically named after a lakefront section of New Orleans, even though Oliver hadn't been home in a decade. He soon sent a lead sheet for the tune to his disciple. "Joe Oliver wrote this tune and we didn't have nothing but one page of the blues he had on there," Armstrong said.[5] Armstrong and his men sketched out a routine for the recording, but needed a way to start it. "So, this introduction, we had to make one and that's what it was, that introduction I put onto 'West End Blues,'" Armstrong stated matter-of-factly in 1956.

The "introduction" turned out to be an unaccompanied trumpet cadenza that would soon take its place as one of the most iconic moments of twentieth-century music. In about 13 seconds, Armstrong drew on nearly everything that had inspired him up to this point in his career: the blues he immersed himself in in New Orleans, the tone of Bunk Johnson, the chromaticism of Buddy Petit, the classical patterns shown to him by Lil Hardin, the high notes of Kid Rena and B. A. Rolfe, the operatic stylings of Enrico Caruso, the drama of everyday life itself, the strength garnered from working on the coal cart, the hunger forged from not knowing where his next meal was coming from, all coming together to service a composition by Joe Oliver.

Those present in Armstrong's life had different theories as to when and where he came up with the "West End Blues" cadenza. The seeds could be heard in earlier Armstrong outings such as the double-timed break on "Changeable Daddy of Mine" in 1924 or his solo on "Once in a While" the previous December, but this was something different. Despite later claims from cornetist Muggsy Spanier, it did not come from Oliver. "Joe Oliver never played the 'West End' cadenza," Lil stated. "That came from some of the classical stuff that [I] taught Louis."[6] Zutty Singleton said, "That was Louis's idea of it. We rehearsed it in his front room, just once."[7] Upon hearing it during rehearsal, Earl Hines was skeptical. "I told Louie that I didn't want him to make that introduction because he was the type of fella that sometimes he'd feel like playing and sometimes he wouldn't and when he didn't feel like playing, he'd say, 'Earl, make the introduction,'" Hines said. "I told him I wasn't going to make nothing like that. So I said, 'Now, if you're going to make this introduction, be sure you'll be able to do it when you make a public appearance.'"[8]

Aside from the cadenza—which he apparently had to play multiple times because Singleton ruined several takes—Armstrong continued to play lead for the solemn first chorus, sticking to Oliver's melody and climaxing it with an arpeggio up to a high concert B♭. He then handed it over to Robinson for a mournful trombone solo atop some rumbling Hines tremolos, followed by another soon-to-be immortal moment: a chorus of Strong's low-register clarinet in conversation with Armstrong's delicate scat singing. Hines kept the momentum going with what Armstrong felt was his "best solo" on record.[9] As with Armstrong's opening cadenza, it serves as a perfect summation of Hines's style in 12 bars: there's his consistently shifting left hand, punctuating steady stride with jarring off-the-beat accents, while his right hand unleashed both "trumpet style" octaves and mesmerizing single-note lines; both hands even come together for an ascending chordal run that never fails to surprise.

Fully rested, Armstrong came back for the final chorus with "full force," as Hines put it, hitting and holding a high B♭ for four long bars, his vibrato throbbing with intensity as Hines, Robinson and Strong surge beneath him. He repeats a series of slashing, descending four-note arpeggios, his phrasing growing more operatic as he finishes the chorus, but according to Hines, they hadn't worked out an ending. "We got to the end of it and Louis looked at me and I thought of the first thing I could think of, a little bit of classic thing that I did a long time ago and I did it five times," Hines said, "and after I finished that I held the chord and Louis gave the downbeat with his head and everybody hit the chord on the end."[10] Singleton got the last word in, ending the record with a "clop" of his hand cymbals, closing the lid of a time capsule containing one of the century's most lasting performances.

The members of the new Hot Five had time to knock off one more tune—the far less reverent "Sugar Foot Strut," with lyrics alluding to yams and cinnamon rolls—and then went back to their regular evening engagements, quickly forgetting about the sides they just made. "Well, I remember Louie and I, when we made this ['West End Blues'], we had no idea it was gonna have the effect that it did have," Hines recalled.[11] That effect was still a couple of months away, but its reverberations would be felt for the rest of their lives and beyond.

OKeh's Chicago studio was the place to be on July 5, 1928. The new Hot Five reassembled to record Lil's new composition, "Knee Drops," but more important, the full Carroll Dickerson Orchestra also cut two sides with Hines guesting in the piano chair. The results, "Symphonic Raps" and "Savoyager's Stomp," were spectacular, emanating from a different world from the Hot Five. This was big band music, with hip whole-tone harmonies on the former, Singleton playing the soon-to-be-standard "ride cymbal" pattern behind Hines on the latter, and Armstrong in peak virtuosic Savoy Ballroom form on both selections. However, Rockwell seemed to only want the Hot Five sound for the time being, rejecting the titles in the United States and only releasing them in Argentina.

That same day in the same studio, OKeh also recorded two sides by Frankie Traumbauer and His Orchestra featuring Bix Beiderbecke, then in town with Paul Whiteman's Orchestra. Whiteman was in the middle of a week's engagement at the Chicago Theater and Armstrong wasn't about to miss it. He had never seen Beiderbecke in "such a large hellfire band as Mr. Whiteman's" and was especially impressed with his playing on "From Monday On." "My, my what an arrangement that was," Armstrong wrote. "They swung it all the way... and all of a sudden Bix stood up and took a solo . . . and I'm tellin' you, those pretty notes went all through me." Armstrong also admired how Beiderbecke's "pure tone" cut through the "shooting cannons, ringing bells, [and] sirens" Whiteman set off during the closing performance of the 1812 Overture.[12]

Later that evening, Beiderbecke joined Armstrong at the Savoy after the venue was closed to the public. "Then we would lock the doors," Armstrong recalled. "Now you talking about jam sessions. . . . huh . . . . those were the things . . . with everyone feeling each other's note or chord, etc. . . . and blend with each other instead of trying to cut each other . . . nay, nay, we did not even think of such a mess . . . we tried to see how good we could make music sound which was an inspiration within itself."[13] Beiderbecke would eventually call it quits to get enough rest before the morning show at the Chicago Theater. Armstrong wrote, "He and I had a big laugh concerning the same subject . . . we both agreed that if you *don't* get a certain amount of sleep while playing one of the theaters and when you *do* hit that stage, those footlights look like they are going to *come up* and slap you right square in the face . . . . ha ha . . . oh, he and I had many laughs together . . . my man."[14]

Though alcohol would cut Beiderbecke's life short in 1931, it's quite possible he and Armstrong shared their laughs over another mind-altering substance: marijuana. "It was actually in Chicago when I first picked my first stick of gage," Armstrong wrote, using a slang term for the drug. "And I'm telling you, I had myself a Ball." He remembered he was introduced to the still legal drug by "the white young musicians coming every night to this swell night club where I was playing and although they had just finished their jobs, they still looked fresh-neat and very much contented."[15] Armstrong's friend

Charles Carpenter, then still in high school, recalled, "It was at the Savoy Ballroom that Louis was introduced to pot." According to Carpenter, "a white arranger" told Louis, "I got a new cigarette, man," and told Louis how it had helped cure a recent bout with pneumonia.

"So this guy lit it up, took a drag or two, and passed it around, and nobody would take it," Carpenter said.

"Let me try it," Louis finally said.

"So he tried it," Carpenter said. "It was pure marijuana, direct from Mexico, and it had an attractive odor, a little like the smell of those cigarettes people with asthma smoke."[16]

It was the beginning of a lifelong love affair with the herb. "I smoked it a long time," Armstrong wrote in 1959. "And I found out something. First place it's a thousend [*sic*] times better than whiskey ...It's an Assistant- a friend, a nice cheap drunk if you want to call it that."[17]

Armstrong continued befriending white musicians as 1928 progressed, most likely to the consternation of Dave Peyton. Peyton had dropped his championing of Reuben Reeves and settled firmly in Armstrong's corner, referring to him as "King Menelik," a reference to Menelik II, the longtime king of Shewa and later emperor of Ethiopia. "One of my most valued friends is King Menelik, who is none other than the great Louis Armstrong, the jazz cornet wizard, who has slaughtered all of the ofay jazz demons appearing at the Savoy recently," Peyton wrote the week after Beiderbecke's visit.[18] Peyton's reference to the "ofay jazz demons" had been expanded on in an earlier column. "What we are up against is the fact that our music, our rhythm, our humor, has been pirated by the other races, and they are doing our stuff which was ours exclusively once," Peyton wrote in February, adding, "We should feel ashamed of ourselves and should take the present situation as a warning."[19]

As at the Sunset, Armstrong paid such warnings no mind at the Savoy. "I hung out with Louis every day for years on the South Side," Art Hodes said, "and he opened all the doors for me. When he found out how I felt about the blues, he started showing me where to go to hear the real blues. He taught me a lot—like his incredible joy in playing."[20] "George Wettling and Muggsy Spanier were pals and Louis and I were pals and after the dance we would all go to my house and drink milk and eat some of Marge's lemon pie," Zutty Singleton said."[21]

Armstrong began hanging out—and getting high—with clarinetist Milton "Mezz" Mezzrow, who soon became his marijuana contact. The two often discussed the concept of integrated bands, which Mezzrow admitted "was just a pipedream in those days." "Louis and I used to talk about it all the time—it was our idea of the millennium," he continued. "But Pops, with his great practical wisdom, figured that for a first step, it shouldn't be a colored band taking in a white man, but the other way around, because the privileged should make the first overtures of friendship towards the oppressed."[22]

Armstrong wasn't wrong. He made a few strides toward the "millennium" when he performed a feature with the popular white dance bandleader Benny Meroff at the Savoy in May. "In one number they asked our own Louis Armstrong to play with them," Dave Peyton wrote of Meroff's group. "When they had finished one needed to muffle the ears, so thunderous was the applause."[23]

But it was another white dance band that especially inspired Armstrong at this time: Guy Lombardo and His Royal Canadians. Saxophone sections had been in vogue since the days of Art Hickman, but Lombardo's reeds, with their syrupy intonation and adherence to the melody, had an instantly identifiable sound that soon caught on with the public—including the members of Carroll Dickerson's Orchestra at the Savoy Ballroom.

For Armstrong, it was love at first listen. "Everything they play is perfect," he said. "They can play anything. I sung in choirs, the essence of a whole lot of things I did remind me of Guy Lombardo."[24] There seems to have also been a connection between Lombardo and the early Black dance bands of New Orleans, many of which didn't record. When asked to name his favorite band in the late 1930s, cornetist Manuel Perez, a favorite of the young Armstrong, exclaimed, "Guy Lombardo! I always wanted my bands to sound like that!"[25]

Lombardo's radio broadcasts on WBBM became appointment listening for Armstrong and his bandmates throughout 1928. "As long as he played we'd sit right there, Zutty, Carroll Dickerson and all the band, we don't go nowhere until Guy Lombardo signed off," Armstrong said. "That went on for months."[26] In a later remembrance, Armstrong added further details:

> Guy Lombardo inspired us so much with their sense of timing—their beautiful tone (the most essential thing in music), their beautiful way of phrasing—we stepped right into their footsteps with our big band at the Savoy. . . . We phrased so much like 'em until the patrons of the Savoy . . . they all went for "the sweetest music [this side of heaven]." Meantime, Carroll Dickerson's band (featuring Louis Satchmo Armstrong) played THE HOTTEST MUSIC THIS SIDE OF HELL.... HA, HA, HA... Cute?[27]

The appreciation was not just a one-way street; trumpeter Lebart Lombardo, Guy's brother, caught Armstrong at the Savoy and reported back, "I always thought [Louis] Panico was the greatest. But Armstrong is so good it scares me." On their next Monday night off, Guy and his saxophone-playing brother,

Carmen Lombardo, joined Lebert at the Savoy where they were "thrilled" to meet Armstrong.

Armstrong and Singleton returned the favor in early October, going to see the Royal Canadians at the Granada Cafe. During their intermission, the Granada's owner, Al Quodbach, visited the Lombardo brothers in their dressing room and matter-of-factly announced, "There's two coons outside, call themselves Satch and Zutty, say they want to see you. I told them we don't allow Negroes in here."

Lebert "flew into a frenzy," shouting at Quodbach, "You let the worst scum in the world into your club and try to kick out the best musicians in Chicago. They welcomed us at their place and you're trying to tell them the Lombardos can't welcome them here. I don't know about my brothers, but if you don't go out there and apologize to those men, I'm walking out of here for good."

Quodbach did as told. Armstrong and Singleton paid it no mind. "They treated us so swell I'd be here all night explaining how thrilled Zutty and I were. . . . They introduced us, we sat in, sang and just felt at home."[28]

At the Savoy, as Dickerson's band began mimicking the sound of the Royal Canadians, the results were sometimes mixed. Lombardo regularly featured his brother Carmen's composition "Sweethearts on Parade" on the air, eventually recording it in November 1928. Dickerson became enchanted with this song and purchased a "a big arrangement" with an ending that was part of the big "fad" of the day: the drummer would play an ascending run on a vibraphone, ending on the tonic. "That was beautiful!" Armstrong recalled. "And all them big bands downtown was doing it so we said shit, we gonna do that, too."

Singleton had no experience playing such an instrument, so Dickerson's pianist, Gene Anderson, helped him by putting little pieces of paper on each note he was supposed to hit. "We was ready for these ofay boys who used to come out and hear us, you know," Armstrong said of the white musicians. "Imitating the hell out of us, you know, just blasting." Dickerson was excited to show the white musicians that they could play sweet, too, instead of "just blasting." Before the performance, Armstrong told Singleton, "Man, all them white boys is looking at you, now hit 'em good and solid."

But when it came time to end the song, every note Singleton hit was wrong! "You gave me the wrong notes!" he shouted at Anderson.

"Boy, even the doorman hollered from the front, say, 'What the hell is going on back there!?'" Singleton said. "Cause the brass section went down the dance floor and the reed section broke out of the back, see, and I was left there just with the piano player and I was awful sad."

Armstrong and Singleton laughed uproariously at the memory in early 1971. "You know, it's a funny thing, the band had so much humor," Armstrong said. "If somebody hit a bad note, we had a little pig sitting in front of the band, like a toy pig you'd put money in, nice size. You had to put some money in there if the note you hit was wrong."

"And the pig stayed in front of you until somebody else made a bad note," Singleton added.

"That's right!" Armstrong responded. "And the pig would tell you when something's going wrong. . . . You'd feel *bad*. You got to feel bad."[29]

As the Dickerson band worked on perfecting its "sweeter" elements, over on the opposite bandstand, Clarence Black's Orchestra, which was usually known for being "soft, sweet and scintillating" in the words of Dave Peyton,

Figure 28.2 Carroll Dickerson and His Orchestra at the Savoy Ballroom in Chicago, 1928. In the back row are pianist Gene Anderson, leader Dickerson with his violin, and drummer Zutty Singleton. Front row, left to right: Fred Robinson, Homer Hobson, Louis Armstrong, Mancy Carr, Crawford Wethington, Jimmy Strong, Pete Briggs, and Bert Curry. Note the presence of the toy piggy bank placed in front of Carr's banjo.
Credit: The Frank Driggs Collection, Jazz at Lincoln Center.

turned on the heat with the addition of a trumpeter who would become one of Armstrong's greatest rivals.

In the fall of 1928, Earl Hines noticed that a new Louis Armstrong Hot Five record was on sale: "West End Blues." "Earl Hines, he was surprised when the record came out on the market because he brought it by my house, you know?" Armstrong said. "We had forgotten we had recorded it!"[30] "When it first came out," Hines said, "Louis and I stayed by that recording practically an hour and a half or two hours and we just knocked each other out because we had no idea it was gonna turn out as good as it did."[31]

The record's impact on musicians across the country—and eventually the world—was immediate. "[Armstrong's] records of 'West End Blues' and 'Savoy Blues' were exotic things that brought smiles, excited curiosity and then burned ever so hot," Hoagy Carmichael wrote in 1933. Of Hines, Carmichael said, "His work in 'West End Blues' made him a national reputation as an eccentric pianist that won't be forgot soon."[32]

Over in Baltimore, 13-year-old Eleanora Fagan heard "West End Blues" while running errands for a woman who ran a brothel and was stopped in her tracks by Louis's scat chorus. "And I wondered why he wasn't singing any words," she said. "And he had the most beautiful feeling, you know."[33] A short time later, Fagan began singing under the name Billie Holiday, when she was heard by fellow vocalist Mae Barnes. "She was doing everything that Louis Armstrong was doing," Barnes said of the young Holiday. "She knew his records backwards, every one of them . . . 'West End Blues,' 'Heebie Jeebies,' 'Sweethearts on Parade.' . . . She wasn't imitatin' his style, she was using all his numbers. That was her beginnin' of changing Louis's style to her own, only she used his numbers to do it."[34]

Over at Tuskegee University, pianist Teddy Wilson called "West End Blues" a "record of importance" in his formative years and quickly taught himself how to play Hines's solo. "I don't think there has been a musician since Armstrong who has had all the factors in balance, all the factors equally developed," Wilson later said. "Such a balance was the essential thing about Beethoven, I think, and Armstrong, like Beethoven, had this high development of balance. Lyricism. Delicacy. Emotional outburst. Rhythm. Complete mastery of his horn."[35]

Many of the musicians in New York admitted they hadn't kept up with Armstrong's progress in the years since he'd left Fletcher Henderson's Orchestra, but that all changed after the release of "West End Blues." "We had no idea that the world would accept all of his work as it did until we heard the thing he made in '28 with his small band and those records he made during the same time he made 'West End Blues,'" said multiinstrumentalist Garvin Bushell. "Then we began to feel that Louie would be the top trumpeter of the world. There was no question about it."[36]

Over in England, the Parlophone label began a new "Rhythm Series" of records in 1929, choosing "West End Blues" for its first release, billing it as a "Trumpet Solo." Fifteen-year-old Leonard Feather purchased a copy and had his life changed. "I would never have been in the music world as a musician and critic if it had not been for Louie's original record of 'West End Blues,'" Feather said in 1970. "I heard that when I was at high school in London and it was the first record that really made a profound impression on me. It was one of the most beautiful things I ever heard."[37] Trumpet players, pianists, saxophonists, vocalists, composers, future jazz journalists, white, Black, American, foreign—it seemed that everyone who heard "West End Blues" was affected by it.

The recording might have had a worldwide influence, but now Earl Hines's doubts came to the forefront: could Armstrong replicate it every night at the Savoy? The answer was a resounding yes. Clarinetist Artie Shaw recalled that when he was 18, he drove from Cleveland to the Savoy, "sat right at the front of the bandstand and listened to him play 'West End Blues,' and it was one of the most astonishing musical experiences of my life."[38] "When Louis started blowing the introduction to 'West End Blues' (man, was it mellifluous), everybody in the ballroom started screaming and whistling, and then Louis lowered the boom and everybody got real groovy when he went into the first strains of 'West End,'" drummer George Wettling recalled.[39]

Very few trumpet players could replicate the "West End Blues" cadenza but one who could soon found himself on the opposite bandstand at the Savoy: 19-year-old Cladys "Jabbo" Smith.

Born on Christmas Eve 1908, Smith was a product of the Jenkins Orphanage in Charleston, South Carolina, which was famous for its youth band; numerous professional musicians got their first experience playing jazz with this group. Smith learned to play trumpet and trombone at a young age and toured with the Jenkins Band for several years. He moved up north and became a professional musician while still a teenager, working his way to the pit band for Fats Waller and James P. Johnson's Broadway revue *Keep Shufflin'* in 1928. He was with James P. Johnson's band in Chicago when guitarist Teddy Bunn goaded him about Armstrong: "Man come on down here, this cat can't play nothing!" Smith soon became friendly with Armstrong and Singleton, who invited him to sit in any time he was at the Savoy.

But when Johnson's band broke up, Smith took the job in Clarence Black's band at the Savoy and the gloves came off. "So I went over there with them and that's when they start shouting at each other!" Smith said, referring to the "cutting" contests that ensued. "Yes, we were crazy!"[40]

Of Armstrong, Smith admitted, "I guess he influenced everybody, not only trumpet players, he influenced everybody that plays an instrument, you know." But of their styles, Smith said, "Oh well, we were entirely different, because he played swing and I just played more technical horn. . . . Louie was from New Orleans, but I didn't know anything about New Orleans."[41] "He was the Dizzy Gillespie of that era," bassist Milt Hinton said of Smith. "He played rapid-fire passages while Louis was melodic and beautiful."[42] "So naturally, being new and a kid, people thought I was pretty good, you know?" Smith said. "So I guess I got a pretty good following there."[43]

Naturally, with so many battles between the two, the memories, details, and even verdicts differed from witness to witness. "Jabbo was as good as Louis then," Hinton insisted.[44] "Jabbo had one advantage over a lot of trumpets in that period," according to saxophonist Benny Waters. "He was very, very fast and very, very clean also and he made a lot of notes, but he made them good. But we did never class him in the category of Louie."[45] Those with New Orleans connections remained in Armstrong's camp. "Jabbo Smith came in one night and asked Louis for his horn," Preston Jackson recalled. "He played really well, but then Louis took him."[46] "One time in Chicago, Jabbo Smith came in with blood in his eye for Louis, thinking he would blow him out," said Kid Ory, then also playing with Clarence Black. "When Louis finished playing, Jabbo said, 'I'm gonna get a trombone.'"[47]

Of comparing the two, saxophonist Scoville Brown said, "It's like oranges and apples." Brown offered a vivid account of one of Smith's challenges that inspired Armstrong to call his latest showpiece:

> [Smith] came into the ballroom and he got up on the bandstand and he played and we were all excited because very few people at that time had the audacity, I would say, to challenge Louis. But Jabbo got up and he accounted himself very well. He played beautifully and wonderfully. And then everybody was wondering what was Louis going to do now? You know, he had played so good and he had excited the people. But Louis came back with this song. . . . the "West End Blues," with that wonderful cadenza and he hit down on that, and the place seemed like it was going to come apart. It was bedlam, you know, it was a wonderful night. I mean, I don't think I'll ever forget that. It's very difficult to describe sounds with a voice, but he just about tore the joint up.

Brown added that when Armstrong hit the climactic high note of the cadenza, "the people tried to harmonize by shouting with him. It was a wonderful sound and a wonderful sight. And I was trembling in my little blue suit."[48] Smith later recalled with a laugh, "[Armstrong] had to pull his best shots, he had to pull the 'West End Blues' before he could get anything out!"[49]

But soon, Smith learned to fight fire with fire. "You may not remember, but the most difficult thing Louis ever played was the introduction to 'West End Blues,'" vocalist Floyd Campbell recalled of a night at the Savoy. "Jabbo played that entire song, note for note, just like Louie. Everybody except me was amazed. After that night nobody doubted Jabbo's musical ability."[50] Garvin Bushell also remembered being present when "Jabbo got on the stand and played the 'West End Blues' and he broke up the place just like Louie had played it and nobody else had ever been able to do that. So Jabbo to my mind was the nearest thing to Louis."[51]

"I used to do that 'West End Blues,' you know," Smith recalled. "Of course, the people used to like that, to hear me do it, 'cause nobody was doing it, except him and I." Asked if he interpreted it in his own fashion, Smith responded, "No, I just did it exactly the way he did it. That's the way they wanted to hear it."[52]

Armstrong rarely discussed his battles with Smith, but in 1971 he and Zutty Singleton reminisced about a time that Smith *did* take a chance with the "West End Blues" cadenza. "And this cat started it off right away there, that trumpet introduction *higher* than Louie played it!" Singleton said. "Boy, when he got to that *real* high part, talk about wrestling and scuffling, man, we never did finish, I don't think we ever finished 'West End Blues' that night! Cause he should have made it like Louie made it, you know, but he want to be so big and powerful, he's going to make it in a higher key than Louie started it off."

"And he didn't know his horn either—but he was all the rage!" a still-salty Armstrong recalled. "I don't know, the way he attacked notes and things, you can tell when a cat is trying too hard. He couldn't have played in them brass bands in New Orleans. You got to play with soul and different things like that."[53] Armstrong's views on Smith in the 1920s represent perhaps the first time he looked down on another trumpet player's style for being too technical and not having enough soul. Smith was ultimately unsuccessful in his challenge to Armstrong's throne, but younger trumpeters such as Roy Eldridge and Dizzy Gillespie began listening more to Jabbo than to Louis in the years to come, paving the way for bebop and the sounds of modern jazz—and more similar complaints from Armstrong.

The success of "West End Blues" did make other record labels sit up and take notice and try to mimic the success of the Hot Five with other top Black trumpeters. Vocalion began recording Reuben Reeves—Dave Peyton's favorite—in 1928, Brunswick signed Jabbo Smith in January 1929, and later that year, Victor would begin a series with trumpeter Henry "Red" Allen Jr. of Algiers, Louisiana. But Armstrong and OKeh were one step ahead; by the time these other labels began signing up these other trumpet players to record small group dates, Armstrong was well on his way to becoming a pop star.

29

"Louis Had Changed the Whole World"

1928–1929

Ever since Tommy Rockwell had come to OKeh Records at the end of 1926, he had been tinkering with Louis Armstrong's recordings. E. A. Fearn was content to simply record the Hot Five and hire Armstrong to back the label's various blues singers, but Rockwell saw potential for something different, something bigger. He tried the Hot Seven, which produced timeless music, but was perhaps a little too steeped in the sounds of New Orleans to have an effect in northern markets. He reunited the original Hot Five, but Armstrong's trumpet playing now completely overshadowed the efforts of his elders. He oversaw the recordings of a reconstituted Hot Five in the summer of 1928, adding Earl Hines to the mix, and finally struck pay dirt with "West End Blues."

It should be stressed, though, that up to this point all the records Armstrong made were "race records," marketed squarely at African American audiences around the country. The number of race records sold amounted to a fraction of the number of recordings Whiteman and Lombardo sold regularly. Thousands more people heard Henry "Hot Lips" Busse playing a muted trumpet solo on "When Day Is Done" with Whiteman or Weston Vaughan singing "Charmaine" with Lombardo than heard anything Armstrong did for OKeh in this period. Musicians and singers picked up on Armstrong's innovations and adjusted their styles accordingly, which is why the Hot Five and Seven recordings remain so important today, but Armstrong was still unknown to the vast majority of the population.

African American musicians had been relegated to the world of "race records" since the beginning of the decade, but that was starting to change. In April 1928, clarinetist Fess Williams and his "Jazz Joy Boys," then holding sway at the brand-new Regal Theater, recorded a pair of sides for Vocalion Records that included the aptly named "Drifting and Dreaming" (Sweet Paradise)." "[Vocalion] Manager Jack Kapp says this is the first 'Sweet Record' our musicians have recorded and it was perfect," Dave Peyton reported. "Heretofore our orchestras have been making jazz and hocum [*sic*] numbers, but Fess insisted that if they wanted him to record he would have to be given the same breaks as the white bands were getting and that is making real sweet musical song and dance records. Good for Fess."[1] Though Reuben Reeves contributed a hot muted solo and leader Williams offered up his usual piercing brand of blues clarinet, the side also featured passages for strings and a pronounced two-beat feel in the rhythm section, making it comparable to the sounds created by many of the popular white dance bands of the day.

Rockwell was paying attention. "West End Blues" moved the needle a little bit for Armstrong. While not a runaway pop hit, it did sell better than usual and created a bit of a stir with listeners. Rockwell was now convinced: if Armstrong could just connect with the general public, he had a chance to really become a star. The Hot Five was fun while it lasted but the American popular music scene had moved well past the trumpet-trombone-clarinet-banjo-piano sound that harkened back to New Orleans.

Thus, Rockwell set up a handful of sessions in December 1928 to experiment further. He still didn't want the full Dickerson band; instead, the December sessions would offer something for everyone. Armstrong recorded multiple small group numbers with the same exact personnel as back in the summer, but now the "Hot Five" moniker was retired and the recordings would be attributed to either "Louis Armstrong and His Savoy Ballroom Five" or "Louis Armstrong and His Orchestra." Zutty Singleton was finally allowed to bring in a full drumset, complete with bass drum. Rockwell became enamored with the sound of Singleton's wire brushes, which he had never recorded before. According to Martin Williams, Rockwell "entered the recording studio himself, moved Zutty right on top of the microphone. He had Singleton stand up as Rockwell held his small drum right over the mike while he played. The technique worked."[2]

But most important, Rockwell issued the majority of the December output—and even a few items from the summer sessions—as both "race" and "pop" recordings, his first attempt to see if white audiences would go for this trumpeter with the raspy voice.

Armstrong rose to the occasion with some of the most outstanding trumpet work of his career, especially on the small group recordings of "Basin Street Blues" and "Muggles." On the former, Armstrong unleashes a string of double-timed phrases that would have made Jabbo Smith sit up and take notice, while on "Muggles"—an ode to his newfound love of marijuana—Armstrong enters by confidently swinging a single pitch, attacking it from different angles, and relying on rhythm rather than pyrotechnics. As the tempo settles, he even quotes King Oliver's 1923 solo on "Jazzin' Babies Blues." Oliver was no longer playing trumpet at this time and spent part of December back in Chicago, where Art Hodes remembered him regularly dropping in at the Savoy; perhaps Armstrong's musical gesture was made during this rare reunion, a way of letting Oliver know that his music would live on through his protégé's playing.

The smallest group side of them all was "Weather Bird," a duet between Armstrong and Hines, jokingly referred to by Armstrong as the "Hot Two."[3] During a break in the December 5 session, Armstrong took it upon himself to teach Hines this multistrain piece originally recorded by King Oliver's Creole Jazz Band back in 1923.[4] "We had no music," Hines said. "It was all improvised, and I just followed him. Louis had some ideas and I soon grasped the chord structure."[5] "And I ran it down on the trumpet, see?" Armstrong said. "And it sounded so good, Mr. Fearn said, 'Let's put it on right now.' "[6]

Armstrong had already made a few hundred recordings up to this point, but this time, there would be no big band, no blues singers, no Hot Five, nobody else to back him up but his musical twin, Hines. "Now swing is not an objective word," Teddy Wilson once said, "but *my* conditioning of the swing feeling was the way Armstrong and Hines played on the Hot Five records—not the others, just Armstrong and Hines."[7]

Left to their own devices for three minutes, the pair have a musical conversation, challenging one another, finishing each other's thoughts, collaborating on moments of great beauty—Armstrong's glorious final high C with Hines's shimmering chords under him—and swinging effortlessly from start to finish. Just four short years earlier, King Oliver and Jelly Roll Morton had recorded two duets that showcased the foundational elements of this music but were still rough around the edges and a bit repetitive, even stiff, at times. In the span of a presidential term, the music had progressed to the point where a trumpet-and-piano duet such as "Weather Bird" now represented new, achievable ideals of musical freedom. "We were very close and when we were playing we would steal ideas from each other," Hines once said. "Or, rather, I'd *borrow* an idea from him, and say, 'Thank you.' Then he'd hear me play something he liked, borrow it, and say, 'Thank you.' "[8] If that's the case, then "Weather Bird" is gratitude personified, the feeling extending from the musicians to the listeners.[9]

After those small group affairs, the rest of the December sessions featured arrangements courtesy of Armstrong's old Fletcher Henderson bandmate, Don Redman, now serving as the musical director for McKinney's Cotton Pickers, a popular African American big band from Detroit. "Don is known to make the very best arrangements with the Best of them," Armstrong wrote in 1938. "And I'll go as far as to say he's makes 'Em much better than the best of 'em. . . . He's really my Ideal as a 'first' class swing musician."[10]

While in Chicago to help white drummer Ben Pollack rehearse his band at the Blackhawk, Redman visited the Savoy, where Armstrong invited him to record with him. Once in the studio, Redman brought along a chart for one of his own compositions, "No One Else But You," which transformed "Louis Armstrong and His Savoy Ballroom Five" into a completely modern-sounding entity.

This was the sound Rockwell was looking for; Armstrong sang and played brilliantly, but he was now given a backdrop that was a few steps closer to the popular dance band sound of the period. Redman and Jimmy Strong combined for a creamier reed sound, Singleton's percolating drums drove the proceedings, and the song itself featured a melody the average listener could remember and hum. In this setting, Armstrong's brilliance came to the forefront better than with the Hot Five. "With all the ideas he had, he *also* had a beautiful tone," Hines said of Armstrong. "That's one of the reasons why ordinary people who were not musicians appreciated him so quickly."[11] With "No One Else But You," Rockwell heard a sound that "ordinary people" could enjoy, but it would have to be properly paired and marketed along with something a little more familiar.

Until then, Armstrong would remain content to continue dazzling the musicians who were paying attention, especially on "Beau Koo Jack," another December 5 masterpiece. Armstrong co-composed the tune with pianist Alex Hill, who most likely contributed the hip arrangement, filled with unique breaks and even some forward-looking whole-tone passages. Contemporary recordings by Clarence Williams and even King Oliver used the same chart, as published by the Melrose brothers, but it's the improvisations of Armstrong and Hines, along with the funky drumming of Singleton, that set this record apart.

In his 32-bar solo, Armstrong utilizes every tool in his arsenal: swinging quarter notes, triplets, arpeggios, diminished arpeggios, octave leaps, the blues, flash (the second half of the solo starts with the fluttering of his third valve), chromaticism, motivic development, deep harmonic knowledge, and memorable melodies. "This solo embodies, I think, why Louis Armstrong matters," trumpeter Bria Skonberg said while analyzing the "Beau Koo Jack" solo for a group of students in 2022, summing it up as "flashes of absolute technical brilliance grounded with beautiful melodies."[12]

Rockwell knew that "Beau Koo Jack," unlike "No One Else But You," might be too flashy for the masses, and he issued it as strictly a "race" record. But he approved of the larger sound of the group and invited Redman to return one week later with three more arrangements: Armstrong and Redman's own composition "Heah Me Talkin' to Ya" (the catchphrase of popular Black comedian Marshall "Garbage" Rogers), the first recorded version of "St. James Infirmary," and "Tight Like This," written by McKinney's Cotton Pickers trumpeter Langston Curl.

Where the "West End Blues" cadenza represented all of Armstrong's trumpet influences converging in a matter of a seconds and the "Beau Koo Jack" solo showed off every tool in his toolbox, "Tight Like This" could be viewed as a summary of Armstrong's entire life up to this point. Comedy had been a big part of his personality since he was a kid and it made him a star with Black audiences in Chicago, so it's only fitting that the record includes a running gag of Armstrong and Singleton—the latter using a comedically high-pitched voice—arguing about whether or not "it" really is "tight like that." The song is in a minor key and Armstrong begins his solo in the role of a cantor, the Karnofsky family perhaps on his mind. His playing was authentic enough to impress cantor Samuel Arluck of Buffalo, New York, father of young Hyman Arluck—later known as famed composer Harold Arlen. "Anyway, I played him this record, and there was a musical riff in there—we used to call it a 'hot lick'—that Louis did," Arlen remembered. "And my father looked at me, and he was stunned. And he asked in Yiddish, 'Where did he get it?' Because he thought it was something that *he* knew, you see."[13]

After this Jewish interlude, Armstrong engages in some instrumental comedy; his trumpet makes a meal out of a quote of "The Streets of Cairo," better known as the "snake charmer" song. Eventually the band switches its rhythm to what Jelly Roll Morton dubbed "the Spanish tinge," incorporating a different, but no less important, flavor from his hometown.

But most important, Armstrong's solo tells a story. He would spend the next several decades telling his life's story over and over again, but here he gets to do so over three full choruses, a total of 48 bars, his longest solo outing on record to date. He takes his time, starting quietly and steadily building toward a climax that finds him wailing passionately in the upper register. In many regards, this solo outlined the playbook for nearly all extended improvised solos that would follow: jazz musicians such as Lionel Hampton, Illinois Jacquet, and Roy Eldridge learned this lesson well, but even outside the genre, legends such as B. B. King, Jimi Hendrix, Eddie Van Halen, and countless others who ever started out improvising quietly before building toward a roof-shaking climax were following the blueprint of "Tight Like This."

It was a blueprint that could also make OKeh more money as Armstrong's influence grew, but for that to happen, first Rockwell would have to get Armstrong to New York City.

The rest of the jazz world was finally beginning to catch up on Armstrong's innovations as 1929 began. This included King Oliver, who began a major new recording contract with Victor on January 16, 1929, by recording a remake of "West End Blues" based on Armstrong's version. Oliver fronted Luis Russell's orchestra for the occasion, which featured trumpeter Louie Metcalf. Metcalf remembered Oliver playing Armstrong's record for the band in the studio before they attempted it. "He definitely wanted that introduction," Metcalf said, but Oliver was not in shape to even attempt it himself. "He lost all his teeth," Metcalf said of Oliver. "He wasn't able to carry on." Asked how Oliver felt about Armstrong at the time, Metcalf said, "Oh, he was proud of him. He was proud of him. I mean, King felt like he had born-ed him himself. I think King felt the same way about Louie as Louie felt about me and a lot of other youngsters. There was love in those days."[14]

When it came time to record, Metcalf made it through the cadenza, but not without struggle. "Well, first place it was difficult to even make the introduction," he said. "That was a difficult thing, because I mean, I think he had . . . eight bars without a breath. No, no time for no breathing.[15] "We used to give him hell when he was making that introduction," alto saxophonist Charlie Holmes recalled. "Just before the last note he stopped and taken a breath! Ha-ha-ha!"[16] Metcalf's shakiness aside, "West End Blues" represented the first time an improvised jazz recording was transcribed and scored for a larger ensemble, and it was performed and recorded by Oliver less than six months after Armstrong's version was released. It would be far from the last; less than a month later, on February 15, 1929, Earl Hines's new big band recorded "Beau Koo Jack" for Victor in Chicago, and on that number Armstrong's solo was transcribed, scored, and harmonized for Hines's two trumpeters, Shirley Clay and George Mitchell. Two months later, over in Culver City, California, Paul Howard's Quality Serenaders recorded "Charlie's Idea," with trumpeter George Orendorff taking a solo based on Armstrong's scat episode from "Hotter Than That."

Armstrong's ideas were now being played in recording studios from coast to coast, but ironically, in Chicago, the Savoy began seeing a downturn in business as they celebrated their one-year anniversary at the end of 1928. "All of a sudden, the Regal Theatre opened next door, and business dropped off pretty bad," Charles Carpenter recalled, adding, "Now Louis was getting a hundred dollars a week at the Savoy with Carroll Dickerson, but though he and Zutty were in the band, they weren't drawing flies."[17] Savoy owner I. J. Faggen cut Clarence Black's band and began telling the Dickerson band a "hard luck story" every week. "But look like Mr. Fagan [*sic*] was laying that hard luck story on us a little too often," Armstrong wrote. "And payments on our (Lil +

I) home was *way* past due. And Zuttie and I would talk it over every pay night and we would say to each other—If Fagan comes with no money this week we were sure to quit."[18]

Armstrong did have one option, but he was hesitant to explore it: Tommy Rockwell wanted him to come to New York so he could personally oversee a different type of recording session. "Louis was getting bids from New York, but he didn't like New York," Carpenter said. "He'd been there before with Fletcher Henderson. 'This ain't for me,' he said, and split, and came on back to Chicago."[19] Armstrong truly loved Chicago. "He had friends all along the street," Doc Cheatham recalled. "He couldn't walk on the street. People just crowded him, followed [him] all up and down the streets in Chicago."[20]

Cheatham went to New York in 1928 to join Chick Webb's band and wasn't impressed with the city. "I didn't like New York," he said. "I didn't like the music I was hearing because it was all sophisticated, stiff type of music, see. Coming from Chicago, everything was just real good jazz."[21] Jelly Roll Morton and King Oliver were in New York, but the city wasn't very friendly to New Orleans musicians, according to guitarist Danny Barker. Of Oliver, Barker said, "His laid-back style, that honky tonk style of great jazz playing, didn't fit New York. In fact, New York is populated by very cold black people, very cold white people."[22]

Armstrong decided to take a chance, agreeing to come to New York to play two nights at the Savoy and record for Rockwell at OKeh before heading back to Chicago. Those 48 hours would have repercussions that would last the rest of his life.

He would perform at the Savoy with Luis Russell's band, once again with Louie Metcalf on trumpet. Metcalf had always worshipped Armstrong but had let his own success in New York go to his head. Armstrong would be the featured artist with Russell, but Metcalf would be there, too, sitting on a stool in front of the band—and wearing a crown. "Metcalf took a piece of pasteboard and made a crown," Russell's trombonist, J. C. Higginbotham, recalled. "He put it on his head and said he was the king of trumpeters in New York."[23] "Armstrong didn't do so much in the rehearsals, so Metcalf was confident," Luis Russell told Walter C. Allen.[24]

Things quickly changed the first night at the Savoy. "Then Louis Armstrong played, and Metcalf jumped off the stand," Higginbotham said. "We didn't see him for a while."[25] According to Allen, "[Metcalf] was featured on a number called 'Slue Foot' on which he took three choruses at the end, after which he was pretty tired. Armstrong had arranged it with Russell beforehand to take *six* choruses after Metcalfe [*sic*] had finished his three, which he did with no trouble at all. Metcalfe quickly tore up his crown."[26] "The funniest thing I remember about those two nights was the reaction of Metcalf," Russell recalled. "Up to that time Metcalf fancied himself the hottest trumpet man in New York. After hearing Armstrong, he was ready to throw his horn away."[27] "After that one night when Louie appeared at the Savoy, when I went back to the Rhythm Club—when you go to the Rhythm Club, you have the whole feel of all the jazz musicians, really," guitarist Lawrence Lucie said. "And so the feeling I got when I went back there, Louie had changed the whole world."[28]

There were no hard feelings between Armstrong and Metcalf, though Armstrong did have some advice to share. "So Pops told me, he said, 'Well, you sound good, but the greatest thing is for you to get your own feeling,' " Metcalf said. "And he was so right because nobody could sound like Pops because you didn't have his heart, you know? And so I was thinking, I said, 'Well, maybe he's jealous and he don't want me to copy his style or something like that.' But the man was telling me the truth. 'Go get your own bag.' And I loved him for it." [29]

The two remained friends for the rest of their lives; when Metcalf hit hard times, he remembered Armstrong giving him $1,000 out of his pocket. "I miss him so much," he said after Armstrong passed away. "I almost wish it would have been me that went first instead of him because he helped people. He just believed in helping people. I know all down in New Orleans, the orphan home that he used to go to, he bought instruments for that orphan home every year. And he helped so many churches, so many schools. And man, he did so much, you could almost call him a Jesus, you know. And such a wonderful guy, person. Anybody that didn't like Louis Armstrong, it had to be jealousy. Just plain jealousy."[30]

Aside from Metcalf, the Savoy was filled with important figures from Armstrong's early years. Luis Russell, Paul Barbarin, and Pops Foster were in the rhythm section, associates who went back to his days in New Orleans. A banquet was held in Armstrong's honor after the first night, hosted by Fletcher Henderson. White disciples such as Jack Teagarden and Eddie Condon were present; Condon convinced Rockwell to make Armstrong's first integrated recording, "Knockin' a Jug," that same night.

But most important, Armstrong remembered, "Joe Oliver was there each night," his voice choking up as he remembered it. "And he's always been my inspiration and my idol. He was standing right in front of that trumpet. See what I mean? That was a thrill. Those things he had talked to me about, about my horn just when I was a kid, running errands for his wife, lessons and things—it was coming right out of that horn. Tears coming right out of his eyes, man. Knocked him out. And I laid the good old good ones on him, Pops and killed him. Knocked him out."[31]

One of the songs Armstrong remembered performing for Oliver was "I Can't Give You Anything But Love." This particular number—one of the biggest hits of 1928—had been Tommy Rockwell's main reason for bringing Armstrong to New York in the first place, to see what he could do on a song the public already knew. The result was better than Rockwell could have imagined. With the Russell band repetitively droning the melody in the background, Armstrong both sang and played it in a style unlike any of the various popular versions already on the market. Rockwell knew it was a home run and knew he had the perfect song to pair with "No One Else But You." He released the results on both the race and pop sides along with a heavy marketing campaign and was pleased with the response, working overtime to convince Armstrong to move to New York permanently.

Armstrong didn't need much convincing. "Zutty," he told Singleton upon his return to Chicago. "Man, they had my name in lights at the Savoy, you know. LOUIS ARMSTRONG, you know." "And that knocked him out," Singleton observed.[32] Though his marriage with Lil was on shaky ground and he was spending more time with Alpha Smith, he still looked to Lil for guidance. "And Lil was a big influence," Marge Singleton recalled. "She would commercialize Louis, too, you know. . . . But I know when Rockwell told him how much money he could make, and I know Lil was for that, you know."[33]

Armstrong made up his mind in May, moving to New York—and taking the entire Carroll Dickerson band with him. Once established at Connie's Inn in Harlem, Dickerson ceded the name of the organization to his longtime featured trumpet soloist; they would now be billed as Louis Armstrong and His Orchestra. Not long after, Armstrong became a hit on Broadway with his rendition of "Ain't Misbehavin' " during the revue *Connie's Hot Chocolates.* Rockwell continued releasing Armstrong's recordings as both pop and race records, but by the end of 1929, he had made up his mind: Louis Armstrong was a pop artist.

Not just any pop artist; Armstrong became the first Black pop star. Going back to the earliest days of minstrelsy, the history of American popular music usually followed a pattern of Black innovation inspiring white imitation. Now, for the first time, a Black musician, Armstrong, would infiltrate the lily-white pop world and blow it up from within. He'd use Guy Lombardo's saxophone sound and all the same Tin Pan Alley songs—and sometimes the same arrangements—the white dance bands were using on songs such as "When You're Smiling," "After You've Gone," "Exactly Like You," "I Can't Believe That You're in Love With Me," "I'm Confessin'," "If I Could Be With You," "Body and Soul," "Sweethearts on Parade," "All of Me," "Lazy River," "Star Dust," "I've Got the World on a String," and many others. Once he was finished injecting them

Figure 29.1 Full-page advertisement for Louis Armstrong and His Orchestra from the November 1929 issue of *Melody Maker*, saved to one of Louis and Lil Armstrong's scrapbooks. Left to right: Fred Robinson, Mancy Carr, Homer Hobson, Jimmy Strong, Pete Briggs, Bert Curry, Gene Anderson, Crawford Wethington, Louis Armstrong, Zutty Singleton, and Carroll Dickerson.
Credit: Courtesy of the Louis Armstrong House Museum.

with something unapologetically Black, he had turned pop music on its head and paved the way for all that would follow: swing, rhythm and blues, bebop, rock 'n' roll, soul, funk, hip-hop, and everything in between.

Armstrong's innovations as both a trumpeter and vocalist set the entire soundtrack of the twentieth century in motion. But those innovations didn't come out of nowhere. In some ways, only he could have pulled it off.

He spent the first 28 years of his life soaking up music like a sponge. Growing up in poverty, a generation removed from slavery, he grew up hearing the blues and ragtime and the nascent sounds of jazz and quickly internalized the vernacular sounds of his race. But he also hummed Yiddish lullabies with the Karnofsky family, harmonized on pop tunes with his vocal quartet, sang in church, and bought records by superstars such as Enrico Caruso and John McCormack. He transitioned from Kid Ory's swinging small group to the dance band of Fate Marable, studying the records of Art Hickman and Paul Whiteman as he developed his style. He played hymns and second line specialties in the brass bands, but also read scores and learned the marches of John Philip Sousa. Minstrelsy was in the air, influencing Armstrong's comedic sensibilities through the recordings of Bert Williams, yet he also absorbed a new style of Black comedy pioneered by Bill Robinson, adapting accordingly to inspire laughter in audiences both Black and white. He tangled with Sidney Bechet and perfected the art of the obligato behind the blues singers in New York, while simultaneously getting food for thought from dance band musicians B. A. Rolfe and Vic D'Ippolito while serving as a sideman in Fletcher Henderson's orchestra. When his "Heebie Jeebies" put scat singing on the map, he was accompanying silent movies with a symphony orchestra, trying to not get distracted by Moby-Dick biting into John Barrymore's leg. He played music for dancing and became a dancer himself, demonstrating the Charleston, the Mess Around, and other terpsichorean feats on the Chicago stage. His "West End Blues" changed the sound of jazz at a time when he and his bandmates raced to the radio to hear Guy Lombardo broadcast each night. He idolized pioneers like Joe Oliver and Bunk Johnson, yet made time to encourage his young disciples on and off the bandstand to seek their own original voices. All of this music—and more—was rumbling inside of his soul every time he hit the stage, summarizing all that came before him and making possible all that would follow.

The man they called Pops had become the first King of Pop and nothing would ever be the same.

Epilogue

"I Never Did Leave New Orleans"

It was a long, long journey from his Third Ward upbringing to the Broadway stage, but by 1929, Louis Armstrong was a star. He was only getting started; he would go on to have hit records in every decade of his career, star in over 30 films, break down barriers against his race on radio and television, make thousands of timeless recordings, and became a global icon, embraced around the world as "Ambassador Satch." None of it would have been possible without the support of many of the crucial figures in his life: family, friends, teachers, mentors, fellow musicians, and wives.

Lil Armstrong was the main architect of his stardom, but their marriage had mostly run its course by 1929. The following year, Louis and Lil moved to Los Angeles—as did Alpha Smith. Clarence Hatfield, now 15, was still living with Lil's controlling mother in Chicago at the time of the 1930 census, but when Louis returned to Chicago in 1931, he became determined to remove Clarence from the humiliating environment created by Lil and Decie. He began bringing Clarence over to have dinner with Alpha and her mother, Florence, later writing, "Clarence was so glad over it. Just the idea—he could talk free without some one Hollering at him and ridiculing his Affliction, etc. And he didn't have to put on *Airs* with a certain Spoon for this and a certain fork for that."

"Pops," Clarence told his adopted father, "this is where I should be living instead of staying out there with Lil."

Louis was speechless, but smiled and said, "Yes, Clarence, you are right. And here's where you are going to stay—right here with Mrs. Smith. Not only that—you are going to spend the rest of your life with Mrs. Smith."[1]

Clarence moved in with Florence Smith and her husband, Noah Woods, at 3525 South Parkway. During World War II, Clarence filled out a draft registration card, listing Smith as his "grandmother" and offering the government his new name: Clarence Louis Armstrong. He remained in Chicago until Mrs. Smith passed away in 1953, at which time Louis moved him to the Bronx, even paying a woman named Evelyn Allen to take care of Clarence and serve as his wife. Louis was never embarrassed by Clarence's condition, inviting him to all his concerts and recording sessions in the New York area, and even introducing him and letting him say a few words on a televised episode of *Eddie Condon's Floor Show* in 1949.

Louis and Clarence remained devoted to each other until Louis's passing in 1971. Clarence spent the next several years in the Bronx, watching the New York Mets religiously, but after the death of Evelyn, he was sent to the Hebrew Home for the Aged in Riverdale, New York, where he quietly spent his final years before passing away on August 27, 1998, at the age of 83. By that time, the Louis Armstrong Archives was open at Queens College, with an enlarged photograph of Louis and Clarence greeting visitors in the space's main hallway. Inside the Archives were photos of Clarence, collages Louis made of Clarence, and even tape recordings of Louis and Clarence together, eating Chinese food, talking baseball, and telling dirty jokes. At the end of one such tape, Louis says, "Clarence, you gassed me, Papa"—a beautiful snapshot of a true father-and-son relationship.

On another of his tape-recorded conversations from 1953, Louis again told the story of how Lil treated Clarence and said, "I know Clarence didn't want all that shit from Lil. Lil sees it now, but what the fuck, it's too late. I'm still taking care of her, too."[2] Louis and Lil separated in 1931 and divorced in 1938, but Louis continued to send her money in the decades to come and insisted she keep the properties they had bought together in Chicago and in Idlewild, Michigan, in the 1920s. She decorated both locations with photos and memorabilia from her time with Louis. Lil made it to New York for Louis's funeral in July 1971, but died one month later—in the middle of a performance of "St. Louis Blues" at a memorial concert in Chicago given for her late husband. "She was the soul of Louie," bandleader Sam Wooding once said of Lil. "There's no maybe so, I don't care who followed, she was the soul of Louie."[3]

After Lil, of course, the other major architect of Louis's stardom was King Oliver, who had a last hurrah of sorts in 1929. After taking some time off to have extensive dental work performed, Oliver reemerged in October 1929 with a new set of dental plates, suddenly able to play the hottest, most demanding trumpet of his entire recording career on "Too Late," spending much of his time in the upper register. But "Too Late" was an appropriate title for Oliver's career; later that same month, Wall Street "laid an egg" and the Great Depression began. Oliver claimed to have lost $45,000 in one bank and $18,000 in another; all of the money he had made from his recordings, compositions,

Figure E.1 Lil Hardin Armstrong in the 1960s, posing in front of the home she purchased and lived in with Louis in the 1920s, holding one of his trumpets from that era.
Credit: The Lil Hardin Armstrong-Chris Albertson Collection, Louis Armstrong House Museum.

and performances was gone. Though he had made some popular recordings for the label, Victor chose not to renew his contract the following year.

Oliver settled into a pattern as the 1930s wore on—form a band, go out on tour, watch the tour fall apart, watch the men leave. He followed Armstrong's ascent and remained proud of his protégé, writing to Bunk Johnson on February 15, 1930, "[Armstrong] is some comet player now, Bunk. That bird can hit F and G with ease."[4] But Oliver still had his pride; when Armstrong returned from Europe in the fall of 1932, he no longer had a band of his own and, according to trombonist Otto "Pete" Jones, reached out to Oliver with a proposition. "Louis wanted to take the band over and call it 'Louis and King Oliver,' and make some big money, but King didn't want any of that. He said, 'You know who'd get all the acclaim,' he didn't want any competition."[5]

Oliver ended up stranded in Savannah, Georgia, in 1937 after a proposed tour fell through. He was out of prospects and had to take on work at a fruit and vegetable stand to survive.

In September of that year, Oliver was tapped on the shoulder by a visitor to his stand. He turned around and was shocked to see "Little Louis" standing in front of him.

"Where did you come from, you little gate-mouth son-of-a-bitch?" Oliver said affectionately as he realized it was Armstrong.[6]

"Yes, Louis did bump into him," Frank Dilworth, an associate of Oliver in Savannah, recalled, noting, "Armstrong broke down and cried, gave him money to buy a suit of clothes. I guess King had done a lot for Louis, long ago."[7] "He was just standing there in his shirtsleeves," Armstrong said of this moment.

> No tears. Just glad to see us. Just another day. He had that spirit. I gave him about $150 in my pocket, and Luis Russell and Red Allen, Pops Foster, Albert Nicholas, Paul Barbarin—all used to be his boys—they gave him what they had. And that night we played a dance, and we look over and there's Joe standing in the wings. He was sharp like the old Joe Oliver of 1915. He'd been to the pawn shop and gotten his fronts all back, you know, his suits and all—Stetson hat turned down, high-button shoes, his box-back coat. He looked beautiful and he had a wonderful night, just listening to us—talking.[8]

According to Dilworth, "Louis said he was going to send him twenty dollars a week."[9] Later that year, Duke Ellington's Orchestra passed through Savannah and Oliver reunited with his former reedman Barney Bigard. "He said Louis had been good to him and sent him money to help out from time to time," Bigard said.[10] But it was too late; Oliver's health deteriorated in early 1938, as he began suffering from high blood pressure and heart trouble. He couldn't afford medication, so he took a job sweeping Connie "Pop" Wimberly's pool hall in Savannah for 25 cents a day. Wimberly had lived in New Orleans at the turn of the century and remembered that Oliver used to like to reminisce. "Savannah's all right," Oliver told Wimberly, "but New Orleans—that's my *heart* city!"[11] "You know, before he died," Dilworth said, "he told me that he had such an affection for Louis he wished that in some way he could have been his real son. He sure *cared* for Louis."[12]

Oliver died in Savannah on April 10, 1938. "Most people said it was a heart attack. I think it was a broken heart," Armstrong later said. "Couldn't go no further with grief."[13] The following week, the *Savannah Tribune* ran a headline: "'Daddy' Jazz Music Passes—King Oliver, Noted Band Leader FOUND DEAD IN BED—Was the Discoverer of Louis Armstrong." The *New York Amsterdam News* was more succinct: "King Oliver Dead; Taught Louie." Even in death, Oliver and Armstrong remained connected.

Armstrong traveled from Washington, DC, to attend Oliver's funeral in New York City. He was the only soloist to perform during the service, playing a "funeral dirge" as in the old days of New Orleans. "He started all of us youngsters out," Armstrong said at the time. "And there isn't a riff played today that he didn't play more than 15 years ago."[14]

Armstrong had needed a father. Oliver wanted a son. "Joe Oliver as well as myself felt that we were very close Relatives," Armstrong wrote in 1944, acknowledging a familial connection. "He was always Kind and very Encouraging to me. And willing to help a poor youngster like me out. And until the very last day he drew his last Breath, I stuck right by him."[15]

Armstrong would continue to stick right by Oliver until he drew his own last breath in 1971.

Oliver's unlucky streak followed him to his grave. At the time of his passing, two young white writers, Frederic Ramsey Jr. and Charles Edward Smith, were writing a book on the true story of the birth of jazz, using the words of the pioneers who were still alive. They dispatched 33-year-old William Russell, then living in Chicago, to find Oliver, but his search came to an end when Oliver died.

Instead, the more interviews Russell, Ramsey, and Smith conducted, the more they heard about a mysterious figure named Bunk Johnson and his impact on Louis. Johnson was driving a truck for $1.75 a day in New Iberia, Louisiana, in 1938 and hadn't touched a trumpet since losing his teeth several years earlier. Nobody knew if he was alive and if he was, where he could be found—except Louis Armstrong.

Russell caught up with Armstrong at the Strand Theater in New York in January 1939 and brought up Johnson. "They should talk about that man," Armstrong declared. "What a tone! Man O Man." In his notes on the conversation, Russell wrote, "Louis got all excited and became incoherent." "We saw him all evening in New Iberia this fall," Armstrong shared. "He doesn't play anymore, he's lost his teeth, but why, just to hear him talk sends me!"[16] Armstrong even signed a publicity photo for Johnson, inscribed, "Best Wishes To My Boy 'Bunk.' He's my musical inspiration all my life—yea man. Satchmo, Louis Armstrong."[17]

Armstrong helped Russell connect with Johnson, who had a preternatural talent for taking full advantage of a situation at hand. This came to the forefront in a letter Johnson wrote to Russell that was published in the June 1939 issue of *Down Beat* with a blaring headline: "This Isn't Bunk: Bunk Taught Louis." "The influence of King Oliver upon Louis has been exaggerated," author Park Breck wrote, before quoting "new facts" provided by Johnson himself. "He would fool around with my cornet every chance he got," Johnson said. "I showed him just how to hold it and place it to his mouth, and he did so, and it wasn't long before he began getting a good tone out of my horn."[18]

Figure E.2 Publicity photo of Louis Armstrong, inscribed to Bunk Johnson in 1938: "Best Wishes To My Boy 'Bunk.' He's my musical inspiration all my life—yea man. Satchmo, Louis Armstrong."

Credit: The William Russell Jazz Collection at The Historic New Orleans Collection, acquisition made possible by the Clarisse Claiborne Grima Fund, acc. no. 92-48-L.331.1446.

Ramsey, Smith, and Russell's finished book, *Jazzmen*, was published in the fall of 1939 to rave reviews. "I wanna tell you that it's absolutely Wonderful," Armstrong wrote Russell, offering no corrections. "It really is a Marvelous Book."[19] He also praised Russell's efforts to help Johnson: "I want to thank all the boys whom helped you to help Bunk to go to the Dentist and get his Chops-fixed, for me as well as for Bunk. . . . That was very nice of you boys. . . . Honest-Gate—that's something that we will be talking about the rest of our lives."[20]

The publication of *Jazzmen* turned Johnson into a folk hero overnight. He made his first records in 1942, eventually recording for major labels such as Decca and RCA Victor, and resumed performing in live settings in San Francisco in 1943. His appearance at the Stuyvesant Casino in New York City in 1945 was greeted by an unprecedented wave of publicity, covered by every major newspaper and magazine in town. Yet Johnson's reliance on alcohol often sabotaged his successes; he sometimes showed up too inebriated to perform, was fired by Sidney Bechet after a well-publicized engagement in Boston, and had members of his own band quit after their New York venture.[21]

Johnson finally slowed down and returned home in 1947, rarely performing in public again—except for one last hurrah in 1949 when Armstrong returned home for Mardi Gras. "We played in New Iberia . . . the night before I went into New Orleans to be the King of the Zulus, and Bunk come up on that stand and picked up that horn and played it for an hour," Armstrong said. He was conflicted by the whole saga; part of him felt it was a "wonderful thing . . . to go back and let him have a little more fun before he died," Armstrong said.[22]

But a bigger part of him couldn't help but feel that it should have been Joe Oliver. If Oliver had survived just a little while longer, it would have been Oliver telling his story in *Jazzmen*, Oliver getting a new set of teeth and a new trumpet, Oliver being profiled in *Esquire*, Oliver jamming with him in New Orleans.

The constant mentions of Bunk as Armstrong's teacher—which Armstrong initially helped spur—became part of Johnson's mythology. A few months after their reunion in New Iberia, Johnson died of a stroke on July 7, 1949. It wasn't long before Armstrong unburdened himself of his conflicted feelings, saying, "Bunk didn't teach me shit."[23] There can be no denying that Johnson was one of Armstrong's biggest formative influences, but for the rest of his life, a day seemingly did not pass without him telling anyone who would listen about Oliver. Oliver never got a second chance and Armstrong would do his best to give him one posthumously.

In May 1970, Armstrong recorded "Boy From New Orleans," his autobiographical version of "When the Saints Go Marching In." Ruth Roberts had contributed the lyrics, including a line, "I heard the great Bunk Johnson," which is how Armstrong sang it on the record. But when he began performing it in live settings later that year—including using it as the final song at his final performance at the Waldorf-Astoria in March 1971—Armstrong made a change and now sang, "I heard the great King Oliver." No one, not even Bunk Johnson, could take Oliver's place, in Armstrong's music and in his heart.

Armstrong's final reunion with Bunk Johnson in 1949 occurred the night before one of the biggest moments of his life. "There's a thing I've dreamed of all my life," Armstrong said at the time, "and I'll be damned if it don't look like it's about to come true—to be King of the Zulus' Parade. After that I'll be ready to die."[24]

Armstrong was crowned during a concert at Booker T. Washington High School and Auditorium. "We had a little incident that night," said Zulu Club member Jim Russell. "A woman came up and she wanted to be admitted free, you know, and they wouldn't let her in. So finally she told the people, 'Somebody, go and get Louis Armstrong for me and you tell him Mrs. Louis Armstrong is outside.' " This just led to more confusion as Louis's fourth wife, Lucille Wilson Armstrong, was presently in his dressing room. "So they ran and then they got Louis," Russell continued. "And then Louis came and told them, 'Let her in, let her in, let her in.' And it turned out that was his first wife that he had married before he left home, a woman by the name of Daisy Parker. So they had two Mrs. Louis Armstrongs at the dance that night."[25]

Louis hadn't seen Daisy in quite some time. After Louis had divorced her—without her knowledge—in 1923, Daisy had eventually found out and filed a "Petition to Vacate Decree" in Chicago on February 16, 1925. Daisy claimed that Louis "falsely and fraudulently testified" against her and she probably had a strong case, but decided not to pursue it after talking it over with Louis. "I showed her my Divorce Papers which convinced her immediately," he wrote. "I also told her that I was a changed man since I came to Chicago and married Lil. No more Boisterous—Barrelhouse stuff. Am trying to Cultivate Myself. Now we can be the very best of friends—And if there is anything that I can do within my power I will gladly do it. She said—that's fair enough."[26]

Louis and Daisy became better friends after the divorce than during their tumultuous marriage. "I ran into Daisy several times after that incident," Louis wrote. "And she and I would go to a Tavern and have a few Nips (drinks) together. And she told me that she wouldn't ever stop loving me no matter if we are not together. After all—I'm the only man she'll ever love as long as she live."[27] Louis enjoyed telling a story about a time Daisy heard someone "panning" him in "one of them beat up joints," he said. "And some son-of-a-bitch said something about me that she resented. And we still separated....And she resented it and she and this black son-of-a-bitch stood toe to toe with knives cutting on one another."

"Why, you motherfucker!" Daisy shouted before going on the attack.

"And goddamn, it was a cutting scrape there for hours," Louis said. He was touched by Daisy now wielding her razor in his defense instead of at his throat. "And I hadn't seen her, I mean, you know, intercourse-ly, for a long time!"[28] he joked. Daisy's death in 1950 didn't warrant a full obituary in any major newspapers; to this day, she has not been properly identified in a single photograph, but Louis learned to appreciate her love—intercourse-ly speaking and otherwise—for the rest of his life, too.

After the commotion over Daisy's appearance, the 1949 concert at Booker T. Washington Auditorium was further interrupted by the arrival of another special guest, as remembered by Blaine Kern, the future "Mr. Mardi Gras." "Then [Armstrong] stops playing and all of a sudden, he watches an old man coming down the aisle, walking towards him and Louis spots him," Kern said. "And Louis starts to cry. And the old man walks up on the stage and walks towards him and Louis is positively howling. The old man proceeds to unwrap this towel under his arm and he brings out a battered cornet. It was the first cornet that Louis ever played on in his life. And this old man gave it to him and he fell into the old man's arms and they were crying together. And laughing—it was glorious! The hair went up on the back of my neck. I remember this 50 years later to this day. . . . I witnessed history. Louis being back with his mentor and his first cornet."[29]

The mentor was Captain Joseph Jones of the Colored Waif's Home. Armstrong had stayed in touch with Captain Jones and his wife Manuella over the years, often sending them letters. "I shall never forget the people who has done everything for me," he wrote to them on November 3, 1937. "I feel as though although I am away from the waif's Home I am just on tour from my own home, I feel just that close at all times . . . I've never felt any different . . . Am always proud to tell the world of the place whom started me out as a first class Musician." He added, "I love you people . . . I never get's tired of tellin these people how swell you especially, Mr. Jones were to me when I was a little 'Punk Kid.'" In the same later, Louis referred to, "my Dad, Mr. Jones."[30]

The feeling was mutual. In 1951, Captain Jones finally retired after 43 years of carrying on "a crusade on behalf of neglected and delinquent Negro boys," as the *Times-Picayune* put it.[31] Armstrong was on tour and couldn't attend the ceremony in person, but he sent a telegram, which was answered by Jones. "Dear Son, Just a line from your Pop thanking you for your telegram," Jones opened, before stating, "All the musical cats, both white and colored, ask me to send hello to the king of them all, my favorite son, Louis 'Satchmo' Armstrong. Mom sends special love to you and says you ought to send her your photo. Wishing you continued success, your Pops, Capt. Joseph Jones, New Orleans, Louisiana."[32]

Jones passed away on April 20, 1957, but he left behind an important gift: that same "first cornet" he brought to the concert in 1949, which Manuella Jones donated to the New Orleans Jazz Museum in 1962, where it remains on display today. Asked in 1954 about why he saved it, Jones replied, "I keep it as an example to other Negro boys—to show them that someone who started in the slums of New Orleans has become one of the world's greatest musical artists."[33]

Peter Davis, Armstrong's other major influence at the Colored Waif's Home, also continued to spend many decades at the institution, remaining on staff after it changed its name to the Milne Boys Home. After he retired, Davis continued to teach music to boys there until Milne eventually dropped the music program altogether. "When the boys band was dropped from the music curriculum, Professor Davis was very unhappy," George Kay wrote. "He would drop by the school and talk to Superintendent [Dave] Dalgren about starting up another boys band."[34]

In 1965, Armstrong returned to New Orleans for the first time in a decade. Davis was there to meet him at the New Orleans Jazz Museum, holding a Marceau cornet he claimed was the first one Armstrong played. "When this man was teaching me to play do, re, mi, fa, so, la, ti, do, I had no idea it would end this way," Armstrong told the press. He turned to Davis and said, "You taught us how to get the rudamentals [rudiments]."[35]

But this reunion at the New Orleans Jazz Museum in October 1965 and a television appearance with Armstrong on *I've Got a Secret* in December 1965 marked the last times Davis was seen in public. He became "an elderly recluse with no close family" in the words of Kay; he was eventually admitted to the Prayer Tower Rest Home in 1968. Kay visited him there and brought along a tape recorder, hoping he could record a message to be played for Armstrong, but when he got there, Kay noted, "Peter at 91 could no longer comprehend or speak." No one else in the nursing home knew about Davis's career or the impact he had on young Louis Armstrong and hundreds of boys over the years. As Kay began to leave, a nurse said to him, " 'You know, I didn't dream that he was a music teacher at the Boys Home. He used to look up to me and say 'The boys, the boys, hear the boys?' I would answer, 'Peter, I don't hear any boys.' He would look at me again and say, 'The boys, the boys, don't you hear the boys? Hear them play their music? Hear them sing? They are my boys . . .' "

"You know, Peter Davis was really hearing the boys," Kay told the nurse. "The music he was hearing was definitely for real and it was just possible that he was hearing Little Louis Armstrong."

"Her words heightened our own emotions and I knew that the music that Peter Davis had given to Louis would never die," Kay concluded. "Louie has passed it on to the whole world."[36] Davis died on April 29, 1971, while Armstrong was being held in intensive care in New York City.

The final time Armstrong appeared in New Orleans was a performance at the first Jazzfest in May 1968. Mama Lucy skipped the concert, choosing to go to church instead; after her tough early years as a prostitute, gambler, and occasionally a criminal, she found religion later in life, even getting baptized as an adult. "Jesus sees everything," she told Yoshio Toyama in 1973. "And if you keep that pure heart and keep your hands clean, that's it. God is a clean man. He don't want no filth." But when asked if Louis was as religious as she was, Mama Lucy exclaimed, "That devil, he's never been baptized! He's never been baptized since he was a baby. But he got a better heart than a whole lot of people that done been under."[37]

Though she didn't attend her brother's final New Orleans performance, Mama Lucy did host an afterparty for close friends and family at her small home at 1926 Lesseps Street. Armstrong's clarinetist, Joe Muranyi, attended and recalled, "Louie's sister had a party and she cooked all the food, all the gumbo and the turkey and all that southern stuff. And it was just a marvelous night."

Also in attendance was Louis's half-brother, Henry. "You know, I used to play drums in the 20s and I feel maybe I should have gone to Chicago like Louis," Henry told Muranyi. Later that night, Muranyi said to Louis, "Hey, I talked to your brother Henry about playing the drums. Did he play drums, good drums?" "Ohhhh, come on!" Louis responded. "Are you kidding? He couldn't play at all!" "One of those family things you know, right?" Muranyi concluded, summing up Louis's relationships with Henry, who died in 1991, and with Willie Jr., who lived until 1996.[38]

Mama Lucy traveled to New York when Louis ended up in intensive care after a major heart attack in March 1971 and called to wish him a happy 71st birthday on July 4, 1971, after he returned home. Louis's fourth wife, Lucille, answered, before handing the phone over to Louis, who immediately played the trumpet over it for his sister to hear. "But y'know, honey," later recounted.

"He called me Beatrice, my right name and he never done that before. My poppa did the same thing when he was gettin' ready to die."[39]

After Louis passed away two days later, Mama Lucy traveled to Corona, Queens, for the somber funeral at Corona Congregational Church; it was not a traditional New Orleans funeral in any regard. *Toronto Sun* writer Paul Rimstead asked her, "How come Louis is being buried in New York?" "Mama Lucy looked up, and tears began streaming down her big cheeks," Rimstead reported. "She's his wife y'know," Mama Lucy said of Lucille. "She wants to bury my brother in New York. I can't say nothin' 'bout it."[40]

Lucille was eventually asked the same question and didn't mince words. "Except for his sister, Beatrice, and his half brothers, Henry and William Armstrong, he has nothing in New Orleans," she said at the time of his passing. "He hasn't lived in New Orleans since he was 19, and although he was born there, he considered New York his home. After all, he spent 40 years of his life here."[41]

"I'm his sister, he my brother, by mother, by father, whole," Mama Lucy said after her brother's funeral. "Now I got no more brother. But Jesus is with me, yeah. He's with me, my Lord. He took my momma, my poppa an' my brother. Now I'se all alone."[42] Mama Lucy remained alone, living a quiet life in New Orleans until she passed away in 1987.

But on July 4, 1973, Mama Lucy traveled back to New York to attend the dedication of Louis Armstrong Stadium in Queens, bringing along some important artifacts to give to Lucille: two framed, color-tinted portraits, one of her, Louis, and Mayann, and one of their father, Willie. "I carried it up to New York the Fourth of July," she said in August 1973. "Lucille is going to put it in the Museum. I took it off the wall, she asked for it, you know, going to put it in the museum about Louis."[43]

Lucille Armstrong died in 1983. Twenty years later, the home where she and Louis lived together for 28 years was opened to the public as the Louis Armstrong House Museum. And in 2023, the Louis Armstrong Center opened across the street. The portraits of Louis's mother and father finally took their place in a "museum about Louis" almost 50 years to the day after Mama Lucy brought them to Queens.

The fact that such a museum is located in Queens might be surprising to those accustomed to flying into Louis Armstrong International Airport in New Orleans in the twenty-first century. But as he once put it, Armstrong left New Orleans in 1922 and "got Northern-fied."[44]

In some ways, his true last hurrah in his hometown occurred when he was named King of the Zulus in 1949, the same week he became the first

Figure E.3 Beatrice "Mama Lucy" Armstrong at her home in New Orleans in August 1973, posing in front of a portrait of herself, her mother, and her brother.
Credit: Photo by Yoshio Toyama, courtesy of Yoshio Toyama.

Black jazz musician to grace the cover of *Time*. Yet at the concert at Booker T. Washington Auditorium, Armstrong reached back and performed "Shoe Shine Boy," a song he had introduced on Broadway in 1935, and passionately sang the autobiographical lyrics, the tale of a hard-working shoe-shine boy who works hard all day and has no time to play, yet remains "seldom ever blue" because "You're content with what you've got."

It was Louis—and Mayann's—personal philosophy, in song form, a message to those in the audience—including Daisy, Captain Jones, Mama Lucy, even Grandma Josephine—that perhaps he had become a big star on the cover of a major magazine, but deep down, he was still the same humble kid who sold newspapers and drove a coal cart through the Third Ward. On the eve of living out his boyhood dream of being crowned King of the Zulus, the last thing he was acting like was a king.

But by the late 1950s, Armstrong refused to set foot back home after a law was passed there prohibiting integrated bands from performing in public. "I ain't going back to New Orleans and let them white folks be whipping me on my head," he vented in 1959.[45] Ten years later, lying in intensive care, he bitterly wrote about how his hometown was always "disgustingly segregated."[46]

Yet though Armstrong could distance himself physically from the city of New Orleans, that city's DNA had become so inexorably part of his own DNA, he became a living embodiment of all his hometown had to offer—perhaps sometimes for worse, but far more often, for better.

Guitarist Danny Barker was once asked about what Armstrong got from New Orleans. "The most he got from New Orleans was his attitude," Barker began, before unleashing an insightful, rambling explanation of the effect his hometown had on Armstrong:

> He had a barrelhouse attitude, from the honky tonks to the heights. He never forgot his traits, where he came from or the things that was good to him: good times, to hear good music. . . . He never forgot this atmosphere. . . . And the most humble dish and the most greatest dish you have for anybody is red beans and rice with that ham in it. So he used to write some of his letters, "Red beans and ricely yours, Louis Armstrong." So that's New Orleans. . . . He remembers that, he remembers the good part of New Orleans. He remembers the people that helped him, the Blacks and the whites—he had a lot of white friends here when he was a kid and he never forgot. . . . That's one thing that strike me so much about Louie besides his playing was his benevolence, his goodness. . . . It's just his feel for people. Feel for people. If you see him on the stage, he come out, he could be insulted, he could have been abused or something. When he hit that stage and the spotlight was on him, he give you that smile. Everybody, just people—"Yeaaaaah! Yeah!" They called it Tomming—it wasn't Tomming! He just loved people![47]

Armstrong may have never moved back to New Orleans, but the lessons he learned in that city were present every time he stepped on stage or in a recording studio.

"You know, I never did leave New Orleans," he claimed in 1950. "Right now I keep the essence of New Orleans every time I play."[48]

"They say, 'Where would you live?'" Armstrong asked in a tape-recorded conversation made in 1965. "I said I don't care where, I'm born in New Orleans, that's my hometown. That's it. I don't care where, I'll go to Guadalupe, wherever it is—[I'm a] New Orleans boy, and that's it."[49]

Thus, it was fitting that the last words he sang on stage at the Waldorf in 1971 was the phrase "Boy from New Orleans." Armstrong knew what it meant to miss New Orleans, to love New Orleans, to celebrate New Orleans, to be hurt by New Orleans, and to hate New Orleans—but through it all, he knew that in many ways, he *was* New Orleans, with all of its complexities.

And over 50 years after his passing, he's *still* New Orleans.

Acknowledgments

I first fell under the spell of Louis Armstrong at the age of 15 when a chance viewing of *The Glenn Miller Story* led me to a compilation of Armstrong's 1950s Columbia sessions and the music that truly changed my life. A few months later, my parents bought me a lavish four-cassette boxed set for Christmas, *Portrait of the Artist as a Young Man*, focused on Armstrong's 1923–1934 output. It had received the previous year's Grammy for "Best Album Notes" for the influential essay and track-by-track analysis penned by two folks who became immediate and future heroes, Dan Morgenstern and Loren Schoenberg. With the passing of Dan in 2024, the jazz world lost its biggest advocate and I lost my mentor and friend. As Louis Armstrong said about Dizzy Gillespie, no him, no me.

The more I learned about Armstrong, the more it seemed that everyone agreed about the greatness of his early years; it was after 1928 when the biographers, critics, historians, and fans disagreed regarding his later career path: did he sell out? Did he go commercial? Did he waste his talent? Was he nothing but an Uncle Tom? I knew my response—a resounding no to each of those questions—and sought to learn as much as I could about Armstrong's post-1928 career, interviewing friends of his and the surviving musicians in his band, and eventually listening to all 700+ reel-to-reel tapes compiled by Armstrong himself, now a part of the Louis Armstrong House Museum, where I have served as director of research collections since 2009.

The results were two books, *What a Wonderful World: The Magic of Louis Armstrong's Later Years* and *Heart Full of Rhythm: The Big Band Years of Louis Armstrong*, as well as a slew of CD, LP, and streaming reissues I coproduced and/or wrote notes for, shining a big, broad spotlight on Armstrong's post-1928 career. I toyed with the idea of writing about his early years, but I felt that after his own *Satchmo: My Life in New Orleans* and the work of writers such as Gary Giddins, Laurence Bergreen, Thomas Brothers, Terry Teachout, Brian Harker, Gunther Schuller, and Robert O'Meally, there wouldn't be much more to add to the story.

If I had written about Armstrong's early years first and done the trilogy in strict chronological order, I would only have been able to rehash what had already been in print for many decades. It was never my intention to write the Armstrong saga in reverse chronological order, but it ended up being a blessing thanks to the sudden accessibility of several important sources that turned up in the last decade.

For example, in 2016, Michael Stearns, son of longtime Prentice Hall editor Monroe Stearns, contacted the Louis Armstrong House Museum. Michael was going through his father's late papers and had found an Armstrong-related document—did the Museum want it? The answer was a swift yes! when we discovered that it was a copy of Armstrong's original typewritten manuscript for *Satchmo: My Life in New Orleans.* Armstrong had not used a ghostwriter, though Prentice Hall did edit the book for punctuation and grammar, in addition to toning down the rhetoric at times. Thus, I now had Armstrong's raw, unedited words to pull from, to go along with the thousands of words he spoke on reel-to-reel tape or jotted down in letters and autobiographical manuscripts, all part of the Research Collections of the Museum.

Thus, my first thank-you must go to the staff and board of the Louis Armstrong House Museum for supporting my work and allowing me to oversee, for the last 15 years, the world's largest archive focusing on any single jazz musician. I'd like to single out our executive director, Regina Bain, as well as longtime staff members Hyland Harris, Adriana Carrillo, Junior Armstead, and Pedro Espinosa, not to mention Bruce Harris, Jake Goldbas, Sarah Rose, Brynn White, Ben Flood, Canan Vardal, Sandrine Frem, Charanya Ramakrishnan, Alexis Lubin, Stephen Maitland-Lewis, Jeff Rosenstock, Jay Hershenson, and all of the other wonderful staff members, volunteers, and docents I've been fortunate enough to work with over the years. Special thanks to the late Michael Cogswell and Jerry Chazen, not only for their support of me personally but also for their determination in spearheading the 25-year effort to open the Louis Armstrong Center across from the Armstrong House.

I also must thank Wynton Marsalis, Jackie Harris, and the entire board of the Louis Armstrong Educational Foundation for the ways they have supported my work over the years. My thanks also to the Jazz Department of the Aaron Copland School of Music at Queens College for letting me teach an entire course devoted to Armstrong year after year.

In the 1960s, Lillian Hardin Armstrong was befriended by the Danish jazz writer and historian Chris Albertson. The two began working on Lil's autobiography, which she aborted after only a few chapters because she didn't feel comfortable sharing so many details of her life with Louis when he was still alive. I was fortunate to befriend Chris in his later years and was saddened by his passing in 2019. After he died, the Jazz Foundation of America was able to temporarily move his belongings to a storage unit to which Armstrong House staff had access for exactly one day. It felt like looking for a needle in a haystack, but eventually the unpublished chapters from Lil's autobiography turned up buried in a filing cabinet. I was personally thrilled because now I was certain that Lil's voice would be able to play a bigger role in this story than ever before. Thank you to Hank O'Neal of the Jazz Foundation of America for making this possible.

It was quite a thrill to be involved as a consulting producer for the 2022 documentary *Louis Armstrong's Black and Blues*, produced by Apple TV and Imagine Documentaries. My sincere thanks to director Sacha Jenkins, producers Julie Anderson and Justin Wilkes, executive producer Ron Howard, editors Jason Pollard and Alma Herrera-Pazmiño, and especially tireless archival producer Amilca Palmer for having me along for the ride. It was Amilca who put me in touch with Geoffrey Haydon, who had conducted extensive interviews with both Lil and Louis Armstrong at their respective homes in November 1969—and kept the tapes. Geoffrey was kind enough to share these recordings with me in 2023, giving me access to even more previously unpublished stories from Louis and Lil.

It was also in 2023 that my friend Matthew "Fat Cat" Rivera joined the staff of the Louis Armstrong House Museum for nine months as part of a grant-funded project to hire a temporary archivist. Matt helped contribute to this book in more ways than can adequately be told and I'm forever in his debt for his assistance. At one point, Matthew acquired Zutty Singleton's personal photo collection from our mutual friend Dr. Albert Vollmer and was able to provide incredible scans of many of the photos that appear throughout this book. All hail the Fat Cat!

I first met trumpeter Yoshio Toyama—the "Satchmo of Japan"—and his wife, Keiko, during my first trip to Satchmo Summerfest in New Orleans back in 2008. We have remained very close friends over the years and have even shared the bandstand a few times, but it wasn't until just a few years ago that I learned that Yoshio had interviewed Louis's sister, Beatrice "Mama Lucy" Collins, back in 1973 and had digitized the audio. Yoshio was kind enough to send me a copy of the interview, as well as to grant me permission to publish the striking photo of Mama Lucy that concludes the book. Hearing Mama Lucy's stories for the first time was a life-changing experience and including her voice throughout the text was very important to me. It could not have happened without Yoshio—thanks a million, my friend!

Speaking of New Orleans, Tulane University has been very important to this book in a number of ways. First, I have always respected the work of Bruce Raeburn, longtime curator of Tulane's Hogan Jazz Archive, and am pleased to call him a friend. Some years ago, Bruce helped the Jazz Archive go live with its website "Music Rising," making available hundreds of oral history interviews of the pioneers of jazz, conducted over several decades on behalf of the archive. I spent countless hours with these recordings, allowing these voices from the past into the space to tell their stories of encountering the young Armstrong.

In 2022, I made a trip to Tulane and spent time with Hogan's wonderful current curator, Melissa Weber. This became one of the defining moments of the research process, as Melissa helped me access the research of the late Tad Jones. Let me state this in no uncertain terms: utilizing Tad's research was a complete game changer. I didn't make it to New Orleans until 2008, the year after Tad's untimely passing. Most Armstrong aficionados knew him as the man who'd discovered Armstrong's baptismal certificate, but I also knew that he had been researching the definitive book on Armstrong's New Orleans years. Working in the 1990s without the Internet, armed with only a pen and yellow legal pads, Tad filled up page after page with arrest records, business permits, census information, marriage records, newspaper transcriptions, and much, much more, material that was crucial to my research before much of it finally became available on Ancestry.com. I do hope that someday someone in New Orleans can execute Tad's original vision—he would have written a very different book from this one—and I just wish he was still around so I could thank him in person.

Melissa Weber also graciously set me up with the staff of Tulane University's Special Collections for assistance obtaining digital scans during the pandemic (thank you, Lori Schexnayder) and for obtaining permission to publish some photographs, including the striking one of Black Benny Williams (thank you, Agnieszka Czeblakow). Biggest thanks of all to Melissa herself for her friendship and support!

The Historic New Orleans Collection also provided incredible access to digital scans during the pandemic, especially of William Russell's notes on the interviews he conducted for the 1939 book *Jazzmen*; thank you Eric Seiferth and Rebecca Smith for making that happen. I was also able to publish photos from the William Russell Jazz Collection at the Historic New Orleans Collection; many thanks to Jennifer Navarre for her assistance.

The New Orleans Jazz Museum has always treated me like family and I'm greatly in their debt for allowing me to publish several photos from their astounding archives. Thank you to Greg Lambousy, David Kunian, Michael Leatham, and Erin Patterson specifically for their help. The New Orleans Jazz Museum is also the physical home of Satchmo Summerfest every August. Thanks to the whole French Quarter Festivals team for having me year after year and to Jon Pult for "discovering" me and bringing me down there the first time in 2008.

During a memorable Satchmo Summerfest trip in 2022, I was fortunate to receive a driving tour of Louis Armstrong's New Orleans with one of my favorite trumpeters and human beings on the planet, Wendell Brunious, along with his charming wife, Caroline. They were so gracious as to take me around the West End, the site of the Waif's Home, the Third Ward, and all points in between, a true highlight of the research process (though perhaps only topped by the home-cooked meal Wendell and Caroline made for my wife and me the following year!).

Since Tad Jones passed, no one in New Orleans has made as many groundbreaking discoveries about Armstrong's early years as my friend James Karst. I thank him for his tireless efforts in researching the early life of Armstrong, Buddy Bolden, and other greats from that era. To close my exhaustive New Orleans thank-yous, let me quickly thank Randy Fertel, Gwen Thompkins, the staff at the Louisiana Music Factory, WWOZ Radio, Dan Meyer, John McCusker, Bjorn Barheim, the editors of *64 Parishes*, and every musician who has let me sit in and murder a piano.

Outside of New Orleans, I thank my Institute of Jazz Studies family (there's that word again) at Rutgers-Newark, where I received my master's in jazz history and research 20 years ago with major help from my mentor, Lewis Porter, who continues doing wonderful work now on Substack. Big thanks to Wayne Winbourne, Vincent Pelote, Elizabeth Surles, and Adriana Cuervo for their help at the Institute. Over in New York, Jazz at Lincoln Center has very kindly let me teach various Armstrong-related courses over the years; thanks to Seton Hawkins and Todd Stoll for those opportunities. And extra thanks to Greg Scholl, Nancy Gallegher, and Kay Wolff for their help in obtaining the rights to publish some wonderful images from the Frank Driggs Collection.

While working on this book, my pal Colin Hancock—a marvelous multiinstrumentalist, historian, and all-around genius—recommended me to write the liner notes for a King Oliver boxed set for Archeophone Records. Working with Rich Martin and Meagan Hennessey was a terrific experience, and their feedback strengthened my writing on Armstrong and Oliver. I urge you to check out *Centennial* on Archeophone Records for a perfect soundtrack to this book. And on the subject of record companies, thank you to Scott Wenzel of Mosaic Records and Ken Druker of Verve Records for allowing me to coproduce so many Armstrong reissues over the years—with hopefully more on the way.

When it came time to choose folks to read the manuscript and offer feedback, I looked no further than two of my closest friends in the world, David Ostwald and Michael Steinman. Every paragraph was vetted by David and

Michael and they were not afraid to push back when it seemed like I had lost focus or contradicted myself. I cannot thank them enough for the many, many hours they devoted to helping make this book the best it could possibly be, but more than that, I simply thank them for their friendship.

I have also greatly benefited from getting to know multiple descendants of the Karnofsky family. Judge Jacob Karno, still residing in New Orleans, shared numerous documents on the family's history and was gracious enough to allow me to publish the Karnofsky family photo. In 2019, I had the thrill of showing Karnofsky descendant Rosina Carpantier around the Louis Armstrong House Museum, enthralled by her memories of "Mama" Tillie Karnofsky; Rosina has since passed away but I'm grateful to Roberta Berner for making that visit happen. And Ken Karnofsky not only has become a friend but also, in a true example of fulfilling his family's legacy, donated instruments to the Louis Armstrong House Museum so we could begin offering trumpet lessons to kids on the block—the Armstrong-Karnofsky connection remains strong into the 21st century!

There are so many other people to thank that I just know I'm going to forget someone, but for now, let me just call out a few special people that have been there for me on this journey: Loren Schoenberg, Rob Rothberg, Dan Morgenstern, Bob Borgen, Bob O'Meally, Gary Giddins, Andrew Sammut, Allen Lowe, Jon Faddis, Catherine Russell, Paul Kahn, Steven Lasker, Brad Kay, Marc Caparone, Jonathan David Holmes, Peter Gerler, Richard and Vicki Noorigian, Reno Wilson, Tom Langdon, Alphonso Horne, Bria Skonberg, Ted Gioia, Larry Tye, Maxine Gordon, Tad Hershorn, Stephanie Crease, Ethan Iverson, Donna and Perry Golkin, Maristella Feustle, Jonathan Eig, Jason Moran, Nicholas Payton, Dave Whitney, Mike Persico, Phil Person, Matt Glaser, Rafael Castillo-Halvorssen, David Sager, Emrah Erken, Nick Dellow (who helped with some marvelous photo restorations), Babbette Ory, Bill Stafford, Tim Fitak, Dr. Colleen Clark, Greg Beaman, Sam Irwin, and anyone else who has ever encouraged me during this lifelong endeavor.

I'd also like to just say thank you to two special people who are no longer with us, Jack Bradley and George Avakian. Both men were very close with Louis and I was fortunate to learn so much from them in the years they befriended me. Both also seemed to "check in" during the writing of this book. At one point, when I thought I was finished, I stumbled across a series of handwritten notes in the Jack Bradley Collection at the Louis Armstrong House Museum, filled with quotes and details Bradley jotted down in the 1960s during his many conversations with Louis; I managed to sneak some in at the eleventh hour. But perhaps the craziest story revolves around a series of reel-to-reel tape conversations Avakian had with Armstrong back in 1953.

Avakian found six of these tapes in 1993 and had copies made; David Ostwald was kind enough to share them with me and I've transcribed and studied them all. Before George passed away, his collection was acquired by the New York Public Library, where it was processed by our mutual friend Matt Snyder. In late 2022, Matt contacted me because he found a *seventh* tape from 1953 in a mislabeled box and asked if I would like to hear it. Within seconds, there was Louis talking about the Fisk School in New Orleans! For the interview on this entire "lost" tape, Avakian had a copy of the manuscript to *Satchmo: My Life in New Orleans* and asked Armstrong nothing but questions about his early years. Discovering this tape at the last second was a godsend and I couldn't help but feel that George—and perhaps Louis—wanted to make sure I didn't miss it.

Extra special thanks to my longtime agent, Tony Outhwaite, who took me on as a client after hearing me breathlessly talk about later Armstrong over a meal at the Grammercy Tavern back in 2006 and is still with me three books later. And sincere thanks to my wonderful editor, Lauralee Yeary, who nudged me about doing this book just two months after my previous book was published, and Project Editor Rachel Ruisard who has truly gone above and beyond at every step in the process. Working with Lauralee, Rachel, James Perales, Henry Wilkinson, Bridget Austiguy-Preschel, and the entire publicity team, copyeditors, and staff of Oxford University Press is a dream.

I've used the word "family" multiple times in the previous paragraphs because the jazz world truly does feel like a family sometimes. But I must close by thanking my actual family, who have been with me every step of the way during this crazy journey. Everything begins with my parents, who sensed my deep interest in Armstrong early on and did all they could to support it, taking me to bookstores, record stores, concerts, and everything in between. I think they knew that I was going to write a book before I knew it and I'm thrilled they've been able to see all three books reach the finish line. I couldn't have done it without them. I also must thank my brother (and comedy partner), Jeff, sister, Michele, brother-in-law, Gary, nephews Connor and Nicky, nieces Gianna and Bell for all their support along the way (and we all miss you, Tyler).

Finally, there are my ladies, beginning with my wife, Margaret, who has now stuck with me through thick and thin, during my years as a house painter, through numerous rejections of book proposals, through stressful times at work, and so much more. She's had to shoulder the load with the kids for three separate books and I'm so lucky she is still by my side 20 years later. She's got gaps, I've got gaps, together we fill gaps.

Margaret is also responsible for helping me land the role I really felt born to play, that of a father to three amazing daughters, Ella, Melody, and Lily. My kids were initially disappointed when I told them I was going to write another book so soon after *Heart Full of Rhythm*, with Ella saying, "You just wrote one! You mean we're going to lose you again?" I tried my best not to get "lost" while writing this one but now that it is behind me, I have no immediate plans to write anything else anytime soon, so I'd like to spend as much time as possible laughing with my girls. They bring me more joy than I ever knew was possible.

And let the record show that the same goes for our dogs, Frida and Louie, because once again, if I left them out of the acknowledgments, I would be the one living in the doghouse, not them.

Notes

Epigraph

1. Jack Bradley, "A Symposium on Louis Armstrong," *Saturday Review*, July 4, 1970. This quote comes from the cassette containing the entire original, unedited interview, Jack Bradley Collection, 2005.1.2184, Louis Armstrong House Museum.
2. Beatrice "Mama Lucy" Armstrong, Interview with Yoshio Toyama, 1973. Courtesy of Yoshio Toyama.
3. Frank Hurlock, editor, *Jazz Reprints* (Jazz Pamphlet Society, 1961).
4. Lillian Hardin Armstrong, BBC interview with Geoffrey Haydon, November 10, 1969, courtesy of Geoffrey Haydon.
5. Louis Armstrong, Tape 1987.3.407, recorded May 27, 1970, Louis Armstrong House Museum.

Prologue

1. "Waldorf-Astoria Opens New Empire Room September 18," press release, September 10, 1969, http://waldorfnewyorkcity.com/archive/items/show/630.
2. Louis Armstrong, letter to Dr. Gary Zucker, October 8, 1968, Louis Armstrong House Museum, Corona, NY, 1996.7.2.
3. Louis Armstrong, letter to Dr. Gary Zucker, December 29, 1970, Louis Armstrong House Museum, 1996.7.2.
4. Contract between Louis Armstrong and the Waldorf-Astoria, January 18, 1971, Louis Armstrong House Museum, 1987.10.16.
5. Dr. Gary Zucker, oral history with Michael Cogswell, 1996, Louis Armstrong House Museum, 1996.51.1.
6. John S. Wilson, "Louis Armstrong Takes to Horn in His Comeback at the Waldorf," *New York Times*, March 2, 1971, 60.
7. Earl Wilson, "It Happened Last Night," *Camden Courier-Post*, March 4, 1971, 55.
8. Lil Hardin, *Jazzmen* notes, William Russell Jazz Collection, Historic New Orleans Collection, MSS519.F.14.
9. Eddie Adams, "The Last Trumpet Note," undated Associated Press clipping, Louis Armstrong House Museum, 1987.7.22.
10. Richard Meryman, "Satchmo, the Greatest of All, Is Gone," *Life*, July 16, 1971, 71.
11. Gunther Schuller, *Early Jazz* (New York: Oxford University Press, 1967), 130.
12. Al Rose, *I Remember Jazz* (Baton Rouge: Louisiana State University Press, 1999), 127.
13. Andrea Young, conversation with the author, November 16, 2018.

Chapter 1

1. "World War I Draft Cards: Louis Armstrong," https://www.archives.gov/atlanta/wwi-draft/armstrong.html.
2. "U.S. Social Security Act Application for Account Number," May 25, 1937, Louis Armstrong House Museum, 2001.91.1.
3. Gary Giddins, "Happy Birthday, Pops," *Village Voice*, August 23, 1988, 10.
4. Robert Goffin, *Horn of Plenty* (New York: Allen, Towne & Heath, 1947), 10.
5. "Louis Armstrong's Birthday: The Debate Continues," *Offbeat*, August 2000, 50.
6. Jason Berry, interview with Beatrice "Mama Lucy" Armstrong, 1983, Tad Jones Collection, Hogan Archive of New Orleans Music and New Orleans Jazz, Tulane University.
7. Max Jones, John Chilton, and Leonard Feather, *Salute to Satchmo* (London: I.P.C. Specialist & Professional Press, 1970), 47.
8. Louis Armstrong, "The Armstrong Story," unedited manuscript for *Satchmo: My Life in New Orleans*, Louis Armstrong House Museum, 2016.80.1. Armstrong typed up his own manuscript, which he then sent to Prentice Hall for editing. Armstrong's idiosyncratic typing style has mostly been retained throughout this book, but there have been light edits to remove potentially confusing punctuation marks.
9. "A search for his wife with a revolver in either hand cost George H. Waterman his life last night," the *New Orleans Times-Democrat* reported. "He was shot to death at 9:30 o'clock by his brother-in-law, Albert Duncan, a young mulatto. Duncan put the contents of a double-barrel shotgun, loaded with buckshot, into him, and his death was instantaneous." "Filled with Shot," *New Orleans Times-Democrat*, July 17, 1901, 8.
10. Tad Jones, "Armstrong in New Orleans," 2001 Louis Armstrong Centennial Conference presentation video, Louis Armstrong House Museum 2002.064.03.
11. Jones et al., *Salute to Satchmo*, 49.
12. Michael Steinman, "Louis Eternally," Jazz Lives blog, July 4, 2015, https://jazzlives.wordpress.com/2015/07/04/louis-eternally/. For the sake of completeness, it should also be mentioned that there *was* a homicide on the corner of Tulane Avenue and Rampart Street at 4:30 p.m. on July 3, 1901, when ex–deputy sheriff John McDonell shot and killed current deputy sheriff Alexander Mouledous after an altercation in Sam Bagnetto's saloon. The murder took place one and a half miles away from Jane Alley, which seems to disqualify it from the category of taking place in Mayann's neighborhood, but it did receive much publicity in the press beginning on July 4, so perhaps the buzz over the murder of a deputy sheriff was what Mayann associated with Louis's birth. See "Liquor the Cause," *New Orleans Times Democrat*, July 4, 1901, 6. The full police report can be viewed online at https://cjrc.osu.edu/sites/cjrc.osu.edu/files/new-orleans-1901.pdf.
13. It wouldn't be the first clerical error of this kind. Just in the writing and researching of this book, I have come across wildly differing dates of birth for Armstrong contemporaries such as King Oliver, Baby Dodds, Jelly Roll Morton, and many others. "As someone who spends quite a bit of time in various New Orleans archives every week, I can say that the record keeping around 1900 wasn't always top notch," Greg Beaman, director of research for the Claiborne Avenue History Project and an authority on urban slavery in New Orleans, said in 2015. Beaman, who researches historic properties, added, "If the clerks documenting property transactions worth thousands of dollars got these minor details wrong, who's to say the person documenting the birth of a child from Back of Town got it right?" Greg Beaman, correspondence with the author, July 4, 2015.

14. Tad Jones, interviewed by Peggy Scott Laborde for the WYES documentary *Satchmo in New Orleans*, summer 1990, raw interview transcript, Tad Jones Collection, Hogan Archive of New Orleans Music and New Orleans Jazz. In his 2023 book *Hidden History of Louisiana's Jazz Age*, Sam Irwin posits an interesting theory about why Armstrong would have chosen such a date and how it relates a common practice of poor African Americans choosing a holiday to celebrate their birth because they didn't know the real date; but Louis and his sister's remembrances of celebrating his birthday on the Fourth of July at a young age seem to illustrate that Louis was told he was born July 4 and did not choose it himself. Sam Irwin, *The Hidden History of Louisiana's Jazz Age* (Charleston, South Carolina: The History Press, 2023), 68–87.
15. Geraldine Wyckoff, "Louis Armstrong: Born on the Fourth of July?," *Offbeat*, August 1, 2013, https://www.offbeat.com/articles/louis-armstrong-born-on-the-fourth-of-july/.
16. Dan Vernhettes and Bo Lindstöm, *Jazz Puzzles*, vol. 2 (France: Jazzedit, 2015), 41.
17. "Louis Daniel Armstrong faced the alternatives—an ignominious chase through the streets of New Orleans in Nature's soup-and-fish, or a halt to don his pants, and by delaying, perhaps be caught and thus miss the music lesson?" Bettie Edwards, "Louis—A Study in Brown," *Melody Maker*, January 27, 1934, 22.
18. Marion Gustowski, conversation with the author, March 27, 2024.
19. Armstrong, "The Armstrong Story," 35.
20. Jones et al., *Salute to Satchmo*, 51–52.
21. It should be noted that Josephine Armstrong gave her age as 58 in the 1920 census and when she died in 1950, her death record claimed she was 90 years old, meaning that she added at least four to six years to her age as she got older.
22. New Orleans Health Dept. Death Certificate as kept by the Records of Births, Marriage, and Deaths, vol. 83, p. 733, Tad Jones Collection, Hogan Archive of New Orleans Music and New Orleans Jazz. See also "Vital Statistics," New Orleans *Daily Picayune*, October 1, 1883, 1.
23. Records for an "Ephraim" Armstrong are easy to find in Mobile—the 1870 census lists him as a servant born in 1844 and he was still living there in 1876, operating a cotton press—but nothing turns up from his years in New Orleans. However, later records show that Josephine gave birth to another son in 1896 and named him Ephram—the father of that son is not known but the 1920 census states that Ephram's father was born in Alabama! So it's possible that the younger Ephram was born much earlier than 1896 or Josephine conceived him with another man from Alabama.
24. Book 170, folio 209, Sale John Maltry Sr. to Ms. Florentine Johnson, December 21, 1897, Tad Jones Collection, Hogan Archive of New Orleans Music and New Orleans Jazz.
25. According to their marriage certificate, dated February 18, 1882, Mary Davis took the name Mary Albert. Thomas Johnson was one of the witnesses. Tad Jones Collection, Hogan Archive of New Orleans Music and New Orleans Jazz.
26. Louis's sister, Beatrice, born in 1903, believed the same thing. Asked about Isaac Myles's son Ike, Beatrice told Yoshio Toyama, "That's my mother's sister's child," in other words, Frances Johnson's child. There's also the possibility that young Frances Johnson was Mary Albert's *mother*, giving birth to her after a dalliance with the Albert family living next door in Boutte, and simply posed as an older sister. If the dates are correct, Frances Johnson was born in 1872 and would have been 13 when Mary Albert was born in 1885. Beatrice "Mama Lucy" Armstrong, interview with Yoshio Toyama, August 19, 1973. Interview courtesy of Yoshio Toyama.

27. Bob Rusch, "Louis Armstrong: Interview," *Cadence*, January 1986, 7.
28. For consistency, the spelling "Frances Johnson" and "Isaac Myles" will be used throughout this book, but Frances is also referenced as "Francis," and the "Myles" surname was often spelled "Miles" (including by Louis himself), in addition to typos such as "Myler," "Meyers," and "Mills."
29. John Maltry sold Johnson's promissory note to a man named Alphonse Nobles, who filed suit in Civil District Court on June 7, 1900. By July 20, the *Daily Picayune* offered a "Judicial Advertisement" for "Sale of Improved Property Known As No. 723 Jane Alley." The property was eventually seized by civil sheriff H. B. McMurray and sold at a public auction in early 1901, but the Myles family was able to continue renting the property for at least a couple more years. "Judicial Advertisement," *Daily Picayune*, July 20, 1900, 6.
30. Louis Armstrong, "Louis Armstrong + the Jewish Family in New Orleans, La., the Year of 1907," handwritten manuscript composed by Louis Armstrong between 1969 and 1970, Louis Armstrong House Museum 1987.2.1, 38.
31. "Cozy Single Cottage," *Daily Picayune*, January 6, 1901, 19.
32. Tad Jones, "Armstrong in New Orleans."
33. Goffin, *Horn of Plenty*, 3.
34. Louis Armstrong, "The Armstrong Synopsis," December 5, 1950, Louis Armstrong House Museum, 1987.2.4, 1. Louis's sister, Beatrice, also continued saying "James Alley" as late as the 1973 interview with Yoshio Toyama. Beatrice "Mama Lucy" Armstrong, interview with Yoshio Toyama, August 19, 1973.
35. Louis Armstrong, "The Armstrong Story," 1.
36. Ibid.
37. Rusch, "Louis Armstrong: Interview," 8.
38. Armstrong, "The Armstrong Story," 3.
39. Armstrong, "Louis Armstrong + the Jewish Family," 38.
40. Louis Armstrong and George Avakian, tape recorded conversation, October 24, 1953. Louis Armstrong House Museum, Tape 1993.1.3.
41. The census reports at least five children—Jeremiah, Louise, Sarah, Edward and Flora—but Louis remembered more, listing the full family as "Isaac Miles, Aaron Miles, Jerry Miles, Willie Miles, Louisa Miles, Sarah'ann Miles, and Flora Miles," in addition to "Uncle Ike."
42. Jason Berry, Interview with Beatrice "Mama Lucy" Armstrong, 1983, Tad Jones Collection, Hogan Archive of New Orleans Music and New Orleans Jazz.
43. Armstrong, "Louis Armstrong + The Jewish Family," 38.
44. Armstrong, "The Armstrong Story," 1–2. Josephine supported young Louis with the money she made as a washerwoman. Louis fondly recalled going with his grandmother to her job, playing hide-and-seek with the white kids in the neighborhood as she did the laundry. In a story eventually sanitized for publication, Louis described finding the perfect hiding place: "Immediately, a thought came into my head to make a mad dash, and get up under her dress before the kids could find out where I had gone." Louis finally had to stick his head out after his grandmother farted! As the white kids called him out, a dejected Louis uttered, "Yall' would'nt have 'caught me if grandma hadn't pooted............."
45. Ibid., 2–3.
46. Charles L. Sanders, "The Reluctant Millionaire," *Ebony*, November 1964, 142. When Yoshio Toyama asked Louis's sister, Beatrice, for any memories of her grandmother, she immediately responded, "Our parents' parents was enslaved. See, my mother's folks, my father's folks, they was enslaved, like my mother was." Clearly, slavery was a recurring topic in

conversations with Louis's grandmother and great-grandmother. Beatrice "Mama Lucy" Armstrong, interview with Yoshio Toyama, August 19, 1973.

47. Jack Bradley, handwritten notes on a conversation with Louis Armstrong, October 1967, Louis Armstrong House Museum 2008.3.397.
48. Goffin, *Horn of Plenty*, 18–19.
49. Armstrong, "The Armstrong Story," 1. In the original manuscript, typed by Armstrong, he originally typed "whether Mayann was selling fish" before crossing out those two words and writing "HUSTLING" in the margin. Armstrong expounded on the subject of "whores vs. prostitutes" in a 1953 conversation with George Avakian, saying, "Down in the red light district, what you call the prostitutes, where they get five dollars for a job, the whores where I'm talking about, up in my neighborhood, they get 50 cents to a dollar." Tape 1993.1.3, Louis Armstrong House Museum.
50. "Jealous Negro Shoots," *Daily Picayune*, April 24, 1906, 13.
51. Armstrong, "The Armstrong Story," 3.
52. "Drouth Now Serious," *The Times-Democrat*, June 1, 1906, 5. Tad Jones placed Louis's return to his mother in 1905, believing Mayann was suffering from yellow fever, which wreaked havoc in New Orleans that year, but new research shows Mayann didn't move to 1303 Perdido until after April 1906, around the same time as the drought.
53. Armstrong, "The Armstrong Story," 4.
54. Ibid., 4–5.

Chapter 2

1. Armstrong, "Louis Armstrong + the Jewish Family," 6.
2. Armstrong, "The Armstrong Story," 5–6.
3. Louis Armstrong, private taped conversation with publicist Lloyd Von Blaine, October 1970, Louis Armstrong House Museum 1987.3.430.
4. Ibid.
5. Armstrong, "The Armstrong Story," 29. "You've got the chief of police, all the detectives and judges on one side of the street and on the other side of the street, all this prostitution and carrying on," Tad Jones said. Unsuspecting visitors to the neighborhood would pay the saloonkeepers for drinks, pay a prostitute for action, and if they got arrested and thrown in jail, they'd have to pay a lawyer, and eventually pay a fine. "There was a whole political system, from the government to the saloon owners, that was a wonderful little circle of depriving anyone who came in of all their money," Jones said. Quoted in Michael Jastroch, "In Search of Louis Armstrong's New Orleans," *Offbeat*, August 2005, 46–47.
6. Armstrong, "The Armstrong Story," 7.
7. Armstrong, "The Armstrong Synopsis," 2.
8. Ibid., 3.
9. Jones et al., *Salute to Satchmo*, 53.
10. Quoted in Jastroch, "In Search of Louis Armstrong's New Orleans," 51.
11. Armstrong, "The Armstrong Story," 16.
12. Ibid., 8.
13. Louis Armstrong interview with Willis Conover, Voice of America broadcast, recorded July 13, 1956, Music Library, University of North Texas Libraries, Digital Library, https://digital.library.unt.edu.

14. William Russell, interview with Louis Armstrong for *Jazzmen*, January 18, 1939, MSS 519 F. 16, William Russell Oral History Collection Series, William Russell Jazz Collection, Williams Research Center, Historic New Orleans Collection.
15. For more, see James Karst, "Buddy Bolden's Blues," *64 Parishes*, June 1, 2020, https://64parishes.org/buddy-boldens-blues.
16. Armstrong, "The Armstrong Synopsis," 4.
17. Ibid., 3.
18. Ibid.
19. Armstrong, "The Armstrong Story," 7.
20. Beatrice "Mama Lucy" Armstrong, interview with Yoshio Toyama, August 19, 1973.
21. Armstrong, "The Armstrong Story," 7.
22. Beatrice "Mama Lucy" Armstrong, interview with Yoshio Toyama, August 19, 1973. Not even her brother Louis ever knew the full story. Asked on *The Mike Douglas Show* if he gave her the nickname, Louis replied, "No, she had it when I dug her name the first time!" *The Mike Douglas Show*, May 28, 1970. Audio available at the Louis Armstrong House Museum, Tape 1987.3.407.
23. Private tape made with George Avakian, October 24, 1953. Courtesy of David Ostwald and George Avakian.
24. "The School Board Elects Teachers," *Times-Picayune*, June 30, 1900, 3.
25. Nicholas Bauer, "Annual Report, 1902," Notations on Various Schools, Orleans Parish School Board Collection, Louisiana and Special Collections, Earl K. Long Library, University of New Orleans, 1903–1906, 1909, p. 18.
26. Armstrong, *Satchmo: My Life in New Orleans* (New York: Prentice Hall, 1954), 28.
27. James (b. November 1879); O'donnell (b. July 1882); Casimere (b. June 14, 1884); Walter (b. December 23, 1885); Henry (b. June 12, 1892); Wilhelmina (b. February 15, 1896); Orlenia (b. April 8, 1900); and Alice (b. January 15, 1902).
28. Armstrong, "The Armstrong Story," 12. Armstrong also developed one of his earliest crushes on Wilhelmina Martin, though he never acted on it because "At that time, I had a sort of inferiority complex," he later wrote. In his autobiography, Armstrong lamented that "the poor girl died before I got up the nerve to tell her" his feelings, insinuating perhaps a teenage death, but records show that she passed away on September 20, 1933, at the age of 37, meaning Louis most likely carried a torch for her into his early thirties, possibly even reuniting with her during his 1931 trip back home. Louis Armstrong, *Satchmo: My Life in New Orleans*, 31.
29. Ibid.
30. Private tape made with George Avakian, October 24, 1953. New York Public Library for the Performing Arts, George Avakian and Anahid Ajemian Collection.
31. Drummer Joe Watkins was born on October 24, 1900, and went to Fisk School at the same time Louis did. Asked in 1961 if Fisk had any music program, Watkins responded, "They didn't teach us no music there." Joe Watkins, Interviewed by Richard B. Allen, January 20, 1961, Hogan Archive of New Orleans Music and New Orleans Jazz.
32. *The Mike Douglas Show*, May 25, 1970. Audio available at the Louis Armstrong House Museum, Tape 1987.3.406.
33. Armstrong, "The Armstrong Story," 10.
34. Armstrong, "Louis Armstrong + The Jewish Family," 43.
35. Armstrong, "The Armstrong Story," 11.
36. Ibid.

37. Ibid., 158–160.
38. Meryman, *A Self-Portrait*, 52.
39. "F. D. A. Bans Sweet Spirits of Nitre as Ineffective and Possibly Fatal," in the *New York Times*, October 12, 1980
40. Louis Armstrong with Richard Meryman, *Louis Armstrong: A Self-Portrait* (New York: The Eakins Press, 1971), 52
41. Jones et al., *Salute to Satchmo*, 57.
42. Armstrong, "The Armstrong Story," 10.
43. Beatrice "Mama Lucy" Armstrong, Interview with Yoshio Toyama, August 19, 1973.
44. Armstrong, "The Armstrong Story," 10.
45. Beatrice "Mama Lucy" Armstrong, Interview with Yoshio Toyama, August 19, 1973.
46. Armstrong, "The Armstrong Story," 10–11.
47. Beatrice "Mama Lucy" Armstrong, Interview with Yoshio Toyama, August 19, 1973.
48. Armstrong, "The Armstrong Story," 11.
49. Beatrice "Mama Lucy" Armstrong, Interview with Yoshio Toyama, August 19, 1973.
50. Armstrong, "The Armstrong Story," 11.
51. Armstrong, "Louis Armstrong + the Jewish Family," 8.
52. Ibid.
53. Goffin, *Horn of Plenty*, 20.
54. Beatrice "Mama Lucy" Armstrong, Interview with Yoshio Toyama, August 19, 1973.
55. Goffin, *Horn of Plenty*, 28.
56. Beatrice "Mama Lucy" Armstrong, Interview with Yoshio Toyama, August 19, 1973.
57. Tad Jones, draft of unpublished manuscript, courtesy of Michael Cogswell.
58. Armstrong, "The Armstrong Story," 3.
59. Armstrong, "Louis Armstrong + the Jewish Family," 45.
60. This also contradicts the 1900 and later 1920 censuses, which claimed Mayann could read, as well as Louis's own recollection.
61. Jason Berry, Interview with Beatrice "Mama Lucy" Armstrong, 1983, Tad Jones Collection, Hogan Archive of New Orleans Music and New Orleans Jazz.
62. "Both Men Confident," *New Orleans Times-Democrat*, July 4, 1910, 3.
63. Armstrong, "The Armstrong Story," 14.
64. Armstrong, "The Armstrong Synopsis," 4–5. Armstrong added, "we use to play cow boys and Indians together with the brick bats and stuff around the old delapidated [*sic*] houses." In his typed manuscript, Armstrong sensed the need for a joke to lighten the tension and grabbed a pen to write in the margin, "we were the Indians of course."
65. Armstrong, "Louis Armstrong + The Jewish Family," 30–31.
66. Armstrong, "The Armstrong Story," 15.
67. *The David Frost Show*, with guest host Orson Welles, June 9, 1970.

Chapter 3

1. "Chinatown Fire from Combustion," *New Orleans Times-Democrat*, October 18, 1910, 5.
2. James Karst, "Exclusive: New Details Emerge about Satchmo's Arrest at 9," *The Times-Picayune*, April 30, 2017.
3. "A Juvenile Roundup," *The Daily Picayune*, October 22, 1910, 4.
4. Bob Morris, "Cap Jones," *The Second Line*, May–June 1957, 13.

5. Will Buckingham, "Louis Armstrong and the Waifs' Home," *The Jazz Archivist*, 2011, 3.
6. Morris, "Cap Jones," 13.
7. "To Aid Wayward Child," *New Orleans Times-Democrat*, September 1, 1910, 280.
8. "Joseph Jones" file, Hogan Archive of New Orleans Music and New Orleans Jazz.
9. Jones, *Salute to Satchmo*, 54. Beatrice "Mama Lucy" Armstrong was also emphatic that her brother never went to the Waif's Home more than one time, but she was only seven at the time of this arrest and might have been living with her godmother, making it entirely possible that this incident occurred without her knowledge.
10. Ibid., 53.
11. Armstrong didn't pull this thought out of thin air; in multiple censuses and official documents, the heads of the family listed their birthplace as "Russia." However, their "Petition for Naturalization" lists "Wilky, Russia" and sure enough, the Yiddish word for Vilkija is "Vilky." Family historian Judge Jacob Karno adds, "The name of Karnofsky was derived from a small hamlet known as Karnowo, also located on the Nemunas River between Vilkija and Kovno (today known as Kaunas), Lithuania." Judge Jacob Karno, email to the author, December 22, 2021.
12. Joyce Kay, "Around the World in 80 Years: Migration of the Karnovsky Family," in *Karnofsky Family Reunion* (self-published, 2002), 58. The names of the Karnofsky children were Gussie, Harry Meyer, Morris, Alexander, Hyman, Lillian, David, Sarah, Eva, and Samuel. Louis Karnofsky most likely met other relatives while in New Orleans, such as Rubin Karnofski, who ran a clothing shop first at 640 South Rampart Street and later at 738 South Rampart; Rubin's brother, also named Louis, who ran a secondhand store at 209 South Rampart Street; and Abraham Karnofsky, a "junk dealer" living at 722 Saratoga.
13. Louis Armstrong, letter to Leonard Feather, October 1, 1941, Louis Armstrong House Museum, 1987.9.10.
14. Armstrong, "The Armstrong Story," 39.
15. Louis Armstrong, "Storyville," *True* magazine, November 1947, 32, 100.
16. Goffin, *Horn of Plenty*, 41.
17. Dr. Gary Zucker, interview with Michael Cogswell, January 26, 1996. Louis Armstrong House Museum 1996.51.1.
18. Armstrong, "Louis Armstrong + The Jewish Family," 4, 61.
19. All Karnofsky family documents in this section courtesy of Judge Jacob Karno, with various gaps filled through Ancestry.com searches.
20. The Armstrongs were certainly no strangers to the many Jewish families in their neighborhood; in fact, Beatrice remembered, "You know, my god-father was a white man. I couldn't understand that. He used to have a shop on Magnolia Street. On the corner. Cause I used to go there and he'd give me money. But I didn't know what that money was for. I said, 'How does a white man treat a black baby like me?' " Mama Lucy couldn't remember the man's name in 1983, but Tad Jones identified him most likely as Isaac Rabinowitz, whose World War I Draft Registration card tells us was born on March 23, 1889, and whose shop was at 3316 Magnolia Street. Jason Berry, Interview with Beatrice "Mama Lucy" Armstrong, 1983. Hogan Archive of New Orleans Music and New Orleans Jazz, Tulane University, Tad Jones Collection.
21. Armstrong, "Louis Armstrong + The Jewish Family," 17–18.
22. Ibid., 18.
23. Louis Armstrong, raw interview with Bill Stout of CBS News, July 1970.
24. Armstrong, "Louis Armstrong + The Jewish Family," 35.

25. It must be pointed out that in his manuscript for *Satchmo: My Life in New Orleans*, where Armstrong describes the junk wagon in similar terms, he mentions not Alex Karnofsky but a driver named "Larenzo" (most likely Lorenzo) who blew the tin horn, not Louis. Lorenzo "had an old tin (long) horn, which he used to blow (without the mouthpiece) and he would actually play a tune on the darn thing," Louis wrote. "That, knocked me out to hear him do that . . . He had a soul, too." Armstrong stuck to this tale in an interview with Richard Meryman in 1965. Armstrong biographer Thomas Brothers places the story of Lorenzo early in Louis's life but places the Karnofskys much later when Armstrong was a teenager, which doesn't seem right given the memories of the infants in the home and the details of their residence at 1304 Girod Street, the center of the Karnofsky universe until they purchased a building at 427 South Rampart Street in 1915. Perhaps Louis worked with Lorenzo on a junk wagon at some unspecified time and when he got the chance to work a similar job with Alex Karnofsky, he was excited by the opportunity to blow a tin horn as Lorenzo did. It's all a mystery but there's no denying that the sound of a tin horn on a junk wagon played a crucial role in Armstrong's musical upbringing. Armstrong, "The Armstrong Story," 46. Armstrong with Meryman, *A Self-Portrait*, 11–12.
26. Armstrong, "Louis Armstrong + the Jewish Family," 15.
27. Ibid., 9.
28. Ibid., 14–15.
29. Ibid., 15.
30. "The Karnofskys of New Orleans," undated article, courtesy of Judge Jacob Karno.
31. Armstrong, "Louis Armstrong + the Jewish Family," 61.
32. Goffin, *Horn of Plenty*, 43.
33. Armstrong, "Storyville," 32. Armstrong and his sister weren't initially familiar with the word "prostitute" in that era. In the 1960s, Louis's sister, Beatrice, was confused when a lawyer asked her, "Do you know any prostitutes around there?" "Prostitutes?" Mama Lucy responded, puzzled. "And I forgot," she recounted, "I always called them 'whores.' " Beatrice "Mama Lucy" Armstrong, Interview with Yoshio Toyama, 1973.
34. Armstrong, "Louis Armstrong + the Jewish Family," 20. The Karnofskys still had their share of run-ins with the police. Alex Karnofsky was arrested on June 24, 1914, for "boisterous outcry and peddling within 100 feet of public market." Brother Meyer Karnofsky was arrested for "peddling without license and Boisterous outcry" on July 1, 1908, and for "peddling in market limits during market hours" on June 14, 1912. Morris Karnofsky was arrested multiple times including on January 21, 1913, for causing "traffic" at Canal and South Rampart Street; for peddling without proper license or permit" on August 5, 1915; and for "assault and battery" on February 14, 1917. The latter charge is what might have been alluded to in the following passage from the undated article "The Karnofskys of New Orleans": "Anti-Semitism was also common and after hoodlums from the Irish Channel section of town harassed Jewish shop owners, everyone would say, 'Send for the Karnofskys! . . . Send for the Karnofskys!' Four of the brothers would respond to the call with baseball bats in hand." "The Karnofskys of New Orleans," undated article that is part of "Karnofsky Family Papers" folder at the Louis Armstrong House Museum, 2015.45.1.
35. Armstrong, "Storyville," 100.
36. Louis Armstrong, BBC interview with Geoffrey Haydon, November 17, 1969, courtesy of Geoffrey Haydon.
37. Armstrong, "Louis Armstrong + the Jewish Family," 21.

38. Dalton Anthony Jones, "Louis Armstrong's 'Karnofsky Document': The Reaffirmation of Social Death and the Afterlife of Emotional Labor," *Music and Politics*, Winter 2015, https://quod.lib.umich.edu/m/mp/9460447.0009.105?view=text;rgn=main.
39. Armstrong, "Louis Armstrong + the Jewish Family," 19.
40. Jones, *Salute to Satchmo*, 16.
41. Beatrice "Mama Lucy" Armstrong, Interview with Yoshio Toyama, August 19, 1973.
42. Armstrong, "The Armstrong Story," 161–162.
43. Armstrong, "Louis Armstrong + the Jewish Family," 19.
44. Of the 15 people arrested, 12 were men who were listed as "laborers." The other three arrested were all prostitutes, of whom Mayann was one, giving her name as "Mary Alberts" and her age as 26.
45. Beatrice "Mama Lucy" Armstrong, interview with Yoshio Toyama, August 19, 1973.
46. Meryman, *Self-Portrait*, 13.
47. Beatrice "Mama Lucy" Armstrong, interview with Yoshio Toyama, August 19, 1973.
48. Armstrong, "Louis Armstrong + the Jewish Family," 19.
49. Beatrice "Mama Lucy" Armstrong, interview with Yoshio Toyama, August 19, 1973.
50. Tape 1987.3.256, recorded c. 1951, Louis Armstrong House Museum.
51. *The Mike Douglas Show*, May 28, 1970. Audio available at Louis Armstrong House Museum, Tape 1987.3.407.
52. Meryman, *Self-Portrait*, 7.

Chapter 4

1. Peter Hanley and Lawrence Gushee, "Postscript: The Search Continues," 2005, http://www.doctorjazz.co.uk/portnewor.html.
2. Donald M. Marquis, *In Search of Buddy Bolden: First Man of Jazz* (Baton Rouge: Louisiana State University Press, 2005), rev. ed., 6.
3. Tape 1987.3.218, recorded 1952, Louis Armstrong House Museum.
4. Interview with Albert Nicholas, c. February 1969, William Russell Oral History Collection Series, MSS530, William Russell Jazz Collection, Williams Research Center, Historic New Orleans Collection.
5. Louis Armstrong interview with Willis Conover, Voice of America broadcast, recorded July 13, 1956, Music Library, University of North Texas Libraries, Digital Library, https://digital.library.unt.edu.
6. George "Pops" Foster, interviewed by William Russell, August 24, 1958, Hogan Archive of New Orleans Music and New Orleans Jazz. Wooden Joe Nicholas took about 10 cornet lessons from Johnson but always had trouble finding him. "Bunk would never come home," he said, before giving another possible explanation of Johnson's famous nickname. "That's why they called him Bunk, he'd sleep anywhere. He'd sleep on the old beer barrel if it was [there], knocked out, drunk as a fool. He would never come home right away. That's why they called him Bunk." Wooden Joe Nicholas, interviewed by William Russell, November 12, 1956, Hogan Archive of New Orleans Music and New Orleans Jazz.
7. Louis Armstrong, *Jazzmen* notes, William Russell Jazz Collection, Historic New Orleans Collection, MSS519.F.16.
8. Louis Armstrong interview with Willis Conover, Voice of America broadcast, recorded July 13, 1956, Music Library, University of North Texas Libraries, Digital Library, https://digital.library.unt.edu.

9. Louis Armstrong, acetate disc of April 1950 interview for *The Record Changer*, 2013.70.5, Louis Armstrong House Museum.
10. Oliver's birthplace is also up for debate. His longtime wife, Stella Oliver, stated that her husband was born on the Salsburg Plantation, located two miles southeast of Aben, Louisiana. However, Oliver's half-sister Victoria Davis, who was born in 1877 and claimed to have "nursed [Oliver] when he was a baby," told William Russell that Oliver was born on Dryades Street in New Orleans and grew up in that city's Garden District. Perhaps it was Oliver's mother who worked on the Salsburg Plantation in Aben, one of the frequent moves that took place en route to settling in New Orleans. Stella Oliver, interviewed by William Russell, April 22, 1959, Hogan Archive of New Orleans Music and New Orleans Jazz. Frederic Ramsey Jr., "King Oliver and His Creole Jazz Band." In *Jazzmen*, eds. Frederic Ramsey and Charles Edward Smith, 59. New York: Harcourt Brace, 1939.59.
11. Stella Oliver believed Joe's father was a minister; the census does list a preacher named Nathan Oliver, born in Virginia around 1848 and living in DeSoto Parish in northwest Louisiana in both the 1880 and 1910 censuses. Single in 1880, it appears he never married Jinnie Jones; if he's indeed Joe Oliver's father, then it appears Oliver, like his later protege Louis Armstrong, was similarly a "bastard from the start."
12. Orleans Parish Death Records, vol. 122, p. 721.
13. Ramsey, "King Oliver and His Creole Jazz Band," 59–60.
14. "Emancipation Day," *Times-Picayune*, September 25, 1900, 11.
15. Bassist Wellman Braud remembered Kinchen as a longshoreman; though the 1900 census lists him as a "porter," he did indeed apply for a "Seaman's Certificate of American Citizenship" in 1917.
16. Wellman Braud, *Jazzmen* notes, William Russell Jazz Collection, Historic New Orleans Collection, MSS519.F.20.
17. Ramsey, "King Oliver and His Creole Jazz Band," 60.
18. Stella Oliver, interviewed by William Russell, April 22, 1959, Hogan Archive of New Orleans Music and New Orleans Jazz.
19. Wellman Braud, *Jazzmen* notes, William Russell Jazz Collection, Historic New Orleans Collection, MSS519.F.20.
20. Clarence "Little Dad" Vincent, interviewed by Richard B. Allen, January 21, 1960, Hogan Archive of New Orleans Music and New Orleans Jazz.
21. Stella Oliver, interviewed by William Russell, April 22, 1959, Hogan Archive of New Orleans Music and New Orleans Jazz.
22. Sister Bernice Phillips, interviewed by Richard B. Allen, March 27, 1957, Hogan Archive of New Orleans Music and New Orleans Jazz. It's been stated that Oliver worked in a "shirt factory," but that's not quite true. The Levy brothers announced a new partnership with Simon Gonesnheim and Joseph Gonsehim in October 1903 later "for the purpose and manufacturing and jobbing Gent's Furnishing Goods at 224 and 226 Chartres Street." That address is where the Levy brothers conducted their business, but 2502 Magazine Street was filled with family. "Dissolution—New Firms," *Times-Democrat*, October 11, 1903, 10.
23. Stella Oliver, interviewed by William Russell, April 22, 1959, Hogan Archive of New Orleans Music and New Orleans Jazz.
24. Ramsey, "King Oliver and His Creole Jazz Band," 60.
25. Manuel Manetta oral history, May 10 and 31, 1968, William Russell Oral History Collection Series, MSS 530.2.94, William Russell Jazz Collection, Williams Research Center, Historic New Orleans Collection.

26. Eddie Dawson, interviewed by William Russell, August 4, 1957, Hogan Archive of New Orleans Music and New Orleans Jazz.
27. Richard M. Jones, *Jazzmen* notes, William Russell Jazz Collection, Historic New Orleans Collection, MSS519.F.29.
28. Foster was the one who recommended Oliver to take the cornet chair in the Magnolia Band. Keppard admitted Oliver "did not have no reputation" but gave Oliver the job when the cornetist promised to have a number of dates lined up for the band to play. "We're still waiting to play even the first date that Joe Oliver . . . had in his book," Foster said in 1947. Pops Foster, "Forty-Eight Years on the String Bass," 18.
29. Pops Foster, "Forty-Eight Years on the String Bass," in *The Jazz Record*, March 1947, 18.
30. Louis Keppard, interviewed by William Russell, January 19, 1961, Hogan Archive of New Orleans Music and New Orleans Jazz.
31. Pops Foster, as told to Tom Stoddard, *Pops Foster: The Autobiography of a New Orleans Jazzman* (Berkeley: University of California Press, 1971), 51–52.
32. Louis Keppard, interviewed by William Russell, August 11, 1959, Hogan Archive of New Orleans Music and New Orleans Jazz.
33. Preston Jackson, "King Oliver: Daddy of the Trumpet," *Hot News*, May 1935, 3.
34. Eddie Dawson, interviewed by William Russell, August 4, 1957, Hogan Archive of New Orleans Music and New Orleans Jazz. Louis Keppard agreed that his brother was the first cornetist to play the District, which he said previously only allowed "just string instruments, soft music." But in his version of the story, Freddie Keppard's cornet was added to a trio featuring Johnny Lindsay on bass, his brother Herbert on violin, and their father John on guitar. Louis Keppard also remembered this was at a place called "Hanan's" located on the corner of Iberville (then Customhouse) Street and Marais Street.
35. Foster, as told to Stoddard, *Pops Foster*, 40.
36. Ibid.
37. Eddie Dawson, interviewed by William Russell, August 4, 1957, Hogan Archive of New Orleans Music and New Orleans Jazz.
38. Louis Keppard, interviewed by William Russell, August 11, 1959, Hogan Archive of New Orleans Music and New Orleans Jazz.
39. Eddie Dawson, interviewed by William Russell, August 4, 1957, Hogan Archive of New Orleans Music and New Orleans Jazz. As Oliver and the men in his band began improvising more, occasionally they missed his signal to wrap it up. "When [Oliver] knocked off, they'd be feeling so good, you know, that they couldn't stop, they wouldn't hear him when he knocked off, you see," Dawson said. Eventually, Oliver came up with a solution of his own: "He just got a big brick and when he got ready to knock off, he'd throw the brick up on the music stand and say, 'Well, I guess you heard that,'" Dawson recalled with a laugh.
40. Richard M. Jones, *Jazzmen* notes, William Russell Jazz Collection, Historic New Orleans Collection, MSS519.F.29.
41. Abadie's was originally listed in the 1908 Soards as a grocery run by Mrs. M. Abadie and her son Eugene. But by 1910, the grocery had turned into a saloon run by brothers Eugene and Oliver Abadie, though their mother was still involved; when rumor spread that an African American man was killed after getting in an argument in her place, in 1910, Mrs. Abadie told the press that "her saloon is a resort for whites only, and no negroes had any altercations there." "Saloon for Whites," *Times-Picayune*, December 29, 1910, 4.
42. Richard M. Jones, *Jazzmen* notes, William Russell Jazz Collection, Historic New Orleans Collection, MSS519.F.29.

Chapter 5

1. Armstrong, "Louis Armstrong + The Jewish Family," 42.
2. Ibid., 25.
3. Armstrong, "The Armstrong Story," 3.
4. "Louis Armstrong + The Jewish Family," 32.
5. Louis Armstrong, interview with George Wein, July 23, 1970, https://www.wolfgangs.com/music/louis-armstrong/audio/20020418-15316.html?tid=4845813.
6. Armstrong, "The Armstrong Story," 12.
7. *The Mike Douglas Show*, May 25, 1970.
8. Armstrong, "The Armstrong Story," 38. Trombonist Preston Jackson, born in New Orleans in January 3, 1902, remembered times when the spirit of second lining would lead him a long way from home—and right into Louis Armstrong's dangerous neighborhood. "The Third Ward was supposed to be one of the worst in New Orleans," he recalled. "They called that The Battlefield. See, that's where Louie's from, the Third Ward..... Them gangs, they run you, they get behind you and run you back where you come from. They ask you for a nickel or something and if you didn't give it to them, they'd hit you or anything like that. They had them gangs that used to fight!" Preston Jackson, Interviewed by William Russell, June 2, 1958, Hogan Archive of New Orleans Music and New Orleans Jazz.
9. Beatrice "Mama Lucy" Armstrong, Interview with Yoshio Toyama, August 19, 1973.
10. Private tape made with George Avakian, October 24, 1953. New York Public Library for the Performing Arts, George Avakian and Anahid Ajemian Collection.
11. Ibid.
12. Armstrong, "The Armstrong Story," 13.
13. Ibid.
14. Private tape made with George Avakian, October 24, 1953. New York Public Library for the Performing Arts, George Avakian and Anahid Ajemian Collection.
15. Louis Armstrong, *Jazzmen* notes, William Russell Jazz Collection, Historic New Orleans Collection, MSS519.F.16. Counting Armstrong and occasional substitutes such as future cornetist Louis "Shots" Madison, about six or seven singers passed through Armstrong's "quartet," but he always stressed, "There was always four [singers] whether one was in or out." Private tape made with George Avakian, October 24, 1953. New York Public Library for the Performing Arts, George Avakian and Anahid Ajemian Collection.
16. Goffin, *Horn of Plenty*, 43–44.
17. Henry Rena, *Jazzmen* notes, William Russell Jazz Collection, Historic New Orleans Collection, MSS519.F.36.
18. Goffin, *Horn of Plenty*, 44.
19. Paul Barbarin, interviewed by William Russell and Richard B. Allen, March 27, 1957, Hogan Archive of New Orleans Music and New Orleans Jazz.
20. Richard M. Jones, *Jazzmen* notes, William Russell Jazz Collection, Historic New Orleans Collection, MSS519.F.29.
21. Goffin, *Horn of Plenty*, 45.
22. Studs Terkel, *And They All Sang: Adventures of an Eclectic Disc Jockey* (New York: Norton, 2005), 147.
23. Private tape made with George Avakian, October 24, 1953, Louis Armstrong House Museum, Tape 1993.1.3.

24. Lynn Abbott, "'Play That Barber Shop Chord': A Case for the African-American Origin of Barbershop Harmony," in *American Music* (Champaign, Illinois: University of Illinois Press, 1992), 291.
25. Louis Armstrong, interview with Dave Froh on Club 1520, recorded c. 1955, Louis Armstrong House Museum, Tape 1987.3.55.
26. Terkel, *And They All Sang*, 147.
27. Arvell Shaw, Interview with Phil Schaap, July 2, 1999, WKCR-FM 89.9.
28. Private tape made with George Avakian, October 24, 1953. According to the inflation calculation, $1.50 in 1913 is the equivalent of $47 in 2024, meaning Armstrong would take home the equivalent of $330 a week from just passing the hat with the quartet.
29. Private tape made with George Avakian, October 24, 1953. New York Public Library for the Performing Arts, George Avakian and Anahid Ajemian Collection.
30. Jason Berry, Interview with Beatrice "Mama Lucy" Armstrong, 1983, Tad Jones Collection, Hogan Archive of New Orleans Music and New Orleans Jazz.
31. Billy and Mary McBride, interviewed by William Russell, July 1, 1959, Hogan Archive of New Orleans Music and New Orleans Jazz.
32. Zutty Singleton, "Zutty First Saw Louis in Amateur Tent Show," *Downbeat*, July 4, 1950, 6. Singleton remembered the quartet that night being made up of Red Happy, Little Mack, Louis, "and a guy by the name of Clarence," probably one of their many subs.
33. Sidney Bechet, *Treat It Gentle* (New York: Hill and Wang,1960), 91.
34. Ibid.
35. William Russell, "Louis Armstrong." In *Jazzmen*, eds. Frederic Ramsey and Charles Edward Smith, 120. New York: Harcourt Brace, 1939.
36. Bechet, *Treat It Gentle*, 93.
37. "Louis' Mentors," *H.R.S. Society Rag*, September 1940, 15.
38. Tape 1987.3.14, recorded June 1956, Louis Armstrong House Museum.
39. Louis Armstrong, Interviewed by Steve Allen for BBC's *Be My Guest*, June 1968, Tape 2016.130.11, Louis Armstrong House Museum.
40. Armstrong, "Louis Armstrong + the Jewish Family," 16–17.
41. Ibid., 42.
42. *David Frost Show*, February 10, 1970. Audio available on Tape 1987.3.388.
43. Louis Armstrong, interview with George Wein, July 23, 1970, https://www.wolfgangs.com/music/louis-armstrong/audio/20020418-15316.html?tid=4845813
44. *The Tonight Show Starring Johnny Carson*, March 1, 1971. Audio available on Tape 1987.3.489, Louis Armstrong House Museum.
45. James Karen interview, courtesy of Bob Borgen, email to the author, June 22, 2018.
46. "New Orleans Gives the New Year Greatest and Gladdest Greeting," *Daily Picayune*, January 1, 1912, 13.
47. "Elks Hosts to Thousands," *Times-Democrat*, January 1, 1913, 9.
48. "How the New Year Came to the City," *Daily Picayune*, January 1, 1913, 7.
49. Armstrong, "The Armstrong Story," 13.
50. Ibid., 14.
51. Louis Armstrong, *Swing That Music* (New York: Longmans, Green and Company, 1936), 1.
52. Goffin, *Horn of Plenty*, 57–58.
53. Gray was indeed alive and in touch with Armstrong; in a 1953 conversation with George Avakian, Armstrong mentioned running into him twice in recent years, once in Tuscon, Arizona and once in Texas, where Gray helped fix Armstrong's broken-down band bus.

Private tape made with George Avakian, October 24, 1953. New York Public Library for the Performing Arts, George Avakian and Anahid Ajemian Collection.

54. *The David Frost Show*, August 25, 1970. Audio available on Tape 1987.3.446, Louis Armstrong House Museum.
55. Beatrice "Mama Lucy" Armstrong, interview with Yoshio Toyama, August 19, 1973.
56. Armstrong, "The Armstrong Story," 14.
57. Tad Jones, interviewed by Peggy Scott Laborde for WYES documentary *Satchmo in New Orleans*, summer 1990, raw interview transcript, Hogan Archive of New Orleans Music and New Orleans Jazz.
58. Armstrong, "The Armstrong Story," 14.
59. Armstrong, *Swing That Music*, 6.

Chapter 6

1. Judge Wilson, an "uptown white aristocrat" in the words of Tad Jones, was elected the first judge of the Juvenile Court, beginning his term on January 1, 1909. "So far as the attitude of this court towards the children who may appear before it is concerned, it will be our aim to treat them kindly and considerately," Judge Wilson said on his first day on the bench. Tad Jones, interviewed by Peggy Scott Laborde for the WYES documentary *Satchmo in New Orleans*, summer 1990, raw interview transcript, Hogan Archive of New Orleans Music and New Orleans Jazz. "Andrew H. Wilson, Judge of the Juvenile Court," *Times-Picayune*, February 19, 1912, 52. "Juvenile Court Opens," *The Times-Democrat*, January 3, 1909, 5.
2. Beatrice "Mama Lucy" Armstrong, interview with Yoshio Toyama, August 19, 1973.
3. "Few Juveniles Arrested," *The Times-Democrat*, January 2, 1913, 13.
4. Beatrice "Mama Lucy" Armstrong, interview with Yoshio Toyama, August 19, 1973.
5. The page in the First Precinct Arrest Record is dated "January 4, 1912," and is sourced that way when searching on Ancestry.com. However, a quick scan of the pages before and after illustrate that this was actually the 1913 book and Chief Lewis Rawling must have accidentally misdated it, a common mistake so early in the New Year.
6. Tad Jones, "Waifs' Home Social History," unpublished document, Tad Jones Collection, Hogan Archive of New Orleans Music and New Orleans Jazz.
7. A Reverend Frank Smoot provided religious services for the Home, pronouncing the benediction and offering prayer at a service held there just two months before Armstrong arrived. "Service at Waifs' Home," *The Times-Democrat*, October 14, 1912, 14.
8. Armstrong, "The Armstrong Story," 15.
9. Armstrong remembered two kids who "were so full of body lice and head lice, until, they had to be stripped of their clothings and their clothes were thrown into the fire (underneath the) kettle and burned.....And their heads were shaved off." Armstrong, "The Armstrong Story," 22.
10. Ibid., 18.
11. Ibid., 21–22.
12. *The David Frost Show*, February 11, 1970.
13. Armstrong, "The Armstrong Story," 15.
14. George Kay, interview with Mrs. Joseph Jones, October 1974, Tad Jones Collection, Hogan Archive of New Orleans Music and New Orleans Jazz.

15. "Straight University Ends Successful Year," *The Times-Democrat*, May 30, 1912, 9. Tad Jones, in his unpublished research on the Waif's Home, identified "Miss Spriggins" as Florentine Spriggins, but Florentine was Naomi's younger sister, born a year later in 1892. Florentine did go on to be a public school teacher but isn't listed as such in the Soards's City Directory until 1914; Naomi Spriggins is listed as a teacher in the 1912 edition, making her a more likely candidate to be the teacher when Louis arrived in 1913. Tad Jones, "Waifs' Home Social History," unpublished document, Tad Jones Collection, Hogan Archive of New Orleans Music and New Orleans Jazz.
16. Tape 1987.3.526, Louis Armstrong House Museum.
17. Armstrong, "The Armstrong Story," 18.
18. Both his World War I and World War II draft registration cards list his birthday as October 25, 1890, but when he filled out his social security application, he gave a birthday of October 25, 1888, and when he was interviewed in 1965, he gave it as October 25, 1887. When he died in 1971, obituaries gave his age as 90, meaning he was possibly born as early as 1880.
19. Dr. Robert S. Mikell, "The Legacy of Louis Armstrong's Music Teacher Peter Davis" *The Syncopated Times*, July 27, 2019. "You see when I began, I was playing Cornet in Kid Allen's Jazz Band," Davis said in the early 1950s, most likely referencing the brass band of Henry Allen Sr. of Algiers. Gladys DeVore Williams, "The Man Who Was a Fairy God-Father to Louis Armstrong," in *New Orleans Society Hall*, winter edition, 1950–51.
20. Abbey "Chinee" Foster, interviewed by William Russell and Ralph Collins, March 21, 1961, Hogan Archive of New Orleans Music and New Orleans Jazz.
21. Gladys DeVore Williams, "The Man Who Was a Fairy God-Father to Louis Armstrong," in *New Orleans Society Hall*, winter edition, 1950–51.
22. Ibid.
23. Clay Watson, "50 Golden Years," *The Second Line*, July–August 1965, 89.
24. "Service at Waifs' Home," *The Times-Democrat*, October 14, 1912, 14.
25. Armstrong, *Swing That Music*, 7.
26. Peter Davis, interview with Clay Watson at New Orleans Jazz Museum, May 13, 1965, Tad Jones Collection, Hogan Archive of New Orleans Music and New Orleans Jazz.
27. Ibid.
28. Tape 1987.3.256, recorded c. 1951, Louis Armstrong House Museum.
29. Morris Grossberg Oral History, 1996, Louis Armstrong House Museum, 1996.59.1.
30. Barney Bigard interviewed by Patricia Willard, June 12, 1976, Jazz Oral History Project, Rutgers University.
31. Armstrong, "The Armstrong Story," 16.
32. Henry Armstrong, interviewed by Garry Boulard, September 20, 1983, Tad Jones Collection, Hogan Archive of New Orleans Music and New Orleans Jazz.
33. Ibid.
34. Wesley Jackson, "Music Teacher Recalls Satchmo's Early Years," *Times-Picayune*, August 22, 1962, 14.
35. Peter Davis, interview with Clay Watson at the New Orleans Jazz Museum, May 13, 1965, Tad Jones Collection, Hogan Archive of New Orleans Music and New Orleans Jazz.
36. Ibid.
37. Jones, "Waifs' Home Social History."
38. Jackson, "Music Teacher Recalls Satchmo's Early Years," 14.
39. Armstrong, "The Armstrong Story," 17.
40. Ibid., 16.

41. Ibid., 17.
42. Jackson, "Music Teacher Recalls Satchmo's Early Years," 14.
43. Armstrong, "The Armstrong Story," 17.
44. Jackson, "Music Teacher Recalls Satchmo's Early Years," 14.
45. Armstrong, "The Armstrong Story," 17.
46. Armstrong gave Davis the credit, but later in life, Captain Jones said it was actually his idea to make Armstrong the bugler. "When Louis came to the home, I could tell that he had music in his soul, so I taught him how to play my old bugle," Jones said in 1954. "This wasn't just for Louis' sake, but for the school's. You see, we used to blow police whistles to signal the boys to go to meals and work and classes. But I figured that they'd had enough of police whistles. I thought it would be nice for them to do everything to bugle calls like in the Army. That's the way Louis Armstrong became our first bugler." This seems to be an overreach since Armstrong was not the first bugler, but it's possible Jones told Davis to appoint Armstrong in the role. "Diane Farrell, "Yankee Doodle Dixie," *Dixie*, February 14, 1954, 22.
47. *The David Frost Show*, February 11, 1970.
48. Ibid., 19.
49. Beatrice "Mama Lucy" Armstrong, interview with Yoshio Toyama, August 19, 1973.
50. Armstrong, "The Armstrong Story," 19.
51. Tape 1987.3.526, recorded 1960, Louis Armstrong House Museum.
52. Ibid.
53. Wilbert Tillman, interviewed by Richard B. Allen, January 20, 1966, Hogan Archive of New Orleans Music and New Orleans Jazz.
54. *The Mike Douglas Show*, January 15, 1964.
55. *I've Got a Secret*, December 27, 1965.
56. Armstrong, "The Armstrong Story," 19.
57. Ibid., 20.
58. Beatrice "Mama Lucy" Armstrong, interview with Yoshio Toyama, August 19, 1973.
59. Meryman, *Self-Portrait*, 16.
60. Armstrong, "The Armstrong Story," 20.
61. "Observation of Decoration Day," *Times-Picayune*, May 31, 1913, 13.
62. Rena was sent to the Waif's Home after a dustup with an Italian boy who wouldn't give him a piece of watermelon. Rena hit the boy, who went home and told his mother. She came storming back with other members of the family and found Joseph Rene, Henry's older brother (who retained the family's original spelling of their surname). The family mistook Joseph for Henry and, in his words, "They stomped me to death. Blood out of my mouth and nose and ears and everything." Two policeman intervened and saved Joe Rene's life but when Henry found out what happened, he took a knife and cut one of the women in the Italian boy's family, earning him an extended stay in the Colored Waif's Home. Joseph Rene, Interviewed by William Russell, April 7, 1960, Hogan Archive of New Orleans Music and New Orleans Jazz.
63. John Lucas, "Many Changes Way Down Yonder," *Downbeat*, July 15, 1943, 24.
64. Joseph Rene, interviewed by William Russell, April 7, 1960, Hogan Archive of New Orleans Music and New Orleans Jazz.
65. Goffin, *Horn of Plenty*, 66.
66. Joseph Rene, interviewed by William Russell, April 7, 1960, Hogan Archive of New Orleans Music and New Orleans Jazz.

67. Meryman, *Self Portrait*, 16.
68. Ibid., 20.
69. Kid Ory, interviewed by Neshui Ertegun, April 20, 1957, Hogan Archive of New Orleans Music and New Orleans Jazz.
70. Singleton, "Zutty First Saw Louis in Amateur Tent Show," 6.
71. "Negro Children See Santa Claus," *The Daily Picayune*, December 26, 1913, 4.
72. Ibid.
73. Armstrong, "The Armstrong Story," 22.
74. Williams, "The Man Who Was a Fairy God-Father to Louis Armstrong."
75. "'Nigger' George Makes Last Parade and Answers Roll Call in the Beyond," *The Times-Democrat*, March 6, 1914, 13.

Chapter 7

1. Armstrong, "The Armstrong Story," 23.
2. "Henry Armstrong, Tape #1," transcription of an interview most likely conducted by Tad Jones in the late 1980s. Tad Jones Collection, Hogan Archive of New Orleans Music and New Orleans Jazz.
3. Armstrong, "The Armstrong Story," 23.
4. Jason Berry, interview with Beatrice "Mama Lucy" Armstrong, 1983, Tad Jones Collection, Hogan Archive of New Orleans Music and New Orleans Jazz.
5. Tad Jones transcribed this as "Poydras and South Galvez" but in Goffin, *Horn of Plenty*, Jones, *Salute to Satchmo,* and other sources, the home is described as being at "Poydras and Miro." When Willie Armstrong filled out his World War I card in 1918, he gave the address 1308 South Claiborne Avenue. South Claiborne does intersect with Poydras, but quite a ways away from the 1308 address. In the 1910 census, Willie gave his address as 611 South Roman Street so it's possible he moved his family frequently in those years.
6. "Henry Armstrong, Tape #2," transcription of an interview most likely conducted by Tad Jones in the late 1980s. Tad Jones Collection, Hogan Archive of New Orleans Music and New Orleans Jazz. Asked about the Liberty and Perdido neighborhood's reputation as "The Battlefield," Henry replied, "Yeah, it was bad, too."
7. Armstrong, "The Armstrong Story," 23.
8. Jason Berry, Interview with Beatrice "Mama Lucy" Armstrong, 1983. Hogan Archive of New Orleans Music and New Orleans Jazz, Tulane University, Tad Jones Collection.
9. "Henry Armstrong, Tape #1."
10. Armstrong, "The Armstrong Story," 23.
11. "Henry Armstrong, Tape #1."
12. Obituary for Henry (Baker) Armstrong, *Times-Picayune*, October 13, 1991.
13. "Armstrong, Wizard of the Cornet, Former Item Newsie; Used to Live at Waifs' Home," *New Orleans Item*, June 1931. Clipping found in scrapbook 1987.8.5, Louis Armstrong House Museum.
14. Armstrong, *Swing That Music*, 25.
15. Goffin, *Horn of Plenty*, 72.
16. Armstrong, "The Armstrong Story," 24.
17. Henry Armstrong, interviewed by Garry Boulard.

18. John McLaughlin, "Louis Armstrong's Cornet," *Sky Magazine*, February 2001.
19. Manuel Manetta oral history, March 27, 1957, William Russell Oral History Collection Series, MSS 530.2.2, William Russell Jazz Collection, Williams Research Center, Historic New Orleans Collection.
20. "Henry Armstrong, Tape #2."
21. "Henry Armstrong Tape #3," transcription of an interview most likely conducted by Tad Jones in the late 1980s. Hogan Archive of New Orleans Music and New Orleans Jazz, Tulane University, Tad Jones Collection. In 1962, just a few months after Manuella Jones donated her Armstrong "first cornet" to the New Orleans Jazz Museum, Peter Davis turned up with a cornet he claimed was "the first horn owned by Armstrong." After his death, the cornet came into the hands of cornetist George Finola, who later served as curator for the New Orleans Jazz Museum. Finola regularly displayed Davis's cornet as Armstrong's "first cornet," but after his death in 2000, the cornet that originally was owned by Peter Davis was auctioned by Sotheby's and sold to the Smithsonian for $108,000. Shortly after, an article appeared in the *Historic Brass Society Journal* by three specialists who discovered that Davis's cornet—a Marceau model—did not appear in Sears and Roebuck's catalog until the fall of 1915, meaning that even if it was for sale in early 1915, it would not have been on the market when Armstrong left the Waif's Home in June 1914. It's possible that the Marceau was played by Armstrong when he continued to visit Davis's home for lessons in 1915, but the biggest takeaway is that it is not Armstrong's "first cornet." Jeffrey Nussbaum, Niles Eldredge, and Robb Stewart, "Louis Armstrong's First Cornet?," *Historic Brass Society Journal*, 2003, 355–358.
22. Armstrong, "The Armstrong Story," 24.
23. Jason Berry, Interview with Beatrice "Mama Lucy" Armstrong, 1983. Hogan Archive of New Orleans Music and New Orleans Jazz, Tulane University, Tad Jones Collection.
24. Meryman, *Self-Portrait*, 24–25.
25. Armstrong, "The Armstrong Story," 13.
26. James Karst, "Young Satchmo," in *64 Parishes*, May 31, 2019, https://64parishes.org/young-satchmo. The footage can be viewed on YouTube with the title "B/W people walking on crowded sidewalk / New Orleans 1915 / Petrified Films / Getty Images 280 235," https://youtu.be/NLGrD3aCelk?si=6fTtFaMV_BO8k9gp, Joseph L. Peyton, longtime clerk of court for the Orleans Parish Juvenile Court, told Gary Giddins that Armstrong actually stole the newspapers he was selling. Giddins reported, "That was a 'whites-only' job, [Peyton] says, and whenever Louis was seen leaving a streetcar with papers under his arm, he was arrested and returned to the Waif's Home." This seems unlikely, as Louis was never again mentioned in the Juvenile Court cases regularly covered in the newspapers of the time, plus his sister was adamant that he never went back to the Home. But anything was possible, even stealing newspapers, when it came to helping Mayann make ends meet. Gary Giddins, *Satchmo: The Genius of Louis Armstrong* (New York: Da Capo Press, 2001), 39.
27. Armstrong, "The Armstrong Story, 33.
28. Armstrong, "The Armstrong Story," 34–35. Jason Berry, Interview with Beatrice "Mama Lucy" Armstrong, 1983. Hogan Archive of New Orleans Music and New Orleans Jazz, Tulane University, Tad Jones Collection. Beatrice "Mama Lucy" Armstrong, Interview with Yoshio Toyama, August 19, 1973.
29. Private tape made with George Avakian, October 24, 1953. New York Public Library for the Performing Arts, George Avakian and Anahid Ajemian Collection.

30. *The Mike Douglas Show*, May 25, 1970. On this episode of *The Mike Douglas Show*, Armstrong specifically recalled the routine as being Bert Williams's "How? Fried!," which he recorded for Columbia in 1913. However, Columbia didn't issue the recording until 1922, so either Armstrong's memory was mistaken or it's possible, given Williams's popularity at the time, it was a routine he performed on stage that had reached New Orleans just through cultural osmosis. It's worth noting that Armstrong did recall it with incredible accuracy in 1970, many decades after he initially heard it.
31. Armstrong, "Louis Armstrong + the Jewish Family," 62.
32. Clarence "Little Dad" Vincent, interviewed by Richard B. Allen, January 21, 1960, Hogan Archive of New Orleans Music and New Orleans Jazz.
33. Christopher Hillman, *Bunk Johnson: His Life and Times* (New York: University Books, 1988), 23.
34. Mike Hazeldine and Barry Martyn, *Bunk Johnson: Song of the Wanderer* (New Orleans: Jazzology Press, 2000), 25.
35. Jones, *Salute to Satchmo*, 56.
36. Beatrice "Mama Lucy" Armstrong, interview with Yoshio Toyama, August 19, 1973.

Chapter 8

1. Armstrong, "Louis Armstrong + The Jewish Family," 46.
2. Goffin, *Horn of Plenty*, 72-73.
3. Louis Armstrong, letter to Leonard Feather, October 1, 1941, Louis Armstrong House Museum, 1987.9.10.
4. Cy Shain, "New Orleans Trumpeters," *The Jazz Record*, November 1946, 6.
5. Preston Jackson, "King Oliver: Daddy of the Trumpet," *Hot News*, May 1935, 3.
6. Buddy Christian, *Jazzmen* notes, William Russell Jazz Collection, Historic New Orleans Collection, MSS519.F.21. Armstrong and Christian even remembered almost the same exact personnel, with C. Alvin "Zue" Roberson on trombone and Henry Zeno on drums. The only difference was Christian listed Lorenzo Tio as his clarinetist, while Armstrong recalled it being "Professor Nicholson," most likely a corruption of Wooden Joe Nicholas.
7. Armstrong, "Storyville," 100.
8. Armstrong, "Storyville," 103.
9. Petit was born Joseph Crawford on December 23, 1896, if you believe his World War I draft registration card, August 1895 if you believe the 1900 census, or 1890 if you believe his marriage certificate from 1912. After his father, Alfred Crawford, passed away, his mother, Rose Baptiste, took young Joseph and his siblings to New Orleans, where they took up residence with Joseph Petit, a porter by day who was a pioneering trombonist in some of the early ragtime bands of the era. Joseph Petit became not only a stepfather but also a musical inspiration to young Joseph Crawford, who soon adopted the name Buddy Petit in tribute.
10. Ernie Cagnalotti, interviewed by William Russell and Richard B. Allen, April 5, 1961, Hogan Archive of New Orleans Music and New Orleans Jazz.
11. Edmond Hall, interviewed by William Russell and Richard B. Allen, April 4, 1957, Hogan Archive of New Orleans Music and New Orleans Jazz.
12. Punch Miller, interviewed by Richard B. Allen, April 4, 1960, Hogan Archive of New Orleans Music and New Orleans Jazz.

13. Amos White, interviewed by William Russell, August 23 1958, Hogan Archive of New Orleans Music and New Orleans Jazz.
14. Louis Armstrong, letter to Leonard Feather, October 1, 1941, Louis Armstrong House Museum, 1987.9.10.
15. Louis Armstrong, "The Satchmo Story—2nd Edition," c. 1959 manuscript, Louis Armstrong House Museum, 1987.2.4.
16. In the 1910 census, the Wade brothers were living together at 310 North Liberty Street and were both working as waiters in a saloon. Clerk gave his the year of his birth as 1893, but his grave and the Death Index give a birthday of March 4, 1887. Williams and Bechet were mentioned in William Benbrow, "What's What Down in New Orleans," *The Freeman*, January 9, 1915, 6.
17. Armstrong, "The Armstrong Story," 41.
18. "Seriously Stabbed," *The Daily Picayune*, August 4, 1910, 8.
19. "Negress Is Acquitted," *Times-Picayune*, February 9, 1916, 7.
20. Armstrong, "The Armstrong Story," 41.
21. Ibid., 27.
22. Louis Armstrong interview with Willis Conover, Voice of America broadcast, recorded July 13, 1956, Music Library, University of North Texas Libraries, Digital Library, https://digital.library.unt.edu.
23. Ibid.
24. *The Tonight Show Starring Johnny Carson*, January 25, 1968. Audio available at the Louis Armstrong House Museum Tape 1987.3.659.
25. Louis Armstrong, interview with George Wein, July 23, 1970, https://www.wolfgangs.com/music/louis-armstrong/audio/20020418-15316.html?tid=4845813.
26. Williams, "The Man Who Was a Fairy God-Father to Louis Armstrong."
27. Chester Zardis, interviewed by Tad Jones, April 23, 1989, transcript found in the folder "Armstrong Cornet," Tad Jones Collection, Hogan Archive of New Orleans Music and New Orleans Jazz.
28. "Negro Playground Will Be Dedicated," *Times-Picayune*, August 28, 1915, 14.
29. Lee Collins, interviewed by William Russell, June 2, 1958, Hogan Archive of New Orleans Music and New Orleans Jazz.
30. Marshall Stearns, "The History of 'Swing' Music," *Downbeat*, July 1936, 4.
31. Preston Jackson, interviewed by William Russell, June 2, 1958, Hogan Archive of New Orleans Music and New Orleans Jazz.
32. Armstrong, "The Armstrong Story," 32.
33. Beatrice "Mama Lucy" Armstrong, interview with Yoshio Toyama, August 19, 1973.
34. Armstrong, "The Armstrong Story," 32.
35. Ibid., 33.
36. Ibid., 33–34.
37. Ibid., 32.
38. Christopher "Black Happy" Goldston, interviewed by Richard B. Allen and Margorie Zander, April 11, 1962, Hogan Archive of New Orleans Music and New Orleans Jazz.
39. Dave Bailey, interviewed by Richard B. Allen, October 25, 1959, Hogan Archive of New Orleans Music and New Orleans Jazz.
40. Meryman, *Self-Portrait*, 16–17.
41. R. A. Tiug [pseudonym for Dr. Edmond Souchon], "Historical Glimmer," *The Second Line*, August 1951, 1, 7. Twelve years later, after Manuella Jones donated Armstrong's "first

cornet" to the New Orleans Jazz Museum, Souchon rewrote and republished the same article, this time setting it in 1913 and introducing Jones as the man who brought Armstrong to the pawnshop. It's possible that happened at some point, but the original story, relying on Dave Frank's memory, seems more appropriate for this late 1915–early 1916 part of Armstrong's life.

42. Diane Farrell, "Yankee Doodle Dixie," *Times-Picayune States Boro Magazine*, February 14, 1954, 22.
43. Meryman, *Self-Portrait*, 16.
44. "Armstrong Cornet" folder, Tad Jones Collection,Hogan Archive of New Orleans Music and New Orleans Jazz.
45. Armstrong, "Louis Armstrong + the Jewish Family," 60.
46. Ibid., 25.
47. "Andrews Coal Co. Limited, Moves into New Quarters," *Times-Picayune*, August 29, 1915, 5.
48. Armstrong, "The Armstrong Story," 25.
49. Meryman, *Self-Portrait*, 18.
50. Ricard Alexis, interviewed by William Russell, January 16, 1969, Hogan Archive of New Orleans Music and New Orleans Jazz.
51. Armstrong, "The Armstrong Story," 25.

Chapter 9

1. According to a police report detailing an arrest of Martin in 1918, his real name was Alfred Martin and he lived at 444 South Liberty Street. The police report alludes to a nickname "Buddie" but leaves the "Cocaine" out.
2. Richard D. Woods and Grace lvarez-Altman, *Spanish American Surnames in the Southwestern United States: A Dictionary* (Boston: G. K. Hall, 1978), 110.
3. *Record Book Continuances, Existing Barrooms 1914–1919*, p. 185, #1534, Tad Jones Collection, Hogan Archive of New Orleans Music and New Orleans Jazz
4. "Boogers" is not an easy nickname to track down, but Lawrence Morgan, who lived right in Armstrong's neighborhood at 436 South Liberty, was arrested nearly 20 times between 1907 and 1917 and was often given an alias of "Boogey," "Bogie," or "Boga." The handwriting is often difficult to read on these police reports but on at least one from June 17, 1912, it does appear his alias is spelled "Booger." But to make matters more confusing, Lawrence Morgan had a brother named Frank Morgan who, at the time of the 1920 census, was working as a laborer on the riverfront, which is consistent with Robert Goffin, who had Boogers leaving music and unloading banana boats by the end of the teens. As for the drummer, Barry Ulanov heard Armstrong pronounce his surname as "Gobee," Goffin heard it as "Gaby," Richard Meryman heard it as "Garbee," and Armstrong himself typed it as "Garbie." The closest person to that surname in Armstrong's neighborhood seems to be Sidney Carabi—or Caribee—who was once arrested for "playing an organ." However, later arrest records for Carabi include the alias "Raw Head," who was later listed as one of Armstrong's "Bullies and Trouble Makers." Thus, without concrete proof that Morgan or Carabi were the right men, I will use "Boogers" and "Garbie" henceforth.
5. Armstrong, "The Armstrong Story," 61.
6. Beatrice "Mama Lucy" Armstrong, interview with Yoshio Toyama, August 19, 1973.

7. Armstrong, "The Armstrong Story," 61.
8. Ibid., 25, 92.
9. Private tape made with George Avakian, October 24, 1953, New York Public Library for the Performing Arts, George Avakian and Anahid Ajemian Collection.
10. Armstrong, "The Armstrong Story," 27.
11. Ibid., 28.
12. "Pons Stabbed in Saloonists' Feud," *New Orleans Daily States*, April 8, 1916.
13. Armstrong, "The Armstrong Story," 27.
14. Ibid.
15. "For Larceny of Coal," *Times-Picayune*, December 6, 1914, 40.
16. New Orleans First Precinct Arrest Book, arrest of Isaac Smoot, a "well-known pickpocket," on December 18, 1922.
17. Christopher "Black Happy" Goldston, interviewed by Richard B. Allen and Margorie Zander, April 11, 1962, Hogan Archive of New Orleans Music and New Orleans Jazz.
18. Joseph Rene, interviewed by Richard B. Allen, April 7, 1960, Hogan Archive of New Orleans Music and New Orleans Jazz.
19. James Karst, "The Tragic Life of a Comic Figure in Louis Armstrong's Book," *Times-Picayune*, March 24, 2018.
20. The police record states that both Armstrong and Jackson were given a choice of being fined $15 or going to jail for 30 days; it does not stipulate what they chose. The arrest record also shows Armstrong giving his age as 18, though he was most likely 15 at the time.
21. Meryman, *Self-Portrait*, 22.
22. Louis Armstrong, letter to Larry Amadee, c. 1968, Louis Armstrong House Museum 1987.2.7, 36.
23. "Louis Moore Shot," *Daily Picayune*, September 15, 1907, 2.
24. "First City Criminal Court," *Times-Democrat*, August 29, 1908, 4.
25. "Military Salute Fails to Satisfy, Bullet Follows," *Times-Picayune*, July 17, 1922, 2.
26. Alan Lomax, *Mister Jelly Roll* (New York: Grosset and Dunlap, 1950), 55.
27. "Negro Kills Brother After Family Row," *Times-Democrat*, October 10, 1910, 6.
28. "Two Negro Homicides Here In Day; On Connect With Strange Chain," *Times-Democrat*, August 12, 1911, 2.
29. "First City Criminal Court," *Daily Picayune*, July 6, 1912, 5.
30. "Negro Kills Enemy Who Threatened Him," *Times-Picayune*, July 15, 1915, 12.
31. Private tape made with George Avakian, October 24, 1953, New York Public Library for the Performing Arts, George Avakian and Anahid Ajemian Collection.
32. "Man Stabbed during Encounter in Court," *Times-Picayune*, June 5, 1918, 15.
33. "Two Men Injured in Race Battle," *Times-Picayune*, April 10, 1916, 2.
34. Armstrong, "The Armstrong Story," 55.
35. Ibid.
36. "Claims He Shot in Self-Defense," *Times-Picayune*, December 3, 1917, 15.
37. Armstrong, "The Armstrong Story," 27.
38. Ibid., 28.
39. There are no police records tying Mary Francis together with someone named Alberta, but there are plenty of arrests for fighting of a woman named Alberta, including three times with a prostitute from the neighborhood named Mary Felix, alias "Felice." (Francis and Felix were also arrested once for escaping from the House of Detention!) In two of the fights a man was involved, while in the third another prostitute named Annie Swazer was part of

it. In 1919, Swazer was involved in a knife fight with Alberta Coleman that was covered in the press. Armstrong's recollections of the battle between Mary Francis and Alberta were pretty consistent but he must have witnessed so many similar scrapes it's possible the details blurred together after a few decades.

40. Louis Armstrong and Pops Foster interview, c. summer 1958. Louis Armstrong House Museum, Tape 2001.63a.2.
41. Louis Armstrong, interview with Irwin Johnson, March 6, 1953, Louis Armstrong House Museum, Tape 1996.47.1.
42. Jones et al., *Salute to Satchmo*, 56. Though he was older, Black Benny occasionally sang with Armstrong's vocal quartet. "He could sing, that good ol, baroom tenor, to sweet aderline, or Jefferson Lord-play that barber shop chord," Armstrong wrote, referring to classic barbershop quartet songs "Sweet Adeline" from 1903 and "(Mister Jefferson Lord) Play That Barbershop Chord," the latter a big hit record for Bert Williams in 1910. Armstrong, "The Armstrong Story," 47.
43. George Williams, interviewed by William Russell, March 17, 1959, Hogan Archive of New Orleans Music and New Orleans Jazz.
44. Punch Miller, interviewed by Richard B. Allen, April 1971, Hogan Archive of New Orleans Music and New Orleans Jazz.
45. Ricard Alexis, interviewed by William Russell, January 16, 1969, Hogan Archive of New Orleans Music and New Orleans Jazz.
46. Albert Francis, interviewed by William Russell, August 4, 1961, Hogan Archive of New Orleans Music and New Orleans Jazz.
47. Paul Barbarin, interviewed by William Russell and Richard B. Allen, March 27, 1957, Hogan Archive of New Orleans Music and New Orleans Jazz.
48. Nat Shapiro and Nat Hentoff, *Hear Me Talkin' to Ya: The Story of Jazz by the Men Who Made It* (New York: Rinehart, 1955), 52.
49. "Races Mixed," *Daily Picayune*, February 15, 1912, 12.
50. "Fractured His Skull," *Daily Picayune*, June 30, 1909, 16.
51. "Shooting by Negroes," *Daily Picayune*, September 15, 1913, 4.
52. "First City Criminal Court," *Daily Picayune*, July 9, 1913, 5.
53. "First City Criminal Court," *Daily Picayune*, February 5, 1914, 5.
54. Armstrong, "The Armstrong Story," 31.
55. Ibid.
56. Louis Armstrong, letter to Joe Glaser, August 2, 1955, Louis Armstrong House Museum, 2008.1.43.
57. Armstrong, "The Armstrong Story," 31.
58. Ibid., 29.
59. Ibid.
60. Ibid., 30.
61. Ibid.
62. Charlie Love, interviewed by William Russell, June 19, 1958, Hogan Archive of New Orleans Music and New Orleans Jazz.
63. Charles Chamberlain, "From Tramps to Kings: 100 Years of Zulu," undated press release accompanying 2009 exhibit on the centennial of the Zulu Social Aid and Pleasure Club, mounted at the Presbytere on Jackson Square. Press release can be viewed at https://www.crt.state.la.us/Assets/Museum/onlineexhibits/zulu/Zulu_History.pdf.
64. Leonard Feather, "Satchmo—The Three Lives of Louis Armstrong," *Esquire*, March 1955, 81.

65. Armstrong, "The Armstrong Story," 56.
66. Kid Ory, interviewed by Neshui Ertegun, April 20, 1957, Hogan Archive of New Orleans Music and New Orleans Jazz.
67. Kid Ory, "Louis Was Just a Little Kid in Knee Pants; Ory," *Down Beat*, July 14, 1950, 8.
68. Johnny St. Cyr, interviewed by William Russell, August 27, 1958, Hogan Archive of New Orleans Music and New Orleans Jazz.
69. Shain, "New Orleans Trumpeters," 5.
70. Tape 1987.3.473, recorded c. April 1959, Louis Armstrong House Museum.
71. Meryman, *Self-Portrait*, 22.
72. Armstrong, "The Armstrong Story," 26.
73. Meryman, *Self-Portrait*, 22.
74. "Negro Boy Killed," *Times-Picayune*, August 9, 1916, 8. Thirteen-year-old Chalman Williams, the younger brother of Brown's girlfriend, Hilda, was playing with a gun and shot Brown through the heart, according to a newspaper report.
75. Armstrong, "The Armstrong Story," 37.
76. Ibid., 38.
77. Louis Armstrong, "The Satchmo Story," 1959 manuscript held at the Louis Armstrong House Museum, 1987.2.4, 8.

Chapter 10

1. Armstrong, "The Armstrong Story," 43. In *Satchmo: My Life in New Orleans*, Armstrong tells two very different stories about two very different prostitutes, one only referred to as "Irene," the other as "Nootsy." But in Robert Goffin's *Horn of Plenty*, all such stories revolve around one prostitute named "Nutsie," whom Armstrong eventually calls "Irene," explaining that she's "a lil' gal they calls Nutsie in the Battlefield." It's possible Irene and Nootsy were one and the same but their stories are so different, they will be treated in this text as separate women, as Armstrong described them in his autobiography. Goffin, *Horn of Plenty*, 104.
2. Armstrong, "The Armstrong Story," 43.
3. Ibid., 43–44.
4. Johnny St. Cyr, "Jazz As I Remember It," original unedited manuscript written in 1961 and later published in *Jazz Journal*, MSS 519 F.57, William Russell Jazz Collection, Williams Research Center, Historic New Orleans Collection.
5. Kid Ory and Manuel Manetta, interviewed by William Russell, August 26, 1958, Hogan Archive of New Orleans Music and New Orleans Jazz. Manuel Manetta oral history, March 27, 1957, William Russell Oral History Collection Series, MSS 530.2.2, William Russell Jazz Collection, Williams Research Center, Historic New Orleans Collection. Manuel Manetta oral history, May 31 and June 7, 1968, William Russell Oral History Collection Series, MSS 530.2.95, William Russell Jazz Collection, Williams Research Center, Historic New Orleans Collection. Dr. Edmond Souchon, interviewed by William Russell, February 17, 1962, Hogan Archive of New Orleans Music and New Orleans Jazz.
6. St. Cyr, "Jazz as I Remember It."
7. John McCusker, *Creole Trombone: Kid Ory and the Early Years of Jazz* (Jackson: University of Mississippi Press, 2012), 114.
8. Armstrong, "The Armstrong Story," 41.

9. Louis Armstrong, BBC interview with Geoffrey Haydon, November 17, 1969.
10. Manuel Manetta oral history, March 27, 1957, William Russell Oral History Collection Series, MSS 530.2.2, William Russell Jazz Collection, Williams Research Center, Historic New Orleans Collection.
11. Ibid.
12. Dr. Edmond Souchon, interviewed by William Russell, February 17, 1962, Hogan Archive of New Orleans Music and New Orleans Jazz.
13. Dr. Edmond Souchon, "King Oliver: A Very Personal Memoir," *The Jazz Review*, 1960, 11.
14. Dr. Edmond Souchon, interviewed by William Russell, February 17, 1962, Hogan Archive of New Orleans Music and New Orleans Jazz.
15. Johnny Wiggs oral history, September 17, 1968, William Russell Oral History Collection Series, MSS 530.3.70, William Russell Jazz Collection, Williams Research Center, Historic New Orleans Collection.
16. Johnny Wiggs, interviewed by William Russell, August 26, 1962, Hogan Archive of New Orleans Music and New Orleans Jazz.
17. Alfred Williams, interviewed by Richard B. Allen, February 3, 1961, Hogan Archive of New Orleans Music and New Orleans Jazz. Williams also remembered Armstrong playing the same material Manetta did: the blues, "Sister Kate," and "Wind and Grind," saying of the last one, "That was a nice number! . . . Louis had a good head for making up a number." Alfred Williams, interviewed by Richard B. Allen, October 13, 1961, Hogan Archive of New Orleans Music and New Orleans Jazz.
18. Armstrong, "The Armstrong Story," 41. In addition to Armstrong, Lindsey, Prevost on clarinet, and French on trombone, the group also included Joe Welch on violin, Dominique "T-Boy" Remy on guitar, and Eddie Green on bass.
19. Private tape made with George Avakian, October 24, 1953. New York Public Library for the Performing Arts, George Avakian and Anahid Ajemian Collection.
20. Ibid.
21. Louis Armstrong, interview with George Wein, July 23, 1970, https://www.wolfgangs.com/music/louis-armstrong/audio/20020418-15316.html?tid=4845813.
22. Dr. Edmond Souchon, interviewed by Haywood H. Hillyer III, May 7, 1957, Hogan Archive of New Orleans Music and New Orleans Jazz.
23. Armstrong, "The Armstrong Story," 41.
24. Armstrong, "The Armstrong Story," 41–42.
25. Private tape made with George Avakian, October 24, 1953, New York Public Library for the Performing Arts, George Avakian and Anahid Ajemian Collection.
26. When Harry Houdini escaped from a straitjacket in front of 12,000 onlookers on February 23, 1916, newspapers reported that Frankie Duson's Eagle Band performed "Brown Skin"; one even ran a photo of the group with Buddy Petit on cornet. "Burial Price for Negro Band That Gladdened the Daily Dates Show," *New Orleans Item*, March 1, 1916, 1.
27. Shapiro and Hentoff, *Hear Me Talkin' to Ya*, 57.
28. Ibid., 57–58. Note that this wasn't the first use of the word "jazz" in general; it started showing up in stories about baseball in 1913, before gradually being applied to music. Williams's songs were probably the first uses in New Orleans. For more, see Lewis Porter, "Where Did 'Jazz' the Word Come From," February 26, 2018, https://www.wbgo.org/music/2018-02-26/where-did-jazz-the-word-come-from-follow-a-trail-of-clues-in-deep-dive-with-lewis-porter.
29. "Will Give 'Jas Parade,'" *Times-Picayune*, November 16, 1916, 4.

30. "Steamer Sidney Is Popular," *Times-Picayune*, January 21, 1917, 17.
31. Advertisement for Dugan's Piano Company, *Times-Picayune*, January 28, 1917, 13.
32. "Dixie Jass Band," *Times-Picayune*, February 11, 1917, 49.
33. Advertisement for Maison Blanche, *Times-Picayune*, April 17, 1917, 28.
34. There's evidence that Freddie Keppard and the Original Creole Band had an opportunity to record first but turned it down for a variety of reasons ranging from insufficient payment to Keppard's fear that other cornetists would steal his ideas. Louis Armstrong heard all about it and thought Keppard made a foolish decision. "He was the first one that had the chance to make records," Armstrong said. "He'd cover up his hand [with a handkerchief] and all that, scared somebody gonna steal his stuff. How could you keep me from stealing your stuff if I got ears? Motherfucker should have known that. So he fluffed the date, turned it down and here comes the Original Dixieland Band with all that Larry Shields and that bunch....It should have been Freddie's. I don't know—inferiority complex. Most of our great musicians had one in New Orleans, I always say that." Tape 1987.3.493, Louis Armstrong House Museum.
35. Preston Jackson, "King Oliver: Daddy of the Trumpet," *Hot News*, May 1935, 3.
36. Richard B. Hadlock, liner notes to *The Complete Kid Ory Verve Sessions* (Mosaic Records, 1999), 3.
37. Nick LaRocca, interviewed by William R. Hogan, October 26, 1959, Hogan Archive of New Orleans Music and New Orleans Jazz.
38. Nick LaRocca, interviewed by Richard B. Allen, June 2, 1958, Hogan Archive of New Orleans Music and New Orleans Jazz.
39. Armstrong, "The Armstrong Story," 41.
40. Hadlock, *The Complete Kid Ory Verve Sessions*, 3.
41. Manuel Manetta oral history, May 31 and June 7, 1968, William Russell Oral History Collection Series, MSS 530.2.95, William Russell Jazz Collection, Williams Research Center, Historic New Orleans Collection.
42. Armstrong, "The Armstrong Story," 72.
43. Punch Miller, interviewed by Richard B. Allen, April 4, 1960, Hogan Archive of New Orleans Music and New Orleans Jazz.
44. Private tape made with George Avakian, October 24, 1953, Louis Armstrong House Museum, Tape 1993.1.3.
45. Meryman, *Self-Portrait*, 24.
46. I have chosen not to quote Armstrong's words on the Original Dixieland Jass Band from his 1936 autobiography *Swing That Music*. That book was written with the help of a white ghostwriter, musician/arranger/composer Horace Gerlach. The band was making a comeback at the time that was written, and someone must have thought it would be a good idea to devote an entire chapter to praising the group, but the over-the-top superlatives don't mesh with the more clear-eyed appreciation quoted in this chapter from Armstrong's second book, later interviews, and even private conversations.
47. Armstrong, "Storyville," 101. When Armstrong first told the tale of Lindsey in *True* magazine in 1947, the reformed Lindsey was still alive and had become an influential presence in the church in New Orleans, so Armstrong had to change his name to "Joe Jones."
48. Young trumpeter Amos White heard Armstrong in this band and remembered the undertaker as "Barnes." He also said it was in the winter, meaning most likely January or February 1917. Amos White, Interviewed by William Russell, August 23, 1958, Hogan Archive of New Orleans Music and New Orleans Jazz.

49. Armstrong, “The Armstrong Story,” 44.
50. Louis Armstrong, acetate disc of April 1950 interview for *The Record Changer*, 2013.70.4, Louis Armstrong House Museum.
51. Ibid.
52. Stella Oliver, interviewed by William Russell, April 22, 1959, Hogan Archive of New Orleans Music and New Orleans Jazz.
53. Louis Armstrong, interviewed by Steve Allen for BBC’s *Be My Guest*, June 1968. Tape 2016.130.11, Louis Armstrong House Museum.
54. Armstrong, “The Armstrong Story,” 42.
55. Meryman, *Self-Portrait*, 17.

Chapter 11

1. Brent Staples, “How Italians Became ‘White,’” *New York Times*, October 12, 2019.
2. “Too Many Baby Carriages,” *Daily Picayune*, November 18, 1913, 4.
3. “Shot for a Cigarette,” *Daily Picayune*, September 16, 1909, 4.
4. Armstrong, “The Armstrong Story,” 92.
5. Ibid.
6. Meryman, *Self-Portrait*, 17. In *Satchmo: My Life in New Orleans*, Armstrong placed his Matranga period as after his two weeks in Houma in early 1917, but states, “The first job I went back to [after Houma] was the honky tonk owned by Henry Matranga.” This seems to insinuate that he might have played there before Houma, so it’s also possible he was there in late 1916, shortly after the venue opened for business.
7. Armstrong, “The Armstrong Story,” 49.
8. Private tape made with George Avakian, October 24, 1953, New York Public Library for the Performing Arts, George Avakian and Anahid Ajemian Collection.
9. Meryman, *Self-Portrait*, 23.
10. Jones et al., *Salute to Satchmo*, 57–58.
11. Armstrong, “The Armstrong Story,” 55. In this manuscript, Armstrong tells the prison story and immediately follows with a story about how when he was released, it was Mardi Gras, illustrating “how life can be such a drag one minute and a solid sender the next.” James Karst tried figuring out what Mardi Gras this could be, since there were no Carnival celebrations in 1918 and 1919 because of World War I. Karst leaned toward 1919 because some local parades still took place that year on a smaller scale. If it happened the way Armstrong described it, I personally would argue for 1917, since there was a Mardi Gras that year and “Sore Dick” wasn’t killed until December of that year. However, Armstrong was arrested alongside his family on March 1, 1917, and Mardi Gras was held on February 20, so perhaps he reversed the order of events or mixed it up with a smaller, post–Mardi Gras parade. See James Karst, “When Louis Armstrong Nearly Missed Mardi Gras,” *Times-Picayune*, January 15, 2017.
12. Larry L. King, “Everybody’s Louie,” *Harper’s*, November 1967, 67.
13. Private tape made with George Avakian, October 24, 1953, New York Public Library for the Performing Arts, George Avakian and Anahid Ajemian Collection.
14. *The Mike Douglas Show*, March 24, 1970.
15. Armstrong, “The Armstrong Story,” 36.

16. Ibid.
17. Ibid., 90.
18. Ibid., 36.
19. Ibid., 129. Armstrong then scrawled "AN SISTER" in the margin above this sentence, remembering to give Mama Lucy her respect, too.
20. Private tape made with George Avakian, October 24, 1953, New York Public Library for the Performing Arts, George Avakian and Anahid Ajemian Collection.
21. Armstrong, "The Goffin Notebooks," 82.
22. Ibid.
23. Jones et al., *Salute to Satchmo*, 59.
24. Albin Krebs, "Louis Armstrong, Jazz Trumpeter and Singer, Dies at 71," *New York Times*, July 7, 1971, 41.
25. Armstrong, "The Armstrong Story," 90–94.
26. "Dance Hall Feud Ends in Death of Two Rivals," *Daily Picayune*, March 25, 1913, 1, 6.
27. "Gossip of an Old Timer on Politics Past and Present," *Times-Democrat*, November 2, 1913, 7.
28. "Closing the Cabarets," *Times-Picayune*, March 8, 1915, 2.
29. *Jazz Casual*, broadcast on National Educational Television, January 23, 1963. https://youtu.be/9qT8b6tHL14?si=IOQ2DzM64N6W3S4h
30. Meryman, *Self-Portrait*, 17.
31. Advertisement in *The Freeman*, May 19, 1917, 6. A few months later, a motley crew from the theater was arrested at Billie Mack's home at 1817 Palmyra Street for disturbing the peace. Among the musicians arrested were Joe Oliver, cornetist and violinist Peter Bocage, pianist Arthur Campbell, and violinist Armand John Piron (listed as "Johnny Peron"). Also arrested were Mack, actors Arthur Bruce, Andrew Knox, and Louis Wade, and two prostitutes, Johnnie Covington and Elise Govaux, who were hit with additional charges for being "lewd and abandoned."
32. Manuel Manetta oral history, March 27, 1957, William Russell Oral History Collection Series, MSS 530.2.2, William Russell Jazz Collection, Williams Research Center, Historic New Orleans Collection.
33. Beatrice "Mama Lucy" Armstrong, interview with Yoshio Toyama, August 19, 1973.
34. Ibid.
35. Jones, *Salute to Satchmo*, 58.
36. Bechet, *Treat It Gentle*, 92–93.
37. Armstrong, "The Armstrong Story," 60. Armstrong was even more impressed when, during a previous Labor Day parade, Henry Allen Sr.'s Brass Band was short a cornet and Allen hired Bechet to fill in. Bechet went to Jake Fink's, rented a cornet, and according to Armstrong, "made the whole parade, blowing like crazy."
38. Bechet, *Treat It Gentle*, 93.
39. Emile Barnes, interviewed by William Russell and Ralph Collins, October 1, 1959, Hogan Archive of New Orleans Music and New Orleans Jazz.
40. Paul Barnes, interviewed by June Julian, March 13, 1971, Hogan Archive of New Orleans Music and New Orleans Jazz.
41. Tape 1987.3.262, Louis Armstrong House Museum.
42. *The Mike Douglas Show*, March 24, 1970
43. Armstrong, "The Armstrong Story," 48.

Chapter 12

1. Kay C. Thompson, "Louis and the Waif's Home," *The Record Changer*, July 1950, 43.
2. Herb Morand, interviewed March 12, 1950, Hogan Archive of New Orleans Music and New Orleans Jazz.
3. Albert Nicholas, interviewed February 9, 1967, Hogan Archive of New Orleans Music and New Orleans Jazz.
4. Kay C. Thompson, "Louis and the Waif's Home," *The Record Changer*, July 1950, 43.
5. Ibid.
6. Preston Jackson, Interviewed by William Russell, June 2, 1958, Hogan Archive of New Orleans Music and New Orleans Jazz.
7. Christopher "Black Happy" Goldston, interviewed by Richard B. Allen and Marjorie T. Zander, April 11, 1962, Hogan Archive of New Orleans Music and New Orleans Jazz.
8. Tony Fougerat, interviewed by Richard B. Allen, June 8, 1960, Hogan Archive of New Orleans Music and New Orleans Jazz.
9. Paul Barnes, interviewed by June Julian, March 13, 1971, Hogan Archive of New Orleans Music and New Orleans Jazz.
10. Hughes Panassie, *Louis Armstrong* (New York: Da Capo Press, 1979), 6–7.
11. Bill Matthews, interviewed by William Russell and Ralph Collins, March 6, 1959, Hogan Archive of New Orleans Music and New Orleans Jazz.
12. William "Bebe" Ridgely, interviewed by Richard B. Allen and Marjorie T. Zander, April 11, 1961, Hogan Archive of New Orleans Music and New Orleans Jazz.
13. Hadlock, *The Complete Kid Ory Verve Sessions*, 3.
14. John McCusker, *Creole Trombone: Kid Ory and the Early Years of Jazz* (Jackson: University of Mississippi Press, 2012), 125.
15. Stella Oliver, interviewed by William Russell, April 22, 1959, Hogan Archive of New Orleans Music and New Orleans Jazz.
16. Kid Ory, interviewed by Neshui Ertegun and Bob Campbell, April 20, 1957, Hogan Archive of New Orleans Music and New Orleans Jazz.
17. Paul Barbarin, interviewed by William Russell, Richard B. Allen, and Ralph Collins, March 27, 1957, Hogan Archive of New Orleans Music and New Orleans Jazz.
18. Ibid. There is some debate about when exactly Oliver was crowned "King." "I gave Oliver the name of 'King,'" Kid Ory claimed as early as 1941. Later, Ory said that it was Oliver who had reminded him of that fact during their last conversation at the Savoy Ballroom in 1928, Oliver telling him, "Thanks for naming me King." "Kid Ory, interview by Dave Stuart 1941," The Kid from Laplace: The Kid Ory Archive, https://www.fellers.se/Kid/Kid_Ory_-_Dave_Stuart_1941.html. Kid Ory, interviewed by Neshui Ertegun and Bob Campbell, April 20, 1957, Hogan Archive of New Orleans Music and New Orleans Jazz. But others who knew Oliver in New Orleans, such as Armstrong and Barbarin, never remembered him having that moniker before he left home. "Of course they named Joe - King Oliver, after he made such a wonderful reputation in Chicago," Armstrong wrote. Armstrong, "The Armstrong Story," 101.
19. Ory, "Louis Was Just a Kid in Knee Pants; Ory," 8.
20. Armstrong, "The Armstrong Story," 60.
21. Ory, "Louis Was Just a Kid in Knee Pants; Ory," 8.
22. Ory, "Louis Was Just a Kid in Knee Pants; Ory," 8.
23. Armstrong, "The Armstrong Story," 62.

24. "Cabarets 'Jazz' Their Swansong as Lid Goes On," *Times-Picayune*, July 7, 1926, 26.
25. Armstrong, "The Armstrong Story," 38.
26. Ibid., 54.
27. Manuel Manetta listed himself as a "Musician" on his 1917 draft registration card and officially enlisted on April 27, 1918, spending his time in the service playing with a military band. He was still overseas in September, but perhaps word had reached Armstrong about his musical exploits.
28. Seymore Peck, "Armstrong Remembers New Orleans and Mama," *P. M.*, June 13, 1947, 17.
29. Armstrong, "The Armstrong Story," 54.
30. Ibid., 62.
31. Meryman, *Self-Portrait*, 18.
32. Ibid.
33. "Mother, Aged 31, Carries Bananas," *New Orleans States*, December 8, 1918, 8.
34. Armstrong, "The Armstrong Story," 39.
35. Private tape made with George Avakian, October 24, 1953, New York Public Library for the Performing Arts, George Avakian and Anahid Ajemian Collection.
36. Armstrong, "The Armstrong Story," 59.
37. Advertisement for Cloverlands Dairy Co., *Daily Picayune*, October 6, 1907, 6.
38. Jason Berry, Interview with Beatrice "Mama Lucy" Armstrong, 1983, Tad Jones Collection, Hogan Archive of New Orleans Music and New Orleans Jazz.
39. Myra Menville, "Red Letter Day Finale," *The Second Line*, January–February 1966, 17.
40. Armstrong, "The Armstrong Story," 50–51.
41. Ibid., 53–54.
42. This incident most likely took place in early 1918 as Armstrong clearly remembered Isaac Smoot being there with him. By the time Smoot filled out his draft registration card on August 24, 1918, he listed his home address as 1327 Gravier Street in the Third Ward but under "Name of Employer," gave "State of Maryland, Jessup, Md."—clearly, he was behind bars yet again, this time at the Maryland House of Correction in Jessup.
43. Armstrong, "The Armstrong Story," 54.
44. Tape 1987.3.41, recorded December 25, 1957, Louis Armstrong House Museum.
45. "Big Restaurant for St. Charles Street Planned," *Times-Picayune*, April 9, 1915, 5.
46. Armstrong, "The Armstrong Story," 52.
47. Advertisement for Hibernia Bank and Trust Company, *Times-Picayune*, September 12, 1918, 10.
48. Geo. A. Fuller advertisement, *Times-Picayune*, August 25, 1918, 15.
49. Armstrong, "The Armstrong Story," 52.
50. "Fleet of Boats for Army May Be Built Here," *Times-Picayune*, September 1, 1918, 1.
51. Lee Collins, Interviewed by William Russell, June 2, 1958, Hogan Archive of New Orleans Music and New Orleans Jazz.
52. John McCusker, "Is this Louis Armstrong? Writer calls discovery of historic New Orleans photo 'magical,'" Nola.com, July 30, 2024 https://www.nola.com/entertainment_life/experts-think-its-louis-armstrong-in-old-new-orleans-photo/article_575b4644-49d8-11ef-8e2c-c3ab69548e3c.html. Special thanks to James Karst for the extra detective work in pinning down the date.
53. "Discuss Closing of Every Saloon in Whole State," *Times-Picayune*, October 15, 1918, 1.
54. "Restaurant Waiters Wear Germ Masks," *Times-Picayune*, October 17, 1918, 6.
55. "Drinking Places Must Keep Clean to Remain Open," *Times-Picayune*, October 16, 1918, 1.

56. Armstrong, "The Armstrong Story," 48.
57. Ibid., 35.
58. King, "Everybody's Louie," 68.
59. Armstrong, "The Armstrong Story," 63.

Chapter 13

1. Armstrong, "The Armstrong Story," 64.
2. Ory, "Louis Was Just a Little Kid in Knee Pants; Ory," 8.
3. Armstrong, "The Armstrong Story," 61.
4. Private tape made with George Avakian, October 24, 1953, Louis Armstrong House Museum, Tape 1993.1.3.
5. Louis Armstrong and Pops Foster interview, c. summer 1958, Louis Armstrong House Museum, Tape 2001.63a.2.
6. Armstrong, "The Armstrong Story," 64.
7. Tape 2017.5.1, recorded August 1967, Louis Armstrong House Museum.
8. Armstrong, "The Armstrong Story," 71.
9. "Algiers and Gretna Daily News Budget," *Times-Picayune*, April 5, 1916, 15.
10. Armstrong, "The Armstrong Story," 67.
11. Private tape made with George Avakian, October 24, 1953, New York Public Library for the Performing Arts, George Avakian and Anahid Ajemian Collection.
12. Armstrong, "The Armstrong Story," 67–68.
13. Tape 1987.3.269, recorded c. February 1954, Louis Armstrong House Museum.
14. Armstrong, "The Armstrong Story," 68.
15. Tape 1987.3.269, recorded c. February 1954, Louis Armstrong House Museum.
16. "Negro Woman Stabbed," *Times-Picayune*, March 14, 1919, 10.
17. Armstrong, "The Armstrong Story," 71.
18. Tape 1987.3.269, recorded c. February 1954, Louis Armstrong House Museum.
19. In their eventual divorce papers, the address "2508 Melpomene" is given as Louis and Daisy's former residence, but a search of that property reveals a small, one-story, single-family home nowhere near Saratoga, occupied by Anthony Favaloro in 1919. However, a search of the 1919 Soards's City Directory lists exactly one upholsterer on Melpomene Street, Sidney Butler at 2009 Melpomene. That structure is still standing—now 2009 Martin Luther King Jr. Boulevard—and is exactly how Armstrong described it, a two-story dwelling with multiple "flats," located between Saratoga and South Rampart Streets.
20. Armstrong, "The Armstrong Story," 72–73.
21. Beatrice "Mama Lucy" Armstrong, interview with Yoshio Toyama, August 19, 1973.
22. Armstrong, "The Armstrong Story," 73.
23. Miller gave his birthday as June 10, but his World War I draft registration card—made out to Earnest Burden—lists it as May 10.
24. Punch Miller, interviewed by William Russell and Richard B. Allen, April 9, 1957, Hogan Archive of New Orleans Music and New Orleans Jazz.
25. Punch Miller, interviewed by Richard B. Allen, April 4, 1960, Hogan Archive of New Orleans Music and New Orleans Jazz.
26. Ibid.
27. Meryman, *Self-Portrait*, 24.

28. Advertisement for Victrola, *Times-Picayune*, January 15, 1919, 3.
29. "Galli-Curci Charms Big Audience Here," *Times-Picayune*, April 26, 1919, 2.
30. Noel Straus, "Magic of Caruso Throws Its Spell on New Orleans," *Times-Picayune*, June 27 1920, 6.
31. Ernie Anderson, "Louis Armstrong: A Personal Memoir," *Storyville 148*, December 1, 1991, 125.
32. Louis Armstrong, acetate disc of April 1950 interview for *The Record Changer*, 2013.70.10 Louis Armstrong House Museum.
33. "A Note or Two," *Chicago Defender*, August 9, 1919, 8.
34. "Year in Vaudeville," *Variety*, December 1919, 33.
35. Rose, *I Remember Jazz*, 110.
36. Armstrong, "The Armstrong Story," 62–63.

Chapter 14

1. Tony Catalano, "When Musicians Couldn't Read a Note!," *Down Beat*, June 1938, 8.
2. Verne Streckfus, interviewed by Richard B. Allen, September 22, 1960, Hogan Archive of New Orleans Music and New Orleans Jazz.
3. "Colored Schools," *The Paducah Sun*, June 7, 1907, 4.
4. Beulah Schact, "The Story of Fate Marable," *The Jazz Record*, March 1946, 6.
5. "River Riplets," *The Rock Island Argus*, July 19, 1912, 9.
6. Tape 1987.3.96, recorded March 9, 1953, Louis Armstrong House Museum.
7. Beulah Schact, "The Story of Fate Marable," *Jazz Record*, March 1946, 6.
8. "Steamer Sidney Is Popular," *Times-Picayune*, January 21, 1917, 17.
9. Paul Vandervoot II, "The King of Riverboat Jazz," *Jazz Journal*, August 1970.
10. Albert Francis, interviewed by William Russell, August 4, 1961, Hogan Archive of New Orleans Music and New Orleans Jazz.
11. "Steamer Sidney Excursion Dances," *Times-Picayune*, November 17, 1918, 41.
12. Peter Bocage, interviewed by William Russell, January 29, 1959, Hogan Archive of New Orleans Music and New Orleans Jazz.
13. St. Cyr, "Jazz as I Remember It."
14. Armstrong, "The Armstrong Story," 80.
15. Verne Streckfus, interviewed by Richard B. Allen, September 22, 1960, Hogan Archive of New Orleans Music and New Orleans Jazz.
16. Baby Dodds, in Gara, *The Baby Dodds Story*, 21.
17. Armstrong, "The Armstrong Story," 80.
18. Ibid., 82.
19. Warren "Baby" Dodds, "Oh, Play That Thing," *The Jazz Record*, May 1946, 10.
20. Johnny St. Cyr, interviewed by William Russell, August 27, 1958, Hogan Archive of New Orleans Music and New Orleans Jazz.
21. Ibid.
22. "See It Now: Grandma Moses and Louis Armstrong," December 13, 1955. This is unused outtake from the filming of what became the Edward R. Murrow documentary *Satchmo the Great*. It has been digitized as CBS-SN551213X-228 and can be viewed online at https://commerce.veritone.com/search/asset/48475398.
23. Armstrong, "The Armstrong Story," 86.

24. Johnny St. Cyr, interviewed by Alan Lomax, April 2, 1949, https://archive.culturalequity.org/field-work/new-orleans-jazz-interviews-1949/johnny-st-cyr-449.
25. Captain Joseph Streckfus, "Louie Armstrong—Fate Marable," February 20, 1958, Hogan Archive of New Orleans Music and New Orleans Jazz.
26. Johnny St. Cyr, interviewed by William Russell, August 27, 1958, Hogan Archive of New Orleans Music and New Orleans Jazz.
27. Louis Armstrong, unused outtake from the filming of the Edward R. Murrow documentary *Satchmo the Great*, c. summer 1956.
28. "Steamer Saint Paul Takes Out Two Excursions," *Quad-City Times*, May 5, 1919, 10.
29. Armstrong, "The Armstrong Story," 84–85.
30. Dodds, in Gara, *The Baby Dodds Story*, 28–29.
31. Private tape made with George Avakian, October 29, 1953, Louis Armstrong House Museum, Tape 1993.1.5.
32. Verne Streckfus, interviewed by Richard B. Allen, September 22, 1960, Hogan Archive of New Orleans Music and New Orleans Jazz.
33. *Laughin' Louis*, BBC documentary directed by Russell Davies, 1984.
34. Armstrong, "The Armstrong Story," 80.
35. Pops Foster, interviewed by Nesuhi Ertegun, April 21, 1957, Hogan Archive of New Orleans Music and New Orleans Jazz.
36. Danny Barker, interviewed by Jason Berry, February 4, 1976, Hogan Archive of New Orleans Music and New Orleans Jazz.
37. Armstrong, "The Armstrong Story," 80.
38. Pops Foster, interviewed by Nesuhi Ertegun, April 21, 1957, Hogan Archive of New Orleans Music and New Orleans Jazz.
39. Johnny St. Cyr, "Jazz As I Remember It," original unedited manuscript written in 1961 and later published in *Jazz Journal*, MSS 519 F.57, William Russell Jazz Collection, Williams Research Center, Historic New Orleans Collection.
40. Private tape made with George Avakian, October 24, 1953.
41. Johnny St. Cyr, "Jazz As I Remember It," original unedited manuscript written in 1961 and later published in *Jazz Journal*. MSS 519 F.57, William Russell Jazz Collection, Williams Research Center, Historic New Orleans Collection.
42. Foster, in Stoddard, *Pops Foster*, 118.
43. Marge Singleton, interviewed by Phil Schaap, WKCR-FM 89.9, June 25, 1979.
44. Dodds, in Gara, *The Baby Dodds Story*, 29.
45. Foster, in Stoddard, *Pops Foster*, 119.
46. Johnny St. Cyr, interviewed by Alan Lomax, April 2, 1949, https://archive.culturalequity.org/field-work/new-orleans-jazz-interviews-1949/johnny-st-cyr-449.
47. Ibid.
48. Russell Sanjek, "Zutty," *H. R. S. Society Rag*, November 1940, 6.
49. Bob Shoffner, interviewed by William Russell, September 8, 1959, Hogan Archive of New Orleans Music and New Orleans Jazz.
50. Zutty and Marge Singleton, interviewed by Stanley Dance, Jazz Oral History Project, May 1975.
51. Ed Crowder and A. F. Niemoeller, "St. Louis Jazzmen," *The Jazz Record*, February 1946, 7–8.
52. Pops Foster, interviewed by Nesuhi Ertegun, April 21, 1957, Hogan Archive of New Orleans Music and New Orleans Jazz.
53. Dodds, in Gara, *The Baby Dodds Story*, 22.

54. Greely Walton, interview with Phil Schaap, WKCR-FM 89.9, October 18, 1980.
55. Dodds, in Gara, *The Baby Dodds Story*, 25–26.
56. Jack Bradley, handwritten notes, Louis Armstrong House Museum, 2008.3.393.
57. Armstrong, "The Armstrong Story," 87.
58. Tape 1987.3.188, recorded c. February 1953, Louis Armstrong House Museum.
59. Armstrong, "The Armstrong Story," 96.
60. Ibid., 97.
61. Ibid., 87.
62. Ibid., 97–98.
63. Ibid., 99.
64. Louis Armstrong, as told to Inez Cavanaugh, "Giant of Jazz," *Band Leaders*, January 15, 1945, 18.
65. Manuel Manetta oral history, May 20 and June 10, 1958, William Russell Oral History Collection Series, MSS 530.2.22, William Russell Jazz Collection, Williams Research Center, Historic New Orleans Collection.

Chapter 15

1. Captain Joseph Streckfus, "Louie Armstrong—Fate Marable," February 20, 1958, Hogan Archive of New Orleans Music and New Orleans Jazz.
2. Armstrong, "The Armstrong Story," 74.
3. In Robert Goffin's *Horn of Plenty*, Goffin reported that the prostitute "Nutsie"—"Nootsie" to Armstrong—lived above Gaspar LoCiciero's grocery store. Unless Goffin was confused, by 1920, Nootsy was out and Mayann was in, living there until she moved to Chicago at the end of his life. Goffin, *Horn of Plenty*, 75.
4. "Chronology," document most likely prepared by Tad Jones. Tad Jones Collection, Hogan Archive of New Orleans Music and New Orleans Jazz. And though Louis mentioned taking Clarence with him, on January 19, 1920, the enumerator found five-year-old Clarence Hatfield living at Mayann's old "Brick Row" address of 1303 Perdido Street, as just an anonymous "Boarder" surrounded by a list of unfamiliar names.
5. Jones et al., *Salute to Satchmo*, 59.
6. Tape 1987.3.269, recorded c. February 1954, Louis Armstrong House Museum.
7. Armstrong, "The Armstrong Story," 74–79.
8. Louis Armstrong, "Why I Like Dark Women," *Ebony*, August 1954, 62.
9. Meryman, *Self-Portrait*, 25.
10. "Two Excursions out of Here on Steamer Saint Paul," *Quad-City Times*, May 13, 1920, 10.
11. Armstrong, "The Armstrong Story," 96.
12. Phil R. Evans and Linda K. Evans, *Bix: The Leon Bix Beiderbecke Story* (Bakersfield, CA: Prelike Press, 1998), 47.
13. Norman Mason, interviewed by Paul Crawford, February 6, 1960, Hogan Archive of New Orleans Music and New Orleans Jazz.
14. Jack Pettis, *Jazzmen* notes, William Russell Jazz Collection, Historic New Orleans Collection, MSS519.F.33. For his part, Beiderbecke wrote a letter to his siblings on September 17, 1921, and remarked that he saw "Faite Maribores bunch" perform on the *St. Paul* in Louisiana, Missouri, most likely in July 1921, when Beiderbecke was playing on the *Capitol* with Albert "Doc" Wrixon's Ten Capitol Harmony Syncopaters. However,

some Beiderbecke historians feel the cornetist might have heard a daytime excursion band without Louis and the New Orleans musicians present. Plus, according to newspaper coverage, the *St. Paul* played a dancing excursion for the "Young Zionists' Club" in St. Louis on July 11, the day Beiderbecke was in Louisiana, Missouri, making it less likely that he encountered Armstrong at that time. For more, see Evans and Evans, *Bix*, 70. Bruce Vermazen, "A Floating Seminar: Louis Armstrong and Art Hickman's Orchestra," *Vintage Jazz Mart* 180, Spring 2018, https://www.vjm.biz/fayte-marable.pdf.

15. Johnny St. Cyr, interviewed by Alan Lomax, April 2, 1949, https://archive.culturalequity.org/field-work/new-orleans-jazz-interviews-1949/johnny-st-cyr-449.
16. Louie Metcalf, Interviewed by Phil Schaap, WKCR-FM 89.9, July 1, 1980.
17. Armstrong, "The Armstrong Story," 97.
18. Pops Foster, interviewed by Nesuhi Ertegun, April 21, 1957, Hogan Archive of New Orleans Music and New Orleans Jazz.
19. Warren "Baby" Dodds, "Oh, Play That Thing!" *The Jazz Record*, May 1946, 10.
20. Armstrong, "The Armstrong Story," 94.
21. William Russell, transcription of conversation with Louis Armstrong, November 29, 1953. MSS 536 F. 31, William Russell Jazz Collection, Williams Research Center, Historic New Orleans Collection.
22. Armstrong, "The Armstrong Story," 95.
23. William Russell, transcription of conversation with Louis Armstrong, November 29, 1953. MSS 536 F. 31, William Russell Jazz Collection, Williams Research Center, Historic New Orleans Collection.
24. "Successful Boat Season Closes Oct. 1," *Alton Evening Telegraph*, September 20, 1920, 6.
25. "Steamer Capitol Is Much Admired," *Times-Picayune*, October 10, 1920, 47.
26. "Tired of Jazz," originally published in the *New York World*, syndicated in the *Brown County Democrat*, September 10, 1920, 7.
27. Captain Joseph Streckfus, "Joseph Streckfus," March 18, 1958, Hogan Archive of New Orleans Music and New Orleans Jazz.
28. "Japanese Sandman-Avalon," *Latrobe Bulletin*, November 4, 1920, 1.
29. Captain Joseph Streckfus, "Joseph Streckfus," March 18, 1958, Hogan Archive of New Orleans Music and New Orleans Jazz. Streckfus's memory does present some issues, as he was certain the whole Art Hickman/"Avalon" episode happened on the *Capitol* in Cape Girardeau, Missouri, and Cairo, Illinois, on the steamer's trip back to New Orleans. But "Avalon" wasn't released until late October and the *Capitol* arrived in New Orleans on Wednesday, October 6, meaning this story most likely took place soon after the band arrived in New Orleans.
30. Norman Mason, interviewed by Paul Crawford, February 6, 1960, Hogan Archive of New Orleans Music and New Orleans Jazz.
31. Norman Mason, interviewed by Paul Crawford, February 6, 1960, Hogan Archive of New Orleans Music and New Orleans Jazz.
32. Captain Joseph Streckfus, "Joseph Streckfus," March 18, 1958, Hogan Archive of New Orleans Music and New Orleans Jazz.
33. Norman Mason, interviewed by Paul Crawford, February 6, 1960, Hogan Archive of New Orleans Music and New Orleans Jazz.
34. Dodds, in Gara, *The Baby Dodds Story*, 25.
35. William "Bebe" Ridgely, interviewed by Richard B. Allen and Marjorie T. Zander, April 11, 1961, Hogan Archive of New Orleans Music and New Orleans Jazz.

36. "Anderson's 'Discharge,'" *Times-Picayune*, October 8, 1919, 8.
37. "Jazz Discord Again Blares for Shimmy at Anderson's," *Times-Picayune*, May 23, 1920, 1.
38. Albert Nicholas, interviewed by Richard B. Allen, Lars Edegran, and Hans Lychou, June 26, 1972. Hogan Archive of New Orleans Music and New Orleans Jazz.
39. Albert Francis, interviewed by William Russell, August 4, 1961, Hogan Archive of New Orleans Music and New Orleans Jazz.
40. "Vice War Pressed and Police Raids Lead to Arrests," *Times-Picayune*, June 30, 1921, 1.
41. Armstrong, "The Armstrong Story," 99.
42. Armstrong, "The Goffin Notebooks," 82.
43. Armstrong, "The Armstrong Story," 99.
44. Albert Francis, interviewed by William Russell, August 4, 1961, Hogan Archive of New Orleans Music and New Orleans Jazz.
45. Armstrong, *Swing That Music*, 67.
46. Albert Francis, interviewed by William Russell, August 4, 1961, Hogan Archive of New Orleans Music and New Orleans Jazz.
47. It was also that year when one of the most hotly debated moments of Armstrong's riverboat years occurred—or didn't occur. Marable's band would alternate sets with a white band led by Norman Brownlee in New Orleans, and some of Brownlee's musicians remembered Armstrong engaging in a cutting contest with 18-year-old white cornetist Emmett Hardy. "When Emmet finished his last and best chorus Louis made a deep bow from the opposite stand, raised his hands and yelled 'man, you're the king,'" drummer Monk Hazel recounted. Cornetist Tony Fougerat corroborated Hazel's story and recalled Armstrong telling Hardy, "You're a better man than I." Hazel also claimed that when Hardy died in 1925, Armstrong sent his mother an out-of-character postcard that simply read, "Now that the king is dead, I am the king." Fate Marable came to Armstrong's defense, stating, "I want you to be sure and write that there's no man that ever lived that could cut Louis. It sure makes me mad to hear that some folks are writing that Emmet Hardy made Armstrong throw in the sponge. As far as I know, Louis never even saw Hardy." Armstrong was asked about this moment for the last 30 years of his life and denied it every time. "I am not sure whether I met Emmett Hardy in person or heard him," Armstrong wrote in 1970. "He didn't live long enough for Anyone to pick up on him. Me especially." Bassist Joe Loyacano told a more feasible story, eliminating the cutting contest and instead describing Armstrong hearing Hardy on the boat and remarking, "That's the best I ever heard in my life. Ain't nobody gonna touch that boy when he gets a little older." A one-off line such as that could have been exaggerated and blown up by other white musicians and friends of Hardy, while also being forgotten by Armstrong soon afterward. Dave Dexter Jr., "Story of Emmet Hardy Told by New Orleans Musicians," *Down Beat*, May 15, 1940, 9. Tony Fougerat, interviewed by Richard B. Allen, June 8, 1960, Hogan Archive of New Orleans Music and New Orleans Jazz. Monk Hazel, interviewed by William Russell, July 16, 1959, Hogan Archive of New Orleans Music and New Orleans Jazz. Robert B. Sales, "No Man Ever Cut Louis!," *Jazz Information*, August 9, 1940, 8. Jones, *Salute to Satchmo*, 18–19. Joe Loyacano, interviewed by Richard B. Allen and Paul Crawford, August 20, 1959, Hogan Archive of New Orleans Music and New Orleans Jazz.
48. Hugues Panassie, *Louis Armstrong* (New York: Charles Scribner's Sons, 1971), 9.
49. This most likely took place after the Marable band arrived in St. Louis on May 14, 1921, a time when the Royal Gardens was closed and Oliver had some time before heading to California in June.
50. Armstrong, "The Armstrong Story," 152.

51. Stella Oliver, interviewed by William Russell, April 22, 1959, Hogan Archive of New Orleans Music and New Orleans Jazz.
52. Arthur Murray, "How to Dance the 'Toddle,'" *St. Louis Star and Times*, July 3, 1921, 55.
53. Dodds, in Gara, *The Baby Dodds Story*, 31–32.
54. Streckfus Steamboat Line advertisement, *Vicksburg Evening Post*, September 14, 1921, 4.
55. Armstrong, *Swing That Music*, 68.
56. Albert Francis, interviewed by William Russell, August 4, 1961, Hogan Archive of New Orleans Music and New Orleans Jazz.
57. Shapiro and Hentoff, *Hear Me Talkin' to Ya*, 76.
58. Armstrong, *Swing That Music*, 67–68.
59. Dodds, in Gara, *The Baby Dodds Story*, 32.
60. Tape 1987.3.96, recorded March 9, 1953, Louis Armstrong House Museum.

Chapter 16

1. Armstrong, "The Armstrong Story," 101. Both Armstrong and Zutty Singleton said that Anderson's was closed in this period, leading Armstrong to go with Singleton first at the Orchard Cabaret, but the drummer at Anderson's, Albert Francis, said that Marable and Armstrong "had a humbug so Louie quit and we hired Louie," making it sound like he immediately went to Anderson's. It's quite possible Armstrong alternated between Anderson's and the Orchard for the rest of his time in town.
2. Armstrong, "The Armstrong Story," 101.
3. Russell Sanjek, "Zutty Singleton," *H. R. S. Society Rag*, November 1940, 5.
4. Rudolph Beaulieu, interviewed by William Russell and Ralph Collins, May 31, 1961, Hogan Archive of New Orleans Music and New Orleans Jazz.
5. Zutty and Marge Singleton, interviewed by Stanley Dance, Jazz Oral History Project, May 1975.
6. Armstrong, "The Armstrong Story," 100.
7. Bert Hyde, "Memories Are Rich for 'Butsy,'" *New Orleans States Item*, June 15, 1972.
8. Zutty Singleton, *Jazzmen* notes, William Russell Jazz Collection, Historic New Orleans Collection, MSS519.F.37–38.
9. "Chronology," document most likely prepared by Tad Jones. Tad Jones Collection, Hogan Archive of New Orleans Music and New Orleans Jazz.
10. Circuit Court of Cook County, Louis Armstrong v. Daisy Armstrong, Bill for Divorce, August 30, 1923. Lil Hardin Armstrong-Chris Albertson Collection, Louis Armstrong House Museum.
11. Circuit Court of Cook County, Louis Armstrong vs. Daisy Armstrong, Petition to Vacate Decree, February 16, 1925. Neither Daisy nor Louis was great at remembering dates; thus, it's possible February 15, 1921, refers to the date February 13, 1920, when Daisy took her husband to court, or a failed attempt at reconciliation soon after Daisy withdrew the charges on January 12, 1921.
12. Armstrong, "The Armstrong Story," 102.
13. Private tape made with George Avakian, October 24, 1953. On January 15, 1920, the census enumerator found 12-year-old Willie Mae living with her 14-year-old sister Violet and 33-year-old mother, Mary Wilson, at a boarding house at 1312 Saratoga Street on the corner of Erato, about a block away from Louis and Daisy's residence at 2009 Melpomene. In the

manuscript to *Satchmo: My Life in New Orleans*, Louis mentions that when Daisy adopted Willie Mae Wilson, they were living together in the "white neighborhood" of St. Charles and Clio Street, in the rear of the home of a white family Daisy was working for. Louis never felt comfortable in this neighborhood and after being harassed by an "old geezer" watchman one night, he "immediately found three rooms around Saratoga and Erato Streets" for Daisy, Willie Mae, and himself to move into. Thus, it's possible Louis knew the Wilsons, helped them get set up at that address—Daisy is not mentioned anywhere in the 1920 census—and left soon after, leaving Daisy to raise Willie Mae, whom he would only see during his infrequent reunions with his wife. Armstrong, "The Armstrong Story," 102–103.

14. Armstrong, "The Armstrong Story," 103.
15. Zutty Singleton, *Jazzmen* notes, William Russell Jazz Collection, Historic New Orleans Collection, MSS519.F.37–38.
16. Armstrong, "The Armstrong Story," 101. It's quite possible that Armstrong made his debut with the Tuxedo performing at the funeral of drummer Henry Zeno. Armstrong insisted that Zeno "died in the early part of 1917" but according to the Louisiana Statewide Death Index, Zeno died on November 3, 1921. Armstrong remembered that Zeno "had the largest funeral, of any musician, in the history of music," so it would make sense that the Tuxedo would have performed it, plus a November date gibes with Armstrong's "latter part of 1921" statement.
17. Armstrong, "The Armstrong Story," 101. That was an apt comparison as Louis remembered performing Sousa's "Semper Fidelis" with the Tuxedo Brass Band. Tape 1987.3.257, recorded c. 1952, Louis Armstrong House Museum.
18. Armstrong, "The Armstrong Story," 101.
19. Amos White, interviewed by William Russell, August 23, 1958, Hogan Archive of New Orleans Music and New Orleans Jazz.
20. Joseph "Red" Clark, interviewed by William Russell and Richard B. Allen, January 13, 1959, Hogan Archive of New Orleans Music and New Orleans Jazz.
21. Abbey "Chinee" Foster, interviewed by William Russell, June 29, 1960, Hogan Archive of New Orleans Music and New Orleans Jazz.
22. Rudolph Beaulieu, interviewed by William Russell and Ralph Collins, May 31, 1961, Hogan Archive of New Orleans Music and New Orleans Jazz.
23. Interview with Babe Phillips, March 25, 1957, William Russell Oral History Collection Series, MSS530, William Russell Jazz Collection, Williams Research Center, Historic New Orleans Collection.
24. Louis Armstrong, acetate disc of April 1950 interview for *The Record Changer*, 2013.70.10, Louis Armstrong House Museum.
25. Amos White, interviewed by William Russell, August 23, 1958, Hogan Archive of New Orleans Music and New Orleans Jazz.
26. Louis Armstrong, acetate disc of April 1950 interview for *The Record Changer*, 2013.70.10, Louis Armstrong House Museum.
27. *Heritage*, originally broadcast on PBS, August 2, 1960.
28. Punch Miller, interviewed by Richard B. Allen, August 23, 1960, Hogan Archive of New Orleans Music and New Orleans Jazz.
29. Armstrong, "The Armstrong Story." 104.
30. Ibid., 105.
31. Ibid., 100.

32. Albert Francis, interviewed by William Russell, August 4, 1961, Hogan Archive of New Orleans Music and New Orleans Jazz.
33. Zutty Singleton, *Jazzmen* notes, William Russell Jazz Collection, Historic New Orleans Collection, MSS519.F.37–38. James Karst discovered a *New Orleans Item* article from February 1922 capturing "a quiet night at the old Tom Anderson place in Rampart Street." The article described a band with a cornetist, a violinist, and a pianist, complete with a cartoon depicting the musicians. "The music stops," the *Item* reported. "The plump cornetist, drawing his green eyeshade low upon his face, promptly falls asleep. The pianiste argues about a friend who, it appears, has achieved incarceration in jail." At this point, the article quoted the "plump cornetist" in racist dialect: "Ah tells yu, that niggah's gwine to stay right theah in the parish prison," he was quoted as saying. Though not identified by name, February 1922 is in line with Armstrong's return to Tom Anderson's and the "plump" adjective fits so it's most likely Armstrong's first time being quoted in a newspaper. James Karst, "Fragments of Louis Armstrong when he was on the cusp of greatness," *Times-Picayune*, March 19, 2017.
34. Armstrong, "Storyville," 102.
35. Lucille Armstrong, interview with Steve Allen for BBC Radio 2 documentary series *Satchmo: The Life of Louis Armstrong*, 1974.
36. "Negro Shot by Negress," *New Orleans Item*, October 1, 1923, 9.
37. Armstrong, "The Armstrong Story," 103.
38. Max Jones and John Chilton, *Louis: The Louis Armstrong Story, 1900–1971* (Boston: Little, Brown, 1971), 228.
39. "Negro Jazzers Stir WGV Fans; Miss Dove Star," *New Orleans Item*, April 22, 1922, 1.
40. "OKeh Record Artist Has Rapid Rise to Stardom," *Chicago Defender*, July 21, 1923, 6.
41. Ibid.
42. "Colored Singers and Players to Fame and Fortune by Disc," *Variety*, August 2, 1923, 5.
43. "Ethel Radiates," *Chicago Defender*, April 29, 1922, 7.
44. Fletcher Henderson, "Henderson 'Had to Get Louis' for Roseland Ork," *Down Beat*, July 14, 1950, 4.
45. Fletcher Henderson, "He Made the Band Swing," *The Record Changer*, July–August 1950, 15.
46. Albert Francis, interviewed by William Russell, August 4, 1961, Hogan Archive of New Orleans Music and New Orleans Jazz.
47. Henderson, "He Made the Band Swing," 15.
48. Henderson, "Henderson 'Had to Get Louis' for Roseland Ork," 4.
49. Louis Armstrong, acetate disc of April 1950 interview for *The Record Changer*, 2013.70.8, Louis Armstrong House Museum.
50. Zutty and Marge Singleton, interviewed by Stanley Dance, Jazz Oral History Project, May 1975.
51. Louis Armstrong, acetate disc of April 1950 interview for *The Record Changer*, 2013.70.8, Louis Armstrong House Museum.
52. Tape 1987.3.96, Louis Armstrong House Museum.
53. Lil Armstrong, "Lil Tells of First Time She Met Louis," *Down Beat*, July 14, 1950, 18.
54. Lillian Hardin Armstrong, BBC interview with Geoffrey Haydon, November 10, 1969.
55. Dodds, in Gara, *The Baby Dodds Story*, 34.
56. "Ragtime" Billy Tucker, "Coast Dope," *Chicago Defender*, April 29, 1922, 8.

57. Bookman's name is consistently given as Bertha Gonsoulin and online resources list a birthday of November 11, 1883. There was a Bertha Gonsoulin born in Loreauville, Louisiana, on that date who spent her final years in New Iberia, Louisiana, but that's not the musician. The 1900 census lists the "Gonzalin" family at 625 Seguin Street in New Orleans with Bertha born August 1887, living with father, Henry, mother, Martha, and brother, Phillip. She moved to San Francisco and married a man named Frank Bookman. In the 1920 census, both Bertha and Frank Bookman are listed as being 29 years old, with Bertha's occupation listed as "piano player." She used the name Bertha Bookman during her time with Oliver. She is later listed as "widowed"; she went back to using the name Bertha "Gonsouland" or Bertha "Gonsoland" but seemingly never used "Gonsoulin" as it is consistently given in the history books. According to the death index, "Bertha Bookman [Bertha Gonsoland]" died in San Francisco on August 31, 1947.
58. Alexander Bigard, interviewed by Richard B. Allen, April 30, 1961, Hogan Archive of New Orleans Music and New Orleans Jazz.
59. George Mitchell, interviewed by William Russell, July 1, 1959, Hogan Archive of New Orleans Music and New Orleans Jazz.
60. Armstrong, "The Armstrong Story," 105.
61. Paul Mares, *Jazzmen* notes, William Russell Jazz Collection, Historic New Orleans Collection, MSS519.F.31.
62. "Police Begin New Vice Crusade," *New Orleans States*, July 3, 1922, 13.
63. Maurice Durand, interviewed by William Russell, August 22, 1958, Hogan Archive of New Orleans Music and New Orleans Jazz.
64. Tape 1987.3.123, Louis Armstrong House Museum.
65. *Satchmo: The Wonderful World of Louis Armstrong*, BBC radio documentary, aired January 5, 1975.
66. During the parade, Armstrong asked to try his mouthpiece, leading them to swap. Durand paid Armstrong off at the conclusion of the parade and Armstrong thanked him, saying, "Well, I'll see you, I gotta go to work tonight"—taking Durand's mouthpiece with him. "And the next day he went to Chicago!" Durand lamented, as he had never gotten it back. Maurice Durand, interviewed by William Russell, August 22, 1958, Hogan Archive of New Orleans Music and New Orleans Jazz.
67. Albert Francis, interviewed by William Russell, August 4, 1961, Hogan Archive of New Orleans Music and New Orleans Jazz.
68. *Satchmo: The Wonderful World of Louis Armstrong*, BBC radio documentary, aired January 5, 1975.
69. Hyde, "Memories Are Rich for 'Butsy.'"
70. Armstrong, "The Armstrong Story," 106.
71. Albert Nicholas, interviewed February 9, 1967, Hogan Archive of New Orleans Music and New Orleans Jazz.
72. Meryman, *Self-Portrait*, 27.
73. Punch Miller, interviewed by Richard B. Allen, April 1971, Hogan Archive of New Orleans Music and New Orleans Jazz. Miller hinted that the only reason Armstrong got the call was because Oliver was romantically linked with Mayann, of which there is no evidence.
74. *The David Frost Show*, February 11, 1970.
75. Armstrong, "The Armstrong Story," 106.
76. Danny Barker, interviewed by Jason Berry, February 4, 1976, Hogan Archive of New Orleans Music and New Orleans Jazz.
77. Armstrong, "The Armstrong Story," 107.

Chapter 17

1. Louis Armstrong, "Chicago, Chicago, That Toddlin' Town," in *Esquire's 1947 Jazz Book* (New York: Conde Nast, 1947), 40. Saturday, July 8, was clearly a memorable date to Armstrong, but did it represent the date he received the telegram from Oliver, the date he left New Orleans, or the date he arrived in Chicago? The pianist in Oliver's band, Bertha Bookman, told William Russell "the telegram asking Louis Armstrong to join the Oliver band was sent to him on a Sat. evening and he replied Sunday eve. Louis arrived on Tuesday eve., carrying his cornet wrapped in a black bag." That would mean Armstrong got the telegram July 8, played the funeral and any last engagements on July 9, and embarked on the 25-hour train ride on July 10, arriving on Tuesday, July 11. But trombonist Preston Jackson said he was "sitting on the stand when Louis walks in there [at the Lincoln Gardens]. . . . on a Sunday night when he first came in." That would mean that Armstrong boarded the train on July 8 and arrived in Chicago on Sunday, July 9. William Russell, "Bertha Gonsoulin 1940s," handwritten notes from "California Notes," MSS 536 F15, William Russell Jazz Collection, Williams Research Center, Historic New Orleans Collection. Preston Jackson, Interviewed by William Russell, June 2, 1958, Hogan Archive of New Orleans Music and New Orleans Jazz.
2. Armstrong, "The Armstrong Story," 107.
3. Ibid.
4. Ibid., 108.
5. Armstrong, "Chicago, Chicago, That Toddlin' Town," 40.
6. George Wettling, "Lincoln Gardens," *H. R. S. Society Rag*, December 1940, 25.
7. Preston Jackson, interviewed by Richard B. Allen, September 7, 1973, Hogan Archive of New Orleans Music and New Orleans Jazz.
8. Armstrong, "The Armstrong Story," 109.
9. Clyde Bernhardt, interviewed by Phil Schaap, WKCR-FM 89.9, August 17, 1976.
10. William Russell, "Bertha Gonsoulin 1940s," handwritten notes from "California Notes," MSS 536 F15, Williams Research Center, Historic New Orleans Collection.
11. Armstrong, "The Armstrong Story," 109.
12. "King Jones in from Chicago to Welcome 'Fess' Williams," *New York Amsterdam News*, January 26, 1927, 12.
13. "King Jones," *Chicago Defender*, August 7, 1926, 7.
14. Armstrong, "The Armstrong Story," 110..
15. Ibid.
16. Ibid, 111.
17. Ibid., 112.
18. Tape 1987.3.123, recorded c. 1951, Louis Armstrong House Museum.
19. Armstrong, "The Armstrong Story," 121.
20. Ibid.
21. Dodds, *The Baby Dodds Story*, 37.
22. Armstrong, "The Armstrong Story," 121.
23. Ibid., 122.
24. Armstrong, "Chicago, Chicago, That Toddlin' Town," 40.
25. Ibid., 40–41.
26. Preston Jackson, interviewed by William Russell, June 2, 1958, Hogan Archive of New Orleans Music and New Orleans Jazz.
27. David Sager, liner notes to *King Oliver, Off the Record* (ARCH OTR-MM6-C2, 2006), 14.

28. Paul Mares, *Jazzmen* notes, William Russell Jazz Collection, Historic New Orleans Collection, MSS519.F.31.
29. Preston Jackson, "King Oliver: Daddy of the Trumpet," *Hot News*, May 1935, 3.
30. Dodds, in Gara, *The Baby Dodds Story*, 25.
31. Louis Armstrong, interviewed by Phil Elwood, c. January 1963, Louis Armstrong House Museum, Tape 1995.28.1
32. Dixon Gayer, " 'Chicago Style' All Bunk Bud Freeman Asserts,' 'Ain't No Such Animal,' " *Down Beat*, December 1, 1942, 4.
33. Muggsy Spanier, interviewed by William Russell, February 2, 1961, Hogan Archive of New Orleans Music and New Orleans Jazz.
34. Clyde Bernhardt, interviewed by Phil Schaap, WKCR-FM 89.9, August 17, 1976.
35. Happy Caldwell, interviewed by Phil Schaap, WKCR-FM 89.9, August 2, 1973.
36. Clyde Bernhardt, interviewed by Phil Schaap, WKCR-FM 89.9, August 17, 1976.
37. Armstrong, "The Armstrong Story," 125.
38. Dave Peyton, "Things in General: Creole Musicians," *Chicago Defender*, November 19, 1927, 6.
39. Preston Jackson, interviewed by William Russell, June 2, 1958, Hogan Archive of New Orleans Music and New Orleans Jazz.
40. Lester Boone, interviewed by Phil Schaap, WKCR-FM 89.9, July 16, 1983.
41. Louis Armstrong, acetate disc of April 1950 interview for *The Record Changer*, 2013.70.8, Louis Armstrong House Museum.
42. Dodds, in Larry Gara, *The Baby Dodds Story*, 35.
43. Armstrong, "The Armstrong Story," 124.
44. Glover Compton, interviewed by William Russell, June 30, 1959, Hogan Archive of New Orleans Music and New Orleans Jazz.
45. Louis Armstrong, acetate disc of April 1950 interview for *The Record Changer*, 2013.70.8, Louis Armstrong House Museum.
46. Armstrong, "The Armstrong Story," 123.
47. Ibid.
48. Tape 1987.3.210, recorded c. 1951, Louis Armstrong House Museum.
49. Armstrong, "The Armstrong Story," 123–124.
50. Ibid., 124.
51. Tape 2017.5.1, recorded August 1967, Louis Armstrong House Museum.
52. Armstrong, "Louis Armstrong + the Jewish Family," 56.
53. Dodds, *The Baby Dodds Story*, 40.
54. Clyde Bernhardt, interviewed by Phil Schaap, WKCR-FM 89.9, August 17, 1976. Berhnardt remembered Oliver telling a sideman, "You look like a goddamned snapping turtle," only to be told "You look like a damn big bullfrog" in return.
55. Baby Dodds, interviewed by William Russell, May 31, 1958, Hogan Archive of New Orleans Music and New Orleans Jazz.
56. Johnny Simmen, "A King—No Doubt!," *Storyville,* vol. 46, April–May 1973, 148.
57. Clyde Bernhardt, interviewed by Phil Schaap, WKCR-FM 89.9, August 17, 1976.
58. Freddie Moore, interviewed by Phil Schaap, WKCR-FM 89.9, August 17, 1976.
59. Preston Jackson, interviewed by William Russell, June 2, 1958, Hogan Archive of New Orleans Music and New Orleans Jazz.
60. Stella Oliver, interviewed by William Russell, April 22, 1959, Hogan Archive of New Orleans Music and New Orleans Jazz.

Chapter 18

1. All quotes in this chapter, unless otherwise noted, are from Lillian Hardin Armstrong's unpublished autobiographical manuscript, "Memphis to Paris on a Piano Stool," written c. 1962 with the help of Chris Albertson, Louis Armstrong House Museum.
2. Lillian Hardin Armstrong, BBC interview with Geoffrey Haydon, November 10, 1969.
3. "Gone West," *Chicago Defender*, December 2, 1922, 6.
4. Armstrong, "The Armstrong Story," 122.
5. Lillian Hardin Armstrong, BBC interview with Geoffrey Haydon, November 10, 1969.
6. Armstrong, "The Goffin Notebooks," 86.
7. Armstrong, "The Armstrong Story," 125–126.
8. Ibid., 128.
9. Armstrong, "The Goffin Notebooks," 87.
10. Armstrong, "The Armstrong Story," 128–129.
11. Ibid., 129–130.
12. Armstrong, "The Goffin Notebooks," 88.
13. Ibid., 86.
14. LP, catalog no. 12-120, Lil Armstrong, *Satchmo and Me* (New York City: Riverside Records, 1957).
15. Hoagy Carmichael, *The Stardust Road* (Bloomington: Indiana University Press, 1982), 53.

Chapter 19

1. Regarding the date(s) of the session(s), Baby Dodds said, "We journeyed from Chicago to Richmond by train and we did all that recording in one day because none of us had quarters to sleep in Richmond. We went in the morning and came back at night." However, according to Gennett's recording ledgers, the Oliver band recorded five selections on April 5 and four more on April 6. Perhaps Dodds forgot about staying overnight. It's also possible the session began on the evening of April 5 and finished in the early hours of April 6. George W. Kay, "Those Fabulous Gennetts," *Record Changer*, June 1953, 7.
2. Dodds, in Gara, *The Baby Dodds Story*, 69.
3. Ibid.
4. *Jazz Casual.*
5. Lillian Hardin Armstrong, interviewed by William Russell, July 1, 1959, Hogan Archive of New Orleans Music and New Orleans Jazz.
6. "Gennett Records" blank contract, "King Oliver" folder, Frederic Ramsey Jr. Papers, MSS 559, F. 45, Williams Research Center, Historic New Orleans Collection.
7. Zutty Singleton, *Jazzmen* notes, William Russell Jazz Collection, Historic New Orleans Collection, MSS519.F.37–38.
8. Louis Armstrong, acetate discs of April 1950 interview for *The Record Changer*, 2013.70.7 and 2013.70.8, Louis Armstrong House Museum.
9. Interview with Alberta Hunter and John Hammond, 1983, raw footage digitized by Historicfilms.com, https://historicfilms.com/search/?q=alberta+hunter+john+hamm.
10. Sidney Bechet, *Jazzmen* notes, William Russell Jazz Collection, Historic New Orleans Collection, MSS519.F.20.

11. Louis Armstrong interview with Willis Conover, Voice of America broadcast, recorded July 13, 1956, Music Library, University of North Texas Libraries, Digital Library, https://digital.library.unt.edu.
12. Though Manuel Manetta remembered playing it with the Ory and Oliver band in 1917, Bill Johnson said, "Louis composed the 'Dippermouth [Blues] at the Royal Gardens at that period. Louis was called Dippermouth then." When asked about it directly, Armstrong was vague, saying they worked it up "after we got together. We'd make up those things and then he'd put [my name] on it. He didn't have to, of course." Bill Johnson, *Jazzmen* notes, William Russell Jazz Collection, Historic New Orleans Collection, MSS519.F.28. Private tape made with George Avakian, October 24, 1953. For more on the composition of this piece, see Lewis Porter, "King Oliver and Louis Armstrong in 1923, Part 4: Who Wrote 'Dipper Mouth' Blues," August 12, 2023, https://lewisporter.substack.com/p/king-oliver-and-louis-armstrong-in.
13. Shain, "New Orleans Trumpeters," 6.
14. Dodds, in Gara, *The Baby Dodds Story*, 69–70.
15. Oliver listed himself as the composer, even though New Orleans clarinetist Alphonse Picou claimed it was his piece. Oliver would make it up to Picou by recording three of his compositions, "Alligator Flop," "Olympia Rag," and "Onzanga Blues," though they were issued as Picou-Oliver compositions "Alligator Hop," "Chattanooga Stomp," and "New Orleans Stomp," respectively.
16. Richard B. Hadlock, *Annals of Jazz* broadcast, August 3, 2008, featuring an interview Hadlock conducted with Armstrong in San Francisco on January 17, 1962.
17. Roy Palmer, interviewed by William Russell, September 22, 1955, Hogan Archive of New Orleans Music and New Orleans Jazz.
18. Bill Johnson, *Jazzmen* notes, William Russell Jazz Collection, Historic New Orleans Collection, MSS519.F.28.
19. "Local Music House Head Wins Honors at National Meeting," *Herald-Palladium*, June 12, 1923, 4.
20. "Picked Up around the Drake Lobby," *Talking Machine World*, June 15, 1923, 73.
21. "From Our Chicago Headquarters," *Talking Machine World*, August 15, 1923, 103.
22. Clyde Bernhardt, interviewed by Phil Schaap, WKCR-FM 89.9, August 17, 1976.
23. Punch Miller, interviewed by Richard B. Allen, April 4, 1960, Hogan Archive of New Orleans Music and New Orleans Jazz.
24. Lil Armstrong, *Satchmo and Me*.
25. Lillian Hardin Armstrong, BBC interview with Geoffrey Haydon, November 10, 1969.
26. Circuit Court of Cook County, Louis Armstrong v. Daisy Armstrong, Bill for Divorce, August 30, 1923, Lil Hardin Armstrong-Chris Albertson Collection, Louis Armstrong House Museum.
27. Circuit Court of Cook County, Chancery, Armstrong vs. Same, Order of Default, October 18, 1923. Lil Hardin Armstrong-Chris Albertson Collection, Louis Armstrong House Museum.
28. "Complete Plans for Big Parade," *The Richmond Item*, October 5, 1923, 8.
29. "Spectacular Array Presented by Klan in Mamoth [*sic*] Parade," *The Richmond Item*, October 6, 1923, 1, 2.
30. "Mabel's Dream" also offers evidence of the techniques he picked up from Walt Roesner, Art Hickman's lone trumpeter, who often played similar second parts on the records Armstrong had to learn with Fate Marable. According to pioneering research by Bruce

Vermazen, Roesner often played second parts to Hickman's violin and reeds in a fashion similar to Armstrong's on "Mabel's Dream." "I am not suggesting that Armstrong copied Roesner," Vermazen concluded, "but only that he may have heard in Roesner's 'second' parts, which Streckfus obliged him to reproduce (or more likely only approximate), an approach that he could develop and transform into his own, unique second-part style, in the way that he took Oliver's lead playing and developed it into his own, unique lead style." Bruce Vermazen, "A Floating Seminar: Louis Armstrong and Art Hickman's Orchestra," *Vintage Jazz Mart* 180, Spring 2018, https://www.vjm.biz/fayte-marable.pdf.

31. Louis Armstrong interview with Willis Conover, Voice of America broadcast, recorded July 13, 1956, Music Library, University of North Texas Libraries, Digital Library, https://digital.library.unt.edu. In 1951, Armstrong made up for it on one of his reel-to-reel tapes from 1951, playing trumpet along with "Tears" and stating his beautiful melody.
32. Leonard Kunstadt, "The Story of Louie Metcalf," *Record Research*, October 1962, 5.
33. Stunning new restorations of the King Oliver Creole Jazz Band sides were released in 2024 on the boxed set *Centennial*, produced by Rich Martin and Meagan Hennesey for Archeophone Records. To learn more about this set, visit https://www.archeophone.com/catalogue/king-oliver-centennial/
34. Preston Jackson, "King Oliver: Daddy of the Trumpet," *Hot News*, May 1935, 3.
35. Lillian Hardin Armstrong, BBC interview with Geoffrey Haydon, November 10, 1969.
36. Dodds, in Gara, *The Baby Dodds Story*, 48.
37. Interview with Jerry Blumberg, undated, William Russell Oral History Collection Series, MSS530, William Russell Jazz Collection, Williams Research Center, Historic New Orleans Collection.
38. Armstrong, "The Armstrong Story," 133.
39. Ibid., 133–136.
40. Music was provided by cornetist Oscar "Bernie" Young's seven-piece "Creole Jazz Band," which included reedman Stump Evans and young trombonist Preston Jackson. The same week as the reception, Paramount Records released the three Oliver sides they recorded in December 1923. Needing a fourth side to even it out, the label chose "Dearborn Street Blues" by Bernie Young's Creole Jazz Band.
41. Armstrong, "The Goffin Notebooks," 89–90.
42. Mae Tinee, "The Greatest Film Is the Greatest," *Chicago Tribune*, February 4, 1924, 21.
43. "The Birth of a Nation," *Chicago Tribune*, February 6, 1924, 8.
44. Louis Armstrong, interview with Joe Delaney, Las Vegas, January 1971. Courtesy of Joe Muranyi.
45. "Miss Lillian Hardin Is Bride of Louis Armstrong," *Chicago Defender*, February 16, 1924, 9.
46. Charles Chilton, "Jackson and the Oliver Band," *Jazz News*, vol. 3, no. 6, 1947, 5.
47. Armstrong, "The Armstrong Story," 131.
48. "Sensational Jazz Music by Oliver's Band Friday Night," *The Gazette*, March 10, 1924, 5. This was corroborated in Karl Kramer's 1961 article "MCA Booked Oliver in 1924," *The Second Line*, November–December 1961, 13.
49. Armstrong, "The Armstrong Story," 131.
50. Chilton, "Jackson and the Oliver Band," 6.
51. Albert Nicholas, interviewed by Richard B. Allen, Lars Edegran, and Hans Lychou, June 26, 1972, Hogan Archive of New Orleans Music and New Orleans Jazz.
52. Paul Whiteman, "What Is Jazz Doing to American Music?," *The Etude*, August 1924, 523.
53. Dr. Edmond Souchon, interviewed by William Russell, February 17, 1962, Hogan Archive of New Orleans Music and New Orleans Jazz.

54. "Ross Franklin Orchestra Here," *The South Bend Tribune*, April 21, 1924, 6.
55. Armstrong, "The Armstrong Story," 133.
56. Louis Armstrong, acetate disc of April 1950 interview for *The Record Changer*, 2013.70.8, Louis Armstrong House Museum.
57. Chilton, "Jackson and the Oliver Band," 6.
58. Armstrong, "The Goffin Notebooks," 92.

Chapter 20

1. Lillian Hardin Armstrong, BBC interview with Geoffrey Haydon, November 10, 1969.
2. Chilton, "Jackson and the Oliver Band," 6.
3. Lillian Hardin Armstrong, BBC interview with Geoffrey Haydon, November 10, 1969.
4. Tape 1987.3.424, recorded August 15, 1970, Louis Armstrong House Museum.
5. Tape 1987.3.262, recorded c. March 1952, Louis Armstrong House Museum.
6. Tape 1987.3.424, recorded August 15, 1970, Louis Armstrong House Museum.
7. Ralph Gulliver, "The Band from Columbus," *Storyville 48*, August–September 1973, 214.
8. Albert Wynn, interviewed by William Russell, May 29, 1959, Hogan Archive of New Orleans Music and New Orleans Jazz.
9. Dempsey J. Travis, *An Autobiography of Black Jazz* (Chicago: Urban Research Institute, 1983), 65.
10. Tape 1987.3.36, recorded c. 1954, Louis Armstrong House Museum.
11. Jones et al., *Salute to Satchmo*, 97.
12. Lillian Hardin Armstrong, BBC interview with Geoffrey Haydon, November 10, 1969.
13. Tape 1987.3.36, recorded c. 1954, Louis Armstrong House Museum. Interestingly, on some level, Stewart might have known Armstrong represented an important new ingredient in the music's development. In August 1924, he hired a hot trumpet soloist from Chicago in Eugene Hutt and even recorded some Oliver-inspired two-cornet breaks on "My Man Rocks Me" that same month.
14. Lil Hardin, *Jazzmen* notes, William Russell Jazz Collection, Historic New Orleans Collection, MSS519.F.14. While conducting interviews for *Jazzmen*, William Russell spoke with Richard M. Jones, who gave more credit to Oliver, stating, "Used to help Louis with fingerings, reading and all that stuff, Oliver did." Jones then uttered one line—"Louis studied with a German teacher in Kimball Hall"—and resumed talking about Armstrong and Oliver. The importance of Armstrong studying with a German teacher has become somewhat inflated in this writer's opinion. Neither Louis nor Lil ever mentioned it, unlike Kid Ory, who detailed his studies with trombonist Jaroslav Cimera of Bohemia, or Buster Bailey, who studied with German clarinetist Franz Schoepp. Russell only jotted down that one line and didn't ask for any follow-ups, so even if Armstrong studied with a German teacher, it's not clear when or for how long. The fact that he never mentioned it in any of his writings or interviews does seem to minimalize any impact it may have had, especially compared with what he learned from Oliver and Hardin. Richard M. Jones, *Jazzmen* notes, William Russell Jazz Collection, Historic New Orleans Collection, MSS519.F.29.
15. Lil Hardin, *Jazzmen* notes, William Russell Jazz Collection, Historic New Orleans Collection, MSS519.F.14.
16. Lil Armstrong, *Satchmo and Me*.
17. Lil Hardin, *Jazzmen* notes, William Russell Jazz Collection, Historic New Orleans Collection, MSS519.F.14

18. Private tape made with George Avakian, October 24, 1953, New York Public Library for the Performing Arts, George Avakian and Anahid Ajemian Collection.
19. Fascinatingly, at the time of this arrest, Williams gave his address as 122 North Liberty Street. In her response to Louis's divorce papers, Daisy Parker Armstrong claimed that at the time Louis filed for divorce in August 1923, she was living at 122 North Liberty Street! And Black Benny's arrest on November 15, 1923, was the same date Mayann Armstrong was arrested, though it is not known if these were connected or separate instances. The world of Armstrong's characters back home indeed was a small one.
20. Report of Homicide, Department of Police, First Precinct, New Orleans, July 10, 1924.
21. James Karst, "The Life and Death of Early Jazz Drummer Black Benny Williams," *Times-Picayune*, January 24, 2016.
22. Joe Watkins, interviewed by William Russell, March 16, 1960, Hogan Archive of New Orleans Music and New Orleans Jazz.
23. Private tape made with George Avakian, October 24, 1953, New York Public Library for the Performing Arts, George Avakian and Anahid Ajemian Collection.
24. Ramsey, "King Oliver and his Creole Jazz Band," 75.
25. Lillian Hardin Armstrong, BBC interview with Geoffrey Haydon, November 10, 1969.
26. The saga of Armstrong squaring off against Johnny Dunn quickly grew into legend, discussed by musicians who weren't even there, some of whom placed it in 1923 when Armstrong was with Oliver, while others believed it happened later in the decade at the Sunset Café; clarinetist Albert Nicholas thought it happened at the Plantation Café, where Armstrong did not perform. But the truth resides in Armstrong's own versions of the story, which share three crucial details: it occurred in the Dreamland Cafe, Dunn was there with members of a big show from New York, and the dancers Brown and McGraw were also on the bill. Taking into account those elements, August 1924 fits from both a logical and logistical standpoint; after his run-in with Dunn, Armstrong would be ready for his next major career move.
27. Doc Cheatham, interviewed by Phil Schaap, WKCR-FM 89.9, April 11, 1977.
28. Punch Miller, interviewed by Richard B. Allen, April 4, 1960, Hogan Archive of New Orleans Music and New Orleans Jazz.
29. Ibid.
30. "Johnny Dunn Plays," *Chicago Defender*, June 14, 1924, 6.
31. Leonard Kunstadt, "The Story of Louie Metcalf," *Record Research*, October 1962, 6.
32. "A Note or Two," *Chicago Defender*, August 23, 1924, 7.
33. Louis Armstrong and Zutty Singleton in conversation at the Hotel Woodward, New York City, February 1971, Tape 2005.1.2209, Louis Armstrong House Museum.
34. Louis Armstrong, acetate disc of April 1950 interview for *The Record Changer*, 2013.70.6, Louis Armstrong House Museum.
35. Louis Armstrong and Zutty Singleton in conversation at the Hotel Woodward, New York City, February 1971, Tape 2005.1.2209, Louis Armstrong House Museum.
36. Darnell Howard, interviewed by Nesuhi Ertegun and Robert Campbell, April 21, 1957, Hogan Archive of New Orleans Music and New Orleans Jazz.
37. Louis Armstrong and Zutty Singleton in conversation at the Hotel Woodward, New York City, February 1971, Tape 2005.1.2209, Louis Armstrong House Museum.
38. Darnell Howard, interviewed by Nesuhi Ertegun and Robert Campbell, April 21, 1957, Hogan Archive of New Orleans Music and New Orleans Jazz.

39. Louis Armstrong and Zutty Singleton in conversation at the Hotel Woodward, New York City, February 1971, Tape 2005.1.2209, Louis Armstrong House Museum.
40. Louis Armstrong, acetate disc of April 1950 interview for *The Record Changer*, 2013.70.6, Louis Armstrong House Museum.
41. Darnell Howard, interviewed by Nesuhi Ertegun and Robert Campbell, April 21, 1957, Hogan Archive of New Orleans Music and New Orleans Jazz.
42. Louis Armstrong and Zutty Singleton in conversation at the Hotel Woodward, New York City, February 1971, Tape 2005.1.2209, Louis Armstrong House Museum.
43. Henderson, "He Made the Band Swing," 15.
44. W. E. Burghardt DuBois, "The Talented Tenth," in *The Negro Problem* (New York: James Pott, 1903), 33.
45. Black Swan Phonograph Company, Inc. advertisement, *The Crisis Advertiser*, January 1923, 139.
46. On September 13, 1923, a Henderson-led small group recorded "The Dicty Blues" for Columbia, leaning into the word associated with the highbrow groups such as Sammy Stewart's. But instead of a polite dance recording, Henderson seemed to burlesque the southern sounds of groups such as King Oliver's, the very opposite of "Dicty"; the arrangement references both Lil Hardin's solo from "Chimes Blues" and the melody to "Royal Garden Blues." It's a spirited performance, though more a satire of New Orleans music than the real thing.
47. "Prof. Piron Arrives," *Chicago Defender*, September 9, 1922, 9.
48. "Cabarets," *Billboard*, July 23, 1924, 39.
49. Louis Armstrong and Pops Foster interview, c. summer 1958. Louis Armstrong House Museum, Tape 2001.63a.2.
50. Advertisement, *Chicago Defender*, September 6, 1924, 6.
51. While in New York, Oliver took part in a recording session with Butterbeans and Susie that produced "some almost perfect Joe Oliver" in the words of cornetist Johnny Wiggs. "That's the only place I ever heard Joe Oliver on records where he sounds like Joe Oliver." Johnny Wiggs oral history, July 14, 1957, William Russell Oral History Collection Series, MSS 530.3.63, William Russell Jazz Collection, Williams Research Center, Historic New Orleans Collection.
52. Lee Collins, interviewed by William Russell, June 2, 1958, Hogan Archive of New Orleans Music and New Orleans Jazz.
53. "Considerable Band Music in Air Monday Night; Little Novelty," *Variety*, July 30, 1924, 36. *Variety* reported Henderson playing "O Sole Mio" in waltz time and two recent pop tunes, "Limehouse Blues" (recorded by Paul Whiteman in April 1924) and "After the Storm."
54. Henderson, "Henderson 'Had To Get Louis' for Roseland Ork," 4.
55. Armstrong, "The Goffin Notebooks," 89.
56. Henderson was not alone in his interest in Armstrong. Pianist Sam Wooding was a member of Johnny Dunn's band between 1921 and 1923 and was now leading an orchestra of his own at the Club Alabam in New York. Wooding was also looking to add a "punch man" on third trumpet after receiving an offer to take his band to Europe in 1925 and approached Armstrong, but by that time Armstrong had accepted Henderson's offer. "I know he did the right thing by going with Fletcher Henderson than with me because that was the type of thing where he stayed in America and became a great man," Wooding admitted; Sam Wooding, interviewed by Phil Schaap, WKCR-FM 89.9, October 6, 1980.

Chapter 21

1. Don Redman, "Don Redman," *The Jazz Review*, November 1959, 6.
2. Howard Scott, interviewed by Chris Albertson, Jazz Oral History Project, March 8, 1979.
3. Kaiser Marshall, "When Armstrong Came to New York," *Jazz Record*, April 1, 1943, 4.
4. Howard Scott, interviewed by Chris Albertson, Jazz Oral History Project, March 8, 1979.
5. Louis Armstrong, interview with Joe Delaney, September 1970. Tape 1987.3.432, Louis Armstrong House Museum.
6. Louis Armstrong, acetate disc of April 1950 interview for *The Record Changer*, 2013.70.26, Louis Armstrong House Museum.
7. Louis Armstrong, interview with Joe Delaney, September 1970. Tape 1987.3.432, Louis Armstrong House Museum.
8. Ibid.
9. Kaiser Marshall, "When Armstrong Came to New York," *Jazz Record*, February 1947 12.
10. Henderson, "Henderson 'Had To Get Louis' for Roseland Ork," 4–5.
11. Ibid.
12. Meryman, *Self-Portrait*, 32.
13. Marshall, "When Armstrong Came to New York," 4
14. Howard Scott, interviewed by Phil Schaap, WKCR-FM 89.9, October 13, 1975. In a letter to his wife, Lil, from February 1925, Louis recounted some of the bills he was paying and noted, "Also sent in the monthly payments on the cornet." It's possible he was still using the word "cornet" from force of habit after over a decade of playing one or it's possible Scott was mistaken and Armstrong bought a new cornet, instead of a trumpet, once in New York. The photos of Armstrong that survive from this period do not offer a clear glimpse of his instrument, though trumpeter Yoshio Toyama has made a convincing case that Armstrong can be seen holding the same Beuscher trumpet in his photos with Henderson that he held in his later photos with the Hot Five in Chicago; correspondence with the author, February 26, 2024. The question may never be completely answered, but Louis's letter does make it clear that he was playing—and paying for—a new horn of some kind after joining Henderson. Louis Armstrong, letter to Lillian Armstrong, February 8, 1925, https://www.liveauctioneers.com/item/40361043_louis-armstrong-letter-to-his-wife-feb-8-1925.
15. Louis Armstrong, acetate disc of April 1950 interview for *The Record Changer*, 2013.70.26, Louis Armstrong House Museum.
16. Garvin Bushell, interview with Phil Schaap, WKCR-FM 89.9, June 25, 1980.
17. Ibid.
18. Howard Scott, interviewed by Chris Albertson, Jazz Oral History Project, March 8, 1979.
19. Ibid.
20. Meryman, *Self-Portrait*, 32.
21. Walter C. Allen, *Hendersonia,* Jazz Monographs no. 4 (Highland Park, NJ,Walter C. Allen, 1973), 126.
22. Louis Armstrong, acetate disc of April 1950 interview for *The Record Changer*, 2013.70.26, Louis Armstrong House Museum.
23. Howard Scott, Interviewed by Phil Schaap, WKCR-FM 89.9, October 13, 1975.
24. Henderson, "He Made the Band Swing," 15.
25. Shapiro and Hentoff, *Hear Me Talkin' to Ya*, 208.

26. Robert Goffin, "Jazzmen's Greatest Kicks," *Esquire*,August 1944, 142.
27. Antonio Hart, conversation with the author, February 14, 2021.
28. Allen, *Hendersonia*, 128.
29. Russell Procope, interview with Phil Schaap, WKCR-FM 89.9, June 17, 1980. Of that nickname, Procope simply explained, "At that time they used to call him 'Fat' Armstrong—I suppose because he was fat at that time."
30. Kunstadt, "The Story of Louie Metcalf," 6.
31. Russell Procope, interview with Phil Schaap, WKCR-FM 89.9, June 17, 1980.
32. Howard Scott, interviewed by Chris Albertson, Jazz Oral History Project, March 8, 1979.
33. Shapiro and Hentoff, *Hear Me Talkin' to Ya*, 205–206. The precise date of this moment at the Lafayette has been a mystery for decades. Louis Metcalf was likely at the Lafayette as a member of Johnny Hudgins's "Club Alabam Revue" in January 1925, but both he and pianist Louis Hooper referred to it as Armstrong's "introduction" to New York, which seems late. Still, given Henderson's infrequent performances for Black audiences, it might have very well been the first time Armstrong set foot on a Harlem theater stage. Louis Hooper, "Harlem in the Twenties," *Record Research,* June 1966, 3.
34. Rex Stewart, "Boy Meets King," *Down Beat*, July 15, 1965, 23, 25.
35. Duke Ellington, "Jazz as I Have Seen It," *Swing: The Guide to Modern Music*, July 1940, 10.
36. Tape 1987.3.424, Louis Armstrong House Museum.
37. Dan Morgenstern, "Portrait of the Artist as a Young Man," in *Living with Jazz* (New York: Pantheon, 2004), 25.
38. Louis Armstrong interview with Willis Conover, Voice of America broadcast, recorded July 13, 1956, Music Library, University of North Texas Libraries, Digital Library, https://digital.library.unt.edu.
39. Tape 1987.3.424, Louis Armstrong House Museum.
40. Henderson, "Henderson 'Had To Get Louis' for Roseland Ork," 4.
41. Tape 1987.3.424, Louis Armstrong House Museum.
42. Floyd G. Snelson, "Society and Stage Mingle Delightfully at Benefit," *The Pittsburgh Courier*, November 22, 1924, 1.
43. Louis Armstrong, notes on *World's Great Men of Color*, 1987.2.19, Louis Armstrong House Museum.
44. Floyd G. Snelson, "Theatrical Comment," *The Pittsburgh Courier*, December 6, 1924, 10.
45. Shapiro and Hentoff, *Hear Me Talkin' to Ya*," 206–207.
46. Tape 1987.3.424, Louis Armstrong House Museum.
47. Paramount producer J. Mayo Williams reached out to Henderson to put a band together for the date and remembered Henderson telling him, "I can't give you my first trumpet player, but I'll give you my second trumpet player." "And you know who the second trumpet player was?" Williams asked in 1970. "Louis Armstrong." Interview with Mayo Williams, 1970 November 20, William Russell Oral History Collection Series, MSS 530.4.56, William Russell Jazz Collection, Williams Research Center, Historic New Orleans Collection.
48. Lillian Borgeson, interview with Ralph Peer, Southern Folklife Collection, University of North Carolina, Chapel Hill.
49. Marshall, "When Armstrong Came to New York," 12.
50. Vic Berton, as told to Charlie Emge, "Behind the Drums from Ragtime to Swing," *Tempo*, July 1936, 6.

51. Louis Armstrong interview with Willis Conover, Voice of America broadcast, recorded July 13, 1956, Music Library, University of North Texas Libraries, Digital Library, https://digital.library.unt.edu.
52. Armstrong, "The Armstrong Story," 134. However, after recording that take, Henderson called another at a slightly slower tempo—just slow enough to end before Armstrong's spoken interlude. And it was this take that became the more common one, released on the Regal label under Henderson's name. The version with Armstrong's voice was eventually issued on the cheaper Domino label with a pseudonym, "Hal White's Syncopators," on the label.
53. Louis Armstrong, interviewed by Phil Elwood, c. January 1963, Louis Armstrong House Museum, Tape 1995.28.1.
54. Armstrong, "The Armstrong Story," 132–133.
55. John Chilton, *Sidney Bechet: The Wizard of Jazz* (New York: Oxford University Press, 1987), 68.
56. Clarinetist Evan Christopher has argued that on the OKeh version, Bechet simply falls back to keep the melody going in standard New Orleans fashion, happy to let Armstrong knock himself out. The late historian Phil Schaap felt that people who said Bechet "won" the first recording and Armstrong "won" the second are only fooled because of who takes the last break on each recording.
57. Bechet, *Treat It Gentle*, 91.
58. Lil Hardin, *Jazzmen* notes, William Russell Jazz Collection, Historic New Orleans Collection, MSS519.F.14

Chapter 22

1. Interview and cornet lesson with Johnny Wiggs, August 25, 1957, William Russell Oral History Collection Series, MSS 530.3.68, William Russell Jazz Collection, The Williams Research Center, Historic New Orleans Collection.
2. Marshall Stearns, "The History of Swing," *Downbeat*, March 1937, 8.
3. Nat Hentoff, "Garvin Bushell and New York Jazz in the 1920's," *The Jazz Review*, February 1959, 9.
4. Johnny Wiggs, interviewed by William Russell, August 26, 1962, Hogan Archive of New Orleans Music and New Orleans Jazz.
5. Advertisement for The Plantation Cafe, *Chicago Defender*, November 29, 1924, 6.
6. Sidney Bechet, *Jazzmen* notes, William Russell Jazz Collection, Historic New Orleans Collection, MSS519.F.20.
7. Garvin Bushell, interview with Phil Schaap, WKCR-FM 89.9, June 25, 1980.
8. This time, the quote didn't come from Lil, who recalled "some woman violinist played it once at the same concert [Louis] was playing at, and he heard it once and remembered it." Lil Hardin, *Jazzmen* notes, William Russell Jazz Collection, Historic New Orleans Collection, MSS519.F.14.
9. Louis Armstrong interview with Willis Conover, Voice of America broadcast, recorded July 13, 1956, Music Library, University of North Texas Libraries, Digital Library, https://digital.library.unt.edu.
10. Red Nichols, "Jazz Hit Its Highest Peak to Date on My Mid-'20s Records: Nichols," *Downbeat*, September 7, 1951, 2.
11. Louis Armstrong interview with Willis Conover, Voice of America broadcast, recorded July 13, 1956, Music Library, University of North Texas Libraries, Digital Library, https://digital.library.unt.edu.

12. Ibid.
13. Cornet and trumpet virtuosos were tremendously popular in the late 1800s and early 1900s, perhaps best typified by the popularity of Herbert L. Clarke, who spent many years in John Philips Sousa's band. This tradition was not lost on Armstrong; he owned many of Clarke's records and upon dubbing some in the 1950s, remarked on tape, "I admired this man ever since I was a child." Tape 1987.3.227, Louis Armstrong House Museum.
14. Louis Armstrong interview with Willis Conover, Voice of America broadcast, recorded July 13, 1956, Music Library, University of North Texas Libraries, Digital Library, https://digital.library.unt.edu.
15. Tom Lord, *Clarence Williams* (Essex, UK: Storyville, 1976), 30–31.
16. Alberta Hunter, interviewed by Chris Albertson, Jazz Oral History Project, December 17, 1976. Hunter was also from Tennessee but the light complexion of her skin might have also gone over better with the "dicties."
17. Richard B. Hadlock, *Annals of Jazz* broadcast, August 3, 2008, featuring an interview Hadlock conducted with Armstrong in San Francisco on January 17, 1962.
18. Louis Armstrong interview with Willis Conover, Voice of America broadcast, recorded July 13, 1956, Music Library, University of North Texas Libraries, Digital Library, https://digital.library.unt.edu.
19. *Jazz Casual.*
20. The impact of "Cold in Hand Blues" was especially felt in Texas, where Jack Teagarden was still playing with pianist Peck Kelly's band. "Bessie singing 'Cold in Hand Blues' with Louis playing—there's something really pretty," Teagarden said. "Peck Kelly used to play that and cry like a baby." Leonard Feather, "I Never Did Like Duke," *Metronome*, April 1947, 29.
21. Louis Armstrong interview with Willis Conover, Voice of America broadcast, recorded July 13, 1956, Music Library, University of North Texas Libraries, Digital Library, https://digital.library.unt.edu.
22. George Avakian, conversation with the author, February 22, 2007.
23. Meryman, *Self-Portrait*, 32.
24. Howard Scott, interviewed by Chris Albertson, Jazz Oral History Project, Rutgers University, March 8, 1979.
25. Louis Armstrong, interview with Joe Delaney, Las Vegas, January 1971.
26. Chip Deffaa, "Joe Tarto: Last of the Five Pennies," *Mississippi Rag*, February 1985, 2.
27. Neither Armstrong nor Redman ever talked about why it was renamed but it's interesting to point out that the *Chicago Defender* mentioned "The Sugar Foot Sam from Alabam Minstrels" in both its May 16 and May 23, 1925, issues, the latter article under the headline "Sugar Foot Bunch." Given the popularity of the *Chicago Defender* in African American communities, including in New York, one wonders if Redman saw the multiple mentions of "Sugar Foot" on May 16 and 23 and thought it might make a fun title for the May 29 recording.
28. Allen, *Hendersonia*, 134.
29. Ibid.
30. "Modern Eve," *The Lincoln Star*, August 30, 1925, 102.
31. Advertisement for The Starr Piano Company, Richmond *Palladium-Item*, July 29, 1925, 4.
32. "Floyd G. Snelson Jr., "Harlem Limited, Broadway Bound," *The Pittsburgh Courier*, June 13, 1931, 18.
33. "Latest Records in the World of Music," *St. Louis Globe-Democrat*, April 5, 1925, 25.
34. Bucklin Moon, "Louis and the Blues," *The Record Changer*, September 1953, 9.

35. Advertisement for the Columbia Music Shop, *The Buffalo American*, July 2, 1925, 2.
36. Advertisement for George M. Wood, *Pittsburgh Courier*, March 14, 1925, 15.
37. Louis Armstrong, letter to Lillian Armstrong, February 8, 1925, https://www.liveauctioneers.com/item/40361043_louis-armstrong-letter-to-his-wife-feb-8-1925.
38. Marshall, "When Armstrong Came to New York," 5.
39. Lil Armstrong, *Satchmo and Me*.
40. "Armstrong Toots a Wicked Cornet," *Chicago Defender*, May 30, 1925, 6.
41. Clyde Bernhardt, interviewed by Phil Schaap, WKCR-FM 89.9, August 17, 1976.
42. Lorraine Lion, "Mr. Armstrong and Mr. Robbins," *The Jazz Record*, December 1947, 10.
43. Tape 1987.3.424, Louis Armstrong House Museum.

Chapter 23

1. Travis, *An Autobiography of Black Jazz*, 67–68.
2. Lillian Hardin Armstrong, BBC interview with Geoffrey Haydon, November 10, 1969.
3. Louis Armstrong, BBC interview with Geoffrey Haydon, November 17, 1969.
4. "Lil's Dreamland Orchestra," *Chicago Defender*, city edition, October 31, 1925, 6.
5. Lillian Borgeson, interview with Ralph Peer, Southern Folklife Collection.
6. Louis Armstrong, "Jazz on a High Note," *Esquire*, December 1951, 209.
7. Kid Ory, as told to Lester Koenig, "The Hot Five Sessions," *The Record Changer*, July–August 1950, 17.
8. Dave Peyton, "Louis Armstrong Coming Back," *Chicago Defender*, November 7, 1925, 7. Lil had continued planting items in the press about Louis's return, though now she told writers that her husband had traveled from a slightly more exotic place than Roseland in New York City. "Louis Armstrong, trumpeter, recently returned from Germany where he played with a very snappy orchestra for several weeks," one article with the headline "Home at Last" reported, complete with a picture of Louis and a fake quote: "Like all travelers, I can say 'I'm glad to get back.' State Street looks mighty good to me." "Home at Last," undated clipping, c. November 1925, Scrapbook 1987.8.83, Louis Armstrong House Museum.
9. Chip Deffaa, "Doc Cheatham: Chicago Memories," *Mississippi Rag*, July 1990, 18.
10. Garvin Bushell, interview with Phil Schaap, WKCR-FM 89.9, June 25, 1980.
11. Louis Armstrong interview with Willis Conover, Voice of America broadcast, recorded July 13, 1956, Music Library, University of North Texas Libraries, Digital Library, https://digital.library.unt.edu.
12. Tape 1987.3.571, recorded January 1953, Louis Armstrong House Museum.
13. Stewart, "Boy Meets King," 23–25.
14. Lil Armstrong, *Satchmo and Me*.
15. Lillian Hardin Armstrong, BBC interview with Geoffrey Haydon, November 10, 1969.
16. Tape 1987.3.424, recorded August 15, 1970, Louis Armstrong House Museum.
17. Lillian Hardin Armstrong, BBC interview with Geoffrey Haydon, November 10, 1969.
18. Dave Peyton, Undated clipping from c. November 1925, Scrapbook 1987.8.83, Louis Armstrong House Museum.
19. Lil Armstrong, *Satchmo and Me*.
20. Johnny St. Cyr, interviewed by William Russell, August 27, 1958, Hogan Archive of New Orleans Music and New Orleans Jazz.
21. Tape 1987.3.49, recorded c. 1951, Louis Armstrong House Museum. Armstrong was eventually paid royalties for the Hot Five recordings after his manager, Joe Glaser, negotiated a

new deal with producer George Avakian to have Armstrong begin making new recordings for the label in 1954.

22. *Jazz Casual.*
23. Ory, "The Hot Five Sessions," 45.
24. Interview with Johnny St. Cyr, 1958 August 27, William Russell Oral History Collection Series, MSS530.3.56, William Russell Jazz Collection, Williams Research Center, Historic New Orleans Collection.
25. Ory, "Louis Was Just a Kid in Knee Pants; Ory," 8.
26. Louis Armstrong interview with Willis Conover, Voice of America broadcast, recorded July 13, 1956, Music Library, University of North Texas Libraries, Digital Library, https://digital.library.unt.edu.
27. Johnny St. Cyr, "The Original Hot Five," *The Second Line*, September–October 1954, 2.
28. Ibid.
29. Louis Armstrong, private taped conversation with publicist Lloyd Von Blaine, October 1970, Louis Armstrong House Museum 1987.3.430.
30. St. Cyr, "The Original Hot Five," 2.
31. "Dreamland Once Again in Full Bloom," undated clipping, c. November 1925, Scrapbook 1987.8.83, Louis Armstrong House Museum.
32. Ory, "The Hot Five Sessions," 17.
33. Dave Peyton, "The Musical Bunch: The Career of Erskine Tate," *Chicago Defender*, April 24, 1926, 6.
34. Minnie Adams, "Musical and Dramatic," *Chicago Defender*, November 2, 1912, 5.
35. "Vendome Symphony Orchestra," *Chicago Defender*, May 10, 1919, 8.
36. Scoville Brown, Interview with Phil Schaap, WKCR-FM 89.9, October 18, 1980.
37. "Vendome Symphony Orchestra," *Chicago Defender*, May 10, 1919, 8.
38. Armstrong, "The Goffin Notebooks," 95.
39. Lillian Hardin Armstrong, BBC interview with Geoffrey Haydon, November 10, 1969.
40. Armstrong, "The Goffin Notebooks," 95.
41. Lillian Hardin Armstrong, BBC interview with Geoffrey Haydon, November 10, 1969.
42. Dave Peyton, "The Musical Bunch: The Origin of Jazz," *Chicago Defender*, December 12, 1925, 7.
43. Louis Armstrong interview with Willis Conover, Voice of America broadcast, recorded July 13, 1956, Music Library, University of North Texas Libraries, Digital Library, https://digital.library.unt.edu.
44. Stanley Dance, *The World of Earl Hines* (New York: Scribner, 1977), 35.
45. Louis Armstrong interview with Willis Conover, Voice of America broadcast, recorded July 13, 1956, Music Library, University of North Texas Libraries, Digital Library, https://digital.library.unt.edu.
46. Ibid.
47. Armstrong, "The Goffin Notebooks," 95.
48. Armstrong, "Louis Armstrong + the Jewish Family," 59.
49. Louis Armstrong, Interviewed by Steve Allen for BBC's *Be My Guest*, June 1968, Tape 2016.130.11, Louis Armstrong House Museum.
50. "Classic Faves—2 Pops Armstrong," *Down Beat*, July 16, 1952, 4. The list opened with a statement from Armstrong: "Each selection that I've picked I was fortunate enough to have the opportunity to play in Erskine Tate's Vendome Theatre Orchestra on the South Side of Chicago in 1925, playing for silent films, which was one of the greatest thrills of my life. Yours, Louis Armstrong."

51. Tape 1987.3.279, Louis Armstrong House Museum.
52. Louis Armstrong interview with Willis Conover, Voice of America broadcast, recorded July 13, 1956, Music Library, University of North Texas Libraries, Digital Library,https://digital.library.unt.edu.
53. Lillian Hardin Armstrong, BBC interview with Geoffrey Haydon, November 10, 1969.
54. Tape 1987.3.424, recorded August 15, 1970, Louis Armstrong House Museum.
55. Lillian Hardin Armstrong, BBC interview with Geoffrey Haydon, November 10, 1969.
56. Louis Armstrong, raw interview with Bill Stout, *CBS News*, July 1970.
57. The Baltimore *Afro-American* originally mocked "Gut Bucket Blues" based on its title alone, writing on January 2, "A few of the titles selected for records released by a leading record company indicates that the title writers of the songs have exhausted their lists in naming songs; or that there is the mistaken belief that 'lowdown' titles are selling points for the colored trade. For instance there is: 'Adam and Eve Had the Blues,' 'Gut Bucket Blues,' 'Don't Lose Your Head and Put Your Hands on Me,' 'Put It Where I Can Get It.' The former are among the January numbers." "'Blue' Titles Seem Scarce," Baltimore *Afro-American*, January 2, 1926, 4.

Chapter 24

1. St. Cyr, "The Original Hot Five," 1.
2. Johnny St. Cyr, interviewed by William Russell, August 27, 1958, Hogan Archive of New Orleans Music and New Orleans Jazz.
3. Louis Armstrong interview with Willis Conover, Voice of America broadcast, recorded July 13, 1956, Music Library, University of North Texas Libraries, Digital Library, https://digital.library.unt.edu.
4. Private tape made with George Avakian, October 29, 1953, Louis Armstrong House Museum, Tape 1993.1.5.
5. George Avakian, liner notes to *King Louis*, Columbia Records C-28, 1940.
6. Ory, "The Hot Five Sessions," 17.
7. St. Cyr, "The Original Hot Five," 1–2.
8. Lil Armstrong, *Satchmo and Me*.
9. Louis Armstrong and George Avakian, tape recorded conversation, October 24, 1953. Louis Armstrong House Museum, Tape 1993.1.3.
10. Louis Armstrong interview with Willis Conover, Voice of America broadcast, recorded July 13, 1956, Music Library, University of North Texas Libraries, Digital Library, https://digital.library.unt.edu.
11. Armstrong, *Swing That Music*, 85.
12. Mezz Mezzrow and Bernard Wolfe, *Really the Blues* (New York: Random House, 1946), 120.
13. *Laughin' Louis*, BBC documentary directed by Russell Davies, 1984.
14. Louis Armstrong interview with Willis Conover, Voice of America broadcast, recorded July 13, 1956, Music Library, University of North Texas Libraries, Digital Library, https://digital.library.unt.edu.
15. Tape 2003.197.18, recorded c. 1952, Louis Armstrong House Museum.
16. For more information on the "clarinetisms" in Armstrong's playing, see Brian Harker, *Louis Armstrong's Hot Five and Hot Seven Recordings* (New York: Oxford University Press, 2011).

17. Louie Metcalf and Doc Cheatham, interview with Phil Schaap, WKCR-FM 89.9, July 1, 1980.
18. Jonah Jones, interview with Phil Schaap, WKCR-FM 89.9, May 11, 1988.
19. Roy Eldridge, interview with Phil Schaap, WKCR-FM 89.9, December 16, 1987. It would take some time for Eldridge to fully appreciate Armstrong, but by 1950, French pianist Claude Bolling recalled, "At that period . . . Roy was crazy about Louis Armstrong, particularly on the beauty of 'Cornet Chop Suey.'" John Chilton, *Roy Eldridge: Little Jazz Giant* (London: Continuum, 2002), 180.
20. Fred Higginson, "Jack, Peck, Peewee, Snoozer, Tim," *Metronome*, November 1941, 22.
21. Joe Sullivan, "My Favorite Records," *Hollywood Note*, June 1946, 16.
22. George Hoefer, "George Barnes Settles Perennial Problem," *Down Beat*, June 16, 1950, 13.
23. Preston Jackson, "King Oliver: Daddy of the Trumpet," *Hot News*, May 1935, 3.
24. John Lucas, "Reminiscing with Red," *The Record Changer*, December 1954, 6.
25. Tape 1987.3.423, recorded July 1970, Louis Armstrong House Museum.
26. William "Bebe" Ridgely, interviewed by Richard B. Allen and Marjorie T. Zander, April 11, 1961, Hogan Archive of New Orleans Music and New Orleans Jazz.
27. Alfred Williams, interviewed by Richard B. Allen, October 13, 1961, Hogan Archive of New Orleans Music and New Orleans Jazz.
28. Punch Miller, interviewed by Richard B. Allen, September 25, 1959, Hogan Archive of New Orleans Music and New Orleans Jazz.
29. Nonetheless, it still became another favorite of Jack Teagarden and another trumpeter out of New Orleans, Wingy Manone. "We used to play records a lot, including those great platters by Louis," Manone wrote. "They sure used to knock Jack out. He was gone on one record particularly, a tune called 'Oriental Strut.' When I played that for Jack he thought it was the end. He decided nobody else could ever top that, and said we ought to put it away someplace to preserve it for posterity. We had heard that if you buried things out there on the mesa they would be petrified like all the old trees and stuff that had turned to stone. So one day Jack and I took Louis' record of 'Oriental Strut' and drove out on the mesa with it. We dug a big hole and laid that record away, and as far as I know it is still there today." Wingy Manone, *Trumpet on a Wing* (New York: Doubleday, 1948), 68–69.
30. Martin Williams, *Jazz Masters of New Orleans* (New York: Macmillan, 1967), 211.
31. Kid Ory, "How I Wrote Muskrat Ramble," liner notes to *Kid Ory's Creole Jazz Band 1954* (Good Time Jazz L-12004), 1954.
32. Louis Armstrong interview with Willis Conover, Voice of America broadcast, recorded July 13, 1956, Music Library, University of North Texas Libraries, Digital Library, https://digital.library.unt.edu.
33. According to Ralph Berton, "Though credited by long-standing common consent to Kid Ory, Bechet assured me, years ago, that in New Orleans, in the days when Ory and Bechet were both in knee pants, this very same tune was already a standard march known to old-timers as 'The Old Cow Died.'" Ralph Berton, "Records Old and New," *Jazz Information*, July 1945, 12. A search of newspapers.com turns up hundreds of mentions of "The Tune the Old Cow Died From," apparently of Irish origin and known for having many variations. It was often mentioned in New Orleans newspapers. See "The Tune the Old Cow Died On," *Times-Picayune*, August 19, 1888, 6.
34. Tape 1987.3.123, recorded c. 1951, Louis Armstrong House Museum. Trumpeter Doc Cheatham arrived in Chicago in 1924 and later noted, "I heard 'Muskrat Ramble' before it was named 'Muskrat Ramble.' I heard that in 1924 on a visit to Chicago. I didn't know what

it was until years after they named it 'Muskrat Ramble.'" Doc Cheatham, Interview with Phil Schaap, WKCR-FM 89.9, June 13, 1985.

35. Lillian Hardin Armstrong, BBC interview with Geoffrey Haydon, November 10, 1969.
36. Private tape made with George Avakian, November 1, 1953, New York Public Library for the Performing Arts, George Avakian and Anahid Ajemian Collection.
37. Armstrong, "The Goffin Notebooks," 97.
38. Private tape made with George Avakian, November 1, 1953, New York Public Library for the Performing Arts, George Avakian and Anahid Ajemian Collection.
39. Armstrong, "The Goffin Notebooks," 97.
40. Ibid., 95.
41. Interview with Albert Nicholas, c. February 1969, William Russell Oral History Collection Series, MSS530.4.42, William Russell Jazz Collection, Williams Research Center, Historic New Orleans Collection.
42. Barney Bigard, Interview with Phil Schaap, WKCR-FM 89.9, August 22, 1976.
43. Interview with Albert Nicholas, c. February 1969, William Russell Oral History Collection Series, MSS530.4.42, William Russell Jazz Collection, Williams Research Center, Historic New Orleans Collection.
44. Meryman, *Self-Portrait*, 35.
45. Dave Peyton, "The Musical Bunch: Clarence Cameron White," *Chicago Defender*, April 10, 1926, 6.
46. Dance, *The World of Earl Hines*, 45.
47. Louis Armstrong, letter to Slim Evans, September 31 [*sic*], 1967. 2008.1.32, Louis Armstrong House Museum.
48. Dance, *The World of Earl Hines*, 45.
49. Dave Peyton, "The Musical Bunch: Career of W. C. Handy," *Chicago Defender*, April 17, 1926, 6.
50. Dave Peyton, "The Musical Bunch: Successful Musicians," *Chicago Defender*, August 21, 1926, 6.

Chapter 25

1. Dave Peyton, "The Musical Bunch: Career of W. C. Handy," *Chicago Defender*, April 17, 1926, 6.
2. Eddie Condon, *We Called It Music: A Generation of Jazz* (London: Peter Davies, 1948), 133.
3. Doc Cheatham, interview by Phil Schaap, WKCR-FM 89.9, April 11, 1977.
4. Dance, *The World of Earl Hines*, 47.
5. Muggsy Spanier, "Louis My Idol and Inspiration: Spanier," *Down Beat*, July 14, 1950, 4.
6. Interview with Natty Dominique, 1955, William Russell Oral History Collection Series, MSS530.3.12, William Russell Jazz Collection, Williams Research Center, Historic New Orleans Collection.
7. Kapp initially tried to record the Hot Five on April 20, recording two songs credited to "Lillian Armstrong's Serenaders," but the results were rejected, possibly for technical reasons since Vocalion was still getting accustomed to making electric recordings with microphones.
8. Johnny St. Cyr was in the same boat and had a vivid memory of this date, saying he performed at the Dreamland Cafe from 8 to 12 p.m. and then played the Apex Club from 1

to 6 a.m., didn't go to sleep, and headed to the studio at 10 a.m. to record with Armstrong, when he was also asked to record with Tate, finishing by 1 p.m. If Armstrong was following a similar schedule, it would explain the imperfections in his playing. Interview with Johnny St. Cyr, 1958 August 27, William Russell Oral History Collection Series, MSS530.3.56, William Russell Jazz Collection, Williams Research Center, Historic New Orleans Collection.

9. Matrix numbers are rarely wrong and Vocalion's show that the Tate numbers were recorded first, which might have emptied Armstrong's gas tank. However, both Johnny St. Cyr and Lil Armstrong remembered recording the Lil's Hot Shot sides first, at which point Lil went home and St. Cyr was asked to sit in on the Tate sides.
10. Dance, *The World of Earl Hines*, 49.
11. George Avakian, "Collectors' Corner," *Tempo*, December 25, 1939, 12.
12. Louis Armstrong, letter to Slim Evans, September 31st [*sic*], 1967, Louis Armstrong House Museum, 2008.1.32.
13. Private tape made with George Avakian, October 29, 1953, Louis Armstrong House Museum, Tape 1993.1.5.
14. Armstrong, "Chicago, Chicago, That Toddlin' Town," 43.
15. "Carroll Dickerson and Sunset Cafe: A Great Combination," undated newspaper clipping found in Scrapbook 1987.8.83, Louis Armstrong House Museum.
16. Warren 'Baby' Dodds, "Drums in the Twenties," from *Footnotes to Jazz, Vol. 1: Baby Dodds Talking and Drum Solos* (Folkways FW02290_101, 1951), recorded 1946.
17. Dance, *The World of Earl Hines*, 48.
18. Dave Peyton, "The Musical Bunch: Standard Music," *Chicago Defender*, June 5, 1926, 6. Dave Peyton, "The Musical Bunch: Professional Jealousy," *Chicago Defender*, July 31, 1926, 6.
19. Dave Peyton, "The Musical Bunch: Terrible Teddy," *Chicago Defender*, June 19, 1926, 6.
20. Advertisement for "Cornet Chop Suey," *Chicago Defender*, July 3, 1926, 6.
21. "Consolidated Music Publishing House," advertisement, *Chicago Defender*, June 12, 1926, 6.
22. This recording has never turned up, leading some, such as Gene Anderson, author of *Original Hot Five Recordings of Louis Armstrong,* to assume that the record demonstration never took place. But New Orleans trombonist Oscar "Chicken" Henry was on the bill and specifically remembered, "And after one band would come on, another one and another one until Louis Armstrong came on last and made the records." Oscar "Chicken" Henry, interviewed by William Russell and Ralph Collins, July 11, 1959, Hogan Archive of New Orleans Music and New Orleans Jazz.
23. Schuller, *Early Jazz*, 102.
24. George Avakian, liner notes to David Ostwald's *Blues in Our Heart*, Nagel Heyer CD 051, 1999.
25. Tape 1987.3.123, Louis Armstrong House Museum.
26. Dave Peyton, "The Musical Bunch: Things in General," *Chicago Defender*, October 9, 1926, 6.
27. OKeh advertisement for "Big Fat Ma and Skinny Pa," *Chicago Defender*, July 24, 1926, 6.
28. Louis Armstrong, letter to Lil Armstrong, July 20, 1926, https://www.invaluable.com/auction-lot/louis-armstrong-letter-to-wife-july-20-1926-38-c-2e14b82b2a.
29. Louis Armstrong, letter to Lil Armstrong, July 21, 1926, https://www.liveauctioneers.com/item/40361051_louis-armstrong-letter-to-wife-july-21-1926.

30. Undated news clipping found in Scrapbook 1987.8.83, Louis Armstrong House Museum.
31. Louis Armstrong and Zutty Singleton in conversation at the Hotel Woodward, New York City, February 1971, Tape 2005.1.2209, Louis Armstrong House Museum.
32. Lillian Hardin Armstrong, interviewed by William Russell, July 1, 1959, Hogan Archive of New Orleans Music and New Orleans Jazz.
33. Armstrong, "The Goffin Notebooks," 97.
34. "Louis Armstrong's 'Hot Five' Orchestra," unidentified clipping published July 24, 1924, found in Scrapbook 1987.8.83, Louis Armstrong House Museum.
35. " 'Messin' Aroun' and 'Heebie Jeebies' Song Thrills Vendome Fans," undated news clipping found in Scrapbook 1987.8.83, Louis Armstrong House Museum.
36. " 'Bo' Adopts 'Heebies,' " undated news clipping found in Scrapbook 1987.8.83, Louis Armstrong House Museum.
37. Stewart, "Boy Meets King," 26.
38. Undated news clipping, found in Scrapbook 1987.8.2, Louis Armstrong House Museum.
39. "Armstrong Will Preach at Vendome," undated news clipping, found in Scrapbook 1987.8.83, Louis Armstrong House Museum.
40. "Luis Armstrong Scores Heavily with 'My Baby Knows How' at Vendome," undated news clipping found in Scrapbook 1987.8.83, Louis Armstrong House Museum.
41. Allan Fritzsche, letter to E. A. Fearn, September 3, 1926, Scrapbook 1987.8.83, Louis Armstrong House Museum.
42. Louis Armstrong and Zutty Singleton in conversation at the Hotel Woodward, New York City, February 1971, Tape 2005.1.2209, Louis Armstrong House Museum.
43. Ibid.
44. Interview with Natty Dominique, 1955, William Russell Oral History Collection Series, MSS530.3.12, William Russell Jazz Collection, Williams Research Center, Historic New Orleans Collection
45. Interview with Natty Dominique, 1955, William Russell Oral History Collection Series, MSS530.3.12, William Russell Jazz Collection, Williams Research Center, Historic New Orleans Collection.
46. Tape 1987.3.493, Louis Armstrong House Museum.
47. Morgenstern, "Portrait of the Artist as a Young Man," in *Living with Jazz*, 30.
48. Interview with Natty Dominique, 1955, William Russell Oral History Collection Series, MSS530.3.12, William Russell Jazz Collection, Williams Research Center, Historic New Orleans Collection.
49. Armstrong, "Chicago, Chicago, That Toddlin' Town," 43.
50. Schuller, *Early Jazz*, 103–104.
51. And as author Brian Harker has argued, it's quite possible that this was part of the routine Armstrong had worked out with the dancers Brown and McGraw. What started with Armstrong putting notes to Brown and McGraw's dancing back at the Dreamland Café in 1924 had now expanded into a 45-minute act as part of the latest Sunset Café revue, according to Natty Dominique. Earl Hines confirmed that "Big Butter and Egg Man" was "a number Brown and McGraw used to do, too." Dance, *The World of Earl Hines*, 49. For more on "Big Butter and Egg Man" and Dance, see Brian Harker, *Louis Armstrong's Hot Five and Hot Seven Recordings* (New York: Oxford University Press, 2011).
52. Adolphus "Doc" Cheatham, interviewed by Chris Albertson, April 1976, Jazz Oral History Project.

53. Chip Deffaa, "Doc Cheatham Part II: Chicago Memories," *Mississippi Rag*, July 1990, 18.
54. Interview with Natty Dominique, 1955, William Russell Oral History Collection Series, MSS530.3.12, William Russell Jazz Collection, Williams Research Center, Historic New Orleans Collection.
55. Undated news clipping found in Scrapbook 1987.8.83, Louis Armstrong House Museum.
56. Tyree Glenn, "Unforgettable 'Satchmo,'" *Reader's Digest*, 82.
57. Pops Foster, interviewed by William Russell, August 24, 1958, Hogan Archive of New Orleans Music and New Orleans Jazz.
58. Dance, *The World of Earl Hines*, 49.
59. *Satchmo: The Story of Louis Armstrong*, BBC Radio 2 documentary, January 12, 1975.
60. Louis Armstrong, Letter to Oscar Cohen, January 21, 1970, reproduced in *Jazz* auction catalog (Guernsey's, 2005), 13.
61. Undated news clipping found in Scrapbook 1987.8.2, Louis Armstrong House Museum.

Chapter 26

1. Louis Armstrong, acetate disc of April 1950 interview for *The Record Changer*, 2013.70.6, Louis Armstrong House Museum.
2. Louis Armstrong and George Avakian, tape recorded conversation, October 24, 1953, Louis Armstrong House Museum, Tape 1993.1.3.
3. Louis Armstrong, acetate disc of April 1950 interview for *The Record Changer*, 2013.70.6, Louis Armstrong House Museum.
4. Louis Armstrong, Interview with Joe Delaney, Las Vegas, January 1971. Courtesy of Joe Muranyi.
5. Dave Peyton, "The Musical Bunch: Organist for Vendome," *Chicago Defender*, March 19, 1927, 8, 10.
6. Dave Peyton, "The Musical Bunch: Things in General," *Chicago Defender*, October 23, 1926, 6.
7. George Wettling, *Jazzmen* notes, William Russell Jazz Collection, Historic New Orleans Collection, MSS519.F.40.
8. Spanier, "Louis My Idol and Inspiration: Spanier," 4.
9. Dance, *The World of Earl Hines*, 48.
10. Louis Armstrong, raw interview with Jim Grover, January 8, 1970, Tape 1987.3.423, Louis Armstrong House Museum.
11. Richard M. Sudhalter and Philip R. Evans, *Bix: Man and Legend* (New York: Schirmer Books, 1975), 192.
12. Bill Challis, interview with Phil Schaap, WKCR-FM 89.9, March 10, 1973.
13. Larry Kiner and Philip R. Evans, *Tram: The Frank Trumbauer Story* (New Brunswick, NJ: Rutgers Institute of Jazz Studies/Scarecrow Press, 1994), 61.
14. Louis Armstrong, raw interview with Jim Grover, January 8, 1970, Tape 1987.3.423, Louis Armstrong House Museum.
15. Jim Grover, *Bix: A Series of Nineteen One-Half-Hour Original Tape-Recorded Radio Programs on the Life and Music of Leon Bix Beiderbecke* (Oxford, OH: Miami University Press, 1971).
16. George Hoefer, "The Hot Box: Will the Louis Sides on Cylinder Ever Turn Up?," *Down Beat*, July 14, 1950, 11.

17. Between 1974 and 2002, Swedish trumpeter Bent Persson recorded several albums on which he performed Armstrong's transcribed solos and breaks in full-band settings. The project was spearheaded by producer Gösta Hägglöf, who eventually released the complete sessions on compact disc on the Kenneth label.
18. Dave Peyton, "The Musical Bunch: Things in General," *Chicago Defender*, April 16, 1927, 6. The extra money earned from the books allowed Louis to splurge on a car. "I sold a book of trumpet exercises to Melrose and bought a cute little Hupmobile," he later said. Dave Peyton even picked up on it, writing, "The Melrose Music Co. is publishing both books for Louis who is all smiles nowadays riding around in his brand new Hupmobile eight." Meryman, *Self-Portrait*, 39.
19. Richard M. Jones "resigned the dictatorship of the Race record department of the Chicago Consolidated Music company," as the *Chicago Defender* put it in February, shortly after Rockwell's arrival. Dave Peyton, "The Musical Bunch: Things in General," *Chicago Defender*, February 19, 1927, 6.
20. Tommy Rockwell, letter to E. A. Fearn, January 7, 1927, Louis Armstrong House Museum.
21. Tape 1987.3.96, Louis Armstrong House Museum.
22. Richard B. Hadlock, *Annals of Jazz* broadcast, August 3, 2008, featuring an interview Hadlock conducted with Armstrong in San Francisco on January 17, 1962.
23. "Wild Man Blues" was a Jelly Roll Morton composition originally known as "Ted Lewis Blues," but with Armstrong's *50 Hot Choruses* books due to hit the market, the Melrose brothers added Armstrong as cocomposer, hoping the popularity of his name would generate more interest in the tune. Generations of jazz fans fantasized over the notion of Armstrong and Morton collaborating on the song, but when directly asked about it, Armstrong admitted, "I didn't write none of that, I just played it." William Russell, "Louis Armstrong Phone Interview N.Y.C.," May 5, 1970, MSS 519F1, William Russell Jazz Collection, Williams Research Center, Historic New Orleans Collection.
24. Louis Armstrong, Interview with Joe Delaney, Las Vegas, January 1971.
25. Armstrong, "Jazz on a High Note," 212.
26. Avakian also discovered an anomaly, "Chicago Breakdown," the one and only recording by Louis Armstrong and His Stompers, Armstrong's Sunset Café group. It's a riveting performance with some excellent Earl Hines, a percolating Armstrong solo with only guitar backing, and a freewheeling rideout chorus, topped by some surprising harmonies at the end. But again, OKeh rejected this effort and instead focused on Armstrong's small group work.
27. Louis Armstrong, acetate disc of April 1950 interview for *The Record Changer*, 2013.70.23, Louis Armstrong House Museum.
28. Matt Glaser, "Satchmo, the Philosopher," *Village Voice*, June 5, 2001, https://www.villagevoice.com/2001/06/05/satchmo-the-philosopher/.
29. Some musicians paid attention—a lick Louis originally played on "Tears" with King Oliver and used again here would be transcribed and scored in a 1931 arrangement of "I'm Crazy 'Bout My Baby" by Ted Lewis's Orchestra, featuring Sunset Café regulars Benny Goodman, Muggsy Spanier, and Fats Waller.
30. Armstrong, "Jazz on a High Note," 209.
31. Dave Peyton, "The Musical Bunch: Things in General," *Chicago Defender*, December 18, 1927, 6.

32. Listening to the recording in 1960, drummer Paul Barbarin remarked, "That's his idea, that introduction, all that's Oliver's. That guy had a lot of ideas, man, gee whiz, man. He was a gift, God's gift, that's right. Lost a great man when you lost him. When he passed away, we lost a great man. Ideas!" Paul Barbarin, interviewed by Richard B. Allen, January 28, 1960, Hogan Archive of New Orleans Music and New Orleans Jazz.
33. Laurie Wright, *King Oliver* (Essex, UK: Storyville, 1987), 67.
34. Louis Armstrong, acetate disc of April 1950 interview for *The Record Changer*, 2013.70.7, Louis Armstrong House Museum.
35. Preston Jackson, interviewed by Richard B. Allen, September 7, 1973, Hogan Archive of New Orleans Music and New Orleans Jazz.
36. Wild Bill Davison, interviewed by Hal Willard, January 2–4, 1980, Jazz Oral History Project.
37. Louis Armstrong, acetate disc of April 1950 interview for *The Record Changer*, 2013.70.6, Louis Armstrong House Museum.
38. Sam A. Tucker, "As I View the Things," *Herald and Review*, April 8, 1927, 6.
39. King, "Everybody's Louie," 68.
40. To add insult to injury, Ellington's "jungle" band was inspired heavily by Oliver, especially in the muted work of trumpeter "Bubber" Miley, who heard Oliver in Chicago several years earlier. Ellington took Oliver's blues chorus based on "The Holy City" and put it in a minor key, calling it "Black and Tan Fantasy." When reedman Rudy Jackson joined Ellington, he brought over a solo he used to play with Oliver on "Camp Meeting Blues," which turned into Ellington's "Creole Love Call." Bigard would eventually leave Oliver and join Ellington, too, staying until the 1940s and becoming a star in his own right.
41. Louis Armstrong, acetate disc of April 1950 interview for *The Record Changer*, 2013.70.7, Louis Armstrong House Museum.
42. A 39-year-old African American washerwoman named "Mary Armstrong" was also arrested for being in possession of "lottery paraphernalia" and "acting as an agent" on April 5, 1927, but this Mary Armstrong gave a home address of 1414 Congress and was arrested at nearby North Villere Street, over three miles away from Mayann's usual Third Ward neighborhood. Thus, unless she moved at the very end to a different part of town, I'm assuming this is most likely a different Mary Armstrong.
43. Armstrong, "The Goffin Notebooks," 90.
44. Dave Peyton, "The Musical Bunch: Things in General," *Chicago Defender*, April 23, 1927, 6.
45. Louis Armstrong interview with Willis Conover, Voice of America broadcast, recorded July 13, 1956, Music Library, University of North Texas Libraries, Digital Library, https://digital.library.unt.edu.
46. Armstrong, "The Goffin Notebooks," 90.
47. Ibid.
48. Beatrice "Mama Lucy" Armstrong, interview with Yoshio Toyama, August 19, 1973.
49. Beatrice "Mama Lucy" Armstrong, interview with Jason Berry, 1983, Tad Jones Collection, Hogan Archive of New Orleans Music and New Orleans Jazz.
50. Armstrong, *Swing That Music*, 86.
51. Armstrong, "The Goffin Notebooks," 90.
52. Meryman, *Self-Portrait*, 31.
53. Tape 1987.3.472, Louis Armstrong House Museum.
54. Armstrong, "The Goffin Notebooks," 90.

Chapter 27

1. Dave Peyton, "The Musical Bunch: Things in General," *Chicago Defender*, May 28, 1927, 6.
2. Dave Peyton, "The Musical Bunch: Things in General," *Chicago Defender*, September 17, 1927, 6.
3. Dave Peyton, "The Musical Bunch: Things in General," *Chicago Defender*, September 3, 1927, 6.
4. Dave Peyton, "The Musical Bunch: Things in General," September 17, 1927, 6.
5. Without anything else to choose from, Rockwell released the final two Hot Seven sides, "Weary Blues" and "That's When I'll Come Back to You," at the end of the year, fudging the label and crediting each side to the Hot Five, probably another attempt to cash in on the success of the brand.
6. Jones, *Salute to Satchmo*, 87. Louis never claimed any of Lil's other credited compositions and once told friends that unlike other bandleaders, he felt it was "corny" to put his name on songs he didn't compose. Tape 2017.5.1, recorded August 1967, Louis Armstrong House Museum.
7. *Jazz on a High Note*, 212.
8. Ibid.
9. Ralph Berton, "Reviews: Books," *The Jazz Review*, April 1959, 32.
10. Dance, *The World of Earl Hines*, 54. The three principals immediately pooled their money together to buy a yellow Ford for less than $100. "Louis was very proud of it," Hines said. "He'd ride to church in it, sitting up there just as big and proud as you like." Hines, though, didn't feel the same way. "It was such a terrible looking thing, we called it 'The Covered Wagon,'" he said. The press even picked up on it, reporting, "Louis Zuddy [*sic*] Singleton and Earl Hines were touring around town in a Yellow Ford roadster. Earl was asked to crank the Ford, but he preferred walking—and he walked." Unidentified newspaper clipping, found in Scrapbook 1987.8.2, Louis Armstrong House Museum.
11. On December 13, 1927, the same day as the final original Hot Five session, Louis spent his free time with Alpha, giving her a gag card, which she filled out and included in her scrapbook. It read: "SAFETY FIRST GUARANTEE THIS CERTIFIES that I, the undersigned, a female about to enjoy sexual intercourse with Louis Armstrong am above the age of consent, am in my right mind, and not under the influence of any drug or narcotic. Neither does he have to use any force, threat or promise to influence me. I am in no fear of him whatever, do not expect or want to marry him; don't know whether he is married or not and don't care. I am not asleep or drunk and am entering into this relation with him because I love it and want it as much as he does, and if I receive the satisfaction I expect I am willing to play an early return engagement. Furthermore, I agree never to appear as a witness against him, or to prosecute him under the Mann White Slave Act. Signed before going to bed this Dec. 13 day of 1927 Name Alpha Smith." Scrapbook 1987.8,2, Louis Armstrong House Museum.
12. Zutty Singleton, *Jazzmen* notes, William Russell Jazz Collection, Historic New Orleans Collection, MSS519.F.37–38.
13. George D. Tyler, "Savoy Ball Room Opens Its Doors," *Afro-American*, December 3, 1927, 8.
14. "Louis Armstrong's Dance," *Chicago Defender* (local edition), December 17, 1927, 12.
15. Zutty and Marge Singleton, interviewed by Stanley Dance, May 1975, Jazz Oral History Project.

16. Louis Armstrong, interview with Richard B. Hadlock in San Francisco, January 17, 1962, featured on Hadlock's *Annals of Jazz* broadcast, August 3, 2008.
17. Dave Peyton, "The Musical Bunch: Imposing Leaders," *Chicago Defender*, December 31, 1927, 6.
18. Zutty Singleton, *Jazzmen* notes, William Russell Jazz Collection, Historic New Orleans Collection, MSS519.F.37–38.
19. Zutty and Marge Singleton, interviewed by Stanley Dance, May 1975, Jazz Oral History Project.
20. Louis Armstrong, "Forward" to unpublished joke book, c. 1943, Louis Armstrong House Museum, 1987.2.20, 4.
21. Whitney Balliett, "Sunshine Always Opens Out," in *American Musicians II* (New York: Oxford University Press, 1996), 102.
22. Louis Armstrong, "Forward" to unpublished joke book, c. 1943, Louis Armstrong House Museum, 1987.2.20, 4.
23. Dave Peyton, "The Musical Bunch: Fess Williams," *Chicago Defender*, February 11, 1928, 6.
24. Zutty Singleton, *Jazzmen* notes, William Russell Jazz Collection, Historic New Orleans Collection, MSS519.F.37–38.
25. Ibid.
26. "Stage Shows: Chicago Metropolitan," *Exhibitors Herald and Moving Picture World*, February 25, 1928, 41.
27. Armstrong, "Chicago: That Toddlin' Town," 43.
28. "Stage Shows: Chicago Metropolitan," 41.
29. George D. Tyler, "In Chicago Theaters," *Afro-American*, March 3, 1928.
30. Preston Jackson, *Trombone Man: Preston Jackson's Story as Told to Laurie Wright* (England: L. Wright, 2005), 87.
31. Dance, *The World of Earl Hines*, 54.
32. Dave Peyton, "The Musical Bunch: We Need Composers," *Chicago Defender*, April 14, 1928, 6.
33. Ibid.
34. "In Chicago Theaters," *Afro-American*, April 28, 1928, 9.
35. Louis Armstrong and Zutty Singleton in conversation at the Hotel Woodward, New York City, February 1971, Tape 2005.1.2209, Louis Armstrong House Museum.
36. Dave Peyton, "The Musical Bunch: Things in General," *Chicago Defender*, May 5, 1928, 6.
37. Travis, *An Autobiography of Black Jazz*, 383–384.

Chapter 28

1. Tape 1987.3.96, recorded March 9, 1953, Louis Armstrong House Museum.
2. Dave Peyton, "The Musical Bunch: Things in General," *Chicago Defender*, June 1, 1928, 6.
3. Tape 1987.3.562, recorded c. July 1960, Louis Armstrong House Museum.
4. George M. Avakian, "Move Over, Stacy and Sullivan—Let Hodes In!," *Down Beat*, December 1, 1939, 7.
5. Louis Armstrong interview with Willis Conover, Voice of America broadcast, recorded July 13, 1956, Music Library, University of North Texas Libraries, Digital Library, https://digital.library.unt.edu.

6. Lil Hardin, *Jazzmen* notes, William Russell Jazz Collection, Historic New Orleans Collection, MSS519.F.14.
7. Zutty Singleton, *Jazzmen* notes, William Russell Jazz Collection, Historic New Orleans Collection, MSS519.F.37–38.
8. *Earl Hines Remembers*, promotional 45-rpm record made for Time-Life's "Giants of Jazz" series, 1978.
9. Louis Armstrong interview with Willis Conover, Voice of America broadcast, recorded July 13, 1956, Music Library, University of North Texas Libraries, Digital Library, https://digital.library.unt.edu.
10. John S. Wilson, liner notes to *Giants of Jazz: Louis Armstrong* (Time-Life, 1978), 38.
11. Tape 1987.3.423, recorded July 1970, Louis Armstrong House Museum.
12. Alicia Armstrong, "Interest in Life of Beiderbecke Still Unflagging after 20 Years," *Down Beat*, March 7, 1952, 13.
13. Ibid. For the rest of his life, Armstrong would place this incident at the Sunset Café, which isn't exactly correct because white musicians, including Beiderbecke, regularly sat in with Armstrong there without much fuss. The Savoy featured an integrated crowd, but the concept of a white musician guesting with a Black band would have been frowned upon.
14. Alicia Armstrong, "How Alcohol Ended Beiderbecke Career," *Down Beat*, March 21, 1952, 13.
15. Louis Armstrong, "The Satchmo Story—2nd Edition," c. 1959 manuscript, Louis Armstrong House Museum, 1987.2.4.
16. Dance, *The World of Earl Hines*, 146.
17. Louis Armstrong, "The Satchmo Story—2nd Edition," c. 1959 manuscript, Louis Armstrong House Museum, 1987.2.4.
18. Dave Peyton, "The Musical Bunch: Things in General," *Chicago Defender*, July 14, 1928, 6.
19. Dave Peyton, "The Musical Bunch: Things in General," *Chicago Defender*, March 24, 1928, 6.
20. Howard Reich, "Born to the Purple," *Chicago Tribune*, March 3, 1991.
21. Sanjek, "Zutty," 9.
22. Mezzrow and Wolfe, *Really the Blues*, 240–241.
23. Dave Peyton, "The Musical Bunch: Things in General," *Chicago Defender*, May 26, 1928, 6.
24. Louis Armstrong, acetate disc of April 1950 interview for *The Record Changer*, 2013.70.16, Louis Armstrong House Museum.
25. Rose, *I Remember Jazz*, 239.
26. Louis Armstrong, acetate disc of April 1950 interview for *The Record Changer*, 2013.70.16, Louis Armstrong House Museum.
27. Louis Armstrong, quoted in Guy Lombardo and Jack Altshul, *Auld Acquaintance* (Garden City, NY: Doubleday, 1975), 78.
28. Ibid., 78–80. The visit even made Dave Peyton's column. "The popular cornetist, Louis Armstrong, and the well-known trap drum artist, Arthur 'Sutie' Singleton, were the guests one night last week of Guy Lombardo and his orchestra at the Granada cafe, Chicago," Peyton wrote. "Louis says he was never lauded and treated any better anywhere in his life as he was by this famous orchestral group." Dave Peyton, "The Musical Bunch: Things in General," *Chicago Defender*, October 13, 1928, 6.
29. Louis Armstrong and Zutty Singleton in conversation at the Hotel Woodward, New York City, February 1971, Tape 2005.1.2209, Louis Armstrong House Museum.

30. Louis Armstrong interview with Willis Conover, Voice of America broadcast, recorded July 13, 1956, Music Library, University of North Texas Libraries, Digital Library, https://digital.library.unt.edu.
31. John S. Wilson, liner notes to *Giants of Jazz: Louis Armstrong* (Time-Life, 1978), 38.
32. Hoagy Carmichael, "The Jazz Pioneers Are Passing," *Metronome*, August 1933, 22.
33. *Night Beat*, Dumont television program, November 8, 1956, https://lewisporter.substack.com/p/billie-holiday-the-improviser-part.
34. Donald Clarke, *Wishing on the Moon: The Life and Times of Billie Holiday* (New York: Viking, 1994),
35. Tom Scanlan, "The Impeccable Mr. Wilson," *Down Beat*, January 22, 1959, 19.
36. Garvin Bushell, Interview with Phil Schaap, WKCR-FM 89.9, June 25, 1980.
37. Tape 1987.3.423, recorded July 1970, Louis Armstrong House Museum.
38. Artie Shaw, interview with Steve Allen for *Satchmo: The Life of Louis Armstrong*, BBC Radio 2 documentary series, 1974.
39. George Wettling, "Happy Birthday Louis from . . . ," *Down Beat*, July 14, 1950, 2.
40. Jabbo Smith, interviewed by John Steiner, March 1979, Jazz Oral History Project.
41. Jabbo Smith, interviewed by Phil Schaap, WKCR-FM 89.9, September 13, 1980.
42. Shapiro and Hentoff, *Hear Me Talkin' To Ya*, 135.
43. Jabbo Smith, interviewed by Phil Schaap, WKCR-FM 89.9, September 13, 1980.
44. Shapiro and Hentoff, *Hear Me Talkin' To Ya*, 135.
45. Benny Waters, interviewed by Phil Schaap, WKCR-FM 89.9, June 2, 1980.
46. Jackson, *Trombone Man*, 87.
47. Richard Hadlock, "Kid Ory," *Down Beat*, January 8, 1959, 17.
48. Scoville Brown, interviewed by Phil Schaap, WKCR-FM 89.9, October 18, 1980.
49. Jabbo Smith, interviewed by John Steiner, March 1979, Jazz Oral History Project.
50. Travis, *An Autobiography of Black Jazz*, 242.
51. Garvin Bushell, interviewed by Phil Schaap, WKCR-FM 89.9, June 25, 1980.
52. Jabbo Smith, interviewed by Phil Schaap, WKCR-FM 89.9, September 13, 1980.
53. Louis Armstrong and Zutty Singleton in conversation at the Hotel Woodward, New York City, February 1971, Tape 2005.1.2209, Louis Armstrong House Museum.

Chapter 29

1. Dave Peyton, "The Musical Bunch: We Need Composers," *Chicago Defender*, April 14, 1928, 7.
2. Martin Williams, *Jazz Masters of New Orleans* (New York: Da Capo Press, 1978), 92.
3. Louis Armstrong interview with Willis Conover, Voice of America broadcast, recorded July 13, 1956, Music Library, University of North Texas Libraries, Digital Library, https://digital.library.unt.edu.
4. The 1923 Oliver recording listed Armstrong as the composer, but OKeh's 1928 release recordings attributed the composition to King Oliver. Louis wrote out a lead sheet and submitted it to the Library of Congress on January 2, 1929, listing himself as composer. To add to the confusion, in a 1956 interview, Armstrong remembered playing it with Fate Marable and that Marable wrote "a big arrangement" of it. The melody does sound more like Armstrong than Oliver, but perhaps this mystery will never be solved. Louis Armstrong

interview with Willis Conover, Voice of America broadcast, recorded July 13, 1956, Music Library, University of North Texas Libraries, Digital Library, https://digital.library.unt.edu.

5. Stanley Dance, liner notes to *Giants of Jazz: Earl "Fatha" Hines* (Time-Life, 1980), 36.
6. Louis Armstrong interview with Willis Conover, Voice of America broadcast, recorded July 13, 1956, Music Library, University of North Texas Libraries, Digital Library, https://digital.library.unt.edu.
7. Scanlan, "The Impeccable Mr. Wilson," 19.
8. Dance, *The World of Earl Hines*, 52.
9. However, it would take a few years before listeners had the opportunity to even hear "Weather Bird." Rockwell shelved "Weather Bird" for the time being, waiting until Armstrong recorded a similar duet with pianist Buck Washington on "Dear Old Southland" and pairing the two songs in late 1930.
10. Louis Armstrong, letter to Jim Allison, May 12, 1938, courtesy of Cameron Nelson.
11. Dance, *The World of Earl Hines*, 52.
12. Bria Skonberg, conversation with the author, February 14, 2022.
13. Max Wilk, *They're Playing Our Song* (Westport, CT: Easton Studio Press, 2008), 166.
14. Louie Metcalf, interviewed by Phil Schaap, WKCR-FM 89.9, July 1, 1980.
15. Ibid.
16. Charlie Holmes, interviewed by Albert Vollmer, October 9, 1982, Jazz Oral History Project.
17. Dance, *The World of Earl Hines*, 146.
18. Armstrong, "The Goffin Notebooks," 103.
19. Dance, *The World of Earl Hines*, 146.
20. Doc Cheatham, Interviewed by Phil Schaap, WKCR-FM 89.9, July 1, 1980.
21. Doc Cheatham, Interviewed by Phil Schaap, WKCR-FM 89.9, April 11, 1977.
22. Interview with Danny Barker, December 21, 1985, William Russell Oral History Collection Series, MSS530.4.9, William Russell Jazz Collection, Williams Research Center, Historic New Orleans Collection.
23. J. C. Higginbotham, "Cross Section," *Down Beat*, January 8, 1959, 13.
24. Walter C. Allen, "Luis Russell," *Playback*, June 1949, 6.
25. Higginbotham, "Cross Section," 13.
26. Allen, "Luis Russell," 6.
27. George Hoefer, "Luis Russell," *Down Beat*, November 8, 1962, 44.
28. Lawrence Lucie, interviewed by Phil Schaap, WKCR-FM 89.9, July 1980.
29. Louie Metcalf, interviewed by Phil Schaap, WKCR-FM 89.9, July 1, 1980.
30. Ibid.
31. Louis Armstrong, acetate disc of April 1950 interview for *The Record Changer*, 2013.70.3, Louis Armstrong House Museum.
32. Zutty and Marge Singleton, interviewed by Stanley Dance, 1975, Jazz Oral History Project.
33. Ibid.

Epilogue

1. Armstrong, "The Goffin Notebooks," 97–98.
2. Private tape made with George Avakian, November 1, 1953, New York Public Library for the Performing Arts, George Avakian and Anahid Ajemian Collection.

3. Sam Wooding, interviewed by Phil Schaap, WKCR-FM 89.9, October 6, 1980.
4. Joe Oliver, letter to Bunk Johnson, February 15, 1930, Frederic Ramsey Jr. Papers, MSS 559 F.45, Williams Research Center, Historic New Orleans Collection.
5. Wright, *King Oliver*, 336.
6. "Louis . . . by His Friends," *Storyville 59* (June–July 1975): 182.
7. Frederic Ramsey Jr., "King Oliver in Savannah," *Saturday Review*, March 17, 1956, 31.
8. Meryman, *Self-Portrait*, 48–49.
9. Ramsey, "King Oliver in Savannah," 31.
10. Biarney Bigard, *With Louis and the Duke: The Autobiography of a Jazz Clarinetist*, edited by Barry Martyn (New York: Oxford University Press, 1986), 33–34.
11. Ramsey, "King Oliver in Savannah," 31.
12. Ibid.
13. Meryman, *Self-Portrait*, 49.
14. "King Oliver Dead; Taught Louie," *New York Amsterdam News*, 24.
15. Armstrong, "The Goffin Notebooks," 87.
16. Louis Armstrong, *Jazzmen* notes, William Russell Jazz Collection, Historic New Orleans Collection, MSS519.F.16.
17. Vicky Branton, "Jazz Heritage Turns 20," *The Daily Iberian*, May 20, 2018, https://www.thedailyiberian.com/people/jazz-heritage-turns-20/article_60d5bc92-5bb2-11e8-b76b-fff331e5c16d.html.
18. Park Breck, "This Isn't Bunk: Bunk Taught Louis," *Downbeat*, June 1939, 4.
19. Louis Armstrong, Letter to William Russell, October 3, 1939, MSS536.F.4, William Russell Jazz Collection, Historic New Orleans Collection.
20. Ibid.
21. Hal Smith, "Bunk Johnson," https://exhibits.stanford.edu/sftjf/feature/bunk-johnson.
22. Louis Armstrong, Interviewed by Dan Morgenstern and Jack Bradley, May 22, 1965, Tape 2002.37.1, Louis Armstrong House Museum.
23. Tape 1987.3.218, Louis Armstrong House Museum.
24. "Louis the First," *Time*, February 21, 1949, 52.
25. *Satchmo in New Orleans*, WYES-TV, 1990.
26. Armstrong, "The Goffin Notebooks," 91.
27. Ibid.
28. Tape 2017.5.1, recorded August 1967, Louis Armstrong House Museum.
29. Blaine "Mr. Mardi Gras" Kern, "What Does Louis Armstrong Mean?," *Offbeat*, August 2001, 47.
30. "Louis Armstrong's Letter to His 'Daddy,'" *The Second Line*, July 1976, 13–15.
31. "'Captain' Jones Is Presented Chair as Token of Services to Community," *Times-Picayune*, June 30, 1951, 3.
32. Tape 1987.3.49, Louis Armstrong House Museum.
33. Diane Farrell, "Yankee Doodle Dixie," *Dixie: Times-Picayune States Roto Magazine*, February 14, 1954, 22.
34. George Kay, "The Finding of Peter Davis," *The Second Line*, Spring 1971, 39.
35. "Homecoming 'Like a Dream' Says Famed N.O. Jazzman," *Times-Picayune*, November 1, 1965.
36. Kay, "The Finding of Peter Davis," 39–41.

37. Beatrice "Mama Lucy" Armstrong, interview with Yoshio Toyama, August 19, 1973. Courtesy of Yoshio Toyama.
38. Joe Muranyi, interviewed by Phil Schaap, WKCR-FM 89.9, October 19, 1980.
39. Paul Rimstead, "Talking with Satchmo's Sister," undated news clipping from *Toronto Sun*, held at the Louis Armstrong House Museum, 2003.80.78
40. Ibid.
41. "New Orleans Not Final Resting Place for Satchmo; Some Disappointed," *Jet*, July 22, 1971, 17.
42. Rimstead, "Talking with Satchmo's Sister."
43. Beatrice "Mama Lucy" Armstrong, interview with Yoshio Toyama, August 19, 1973.
44. *The Dick Cavett Show*, July 29, 1970.
45. Max Jones, "The World of Jazz: Louis Blasts Jim Crow," *Melody Maker*, December 12, 1959.
46. Armstrong, "Louis Armstrong + the Jewish Family," 69.
47. Danny Barker, raw interview for WYES documentary *Satchmo in New Orleans*, 1990, 2009.1.80, Louis Armstrong House Museum.
48. Louis Armstrong, acetate disc of April 1950 interview for *The Record Changer*, 2013.70.28, Louis Armstrong House Museum.
49. Tape 1987.3.667, recorded February 1965, Louis Armstrong House Museum.

Index

For the benefit of digital users, indexed terms that span two pages (e.g., 52–53) may, on occasion, appear on only one of those pages.

Figures are indicated by an italic *f*.